LAW AND LITERATURE

CURRENT LEGAL ISSUES 1999

Volume 2

LAW AND LITERATURE

CURRENT LEGAL ISSUES 1999
Volume 2

Edited by

MICHAEL FREEMAN
Professor of English Law
University College London

and

ANDREW D. E. LEWIS
Senior Lecturer in Laws
University College London

OXFORD
UNIVERSITY PRESS

This book has been printed digitally and produced in a standard specification
in order to ensure its continuing availability

OXFORD
UNIVERSITY PRESS

Great Clarendon Street, Oxford OX2 6DP

Oxford University Press is a department of the University of Oxford.
It furthers the University's objective of excellence in research, scholarship,
and education by publishing worldwide in

Oxford New York

Auckland Bangkok Buenos Aires Cape Town Chennai
Dar es Salaam Delhi Hong Kong Istanbul Karachi Kolkata
Kuala Lumpur Madrid Melbourne Mexico City Mumbai Nairobi
São Paulo Shanghai Taipei Tokyo Toronto

Oxford is a registered trade mark of Oxford University Press
in the UK and in certain other countries

Published in the United States
by Oxford University Press Inc., New York

ISBN 0-19-829813-7

Printed in Great Britain by
Antony Rowe Ltd., Eastbourne

CONTENTS

PREFACE

This book—the product of University College London's second interdisciplinary colloquium—brings together the revised papers of the colloquium held on 29 and 30 June 1998. It was an occasion to savour and one that can be lived and relived. We were fortunate in being able to attract leading thinkers from the United States and Canada as well as from the Netherlands and Australia. The annual Margaret Howard Memorial Lecture on Law and Literature, given by Germaine Greer, was incorporated within the colloquium, though Professor Greer's text is not reproduced in this collection.

The book begins with the doyen of law and literature scholars, James Boyd White, interpreting a poem about eating plums. It would be invidious of us to pick the plums in this collection. There are essays on law in literature, on law as literature, on the relationship of the disciplines (and others), on the confrontation between law and literature (defamation, blasphemy, plagiarism, etc.), on methods of interpretation of legal and literary texts. Texts analysed range from drama (Shakespeare and Ibsen), to novels (Scott, Hardy, Edgar Allen Poe, Angela Carter), to film and musical performance and interpretation, to the Bible. Trials dissected include the Eichmann case, M'Naghten, the treason trial of Elizabeth Barton and witchcraft trials in Guernsey. The range of subjects includes legal ethics, punishment, responsibility, constitutions and constitutional morality, colonialism, violence, and feminism. Theoretical insights, demonstrating the breadth of contemporary jurisprudence, are to be found throughout.

The colloquium was convened by Michael Freeman. The administrative burden of running it and putting together this book was undertaken by Andrew Lewis. Both shared the editorial responsibilities. The colloquium was facilitated by generous support from the British Academy and by contributions from the Faculty of Laws Research Fund and University College London's Graduate School. We are most grateful to them, and also to Gillian Howard who sponsored the lecture in her mother's memory and hosted a memorable dinner. We are also most grateful to Anthony Julius for agreeing to write the introduction to this book.

The colloquium and the book were serviced throughout by Jacqui Bennett. Her commitment to the project went far beyond the call of duty. Our indebtedness to her cannot be adequately expressed, but simply without the Jacquis of this world colloquia would not take place. She was assisted at various stages by Deborah Harris, Ruth Redfern and Ceri Higginbottom and to them also we are very grateful.

We hope *Law and Literature* will give scholars and students as much pleasure as we have had in organizing the colloquium and producing the book.

Future colloquia are planned: in 1999 on Law and Medicine and in 2000, appropriately, on Law and Religion. Further details of these colloquia and the ongoing programme may be sought from Andrew Lewis at UCL, Endsleigh Gardens, London, WC1H 0EG, or by fax (0171–387 9597) or e-mail (uctladl@ucl.ac.uk).

Michael Freeman and
Andrew Lewis

INTRODUCTION

Anthony Julius

Like most interdisciplinary undertakings, law and literature studies has both a history and a pre-history. Its history opens with the publication in 1973 of James Boyd White's *The Legal Imagination*, which set out to retrieve the study and practice of law from an impoverishing, but pervasive, legal formalism.[1] The pre-history begins with Plato's disparagement of both sophists and poets and Aristotle's inquiries into rhetoric and poetics. Certain cultural continuities relate the Greek philosophers to the American jurist, chief among which is the work of Shakespeare, and its reception.

This is not surprising. In the sheer density of their language, their complexity of meaning and their severity of form, in the range of their reference and the breadth of their ambition, Shakespeare's plays are at the centre of the literary canon. To engage with literature is necessarily to encounter Shakespeare; all the great English literary critics wrote extensively on his oeuvre. And of course, the sheer plenitude of references to law and legal processes in the plays and poems invite explication by readers familiar with the world from which they are drawn. So far from trespassing when they approach the plays or the poems, lawyers are (on occasion, at least) needed as guides.[2]

What is perhaps somewhat surprising, however, but critical if one is to understand the course taken by law and literature studies, is that while Shakespeare's work takes up a generally adversarial stance in relation to law, its reception by lawyers has always been very positive (some lawyers even claim him as one of their own).[3] The plays, broadly speaking, display a disrespect for law

---

[1] See the Preface to the abridged edition of the book (Chicago, 1985), xi–xvi.
[2] See, e.g., Sir Dunbar Plunket Bertin, *Shakespeare and the Law* (New York, 1929); George W. Keeton, *Shakespeare's Legal and Political Background* (London, 1967); O. Hood Phillips, *Shakespeare and the Lawyers* (London, 1972).
[3] See, e.g., John Lord Campbell, *Shakespeare's Legal Acquirements* (London, 1859), and a sceptical response, William C. Devecmon, *In Re Shakespeare's 'Legal Acquirements'* (New York, 1899).

and legal processes. There is in Shakespeare a certain aesthetic opportunism, one which makes use of law and legal categories for their literary value, without regard to propriety of context or accuracy of content. (One might put it thus: legal language is exploited as one resource among others, part of the material available to the playwright-*bricoleur*.) There is also a complementary aesthetic integrity, which refuses to give the last word to any position, a perspectivism which denies the law's claims to conclusiveness.

Shakespeare offers a subversive, critical account of law and legal processes, one which entails the scaling down of law's pretensions. Against the tendency of law to present itself as the master discourse, a discourse of command to which other discourses must subordinate themselves, Shakespeare places his plays and his poems. The plays, for example, are realistic in their acknowledgement that law has its origin in political power and is used for political ends. They thus comprise a series of defeats and subjugations of law. Rarely does law triumph. All in all, this comprises what might be termed the Shakespearean *anti*-jurisprudence.

However, and notwithstanding this (perhaps, even, *because* of this), many of Shakespeare's editors, and a number of his early critics, were lawyers or had legal training. And beyond this committed and professional attention, one can identify a general, diffuse enthusiasm for Shakespeare by lawyers. The eighteenth-century lawyer Erskine is said to have been so familiar with Shakespeare that he could carry on a conversation for days on all subjects in the language of his characters. Certain lines have become legal stock phrases; Shakespeare is frequently cited in legal argument. Daniel Kornstein's *Kill all the Lawyers?*[4] commends Shakespeare's work as 'the greatest law school of them all'. Literature can make lawyers more empathetic; 'great literature is seldom repressive'. Reading literature teaches good writing. Literature can expose the harshness of legal doctrines. And it offers a method by which 'we can set up a situation and work out its consequences'. 'Scientific' lawyers regard literature as remote from law's theory and practice, one of imperative commands,

---

[4] Daniel J. Kornstein, *Kill All the Lawyers?: Shakespeare's Legal Appeal* (Princeton, 1994).

coercion, reason, and analysis, whereas 'humanist lawyers' regard law as an art of persuasion, a cultural practice. And, in the present volume, Ian Ward argues that Shakespeare's 'treatment of constitutional theory will enrich our understanding of constitutionalism'.

This odd, unreciprocated regard, in which lawyers might be said to embrace works which are (at the very least) in places scornful of their own language, practices, and professional ethic, is symbolic of a general asymmetry of esteem between the legal and the literary. As with law and Shakespeare studies, so with law and literature studies in general. And this is an asymmetry which belies the phrasing of the undertaking, 'law and literature studies', suggestive instead of an equality, a harmony, and an identity of relation, between the two terms, 'law' and 'literature', their relation a constant across all of its instances.[5]

The project of relating law to literature, as an interdisciplinary undertaking (or 'activity')[6] with institutional support, is commonly taken to have four elements. There is the study of the law relating to literature (the law of literature). There is the study of the literary properties of legal texts (law as literature—as a 'branch of literature').[7] There is the study of the methods of interpretation of legal and literary texts (legal and literary hermeneutics). Last, there is the study of the representation of law and legal processes in literature (law in literature). Practically all the essays in this collection fall within one or other of these categories.

The law of literature: There is no discrete body of law relating to literature. There is instead a miscellany of laws regulating literature, some statutory, some judge-made, some criminal, others civil. The law of defamation, copyright law, laws prohibiting obscenity and blasphemy, bear—in variously restrictive and overlapping

---

[5] For an example of just how the relation changed, across a relatively short period in the United States, see Brook Thomas, *American Literary Realism and the Failed Promise of Contract* (Berkeley, 1997), ix–x, in which Thomas comments on how the differences in that relation between the pre-Civil War period (examined in his earlier *Cross-examinations of Law and Literature* (New York, 1987)), and the late nineteenth, and early twentieth, centuries (the period examined in this second book), made it necessary for him to change his approach to 'law and literature'.

[6] Thomas Morawetz, 'Law and Literature' in D. Patterson (ed.), *A Companion to Philosophy of Law and Legal Theory* (Oxford, 1996), 450.

[7] Sanford Levinson, 'Law as Literature' in S. Levinson and S. Mailloux (eds.), *Interpreting Law and Literature: A Hermeneutic Reader* (Chicago, 1991), 162.

ways—on literary creativity. But there is no legal code which takes literature as its subject; the 'law of literature' lacks coherence, it is without system or structure. It is in a state of disarray; it oppresses without bringing order. In this volume, Eric Barendt attempts to bring order to defamation law; inevitably, this leads him to call for reform of 'fundamental aspects' of the law.

There is a tendency in law and literature studies to promote a false essentialism about both 'law' and 'literature', to encourage the belief, that is, that each exists as a sovereign, independent, discourse. The 'law of literature' aspect, which examines the relation between the two at its most distant and antagonistic, is thus the most open to this error. What therefore is most impressive about, say, Simon Petch's paper is precisely his sensitivity to the interpenetration of legal and literary discourses.

Law as literature: In a novel twist to 'law as literature' inquiries, Guyora Binder subjects those very inquiries to a literary analysis, treating them as instances themselves of a literary genre ('The Law-as-Literature Trope'). And while Jill Tomasson Goodwin's paper offers a more mainstream, though illuminating, example of how a work of literary criticism (in this case, Barbara Herrnstein Smith's *Poetic Closure*) may be applied to closing arguments, the contribution by J. M. Balkin and Sanford Levinson encourages the conclusion that we are moving away from a specific law–literature nexus, and toward a conception of 'law as a performing art':

We believe that the comparison between law and the literary text interpreted by an individual reader is inadequate in important respects. A much better analogy, we think, is to the performing arts—music and drama—and to the collectivities and institutions that are charged with the responsibilities and duties of public performance. In other words, we think it is time to replace the study of law as literature with the more general study of law as a performing art.[8]

This gradual extending of law and literature studies to comprise 'law, literature, and philosophy' studies or 'law, literature, and theology' studies risks dissolving the specificity of the original interdisciplinary undertaking. James Boyd White's paper, and Adam Gearey's paper, point the way here, while Wai Chee Dimock's paper is an especially remarkable synthesis of jurisprudence,

---

[8] This is an especially important statement, given Levinson's own earlier position (see 'Law as Literature', n. 7 above, 155–73).

physics, philosophy and autobiography.[9] The tendency towards greater interdisciplinarity—evidence of that 'blurring of the genres' noticed by Clifford Geertz[10]—may ultimately lead to a general reconfiguration of genres in which 'law' disappears as a distinct discipline. In this sense, the 'interdisciplinary' is merely evidence of a transition from one matrix of disciplines to another.

Legal and literary hermeneutics: Comparative legal and literary hermeneutics asks two questions. What can the interpreters of (say) statutes and (say) novels learn from each other? And: can we better understand how judges develop case law if we study how certain literary forms are developed by *their* practitioners? The first question is concerned with the understanding of individual texts, the second, with how texts relate to each other within a specific tradition of such texts.

However, answers to the first question tend to founder on the fact that while ambiguity is the delight of literary criticism it is the enemy of legal analysis. The former welcomes it; the latter hunts it down in order to eliminate it. And answers to the second question—when they do not simply descend into the bad humour of (say) the Dworkin–Fish exchanges on the subject of the politics of legal interpretation[11]—tend to founder on the resistance of both the common law and literary tradition to comparative analysis. Each has its integrity, its specific and defining characteristics, which makes analogies glib, shallow.[12]

---

[9] See also her *Residues of Justice: Literature, Law, Philosophy* (Berkeley, 1996).

[10] C. Geertz, 'Blurred Genres' in *Local Knowledge* (London, 1993), 19–35. But cf.: 'Despite the recent millenarian calls to interdisciplinarity, disciplines will prove remarkably resilient and difficult to kill' (Stanley Fish, 'Almost Pragmatism: The Jurisprudence of Richard Posner, Richard Rorty, and Ronald Dworkin' in *There's No Such Thing as Free Speech . . . and It's a Good Thing Too* (Oxford, 1994), 220).

[11] See W. J. T. Mitchell (ed.), *The Politics of Interpretation* (Chicago, 1983), 249–314.

[12] T. S. Eliot went about as far as one can usefully go, I think: 'There is a logic of the imagination as well as a logic of concepts. People who do not appreciate poetry always find it difficult to distinguish between order and chaos in the arrangement of images; and even those who are capable of appreciating poetry cannot depend on first impressions. I was not convinced of Mr. Perse's imaginative order until I had read the poem five or six times. And if, as I suggest, such an arrangement of imagery requires just as much "fundamental brainwork" as the arrangement of an argument, it is to be expected that the reader of a poem should take at least as much trouble as a barrister reading an important decision on a complicated case' (Preface to St John Perse, *Anabasis* (London, 1959), 10).

The law in literature: The law and literature canon is a rather heterogeneous group, comprising works by Sophocles, Shakespeare, Dickens, Melville, Kafka, and others. These add up to not much more than a themed subset of the received canon of Western literature, though a number are pre-eminent in the canon. (Harold Bloom, for example, rates Dickens as 'stronger' than any other 'nineteenth century novelist' and *Bleak House* as his 'central work'.)[13]

Before the advent of law and literature studies, reading novels (and plays or poems for that matter) for their representations of legal processes and lawyers encouraged two kinds of *mis*reading. It promoted interpretations that were either naively referential or equally naively symbolic, so that the question for consideration became *either*: how accurate is the account the work gives of this or that aspect of the legal system? *or*, what does law stand for in the work, what larger subject does it represent? Dickens and Kafka were the chief victims of these misreadings, trapped between a banal literalism on the one hand and an often fanciful symbol-mongering on the other. Law and literature studies expressly repudiates such misreadings: 'it would be bizarre to propose that any clear prescriptions for law reform could emerge from reading plays and it would be equally crazy to suggest that works of literature could be improved if their grasp of legal principle were to be made firmer' as John Stanton-Ife argues.

Now, however, the practice tends to be to deploy literature in rebuke to law (or endorses literature's own rebukes: Richard Weisberg's *The Failure of the Word* was an early, sophisticated instance of this approach).[14] Marie Hockenhull Smith, in her paper on *The Heart of Midlothian*, praises Scott's novel for its 'resistance to the coercion of subjective lives into objective legal

---

[13] Harold Bloom, *The Western Canon* (London, 1994), 311.

[14] '[The] book situates the source of modern literature's holocaustic predictions and postmortems in the futile wordiness of legalistic protagonists' (*The Failure of the Word* (New Haven, 1984), xi). In his Preface to the book's second edition, however, Weisberg is keen to defend himself against the charge of antinomianism: 'The restoration of a sounder culture . . . will assure the preeminence of law (even "legalism") as the best way to organise human interaction' (xiii). Note also Ian Ward: 'One of the purposes of this particular book, indeed perhaps its primary purpose, is to suggest that students might better enjoy, and thus inevitably better understand . . . the inadequacies of rape law by reading *The Handmaid's Tale*' (*Law and Literature: Possibilities and Perspectives* (Cambridge, 1995), ix).

categories'. Melanie Williams argues that Hardy's *Tess of the d'Urbervilles* 'makes a prescient case . . . for . . . expansion of the doctrine [of provocation in the law of homicide], overcoming the prior partiality of the doctrine and culture for certain "criminals"; it also demands acknowledgment of the cultural production of *the crime*'. The novel makes possible a 'critique' of the law, 'primarily because it *upbraids*' it. Likewise Jan-Melissa Schramm, in her paper on the nineteenth-century debate about the licence of counsel (how may the guilty be defended?) addresses the 'extent to which literature can act as a moral commentary on the excesses of the law'.[15] And Thomas Morawetz demonstrates how certain American short story writers examine the lawyer's conscience 'in troubling ways'.

The law and literature movement is largely confined to law faculties and does not tend to figure in general accounts of modern literary theory. Until Stanley Fish's contributions[16] (and some would say, even after them) the principal law and literature writers have been lawyers rather than literary critics. While courses on the relations between law and literature are multiplying, they tend to be addressed to law, and not literature, students. What is more, in law and literature studies, law defers to literature.

Academic lawyers tend to think that their students *need* literature. As Jane Baron remarks, '[m]uch of law and literature addresses the question of why lawyers should read literature, of what it is that literature teaches. Literature, in short, is a source of values otherwise missing from the law.' Morawetz likewise has written of 'the lure of literature as a moral resource'.[17] This valorizing of literature is nothing new, of course. The social mission of English criticism in the second half of the nineteenth

---

[15] See Robin West, *Narrative, Authority, and Law* (Ann Arbor, 1993), 12–13.

[16] See, e.g., Stanley Fish, *Doing What Comes Naturally* (Oxford, 1989), chs. 4–6, and 13; *There's No Such Thing as Free Speech*, n. 10 above, *passim*; H. Aram Veeser (ed.), *The Stanley Fish Reader* (Oxford, 1998), chs. 6–7. The literary critic Christopher Norris has also intervened in some jurisprudential controversies: see Costas Douzinas and Ronnie Warrington with Shaun McVeigh, 'Law (un)like Literature: Who is afraid of pragmatism?' in *Postmodern Jurisprudence: The Law of Text in the Texts of Law* (London, 1993), ch. 8, and the essays cited in the footnotes to the chapter.

[17] 'Law and Literature' in Patterson, n. 6 above, 456. And so, naturally, anthologies are now being compiled of 'law/lit' texts for law students: see, e.g., Lenora Ledwon (ed.), *Law and Literature: Text and Theory* (New York, 1996).

century and the first quarter of the twentieth, has been written up by Chris Baldick; if Richard Rorty is to be taken as representative of our present cultural moment, then this conviction that literature has a 'mission' is still with us.[18] Much, but by no means all,[19] of law and literature studies reflects just this conviction: see, for example, Ian Ward's paper: 'art is the only means by which the ideal of democracy can be reinvigorated and given meaning in modern society.'[20]

For the 'legal narrative' academics (a grouping within the law and literature movement) the need is not narrowly for literature but for stories in general as a means of redeeming law.[21] In their professional lives, lawyers encounter two kinds of story. There are the stories that are told in court by witnesses, and then there is the story told by the judge in his decision. There are stories, then, and there is the Story, the latter an authoritative, selective restatement of the former. The litigants and their advisers apart, however, lawyers tend not to be especially interested in these stories. They disregard the first kind because of their incompleteness and unreliability, and they discount the second as merely preambular to the legal principle articulated in the judgment, the *ratio* of the case.

Therefore, to be told that stories are important in law is likely to be received with incredulity by lawyers. Surely it is principles that matter in the law, not stories? Both the storytellers and their stories are governed by legal rules. Substantive criminal law brings a defendant to trial; the law of evidence will determine what he is allowed to say in his defence. Stories, in this story of the criminal

[18] Chris Baldick, *The Social Mission of English Criticism 1848–1932* (London, 1983); Richard Rorty, *Contingency, Irony, and Solidarity* (Cambridge, 1989), 94 (of course, Rorty is quick to point out that this is only one of the things that literature can do).

[19] Cf.: (a) Richard Weisberg's qualified dissent on this point in his 'Literature's Twenty-Year Crossing into the Domain of Law' (b) Christine L. Krueger's semi-humorous praise of 'law and literature' as a 'heady blend of imagination and social activism—a combination which probably attracted many of us to our field of study and might promise to return literature from its exile on the margins of hedonistic consumerism' ('Victorian Narrative Jurisprudence') (c) 'the effects of literature on law have not always been benign. Arguably, much popular literature dehumanizes criminals, reinforces racial and ethnic stereotypes . . .' etc. etc. (Morawetz, in Patterson, n. 6 above, 453).

[20] Ward is probably summarizing Iris Murdoch here (see his fn. 12), but without demurring from her views.

[21] See Peter Brooks and Paul Gewirtz (eds.), *Law's Stories: Narrative and Rhetoric in the Law* (New Haven, 1996).

process, are necessary, certainly, but also subordinate. They are necessary because without them there would be nothing for the court to adjudicate upon. They are also necessarily subordinate because unless brought under principles, there would be no means by which they could be assessed.

The radical advocates of legal storytelling answer: to conceive of law as a complex of rules is to misunderstand the nature of law; operating a legal system under this mistaken assumption has the effect of excluding those who are predisposed to express themselves in narrative rather than casuistry. In Christine L. Krueger's succinct formulation, 'narrative jurisprudence critiques legal formalism'. And, as Binder points out, 'lawyers and legal scholars tend to value foreign disciplines as tools for apprehending subjectivity'.

This may in part be attributed to a certain tendency of lawyers to defer to other academic discourses. This professional humility perhaps derives from a sense of law as merely an applied discipline (and perhaps also in response to tacit pressure from vocationally oriented students).[22] So while H. L. A. Hart's remark that 'jurisprudence trembles . . . uncertainly on the margin of many subjects',[23] could just mean that jurisprudence is contiguous with a number of those other subjects, a stronger reading would attribute to the verb just that hesitation before, that deference toward, say, literary or political theory which I am describing here. Law—or in Hart's case, the philosophy of law—*trembles*, a posture quite different from the assertive, imperial stance of other disciplines.[24]

---

[22] William Twining's observation is pertinent here: 'the most persistent pressure point in American law schools is the clash between the interests and expectations of vocationally oriented, fee-paying students and a full time faculty which wishes to be accepted as true academics' (*Blackstone's Tower* (London, 1994), 53). Both the modesty, and the assertiveness, of legal academics in relation to interdisciplinary ventures may be explained, at least in part, by reference to this 'pressure point'. So, for example, two Northern Ireland academic lawyers have suggested that 'the Law and Literature movement . . . was inspired initially by dissatisfaction with legal education's preoccupation with technical professional requirements' (John Morison and Christine Bell, 'Introduction', *Tall Stories? Reading Law and Literature* (Aldershot, Hants., 1996), 2).

[23] H. L. A. Hart, *Essays in Jurisprudence and Philosophy* (Oxford, 1983), 49.

[24] Cf.: 'Most academic disciplines suffer from some uncertainty about their boundaries, but legal scholarship, like several others, experiences basic problems with its core identity' (Edward L. Rubin, 'Legal Scholarship', in Patterson, n. 6 above, 562). On the quest for a core, see Twining, n. 22 above, 153–89.

The law and literature movement, Jane Baron comments, has 'defined out of the category "law" almost everything worth having; beauty, sensitivity, emotions, moral lessons—all these and so much more are the province of literature. The province of law is barren of everything but rules, an empty domain of raw power'. Binder concurs: 'The law-as-literature trope is understood to imply that left to lawyers, law is mere Letter: dry, abstract, artificial'. There is thus a tendency for certain law and literature writers (practically all of them lawyers) to caricature law the better to condemn it. One of the more important contributions that the UCL colloquium made to law and literature studies is to have stimulated scholars to offer papers that challenge just this emerging orthodoxy. Binder, for example, argues that 'the literary' should not be regarded 'as something extrinsic to law which corrects or redeems or ornaments it. The literary must be seen as intrinsic to law in so far as law necessarily involves the construction of the characters, personas, and so on 'that compose our social world'.

Such a perspective will often entail an exploration of the ostensibly extralegal properties of legal processes (to return to 'law as literature'). For example, Lawrence Douglas's paper on the Eichmann trial demonstrates how it 'served to destabilize the very boundary between the legal and the extralegal'. That is to say, it taught others, while judging the defendant. This defence of the pedagogic potentialities of the legal process finds in the trial a 'dramaturgy' which has the effect of conferring on the victim-witnesses the 'power to give tortured memory the force of legal evidence'. This implicit defence of the capacities of law against the misrepresentations of the kind described by Baron and Binder needs to be distinguished from, say, the critique of law and literature studies offered by Richard Posner's *Law and Literature*. His work is flawed by a lack of sympathy for the whole project. A more interesting line is pursued by Tony Sharpe in his paper: 'when literature deals with law', he argues, 'it does so with a tendency to confirm its own superiority as a response to reality'. As Binder observes, 'To say that law is literary is also to admit that literature is like law, an arena of strategic conflict.'

It is dispiriting when lawyers have the same low regard for law and legal practices as the least informed (on legal matters, at least) of literary critics. One finds with such critics a certain aestheticism, one which tends to characterize law as merely practical, a denizen of the realm of necessity, hostile to imagination, coercive, and so on. Consider, as typical of this culture, the poet and essayist Craig Raine. Pressed, during a not especially critical interview, about the meaning of one of his poems, Raine responded:

There's no point in arraigning this poem before a court of law and saying 'in the twenty-fifth stanza you said such and such, whereas in the twelfth stanza you said this.' It's much frailer as work of art than that and, if you do that to it, it will just burst into tears in the witness box. Now you have an example of me talking in metaphor, very unfairly, but this is what I do![25]

This is distinguished only by its representativeness (not by any quality of thought). There is a certain scorn for law here, and perhaps some fear, although that has a slightly bogus quality, as if it is being exploited for the pleasure of a sentimentalizing self-pity. There is also the sense conveyed of law, and forensic techniques in particular, being unsuitable for any informed understanding of literature.

Law and literature studies derives in limited measure from academic lawyers' bad conscience about law, and a desire (in Adam Gearey's phrase) 'to think a justice beyond the positive law'. Gary Minda, for example, writes in his paper of 'a general disenchanted condition with the *ethos* of legal discourse'; 'law and literature', he adds, 'must commit itself to understanding the violence of legal discourse'. It is thus, in a related sense, an ally of critical legal studies. It developed in part as a reaction to the 'law and economics' movement, which regards wealth maximization as the legal system's principal objective.[26] Against 'economic man' Robin West, for example, has placed 'literary woman',[27] and Martha Nussbaum has developed a similar—though non-gendered—contrast in her examination of Dickens's *Hard Times*.[28] Law and

---

[25] Clive Wilmer, *Poets Talking* (Manchester, 1994), 73.

[26] See the entry on law and economics by William W. Fisher III in Richard Wightman Fox and James T. Kloppenberg (eds.), *A Companion to American Thought* (Oxford, 1995), 390–1.

[27] 'The literary woman posited by literary legal theorists is coming into her own, and she is at least beginning to operate as a check on the excesses of economic man run wild' (West, n. 15 above, 251).

[28] Martha C. Nussbaum, *Poetic Justice: The Literary Imagination and Public Life* (Boston, 1995).

literature is thus a humanist response to the perceived deficiencies in both law itself and its principal current interdisciplinary partner, economics.[29]

The feminist critique of law and legal institutions has a family relation to law and literature studies: see, for example, Maria Aristodemou's paper on Angela Carter. Judith Resnik's paper identifies an early indifference by law and literature studies both to 'the rich infusion of feminist theory in literature departments' and to 'the claims that feminist jurisprudence was making in law'. According to Michael Thomson, this indifference, which in turn has meant that women's 'voices remain marginalized or excluded', continues to the present time.

A considerable number of the papers in this collection are by American scholars. This is to be expected, for a number of reasons. First of all, the conditions in the United States for a flourishing law and literature movement were more auspicious, from the outset, than in England. The lawyers there tend to be more open to literary influence, in part because American fiction does not hold them (or all of them) in contempt, while the literary critics there tend to have an intuitive understanding of law and legal processes, if only because they are citizens of a law-dominated (at times, one might be forgiven for substituting law-*demented*) State.

The authority and influence of lawyers, as a distinct group, is far greater in the United States than in England. Only in America, when the good fairy appears, does the ordinary Joe growl: 'See my attorney!'[30] (*New Yorker* legal cartoons such as this one, usefully overstate truths about American legal culture.) Many American writers pursued their legal and political careers in parallel with their literary ones (by contrast, our writers have tended to abandon the law for literature). From John Adams to Wallace Stevens, the practice of law frequently enabled the pursuit of literary excellence, and was rarely inconsistent with it. As Robert Ferguson has demonstrated in his magisterial *Law and Letters in American Culture*,[31] lawyers wrote many of the country's first important

---

[29] See Gary Minda, *Postmodern Legal Movements: Law and Jurisprudence at the Century's End* (New York, 1995), 158–9.

[30] *The New Yorker Book of Lawyer Cartoons* (London, 1994), 26.

[31] (Cambridge, Mass., 1984).

novels, plays, and poems. No other vocational group matched their contribution.

The United States, in contrast to England, has a constitutively *legal* culture, finding liberty through law, rather than setting liberty against the law, as we tend to do here.[32] The United States has thus been characterized as a 'law-dependent polity', engaged in a 'law-dependent democratic experiment'.[33] And therefore a crisis in its legal system is a crisis in the polity itself. (Americans, Grant Gilmore remarks in *The Ages of American Law*, both distrust lawyers and yet are enthusiastic about the judges' arrogation of almost unlimited power.)[34] Hence the title and subtitle of a recent, influential book on the American legal scene: Mary Ann Glendon's *A Nation Under Lawyers*, subtitled *How the Crisis in the Legal Profession is Transforming American Society*. Address law in America and one addresses America.

Partly as a result, American literature is broadly sympathetic to lawyers, and even when not, tends to celebrate (however soberly) a legal system integral to the national polity. Consider, for example, the fiction of Twain, of Faulkner, indeed even Gaddis's *A Frolic of his Own*. One imagines American audiences of Miller's *A View from the Bridge* being entirely comfortable with the lawyer Alfieri's role as commentator on the drama's action. We could not expect English audiences to have similar confidence in any English lawyer performing a comparable choric role. And as for English literature itself—there's no place anywhere there for a lawyer to hide. Lawyers thus engage with it in the same manner as they would an adversary. They expect nothing, and cede nothing.

From Langland to Dickens one finds in English literature an hostility to law which goes beyond mere exasperation at an unreformed legal system and unreformable lawyers. It amounts to the embracing of secular versions of an antinomianism which questions the legitimacy of law and subordinates it as a principle to other imperatives—love, war, politics. Not two years before Dickens began serializing *Bleak House*, Hawthorne published *The Scarlet Letter*, a novel which expressly repudiates just that antinomian

[32] Christopher Hill, *Liberty Against the Law* (London, 1996).
[33] Mary Ann Glendon, *A Nation Under Lawyers* (Cambridge, Mass., 1996), 8, 100.
[34] Grant Gilmore, *The Ages of American Law* (New Haven, 1977), 35.

vision on which Dickens's work is predicated.[35] The contrast with the United States could not be starker.

The English legal profession of the present time still awaits its satirist: the 'old school' protecting its privileges in the name of an invariably bogus collegiality, the 'new school' merely trading in law, oblivious to justice. This ugly, exhilarating world, full of bad faith, ambition, energy and fear, needs a Balzac to capture its excitement and its dishonour. Our own novelists can't seem to manage this, probably because *Bleak House* is still too powerful a presence, and the acid of *that* novel despatches its lawyers too summarily. Dickens makes short work of the lawyers; law itself is his target—a target at which no American could aim without also thereby turning his weapon against himself.

Modern, mainstream American jurisprudence, Realism, and its more recent derivatives, is sensitive to law's debt to politics and wise to the extent of judicial creativity. This means that Americans are less self-deceiving than we are here about the judicial process and therefore less likely to be disappointed when it deviates from false standards of objectivity and political neutrality. English lawyers like to think that politics doesn't have much to do with law (to which they would add, literature too).

Last of all, in this series of contrasts, is legal education. In the United States it is a graduate discipline. Coming to the law after their first degree, students tend to be more sophisticated, and better educated, than their English counterparts. Many are likely to have studied literature, history or politics at degree level before putting on law-blinkers. Contrast our own law students, many of whom begin their training at the age of 18 and thereafter never approach a novel or a play (let alone a poem) other than for 'relaxation'. The appellate judge Lord Birkett, speaking—one

---

[35] The rose-bush by the door of the prison where Hester is detained is said, the narrator reports, to have 'sprung up under the footsteps of the sainted Ann Hutchinson'. At the opening of the next chapter, the narrator comments on the possible reasons for a crowd assembling on the plot outside the jail: 'it might be that an Antinomian, a Quaker, or other heterodox religionist, was to be scourged out of town . . .' (Nathaniel Hawthorne, *The Scarlet Letter* (London, 1983), 76–7). Anne Hutchinson, a prominent Antinomian, was banished from Massachusetts and excommunicated for her beliefs. The novel's own complicated adherence to law—its 'Legalism'—is marked at the outset (in chs. 1 and 2) by a reference to Hutchinson and antinomianism which, though sympathetic, establishes its unlawfulness.

feels—for all English lawyers, once confided to an audience, 'I . . . have been a great lover of reading and esteem it one of the major pleasures of life . . . I enjoy occasional reading in bed, with the bolster and the pillows properly arranged . . .' and so on.[36]

The present volume is committed to the principle that literature also makes appropriate daytime reading for lawyers.

[36] Quoted in H. Montgomery Hyde, *Norman Birkett* (London, 1964), 603. Birkett wrote the Foreword to Louis Blom-Cooper's *The Law as Literature: An Anthology of Great Writing in and about the Law* (London, 1961).

NOTES ON CONTRIBUTORS

Maria Aristodemou is a lecturer at Bristol University where she developed and runs one of the first law and literature courses in Britain. She has written several articles on law and literature and law and critical theory and is now working on a book on the subject for Oxford University Press.

J. M. Balkin is Knight Professor of Constitutional Law and the First Amendment and Director of the Information Society Project at Yale Law School. He is the author of *Cultural Software: A Theory of Ideology* (New Haven, 1998) as well as many articles about constitutional law, legal theory, society, and culture.

Eric Barendt has been Goodman Professor of Media Law at UCL since 1990. He is the author of *Freedom of Speech* (1985), *Broadcasting Law* (1993), and *Introduction to Constitutional Law* (1998), all published by Oxford University Press.

Jane Baron is Professor of Law, Temple University School of Law. Her contribution to the colloquium entitled 'The Half-life of Law and Literature in the U.S.' is published in (1999) 108 *Yale Law Journal*, 1059. The contribution to this collection was specially commissioned by the editors.

Guyora Binder is Professor of Law at the State University of New York at Buffalo. He is co-author of *Literary Criticisms of Law* (Princeton, 1999).

Gary Boire has taught at the University of Auckland, NZ, and the University of Kent at Canterbury. He is currently Professor of English at Wilfrid Laurier University in Waterloo, Ontario. He has published on Law and Literature in *Canadian Literature*, *Ariel* and *Mosaic*.

Anthony Bradney is Senior Lecturer in Law in the Faculty of Law at the University of Leicester. He has written widely in the areas of religion and law and legal education. His publications include *The English Legal System in Context* (with Fiona Cownie) (1996) and *Religions, Rights and Laws* (1993).

Wai-Chee Dimock is Professor of English at Yale University. Her most recent publication is *Residues of Justice: Literature, Law, Philosophy* (Berkeley, 1996).

Lawrence Douglas is an Associate Professor in the Department of Law, Jurisprudence, and Social Thought at Amherst College (USA). His book, *The Memory of Judgment: The Holocaust and History at the Nuremberg, Eichmann and Zundel Trials* will be published by Yale University Press.

Jeanne Gaakeer received her Ph.D. from Erasmus University Rotterdam. Her dissertation is a study of the history and development of the law and literature movement, and, more specifically, of the works of James Boyd White. The focus of her writing is on interdisciplinarity in law, and on the development of legal terms and concepts. Her latest book is *Hope Springs Eternal, an introduction to the work of James Boyd White* (Amsterdam, 1998).

Ray Geary is Senior Lecturer in law at the Queen's University of Belfast. He has published 'The Unpardonable Sin' in *Tall Stories? Reading Law and Literature*, edited by John Morison and Christine Bell (1996) and (with John Morison) 'An Illustration of the Literary Approach to the Study of Law' in *One Hundred and Fifty Years of Irish Law*, edited by Norma Dawson, Desmond Greer and Peter Ingram.

Adam Gearey is a Lecturer in law at Birkbeck College, University of London. His most recent publications include 'Finnegans Wake and the Law of Love', *Law and Critique* Vol VIII no 2 and an essay on St Augustine in the forthcoming collection, *Law and Faith* to be published by Hart Publishing in 1999.

Jill Tomasson Goodwin is Associate Professor of Speech Communication at the University of Waterloo, Canada. She has published articles on law and literature and law and language in *Mosaic*, *The Journal of Business and Technical Communication* and *College Literature*.

Anthony Julius is the author of *T. S. Eliot, Anti-Semitism and Literary Form* (Cambridge, 1995), and a consultant at the London law firm of Mischon de Reya.

Christine L. Krueger is Associate Professor of English at Marquette University. She is the author of *The Reader's Repentance: Women Preachers, Women Writers and Nineteenth-Century Social Discourse* (Chicago, 1992) as well as articles in *Mosaic* and *Victorian Studies*.

Sanford Levinson is the W. St. John Garwood and W. St. John Garwood Jr. Regents Chair in Law at the University of Texas Law School. He is the author of *Constitutional Faith* (1988) and *Written in Stone: Public Monuments in Changing Societies* (1998) and is editor or co-editor of *Interpreting Law and Literature: A Hermeneutic Reader* (1988); *Responding to Imperfection: The Theory and Practice of Constitutional Amendment* (1995); and *Constitutional Stupidities/Constitutional Tragedies* (1998).

Anne McGillivray is Associate Professor of Law at the University of Manitoba. With Russell Smandych, Sociology, she is researching Indian childhood in the eurocolonial context, aided by a grant from the Social Sciences and Humanities Research Council.

Matthew McGuinness recently completed his Ph.D. thesis 'Witch Trials in Guernsey: The Year 1617', jointly supervised in the Schools of English and History at Exeter University. He is currently developing internet materials for flexible and distance learning for the School of English.

Gary Minda is Professor of law at Brooklyn Law School in New York. He is the author of *Postmodern Legal Movements: Law and Jurisprudence at Century's End* (New York, 1995) and *Boycott in America: How Imagination and Ideology Shape the Legal Mind* (forthcoming in 1999 from Southern Illinois University Press).

Thomas Morawetz is Tapping Reeve Professor of Law and Ethics, University of Connecticut School of Law.

Simon Petch is Senior Lecturer in the Department of English, University of Sydney. His recent publications include: 'Walks of Life: Legal' in Herbert F. Tucker (ed.), *Blackwell Companion to Victorian Literature and Culture* (Oxford, 1998) and 'Law, Equity and Conscience in Victorian England (1997) 25 *Victorian Literature and Culture*; 'Equity and Natural Law in Browning's The Ring and the Book' (1997) 35 *Victorian Poetry*.

Mary Polito is an Assistant Professor in the department of English at the University of Calgary in Alberta, Canada. Her field of research is early modern drama and the law. She has published this field in a special issue of the journal *Mosaic (Adversaria, Law and Literature)* and in the volume *Comparative Literature Today.*

Judith Resnik is Arthur Liman Professor of Law at Yale Law School. She is the author of *Convergences: Law, Literature and Feminism* (with Carolyn Heilbrun) 99 *Yale Law Journal* 1913 (1990), and of *Changing the Topic,* 7 *The Australian Feminist Law Journal* 95 (1996).

Jan-Melissa Schramm is an Australian barrister and solicitor with a Ph.D. in English literature. She is currently a Research Fellow at Lucy Cavendish College in the University of Cambridge.

Tony Sharpe is Head of the Department of English at Lancaster University and is the author of studies of T. S. Eliot and Vladimir Nabokov (both 1991) and a book on Wallace Stevens is in press. He is currently working on a study of the contexts of British Modernist writing. This paper represents his first foray into the field of Law and Literature.

Marie Hockenhull Smith is currently doing a Ph.D. on the dialogue between legal and literary discourse, 1720–1800, in the English Department of the University of Wales, Aberystwyth. Her first degree was in English Literature, and she has a postgraduate qualification in law.

John Stanton-Ife is Lecturer in Jurisprudence at the Queen's University, Belfast. He is working on a project provisionally entitled 'Justice and Equality in the Allocation of Health Care Resources' and his most recent publication is 'The Kantian Purification of Law and Politics' *Angelaki* 3(1) (April, 1998).

Michael Thomson is a Lecturer in Law at Keele University. His main areas of research are health care law, gender, sexuality and law, and law and literature. He is the author of *Reproducing Narrative: Gender, Sexuality and Law* (1998), and the co-editor of *Feminist Perspectives on Health Care Law* (1998).

Ian Ward, Professor of Law, University of Dundee. Recent publications on Law and Literature include *Law and Literature: Possibilities and Perspectives* (Cambridge, 1996). He is presently working on studies of Shakespeare and the legal imagination, and the literary context of the English constitution.

Richard Weisberg is Flossheimer Professor of Constitutional Law at Cardozo Law School, Yeshiva University, New York, and author of *Poethics* (1994) and *Vichy Law and the Holocaust in France* (1996; French edn 1998).

James Boyd White is Hart Wright Professor of Law, Professor of English, and Adjunct Professor of Classical Studies at the University of Michigan. His first book was *The Legal Imagination: Studies in the Nature of Legal Thought and Expression* (1973); his two most recent are: *"This Book of Starres": Learning To Read George Herbert* and *Acts of Hope: Creating Authority in Literature, Law, and Politics*, both published in 1994.

Melanie Williams is a lecturer in law at the University of Wales, Aberystwyth; her main research interests are Law and Literature, Medical Law and Ethics, Criminal Law and Gender Issues. Recent publications include 'The Law of Marriage in Jude the Obscure' *Nottingham Law Journal*, 1996; 'Medico-Legal Stories of Female Insanity: Three Nullity Suits' *Feminist Legal Studies* (1998) VI, 1; 'Euthanasia and the Ethics of Trees: Law and Ethics through Aesthetics' 10 *Australian Feminist Law Journal* (1998).

Willem J. Witteveen is Professor of Jurisprudence at Tilburg University, the Netherlands. His research focuses on classical rhetoric, law and literature, legal and political theory, and constitutional law. He has written on the relevance of classical rhetoric for modern law, on the theatre of politics, on the doctrine of the balance of powers, and on approaches to the rule of law. He is an editor of the Law and Literature journal *Karakters*.

WRITING AND READING IN PHILOSOPHY, LAW, AND POETRY

James Boyd White

Introduction

In this paper I will treat a very general question, the nature of writing and what can be achieved by it, pursuing it in the three distinct contexts provided by philosophy, law, and poetry.

My starting-point will be Plato's *Phaedrus*, where, in a well-known passage, Socrates attacks writing itself: he says that true philosophy requires the living engagement of mind with mind of a kind that writing cannot attain. Yet this is obviously a paradox, for Socrates' position is articulated and recorded by Plato in writing. How then can we make sense of what Plato is saying and doing? What kind of writing, for example, does he think he is himself engaged in? What, according to him, is good philosophical writing more generally, if such a thing exists? This will be my first question.

Next I shall turn to the law, where it seems that writing is both utterly necessary and, as we shall see, often hopeless as a guide to the decision of actual cases. I shall look in particular at the first amendment to the Constitution of the United States and a case arising under it, asking what we can hope writing can achieve in this context. What is good *legal* writing, if such a thing exists, and what can be attained by it? Finally, I shall turn to poetry, using a poem by William Carlos Williams as my example, to define more fully the conception of writing, and of writing well, towards which I am working, in the hopes that we can then carry it back to what we have already done in philosophy and law. In all of this I shall be trying to give content to a rather simple and traditional idea—that reading and writing can be seen as forms of conversation—by working it out in three rather different situations.

Philosophy

First, then, Plato's *Phaedrus*. Towards the end of this dialogue the conversation turns from the nature of the soul and of love, its ostensible subjects, to the rather more mundane subject of writing. In this connection Socrates tells a story, supposedly from Egypt, which runs roughly this way:

The god Theuth, the inventor of astronomy and geometry and arithmetic and other sciences, comes to Thamus, the king of Egypt, to offer him his various inventions. He presents them to the king, one by one; Thamus, a kind of technological sceptic, examines each, asking what it is good for and what dangers it presents, before deciding whether to accept it. The conversation is intense and extended, as the merits of each invention are discussed in detail. The god Theuth is perhaps a bit deflated by Thamus' critical responses, but when he comes to the gift of writing his spirits are restored: he expresses the greatest confidence that this is a great invention, one that will surely make the Egyptians happy, for it will improve their memories. In writing he has found, he says, a magic charm for wisdom and memory. But Thamus disputes this claim, claiming that writing will in fact have the opposite effect from that predicted: since people will rely upon writing rather than their memories it will stimulate forgetfulness, not memory; and since they will be calling upon something external to themselves, not what is in their minds, it will create the false appearance, not the reality, of knowledge and wisdom.

Socrates then goes on to say, in his own voice, that writing is to speaking as a painting is to a person: it creates the image of meaning, but is wholly unable to answer when questioned. The written text just keeps repeating the same thing over and over, unable to adjust or respond to questions, doubts, or new ideas. For this reason, he says, we should take rather little satisfaction in what we write, even the best things we can do. This sceptical view of the value of writing is reaffirmed in Plato's seventh letter where he says that his philosophy is not to be found in any of his writings, but exists only in the living engagement of the mind.[1] Writing is at best a kind of play or game; the real thing, that about which we

---

[1] Plato, *Seventh Letter*, 341C–D, 344C.

should really be concerned, lies elsewhere, in actual conversation between minds taking place in what we might call 'real time'.

As I said above, there is an obvious paradox here, for both of the Platonic strictures against writing take place in writing. Without writing, indeed, we should have virtually no access to Plato's mind, or the mind of Socrates either for that matter, nor any sense of what Plato meant when he said that philosophy lay not in writing but in conversation. In fact, our best examples of the kind of living interaction between mind and mind that he admires are themselves in writing, as in this very dialogue. It is impossible to believe that Plato, one of the world's best writers, did not value highly his achievement of this kind.

What sense, then, can we make of Plato's attack on writing? To pursue this question will perhaps help us think about the merits and demerits of writing in our own world, and about the kind of education that will enable us to write well, and read well, including in the law.

READING THE *PHAEDRUS*

A natural place to begin is with our experience of reading the writing that is the text of the *Phaedrus*. The first thing that is likely to leap out at the reader is that this text, like so many other of the Platonic dialogues, is neither an argument written to support a particular set of propositions, nor a disquisition upon a particular subject. Rather, it is a story; a drama; a conversation; a dialogue, beginning with the meeting of Socrates and Phaedrus outside the walls of Athens and ending with their going back into the city together. Something happens between those two points; the creation of that happening between the speakers, and the corresponding happening in the life of the reader, is certainly one aim, perhaps the true aim, of the text.

I will not try to summarize the whole thing, but it may help if I say this much about what happens: Phaedrus and Socrates meet outside the city walls; Phaedrus talks about a party he has just recently left, at which the orator Lysias read a very clever speech; Phaedrus has borrowed a copy of this speech, which he has been planning to commit to memory; now seeking a place to discuss the speech, Socrates and Phaedrus find the cool and shaded atmosphere of the river-trees, commenting in detail on their surroundings.

Phaedrus then reads aloud the speech of Lysias, in which a seducer paradoxically argues that the fact that he is not in love is a good reason for his target to yield to his desires; Socrates, spurred on by Phaedrus, gives, in a kind of competition, a speech of his own to the same end, his point being that love is a kind of irrationality and thus inconsistent with the philosophic life. Suddenly visited by his private divine force, however, Socrates realizes that what he has said is awful, for love is a god and must be good; he then delivers a second speech, this one in favour of love, in which among other things he works out the famous image of the human soul as a pair of winged horses, one good, one bad, managed by a charioteer. Human souls once lived in the heavens, he says, but through mismanagement have lost their wings and fallen into an earthly life. Love, Socrates says, is an experience that reminds the soul of what it once had, life in contact with beauty and truth, and it rekindles the desire to attain it. It is one of the greatest gifts of life. When Socrates has finished, he and Phaedrus then speak about various questions raised by the three speeches on love, including the issue whether writing is a good or bad thing.

Even this summary should be enough to show that this dialogue is not, as I say, a sustained conceptual argument, leading by logical progression from one point to another, but a composition far more complex, in which one part answers or responds to another. Its closest analogue may be a play by Shakespeare, where any position Shakespeare has is expressed not by this speech or that, but by the play as a whole, by the way voice answers voice. For Shakespeare's art lies not only in the composition of the speeches but their arrangement: it is here, in the relation of these gestures across time, that Shakespeare can be found. And in Shakespeare as in Plato one finds items of very different kinds, humorous and solemn and farcical and deeply felt.

For the reader of both authors, then, the question is not so much what this all 'means' in a propositional way—as if true understanding meant the capacity to utter a series of true statements that represented what Plato or Shakespeare would have said if they had been smart enough—but what it means in an entirely different way, as an experience of mind and imagination, of thought and feeling. Its end is not persuasion to a set of statements, but something vastly more important and profound, a transformation of the mind and motives and understandings of the reader.

Reading the *Phaedrus* thus requires one constantly to ask exactly how a particular passage is to be taken in light of other passages or other moments. Here the question of tone is crucial. For example, in the central myth about the soul as a pair of winged horses guided by a charioteer, part of the story is that once the soul has fallen from the heavens to the earth, the experience of physical desire for a beautiful body reminds the soul of its own earlier experience of beauty itself, in the heavens, where the Eternal Forms can be directly apprehended; the person thus touched by *eros* starts to feel the itch and pain of his feathers beginning to sprout, in the total intoxication of desire. How are we to read this? I can remember being told that this story was a perfectly serious allegory of the moral nature of the soul, and that the lesson was plain, to develop the rational faculties of the charioteer to control one's baser impulses. But this won't work at all: it is some of the so-called baser impulses that are celebrated here, and the kind of madness they bring about is far from rational control. And in any event such a lead-footed reading is totally dead to what is most wonderful about this myth: its invented, playful quality, comic even to the point of the self-consciously ludicrous, poised as it is against a kind of real seriousness. The speech is both serious and comic, both beautiful and silly, both to be believed and to be disbelieved.

The story about Theuth and Thamus has similar qualities. It is funny, to start with, as the resolutely practical Thamus examines the gifts of the god with a sceptical air and practical intelligence.[2] (I do not think it wholly accidental that their names, at least for me, work as a kind of tongue-twister, leading me to want to lisp the second name, thus, 'Thamuth'.) And, as I suggested before, the apparent message of the story, that writing is bad because it will destroy memory and wisdom, is in plain contradiction to certain of the premises of the text of which it is a part. How then are we to read it?

One possibility—and it is only one—is to start from Socrates' point that the trouble with writing is that it always says the same thing and can thus never respond to questions or criticisms, never

---

[2] This is just what Socrates does not do with the gift of sexual desire, from Eros, and Thamus thus stands as a mild reproach to Socrates' abandonment of reason in telling the central myth.

engage in the conversational process that is the centre of philosophy. Plato is perhaps here telling us why he writes in the form of the dialogue, rather than simply telling us 'what he thinks and why he thinks it'—as though such a thing could be done.

On this view, what the passage about writing suggests is that he, Plato, is trying to write a text that is different from the kind of writing he rejects and instead has some of the essential qualities of conversation. It does not simply say something, and stop; rather, it offers the reader a complex experience, in part consisting of the stimulation of questions—about the myth of horses for example, or this very passage about reading—that the text will not in any obvious or easy way answer, but with respect to which it affords the reader material for thought, if he can grasp and manage it. Here, for example, the question, 'What can Plato mean by these strictures against writing?' leads to the possibility that it is not all writing that he opposes, but writing of a certain kind—or reading of a certain kind—working on certain premises. Moreover, in the way in which Plato renders living conversation between Socrates and Phaedrus one can find some idea of what his own aim is as a writer, and the standards by which he wants his writing to be judged.

I do not want to suggest that this is where the process stops: there are other points about writing, other complications and mysteries here, but this in a sense is the main point: Plato has written a text that does not simply say the same thing always, but says different things as you bring different questions to it. Its aim is to offer its reader a disorienting experience of controlled uncertainty and thus to stimulate independence of mind, in the way that conversation, or dialectic, at its best can do. On this view philosophy is not the exposition of a certain set of propositions about the world, but a mode of life and thought; its end is not a set of statements, but an end of a different kind, the transformation of the mind and imagination of the reader. This is a process that by its nature has no termination until death, and the hoped-for return to the world in which truth and beauty and goodness can be seen simply and clearly for what they are.

THE LIMITS OF LANGUAGE

One reason why Plato wrote this way, rather than proceeding as Euclid was to do in another field, from first principles, or as

Aristotle did, from common knowledge, is that for Plato the language in which he thought and wrote was a large part of the problem he addressed. This was partly a matter of its particular substantive commitments, for example to an idea of justice and 'goodness' that consisted in large part of the power to exercise dominion over others,[3] but partly also a matter of the nature of human language more generally—for there is no language in which the truth can simply be said, and in Plato's view we must train ourselves to accept that fact and to display our awareness of it in our speaking and our writing alike.

The point of Plato's doctrine of the Eternal Forms, then, is not to assert the truth of their existence, which can after all never be observed or known while we live, but to define, by their absence, what human life lacks. This is a way of drawing attention to the important fact of actual human life that such knowledge is denied us. We must live on conditions of radical uncertainty; and it is to show us how this might be done without collapsing into incoherence or despair that the dialogue exists.

The experience of reading Plato may in fact provide us with a method for the reading of philosophy more generally, for it suggests among other things that the language in which philosophy is carried on can, and perhaps should always, be part of its subject. If we start to yield to the desire to create a general philosophic system, as Plato himself often did, the experience of the *Phaedrus* should check us in that course; not to prevent us, necessarily, but to slow us down. If, for example, we find ourselves talking about the 'proper end of life', and defining that as 'happiness', and then defining happiness in terms of the 'fulfilment of human capacities', or if we find ourselves talking about the proper form of political organization, and defining that in terms of 'consent', and consent in terms of the 'will of the majority' as reflected in the ballot, all as though those terms had meanings that were either self-evident or could be stipulated, and as though we occupied a platform somehow above history and culture from which we could speak universal truths on such subjects, the experience of reading Plato should

---

[3] For further discussion see my *When Words Lose Their Meaning: Constitutions and Reconstitutions of Language, Character, and Community* (Chicago, 1984), 95–8. For a fine article on reading Plato as a general matter, see Hayden Ausland, 'On Reading Plato Mimetically' (1997) 118 *American Journal of Philology* 371.

make us pause, and ask how what we are saying might be located in one of his dialogues: poised against what counter-formulations; subject to what dissolutions, as the terms we use are shown not to bear the weight we want to give them; rendered to what degree incomplete or empty, as other related questions are raised to which we have no way of speaking; and so forth.

It is thus one of the monumental achievements of Plato simultaneously to engage in the impulse to systematize and to subject that impulse to criticism.

Law

What bearing if any does this understanding of Platonic philosophy have upon the reading and writing of the law? At first it may seem none at all: the whole point of written laws in our system is that they be clear and publicly available; only then, after all, can the citizen who is subject to them conform his or her conduct to their requirements, and only then can the official who interprets and applies them be subject to the constraint we think of as government under law. Uncertainty of law is a recipe for official corruption, for the denial of the fundamental principle of notice, and for violation of the ideal that like cases are to be treated alike. We therefore demand that the law be clear, in America making a constitutional principle of it. We in fact want the law to do just what Socrates complains that writing does, namely to say the same thing always. We do not want law to be dialectical or conversational; we want clarity, fair notice, obedience, equal treatment.

READING LAW

But all this is far easier to say in general terms than it is to work out in practice, as any look at a statute book or constitution or a set of judicial cases will show. The main provisions of the first amendment to the American Constitution, for example, are on the surface plain enough: 'Congress shall make no law respecting the establishment of religion, or prohibiting the free exercise thereof; or abridging freedom of speech, or of the press.' When we read this we understand in a general way the values that the framers are articulating, and we know that they want to be read as meaning business. But when we come to the application of such a standard, serious problems emerge: is it an establishment of religion, for example, for a legislature to begin its sessions with prayers led by a chaplain paid by tax dollars? For the armed services to employ chaplains? For a state to exempt religious organizations from its tax laws? For a city to have a Christmas display that includes a nativity scene?

Deciding those questions is not merely a matter of looking at the words and seeing what they mean, for different people will have different readings of the same language—different, reasoned, and decent readings. The question the law faces, here as elsewhere, is what to do about the fact that we do reasonably differ, including on the most important matters, and that there is no obviously right way to resolve our differences.

This means that the ideal of clear language applied the same way every time is simply out of reach. In the law the meaning of the language in which authoritative directions are given is itself always in question. Much in the same way that Plato sees that the central terms of his language are uncertain in meaning and call for new definition, the lawyer comes to see that the same is true of the central terms in her discourse: terms such as 'religion' and 'speech' and 'establishment' and 'free exercise' in the first amendment, for example. The lawyer should not simply use her language as a given, then, but see it as the proper subject of critical attention and transformation.

Likewise, the lawyer should know what Plato reveals, that there is no such thing as purely neutral, unsituated, abstract, or disinterested thought or speech: no way, except in the heavenly life Plato imagines to precede and follow our earthly one, in which one can see beauty and truth and justice for what they are, unchanging and eternal essences. Rather, every effort at thought and expression is located in an historical moment and a particular set of social relations, and these circumstances affect the meaning of what is said. This is true of the *Phaedrus* itself, which is a conversation between Socrates and Phaedrus; and true of the lawyer who always thinks and speaks as the representative of a particular client—the citizen who wants the nativity scene removed for example, or the city that wants it to remain—or, if he is a judge, as one trying to resolve the particular dispute before him. For both lawyer and judge, the materials of meaning with which they work are to a large degree given them by others, in the constitutions, statutes, regulations, contracts, judicial opinions, and other texts that speak to the particular event. This material will not and should not say the same thing always; it will in fact yield different meanings to different minds in different situations, differences that themselves become the topic of thought and argument.

For the lawyer, as for Plato, every discovery, every conclusion, is provisional, open to question and perhaps to repudiation in a later conversation—think of Socrates, who in the *Phaedrus* made one speech against love, another one in praise of it, and then changed the subject entirely. And it is common for a Platonic dialogue to end with Socrates in a kind of perplexity, or if not that, by reaching a conclusion that is still, in the terms established in the dialogue itself, open to doubt.[4] Likewise each performance in the law is the best we can do at the time, but it is always open to revision: by appeal, by distinction, by overruling, by amendment.

The life of the law, like the life of philosophy, lies then in the activity by which a problem is defined and approached, not in any solution to it. This activity is what we learn and what we teach. The part of this activity that we call 'reading' has much of the character of a conversation with the ruling texts of the law, and 'writing' takes the form of conversation too, between judge and lawyer, among lawyers, between lawyer and client, and so on.

Let me give you an example of what I mean, in the form of a much simplified version of a real case, *Lee v. Weisman*.[5] The question is whether it is an improper establishment of religion for a public high school to invite a local pastor or rabbi to give a prayer as part of the graduation exercises. We can assume that the prayer in question is as non-sectarian and vague as they usually are, perhaps as simple as this: 'God of the Free, Hope of the Brave, for the legacy and liberty and destiny of America we thank you. May these young people fulfill their own hopes and those of their parents and teachers. Amen.' Does this practice violate the Constitution? My guess is that you are likely to have one of two quick reactions, either 'Yes, of course, obviously it does: this

---

[4] See, for example, *Protagoras* and *Crito*.
[5] 505 US 577 (1992).

plainly violates the separation of church and state', or 'No, obviously not: we have had graduation prayers forever, and nothing could be more innocuous than such a thing.'

Notice that the language of the first amendment prohibiting the passage of any law 'respecting the establishment of religion', however plain it may be to those on each side of the dispute, does nothing to resolve the difference between them. It sits there, as Plato says, reiterating itself and unable to respond to the questions we have of it. But in the law we have more than the amendment: we have the cases decided under it, and these complicate the question by providing two somewhat inconsistent lines of authority.

First, the Supreme Court has decided a series of cases, beginning with *Engel* v. *Vitale* in 1962, that prohibited the use of prayers as part of the public school curriculum. Later cases have similarly struck down Bible readings in school, recitations of the Lord's Prayer, moments of silence meant as moments of prayer, and the like.[6] These cases would support the conclusion that the graduation prayer is invalid.

But there is a contrary line of authority, partly judicial, partly rooted in the practice of other branches: Congress begins its sessions with a prayer made by a chaplain paid with public funds; there are chaplains in the military; high national officers are sworn in on the Christian Bible; the President often includes a prayer as part of his inaugural address; the Thanksgiving Proclamation is typically in the form of a prayer, at least in part; and, most recently, the Court held that the Nebraska legislature does not violate the amendment by beginning its sessions with prayers made by chaplains paid with state funds, even though some of these prayers are highly sectarian in content.[7] In the same vein, within recent years the Court approved the inclusion of a nativity scene in a municipal Christmas display. These precedents would support the validity of the graduation prayer.

So what is the Court in the graduation prayer case to do? Distinctions can be drawn, focusing for example on the degree of compulsion present in school prayers, or the impressionable age of the children in those cases; similarly, one can try to work out

---

[6] See *Engel* v. *Vitale*, 370 US 421 (1962); *School District* v. *Schempp*, 374 US 203 (1963); *Wallace* v. *Jaffree*, 472 US 38 (1985).
[7] *Marsh* v. *Chambers*, 463 US 783 (1983).

'tests' of various sorts for the resolution of this and similar cases. I do not want here to pursue the various lines of argument in detail but only to make the rather simple point that the task of the lawyer, as he reads the amendment in the context of the cases briefly outlined above, and in the context too of the particular facts of the case, is a form of conversation, with a set of texts none of which will say the same thing always. The language of the amendment stimulates a conversation with its various contexts in which it says not one but many different things, among which choices have to be made. In fact, the law does not so much 'say things' as create the conditions for a complex process of thought and conversation, highly dialogic in character; it is this process of thought that we learn, and teach, and practise as lawyers; this process is, in an important sense, the law itself.

WRITING THE LAW

To think now about the problem of writing from the perspective of the writer of laws—whether they take the form of statutes, regulations, contracts or opinions—it should be plain that one cannot proceed simply by saying what one means clearly and plainly. This is partly a matter of the inherent vagueness of language in certain contexts. Think, for example, of the definition of crime. This requires an element of 'intention' or 'wrongfulness'—for we all surely would distinguish for purposes of criminal punishment between accidental and deliberate injury of another—but no one can specify states of mind with clarity and precision. Sentencing and custody disputes are similar cases: one simply cannot articulate rules that wholly capture the considerations that one thinks ought to influence the judgment in a particular case.

But the difficulty is not confined to cases where the law is forced to use uncertain terms. The larger point rather is that the way legal texts are used in our system—placed now in this factual context, now another, placed now in this composition of other texts, now another—gives all legal texts a kind of inherent uncertainty, which in turn gives rise to the necessity for the kind of legal thought I have described. Legal texts do not and cannot say the same thing always, and it is unrealistic in the extreme for the writer to hope they can.

How then is one to think of the process of writing law, or to teach it, if not as the communication of commands in clear and direct language? The heart of it I think is this: the lawmaker should recognize that the application of his text depends on the action and judgment of others. It is thus a social and cooperative activity, and part of the lawmaker's task and opportunity is the management of the social relations through which his statute (or other text) will work. He is engaged in a conversation with his audience and should try to speak to them about the task which he has given them in some way other than by simply reiterating his commands. He should thus write a text that does not simply say the same thing always, but invites and responds to questions; a text that has some of the quality of a dialogic partner.

The writing task is made all the more difficult when one realizes that there is not one audience for legislative and legal texts but multiple audiences, ranging from citizens to jurors to lawyers and judges. In each case the legislator must try to attune himself to the situation of his audience, understanding the context against which they will read this gesture, and do his best to produce a text that will speak well to them all. An impossible but necessary task.

How this might be done, in particular cases or more generally, is the topic of another talk, or of a course.[8] For present purposes it is enough to see that this kind of writing is not mechanistic, dull, or easy, but hard, complex, a full challenge to the mind.

Thus the best writing in the law and in philosophy alike does not, as one might first think, strive to say the same things always, but offers the reader an experience like that of conversation: it stimulates questions, and responds to them; these responses invite further questions, and lead the reader to a deepened understanding bounded by uncertainty. It is not in what Socrates 'says' or what Phaedrus 'says' that we are to find the philosophy of Plato, but in what the dialogue as a whole offers its reader, the experience of our engagement with it. Likewise it is not in what the Constitution—or a statute, or a judicial opinion—'says' that we find the law, but in the activity of reading and writing that these texts simultaneously stimulate and reward.

The experience of the law can thus be seen to reinforce the complex point of Plato's passage on writing, especially when it is coupled with his own performance as a writer. He tells us that we

---

[8]   It is the subject of my *The Legal Imagination: Studies in the Nature of Legal Thought and Expression* (Boston, 1973; Chicago, 1986).

should not strive for writing that simply states its position in plain words and stops, for such a thing is neither desirable nor possible. Words do not carry meanings like freight cars and cannot be made to do so; instead, we should understand that every act of language is a performance, a gesture against a background of other gestures, and that it asks to be understood as such by both speaker and audience, by both writer and reader. Every performance is by a situated speaker to a situated audience, and its conclusions must always be provisional. No final and universal statements of truth are possible for us here on earth but only, as Plato says, in the heavens, where we can see truth and beauty and justice directly— an image the whole point of which is to distinguish it from the conditions on which we live.

Poetry

Such are some connections between writing—and reading—in philosophy and in law. How about the third form, poetry?

My thought here is that the sense of writing worked out above, as an activity of mind—as an engagement with the nature of language and the limits of human understanding that cannot resolve itself into propositions assumed to be stable, but must renew itself, again and again, whenever we speak or write—is an essentially literary or poetic one. It might help, then, to work through a poetic example, both as a way of making clearer what I mean to say about philosophy and law, and as a way of suggesting a resource to which as lawyers and philosophers we might turn to learn more fully about the nature of the activity in which we are engaged when we write.

For it is much easier to see that a poem or a novel does not simply carry a message than it is to read a legal or philosophic text in such a manner; much easier to see of the literary text that much of its meaning lies in its tones of voice and their transformations, its ways of imagining the world and the speaker within it, its definition and management of relations between speaker and audience, its metaphors and images, its ways of meeting and upsetting expectations as to form, and so on. Literary texts are more obviously dramatic texts, explicit performances with language and with social relations, and to learn to read them may help us be more alert to what might be called the literary aspects of apparently non-literary texts. In particular, poetic texts are commonly founded on a tension, or a contradiction, between different ways of thinking or feeling or acting or imagining the world, which they may not resolve at all, or only partly. The truth that such a text asserts is thus not reducible to one position, one voice, one way of thinking, but lies in the fact that both opposing elements have weight and validity.

As an example I have deliberately chosen a poem that may not look or sound much like a poem at all, and one that in fact may seem reducible to a message. It is William Carlos Williams's poem about taking the plums from the icebox,[9] which reads this way:

THIS IS JUST TO SAY

I have eaten
the plums
that were in
the icebox

and which
you were probably
saving
for breakfast

Forgive me
they were delicious
so sweet
and so cold

When you first read this poem, or hear it read aloud, I think you are likely to have one or two rather strong reactions (just as was the case with the graduation prayer case): either that this is a beautiful poem, special in some as yet unknown way, or that it is trivial and empty. In my own experience this was true of a group of friends, all good readers, who divided in exactly that way and engaged in heated dispute over the question that divided them.

On the negative side, it seems true that the poem does not have the kind of dramatic and intense and clearly-shaped imagery of a poem, like Wallace Steven, 'Thirteen Ways of Looking at a Blackbird',[10] which begins this way:

---

[9] 'This is just to say' in *The Collected Poems of William Carlos Williams* (A. Walton Litz and Christopher MacGowan (eds.), New York, 1986), 372. [William Carlos Williams, 'This is Just to Say' from *Collected Poems: 1909–1939*, Volume 1, copyright © 1938 by New Directions Publishing Corp., reprinted by permission of the publishers, Carcanet Press Ltd. and New Directions Publishing Corporation.]

[10] 'Thirteen Ways of Looking at a Blackbird' in *The Collected Poems of Wallace Stevens* (New York, 1971), 92.

Among twenty snowy mountains
The only moving thing
Was the eye of the blackbird.

By comparison, the language 'and which you were probably saving for breakfast' seems cluttered and awkward and utterly ordinary, devoid of visual force. In addition, those who take the negative view might add that this is a poem that is indeed reducible to a mere proposition: I have eaten your plums, and apologize. That is all there is to it.

But is that so? To test that we might ask what, if anything, the poem does that such a message does not. Here imagine that you are the poet's spouse—or perhaps room-mate or partner or host—and that you found this note on the icebox door: 'I ate your plums; sorry about that.' How would that be different from this poem?

Part of it is formal. You will probably not have noticed this when you read the poem, but, as one of my friends observed in the disputation referred to, there are patterns of sound that run through the poem, all leading up to a strong emphasis on the last line, 'so sweet and so cold'. 'Sweet' for example picks up the end rhymes of 'eaten', 'probably', and 'me'; 'and so cold' picks up the *d* and *l* from 'delicious', the *l* from 'plums', the *k* sound from the last line of each of the other stanzas, and, most of all, the enormously strong open *o*, which we have seen foreshadowed in weaker form in 'forgive' and 'icebox' and 'probably'. As my friend put it, these sounds 'have been laid out, given prominence, and anticipated, all as carefully as a key and scale in music'.[11]

But even if you assume that we could go on at length in this vein, establishing the formal complexity and coherence of what seems at first a purely ordinary statement, there remains the question to what end this formal composition exists. It could still be at bottom an empty expression, however mathematically or musically complex its organization of sounds. As the recipient of such an apology you might feel that it was ingenious, reflecting a lot of skill and effort, but still not very different in the end from 'sorry about that'.

This brings us to the heart of the poem, which is the definition

---

[11] The friend referred to is my colleague A. L. Becker, whom I thank for his help.

of feelings and social relations achieved in its tones of voice. Take, to begin with, the phrase, 'I have eaten', which stands as its own line at the very beginning of the poem. It is hard for anyone educated in the Western tradition not to hear behind this simple phrase echoes of the Garden of Eden: 'And hast thou eaten of the tree whereof I commanded that thou shouldst not eat?' This allusion is reinforced by the later isolation of the word 'saving' in a single line, and by the force of the phrase, again in a single line, 'Forgive me'.

What does the speaker do with this allusion? It could work in ways that are heavy-handed, portentous, mechanistic; but in fact it is quite delicate, precise, at once amusing and touching. See how it plays against the self-depreciating title—'This is just to say'—to create a real tension, the subject of which is the poem itself: is this poem a trivial, minor, quotidian gesture, or is it serious, even too serious?

The biblical reference is reinforced by the fact that what is eaten here turns out to be a fruit; but at the same time it is made less heavy-handed or merely allegorical by the fact that the fruit here is not the apple of tradition but a plum—far more delicious and tempting, and far more ordinary at least than that traditional fruit, in part because it is located, we learn, in the 'icebox'.

Yet, despite the clarity of these allusions, a voice within us wants to say that this simply cannot be an instance of the Fall; it is far too quotidian or trivial. To think of this event in such a grand way is ludicrous. But eating an apple is trivial and quotidian too; and in the second stanza the poem makes plain that the eating of the plums was an act with real moral significance, not simply as a matter of doctrine or theology, but as a matter of actual human relations, for they were not his but someone else's, and he did not eat just one but all of them. Once more we face the peculiar tension that it is the characteristic of this poem to stimulate: we are bound to feel, in part, that this is simply not a big deal, perhaps once more finding ourselves using the word 'trivial'; but it is not an entirely small thing either, and if a marriage or other relation were regularly marked by such transgressions it would be full of difficulty. (Just imagine what Jane Austen would make it mean.) And if the Fall means anything it will show up in the smallest details of life.

The speaker has in fact wronged his wife (let us assume), on however small a scale and no matter how understandable the temptation; what does he do about this fact? He acknowledges that the plums were themselves not trivial, but important to her; he also shows, especially in the 'probably', that he knows her, her tastes and values. This at once makes his offence the more serious and the poem a more adequate recompense, for this is not a stereotyped apology, any man to any woman, but one addressed to her. He shows that he knows her.

His acknowledgement is the initial point of the note itself— 'This is just to say'. But why 'just'? He is here minimizing both the expression and the wrong that gave rise to it; this is part of what leads some readers to take the poem as trivial. But he does not stop with the sentence begun in the title, and the sentiments upon which that sentence was based, but comes to see the need to go on, to take another step. And this is far from a small one: 'Forgive me'.

This is still not the end. Now he reaffirms the original act, at least in part, by making the temptation seem practically irresistible, indeed by trying to elicit his reader's imaginative sympathy, even complicity, to confirm what he has done. This is the significance of what we noticed earlier, the great emphasis and intensity given to 'so sweet and so cold'.

The speaker thus begins with a gesture designed to trivialize both what he has done and his present expression; but he finds he cannot do this; he recognizes that the wrong, however small, was real—she was saving the plums for breakfast. He then asks for forgiveness, at first on the basis of his repentance; but he discovers that this too will not work, for the repentance is not and cannot be entirely sincere; he is still in the temptation and cannot deny it. Then he asks for forgiveness, implicitly, on quite a different ground, that it is his nature—and ours too: we confirm it in our response to the last line—to yield to such temptations.

The poem ends with real sweetness, in his confidence that he will be forgiven. This is an enactment of trust, part of what makes it a love poem. (The other part is his knowledge of her.) But it also ends with a real coldness, in the inescapably fallen nature of his being and ours. Yet it is this coldness that makes the sweetness possible: the sweetness is the blessing that he knows that with all his faults, he loves and is loved after all.

To return now to the question whether this really is a poem, or really any good: you can see that I think that the answer to both questions is yes. On the other hand, the negative judgments I describe are not without basis, for the poem itself is perpetually creating a tension between the view that it, and the events it speaks of, are crucial, important, aspects of eternal human truth, and the view that it is all too trivial, ordinary, quotidian to count for much. Both parts, the claim of meaning and the self-depreciation are parts of the poem, and important parts: indeed this is the tension at the centre of the piece.

In this the poem captures a tension present in our own everyday life including as lawyers: are the details of our lives merely quotidian and trivial? Or do they make up a moral and aesthetic drama of real importance? This is a question to which law itself speaks. The truth that grandeur can be found in the ordinary, the great in the small, is in this poem placed against the truth that the ordinary is truly ordinary; what the poem represents is thus a crucial and unresolvable uncertainty at the heart of human life. It holds itself out as a response to be imitated, finding a kind of redemption in the tones of voice with which it speaks, at once serious and comic, overstated and understated, claiming and disowning meaning, all in a gesture of love and trust.

Let me briefly make it plain that the question at the heart of this poem is also at the heart of the law. Something happens in the client's life, say an unwanted pregnancy, or an arrest for drunkenness, or a restriction in the use of his land: does this mean anything, does it matter? These are the questions for the lawyer, whose task it is to see that it does matter and to give it meaning in the language of the law. We live our lives on the faith that this can be done, that law can convert the raw material of human experience—the pain, the fury, the loss—into the material of meaning, and in such a way as to permit or invite or enable meaningful action in response. Philosophy too, at least as Plato does it, lives out these questions: does it matter that Phaedrus is infatuated with the rhetoric of Lysias? What does it mean?

Williams's poem can be taken as an instance of a text that does not say the same thing always, but offers its reader a drama, an experience of discovery, that has many of the qualities of a conversation. I have offered one version of this poem, but it is only one version and surely not complete; what is more, I respect the views of my friends who read and judge it very differently.

This poem is at heart the occasion for an activity of thought and reflection and argument, in principle not reducible to an outcome, which it stimulates and rewards. Its value is the value of that activity. In this it is like the best of philosophy and the best of law.

In all three fields it is a mistake—a denial of life—to try to write a text that will say the same thing always, or to read a well-written text as if that were the writer's goal. Philosopher, lawyer, poet—all three do their real work in the conversations they establish with their reader, or among their readers. This is where the life and meaning are. There is a side of each of us that wants to forget this, and to live in a simpler world of statements that are true or false, rules that are just or unjust, poems that are beautiful or ordinary, denying our responsibility to face the uncertainties and tensions with which even the best work—especially the best work—presents us. But this will not do: the best work in each field teaches us otherwise; and in each field we are constantly in need of the education offered by the others.

INTERDISCIPLINARY LEGAL SCHOLARSHIP AS GUILTY PLEASURE: THE CASE OF LAW AND LITERATURE

Jane B. Baron

Legal scholarship has increasingly borrowed from other, non-law, disciplines; as it has done so, legal scholars have taken increasing interest in the possibilities and limits of interdisciplinarity. Tellingly, virtually all discussions of interdisciplinary scholarship call upon two related metaphors. The first is a metaphor of border-guarding. This is an immigrant–emigrant scholarship, employing tropes of insiders and outsiders, residents and aliens; it relies on images of imperialism, scavenging, and parasitism. The second metaphor is one of fidelity. This metaphoric realm employs tropes of seduction, enchantment, betrayal, faithlessness and abandonment, calling on images of marriage, adultery, and divorce. The two metaphors are linked by a common theme, the theme of boundaries that can be respected or crossed.

The 'interdiscipline' of law and literature is no exception to this rule. Literature is sometimes offered as a rich, humanist supplement to dry, technical law. What will result from their mixing is an alliance beneficial to both parties: law will be improved by moral and psychological lessons from literature, while literature will gain force from application in the world of practical affairs. Here is a happy marriage.

But the connections between literature and law might not always or necessarily be positive. In the legal setting—famously described by Robert Cover as the 'field of pain and death'[1]—the

---

[1] Robert Cover, 'Violence and the Word' (1986) 95 *Yale Law Journal* [*Yale LJ*] 1601.

use of interpretive techniques borrowed from literature can be dangerous. It has been argued, for example, that judges employing the freedom and creativity of contemporary literary theorists could easily betray their proper role as appliers, not makers, of law.[2] Interdisciplinarity here is transgression, the *over*stepping of important boundaries.

Border metaphors raise questions about the legitimacy of discipline-traversing scholarship. What does a scholar from one discipline need to know in order to 'employ' another discipline? Can we really learn another discipline (late in life? without formal training?)? And if we cannot, what is it we borrow from the other discipline? Facts? Theories? The formulation of questions or the organization of research problems? What kinds of interdisciplinary work represent 'rigorous' scholarship, as opposed to what one sceptic has called 'intellectual voyeurism'?[3] Most importantly, what are the underlying ways in which we categorize knowledge?

Curiously, much of the writing on 'law and', by lawyers and non-lawyers alike, ignores these questions and assumes the integrity of 'law', 'philosophy', 'history', 'literature', and the like as separate disciplines. This assumption of separateness underlies some of the more powerful critiques of attempts by legal scholars to enlist other disciplines in the service of legal arguments. Critiques of law and history, law and philosophy, and law and humanities share a common structure. In each area, the non-law discipline is presented as having serious, 'rigorous' standards. Legal scholars are presented as lacking the knowledge, commitment, background, interest, energy, and common decency required to learn those standards, so their work does not conform to them. Indeed, legal scholars are said to 'abuse' the non-law discipline, enlisting it toward ends for which it is not suited. These critiques invoke both the border-guarding and fidelity metaphors; legal scholars are accused of transgressing into foreign domains they do not truly understand, and also of adulterous style couplings serving solely the selfish needs of the lawyer.

These arguments seem to assume that there really *are* ends to law or legal scholarship and that those ends really *are* different

---

[2] R. A. Posner, *Law and Literature* (revised edn, Cambridge, Mass., 1998), 237.

[3] Brian Leiter, 'Intellectual Voyeurism in Legal Scholarship' (1992) 4 *Yale Journal of Law and Humanities* [*Yale JL & Hum.*] 79, 80.

from those of philosophy or history. In the compare-and-contrast strategy of interdisciplinary critique, law is depicted as a place, a bounded space, filled only with rules. Nowhere is this more true than in the case of law and literature, where 'law' tends to be portrayed in stereotypical terms as wholly technical, analytical, non-emotional and—above all—doctrinal. This picture is so hackneyed, so caricatured, as to suggest an unacknowledged rhetorical investment in keeping law's borders drawn tightly around the domain of rules. Such an investment is of great cultural significance, revealing a curious attachment to a vision of law that ostensibly has been discredited in the United States for over fifty years, the Langdellian vision of law as autonomous.

The border and fidelity metaphors tell a disconcerting, sexualized, story in response to this paradox. Ideally, the couplings of law and other disciplines are healthy and natural, satisfying on both sides. But, like border crossings, the couplings of 'law and' can be dangerous, involving compromises—of standards, of integrity—demeaning to each partner. It may be that knowledge, in its 'best' form, is pure. This is why, some argue, scholars should remain faithful to their disciplines of original training; they should commit themselves rather than skittishly playing the field. Purity also requires internal consistency; it cannot be contaminated with other strains of thought, with foreign blood or cultural difference. The pleasures of interdisciplinarity, then, are guilty ones, and the pure scholar may need to forego them.

Langdellian Orthodoxy and the Creation of Law as a Place

To understand the conceptualization of law as a place filled with rules, one must start with Christopher Columbus Langdell. Leading historical accounts agree that the 'professionalization' of American legal education began in 1870 when Langdell became Dean at Harvard.[4] Langdell's contribution was the 'case method', pursuant to which students would read cases in an area of law and extract, deduce, or infer (the proper verb is highly contested) from them the transcendent principles of that legal field. The principles

---

[4] See, e.g., R. Stevens, *Law School: Legal Education in America From the 1850s to the 1980s* (Chapel Hill, NC, 1983); R. F. Ferguson, *Law and Letters in American Culture* (Cambridge, Mass., 1984).

could be classified and organized 'scientifically'. Subsequent cases could then be criticized for failing to conform to those principles or praised for properly applying them. (As to how one knew which cases correctly expressed the principles and which perverted those principles, well, never mind that small difficulty.)

It is worth pausing to consider Langdell's vision, sometimes called 'orthodox' or 'classical' legal thought:

> Classical orthodoxy was a particular kind of legal theory—a set of ideas to be put to work from *inside* by those who operate legal institutions, not a set of ideas about those institutions reflecting an *outside* perspective, whether a sociological, historical or economic explanation of legal phenomena.[5]

Langdellians 'treated law as an intellectual discipline independent of theology, moral philosophy, economics, or political science, one that involved the application of scientific methods to common law materials'.[6] To a classicist, law should be *formal, systematic*, and *autonomous*, that is, 'its principles derived from distinctively legal materials, not resting on politically or philosophically controversial claims or methods'.[7]

To restate this point in a slightly different way, there was no 'and' to law in its Langdellian form. Indeed, this lack of 'and' was what made law law. Putting the point still another way, the Langdellian vision of law as autonomous created distinct borders that separated what was part of or 'inside' law (legal principles) from what was outside (everything else).

Langdell's view of law as formally connected, logically inferable principles immanent in cases, complete in itself and requiring resort to nothing 'outside', was almost immediately contested. Legal progressives, for example, argued that law should not be 'idealized as an abstract and autonomous system of norms', but instead should be 'seen as a means to an end, a socially embedded and purposive set of activities aimed at satisfying human wants collectively expressed as public policies'.[8] Legal realists similarly

---

[5] Thomas C. Grey, 'Langdell's Orthodoxy' (1983) 45 *University of Pittsburgh Law Review* 1, 6.

[6] Thomas C. Grey, 'Modern American Legal Thought' (1996) 106 *Yale LJ* 493, 495 (book review).

[7] Grey, n. 6 above, 496.

[8] Grey, n. 6 above, 498. For more on 'Progressivism', see G. Edward White, *Patterns of American Legal Thought* (Indianapolis, Ind., 1978), 99–135.

resisted Langdellian formalism, arguing, *inter alia*, that legal principles alone could neither dictate nor explain outcomes.[9] This particular challenge survives to the present day, in the form of the indeterminacy critique for which critical legal studies (CLS) is (in)famous.[10]

While progressivism, realism, and CLS obviously do not exhaust the field of intellectual movements within American law, they are typical and noteworthy in taking as central the question of law's autonomy and in conceptualizing that question in terms of what is inside and what is outside law. These issues have remained central in American legal discourse, as is illustrated by Judge Richard Posner's famous essay, *The Decline of Law as an Autonomous Discipline: 1962–1987*.[11] Posner begins by describing his experience as a student at Harvard Law School in the early 1960s, an experience confirming that, a century after Langdell came to Harvard, law was still being treated as at least relatively autonomous:

The faculty believed, or at least appeared to believe, that the only thing law students needed to study was authoritative legal texts—judicial and administrative opinions, statutes, rules—and that the only essential preparation for a legal scholar was the knowledge of what was in those texts . . . The difference from Langdell's day—a difference that was the legacy of Holmes and the legal realists—was that law now was recognized to be a deliberate instrument of social control, so that one had to know something about society to be able to understand law, criticize it, and improve it. The 'something,' however, was what any intelligent person with a good general education and some common sense knew; or could pick up from the legal texts themselves . . . : a set of basic ethical and political values, some knowledge of institutions, some acquaintance with the workings of the economy.[12]

---

[9] See, e.g., Felix Cohen, 'Transcendental Nonsense and the Functional Approach' (1935) 35 *Columbia Law Review* 809. On legal realism generally, see L. Kalman, *Legal Realism at Yale 1927–1960* (Chapel Hill, NC, 1986), W. Twining, *Karl Llewellyn and the Realist Movement* (London, 1973), and N. Duxbury, *Patterns of American Jurisprudence* (Oxford, 1995).

[10] On the indeterminacy critique generally, see M. Kelman, *A Guide to Critical Legal Studies* (Cambridge, Mass., 1987), 257–62. On the legacy of realism to critical legal studies, see Joseph William Singer, 'Legal Realism Now' (1988) 76 *California Law Review* 465; David Kairys, 'Introduction' in D. Kairys (ed.), *The Politics of Law* (3rd edn, New York, 1998), 3–6.

[11] (1987) 100 *Harvard Law Review* [*Harv. L. Rev.*] 761.

[12] Posner, n. 11 above, 763.

The remainder of the article examines why the belief in law's autonomy has eroded. Posner cites several factors,[13] but more interesting than the reasons themselves is Posner's complete certainty that, by the time of his writing, law *had* in fact declined as an autonomous discipline.[14] Certainly law and economics, which Posner in many senses pioneered, has made great, and probably enduring, inroads into legal education and theory.[15] But

---

[13] The political consensus that once characterized the academy had shattered, so that two equally distinguished legal thinkers facing the same legal problem might come up with two incompatible solutions. Posner, n. 11 above, 766–7. There had been a boom in disciplines 'that are complementary to law, particularly economics and philosophy' (769). Confidence in lawyers' ability to solve the major problems of the legal system had collapsed (772). The rise in the prestige and authority of scientific and other exact modes of inquiry in general had made conventional legal analysis look *passé* (773). Finally, the constitution and statutes (as opposed to common law) had become increasingly important sources of law, but legal education, still centred on case analysis, did not train students to interpret these sources (777).

[14] Of course, Posner is not the only scholar to have argued that law's autonomy has substantially eroded. See, e.g., Marc Galanter and Mark Alan Edwards, 'Introduction: The Path of the Law Ands' (1997) *Wisconsin Law Review* [*Wis. L. Rev.*] 375, 376 (arguing that 'a consensus that legal activity was to be explained and understood as the product of exogenous forces [has] displaced the long-challenged but resilient faith that law was an autonomous realm . . .'). But see n. 18 below and accompanying text.

[15] There does seem to be consensus that law and economics has been influential in a way that no other 'law and' has. See, e.g., Robin West, *Caring for Justice* (New York, 1997) 180–1 (describing how law and economics has been influential in ways in which law and literature has not approached). Nonetheless, many of the points made below with respect to other non-law fields could be made about economics as well. Many economists would no doubt criticize particular legal economic arguments as 'bad' economics, i.e., as economic treatments that are not 'rigorous' and do not conform to the 'standards' of professional economists. So the two fields have by no means merged.

Still, the 'and' relationship in law and economics seems different from the 'and' relationships in the other 'law ands'. A complete and authoritative explanation of that difference is well beyond the scope of this essay. One very tentative theory can be offered. The thesis of the first wave of law and economics theories was that common law decision making was already guided by an unstated (and possibly unconscious?) commitment to the goal of efficiency. See, e.g., Maxwell L. Stearns, 'Restoring Positive Law and Economics: Introduction to the Public Choice Issue' (1998) 6 *George Mason University Law Review* 709; R. A. Posner, *Economic Analysis of Law* (1st edn, Boston, 1972), 98. This first wave, that is, purported to be descriptive. So in developing law and economics, Posner and his compatriots did not have to ask courts to do anything new, think in different ways, etc. They simply had to tell courts to do what they were already doing—but they had to make the judges do it more explicitly, and with better understanding of how to determine efficient results. If legal analysis always *was* economic, then economics was never something that had to be added.

Of course, now, many have argued, law and economics has turned from

what is striking if one reads articles about the other 'law and' fields—law and society, law and history, and so forth—is their absolute confidence that law *remains* an autonomous discipline. Indeed, a major complaint in scholarship reflecting on various 'law ands' is how little impact the 'and' field has had.

Typical and illustrative in this regard are the assessments of the law and society movement, one of the oldest 'law ands',[16] on the state of interdisciplinarity in the American legal academy. Law and society scholars are diverse in methods and outlook, but they share 'a general commitment to approach law with a vision and with methods that come from outside the discipline itself; and they share a commitment to explain legal phenomena (though not necessarily all legal phenomena) in terms of their social setting'.[17] Even the movement's most ardent supporters concede that it has had but limited impact.[18] Consider the following reasons offered to explain the movement's minimal influence:

The whole thrust of legal education goes against the grain of law and society. Law school tries to empty the mind of all 'extraneous' matter, the better to develop legal skills. The finest products of the process, of course, end up as teachers.

The law and society movement stresses the importance of what is happening in society, as opposed to exclusive attention to what is 'inside' the system. This means, first of all, that one has to know something about the surrounding society—things lawyers are unlikely to know, in any systematic way.[19]

A striking aspect of this analysis is its dependence on the inside–outside metaphor. There are methods internal to the legal discipline, and methods that come 'from outside the discipline

---

description to prescription, but I will not prolong this digression by seeking to elaborate a theory that would explain its continuing force. Law and economics may well be different from other law ands, but for simplicity's sake I will not clutter the text below by a string of clauses explicitly excepting law and economics from the discussion.

[16] See Galanter and Edwards, n. 14 above, at 376 ('Law and society and law and economics are the oldest and most institutionalized' of the 'law ands'.).

[17] Lawrence M. Friedman, 'The Law and Society Movement' (1986) 38 *Stanford Law Review* [*Stan. L. Rev.*] 763.

[18] See, e.g., Galanter and Edwards, n. 14 above, 380 ('even supporters concur with the judgment . . . that law and society has been unable to gain more than a toehold in the legal academy') (internal quotations omitted).

[19] Friedman, n. 17 above, 774–5.

itself'. Similarly, there is whatever is 'inside' the legal system, and then the '[outside] surrounding society'. Moreover, the attitude from 'inside' law is one of complete indifference to skills that are not distinctly legal; they are not skills lawyers need to have, because they do not relate to what lawyers *do*. Putting this point another way, since lawyers work inside the realm of law, they do not need to know how to do things outside that realm.

John Henry Schlegel, who has studied how empiricism has been received in legal education since the realist period, reaches conclusions strikingly similar to those suggested above. Here is his explanation of why empirical legal research never took hold in law schools:

[A]lthough there may have been a great deal of talk about teaching people to think like a lawyer, whatever that might be, the real subject matter was going to be law as rule, the rules of law. . . . If one was going to take a broader, or even a different view of law . . . then one was going to teach political science or history or economics or what have you, not law.[20]

Schlegel is convinced that lawyers and law professors see the 'main business of doing law' as 'doing rules'.[21] Rules, indeed, are what the 'inside' of law consists of. Empirical social science is therefore downright threatening to 'the professional identity of the law professor', for it suggests 'that the words of law might not be too important, that the special preserve of the law professor might not be too special and that, since law was not just rules, the rule of law might not be just a matter of following rules either'.[22]

Notice here how 'professional identity' is tied to a Langdellian vision of law as autonomous, and this is the source of resistance to methodology or information from 'outside' law. Although Schlegel concludes by conceding that the norms of scholarship and the identity of the law professor have shifted somewhat over time in the direction of policy analysis, he asserts that in this form of policy analysis 'empirical knowledge is always relevant but never determinative; policies can always trump facts or make them irrelevant. And so it is the rule that remains the centerpiece of discussion'.[23]

Law emerges in these discussions as a *place*, a realm, a territory

[20] J. H. Schlegel, *American Legal Realism and Empirical Social Science* (Chapel Hill, NC, 1995), 253.   [21] Schlegel, n. 20 above, 255.
[22] Schlegel, n. 20 above.   [23] Schlegel, n. 20 above, 256.

with boundaries. And it is a particular sort of place. It is a place of *rules*. Xenophobically suspicious of influences from outside its borders, and solipsistically disinterested in examining the actual impact of rules, the place in which law resides is enclosed, walled, sealed off. In a curious and surprising return to its classical origins, law in its powerful resistance to other disciplines declares itself as precisely the autonomous discipline Langdell sought to create.

Borders as Sites of Possibility and Danger

Places are demarked and defined by borders; they have boundaries. While boundaries separate one place from another, they can also be sites of connection, the *loci* of alliances and cross-cultural exchanges. *Because* there is a divide between law and other disciplines, law can be connected to those other disciplines through some sort of 'and' relationship. Thus, the independence of law from other disciplines creates the possibility of interdisciplinarity. Periodically, scholars from non-law fields have offered to create interdisciplinary cross-cultural exchanges with law, proffering learning from 'outside' law's borders to enrich the life within.

In a 1993 article, Martha Nussbaum made such a case for philosophy.[24] First, she argued, philosophy could shed light on basic concepts used in legal arguments all the time, concepts (such as justice, equality, liberty, free will, and the like) 'to the understanding of which professional philosophers have devoted a lot of effort'.[25] Second, philosophers' 'systematic and detailed inquiries' about 'what belief and knowledge are, what rationality is, what interpreting a text is, what methods are and are not conducive to understanding' had much to offer the law, 'which inevitably talks about evidence and knowledge, about interpretation and objectivity, and about the nature of rationality'.[26] Finally, Nussbaum suggested, Socratic questioning in the law school classroom, however searching, seeks neat conclusions, but philosophical exploration of the complexity of the underlying

---

[24] Martha C. Nussbaum, 'The Use and Abuse of Philosophy in Legal Education' (1993) 45 *Stan. L. Rev.* 1627.
[25] Nussbaum, n. 24 above, 1630.
[26] Nussbaum, n. 24 above, 1637.

issues could counteract this tendency toward oversimplification.[27]

Nussbaum was careful to note the difficulties that might attend efforts to conjoin law and philosophy. 'Philosophy', she noted, 'is sometimes too indifferent to empirical fact, to science, to history, to psychology. This defect, bad enough when philosophy is on its own, is absolutely fatal if it wishes to speak effectively to lawyers.'[28] In addition, 'because of its concern for open-ended investigation, for wonder in the best sense, philosophy is often slow to move to a determinate solution. . . . But lawyers want and need definite outcomes'.[29] Finally, there will be times when the philosophically best solution to a problem cannot be implemented within the current institutional structure: 'Judges are never free to go for the best. They are constrained by history, by precedent, by the nature of legal and political institutions.'[30]

Notice how both Nussbaum's affirmative case and the caveats she notes presuppose real differences between law and philosophy. Philosophy must 'speak' to lawyers; it must meet lawyers' needs, which presumably are not philosophy's needs. Law students 'can use the insights of philosophers', but the goal is not for them to *be* philosophers—they are training, after all, to be lawyers.[31] For their part, philosophers need to retain their connection to their own 'disciplinary base'.[32] In Nussbaum's vision, law and philosophy can be joined together, but they cannot be integrated. Rather, they remain separate disciplines, useful to one another despite fundamental differences in their conventions and aims.

A certain, rather hopeful, picture of interdisciplinarity emerges from Nussbaum's consideration of the relation between law and philosophy. In this picture, the separate, independent territories—places—of law and philosophy will be connected, producing two adjacent realms each of which is stronger for alliance with the other. Interdisciplinarity, in this view, is supplementation, enrichment,

---

[27] Nussbaum, n. 24 above, 1640. Nussbaum sought to encourage in law school classrooms 'wonder of the Socratic sort', i.e., 'a concerted rigorous inquiry into the subtleties of some foundational issue, informed by the relevant empirical information'. [28] Nussbaum, n. 24 above, 1642. [29] Nussbaum, n. 24 above. [30] Nussbaum, n. 24 above, 1643. [31] Nussbaum, n. 24 above. ('The aim should not be to produce students who think like philosophers; the aim should be to produce students who can use the insights of philosophy in a flexible way in grappling with the practical problems they encounter.') [32] Nussbaum, n. 24 above, 1644.

enhancement. Each discipline retains its separate identity, but that identity is improved by its encounter with the alien other.

Although borders may be sites of great possibility, as Nussbaum suggests, they can also be sites of great danger, places of imperialistic trespass. The very independence that creates the possibility of interdisciplinarity paradoxically provides law the power to resist, hijack, distort, and abuse other disciplines. Nussbaum's optimism over the possibilities for fruitful interdisciplinary connection between law and other fields is not widely shared. Most assessments of attempts by legal scholars to use learning from non-law disciplines are deeply critical.

One scholar has dubbed legal scholars' use of philosophy, for example, 'intellectual voyeurism': a 'class of sub-standard interdisciplinary work' characterized by 'superficial and ill-informed treatment of serious ideas, apparently done for intellectual "titillation" or to advertise, in a pretentious way, the "sophistication" of the writer'.[33] Primarily a 'forum for posturing and the misuse of knowledge', the paradigmatic traits of intellectual voyeurism are a misunderstanding of the philosophical ideas at issue; a lack of critical knowledge of the relevant secondary literature; and a pretence of intellectual sophistication.[34] Legal scholars with intellectual integrity would 'engage in a deeper study of the other disciplines before rushing into print', that is, they would be 'more rigorous'.[35]

Obviously, work can only be 'sub-standard' as compared to a standard; the allegation of 'misuse' of philosophy implies a proper use; the 'standard' to which scholars should be held will involve 'rigour' and 'real intellectual encounters'.[36] The presumption is clear: philosophy *is* a discipline, as bounded in its own way as

---

[33] Brian Leiter, n. 3 above, 80. In fairness, Nussbaum primarily addressed the question of how philosophy and law *could* in the ideal case be used to enhance one another. As to the *actual* use of philosophy by lawyers, she was not impressed: 'Most of what I have read on emotion and empathy in the law, for example, would not even get a very high grade as undergraduate paper written for a course of mine at Brown; it bears no interesting relation to the professional literature in the discipline.' Nussbaum, n. 24 above, 1644.

[34] Leiter, n. 3 above, 80. See also Charles W. Collier, 'Interdisciplinary Legal Scholarship in Search of a Paradigm' (1993) 42 *Duke Law Journal* [*Duke LJ*] 840, 852 ('The "citation" of philosophers and their nonlegal theories is primarily an attempt to import greater intellectual authority to an area of law that seems to lack or need it.').   [35] Leiter, n. 3 above, 80.

[36] Leiter, n. 3 above, 104.

law. One should not toy with philosophy, but should learn it. Otherwise, one should leave it alone.

'Rigour' and 'standards' are themes that surface again, and again, in discussions of legal scholars' use of history. Interest in the 'and' of law and history has focused on how legal scholars (and sometimes judges and lawyers) enlist historical sources in support of claims about law. In theory, the claims could be about any area of law at all, but the claims that have attracted attention most recently have been claims about constitutional law. More specifically, the claims have concerned the role of 'civic republicanism' in constitutional theory.[37]

Reviews of lawyers' use of historical sources in support of their arguments for civic republicanism are unremittingly negative. Law professors are accused of 'ransacking' or 'scavenging' the past 'to find arguments for whatever vision of the social order they wished to promote'.[38] Civic republicans' use of history has been further characterized as 'one-sided', 'highly selective', and insensitive to context.[39]

The problems with civic republicans' use of history echo long-standing concerns about how legal scholars employ history generally, in contexts other than discussions of republicanism. Legal scholars, it is said, do not really produce history, but 'law office history' or 'lawyer's history'.[40] Law office history is not history 'according to the canons of the academic historical method', that

---

[37] On civic republicanism generally, see 'Symposium: The Civic Republican Tradition' (1988) 97 *Yale LJ* 1493. Civic republicanism can be understood as an alternative political theory, and not as political or constitutional history. See Jane B. Baron and Jeffrey L. Dunoff, 'Against Market Rationality: Moral Critiques of Economic Analysis in Legal Theory' (1996) 17 *Cardozo Law Review* 431, 452 n. 89. But some civic republicans have sought support for their arguments in historical sources, and it is this attempt to ground civic republicanism in the historical record that has made historians apoplectic. For an overview of the controversy, see Nomi Maya Stolzenberg, 'A Book of Laughter and Forgetting: Kalman's "Strange Career" and the Marketing of Civic Republicanism' (1998) 111 *Harv. L. Rev.* 1025 (book review).

[38] The metaphor of 'ransacking', and the remainder of the quote, is from L. Kalman, *The Strange Career of Legal Liberalism* (New Haven, 1996). The metaphor of 'scavenging' is from Kathryn Abrams, 'Law's Republicanism' (1988) 97 *Yale LJ* 1591.

[39] Martin S. Flaherty, 'History "Lite" in Modern American Constitutionalism' (1995) 95 *Columbia Law Review* 523, 567–79.

[40] The term was coined by Alfred H. Kelly in 'Clio and the Court: An Illicit Love Affair' (1965) *Supreme Court Review* 119.

is, it is not used to ascertain truth but as a form of advocacy.[41] It asks questions of the past that the past cannot answer, in that it seeks to use the past to answer questions that were not thought of at the time; it thus abuses historical method.[42] It is selective, emphasizing facts supportive of a claim and disregarding those that might conflict with or undermine the claim.[43]

The fundamental idea of this critique is identical to that of the critique of lawyers' use of philosophy. It is that historians have standards for 'doing' history that legal scholars tend not to meet.[44] One of the basic standards legal scholars consistently violate 'is simply getting the elementary facts straight'.[45] Another is 'the necessity of thorough reading, or at least citation, of both primary and secondary source material generally recognized by historians as central to a given question'.[46] Nor do lawyers meet the procedural standard of 'viewing, or at least attempting to view, events, ideas, and controversies in a larger context'.[47]

The parallels between the critiques of law and history and those of law and philosophy are clear. Each non-law discipline is presented as an integral, independent realm—a separate place— with its own 'rigorous' internal standards. Legal scholars (who come, after all, from a different place) are presented as unable or unwilling to learn those standards.

This point is often underscored by a strategy of compare-and-contrast, whereby 'real' philosophy or history (etc.) is juxtaposed against philosophy or history as employed by legal scholars. 'For all their excursions into other disciplines', one historian writes, 'historians still favor context, change, and explanation. Despite their acquaintance with Bailyn, Wood, and others, authors of

---

[41] John Phillip Reid, 'Law and History' (1993) 27 *Loyola LA Law Review* 193, 201.   [42] Reid, n. 41 above, 202–3.

[43] Reid, n. 41 above, 197.

[44] Flaherty, n. 39 above, 551 ('Among the academics and professionals who make up the audience which constitutional theorists seek to persuade, it is axiomatic that any argument drawing from another established discipline is convincing to the extent that it abides by the conventions of that discipline.').

[45] Flaherty, n. 39 above, 553. But see Mark Tushnet, 'Interdisciplinary Legal Scholarship: The Case of History-In-Law' (1996) 71 *Chicago-Kent Law Review* 909, 932 ('[O]ne might think that legal scholars using history in law would perform badly if they got the facts wrong. One might think that, but one would be wrong.')(footnotes omitted).   [46] Flaherty, n. 39 above, 553.

[47] Flaherty, n. 39 above, 554.

lawyer's legal history value text, continuity, and prescription.'[48] In a similar vein, another commentator suggests that philosophical sources are used entirely differently 'inside' the humanities from the way they are used in law. 'Authority' within the humanities is 'earned'; sources such as Plato and Aristotle have 'garner[ed] support through centuries of reasoned debate and intellectual assessment'.[49] But 'authority' within law is 'institutional': 'the mere fact that a case has been decided one way rather than another, or that a judge has made a particular pronouncement, provides grounds ("authority") for deciding another case similarly or in conformity with the judge's pronouncement—whatever it may be'.[50] When legal scholars discuss Nietzsche, Saussure, or Foucault they commit something akin to a category mistake: they 'attempt to bring greater "intellectual authority" to a form of scholarship that, nevertheless, remains intractably dependent upon and derivative of the "institutional authority" of the judiciary'.[51]

Given lawyers' routine misunderstanding and misuse of learning from other fields, the sort of interdisciplinarity that Nussbaum proposed would be downright foolhardy. It is no accident that the term 'border-guarding' is used openly in the scholarship critiquing lawyers' use of non-law disciplines.[52] Who would want to confederate or ally with people ignorant of and indifferent to important aspects of one's own professional identity? Indeed, if legal scholars cannot or will not assimilate the conventions and aims of other fields, interdisciplinarity is dangerous. More accurately, interdisciplinarity is just a cover for encroachment, colonization, or other acts of piracy by which non-law disciplines are selfishly and faithlessly deployed for distinctly legal purposes.

[48] Kalman, *Strange Career*, n. 38 above, 180. Kalman argues that while legal scholars seek to use the past as authority, historians do not consider the past authoritative; 'to the historian, there are no "lessons from the past" '.

[49] Charles W. Collier, 'The Use and Abuse of Humanistic Theory in Law: Reexamining the Assumptions of Interdisciplinary Legal Scholarship' (1991) 41 *Duke LJ* 191, 220.

[50] Collier, n. 49 above, 219.

[51] Collier, n. 49 above, 205. Putting this point another way, 'the "citation" of philosophers and their nonlegal theories . . . is not an attempt to engage these philosophical theories on their own terms or according to the nonlegal canons of discussion and professional criteria proper to them'. Collier, Interdisciplinary Legal Scholarship, n. 34 above, 852.

[52] See, e.g., Laura Kalman, 'Border Patrol: Reflections on the Turn to History in Legal Scholarship' (1997) 66 *Fordham Law Review* 87.

Interdisciplinarity in Legal Scholarship

The critiques of ostensibly 'law and' scholarship raise the question whether interdisciplinarity is truly possible. If each discipline is, like law, a self-enclosed independent space, with methodologies, standards, and aims more or less unique, then attempts at interdisciplinarity seem doomed to failure. The critiques suggest that at any given moment, one can be doing law *or* one can be doing history (*or* philosophy, etc.), but never both.

But what if disciplines are not hermetically sealed territories? The force of the critiques of legal interdisciplinarity seem to depend critically on assumptions about 'disciplinarity' that are themselves questionable. The critiques of interdisciplinarity have led, in their turn, to consideration of whether 'disciplines' are indeed separate spaces and of how the notion of 'interdisciplinarity' should be conceptualized.

One theory is that the discipline of law has never seriously tried to make 'interdisciplinary' connections to other disciplines. Mark Tushnet has made this argument in the context of law and history.[53] Like the historians we have just encountered, Tushnet believes that 'history is a practice' with distinct aims, and that it makes sense to ask questions such as 'What constitutes a good performance within that practice? Who determines what constitutes good historical practice?'[54] Like other historians, Tushnet asserts that legal scholars are not doing 'history'. They are engaging in 'their own genre of scholarship, which I call history-in-law (instead of history). I believe that history functions in that genre as decoration rather than authority.'[55]

If Tushnet were following in the footsteps of the historians described above, this observation about history-as-decoration would be offered as a critique—a 'there they go, misusing the past again' type of charge. But instead Tushnet makes a leap, suggesting that 'the criteria for determining whether someone has done well at the practice of history-in-law may be different from those for determining whether someone has done well at the practice of

---

[53] Tushnet, n. 45 above.
[54] Tushnet, n. 45 above, 917. In Tushnet's view, 'historians try to emphasize the pastness of the past. They take up particular events, ideas, and institutions as they were in the past, and situate them in as full a context as they can' (916).
[55] Tushnet, n. 45 above, 914.

history, and they may be developed and applied by lawyers and legal academics rather than historians'.[56] In other words, history-in-law is not the practice of the discipline/field of history, it is a practice of the discipline/field of law.

This conceptualization keeps the divisions between disciplines intact. The very practices that the other historians condemn because they are not truly 'history' Tushnet forgives precisely because they are not truly 'history'. As long as we understand that legal scholars are just doing *law*, Tushnet seems to say, where is the problem? His conclusion makes this point explicit:

Law-office history is a legal practice, not a historical one. The criteria for evaluating it, for determining what is a successful performance, must be drawn from legal practice rather than from historical practice. *I believe that the same conclusion can be drawn about interdisciplinary legal scholarship generally* (emphasis added).[57]

That last sentence is quite interesting. Law and history (and philosophy, and empirical research, etc.) are independent disciplines, separate practices. When lawyers 'do' history (philosophy, etc.) they do not actually engage in the practices that belong to the discipline of history (philosophy, etc.), but really engage in practices that belong to the discipline of law. It is not that legal scholars *cannot* meet the standards of other disciplines, it is that they are not even trying to meet them. So what is happening when lawyers use/abuse/employ/etc. these other fields is just not interdisciplinary. Interdisciplinarity, in short, simply isn't happening.

Another legal historian, G. Edward White, begins from premises quite similar to Tushnet's, but reaches a quite different conclusion: the failure of legal scholars to produce truly interdisciplinary work reveals that the very idea of a disciplinary perspective or concept has become unintelligible.[58] Like Tushnet, White thinks that scholars engaged in purportedly interdisciplinary work actually are engaged in a distinctly legal practice, which he sees as the practice of shedding light on 'contemporary public policy

---

[56] Tushnet, n. 45 above, 917.
[57] Tushnet, n. 45 above, 934–5.
[58] G. Edward White, 'Reflections on the "Republican Revival": Interdisciplinary Scholarship in the Legal Academy' (1994) 6 *Yale JL & Hum.* 1.

debates'.[59] White recognizes the potential for abuse when one discipline is enlisted to serve the agendas of a very different discipline,[60] but, White argues, the 'distortion' that abuse theorists worry about is only a problem if each field truly has its own distinct standards, rules, practices, etc. In light of postmodern thinking, that assumption is, White notes, quite essentialist and quite naive:

The Kuhnian dilemma, that no discipline could achieve a truly objective, universalistic research design for its practitioners and therefore assure that its scholars would be properly 'disciplined,' could be said to exist everywhere in academic life. 'Economics,' 'literature,' 'history,' and other scholarly fields had no transcendent body of data and research techniques that superseded the ideological leanings of scholars.[61]

'What, then', White asks, have been 'the governing assumptions of "law and" scholarship?'[62]

Practitioners of 'law and' did not set out to supplant the traditional scholarly orientations of the legal professorate, since the extralegal disciplines they drew upon were enlisted in the service of those orientations, contemporary doctrine and policy. Instead, those practitioners seemed to be making an implicit concession that the traditional scholarly orientations of the legal academy, if conducted exclusively within an intraprofessional framework, produced unstimulating work, . . . 'Interdisciplinary' scholarship allegedly reinvigorated the research design of the legal academy by bringing in fresh, extraprofessional perspectives, the perspectives of other 'disciplines.' But in the process . . . the intelligibility of a disciplinary perspective, indeed the concept of an academic discipline, became elusive.[63]

---

[59] White, n. 58 above, 24 ('[Existing "law ands"] start from the assumption that 'legal' scholarship of any kind is ultimately relevant to the discussion of contemporary policy issues that concern the legal profession. They then ask what light other disciplines can shed on those issues.').

White is by no means alone in the view that the purpose of legal scholarship is to elucidate policy issues. See, e.g., Edward L. Rubin, 'Law And and The Methodology of Law' (1997) *Wis. L. Rev.* 521; Edward L. Rubin, 'The Concept of Law and the New Public Law Scholarship' (1991) 89 *Michigan Law Review* [*Mich. L. Rev.*] 792 (both arguing that the purpose of legal scholarship is to frame recommendations to responsible decision-makers).

[60] White, n. 58 above, 26 ('How can the legal scholar avoid distortion of the perspectives of the other discipline purportedly being used as a source of insights if that discipline is used only in the service of contemporary legal doctrine and policy?').   [61] White, n. 58 above, 28.

[62] White, n. 58 above.   [63] White, n. 58 above, 28–9.

Again, interdisciplinarity isn't happening, but now for an entirely different reason. The attempt to invigorate one discipline by resort to another shows how contingent and ideological disciplinary boundaries have always been. Interdisciplinarity isn't happening, in White's view, because, increasingly, the idea of disciplinary coherence has broken down.[64]

Where White believes that disciplinary coherence is disintegrating under the pressure of anti-foundationalist attacks, Stanley Fish regards those antifoundationalist attacks as effectively undoing themselves; followed to their logical conclusion they suggest not that disciplines are breaking down but rather that they are inescapable:

> Partiality and parochialism are not eliminated or even diminished by the exposure of their operation, merely relocated. The blurring of existing authoritative disciplinary lines and boundaries will only create new lines and new authorities; the interdisciplinary impulse finally does not liberate us from the narrow confines of academic ghettos to something more capacious: it merely redomiciles us in enclosures that do not advertise themselves as such.[65]

Those who purport to be doing interdisciplinary tasks are actually doing one of three possible things:

> either they are engaging in straightforwardly disciplinary tasks that require for their completion information and techniques on loan from other disciplines, or they are working within a particular discipline at a moment when it is expanding into territories hitherto marked as belonging to someone else . . . ; or they are in the process of establishing a new discipline, one that takes as its task the analysis of disciplines, the charting of their history and of their ambitions.[66]

Now interdisciplinarity isn't happening because such a thing is simply conceptually impossible. All thinking within or about disciplines must be done from 'inside' a discipline—if only the new discipline of thinking about disciplines.

---

[64] White, n. 58 above, 32 ('the [republican] revival episode reveals that both the community of historians and the community of legal scholars are having grave difficulties defining, let alone agreeing upon, the precise content of their scholarly missions'). See also at 31 (all disciplines are susceptible to 'the Kuhnian virus—the difficulty of formulating a transcendent body of research techniques that truly constrains the normative agendas of scholars within a discipline').

[65] Stanley Fish, *There's No Such Thing as Free Speech, and It's a Good Thing, Too* (New York, 1994), 237.   [66] Fish, n. 65 above, at 242.

Jack Balkin reaches a similar conclusion about the basic impossibility of interdisciplinarity, but is careful to limit his case to law.[67] Balkin argues that law is particularly resistant to being changed by any ideas 'on loan from other disciplines' because 'law is less an academic discipline than a professional discipline. It is a skills-oriented profession, and legal education is a form of professional education.'[68] Because law is not truly an academic discipline but rather a professional practice, it has no 'academic methodology that might be subverted or replaced'.[69] For the purposes of Balkin's argument, the theoretical possibility or impossibility of interdisciplinarity is almost irrelevant. Interdisciplinarity cannot happen for law because law was not and is not a 'real' discipline anyway.[70]

As these debates reveal, interdisciplinarity is a hotly contested topic in the American academy at this time. Law is fertile ground for this sort of contest. If law is a separate place, its own domain, it *should* be possible to connect it to other disciplinary places, to create meaningful interdisciplines combining law with other fields. If this possibility is not being realized—and there seems to be consensus that it is not—then maybe we just do not share a vision of what the discipline of law truly is.

Law, Literature, and Interdisciplinarity

Where does the law and literature movement fit in to the ongoing debates about interdisciplinarity? On one level, discussions of the

[67] J. M. Balkin, 'Interdisciplinarity as Colonization' (1996) 53 *Washington & Lee Law Review* 949.   [68] Balkin, n. 67 above, 964.
[69] Balkin, n. 67 above, 966.
[70] Curiously, some who share Balkin's view of law as a relatively weak discipline see in that weakness a reason why law *must* turn to other disciplines. These scholars argue that the 'realist revolution' that led to the 'broader understanding' of law and legal doctrines as 'instruments of social policy' left law reliant on other disciplines, for law itself possesses no 'internal metric' for determining effects. George L. Priest, 'The Growth of Interdisciplinary Research and the Industrial Structure of the Production of Legal Ideas: A Reply to Judge Edwards' (1993) 91 *Mich. L. Rev.* 1929, 1931–3. *Accord* Rubin, 'Law and', n. 59 above, at 553 ('legal scholarship must rely on other disciplines to characterize external events and effects'. But the reliance referred to here is the use of other disciplines *in the service of law*. 'What is being sought . . . cannot be a method for legal scholarship itself, for no other discipline addresses the same issues and adopts the same stance toward them.' This sort of turn to other disciplines is not, then, an instance of interdisciplinarity, but of law being law (and using—and abusing—other disciplines for law's own distinct purposes).

relation of law to literature seem remarkably disconnected from the controversy. The enterprise of law and literature is, in many cases, simply assumed to be, and praised for being, interdisciplinary,[71] without much explicitly being said about what interdisciplinarity truly consists of. On another level, however, discussions of the lessons of literature for law instantiate and replicate the conflicts over 'real' interdisciplinarity, and provide insight into the border metaphor in which so much of the debate is couched.

Much of law and literature addresses the question of why lawyers should read literature, of what it is that literature teaches.[72] The humanist strand of the law and literature movement answers that lawyers should read literature for 'moral uplift'.[73] In this view, literature is a source of knowledge about human nature—especially about people different from lawyers themselves.[74] It can also help correct lawyers' tendency to rely excessively on abstract reason over forms of understanding that are emotional, intuitive, and concrete.[75] Finally, literature, it is said, can provide training in making the moral judgments with

[71] See, e.g., Richard Weisberg, 'Literature's Twenty-Year Crossing into the Domain of Law: Continuing Trespass or Right by Adverse Possession' (in this book).

[72] Unfortunately, there is no consensus on the answer to this question. Rather, the movement divides into three separate strands, one 'humanist', another 'hermeneutic', and a third 'narrative'. For a description of these strands, see Jane B. Baron, 'Law, Literature, and the Problems of Interdisciplinarity' (1999) 108 *Yale LJ* 1059. For a slightly different description of the 'genres' of law and literature, see Guyora Binder, 'The Law-as-Literature Trope' in this book. A more conventional approach divides the movement into 'law in literature' and 'law as literature'.

[73] J. B. Baron and J. Epstein, 'Language and the Law: Literature, Narrative, and Legal Theory', in D. Kairys (ed.), *The Politics of Law*, n. 10 above, 662–4.

[74] See, e.g., Martha C. Nussbaum, *Poetic Justice: the Literary Imagination and Public Life* (Boston, 1995), 5–6 ('[L]iterary works typically invite their readers to put themselves in the place of people of many different kinds and to take on their experiences . . .'); John H. Wigmore, 'A List of Legal Novels' (1908) 2 *Illinois Law Review* 574, 579 ('[T]he lawyer must know human nature . . . For this learning . . . he must go to fiction, which is the gallery of life's portraits.').

[75] See, e.g., Paul Gewirtz, 'Aeschylus' Law' (1988) 101 *Harv. L. Rev.* 1043, 1050 ('Literature makes its special claims upon us precisely because it nourishes the kinds of human understanding not achievable through reason alone but involving intuition and feeling as well. If . . . law engages nonrational elements and requires the most comprehensive kinds of understanding, literature can play an important part in the lawyer's development.'). See also W. C. Dimock, *Residues of Justice: Literature, Law, Philosophy* (Berkeley, Calif., 1996), 10 (literature transposes the 'clean abstractions' of law 'into the messiness of representation'.).

which lawyers are faced all the time.[76] Literature, in short, is a source of values otherwise missing from the law.

This argument rests on a vision of law as inherently empty or ignorant of moral values, which must be supplied from 'outside' law. This vision is reinforced by frequent contrasts drawn by proponents of humanist law and literature between dry, technical, rule-governed law and nuanced, emotional, complex literature.[77] Such contrasts both rely on and entrench the concept of law we have previously encountered, the concept of law as a separate place, filled only with rules.

The role envisioned for literature in enriching the barren territory that is law calls upon the hopeful picture of interdisciplinarity as supplementation by alliance. Literature and law are separate and different—law being abstract where literature is concrete, law dealing in general principles where literature deals with specific contexts, etc. But they can be connected in a basically positive fashion: law is better for its assimilation of the lessons of literature, while literature is made stronger and more worthy of respect as a discipline by being given practical effect in the real world in which law operates.

Where humanist law and literature regards the borders between law and literature with hope and optimism, hermeneutic law and literature, which seeks to apply to law interpretive methodologies

---

[76] See, e.g., Linda R. Hirshman, 'Bronte, Bloom, and Bork: An Essay on the Moral Education of Judges' (1988) 137 *University of Pennsylvania Law Review* [*U. Pa. L. Rev.*] 177, 179: 'Literature trains people in the reflection, consciousness, choice, and responsibility that makes up the ability to engage in moral decision-making. It does so by presenting artificial, but concrete, universes in which premises may be worked out in conditions conducive to empathy but ambiguous enough to allow for the formation of moral judgment.'

See also Richard Weisberg, 'Coming of Age Some More: "Law and Literature" Beyond the Cradle' (1988) 13 *Nova Law Review* 107, 123–4 ('Rightness—virtue—can be understood through literature. Pedagogically, I am convinced that literature is a better medium for lawyers than is, say, moral philosophy, from which to learn about rightness. It delights as it instructs. It places the inquiry on virtue into a dynamic framework and allows the reader to reason inductively from the cases described to her own experience and thoughts.').

[77] See, e.g., Elliott M. Abramson, 'Law, Humanities and the Hinterlands' (1979) 30 *Journal of Legal Education* 27, 29 ('professional training narrows by omitting', but 'the humanities can broaden and free'); C. R. B Dunlop, 'Literature Studies in Law Schools' (1991) 3 *Cardozo Studies in Law and Literature* 63, 64 ('Fiction gives legal scholars the opportunity to get beyond the technical and circumscribed study of legal rules . . .').

borrowed from literary studies, recalls the transgressive dangers
that attend disciplinary borders. Hermeneutic law and literature
has been preoccupied with the question of whether law's textuality is different from literature's, with many arguing that interpretations of legal texts invoke coercive state power, while
interpretations of literary texts do not.[78] For those who believe
that 'law, including adjudicative law, is imperative', while literature is merely 'expressive',[79] the application of literary theory to
legal interpretation is a category mistake of the most perilous sort:
'[i]f we do not see that the difference between [literary interpretation and adjudication] is the amount of power wielded by the judiciary as compared to the power wielded by the interpreter, then
we have either misconceived the nature of interpretation, or the
nature of law, or both'.[80] Specifically, understanding law as a
species of interpretation 'tie[s] the basis of legal criticism to
communicative texts written or conceived by the community's
collective or not-so-collective past', and thereby precludes 'a truly
radical critique of power: a critique based on the norms and ideals
generated not by the audible voices of our past, but instead by a
"self" who has been trampled, not celebrated, by our history, and
whose vision has been ignored, not expressed, in the collective
communicative texts of our culture's political past'.[81]

This critique of law's use of literary interpretive techniques
echoes in structure and content the critiques of law's use of philosophy and history. The nature and aims of law (coercion,
command) are contrasted to the nature and aims of literature
(expression, artistic delight). The differences having been uncovered, the impropriety of using the methods of the latter ostensibly

---

[78]   See, e.g., Posner, n. 2 above, at 236 ('A poet tries to create a work of art, a
thing of beauty and pleasure . . . A legislature is trying to give commands . . .'). But
see Sanford Levinson and J. M. Balkin, 'Law, Music, and Other Performing Arts'
(1991) 139 *U. Pa. L. Rev.* 1597, 1626–7 (arguing that interpretation outside legal
settings also involves the imposition of significant coercive power and so is not
meaningfully distinct from interpretation in law).

[79]   R. West, *Narrative, Authority, and Law* (Ann Arbor, Mich., 1993), 174.

[80]   West, n. 79 above, 94.

[81]   West, n. 79 above, 96. Where West is concerned that confusing interpretation in law and in literature will preclude radical critique, Judge Posner is
concerned that the confusion will encourage judicial usurpation of the legislature's
law-making role. See text accompanying n. 2 above. In more recent work, West
has conceded that dissents such as hers and Posner's 'did not ring loudly'. West,
Caring For Justice, n. 15 above, 203.

in service of the aims of the former is manifest. Mutually enriching, faithful alliances are one thing, illegitimate border crossings another. Sometimes it is best to stay within disciplinary lines.

But what is *inter*disciplinary about staying inside the boundaries of one's own field? Law enriched by glancing contact with the moral uplift of literature is still, ultimately, a separate place, and it is still a place of rules. But where is this place? Who made it a place of rules?

Let us look again at some of the contrasts drawn between law on one side and literature on the other. Is it true that law is only dry and technical rule manipulation, while literature is rich, textured examination of emotions? Surely it is not. As Robert Weisberg has eloquently noted, 'law students are or should be perfectly aware even from conventional case analysis that human pain underlies doctrinal abstraction, that the general rules of common law doctrine live in tension with and are often undone by the particular stories of parties to the case'.[82] Nor—to state the obvious—is literature always emotional; think of the quite heady works of authors such as Frederick Barthelme or Roland Barthes. Neither is it self-evidently true that law is naturally amoral, or immoral, while literature is somehow infused with moral lessons. In the eyes of many, law that is not moral is not law at all, or not law worth having.[83] And literature is by no means reliably moral. 'Those who create literature, no more and no less than those who write legal texts as judges or legislators, have conflicting ethical insights and occasionally none at all . . . Some works of literature may have their value in . . . exemplifying, rather than condemning, dangerous values.'[84] Could it be that the repeated contrasts between law and literature *construct* law as a domain of rules, even as they purport to be discovering that domain?

One's sense that the dice are being loaded is only enhanced when one examines approaches that, rather than contrasting law to literature, treat law as a form of literature. This is most

[82]   Robert Weisberg, 'The Law-Literature Enterprise' (1988) 1 *Yale JL & Hum.* 1, 17–18.
[83]   On the idea that law must be moral, see, e.g., J. Finnis, *Natural Law and Natural Rights* (Oxford, 1980). On the positivist idea that law is the proper and important object of moral criticism, see, e.g., H. L. A. Hart, 'Positivism and the Separation of Law and Morals' (1958) 71 *Harv. L. Rev.* 593.
[84]   Thomas Morawetz, 'Ethics and Style: The Lessons of Literature for Law' (1993) 45 *Stan. L. Rev.* 497, 518 (book review).

famously the approach of James Boyd White, who has argued that 'the life of the law is . . . a life of art, the art of making meaning in language with others'.[85] The 'central concern' of this life, White argues, is 'the kind of relations that we establish with our inherited culture and with each other when we speak its language'.[86] Poetry, philosophy, and law are but specific instances of the general 'cultural and ethical activity of making meaning in relation to others'.[87]

In this view of law as 'literary'[88] in character, law does not require supplementation by anything 'outside' itself, because—given the level of abstraction at which the process of doing law is described—nearly everything that could be outside is actually already 'inside' law. Law, though broadened, remains a self-enclosed discipline. Indeed, the broader and more 'integrated'[89] law is, the less problematic its self-enclosure comes to seem.

It cannot be that law is either everything literature is not or everything literature already is. The law and literature enterprise's tendency to describe law in these ways is itself a phenomenon worthy of examination. Locating emotion and empathy *outside* law, and *inside* literature, as so much humanist law and literature has done, suggests an unacknowledged investment in exactly that vision of cold, mechanical, dehumanized law that literature is supposed to combat. Similarly, locating interpretive power *inside* law, and *outside* literature, as so much hermeneutic law and literature has done, suggests an attachment to exactly that vision of law as uniquely authoritative that attention to textuality is meant to put in question. These investments and attachments are of great cultural interest because they implicate questions of what we want or can envision law to be. They reveal especially the extent to which we seem to *want* law to be distinct from other social institutions.

[85] J. B. White, *Heracles' Bow: Essays on the Rhetoric and Poetics of the Law* (Madison, Wis., 1985), xii.

[86] J. B. White, *When Words Lose Their Meaning: Constitutions and Reconstitutions of Language, Character, and Community* (Chicago, 1984), 273.

[87] White, n. 86 above, 275.

[88] White, n. 86 above, 283.

[89] White emphasizes the importance of 'the integration of parts of our culture, and parts of ourselves, into new wholes', in J. B. White, *Justice as Translation: An Essay in Cultural and Legal Criticism* (Chicago, 1990), 21.

Conclusion

'Law' and 'literature' (and 'philosophy' and 'history') are not natural categories describing disciplines that are just there, pre-existing and pre-defined, and most of those playing the compare and contrast game know it. Comparisons are drawn for a purpose, and getting hold of that purpose will tell us much about our aspirations for law, and for the place of law in our culture. We seem to want law to be a place, a discrete place of rules. We need to know why, but no one is asking.

The question-begging seems particularly obvious in the case of 'law and literature'. The movement has defined out of the category 'law' almost everything worth having; beauty, sensitivity, emotions, moral lessons—all these and so much more are the province of literature. The province of law is barren of everything but rules, an empty domain of raw power.

Is this what law must be? Interdisciplinary explorations such as law and literature *can* be occasions for considering how we categorize knowledge, and why. Within the American legal academy, this promise has gone largely unfulfilled. For all the scorn and ridicule directed over the years at Langdellian orthodoxy, the 'law' of 'law and' is precisely the autonomous realm Langdell envisioned. By holding fast to this vision, we will not learn much from our interdisciplinary 'law and' excursions. But then again, we do not risk much, either. If law is a place of pure rules, it is at least a place we know.

LITERATURE'S TWENTY-YEAR CROSSING INTO THE DOMAIN OF LAW: CONTINUING TRESPASS OR RIGHT BY ADVERSE POSSESSION?

Richard H. Weisberg

If we were to adopt the methodologies of certain competing inter-disciplinary approaches, we practitioners of law and literature might express pride in the accomplishments of the past twenty years or so. Statistics[1] indicate an exponential increase in peda-gogy and scholarship blending two fields that, for most of the earlier part of this century, had been programmatically disjoined by each discipline's self-regard. Today, the field has a vibrancy and a breadth, so that scholars of literature are working in techni-cal legal areas, legal scholars write about hermeneutics, stylistics and stories, judges and playwrights, novelists and practising lawyers participate in discussions and creative enterprises linking artistic vision to social policy and the quest for justice. Historians of legal thought now place law and literature together with critical legal studies, feminist and critical race theories and law and economics as among the leading analytical movements of the last quarter century.[2] In Australia, a large and energetic grouping of scholars, artists and judges has made changes in the law explicitly employing techniques and arguments drawn from literature; the border crossings, in all senses, have also expanded from the

---

[1] E. V. Gemmette, ' "Law and Literature": Joining the Class Action' (1995) 29 *Valparaiso Law Review* 665.

[2] G. Minda, *Postmodern Legal Movements: Law & Jurisprudence at Century's End* (New York, 1995).

United States to Canada, and both in the United Kingdom and on the continent of Europe, remarkable work in law and literature is being produced.

If, as is not typical of us, we were further to indulge in prideful ruminations, we might take note that our particular interdiscipline has advanced in spite of a certain untimeliness in our assumptions. Consider a phrase I just used: 'creative enterprises linking artistic vision to social policy'. By every criterion of postmodernism, such a phrase should not be reduced to print, much less propounded as a programme. We have emerged as a viable interdiscipline during the very years that have been most sceptical of at least one of our major assumptions, the one I want to foreground here: that stories do have perceivable if rarely monolithic meanings that exist, of course, solely in their language, but that may (if discussed with care) contribute to an understanding of the wider world. Lawyers have insisted, when many literary theorists felt embarrassed about the claim, that texts do exist, that they are worth talking about discretely and even from a mildly intentionalist perspective, that they can be taken up comparatively to signal better than any other compendium of sources certain tendencies within a society, certain risks and also certain possibilities. To speak this way was to offend the post-structuralists, although some of us were trained by post-structuralists and did not feel we were violating our training by so proceeding. In my own personal case, several years at the feet of Paul de Man and Geoffrey Hartman while I was in graduate school did not lead me away from the closest readings of literary texts in the service less of 'theory' than of probing social and philosophical inquiry. Many others in the field also resisted the more popular denials of all rational discourse, of specificity, of grand stories, of the very idea that storytelling might be linked to the problems of the real world.

I recall a conference on Herman Melville's *Billy Budd* at Washington and Lee University some years ago.[3] The distinguished grouping, half lawyers, half literary folks, discussed this single story for almost three days. Each morning, the law professors, judges and legal practitioners would dutifully bring their texts (since Harrison Hayford was there, it was the Hayford and Sealts edition); not one professor of literature would bring along a

---

[3] (1989) 1 *Cardozo Studies in Law and Literature* [*CSLL*] 1.

copy of the story, as though to demonstrate through this absence their disdain for the traditional activity of recognizing the distinctiveness of a unique text. Yet they participated, and the event retains a certain symbolic flavour: for twenty or twenty-five years, lawyers interested in stories have sustained the unfashionable position—anathema even or especially to literary theorists—that the single text or collection of texts both exists and can be referenced to the real world.

In the face of such hyperbole, modesty (or at least good taste) rebels, and a reversal of tone here seems mandatory. Going into the interdisciplinary venture some time ago, the handful of so-called 'pioneers' knew that we would meet, what Jean-Pierre Barricelli and I at the time called, a 'special measure of resistance' to this particular interrelation.[4] We believed this less because post-modernist impulses were denying notions of text and meaning, but rather because of something more universal about the two fields. Their inherent closeness, we predicted, would inspire disdain, in much the same way siblings revile reflections of themselves in their brothers and sisters, fleeing to other families, to foreign shores, anywhere except to what is closest to them. We knew that the increasingly hermetic methods of literary discourse would block for some time too keen an attraction to the narrative world of history, law and policy; we felt that legal academicians would also balk before again entwining themselves willingly with their own less scientific—shall we say, less well paid—relatives, balk perhaps at 'the very idea of law and literature', because the idea is so accessible, so familiar, and hence so threatening.

Barricelli and I nonetheless opined that what we divided into the worlds of law-as and law-in literature might entice literary folk, at least, to see that legal sources scanned as narratives offered them new fields of semiotic and rhetorical discovery. This has proved to be true. Law and literature in the graduate schools and the literary journals is now a thriving endeavour, and it is often taught in the undergraduate arts curriculum as well.

We expected resistance 'from both sides of the table', but we knew from reading James Boyd White and a few symposium-length law review numbers already published by 1982 that

---

[4] Jean-Pierre Barricelli and Richard H. Weisberg, 'Literature and Law' in *The Interrelations of Literature* (New York: PMLA, 1982).

lawyers were advancing the field beyond the somewhat amateur-
ish level on which it had been sustained (between the period of
Benjamin Cardozo's seminal essay called 'Law and Literature' in
1925 until White's 1974 book). In passing, though, I would like to
give credit to two of those interim figures, the man who first
divided the field into law-as and law-in (and many recent historians of the field have got this wrong): Ephraim London, a first
amendment lawyer in New York who published the still-available
two-volume set called 'The World of Law', one volume containing
selections from stories about the law, the other his favourite judicial opinions; and J. Allen Smith, who founded the Law &
Humanities Institute.

Barricelli and I could not then have predicted that, over time,
lawyers would more strenuously resist this field than would their
humanistic siblings across the table, particularly since (as I have
noted) literary theory continued to move strongly away from
stories, meanings, and anything remotely akin to law and policy.
But as the 1980s developed, lawyers—mostly law professors but
also a handful of judges—began to object. Perhaps it was the
perseverance of law and literature: the excellent reception of
White's book; the publication of a few other books examining the
representation in stories of law, ratiocination, judicial error,
lawyers and authoritative rhetoric. The debate on *Billy Budd*,
which was to go through several phases, was increasingly publicized. The 1982 *Texas Law Review* volume on interpretation
brought renewed energy to the law-as movement.[5] These were
watershed events, hard to ignore, exciting but also threatening.
Was law being conflated with the humanities instead of drawing
on them in a selective and manageable way? Was law talk either
indeterminate, or—worse—eventually determinable but at that
exact point to be identified with violence, resentment, covertness
and evil? Were judges to aspire to literary craftsmanship in their
opinions, which would mean *writing* their own opinions or at
least confessing that legal rules emerge only within the space of
narrative and form?

Obviously, these threats to ensconced notions of law needed to
be parried. From the right, some might still say the relatively right-
ist right, Richard Posner entered the fray. Here, if I may again be

---

[5] (1982) 60 *Texas Law Review* 373.

forgiven a somewhat personal note that may be of interest to many readers, I believe I helped encourage my former colleague and teacher,[6] who asked me—shortly after he had reviewed my first book quite generously[7]—whether any law review might be willing to accept an essay he would write about law and literature more generally. I assured him that not just *any* but more likely *every* law review in the late 1980s would receive warmly such a contribution, since the field had by then grown to the proportions already discussed earlier in this essay, and since the distinction of the manuscript-writer spoke for itself. There ensued a long essay in the *Virginia Law Review*, and then, after a rather complex exchange of letters between us including Posner's sending me what I considered to be a quite weak and unliterary book-length draft (I frankly told him so), his *Law and Literature: A Misunderstood Relation* appeared.[8]

The gloves were off. The field had progressed sufficiently. It was a threat not only to law and economics but also to a certain ordered perception of legal authority. No matter how much Posner protested that little in the interdiscipline was worth the candle save its attention to judicial style, the compendiousness of his volume on the subject proved its importance to his own professional projects, just as its eventual marketability proved its interest to many other seemingly 'non-literary' lawyers. The field had to be trashed.

There was little literary sensitivity in Posner's book, but there was much of what Robert Batey, writing recently about our debate on Camus' *The Stranger*, describes as follows:

Judge Posner edges up to [an] understanding of the novel. 'It may be possible to regard the work as a commentary on the inherent shortcomings of conceptualization—reason's inability to comprehend passion; for

---

[6] I met Richard Posner in the early 1970s, when I was an assistant professor of French and Comparative Literature at the University of Chicago and Posner, of course, was on the Faculty of Law there. During my time at the University, from which I resigned to practise and teach law, I completed the J.D., partly with the help of some courses from Posner during a year in which I both taught and amassed my final third of law-school credits. Posner was always very generous in discussing with me the then fledgling area of Law and Literature, but I doubt he would have dreamed at the time of ever participating in it.

[7] Posner, review of *The Failure of the Word: the Protagonist as Lawyer in Modern Fiction* (New Haven, 1984), in 96 (1987) *Yale Law Journal* 1173.

[8] (Cambridge, Mass., 1988; 2nd edn, 1998).

we never do learn *why* Meursault pulled the trigger.' Posner, supra, note 19 at 89 (original emphasis)—but [Posner] then skitters off into criticizing Camus for questioning bourgeois values, ultimately damning the novel as an immoral work of fiction, id. at 155. Like Meursault's prosecutor . . . Posner has some insight, but manages to suppress it in order to pursue the role he has chosen, as belittler of literature's significance to law and scourge of Camus' champion, Richard Weisberg. See id. at 151–55. See also [Ernest] Simon . . . (as a critic of *The Stranger* Posner 'takes the part . . . of an executioner').[9]

As Judith Resnik points out (yet again)[10] in this book, Posner's failed attempt to eviscerate the new field nonetheless had the ironic effect not so much of drawing scores of new readers to its debates (Posner wanted this and always told me that—no matter how inaccurate might be his assessments of J. B. White, R. West, and R. Weisberg—it was 'better to be criticized than ignored') as of establishing such an unliterary voice in the forefront of the inquiry. My conclusion is that Posner's authoritative and conclusory voice had a balming effect on many academicians who should have known better but who were handed a way of dismissing some disturbing questions raised by law and literature. For yet others, including one or two of Posner's judicial colleagues, even his grant of the importance of style to law has been too much to bear; so Judge Pierre Leval has been on the hustings recently claiming that literary style (perhaps an aspiration to good writing more generally) is anathema to the judicial function: the appellate opinion, he thinks, should read like the directions you get for putting together a new bicycle.[11] This not terribly edifying view of the quest for justice, combined with Leval's somewhat simplistic faith in language's potential to be straightforward, will not survive the most cursory analysis and should send readers dashing towards their Benjamin Cardozos.[12]

---

[9] Robert Batey, 22 *Legal Studies Forum* 70 (1998), citing Posner, n. 7 above and Ernest Simon in (1990) 2 *CSLL* 111.

[10] Judith Resnik, with Carolyn Heilbrun or on her own, has been making the point for many years that the field's most cited scholar is also its most scathing critic.

[11] See, e.g., Leval's contribution to Gewirtz (ed.), *Law's Stories* (New Haven, 1997). The bicycles I build—despite or because of the directions—tend to work more like wheelbarrows.

[12] See, e.g., Cardozo's masterful and classic 1925 essay, 'Law and Literature' (1925) 14 *Yale Review* 699 and such mere scans upon it as my own 'Cardozo's Judicial Poetics' 1 (1979) *Cardozo Law Review* [*Cardozo L. Rev.*] 283.

These prominent judges, and many of their academic acolytes, cast literature, in almost all of its guises, as a trespasser on the domain of the law. If not firmly rebuffed and actively ejected, stories, style, and hermeneutics might collectively trample turf that has been carefully (if artificially) tilled as somehow unique and 'scientific'. At a minimum, the value of the real estate would be lowered. If law once again were to be reunited with its humane roots, law professors might be salaried like English teachers and judges might lose some of their cloaked and impenetrable auras.

Resistance to 'the very idea of Law and Literature'[13] has come from less authoritarian sources, voices that are less hostile, in theory, and indeed often friendly to the venture of law and literature, but disappointed in the way they feel it has developed. These categories of resistance—one which sees literature less as a trespasser on law than as a yet insufficiently defined shadow—include, each for different reasons, some feminists, some postmodernists, and some whom I shall group under the label 'anti-sentimentalists'. These critics have produced worthwhile and distinctive critiques-from-within, although each is in its own way based on a fallacious understanding, as I see it, of the practice or aims of law and literature.[14] Unlike the kind of resistance Barricelli and I prophesied (fulfilled duly by Posner and by some now diminishing criticism on the literary side of the table),[15] each of these groups has accepted literature into the domain of the law but has wondered aloud at the invader's failure to play its role

[13] The titular phrase was John Ayer's, in a review of my *Failure of the Word* in (1987) 85 *Michigan Law Review* 895.

[14] As I remarked less formally at the outset of my keynote address in June 1998, the phrase 'law and literature' connotes something less unified than my ensuing analysis implies. Even after a full generation of fecund scholarship, many consider it a strength of the field that it lacks a defining text or (to a lesser extent) programme. So in this part of my essay, it is the assumption of certain shared assumptions that may surprise the reader; yet I believe there is now a sufficient 'core' of writing to justify even my use of the Nietzschean pronoun 'we' to modify the identifiable voice of this interdiscipline. Surely, at the very least, it is to redirect this 'we' that the three critical groups I have identified have set their sights.

[15] A documented and significant example of this was the original resistance by the *Billy Budd* community to the notion that legal insights into the story would yield much fruit, partly because it was thought unlikely that Melville intended to ask his reader to pay much attention to the machination of Captain Vere and his hand-picked jury at Billy's trial. But this understandable resistance has yielded. For the full story see, e.g., R. Weisberg, *Poethics* (New York, 1992), ch. 3, n. 34.

effectively. Not only—again—am I respectful of these camps, but I have sometimes set up my tent with them.

For many *feminists* whose minds are turned to law and literature, there has been too much attention paid to the traditional canon. They seem to be saying that a late twentieth-century innovative movement must innovate harmoniously with their own movement's advances. If feminists have been attacking the canon, well, so too must any other new movement, especially one directly connected to literature. This is, of course, fallacious. It would be to insist, say, that Freud have incorporated Marx or else lose his claim to radical relevance. Or that Einstein be attentive to Nietzsche or Heidegger. Or, within a single field, that the neo-realists in law accept the premises of contemporary legal sociologists, or critical race theorists those of law and economics, before proceeding with their own programme. The feminists ask if it is enough for law and literature to develop a destabilizing critique of the law's stories (or of stories about the law) and at the same time employ as major sources texts written by DWEMs.[16] Does it follow that the movement—at the same time it is challenging the Melville industry or *The Merchant of Venice* crowd to reconfigure their approach to the powerful stories whose meaning they control—must also ferret out new sources, programmatically abjuring the classics and leaving them unaltered by effectively radical readings? Indeed, as some feminists continue, should there not (automatically?) be a preponderance of female voices within this new field? With this assumption also unchallenged and presented as an axiom, some of these critics proceed to ignore the fact that scholars such as Judith Koffler, Robin West and Penelope Pether have been there from the origins, performing transformative readings of DWEMs like Dante, Shakespeare and Kafka, not forgetting DWMs like Melville and Twain or merely WMs like Arthur Miller and John Barth.[17] Such a 'canon'—so imploded—

---

[16] Dead-white-European males.

[17] Without Koffler's scathing piece on Antonio's colonial practices in *The Merchant of Venice*, much subsequent scholarship challenging traditional, male-oriented and pro-Christian views of the play would have been impossible. See Judith Koffler, 'Terror and Mutilation in the Golden Age' (1983) 5 *Human Rights Quarterly* 116. Robin West's readings of Kafka pioneered the ongoing attack by Law and Literature scholars upon the seeming intransigence of Law and Economics and partly provoked Richard Posner to write *Law and Literature*, n. 8 above. West, of course, has followed that article with provocative analyses of

reveals the flaws in our culture that may lead to the very anti-feminist structures deplored by our critics. It must be re-examined, not abandoned.

The *postmodernists*, for their part, wonder that law and literature, unlike critical legal studies, sometimes purveys a sense that texts both have a material presence and a discernible meaning. Less playful when touching on questions of 'foundationalism' than they usually are when dealing with any other issue, postmodernists worry when we suggest that justice exists; that law is not normatively corrupt and certainly it is not so just because it is based on some notion of textuality and closure; that language is generated not only to deceive and to play; and that Nietzsche— who stands for all of the propositions in this sentence so far—is a moral and not a hermeneutical radical.[18]

Law and literature seems to the postmodernists anachronistically to reach for and speak of certain foundational notions at the very intellectual moment when all foundationalisms have been rendered suspect. The irony here may be that postmodernist resistance to 'foundationalism' is always everywhere in the situated service of its own regnant foundationalism, which is, of course, that there are no truths, no first causes, no foundationalisms. Anti-foundationalism thus has become a fighting faith, and the tendency of law and literature to be a 'naming' (defining)[19] interdiscipline thus makes it heretical. Everything else is permitted us, but never the possibility of coherence, meaning, law, justice. On a parallel front, postmodernists have only grudgingly perceived that post-war strategies of language have perhaps been wrongly geared as a response to the referential and idealistic 'simplicity' of Hitler's rhetoric, geared in fact to avoid at all costs all referential language, all clarity of speech, all quests for meaning and even for

Twain and Barth. And Penelope Pether, in the pages of *Cardozo Studies in Law and Literature* ((1996) 8 *CSLL* 317) and in the Australian journal she herself helped to found, has linked brilliant analyses of Arthur Miller with probing policy insights into Australian legal developments.

[18] See the work of a very talented postmodernist, Steven Mailloux, at (1989) 1 *CSLL* 83; for my answer to some of Mailloux' positions, see my article in a book he edited, 'Text Into Theory: The Use and Abuse of Nietzsche for Postmodernism' in S. Levinson and S. Mailloux (eds.), *Interpreting Law and Literature* (Evanston, 1988).

[19] So I label it in a recent piece, Editorial Advisory Board Notes, 10th Anniversary Issue (1998) 10 *Yale Journal of Law and Humanities* 395, 396.

law. Now, with new work revealing that the Holocaust emerged at least as much from complex, creative and even deconstructive strategies of oppressive speech (Vichy being the foremost example), law and literature has eschewed any unambiguous alliance with an antifoundationalist program.[20]

A similar irony envelops the oppositional stance of those whom I call the *anti-sentimentalists*. These often highly versed and subtle thinkers include my own namesake and personal Sainte-Beuve, Robert Weisberg. Just as Sainte-Beuve urged Flaubert not to deviate from the themes of his early novels, so Robert Weisberg is constantly trying to get me to return to what he sees as 'the critical bite and moral gravity'[21] of *The Failure of the Word* and to resist the cheerful misapprehension he fears most in what he calls the 'Panglossian . . . all-too happy land of law and literature':[22] that stories (and perhaps particularly 'Great Literature') might actually make legal actors better people.

Now, Robert Weisberg, as well as such other writers as Richard Delgado and Jean Stefancic,[23] have benefited from what amounts to their own fallacious major premise. Law and literature simply does not make any cause-and-effect claims relating to the edification of its practitioners. As one sensitive to the Holocaust, I am only too aware of the paradox that the cold victimization of millions was rendered by the cultured and non-cultured alike, without regard to prior reading lists or taste in music and the other arts. Surely this scepticism about the moral effect of great stories in Western culture also underlies the work of my colleagues Robin West, Judith Koffler, Ian Ward, Daniel Solove, Penelope Pether and most other 'law-in-lit' writers; on the literary side, the profound puzzle of cultured people doing massive evil to others informs the lifelong theoretical project of such thinkers as Geoffrey Hartman, a deconstructionist and sometime law and literature fellow traveller whose 'sentimentalism'—if it exists at all—emerges in an infinite sadness that words have been shown to wreak havoc with human lives.

---

[20] Editorial Advisory Board Notes, n. 19 above, n. 2.
[21] Robert Weisberg, 'Reading *Poethics*' (1994) 15 *Cardozo L. Rev.* 1103.
[22] See Robert Weisberg, review of Barry Schaller (1998) 30 *Connecticut Law Review* 1039.
[23] See their 'Norms and Narratives: Can Judges Avoid Serious Moral Error?' (1991) 69 *Texas Law Review* 1929 at, e.g., 1930 and n. 8. Gyora Binder reiterated and expanded their position at this Law and Literature colloquium, in this book, 63. But the pickings, while there, are slim.

The anti-sentimentalists will get little lasting mileage from their attacks on the movement, if this is the strawman that makes them look inviolable giants. The stress upon literature has little to do with its supposed salutary moral effect on legal actors. Although, as I have discussed here already, we do confess to a structuralist aspiration about the meaning of stories—that is, we believe stories can be discussed intelligently as a source of understanding of law and other human endeavours and emotions—law and literature makes different claims regarding the effects of these discussions on the legal community.

Our first claim as to effect can be summarized in the single word 'disequilibration'. The act of reading the stories many of us have probed during these twenty or twenty-five years is to upset the reader, to make the reader uneasy about the legal assumptions that preceded the understanding of the story. Unlike James Boyd White, as he is usually understood, the scholars I have mentioned and I tend to choose the darker stories about the law, ones that challenge (through plot, character and especially discursive technique) rather than reconfirm our preconceptions. It is hard to find 'sentimentality'—as traditionally understood—in an endeavour akin to the one described by Kafka, who wrote as follows to a friend about his own taste in reading:

it's good when the conscience receives broad wounds, since it thereby becomes more sensitive for every bite. I believe, one should only read books that bite and prick. When a book that we read does not wake us up with a blow to the head, why then do we read the book? In order to make us happy, as you write? My God, we would also be happy without books, and those books that make us happy we could write ourselves if necessary. But we need those books that have the effect of a tragedy which hurts very much like the death of someone whom we loved more than ourselves, like being expelled to forests far away from all people, like a suicide, a book must be the axe for the frozen sea within us.[24]

The anti-sentimentalists thus may be right to accuse us of seeking 'transformation' through stories, but change in the reader of such fiction as Kafka describes—or as we foreground constantly—would require the hardest kind of self-evaluative work. If a medium of disequilibration is largely unavailable to a community, here lawyers and judges, through any other source, than the

---

[24] Franz Kafka, letter to Oskar Pollak (1904).

appeal to stories is justified as iconoclastic work of the highest order. Tales such as *Billy Budd, Noon Wine, The Stranger* and *The Trial* awaken in us a troubling awareness of how language meshes with legal forms to lend an appearance of ineluctable logic to the persecution of the innocent and of the outsider. More even than this, such stories ruthlessly reveal the irrationality—often grounded in the legal authority's religious and moral scruples, hidden from his audience because the law carefully protects him from having to reveal his own subjectivity—of a system that is superficially rational and hence brings a high sense of self-regard to the practitioner.

If Posner persecutes us because we are threatening, the Robert Weisbergs do so because we allegedly add little to the debate. Posner at least is correct. The anti-sentimentalists rely on a false notion of law and literature, perhaps akin to that of the feminists and especially the postmodernists. It will be left to others to decide whether those groups, and especially the critical legal studies component of theoreticians, have added much of real iconoclastic substance to jurisprudence. But if law and literature has done so, it is indeed through an appeal to the disequilibrating stories that have been in our mainstream discourse for almost twenty years now, and, to such a charge of sentimentalism, we plead guilty.

Yet, admittedly, our programme goes beyond disequilibration. It may not be enough to urge on usually reluctant people the very hard task of re-examining their own values. It may not be enough, even when the argument—unlike that of the postmodernists—truly challenges (rather than implicitly reinforces) those values.[25] Law and literature pursues the still more difficult goal of advancing a just programme for law. In this second sense, we move from disequilibration to *synthesis*. Positing legal actors who have been moved to reorient their essential thinking about their own participation in the world of law, we now embrace the notion that a long and subtle process of discovery of structural meanings in the works we read can, indeed, bring those actors to a more just assessment of various issues and of the system as a whole.

If this be 'sentimentality', it is a form of poetic mediation upon

---

[25] For a comparison of deconstructionist tactics to those originally espoused 2,000 years ago by Christian exegetes of the Old Testament, see my article in Levinson and Mailloux, n. 18 above.

the world first identified by Friedrich von Schiller in his masterful 1795 essay *On Naive and Sentimental Poetry*, which I recommend as still the finest and most positive approach to sentimentality we have.[26] Schiller's essay, which I shall join only briefly and so as to lead me back to the title of my essay, identifies two types of sentimentality in literature. The 'satiric' takes as its subject alienation 'from nature and the contradiction between actuality and the ideal'.[27] (So the darker stories about law provide perhaps a unique mediation for the postmodernist mind between justice as an ideal and law as it is practised or theorized about in competing jurisprudential approaches.) The 'elegiac' gets us beyond cynicism to the recapturing of an ideal world through poetic representation. (So the edifying component of dark stories about law—achieved with the utmost, synthetic care—leads us, as the anti-sentimentalists charge, to a positive vision of law.)

Schiller knows that a 'naive', unmediated availability to nature and truth is no longer there for us; but this observation is the beginning and not—as with the postmodernists today—the end of wisdom. Schiller can strive still for the elegiac form of sentimentality, where we find pleasure, rather than satiric bitterness, in harking to the representation of the ideal, lost world. Schiller's argument, a seminally romantic one that I believe has application to late twentieth-century law (always, as it is, in search of such romanticisms as the micro-economic demand curve),[28] posits the unavailability to us moderns of an unmediated appreciation of the natural world. In constant dialogue with his incomparable rival and friend, Goethe, Schiller recognizes that most of us can connect again to nature and truth only through the medium of poetry.

Is our turn to the complexities of stories (our poetic genre *par*

---

[26] F. von Schiller, (Julius A. Elias (trans.)) in *Naive and Sentimental Poetry* (New York, 1967); see also Barbara Benedict, *Framing Feeling: Sentiment and Style in English Prose, 1745–1800* (New York, 1993) and Louis I. Bredvold, *The Natural History of Sentimentality* (Ann Arbor, 1962).

[27] Schiller, n. 26 above.

[28] Whenever I read or listen to Robert Weisberg, whose interest in literature is both sincere and sophisticated, I get the feeling his anti-sentimentalism masks a larger sentimentality—an allegiance to the seemingly 'harder' vision of micro-economic theory. But anyone who has paid the slightest attention to the irksome and counter-intuitive theorems of this stripe of legal economists would turn in a flash to stories for a richer, truer and, finally, harder vision of law.

excellence) in this sense 'sentimental'? Yes! For law and literature practises in both the satiric and elegiac modes of Schiller's descriptive essay. In both modes, we have been treated as a 'trespasser'. As satirists of law, we gain a foothold with the feminists, the postmodernists and even the anti-sentimentalists; but the authoritarians seek to give us the boot. As elegiac strivers after justice, we are greeted with derision even by our fellow-travellers.

But there is no despair in the ranks. Long, unpredictably deep strides have been made as we disequilibrate the world of law by reintroducing the notion of story, sound, significance. The rest of the journey is far more difficult, because it is here that we may need to edify a community either (smugly) committed to its own power or (legitimately but fallaciously) sceptical of all quests for truth, at least such quests as derive from the medium of humane letters instead of micro-economic formulae.

Their scepticism provides yet another proof that our late twentieth-century world is at least as alienated from justice as Schiller, in his generation, claimed people were from nature. The events of this tragic century have more than fulfilled the prophetic signs emerging from Melville, Dostoevsky, and Kafka—that the West was ready for a cataclysm, and that the innocent would suffer horribly during the death throes of the dominant culture.[29] No sentient human being can escape our antisentimentalist critics' fear that talk of justice these days is suspect on its face. You either turn from it (say, to economics) or you work with the mediation of the deeply imaginative stories that prefigured the Fall—you work with them to rebuild.

In the spirit of Schiller, I therefore conclude with a half-dozen 'sentimental' claims for law made through the narratively-attuned medium of the story. Among the bold satiric (disequilibrating) claims are three that can be summarized with the words irrationality, obfuscation, and resentment. They are:

(1) people do not normatively behave as rational economic actors or even in their own best interest as perceived by others; in fact, what is most predictable about human decision-making is its irrationality;

(2) adjudicators and other legal authorities are as prone to irrational

---

[29] See, e.g., my 'Avoiding Central Realities' (1983) 5 *Human Rights Quarterly* 151, and (more recently) 'Why They're Censoring The Tin Drum', 10 *Cardozo Studies in Law and Literature* 161 (1998).

behaviour as most other people even or especially when they claim to be guided by a rational set of formal guidelines; and

(3) the people most likely to be persecuted by even the best (and surely the worst) legal systems are those who speak differently from those who lead, those who challenge by their very being and beliefs the dominant 'forms, measured forms'[30] of legal authority.

But these darker observations are paralleled by three more elegiac (synthetic) literary suggestions that can be summarized by the words empathy, empowerment, and self-scrutiny. They are:

(1) it is necessary and possible for all those in the legal mainstream to try to feel 'irrationally', to feel as most outsiders to the system do;

(2) it is equally necessary for less mainstream players to refine their understanding of the way language works so better to evaluate and parry authoritative law talk while also becoming more rhetorically effective in the service of their own as yet unensconced beliefs; and

(3) law is constantly and inevitably informed by internal forces whose source lies more in religion and myth than in any formalized legal logic.

Stories in their elegiac mode, as Schiller concludes, 'possess the right to mourn only for the infinite'. But modern law has the responsibility to attain it. Our goal, so far unreached, is justice. If stories remain still trespassers along the path to that goal, and if the literary disciplines such as rhetoric, hermeneutics and style seem to some still threatening companions, we who enjoy and are committed to the interdiscipline simply need to work harder over the next twenty years to make literature at least a welcome guest in the domain of law.

---

[30] Captain Vere's cynical but self-describing legal methodology in *Billy Budd, Sailor*.

THE LAW-AS-LITERATURE TROPE

Guyora Binder

The law and literature movement is identified with the analogy of law to literature. This analogy is not a single proposition, but a range of different and possibly incompatible propositions. The analogy may involve a claim that law is like literature in one or several or all possible respects; and that the attributes law shares with literature are more essential, or more important, or more valuable, or simply more worthy of discussion than those that distinguish it from literature.

Yet, if we are to take seriously the claims of legal scholars that they are participants in a literary practice, we should probably not read these claims propositionally. We should read them figuratively, as tropes. If we do so, the law–literature analogy ceases to denote one of several possible incompatible claims and instead connotes them all.

The law and literature movement may be unified less by shared hypotheses than by a shared mood or aesthetic attitude—or a shared sense that contemplation of the relationship between law and literature is an intrinsically edifying pursuit, regardless of what that relationship might turn out to be. To present law as literature is therefore at once to advocate and to model a kind of aesthetic practice. Hence, the law-as-literature trope may have more performative than propositional meaning.

Rather than apprehending the law and literature movement as a theory or a school of thought, let us try to apprehend it as a literary genre by reading its identifying trope, the law-as-literature analogy.

Our first task will be to situate the law–literature trope within the larger semantic field of interdisciplinary analogies. The law and literature movement is part of a larger profusion of interdisciplinary study of society, particularly applying the methods of the humanities to subjects studied by the social sciences. All such interdisciplinary importations share an implicit logic. The host and guest disciplines are in one sense interchangeable—both can illuminate the same phenomena. Yet their powers of illumination differ in quality or quantity. The guest discipline can correct the host's deficiencies, either improving it or displacing it altogether. To import literature into law is therefore to see the two enterprises as potential collaborators or competitors in the same game. What assumptions do we make about society when we view it as the common object of all these disciplines?

I think we make the Weberian or perhaps Foucauldian assumption that there is some connection between the emergence of disciplines of inquiry and the emergence of a modern bureaucratic and commercial society. Thus we probably assume first, that the disciplines that had achieved professional status by the end of the nineteenth century offered themselves as competing modes of apprehending modern society, or—in so far as they interested themselves in the ancient or the 'primitive'—society's evolution towards modernity. Second, that part of what is meant by 'modernity' is the experience of social life as presented by these disciplines—the experience of work as economic activity, the experience of child-rearing and of relationships as psychological processes, and so on. Third, that these disciplines, and the portrait of society they paint, play a role in social order or control. In other words, the disciplines facilitate the bureaucratic and managerial functions of the state and other institutions both by informing these institutions about the populations they regulate and by encouraging these populations to perceive themselves as institutions perceive them. Fourth, that the disciplines perform this dual function of disciplining both social investigators and the objects of social investigation, in so far as they are modes of apprehending subjectivity.

Certainly lawyers and legal scholars tend to value foreign disciplines as tools for apprehending subjectivity. Legal decisions turn on diverse representations of the *will* of legal actors: injunctions, intentions, consents, interests, meanings, needs, expectations, purposes; and also rights, privileges, competences, spheres of liberty and discretion. To lawyers, at least, the disciplines of the humanities and social sciences represent techniques for determining, representing, measuring, and summing desire. The 'modern' society revealed by these disciplines is a field of competing and transacting wills.

What does it mean to represent or experience this social field in a more literary way? To approach this question we need to situate literature and literary criticism within the broader enterprise of apprehending a modern society.

From Letters to Literature

A precondition to the application of literary theory to legal interpretation is their initial separation. Yet it could be said that until the nineteenth century there was no distinct enterprise of literary criticism. Fiction, poetry, and drama were continuous with philosophy, history, and other learned discourses, including the more intellectually ambitious legal writing. All these discursive forms were simply different genres of 'letters'.

A separate category of literature, available for appreciation and criticism, developed only with the emergence of two distinctions we now regard as self-evident. The first was a conceptual distinction between universal and personal perspectives that enabled a division between scientific discourse on the one hand, and expressive discourse on the other. The second was a functional division of letters into the instrumental and the aesthetic, the prosaic and the poetic, the quotidian and the quotable. Taken together, these two distinctions enabled the emergence of a conception of literature as the presentation for aesthetic appreciation of self-expressions.

This new expressive conception of literature is said to have replaced a mimetic conception of literature.[1] According to the older mimetic conception, art's content was supplied by the facts of nature or the truths of revelation, and the artistry consisted in the skilful rendering of a given subject matter.

The very category of literature—writing presented as art—was a creature of romanticism; and in so far as we continue to view literature as an autonomous category of writing or experience, we remain committed to romantic aesthetics. Here are romanticism's basic assumptions, a package of associations evoked whenever we hear the term 'literary'.

---

[1] M. H. Abrams, *The Mirror and the Lamp* (New York, 1953).

First, romanticism celebrated the *imagination* as a form of knowledge. Second, artistic production was identical to imagination, art being an *ideal* product of the mind, rather than a material product of the hand. Third, imagination entailed *innovation*. Imaginative works had to be original, not just skilful renderings of familiar themes. Fourth, the imagination was a distinctively *individual* faculty. Imaginative works had to be authentic to the author. Fifth, great works of art therefore manifested the *genius* of their creators, the extraordinary capacities for innovation entailed by their uniqueness as persons. Sixth, great art exemplified the aesthetic quality of *sublimity*—evoking awe at the infinite, generally through dramatic contrast. Sublime effects were often associated with the depiction or evocation of strong emotion. It was the extraordinary sensibility of the artist, her capacity for unprecedented depths of feeling, that enabled her artistic genius. Seventh, aesthetic experience was nevertheless *contemplative*; it entailed perceiving but not feeling emotion. Eighth, artistic expression was therefore a form of *sublimation*, involving the mastering of great passion and its fashioning into an object for contemplation. In thus disciplining her passions, the artist recreated herself. Ninth, in thus simultaneously determining and expressing herself the artist realized her full human freedom and threw off the restraints of necessity. The faculty of imagination was thus central to the romantic conception of *freedom as self-realization*. Finally, tenth, because aesthetic experience presupposed detachment from the passions, and artistic production entailed the sublimation and control of the passions, romanticism celebrated art as *a realm apart* from the utilitarian pursuit and gratification of desire.[2]

The idea of literature depended on the emergence in society of an aesthetic sensibility for receiving writing—and a contrasting instrumental sensibility. The aesthetic sensibility of romanticism was at once opposed to and bound up with the calculating, instrumental sensibility of commercial capitalism, and the calculating

[2] See S. T. Coleridge, *Biographia Literaria* (London, 1947); R. W. Emerson, 'The Poet' in *Essays, First and Second Series* (New York, 1961); selections from G. W. F. Hegel, 'The Philosophy of Fine Art' in H. Adams (ed.) *Critical Theory Since Plato* (Fort Worth, 1992); I. Kant, *Critique of Judgment* (J. C. Meredith (trans.), Oxford, 1964); J. Mill, 'What is Poetry'; T. Schelling, 'On the Relation of the Plastic Arts to Nature' in Adams (above); P. B. Shelley, 'A Defense of Poetry' in Adams (above); F. von Schiller, *Letters on the Aesthetic Education of Man* (E. M. Wilkinson and L. A. Willoughby (eds.), Oxford, 1967).

instrumental discourse of the utilitarian, the classical liberal, or the legal positivist. If, in the discursive world that emerged in the nineteenth century, literature was an aesthetic discourse of subjectivity, law was an instrumental discourse of subjectivity.

In late nineteenth-century England and America, literature became a subject of instruction in secondary schools, colleges, and research universities. This development reflected a judgment that the romantic aesthetic ideas on which the very category of literature depended were personally edifying and socially useful. Yet as literature became an academic subject, the idea of literature and the practice of literary criticism were also reshaped by the purposes of literary education.

Literary instruction, like the marketing of literature, paradoxically involved the standardization and mass distribution of individuality. Thus the role of literary instruction within a general education in Victorian England and Progressive America tended to suppress the subversive and individualist themes in literary thought and to highlight literature's meliorative, humanizing import. Rather than protesting the alienation attendant upon modernization, literature would alleviate it by providing a common discourse to unite an atomized society, and by providing an inner world of imagination and sensibility to substitute for the lost world of nature and village.[3]

The Risks and Possibilities of the Law-as-Literature Trope

Nineteenth-century ideas about literature suggest the associations evoked when we are exhorted to experience law in a more literary way. We are urged to express our authentic selves and escape alienating roles; to value passion—especially empathy, mercy, love—over reason and rule. Yet we are also urged to be detached rather than engaged, decorous rather than vulgar, gracious rather than grasping, and to value each other aesthetically rather than instrumentally. We must be prepared to decry big institutions as heartless and small ones as petty and provincial. We are encouraged to be inventive, eloquent, and refined. These exhortations may be delivered in the form of a lecture or address, to a 'generalist' audience—lawyers

---

[3] See T. Eagleton, *Literary Theory* (Minneapolis, 1983) 17–53; G. Graff, *Professing Literature* (Chicago, 1987).

rather than professional literary critics—in a milieu like a law review or law school auditorium often devoted to constitutional debate. If so, the context will emphasize the civilizing and morally edifying functions of literature over its message of personal liberation. On occasions commanding piety—graduations, memorial lectures, bicentennials—paeans to the power of imagination may amount to little more than entreaties to suspend disbelief in received truths and tired institutions. On the other hand, the law-as-literature trope may announce an equally ritualized irreverence, a predictable disillusionment with the merely human origins of human arrangements.

Hence the characteristic risks of the law-as-literature trope. First, a sentimentalism in which passion is never cruel or self-indulgent or muddle-headed, invention is never destructive or dishonest, and civility is always inclusive and never elitist. Second, a facile sophistication that mistakes scepticism for criticism and dishonours good causes with bad arguments. Third, a genteel authoritarianism that restricts the aesthetic to the role of ornamenting institutionalized power and becalming the spirit of discontent. While these temptations have different political valences, they all imply reductive characterizations of both literature and law. The law-as-literature trope is understood to imply that left to lawyers, law is mere letter: dry, abstract, artificial, unyieldingly rigid, naively formalistic, cynical, calculating, contentious, profane. Literature, by contrast is a redemptive spirit of unrepressed feeling, anarchic play, or unembarrassed faith.

Although law and literature scholarship is in constant danger of blundering down one of these impasses, it has more promising possibilities. To realize them scholars must apprehend 'the literary' not as something extrinsic to law which corrects or redeems or ornaments it. The literary must be seen to be intrinsic to law in so far as law necessarily involves the construction of the characters, personas, sensibilities, identities, myths, and traditions that compose our social world.

These risks and possibilities may be illustrated by examining a number of discrete genres of literary criticism of law. Each is characterized by the prevalence of certain 'tropes', or rhetorical figures. While all of these genres of course share the law-as-literature trope, each genre hinges this law–literature analogy on a different image of literary activity.

I will discuss five such genres of criticism. The hermeneutic criticism of law, associated with the law-as-interpretation trope, illustrates the risk of scepticism. The narrative criticism of law, associated with the law-as-narration trope, illustrates the risk of scepticism. The rhetorical criticism of law, associated with the tropes of law-as-rhetoric, law-as-persuasion, and law-as-dialogue, illustrates the risk of authoritarianism. The deconstructive criticism of law, associated with the tropes of law-as-signification and law-as-language, illustrates both the sceptical and sentimental risks. Finally, the cultural criticism of law, associated with the trope of law-as-representation illustrates the promise of literary criticism of law to illuminate the role of law in the cultural production of meaning.

The Law-as-Interpretation Trope

One genre is the hermeneutic criticism of law, characterized by the focus on interpretation as the basic mode of literary action. Within this genre, the law-as-literature claim becomes a claim that law is most fundamentally a practice of interpretation.[4] This was the first and remains the most familiar genre of law and literature scholarship. To understand why this genre developed is to understand how legal scholars came to see literary criticism and literary theory as relevant to law.

Between the Revolution and the Civil War, American lawyers developed a sophisticated view of law as an interpretive activity. This hermeneutic model of lawyering faced increasing stresses as the Civil War approached. The collapse of this model interacted with other cultural changes that pushed progressive era lawyers in the direction of seeing themselves more as scientific observers of American society than as authoritative interpreters of American political institutions. Progressive lawyers increasingly identified a

---

[4] Key examples include P. Bobbitt, *Constitutional Fate* (New York, 1982); Robert Cover, 'Violence and the Word' (1986) 95 *Yale Law Journal* [*Yale LJ*] 1601; R. Dworkin, *Law's Empire* (London, 1986); S. Fish, *Doing What Comes Naturally: Change, Rhetoric and the Practice of Theory in Literary and Legal Studies* (Durham, 1989); Owen Fiss, 'Objectivity and Interpretation' (1982) 34 *Stanford Law Review* [*Stan. L. Rev.*] 739; S. Levinson, 'Law as Literature' in S. Levinson and S. Mailbox (eds.), *Interpreting Law and Literature: A Hermeneutic Reader* (Evanston, 1988) 155–75; M. Tushnet, *Red, White and Blue: A Critical Analysis of Constitutional Law* (Cambridge, Mass., 1988).

creative and aesthetic dimension to the judicial observation and representation of society. Yet their firm sense that law properly served prevailing social custom and consensus prevented any great anxiety about the legitimacy of the judicial imagination. Indeed they were more likely to criticize conservative judicial decisions as unimaginative than as overly inventive. Throughout this period, legal interpretation was seen either as a fairly conventional exercise, or as a matter of putting texts to discernible social purposes. Interpretation might require skill but it was not an impossible matter of determining inherently indeterminate meanings.[5]

Only with the civil rights revolution did reformist lawyers lose their confidence that legal interpretation—particularly constitutional interpretation—could be grounded in social custom or majority opinion. If the judicial guardian of minority rights could not be a social scientist, she needed some other identity—a void which the idea of the judge as artist might fill. And if the aspirational meaning of the constitution's vague civil rights clauses could no longer be supplied by social consensus, it would have to be invented. A residual majoritarianism suggested that judges, like artists, could have only persuasive rather than coercive power over the public. Lacking final power, judges could only engage the public and its political representatives in a process of dialogue and hope to win their way by charm.[6]

In the meantime, American literary criticism, partly under the sway of continental influences, had evolved in the direction of celebrating the reader as the true creative source of literary meaning. To American legal scholars, continental 'hermeneutics' and American 'Reader-response theory' seemed suited to explain the new practice of counter-majoritarian constitutional interpretation as a noble and necessary act of literary invention. In his or her role

---

[5] William Blatt, 'A History of Statutory Interpretation: A Study in Form and Substance' (1985) 6 *Cardozo Law Review* [*Cardozo L. Rev.*] 799; R. Ferguson, *Law and Letters in American Culture* (Cambridge, Mass., 1984); R. W. Gordon, 'Legal Thought and Legal Practice in the Age of American Enterprise, 1870–1920' in G. Geison (ed.), *Professions and Professional Ideologies in America* (Princeton, 1983); P. Kahn, *Legitimacy and History: Self-Government in American Constitutional Theory* (New Haven, 1992); F. Lieber, *Legal and Political Hermeneutics* (Boston, 1839); H. Jefferson Powell, 'The Original Understanding of Original Intent' (1985) 98 *Harvard Law Review* [*Harv. L. Rev.*] 885.

[6] A. Bickel, *The Least Dangerous Branch: The Supreme Court at the Bar of Politics* (Indianapolis, 1962).

as constitutional interpreter, the judge became an example of a previously unrecognized type of literary artist: the literary critic. The judge-as-literary-critic metaphor was the central trope of the hermeneutic criticism of law, around which was organized a largely epistemological debate about the legitimacy of legal interpretation. How, if interpretation was unconstrained by text or authorial intent, could it be objective? If not objective, how could interpretation be impartial; and if not impartial, how could it be fair? On the other hand, if constrained by social convention, how could interpretation be fair to the marginalized and despised?

Hermeneutic criticism of law makes two claims about legal language that are sensible but no longer surprising. First, much of it repeats the now familiar objections to empiricist conceptions of linguistic meaning developed by Wittgenstein, Quine and other pragmatist philosophers: that all thought is mediated by language, that language is conventional, that there can be no private language of sensation, that there can be no theory-free description of sense-data, that meaning is use. Generally these ideas are deployed ritually to slaughter imaginary proponents of the view that the meaning of legal texts can be authoritatively fixed by reference to the intentions or other mental states of their authors.

Second, much of the recent legal hermeneutics also repeats the pragmatist attack on rationalist conceptions of linguistic meaning. Thus from the maxim that all thought is in language it follows that concepts are always conventional categories, to be used and interpreted in light of the experiences and expectations of communities of language-users; that the contents of such conventional categories may be linked by historical association rather than any shared characteristic; that the domains of concepts are therefore inherently unstable and their boundaries indeterminate. Generally, legal hermeneutic scholarship applies these points in ritually slaughtering imaginary proponents of the view that the meaning of legal texts is fixed by their language.

From these sensible claims about the indeterminacy of legal meaning, legal hermeneutic scholars frequently derive their third more dubious claim: that the indeterminacy of legal texts undermines the legitimacy of legal interpretation. The more subversive efforts at legal hermeneutics tend to leave off at this point, their critical task completed. The more meliorative efforts proceed with performative demonstrations that sensitivity and imagination can produce persuasive interpretive arguments nonetheless. Yet both share a sense that legal indeterminacy necessitates a legitimation crisis.

I doubt that debate about the validity or justice of legal interpretation can be usefully conducted at the level of generality that has characterized most hermeneutic criticism of law. Most legal interpretation does not raise the fundamental questions about American society that interpretations of the Civil War Amendments must address. Thus a shared sense of interpretive crisis among a community of interpreters of the kind that developed among American constitutional theorists is itself an internal interpretive judgment about discord in a particular institutional tradition. As an interpretive judgment, the identification of such an interpretive impasse cannot be taken as evidence that interpretive judgments are inherently baseless. The debate over the objectivity of legal interpretation therefore provides an example of the sceptical misuse of literary theory.

The Law-as-Narrative Trope

A second genre of literary criticism of law treats the paradigmatic literary activity as the telling of stories.[7] Here, the law-as-literature

---

[7] Key examples include Kathryn Abrams, 'Hearing the Call of Stories' (1991) 79 *California Law Review* 971; Anthony Alfieri, 'Reconstructing Poverty Law Practice: Learning Lessons of Client Narrative' (1991) 100 *Yale LJ* 2107; M. Ball, *The Word and the Law* (Chicago, 1993); P. Brooks and P. Gewirtz (eds.), *Law's Stories: Narrative and Rhetoric in Law* (New Haven, 1996); Robert Cover, 'The Supreme Court 1982 Term, Foreword: Nomos and Narrative' (1983) 97 *Harv. L. Rev.* 4; Anne C. Dailey, 'Feminism's Return to Liberalism' (1993) 102 *Yale LJ* 1265; Richard Delgado, 'Storytelling for Oppositionists and Others: A Plea for Narrative (1989) 87 *Michigan Law Review* [*Mich. L. Rev.*] 2411; Patricia Ewick and Susan Silbey, 'Subversive Stories and Hegemonic Tales: Toward a Sociology of Narrative' (1995) 29 *Law & Society Review* 197; Jack Getman, 'Voices' (1988) 66 *Texas Law Review* [*Tex. L. Rev.*] 577; Christopher Gilkerson, 'Poverty Law Narratives: The Critical Practice and Theory of Receiving and Translating Client Stories' (1992) 43 *Hastings Law Review* 861; Lynn Henderson, 'Legality and Empathy' (1987) 85 *Mich. L. Rev.* 1574; Martha Mahoney, 'Legal Images of Battered Women: Redefining the Issue of Separation' (1991) 90 *Mich. L. Rev.* 1; Carol Rose, 'Property as Story-Telling: Perspectives from Narrative Theory, Game Theory, and Feminist Theory' (1989) 2 *Yale Journal of Law and Humanities* [*Yale JL & Hum.*] 37; Richard Sherwin, 'Law Frames: Historical Truth and Narrative Necessity in a Criminal Case' (1994) 47 *Stan. L. Rev.* 39; R. Weisberg, *Poethics and Other Strategies of Law and Literature* (New York, 1992); R. West, *Narrative, Authority, and Law* (New York, 1993); Lucie White, 'Subordination,

trope takes the more specific form of law-as-narrative. In the narrative criticism of law, 'narrative' tends to connote particularity rather than abstraction, emotional involvement rather than detached rationality, creativity rather than technicality, fluidity rather than rigidity. Often the law-as-narrative trope contrasts a redemptive vision of law as life-giving spirit with an indictment of law's actuality as desiccated letter. In this line of writing, law's redemptive function is to bear witness to the pathos of human suffering. On the other hand, the law-as-narrative trope may play a debunking role, embarrassing law's aspirations to rationality and regularity with an exposure of lawyers' trickery or judges' inconsistency.

The call to view law as narrative tends to be offered as something of a paradox, suggesting that law and narrative are ordinarily opposed. The law-as-narrative trope asserts that contrary to pretence, law is merely a story, one subjective rendering among many; or that it would be better for us all if law were more like narrative literature and less like itself; or that buried within the routines of legal practice lies an element of creativity that can redeem the practice of law or sustain the spirit of its practitioners. Typically, the trope is at once subjunctive in mood, imperative in voice, and wistful in tone: *imagine* law as narrative!

Thus, when lawyers and legal scholars liken law to narrative, they are offering what a linguist might call a performative remark. Rather than denoting similarities between law and narrative, the law-as-narrative trope calls upon the reader to assimilate them *despite their presumed differences*, to make an imaginative leap, to participate in a *fiction*. Thus, scholars and lawyers who use the trope do not mean it literally—indeed, they offer it to oppose what they condemn as the literalism of the law. To understand the trope is already to heed its call, to perform it by imagining immanent within law a hidden character and potential awaiting dramatic realization.

The presumed antinomy of law and narrative is explicit in recent writing about legal themes in narrative literature. Much of this work assumes that law is mechanistic, abstract, rule-bound, and alienating; and that the experience of lawyers and legal actors

Rhetorical Survival Skills, and Sunday Shoes: Notes on the Hearing of Mrs. G.' (1990) 38 *Buffalo Law Review* 6; P. Williams, *The Alchemy of Race and Rights: Diary of a Law Professor* (Cambridge, Mass., 1991).

and the justice of legal decisions would be improved if the abstracted, professional, rationalist voice of law were replaced or complemented by a more human voice.[8] Scholarly writing that implores us to see the human drama obscured by the rules and categories of the law tends to incorporate a sentimental view of literature as antithetical to reason. In such writing, narrative literature stands for human feeling, and is figured as alien to law but inherent in the persons who populate legal settings. Hence narrative represents an insurgent potentiality within law, forever threatening to throw off the robes of reason that confine our passionate natures. This is how the law-as-narrative trope holds in suspense its two seemingly antithetical claims: that narrative is inherent in law, yet that narrative can also redeem or subvert it.

The law-as-narrative trope must be understood as a particularly anti-professional or anti-theoretical version of the law-as-literature trope. Narrative is the aspect of literature most easily appreciated by those who are not technically trained, theoretically informed, or even literate.

Narrative denotes the simple activity of storytelling. To represent a phenomenon in narrative terms is to emphasize change and development. In a story, events are related to one another over time, acquiring meaning from the order in which they happen, or the order in which they are revealed. To experience events as a narrative is to grow or learn. Narratives have beginnings, ends, climaxes, resolutions. They promise suspense, curiosity, entertainment. They are pleasurable and even addictive, inviting us to give up control, so as to experience a childlike credulity and wonder.[9]

Of course, while fiction is always narrative, narrative is not always fictional. Nevertheless, the association of narrative with fiction identifies it with imaginative literature. To call a story a narrative is to emphasize the imaginative activity of a narrator. We expect a 'narrative' account of events, even if factual, to reflect a particular, and often highly imaginative, point of view.

---

[8] Jack Gertman, 'Voices' (1988) 66 *Tex. L. Rev.* 577; Paul Gears, 'Aeschylus' Law' (1988) 101 *Harv. L. Rev.* 1043; B. Thomas, *Cross-Examinations of Law and Literature* (Cambridge, 1987); R. Weisberg, *The Failure of the Word* (New Haven, 1984); R. West, 'Adjudication is Not Interpretation' in *Narrative, Authority, and Law*, n. 7 above, 89–178.

[9] See R. Barthes, *The Pleasure of the Text* (R. Miller (trans.), New York, 1975).

The 'narratives' of interest to non-literary academics may be 'oral histories' or folktales that are told and retold. These narratives are artifacts without necessarily having been self-consciously produced as art and so may be viewed as data, revealing a world view. The academic collector of folk narrative may seek to record and canonize a perspective otherwise unrecognized and suppressed. In so doing, she may reduce official discourse to the status of narrative, just one perspective among many.

If narration is an act of self-definition, and an implicit challenge to some official point of view, then narration seems to promise psychological and political liberation. A patient in psychoanalytic therapy presents her experience or her dreams for analysis in narrative form. For the psychoanalyst Roy Schafer, 'the self is a telling',[10] and the aim of therapy is a 'radically new, jointly authored work'.[11] The therapeutic subject emerges with a new, more aesthetically complete narrative of the self with a beginning (repressed trauma), a middle (neurotic conflict), and an end (self-knowledge, recovery, release).

The political therapy of consciousness-raising has a similar dramatic structure, in which narration triumphs over not only a psychological process of repression but also a social process of 'silencing'. Indeed, to the influential feminist psychiatrist Judith Herman, psychoanalysis and consciousness-raising are just two examples of a more general phenomenon of recovery from trauma, a phenomenon that is always narrative in method and political in significance.[12] In Herman's vision, power consists largely of the capacity to inflict atrocity while silencing protest. At the same time, recovery from the traumatic effects of atrocity depends upon the capacity to integrate the memory of trauma into a coherent narrative of the self, and thereby challenge power. The Recovery Movement that Herman has helped inspire frames both psychological health and political justice in terms of narrative coherence. Whether self-narration is conceived primarily in political or in psychological terms, narrating and revising personal history is increasingly prescribed as the route to an aesthetic transcendence of suffering.

---

[10] Roy Schafer, 'Narration in the Psychoanalytic Dialogue' in W. J. T. Mitchell (ed.), *On Narrative* (Chicago, 1981) 25, 31.

[11] Schafer, n. 10 above, at 31–2.

[12] J. Herman, *Trauma and Recovery: The Aftermath of Violence—from Domestic Abuse to Political Terror* (New York, 1997).

In sum, to liken law to narrative may be to link it to popular culture, the realm of tall tales and twelve-step programmes. The law-as-narrative trope imagines law as literature, but literature that is immediately accessible, unencrypted. Unlike the 'interpretive turn', a 'narrative turn' offers literature without the interdisciplinary middleman of literary theory. It promises not so much interdisciplinarity as extradisciplinarity, an escape from one's own discipline into a literary playground, unpoliced by literary professionals. The turn to narrative is a *return*, a *recovery* of an undamaged inner child beneath the professional shell. The anti-professionalism implicit in the law-as-narrative trope is, therefore, closely related to its sentimentality.

Yet closer attention to literary theories of narrative might discourage sentimental uses of the law-as-narrative trope. First, literary theories treat narrative as the product of imagination working within and upon the constraints of convention. This should discourage us from unreflectively opposing narrative to other social practices as intrinsically more authentic, spontaneous, or sincere. Second, literary scholarship of narrative reveals that the conventions governing narrative are historically contingent—including the very convention that associates narrative with originality and individual self-expression. The characteristics that we now associate with 'narrative' are those of the narrative forms peculiar to modern society—the novel and the national history. These narrative forms presuppose certain legal institutions, which in turn rely on the narrative description of legal subjects and legal institutions that the novel and the academic history exemplify. Law and narrative may thus be mutually complicit rather than antithetical.

The Law-as-Rhetoric Trope

A third genre, the *rhetorical criticism of law*, presents the literary aspect of law as the activities of persuasion and deliberative dialogue. It may find expression in the tropes of law-as-persuasion, law-as-deliberation, law-as-dialogue, and especially 'law-as-rhetoric'.[13] In Classical Greece or Rome, rhetoric was the art of

---

[13] See, e.g., Gerald Wetlaufer, 'Rhetoric and Its Denial in Discourse' (1990) 76 *Virginia Law Review* 1545; James B. White, 'Law as Rhetoric, Rhetoric as Law: The Arts of Cultural and Communal Life' (1985) 52 *University of Chicago Law Review* 984.

persuasion by which public actors sought to channel the natural sentiments of an audience toward proper social behaviour and political practice. The *rhetor* persuaded an audience towards a political goal, often 'modelling' the desired public behaviour by proffering the figure of the speaker as an heuristic example of ethical character. Rhetoric in this sense was not merely a tool of law but was itself a kind of legal order, a personal and public discipline, fusing social authority with personal virtue.[14] For contemporary legal scholars rhetoric is linked to the ideal of a civic republic in which politics engages all citizens but in a disinterested way. According to this ideal the virtuous citizen experiences politics as an intellectual debate or dialogue rather than a contest of opposing interest groups. To refer to legal argument by this classical term is to locate the lawyer in the ancient forum, within a society that valued oratory as a civic responsibility. The law-as-rhetoric trope therefore suggests that the contemporary lawyer is both a noble statesman and a quaint anachronism, the vestige of a more virtuous age.

Yet 'rhetoric's' connotations are not uniformly positive. Plato implied that rhetoric was a superficial technique of verbal and emotional manipulation, at odds with the sincere pursuit of wisdom. To call law rhetoric is therefore to evoke the popular view of lawyers as amoral, venal charlatans. Yet this stuffy, learned term also serves to euphemize and exalt as classical wisdom what the public regards as shallow trickery. It suggests that the gulf of suspicion separating lawyers from the lay public is to the discredit of the public, and reflects the decline of classical literacy and its associated virtues. Yet it offers this veiled defence of law only to those educated to the historically received connotations of 'rhetoric'. Thus the law-as-rhetoric trope offers a tantalizingly concealed defence of law, that persuades by praising as cultivated and wise those capable of unravelling its mystery. In this way the law-as-rhetoric trope is an example of the very art it praises, a performative demonstration of its claim that the art of persuasion depends not on superficial technique, but on cultivation, virtue, and penetrating insight into fundamental truths.

The twentieth-century revival of classical rhetoric has for the

---

[14] See R. Barilli, *Rhetoric* (G. Menozzi (trans.), New York, 1989); I. Worthington (ed.), *Persuasion: Greek Rhetoric in Action* (New York, 1994).

most part been a conservative project.[15] Its leaders have tended to view classical learning as a fragile flame to be kept alight, but sheltered, in the dark age of modernity. They feared that modern culture was constitutively opposed to the essential teaching of the classics that there are objective values, transcending human will and opinion, that are in principle rationally discernible. Some of them allowed that modern culture had good reason to fear this teaching which is easily corrupted into a violently purgative orthodoxy or a corrosive scepticism in the hands of the discontented. Accordingly, those privy to the wisdom of the classics had a special responsibility to conserve both social authority and the higher, but inevitably weaker, authority of reason. This was a delicate task requiring considerable rhetorical skill. It involved instilling piety and deference to authority among those incapable of wisdom; and prudence, patience, and respect for social order, among those qualified for initiation into the secrets of wisdom. The conservative rhetorician did not assume that classical rhetoric could or should again become the everyday currency of public discourse for all. Instead he saw rhetoric as an occult knowledge, a powerful and subtle instrument of persuasion, instruction, and concealment to be deployed by an embattled intellectual and moral elite in addressing different messages to different audiences.

On this conservative rhetorical model, rhetoric serves to check rather than enable popular democracy and personal liberty. But it may be prudent for rhetoric to present itself as a friend to these modern institutions. And so it may speak in the ambiguous language of 'self-governance', encoding a sermon on self-discipline within an apparent endorsement of popular power. Or it may praise tolerance as a salutary form of restraint without conceding that different opinions are of equal authority. But ultimately, conservative rhetoric sees itself as pedagogy, however much it may resemble democratic dialogue.

Can rhetoric nevertheless serve liberal democracy? What would qualify as a liberal rhetoric? It would refigure dialogue as

---

[15] See Robert J. Connors, Linda S. Ede, and Andrea Lunsford, 'The Revival of Rhetoric in America' in R. Connors, L. Ede and A. Lunsford (eds.), *Essays on Classical Rhetoric and Modern Discourse* (New York, 1984); revealing examples include R. S. Crane *et al.* (eds.), *Critics and Criticism* (New York, 1952); H. Jaffa, *Crisis of the House Divided* (New York, 1959); L. Strauss, *Persecution and the Art of Writing* (Glencoe, 1952); R. Weaver, *The Ethics of Rhetoric* (Chicago, 1953).

an egalitarian democratic process, rather than an intrinsically hier-archical process of pedagogy. It might abandon the classical teach-ing that there is an ultimate truth of the matter about questions of value, or it might presume that true values could only be discov-ered through an open-ended and universally inclusive process of rational discussion.

What might be the role of rhetoric in such an egalitarian process? It might be a filter, screening out the expression of views that are intolerant, or that cannot be defended by reference to public reasons.[16] Or it might be a set of conventions specific to a particular community, facilitating collective action by channelling opinion towards a limited number of agenda choices. Or it might reaffirm certain process values important to democratic delibera-tion, like tolerance, willingness to compromise, or trust in the good faith of antagonists in debate. But in calling such an enabling culture of argument 'rhetoric', we invoke a specifically classical cultural heritage at odds with the egalitarian, pluralist, and rela-tivist values of modern liberalism.

Conservative rhetoricians would insist that the idea of a plural-ist or egalitarian rhetoric is inherently confused. They would note that liberal rhetoricians treat tolerance and the equal standing of all participants as intrinsically important process values; they would argue that if any values, including process values, are intrinsic, not all opinions can be equally valuable. They would insist that conversation about value is pointless if there is no truth of the matter and every opinion is as good as any other.

This conservative critique poses a considerable challenge to the project of a liberal rhetoric. The disagreement comes down to this: both liberal and conservative rhetoricians offer rhetoric as a response to the modern faith in the subjectivity of value. To rhetoric's liberal proponents, however, the subjectivity of value is an intractable reality which political discourse must accommo-date. By contrast, for the conservative rhetoricians the modern faith in the subjectivity of value is an irrational prejudice which rhetoric ultimately refutes. The disagreement between liberal and conservative rhetoric is fundamental, but not always perspicuous.

---

[16] See B. Ackerman, *Social Justice in the Liberal State* (New Haven, 1980) and J. Rawls, *Political Liberalism* (New York, 1993) for models of constrained public dialogue.

Because conservative rhetoricians regard the objectivity of value as a dangerous doctrine, corrosive to existing institutions and offensive to the Luddite masses, they teach it with discretion. The result is that we can never be entirely sure whether ostensibly liberal rhetoric is what it professes to be.

This difficulty is particularly apparent where scholars offer *law* as their model of liberal rhetoric.[17] There is something disconcerting about the notion that litigation should be the setting for democratic deliberation, and that we should take judges as our models of democratic citizenship. The implication is that the deliberative discourse enabled by rhetoric is the preserve of a professional elite: 'Have your attorney call my attorney and we'll dialogue.' It sounds like the caption of a *New Yorker* cartoon. If rhetoric is the special competence of experts we get a rather chilling picture of liberal society as a charade of pluralist conflict disguising an inner reality of elite consensus and professional courtesy.

The Law-as-Language Trope

A fourth genre is the *deconstructive criticism of law*. This genre of literary criticism of law takes its inspiration from the work of literary critic and philosopher Jacques Derrida—who in recent years has turned his attention to law.[18] Deconstruction may be thought of as a combination of three elements. First, an adaptation of the anti-essentialist themes of pragmatist epistemology to the practice of reading. Second, a highly original reading strategy designed to produce metaphysical errors in any text by finding essentialism implicit in the use of such unavoidable devices as concepts, generalizations, inferences, conclusions, rhetorical figures, and narratives. Third, characteristically Derridean targets of critique largely consisting in various forms of romantic populism, which Derrida sees as expressions of a metaphysically essentialist ideal of authenticity, with totalitarian implications. The ultimate target of Derrida's deconstruction is not the metaphysics

---

[17] See L. Bollinger, *The Tolerant Society* (New York, 1986); Frank Michelman, 'Traces of Self-Government' (1986) 100 *Harv. L. Rev.* 3; J. Vining, *The Authoritative and the Authoritarian* (Chicago, 1986); J. B. White, *When Words Lose their Meaning* (Chicago, 1984).

[18] See especially, Jacques Derrida, 'Force of Law: The Mystical Foundation of Authority' (1990) 11 *Cardozo L. Rev.* 919.

but the *politics* of 'presence', the politics of popular sovereignty which, he fears, tends to exclude all that can be seen as foreign, cosmopolitan, sophisticated, artificial, or intellectual.

Most practitioners of deconstruction in law have identified with the left wing of the legal academy, either as 'critical legal scholars' or feminist scholars. Deconstructive criticism treats law as no more and no less literary than any other use of language. One of its recurrent tropes is law-as-language. However it draws an additional trope from Derridean deconstruction: language-as-literature. Deconstructive critics treat all language use, or 'signification', as figurative rather than literal. Thus, deconstructive criticism represents law as an inherently literary practice of signification. In deconstructive criticism of law, the fact that signification is figurative is often treated as an indictment: language distorts or obscures what it represents. Above all it reduces the richness and complexity of the experienced world. Law, as a form of signification—as the letter—is therefore inherently reductive. This charge of reductiveness generally takes two forms, one epistemological and one ethical.

The epistemological version usually appears as part of an argument that legal rules do not have clear or determinate implications for future cases. Legal standards condition results on 'subjective' mental states, but these can only be known through inherently reductive 'objective' indicia. The law's inevitable gap between rule and purpose, letter and spirit, is a recurrent source of (presumably undesirable) flexibility. Critical legal scholars in particular interested themselves in deconstruction as the latest model of imported epistemological critique. They accordingly invoked the sceptical implications of deconstruction to buttress their critical accounts of 'liberal' legal doctrine as indeterminate and fatally contradictory.[19]

---

[19] Some examples include Jack Balkin, 'Deconstructive Practice and Legal Theory' (1987) 96 *Yale LJ* 743, James Boyle, 'The Politics of Reason: Critical Legal Theory and Local Social Thought' (1985) 133 *University of Pennsylvania Law Review* 685; Clare Dalton, 'An Essay in the Deconstruction of Contract Doctrine' (1985) 94 *Yale LJ* 997; Gerald Frug, 'The Ideology of Bureaucracy in American Law' (1984) 97 *Harv. L. Rev.* 1277; David Kennedy, *International Legal Structures* (Baden-Baden, 1987); Duncan Kennedy, 'A Semiotics of Legal Argument' (1991) 42 *Syracuse Law Review* 75; Gary Peller, 'The Metaphysics of American Law' (1985) 73 *California Law Review* 1152; Pierre Schlag, ' "Le Hors de texte, c'est moi": The Politics of Form and the Domestication of Deconstruction' (1990) 11 *Cardozo L. Rev.* 1631.

Much of this criticism amounted to facile scepticism. Because it applies equally to all legal standards and institutions, such epistemological deconstruction cannot effectively criticize any particular institution. Moreover, because it portrays legal language as always equally conflicted and incoherent, such deconstruction cannot explain why legal actors sometimes experience legal language as in crisis and sometimes do not.

Ethical deconstruction finds different implications in the reductiveness of legal language. First, that representations of the public interest or of society in legal settings will always be partial and partisan. Second, that the groups or 'voices' excluded from representation will often be the weakest and most oppressed. Deconstruction can be used to show that such voices have been excluded and to challenge such exclusion as itself oppressive 'violence'. Thus feminist legal scholars have tended to see a humane, ethical message in deconstruction's demonstrations that categorical thought is reductive and exclusive of 'difference'.[20] In deconstructive thought 'difference' usually means the distinguishability and comparability of particulars that enables their variable categorization. In feminist deconstruction, however, 'difference' also means the deviance ascribed to women and other underprivileged groups. Thus the exclusion of difference becomes the exclusion of the underprivileged from political representation. The difficulty is that deconstructive premises imply that the 'exclusion' of difference is inevitable in any use of language, so that there can be no ethical imperative to be all-inclusive. Because ethical deconstruction of law often presumes that law always should—but never can—recognize the full particularity of its subjects, it exemplifies the risk of sentimentalism. Deconstruction appears to be at best an ornament if not an actual impediment to arguments for greater political participation by the underprivileged.

In its home terrain of France and its home field of literature, deconstruction opposes as totalitarian a radical tradition associated

---

[20] Examples include D. Cornell, *The Philosophy of the Limit* (New York, 1992); D. Cornell, *Beyond Accommodation: Ethical Feminism, Deconstruction and the Law* (New York, 1991); Christine Desan, 'Expanding the Legal Vocabulary: The Challenge Posed by the Deconstruction and Defense of Law' (1986) 95 *Yale LJ* 969; Z. Eisenstein, *The Female Body and the Law* (Berkeley, 1988); Joan Scott, 'Deconstructing Equality-Versus-Difference: Or the Uses of Post-Structuralist Theory for Feminism' (1988) 14 *Feminist Studies* 33; I. M. Young, *Justice and the Politics of Difference* (Princeton, 1990).

with Marxism. But in the United States, deconstruction is merely the latest representative of the post-Kantian critical tradition in continental thought that for over thirty years has offered a discreet cover for affiliation with a genteel and humane Marxism. Thus in the United States the invocation of deconstruction signals a vague identification with the New Left themes of community and participatory democracy, notwithstanding an explicit repudiation of these values in deconstruction's canonical texts. The reason is that the political identification of American intellectual work has long since ceased to depend upon its normative conclusions. The intellectual American left has so long had to hide its hunted, heretical politics beneath the enigmatic rhetoric and epistemological scepticism of continental philosophy that it has come to see politics as a matter of writing style.

The Law-as-Representation Trope

We have thus far considered four genres of scholarship—the hermeneutic, narrative, rhetorical and deconstructive criticism of law—organized around four variants of the law-as-literature trope—law-as-interpretation, law-as-narration, law-as-persuasion, and law-as-signification. These four genres pretty well exhaust the first wave of scholarship developing the law-as-literature analogy. Some of this scholarship was aimed at defending counter-majoritarian judicial discretion and informing its exercise with Kantian liberal ideals of personal autonomy and dignity in the face of the increasing influence of law and economics. Some of this scholarship instead articulated a scandalized 'discovery' that the legitimacy of adjudication could not be placed upon objective foundations. Overall, these genres of scholarship reveal certain risks associated with the law-as-literature trope: the risks of sentimentalism, scepticism, and authoritarianism.

These risks have as much to do with the way we view law as with the connotations of the literary. A familiar view of law in modern society presumes that the coercive force of the state must be justified by consent: the consent of individuals to private arrangements or the consent of populations to public policies. Legal judgment, then, polices the disputed boundaries between public and private, mine and thine, consent and coercion. The fundamental operation of law is to identify legal persons, entitlements, and preferences; when law has identified all of these, it has fully represented society. On this view of law, authority is vested solely in human will, and it is the essentially mimetic task of law to reflect and enforce that will.

Much critical scholarship in law accepts the premise that law should mimic social will, but then argues that law either does not or cannot do so. It is argued that the lines between public and private, mine and thine, and consent or coercion are arbitrary and cannot themselves be based in consent. Accordingly, it is the personal interests or contestable value judgments of officials, not the preferences of society, that resolve legal disputes. The only defence against this official discretion is a system of formal rules. Yet, the argument continues, these rules yield arbitrary results. By blinding legal decision-makers to nuances of social context, rule formalism achieves results that popular will would reject as irrational; it distorts or ignores the preferences of affected parties and presents this indifference to its human consequences as a virtue.

This style of criticism courts the twin dangers of scepticism and sentimentalism. Criticism is egregiously sceptical when it treats practices as presumptively illegitimate unless they rest on a foundation of epistemological certainty. Since subjective judgment and reductive formalism are both useful tools of practical reasoning, they should not by themselves discredit legal decision-making. Criticism is egregiously sentimental when it assumes that subjective judgment and reductive formalism, even if necessary to practical reasoning, are always inappropriate when applied to human beings. *How* human beings should be represented in social thought is a pressing moral question; but *whether* they should be represented is not. Criticism that can be dismissed as egregiously sceptical or sentimental ill serves the values that motivate it.

The dangers of scepticism and sentimentality are endemic to criticism that accepts the mimetic ideal of law as the accurate depiction of social will. It only makes sense to criticize law for inaccurately representing individual or collective preferences if preferences have a determinate character independent of their legal representations. A more sophisticated and less fragile critique recognizes that social will may not be independent of its legal representation. Individual preferences depend upon socially conferred identities and socially distributed resources; collective preferences depend on the method by which they are measured and the order in which alternatives are posed. Because all of these conditions affecting preferences are themselves influenced by law, law cannot simply reflect but must also help compose society and its characters.

Thus, the legal representation of social will bears little resemblance to scientific observation. It is more like the literary representation of such generic themes as 'the pastoral' and 'the sublime', familiar myths such as Faust and Don Juan or stock characters such as Reynard the Fox and the hard-boiled gumshoe. Like preferences, none of these entities exists independent of its representations. These representations are judged aesthetically rather than epistemologically: they are judged according to the experience they enable rather than their truth to past experience. So too we can judge law aesthetically, according to the society it forms, the identities it defines, the preferences it encourages, and the subjective experience it enables. We can 'read' and criticize law as part of the making of a culture.

Thus, the most promising literary criticisms of law are not particularly aimed at defending legal interpretation against majorit-arian politics or defending human dignity against utilitarian rationality. Instead they interpret law as a cultural datum and analyse legal processes as arenas for the production of cultural meaning. In such 'cultural studies' of law, the fixed preferences of economic analysis and the stable self-sufficient persons of Kantian ethics give way to a more complex and contingent picture of the self. Our desires are not simply our own, given in advance of the political, economic, and legal institutions that recognize them or the cultural media available for expressing them. Instead, our preferences and interests depend upon the identities socially and culturally available to us. Although socially recognized, these identities are not simply dictated by class or gender or any other invariant social structure. They are never more than temporary settlements of ongoing struggles and negotiations among social actors engaged in projects that are at once strategic and aesthetic, instrumental and expressive. Often these struggles over meaning are legal struggles waged in legal fora.

This genre of criticism treats legal disputing and transacting as occasions for the representation of self, others, and society. It equates the literary with the depiction of character and the delineation of a social landscape. In this way, the cultural criticism of law metaphorically extends the concept of literature from the presentation of such depictions for aesthetic consumption to the everyday practical activity of staking claims to desirable roles and identities or interpreting those roles in advantageous ways.[21] Law, then, is literary in so far as it involves claiming, exchanging and distributing not just resources, but also cultural meanings. Law-as-representation is its constitutive trope. It draws on the structuralism of Michel Foucault, the pragmatic cultural sociology of Pierre Bourdieu, the normative aestheticism of Nietzsche, and the recent Cultural Studies and New Historicism movements in literary studies.[22]

For the most part, cultural criticisms of law have examined cultural representation in two sorts of legal settings. First, they have read the representations of parties in disputes that take on

---

[21] See Guyora Binder, 'Representing Nazism: Advocacy and Identity at the Trial of Klaus Barbie' (1989) 98 *Yale LJ* 1321; Guyora Binder and Robert Weisberg, 'Cultural Criticism of Law' (1997) 49 *Stan. L. Rev.* 1149; J. Clifford, *The Predicament of Culture: Twentieth Century Ethnography, Literature and Art* (Cambridge, Mass., 1988), 277–346; Janet E. Halley, 'Reasoning about Sodomy: Act and Identity In and After Bowers v. Hardwick' (1993) 79 *Virginia Law Review* 1721; Janet E. Halley, 'Equivocation and the Legal Conflict Over Religious Identity in Early Modern England' (1991) 3 *Yale JL & Hum.* 33; Janet Halley, 'The Politics of the Closet: Towards Equal Protection for Gay, Lesbian and Bisexual Identity' (1989) 36 *UCLA Law Review* 915; H. Horwitz, *By the Law of Nature: Form and Value in Nineteenth Century America* (New York, 1991); J. Katz, *The Seductions of Crime* (New York, 1988); G. E. Marcus with P. D. Hall, *Lives in Trust: The Fortunes of Dynastic Families in Late Twentieth Century America* (Boulder, 1992); W. B. Michaels, *The Gold Standard and the Logic of Naturalism* (Berkeley, 1987); W. I. Miller, *Bloodtaking and Peacemaking: Feud, Law and Society in Saga Iceland* (Chicago, 1990); M. Shell, *Money, Language and Thought: Literary and Philosophical Economics from the Medieval to the Modern Era* (Berkeley, 1982); M. T. Taussig, *The Devil and Commodity Fetishism in South American* (Chapel Hill, 1980), Robert Weisberg, 'Commercial Morality, The Merchant Character, and the History of the Voidable Preference' (1986) 39 *Stan. L. Rev.* 3.

[22] P. Bourdieu, *Outline of a Theory of Practice* (R. Nice (trans.), Cambridge, 1977); P. Bourdieu, *The Logic of Practice* (R. Nice (trans.), Cambridge, 1990); P. Bourdieu, *Language and Symbolic Power* (J. B. Thompson (ed.), G. Raymond and M. Adamson (trans)., Cambridge, Mass., 1991); M. Foucault, *Discipline and Punish* (Alan Sheridan (trans.), New York, 1977); M. Foucault, *The Order of Things* (New York, 1970); M. Foucault, *The History of Sexuality* (Robert Hurley (trans.), New York 1978); S. Greenblatt, *Shakespearian Negotiations* (Berkeley, 1988); S. Greenblatt, *Renaissance Self-Fashioning: From More to Shakespeare* (Chicago, 1980); A. Nehamas, *Nietzsche: Life as Literature* (Cambridge, Mass., 1985); L. Grossberg, C. Nelson and P. Treichler (eds.), *Cultural Studies* (New York, 1992); B. Thomas, *The New Historicism: and Other Old-Fashioned Topics* (Princeton, 1991); A. A. Veeser (ed.), *The New Historicism* (New York, 1989).

expressive meaning against a background of legal and social norms regulating or recognizing statuses and identities. These norms enable actors to define themselves and one another, or to subvert those definitions. Second, they have examined the representation of character, credit and value in commercial and financial law. The premise of such studies is that commercial capitalism is not only a system of economics, but also a system of representation. The mobilization of resources for production depends upon the cultural work of representing them as commodities, while the disposition of what is produced depends upon the cultural work of constructing the characters who will make investment and consumption decisions. Thus the legal forms of wealth and exchange may mark the shifting, often contested boundaries between community and commerce, between intrinsic and instrumental worth.

Critical scholarship treats law as a dimension of culture in so far as it:

(1) views law as an arena for the performance and contestation of representations of self and as an influence on the roles and identities available to groups and individuals in portraying themselves;

(2) interprets self-portrayal as a project that, whatever its instrumental pay-offs, also has aesthetic and expressive import;

(3) treats the interests and preferences that motivate instrumental action as dependent upon the identities actors assume.

This genre of criticism may be seen as part of the emergent interdisciplinary movement of cultural studies. This movement has blurred the boundaries between the humanities and the social sciences by viewing the phenomena studied by political scientists, sociologists, economists, and historians as social 'texts' available for interpretation and criticism. It has also extended the domain of ethnographic method from the study of traditional non-Western societies to modern Western societies, thereby both expanding anthropology and raising critical questions about the cultural assumptions that have confined it in the past. The closely aligned movement in literary studies, the 'new historicism', has in essence made literary criticism an instrument of the ethnography or archaeology of modernity by treating literary texts as cultural artifacts. But my proposal is not just that legal phenomena be viewed as cultural artifacts or 'social texts' like any others. It is that legal forms and legal processes play a compositional role in modern culture—that cultural criticism must attend to the legal dimension of culture or remain superficial.

Cultural criticism of law has rich implications for descriptive and normative legal theory. While much law and literature scholarship has opposed the literary to the instrumental analysis that dominates contemporary legal discourse, cultural criticism of law rejects this dichotomy. Instead, it implies that far from excluding aesthetic or expressive considerations, such instrumental policy analysis has a constitutively important expressive dimension that literary reading can illuminate. The best cultural studies of law reveal how policy decisions may reshape the expressive possibilities and social identities available to individuals, thereby conditioning the preferences considered by conventional policy analysis.

In striking contrast to the early law and literature scholarship, the newer cultural criticism implies that civil libertarian policies cannot be adequately delineated or defended by reference to the natural rights of individuals to personal autonomy or integrity. If identity is the contingent outcome of socially conditioned strategic choices, it is neither natural nor, in the traditional sense, 'personal'. Cultural criticism of law demands that normative argument defend institutions on the basis of the kind of identities they will cultivate rather than their protection or accurate representation of existing personalities. Such criticism may be seen as part of a broad movement away from mimetic justification, already well established in aesthetics and epistemology, but only now emerging in ethics and politics.

If law is inevitably literary, the call to make it so is not just pointless but deceptive: it implies that if only law becomes more literary, criticism of law will no longer be necessary. To recognize the constitutively literary dimension of law is not to commend law as inevitably humane or redemptive, however. Law's constructions may starve the poor or demean the weak; they may arise out of struggle, strategy, and violence. They demand critical evaluation. Nevertheless laws, legal judgments, legal arguments, legal transactions all have expressive meaning; and to miss law's meaning is to miss a part of what needs criticism.

There is no reason why the literary reading of law must be laudatory. To say that law is literary is also to admit that literature is like law, an arena of strategic conflict. Indeed, some of the most illuminating contemporary criticism of imaginative literature recognizes that literature is a social practice conditioned by institutional conventions, social power, and practical aims. Literature may be a realm of artifice and invention but so is the confidence game—not every expression of creativity exalts the human spirit. Whether any particular literary work is redemptive or humane must be an open question if reading is to qualify as honest inquiry. Similarly, the redeeming qualities of any legal institution must remain in question if the literary criticism of law is to be an honest job.

(PER)VERSIONS OF LAW
IN LITERATURE

Tony Sharpe

In this paper I consider some of the ways in which law has been misunderstood or misrepresented in literature, and speculate why this has been so. My belief is that when literature deals with law, it does so with a tendency to confirm its own superiority as a response to reality, which it achieves by means of a partial or distorting view of law's premises, operations, and consequences. Neither 'law' nor 'literature' can be exactly delimited terms; but by 'literature' I mean that body of poems, plays, and prose fiction in which the creative imagination is manifested in language; and by 'law' I denote the bodies of writing which constitute its basis, and also the systems by which illegality is detected, judged, and punished. I concede that this is a large definition, but it does not seem to me that, typically, literature visualizes law with any great specificity; rather, its recourse to law depends, I am suggesting, on an advantageous selectivity of vision. I wish to develop this with regard to two principal aspects: literature *as* law, and law *in* literature. The first is a kind of competitive emulation of law by literature, and the second involves, not the reflection of specific legal issues in fiction, so much as the implicit (or explicit) comparison within a literary text, between legal methodology and its own ways of working. Such a comparison tends to construct law as a clumsily inflexible system which is incapable of making the kinds of sensitive discrimination that are the province of literature alone.[1]

---

[1] My purpose is to provoke thought, rather than to present an irrefutable case: the general scope of my argument could hardly be substantiated by a less-than-encyclopaedic marshalling of evidence. My tendency to present 'literature' as a kind of homogeneous personification is in some respects outrageous, but is a necessary simplification of a complex matter—even though it lays me open to the charge of treating literature with the presumptuous selectivity with which I allege it tends to treat law. I am not a legal specialist, and therefore my views of law have

Literature as law

My first category, literature *as* law, is not necessarily concerned with making sensitive discriminations as a means of differentiating itself from law, so much as with setting itself up in rivalry. In *Law, Fact and Narrative Coherence*, Bernard Jackson has written that for many people 'adjudication in court' figures as 'the paradigm of legal activity';[2] and the visible achievement of certitudinous judgment is what is aimed at here: in a kind of literary simulation of juridical process, justice must be seen to be done. This is the sort of book Miss Prism wrote, in *The Importance of Being Earnest* (1895), and which she summarized thus: 'The good ended happily, and the bad unhappily. That is what Fiction means'.[3] Her three-decker was never published, even in make-believe; but her viewpoint had some distinguished, if more sophisticated, antecedence. For centuries, writers had chafed at their exclusion by Plato from his ideal society in *The Republic*; and one way of challenging his verdict has been to stress the ethical necessity of literature. Albeit more stately in expression and more weighty in substance, Ben Jonson's musings on the matter in *Timber, or Discoveries* (1640) also insist on the writer's responsibility for just discernment of right and wrong:

I could never thinke the study of *Wisdome* confined only to the Philosopher: or of *Piety* to the *Divine*: or of *State* to the *Politicke*. But that he which can faine a *Common-wealth* (which is the *Poet*) can governe it with *Counsels*, strengthen it with *Lawes*, correct it with *Iudgements*, informe it with *Religion, and Morals*; is all these. Wee do not require in him meere *Elocution*; or an excellent faculty in verse, but the exact knowledge of all vertues, and their Contraries, with ability to render the one lov'd, the other hated, by his proper embattaling them.[4]

---

to rest on the definitions of those who are; there seems to me some truth in Richard Posner's assertions that literature's use of law is often 'metaphorical or . . . highly general', in *Law and Literature: A Misunderstood Relation* (Cambridge, Mass., and London, 1988), 16. The argument against Posner's overall position was forcefully stated by James Boyd White in his review of the book: 'What Can a Lawyer Learn from Literature?' (1989) 102 *Harvard Law Review* 2014–47.

[2] Bernard S. Jackson, *Law, Fact and Narrative Coherence* (Liverpool, 1988), 1.

[3] *Complete Works of Oscar Wilde* (London and Glasgow, 1966), 341.

[4] *Ben Jonson*, Vol.VIII, (C. H. Herford and Evelyn Simpson (eds.), Oxford, 1947), 595.

Jonson is notable as a very early example of the self-constituting man of letters, actually overseeing, in 1616, a published collection of his works. In the account just quoted, qualities of literary craftsmanship are subordinated to qualities of legislative and adjudicative discrimination ('mere' verbal dexterity seems inferior to 'exact knowledge'); and the claims made on behalf of 'the poet' are bold: far from being Platonically surplus to requirements, he is fundamental to the state's well-being, and it seems a short step from the commonwealth he has 'feigned' to the one in which he happens to live.[5] In this tradition, literature embodies justice, in its instructional perceptions; and to see how this might occur in a writer less rebarbative than Jonson, I want to turn to the closing chapter of Jane Austen's *Mansfield Park* (1814), in which, conforming to Prismatic prescription, the good end happily, and the bad end unhappily.

This process begins with a famously concessive note ('Let other pens dwell on guilt and misery'), and an announcement of the authorial desire to restore all approximately deserving characters to 'tolerable comfort', and 'to have done with all the rest';[6] yet it turns out that 'having done' with the unworthy cannot be so perfunctory a process as is initially implied, but instead requires their standing in the dock to have sentences passed. These vary from the conditional discharge that falls to Tom Bertram ('He had suffered, and he had learnt to think'), through more judicious gradations—as in the case of Mr Rushworth, who has not learnt to think: 'The indignities of stupidity, and the disappointments of selfish passion, can excite little pity. His punishment followed his conduct, as did a deeper punishment, the deeper guilt of his wife' (*née* Maria Bertram, who had committed adultery with Henry Crawford). Her fate is to be consigned to a purdah intensified rather than alleviated by her Aunt Norris 'where, shut up together with little society, on one side no affection, on the other, no judgment, it may be reasonably

---

[5] A later exemplar of moral centrality would of course be Pope, claiming as his incitement 'The strong antipathy of Good to Bad'. See 'Epilogue to the Satires: Dialogue II', l. 198 *et seq.*, in *The Poems of Alexander Pope* (John Butt (ed.), London, 1963), 701.

[6] I wish not to encumber a reader with footnotes or pseudo-scholarliness. For the sake of consistency, wherever possible references to works of prose fiction will cite the easily-accessible Penguin editions. The quotations in this paragraph come from *Mansfield Park* (Tony Tanner (ed.), Harmondsworth, 1966), 446, 447, 449, 450, 451, 452, 453.

supposed that their tempers became their mutual punishment'. Aunt Norris, the wicked witch of the story, even receives what reads like a covert death-sentence: we learn that '[n]ot even Fanny had tears for Aunt Norris—not even when she was gone for ever'. As for Henry Crawford, arraigned for 'cold-blooded vanity', we are told that the 'public punishment of disgrace' that should equally attend his conduct as it has Maria's will not do so, as this world's imperfect justice goes;[7] but by the powers invested in her as author of the book, Jane Austen is able to assure us of a not inefficacious system of retribution:

We may fairly consider a man of sense like Henry Crawford, to be providing for himself no small portion of vexation and regret—vexation that must rise sometimes to self-reproach, and regret to wretchedness—in having so requited hospitality, so injured family peace, so forfeited his best, most estimable and endeared acquaintance, and so lost the woman whom he had rationally, as well as passionately loved.

Notwithstanding the chapter's opening declaration, the space it allots to the unhappiness of the bad is considerably in excess of that which it devotes to the happiness of the good. The paragraph in which the novel's central narrative thrust finds culmination is notoriously concise:

I purposely abstain from dates on this occasion, that every one may be at liberty to fix their own, aware that the cure of unconquerable passions, and the transfer of unchanging attachments, must vary much as to time in different people.—I only intreat everybody to believe that exactly at the time when it was quite natural that it should be so, and not a week earlier, Edmund did cease to care about Miss Crawford, and became as anxious to marry Fanny, as Fanny herself could desire.[8]

Within seven paragraphs the book has ended. The perfunctory levity of the passage just quoted hardly disguises the fact that greater animation has been called forth by analysing and describing the various gradations of guilt and misery, greater imaginative specificity has been involved, than in delineating the fulfilment of Fanny's happiness. What predominates in this last chapter is a

---

[7] 'But by G—if she belonged to me, I'd give her the rope's end as long as I could stand over her. A little flogging for man and woman too, would be the best way of preventing such things'—thus Fanny's father, on learning of the adultery: in this respect, at least, aligning himself with narratorial views on equality of treatment (*Mansfield Park*, 428).   [8] *Mansfield Park*, 454.

tone akin to what Burke called the cold neutrality of an impartial judge (*Preface to Brissot's Address to his Constituents* (1794)), in which forensic atmosphere Jane Austen situates the reader as complicit in the act of judgment. In so far as what we witness is a world regulated, in which just consequences are seen to follow certain courses of action, the restoration of balance by the visible apportionment of punishment in the novel closely resembles the culmination of legal process in the paradigmatic act of adjudication. Such resemblances are of course implicit in the closural manoeuvres of a great many more-or-less conventional works of fiction; but it is fair to say that in *Mansfield Park* the effect is heightened. Yet the congruence between process of law and process of literature, thus highlighted, is simultaneously the point at which the differences are most discernible: for if literature dreams of actual rather than virtual power, of poets becoming acknowledged rather than unacknowledged legislators, its relative impotence becomes clearest in the issue of judging.

The act of adjudication is paradigmatic, because at that point the narrative which has been constructed in a court of law takes effect beyond language; the imposition of punishment on guilty parties is what, to most people, makes manifest the actuality of law's power. Hamlet's players can only murder 'in jest'; literature can only punish 'in jest':[9] *Mansfield Park* is both more absolute and more impotent than the legal process it resembles. More impotent, in that its narrative, however magisterial, has no executive issue beyond the story as constructed; more absolute, in that the panoptic survey available to author and readership in the final chapter, which can predict the future and penetrate the states of mind of those within its purview, clearly avails itself of qualities of knowledge unavailable to any actual judge or juror in actual court: the narratorial evidence is unassailable. Miss Prism's dictum, which finds embodiment in the somewhat formulaic structure of Jane Austen's final chapter, denotes a similar purposiveness in literature as in law: that being, the achievement of justice, in which both legal and fictional narratives are resolved. But it is the nature and the meaning of such resolution that shows up the clearest difference: for the tariff of rewards and (principally)

---

[9] '[T]hey do but jest—poison in jest. No offence i' th' world'; *Hamlet*, III. ii, l. 229.

punishments in which the final chapter consists enacts, in its mechanistic ritual, the extinction of fiction in the achievement of justice.

I will say more on this shortly, but before doing so I want to consider another generic sub-type of 'literature *as* law', which concerns itself slightly less with the dispensation of final judgment, than with the processes by which wrong-doing is established and exposed. As Umberto Eco has written, in his gnomic musings on *The Name of the Rose*, 'the fundamental question of philosophy (like that of psychoanalysis) is the same as the question of the detective novel: who is guilty? To know this (to think you know this), you have to conjecture that all the events have a logic, the logic that the guilty party has imposed on them'.[10] The tale that I want to consider is a very early example of the genre, Edgar Allan Poe's 'The Murders in the Rue Morgue', first published in April 1841 in *Graham's Magazine*; and it is interesting to me because, despite its earliness, it seems already subversive of the apparent affinities with law as outlined by Eco. In it, the question 'who is guilty?' receives an answer factually unambiguous and morally ambivalent.

Poe defined this as a 'tale of ratiocination'; its amateur sleuth, Dupin, would father an inordinate fictional progeny, and for the narrator he is a type of 'the analyst [who glories] in that moral activity which *disentangles*'.[11] The point of the tale was to establish the superiority of this 'analytic ability' over mere ingenuity, in a hierarchy which is expressly compared to the difference between 'imagination' and 'fancy'. The principal events of the tale, it will be recalled, are set in motion by the discovery of the mutilated corpses of a mother and her daughter, who had lived secludedly in a Parisian side street. The daughter's body had with great violence been stuffed feet-first up a chimney in their apartment, and the mother's virtually decapitated body flung down into the little courtyard. The events are reported in a newspaper, followed the next day by depositions from the various witnesses (principally auditory); the Parisian police have dutifully arrested the wrong man, under suspicion. Dupin's analytical powers and intuitive

---

[10] Umberto Eco, *Reflections on The Name of the Rose* (London, 1985), 54.

[11] *Edgar Allan Poe: Selected Writings* (David Galloway (ed.), Harmondsworth, 1967), 189.

brilliance lead him to the right conclusion, which is that the culprit is an orang-outang, escaped from the custody of its owner, a sailor who had hoped to make money by it. On demonstrating this to the authorities, the suspect is released—and to that extent, justice is done.

But in the main, justice is not done because, this being post-Enlightenment Paris rather than medieval France, animals are not legally accountable; in fact, notwithstanding the tale's lurid title, no murder has been committed. The particular subversiveness of Poe's model, here, is not only that the first and last terms of the question 'Who is guilty?' are undermined by what the narrative discloses; it is also that the process of solution—Dupin's brilliant disentanglement and intuitive assemblage of the various items of evidence—does not in any significant way interact with those legal or moral dimensions of the plot implicit in words such as 'murder' or 'guilt'. The degrees of implausibility attaching to various aspects of Dupin's deductive sequence reinforce the flagrancy with which it fails to conform to the requirements it appeared to set out to meet: it is a narrative of culpability in which, to borrow from *King Lear*, 'none does offend' (III.vi.170). If one of the motive forces behind both legal and literary process in detective fiction is the production of a guilty party, then Poe's tale marks the beginning of difference.[12] Yet we are left with a solved, and not an unsolved, mystery: albeit one in which the brutal termination of two lives has no issue—is, indeed, irrelevant to what the tale turns out to have been 'about'. The plot is instigated by bestial killing, and duly discloses a beast as perpetrator; we are able to deduce what happened, but that knowledge is our only prize; outside its sphere lie the mangled corpses and what Yeats termed the 'uncontrollable mystery on the bestial floor'.[13]

What the tale fails to do is to close the narrative circle, in the

---

[12] 'What, indeed, does detective fiction do? It creates a problem, a "concrete effect"—the crime—and declares a sole cause relevant: the criminal'—from the essay 'Clues' in Franco Moretti, *Signs Taken For Wonders* (London, 1983), 144. Moretti stresses what might be called the 'end-orientedness' of detective fiction; and although Poe too asserted that 'it is only with the *dénouement* constantly in view that we can give a plot its indispensable air of consequence', the ending of this tale both satisfies and subverts such demands. See his essay 'The Philosophy of Composition' in *Selected Writings*, n. 11 above, 480.

[13] See his poem 'The Magi', in *Yeats's Poems* (A. Norman Jeffares (ed.), London, 1989), 229.

way that *Mansfield Park* does: balance is not restored, the breach
in nature (which had seemed to be a breach in law) is unhealed;
the murders which turn out to have been mere killings turn out,
also, to be incidental to the real meaning of the story told. The
revelation of agency at the same time discloses the irrelevance of
law and the impossibility of restitutive or retributory justice in
respect of the events described. In spite of the apparent congruence between this tale's intentions and procedures and those
appropriate to law, the differences are profound. Poe's particular
achievement here lies in constructing a narrative so diverse in its
appearance and its essence: superficially simulating the law-driven
process of discovery, while dissimulating its subversion of the
premises of legal inquiry. For if a function of law, in its visible
administration of justice, is to make any kind of aberrant behaviour containable within its process, and therefore to that degree
conformable to its construction of reality and its regulation of
society, then it is a universalizing procedure. The man who hacks
his wife to death, the woman who deliberately crushes a hated
rival under her car, the assassin who shoots his victim with a
poison dart, can all, whatever the diverse specifics of their deeds,
fall within the generalizing category of 'murderer' and, when
brought to justice, receive the punishment appropriate to that
category. The individual irregularities of their conduct are as it
were brought into conformity with the law's overarching definition of that type of crime, and so justice becomes impersonal, and
the rent in the social fabric is to some extent mended. Poe's tale,
however, moves not from particulars to universals, but in exactly
the opposite direction: it commences (literally so, in its title) with
the universalizing concept of 'murders', but progresses to the
parodically unique circumstance of the orang-outang—whose
production disables the entire legal machinery attendant on the
crime's solution.[14]

Although in their different ways both *Mansfield Park* and 'The
Murders in the Rue Morgue' seem to be types of 'literature *as*
law', in each case what is finally established is an incongruence:

---

[14] Two further quotations from 'Clues' (trans. Susan Fischer) are suggestive:
'The difference between innocence and guilt returns as the opposition between
stereotype and individual. Innocence is conformity, individuality, guilt'; 'Detective
fiction . . . exists expressly to dispel the doubt that guilt may be impersonal, and
therefore collective and social'—in Moretti, n. 12 above, 135.

because law aims at obviating or annulling the circumstances in which fiction originates.[15] For it is in depicting the existence of conflict, of imbalance, that fiction comes into being; and even if it moves toward resolving conflict and restoring order in a way that can resemble the procedure of law, we should not set aside the Aristotelian beginning and middle of the plot, in favour of the end alone. If law finds affirmation in the restoration of balance, fiction finds, oddly, its own exhaustion and non-existence. As the critic D. A. Miller pointed out in *Narrative and Its Discontents*, fiction depends on an imbalance as its point of departure; and although the comic plot, such as Jane Austen uses, typically moves toward resolution of an initial problem, in resolution lies its own extinction, and in elaboration of the problem and its consequences it has its being. Therefore the end at which law aims, and which the ending chapter of *Mansfield Park* simulates, is the restoration of balance in the triumph of justice; yet at that point fiction loses energy—as is perhaps enacted in the uninterested judiciality of that last chapter. Like *Mansfield Park*, Poe's tale knows that its termination is its death, and therefore provides a conclusion in which nothing is concluded, in which the processes of fiction are gleefully unaccountable to the processes of law, and Dupin turns out to be a kind of sublimely irresponsible artist.[16]

Law in Literature

I move from my first to my second category ('law *in* literature') by means of a quotation from Saul Bellow's first novel *Dangling Man* (1944), implicitly stating the case against literature as a means to judgment—understanding 'judgment' to imply the sort of conclusive assessment leading to moral quantification, that is analogous to legal adjudication. The narrator is speaking of himself in the third person:

Theories of a wholly good or a wholly malevolent world strike him as foolish . . . For him, the world is both, and therefore it is neither. Merely

---

[15] 'Law's aim is to mediate, often to diffuse, but rarely if ever to aggravate, conflict'; Posner, n. 1 above, 79. Law, then, would prefer the novel of chastity to the novel of adultery, the happy families that (according to Tolstoy) are all alike, to the individualistically unhappy ones that are interesting to read about.

[16] D. A. Miller in *Narrative and Its Discontents* (Princeton, 1981), quotes Flaubert's dictum: 'L'ineptie consiste à vouloir conclure' (191).

to make a judgement of that kind is, to representatives of either position, a satisfaction. Whereas, to him, judgement is second to wonder, to speculation on men . . . In a sense, everything is good because it exists. Or, good or not good, it exists, it is ineffable, and, for that reason, marvellous.[17]

Judgment is here constituted as inimical to 'wonder', 'speculation', or a due appreciation of the ineffably marvellous qualities of 'the world that is the case'—to appropriate Wittgenstein. And it is with all these, reliant on a suspension of judgment, that literature is most characteristically concerned—so the argument would run. Miss Prism and those sympathetic to her formula would disagree; but the play in which she is a character does not, of course, support her view of the meaning of fiction; and when Wilde quipped that one would have to have a heart of stone not to laugh at the death of Little Nell (in *The Old Curiosity Shop*), he was reproving Dickens for a sentimentality that had blurred the boundaries between art and life, for writing a fiction that had forgotten the cardinal importance of being not in earnest.

A kind of blinkered earnestness, by contrast, is often attributed to law, by a literature keen to establish its nutritive differences. Judge Hiller B. Zobel, deciding on the various motions consequent upon the verdict in the trial of the British *au pair* Louise Woodward, opened with these words: 'The law, John Adams told a Massachusetts jury . . . is inflexible, inexorable, and deaf: inexorable to the cries of the defendant; "deaf as an adder to the clamours of the populace" '.[18] Adams's definitions of law read like a reverse image of what some writers have regarded as desirable in literature. Remaining in Massachusetts, let us consider the picture painted by Nathaniel Hawthorne in *The Scarlet Letter* (1850)—a book written, he half-suggests, to atone for the judicial bloodthirstiness of his ancestors William and John Hathorne, the first a 'legislator, judge' and 'bitter persecutor', whose son—the

---

[17] Saul Bellow, *Dangling Man* (Harmondsworth, 1963), 24. This quotation was brought to my attention by Tony Tanner in *The Reign of Wonder* (Cambridge, 1965), to which I am indebted.

[18] Superior Court Memorandum and Order, 10 November 1997, *Commonwealth of Massachusetts* v. *Louise Woodward*. This case and its aftermath provoked great interest in Britain, and achieved a high profile in the United States. Judge Zobel's innovative—if, in the event, jinxed—action in simultaneously publishing his decision on the Internet probably made this the most widely-read judicial opinion of the century.

second—presided over the infamous Salem witchcraft trials in 1692. Thus much is contained in the prefatory material ('The Custom-House'), and in the tale proper we almost immediately encounter a familiar opposition, in which a vulnerable human is subjected to the inexorable machinery of justice. The 'heavily timbered' prison door, 'studded with iron spikes', is to be contrasted with the 'young woman' with 'dark and abundant hair', 'beautiful' and 'lady-like', who emerges from it with her baby daughter to endure her decreed humiliation on the scaffold in the market-place—a scaffold described by Hawthorne as part of 'a penal machine' that also included a pillory.[19] A 'penal machine', of course, is the most violent and visible result of the disciplinary ambitions of what Michel Foucault has termed a 'carceral society' (*Discipline and Punish* (1975)), keen to imprint its judgments on the bodies of the guilty. The contrast between the insentient inexorability of such machines and the complex receptivity to pain of the flesh on which they operate, is a culminating image of the necessary insensibility of law to human frailties. Both the import and the execution of such punishments alike emphasize the differences between law's powers and literature's, between its aims and literature's areas of interest, concerned more to explore the variousness of being than to promote conformity.[20]

'A blessing on the righteous Colony of the Massachusetts', cries the beadle in Hawthorne's tale, 'where iniquity is dragged out into the sunshine! Come along, Madam Hester, and show your scarlet letter in the market-place!' Part of the fictional strategy of what follows is to differentiate between the rectitudinous absoluteness of those who suppose they can discern and punish 'iniquity', and the relativities and *in*omniscience embodied in Hawthorne's

---

[19] Nathaniel Hawthorne, *The Scarlet Letter* (Harmondsworth, 1983), 75, 80, 81, 82.

[20] '[T]he crowd were pushing, quarrelling, joking. Everything told of life and animation, but one dark cluster of objects in the centre of all—the black stage, the cross-beam, the rope, and all the hideous apparatus of death'; so ends the penultimate chapter of *Oliver Twist* (1838), and as with the evocation of the guillotine in the last chapter of *A Tale of Two Cities* (1859) as 'the crashing engine that constantly whirrs up and falls', it is appropriate that such images, in which fiction gazes with fascinated horror on its opposite, occur at the end of narratives. For these machines, in their Procrustean relentlessness, embody everything that law is that literature, as it likes to think, is not. Page references for these quotations are respectively *Oliver Twist* (Harmondsworth, 1966), 475; *Tale of Two Cities* (Harmondsworth, 1970), 402.

'romance'—as he termed it—about Hester Prynne. If the scarlet
letter displayed in the sunshine is intended as an unambiguous
signifier of 'Adulteress' to its onlookers, the ensuing story as
embroidered by Hawthorne multiplies the possible significations
of that letter, without ever defining any of them. The suggestive
capaciousness of the fictional structure, as opposed to 'the whole
dismal severity of the Puritanic code of law', is repeatedly
enforced.[21] Hawthorne interestingly revises the pattern I have
previously suggested, where the establishment of guilt and its
attendant punishment entail the conclusion of narrative: for
Hester excites interest at precisely the moment her punishment
takes public effect, in refutation of the closural assumptions inherent in the pronouncement of sentence; and the story moves ever
further away from the certainty embodied in that initial act of
adjudication. Thus, in part like 'The Murders in the Rue Morgue',
The Scarlet Letter concerns itself with matters highly pertinent
to—and highly conscious of—a legal framework, only to suggest
that finally they lie beyond the bounds of jurisdiction.

Poe's Dupin benefits from being contrasted with the Parisian
police, as the writer of *The Scarlet Letter* benefits from the
comparison with the Puritan zealotry and its notions of law. These
kinds of contrast are also to be observed in Herman Melville: in
Billy Budd, Sailor (c. 1888), where the definitions of law seem
unable to accommodate the realities of being of such a one as Billy
(or of Claggart); and in 'Benito Cereno' (1855), where the legal
depositions at the end (derived from Melville's source) contrast
with the dominant tone of this tale of perplexity. Unlike these two
later tales, 'Bartleby, the Scrivener' (1853) does not culminate in a
trial, but concerns itself with law in its textual rather than its judicial manifestation. The anonymous narrator is 'a rather elderly
man' who defines himself as 'one of those unambitious lawyers
who never addresses a jury, . . . but in the cool tranquillity of a
snug retreat, do a snug business among rich men's bonds, and
mortgages, and title-deeds'.[22] Into this smug office routine pene-
trates the unemphatically disruptive Bartleby, who is the only

---

[21] *The Scarlet Letter*, n. 19 above, 82, 80.
[22] Herman Melville, *Billy Budd, Sailor & Other Stories* (Harold Beaver (ed.),
Harmondsworth, 1967), 59, 60. I identify this tale by the title it bore on its first
appearance in *Putnam's Monthly Magazine*; Melville later shortened it to
'Bartleby' for inclusion in his collection *The Piazza Tales* (1856).

character in the story with a name that is neither a cognomen nor parodically indicative of his function. Although initially he seems to be a perfect scrivener, the tale explores the gulf concealed by the comma between name and function in its title, in recounting Bartleby's gradual withdrawal from work and then from life itself, each stage prefaced by the implacably courteous formula 'I would prefer not to'. The narrator at last vacates his own office, in which he had discovered Bartleby to have been living, the landlord causes him to be removed to prison as a vagrant, and there he ceases eating and dies, clucked over by his perplexed former employer, who then speculates that Bartleby's self-destructive melancholia may have been induced by previously working as clerk in the dead-letter office, perceiving there a communicative futility that grew to colour his perception of life itself. 'Ah, Bartleby!' the tale concludes, 'Ah, humanity!'.

Yet it is precisely in this generalizing conclusion, which attempts to fit the pale clerk into a sedatively universalist category, that we see the old lawyer lose any grip on Bartleby's quiddity, the uniqueness of his presence, as of his absence. He cannot do justice to his former clerk's existence; and my metaphor here is intentional, in that Melville seems to have connected this imaginative disability to his narrator's 'avocation' in the law, which he relates to dully categorical habits of perception. The incompatibility of legal and literary sensibilities is touched upon in the tale: 'I cannot credit that the mettlesome poet, Byron, would have contentedly sat down with Bartleby to examine a law document of, say, five hundred pages, closely written in a crimpy hand',[23] declares the narrator, when trying with elephantine humour to define the attributes of a good scrivener. It can be deduced that the painstaking exactitude that must attend the scrivener's copying is dependent on his ability not to introduce into a legal document even the tiniest inflection it does not already contain; in other words, no trace of his individual intermediation must result from copying. Bartleby takes to a logical extreme the self-effacement implicit in the scrivener's task: reduced to no more than an agent of mechanical reproduction, the work consists in the systematic repression in himself of what poet-lawyer Wallace Stevens memorably termed 'the accent of deviation in the living thing/That is its

---

[23] *Billy Budd*, n. 22 above, 67.

life preserved'.[24] Small wonder that the narrator wishes not to see the part his own employment might have played in Bartleby's self-extinction, and that he cannot fathom the challenge offered to his systems of belief.

Bellow's word 'wonder' is useful, because in a state of wonderment purposive activity is arrested; it obviously corresponds to Keats's definition of 'Negative Capability': 'when a man is capable of being in uncertainties, Mysteries, doubts, without any irritable reaching after fact & reason'.[25] Thus, literary 'wonder' would contrast with law's tendency to proceed to consequences, even when to do so entails simplification or abridgement. In *The Scarlet Letter*, as in 'Bartleby, the Scrivener' and *Billy Budd*, law is constructed as a systematic negligence of the profounder recesses of the central characters, whose accents of deviation it would coercively correct: law becomes that process for excluding the differentiations by which individuality maintains itself. So, too, in *The Adventures of Huckleberry Finn* (1884), Huck's philosophical and moral problem—which underlies the various intensely practical problems he and Jim encounter on their journey down the Mississippi—is how to square the democratic human regard he develops for Jim with the definitions his society offers: whether linguistic, as 'nigger', or legal, as chattel slave. Clemens subsequently glossed this as the struggle between Huck's 'sound heart' and his 'deformed conscience';[26] and certainly Huck's decision not to betray Jim's whereabouts, in the letter to Miss Watson he writes and then tears up, sets him against a legal and moral framework from whose premises he does not consciously dissent. But 'wonder' makes nothing happen. The seductive implicit purposiveness of their time together on the raft, and the attractiveness of Huck's slow self-cleansing from the poison of racism, incline readers to believe that these have been causes, culminating in the grand effect of Jim's freedom. But it is not so: Huck's 'sound heart' has had nothing to do with Miss Watson's decision to manumit Jim, and has no consequence in the legal arena where such matters are

---

[24] See his poem 'A Discovery of Thought' in *The Palm at the End of the Mind* (Holly Stevens (ed.), New York, 1971), 366.
[25] From a letter dated 21, 27 (?) Dec. 1817, in *Letters of John Keats* (Robert Gittings (ed.), Oxford, 1970), 43.
[26] Mark Twain, *The Adventures of Huckleberry Finn* (Peter Coveney (ed.), Harmondsworth, 1966), 31.

decided. The novel's persuasive depiction of Huck's human development conceals an allegory of his powerlessness, that perhaps
extends to the book itself: for in taking slavery as subject it
addresses—not unlike *Bleak House*—a legal issue no longer
current at the time of writing.

Literature, then, has been able to represent itself as superior to
law and its systems, by staking a claim to virtual realities, the
'golden' world Sidney asserted (*The Defence of Poesy* (1595))
was the poet's domain, as opposed to the 'brazen' one of nature
(and, presumably, of Hobbesian law): secure as the realm in which
'sound heart' can operate, it leaves to law deformities of
conscience as appropriate satisfaction. One of the more chilling
evocations of the institutionalization of law leading to deformity
of conscience occurs in H. G. Wells's dystopian fable *The Island
of Dr Moreau* (1896). The island in question is a remote one, on
which the story's eponym, a megalomaniac vivisectionist, tortures
animals into a semblance of humanity and presides over the
results. At one point the narrator, having misunderstood the
precise nature of Moreau's experiments and fearing he himself is
intended as a subject of them, takes refuge among the beast-
people, who insist on instructing him in the recitation of their
'Law':

The voice in the dark began intoning a mad litany, line by line, and I and
the rest [had] to repeat it. As they did so, they swayed from side to side,
and beat their hands upon their knees, and I followed their example . . .

'Not to go on all-Fours; *that* is the Law. Are we not Men?'
'Not to suck up Drink; *that* is the Law. Are we not Men?'
'Not to eat Flesh nor Fish; *that* is the Law. Are we not Men?'
'Not to claw the bark of Trees; *that* is the Law. Are we not Men?'
'Not to chase other Men; *that* is the Law. Are we not Men?'

And so from the prohibition of these acts of folly, on to the prohibition of
what I thought then were the maddest, most impossible, and most inde-
cent things one could well imagine.[27]

In this lurid picture of animals, surgically adjusted and compelled
(under threat of readmission to the dreaded 'House of Pain') to
deny their true natures, Wells offers his reader a sufficiently
pointed allegory. Moreau's ambitions, as later clarified to the

[27] H. G. Wells, *The Island of Dr Moreau* (Harmondsworth, 1962), 84–5.

narrator, are merely a version—albeit magnified by lunacy—of that hostility to randomness inherent in any codified behavioural system:

It's afterwards as I observe them that the persuasion fades. First one animal trait, then another, creeps to the surface and stares out at me . . . But I will conquer yet. Each time I dip a living creature into the bath of burning pain, I say, this time I will make a rational creature of my own.[28]

Moreau, although primarily a disgraced scientist, exhibits here the Apollonian frenzy that literature tends to associate with creators and enforcers of the law; a travesty to which can then be opposed its own permissive magic, happily able to accommodate what Louis MacNeice memorably termed 'the drunkenness of things being various'.[29]

How unfair is this to law? Even Posner concedes that 'Law, a bastion of Apollonian values, is problematic for anyone whose outlook is Dionysian'; but this is not the same as ascribing to law an inflexibility of intention and operation. In rebuttal of some of literature's favourite imagery, Posner argues that law is 'the *art* of governance by rule, not just an automated machinery of enforcement';[30] and to see this in action we could recall that the image of inflexible inexorability invoked by Judge Zobel at the outset of his ruling was modified at the outcome. There he announced his 'determination, guided by my reason, my conscience, and the established precedents and principles, that the interests of justice are best served here by my exercising my informed discretion and lowering the degree of guilt attributable': in which we observe justice tempered, not by mercy, but by duly Apollonian process that turns out to be less obdurate than sometimes represented.[31]

It is probably true to say that for many British viewers the obduracy and inflexibility of law were emphasized by newsreel

---

[28] *Dr Moreau*, n. 27 above, 112.
[29] See the poem 'Snow' in *Louis MacNeice: Collected Poems* (London, 1979), 30.
[30] Posner, n. 1 above, 155, 109.
[31] Zobel, n. 18 above. There is of course an argument that Judge Zobel opened by alluding to the inflexibility of law, as a rhetorical strategy to deflect attention from the fact that he was about to operate flexibility; and that his stress on precedent, while obviously a routine aspect of judicial summary, was the greater in that what he actually did was, in the eyes of many commentators, virtually unprecedented. His decision has since been confirmed by a majority vote of the highest court.

footage of the teenage defendant being delivered fettered and manacled to Judge Zobel's court in Boston. As with the scaffold on which Hester Prynne is exhibited, such literally forceful manifestations of law's ability to discipline and restrain are a minatory expression of its latent power.[32] Establishing public control over what the individual has been apt to consider the intrinsically private property of her body seems the first step in a correctional process that has in its sights the ultimate regulation not just of physical but also of mental behaviour. The proscriptive and prescriptive inherencies of literature, however didactic, are much less susceptible of demonstration or enforcement. As Robin West has argued: 'Adjudication is in form interpretive, but in substance it is an exercise of power in a way that truly interpretive acts, such as literary interpretation, are not'.[33] Thus it is, of course, that a work like *The Scarlet Letter* sets its interpretative multiplicitousness against the tunnel vision of its Puritan legislators; and so it comes about that literature can imagine law as set of potentially life-denying codes (as with the litany on Moreau's island), capable of enforcement to the point of brutality, all-too-indistinguishable from the infernal machines by which its final authority is expressed and enacted. Implicit in West's formulation cited above, is that the relative powerlessness of literature is part of what guarantees its *bona fides*. 'Poetry makes nothing happen', declared Auden in his elegy for Yeats; and there he urged that poetry embody what he termed an 'unconstraining voice'—clearly distinct from the kinds of constraint or restraint available to law, which is precisely there to make things happen or prevent them from doing so.[34]

---

[32] 'The court's physical control over the defendant's body lies at the heart of the criminal process': Robert Cover, 'Violence and the Word' in Martha Minow, Michael Ryan, Austin Sarat (eds.), *Narrative, Violence, and the Law* (Ann Arbor, 1993), 211n.

[33] Robin West, *Narrative, Authority, & Law* (Ann Arbor, 1993), 93. Also relevant is Cover, n. 32 above: 'Legal interpretation takes place in a field of pain and death ... A judge articulates her understanding of a text, and as a result, somebody loses his freedom, his property, his children, even his life. Interpretations in law also constitute justifications for violence which has already occurred or which is about to occur. When interpreters have finished their work, they frequently leave behind victims whose lives have been torn apart by these organized, social practices of violence' (203).

[34] 'In Memory of W. B. Yeats' in *The English Auden: Poems, Essays and Dramatic Writing 1927–1939* (Edward Mendelson (ed.), London, 1978), 242, 243. As James Boyd White asserts: 'Texts of this [literary] sort are not coercive of their reader, but invitational' (n. 1 above, 2018).

A Frolic of His Own

The last book I want to discuss is the most specific in its legal
visualization; almost everything that occurs in terms of plot relates
to the prospect, process, or outcome of lawsuits taking place 'off-
stage'. William Gaddis's 1994 novel *A Frolic of His Own* seems to
concede the deadening restrictiveness of the letters of the law,
whilst reserving judgement on whether literature offers any salvation.[35] Almost all the characters are engaged in or about to engage
in litigation; but although in many ways lawyers seem to be to
Gaddis what doctors were to Molière, writers and artists also
come in for some adversarial scrutiny.

The book's major plot concerns the battle entered upon by
Oscar Crease, untenured college history teacher and decaying
scion of a distinguished family of jurists, to obtain redress for
infringement of his authorial rights by the release of a Hollywood
blockbuster about the Civil War in which, he alleges, key elements
derived from his own drama 'Once in Antietam'—which has never
been performed or published, but had formerly been submitted for
consideration to the film's producer. A subsidiary plotline
concerns the legal travails involving Oscar's father, nonagenarian
Judge Thomas Crease, presiding over lawsuits provoked by the
erection of a massively ugly steel sculpture in a small Virginian
town, and by the drowning of a boy during immersive baptism (in
a river in spate) by a fundamentalist minister (for which Judge
Crease considers God to be legally accountable). Various other
legal proceedings hover in the air of this novel, which includes
Japanese car manufacturers appropriately named 'Sosumi' and
'Isuyu', and a case hinging upon the fact that 'Pepsi-Cola' is an
anagram of 'episcopal'. At the very end Oscar has achieved a
Pyrrhic victory, not only because by it is revealed his late father's
indifference toward him, and because any damages seem likely to
evaporate or be consumed in other lawsuits; but principally
because the legal grounds for the victory, hinging on the distinction between 'originality' and 'novelty' in art, seem negligent of
precisely those aspects of his play he himself most values.

---

[35] William Gaddis, *A Frolic of His Own* (Harmondsworth, 1995). I believe
that in the case of this novel it will be clearest for the reader if I incorporate page
references in my running text, following the quotations.

I want to focus on two principal aspects of this complex and comic novel: of law as waste, and of art as possible redemption. 'What do you think the law is, that's all it is, language' (284), Christina (Oscar's half-sister) is told by her husband Harry, a lawyer, who further adds that 'it all evaporates into language confronted by language turning language itself into theory until it's not about what it's about it's only about itself turned into a mere plaything' (284–5). Law is presented as a process whose aim is the preservation of its own discourse: Harry tells Christina that her father the judge is '[t]rying to rescue the language'; and this seems not to be a case of purifying the dialect of the tribe so much as preserving the shared idiolect of an elite. This is made clearest when Oscar learns why his father, whom he has disappointed, intervened to his advantage in the lawsuit against Hollywood he had lost at first judgment. Judge Crease is revealed by the old law clerk, his executor, to have acted in typically austere character. He tells Oscar, 'he didn't draw up that appeal for love of anybody, not you or anybody no. It was love of the law' (559). This inhuman fixity of purpose in the judge is a kind of legalist's myopia, hinted at in the novel's opening remark, by Harry to his wife: 'Justice?—You get justice in the next world, in this world you have the law.' (11). Law, then, is the machinery by which justice may—or may not—be done, and whether it is at all correct to posit justice as the end at which law should aim has been a matter of profound debate. In their later conversation, Harry recounts the anecdote of Judge Learned Hand's exhorting Judge Oliver Wendell Holmes Jr to 'do justice', and of Holmes replying it was not his job to do justice but 'to apply the law' (285). When Oscar's father dies, his obituary places him squarely in the Holmes tradition; less admiring is Christina's definition of him as 'one of the most selfish men who ever lived, the law was the only thing that was alive for him people were just its pawns' (487). As Burke somewhere remarks, it is possible to love systems rather than the truth; it is possible to love law rather than justice.

A Frolic of His Own does not, however, seem inclined to establish literature as the truest court of appeal; although it does suggest a difference between literature and law, implicit in its title-phrase. This indicates something done by a servant or employee in the course of his duties, for which the master or employer cannot be held liable, because it was an unforeseeable and unsanctioned

free act without relation to correct performance of the service or
employment in question (398, 429). I suppose it might be said that
irrelevance here is the basis for legal defence; or at least, that in a
novel wherein taking somebody to court is the tarbaby easily
embraced but difficult to disengage from, it gestures toward a
realm secured from litigation, which seems like an Eden of unac-
tionable *actes gratuits*. The book almost suggests that in prolifer-
ating civil actions American citizens are perpetuating a series of
individualized civil wars ('whole society's based on an adversary
culture what America's all about'—485–6). In an important if
inebriated perception of Christina's, she attributes the artistic
impulse to a freedom from those kinds of motivation:

—I mean, but I mean isn't that really what the law is all about? and she
straightened up as though to disown the slur in her voice setting her glass
down emptied—where it's all laws, and laws, and everything's laws and
[Oscar]'s done something nobody's told him to, nobody hired him to and
gone off on a frolic of his own I mean think about it Harry. Isn't that
really what the artist is finally all about? (399)

It is not clear that the world of art can so securely be separated
from what Henry James termed 'clumsy Life';[36] for Gaddis's own
text is subject to repeated 'invasion' by modes of discourse other
than its own, embracing long extracts from Oscar's play, newspaper reports, insurers' letters, and a variety of legal documents
including a formally recorded interview, judge's instructions to
jury, and judicial opinions: their difference from the main body of
the text is accentuated not only by differences of lexis and register,
but differences of typeface as well. They are, thus, ambiguously
part of and apart from the book they are included in. While it
could not be easily proved that the elevated language of the opinions—where proper citation of precedents does not preclude the
deployment of wit—is intrinsically inferior to the halting and
cross-purposed dialogue that constitutes a great proportion of the
rest of the novel, it may be that the very effort made by legal
discourse to exclude that haphazardness elsewhere so evident, is

---

[36] This phrase comes from the preface to *The Spoils of Poynton* James
composed for the New York edition of his works; in this, he opposes the 'sublime
economy' of art to the 'splendid waste' of life. See the prefaces as gathered
together—with an introduction by R. P. Blackmur—as *The Art of the Novel* (New
York, 1934), 120, 121.

what ensures its inadequacy, and highlights the literal and metaphorical arbitrariness of its closure. For events suggest that however stately are the periods and impressively massive the citations of the judgments, adjudication is only ever an illusorily final act, invariably subject to appeal or to substantive alterations in effect. To this degree, then, the law is infected by the randomness of the surrounding world, as the embedding text is invaded by these legal interpolations.

There is nonetheless a sense, in Gaddis, that artists who resort to law are acting in bad faith. This can be seen in the zealously litigious Oscar, as well as the sculptor Szyrk, whose 'notorious outdoor sculpture known as Cyclone Seven' has caused a furore amusingly reported in the press. The initial perplexed hostility of the citizens of Tatamount is intensified when a local boy's puppy becomes ensnared in the structure; they propose to free it using oxyacetylene torches. The sculptor opposes this, mounting 'a fierce defense of its artistic integrity', but before the case is decided lightning strikes the steel sculpture, electrocuting 'Spot'. Next the 'Village' wins a court order for the removal of Cyclone Seven, against its creator's assertion of its 'site specific status'; but subsequent publicity and ensuing financial opportunities provoke mutual reassessment of advantage, as the newspaper drily notes:

The matter is again before the courts where each side has reversed its position. The sculptor, Mr R Szyrk of New York, now demands the Village pursue its mandated course permitting the structure's removal, claiming his constitutional right to its eventual disposition as embodying a protected statement under the First Amendment. Pending the outcome of its petition for Landmark status the Village has refused removal or altering of the unique creation which has 'put Tatamount on the map' bringing substantial tourist revenues and jobs to this chronically depressed area where unemployment runs thirty nine percent among whites and double that for blacks, with a twenty six percent overall literacy rate. Since the plaintiff resides out of state the case will be heard in Federal district court by Judge Thomas Crease, who has already been subjected to vilification and abuse relating to lawsuits spawned by Cyclone Seven and is currently embroiled in his nomination to the U.S. Court of Appeals being vigorously opposed by Senator Orney Bilk, a native of nearby Stinking Creek, who is reported to have called for his impeachment. (392–3)

Something of the novel's persistent mordancy of humour is audible here; but so too is the darker tone deriving from its imagery of entrapment and embroilment. Yet it is notable that these images do not attach exclusively to legal process. If the law is a machine that lethally entangles so, in this novel is art—at least as embodied in the 'serrated steel' labyrinth that is Szyrk's contribution to the gaiety of nations. 'Trapped by the words' (page 460) is a phrase that occurs, and could apply equally to law or literature, both embodied in the ineluctable modality of language.

Whatever their similarities, however, *A Frolic of His Own*, thoroughly imbued with law, implies difference—clear-sighted as it nonetheless is about the impossibility of achieving any essentialist definition of literature. Whether law aim at justice or at rescuing its own language, the having such an aim at all may be chief ground for differentiation. If we follow Christina in associating art-activity with the novel's title (she is drunk at the time, but *in vino veritas*), then the implication is that the creativity licensed by art's very *un*purposiveness—the 'frolic' as opposed to being about his master's business—is paramount. The local difficulty that there is not in the novel any artist who exemplifies that kind of disinterest, is recuperated if we understand that this is what the novel itself exemplifies, able to accommodate a textual polyphony, and free of what Keats called 'a palpable design' on its readers.[37] Thus it remains alert to the perception embodied in its epigraph, from Thoreau: 'What you seek in vain for, half your life, one day you come full upon, all the family at dinner. You seek it like a dream, and as soon as you find it you become its prey'. In keeping unclosed the circle of seeking and finding—which is another way of preserving 'Negative Capability'—literature is intrinsically different from law. This does not mean that stories do not end, but that their endings may be of less consequence than *how* they have been reached: the happy marriages in the last act of *A Midsummer Night's Dream* are of less moment than the magical transformativeness by which they have been rendered possible. A different energy is at work.

Robin West has differentiated literature's 'expressive' function from law's 'imperative' one—embedded in which is the contrast between (desirable) individualism and (undesirable) centralism.[38] Another way of stating this difference could be to say that law is

---

[37] 'We hate poetry that has a palpable design on us'; letter of 3 February 1818 in *Letters of John Keats* (n. 25 above), 61.

[38] Robin West, n. 33 above, 174.

designed and obliged to regulate situations, where literature can remain sublimely irresponsible, and therefore unaccountable.[39] Many of the writings touched upon are apt to contrast a certain leadenness in the law with their own lightness of being; and some have done so by ignoring those aspects in which law functions as an enabling process (in securing and protecting rights), or is less absolute and more flexible than is depicted. But am I being fair to literature? It might be appropriate to end on a conciliatory note, or at least one which suggests literature's capacity to know more about itself than my arraignment of its unfairness to law has implied. Kafka's tale *In the Penal Settlement* (1919), which centres round an implement of judicial torture and execution, seems to offer a chilling parable of the potential monstrousness of law. Yet this sadistically-designed if ultimately inefficient machine could as easily be read as a metaphor for literature, as for law. For although part of its function is to inscribe and reinscribe the infracted article of law upon the living flesh of the condemned, this writing only takes place around the trunk of the body, whose extremities are incised with curlicues and embellishments that are purely aesthetic in design, although doubtless no less painful to endure. As an infernal writing-machine, then, it suggests the futility of attempting to understand or plot the physiological modes of transmission, whereby the meaning of a text, which has an objective existence as ink on a page, is received by the mind of its reader; and furthermore, that there will always be an unaccountable aesthetic residuum that lies beyond the 'meaning' as strictly defined, but which nevertheless incalculably contributes to it. This interlinkage of punishment, decoration, and meaning is also present in Hester Prynne's ingeniously-embroidered scarlet letter, offered in defiance of the totalitarian impulse of a judicial system that seeks not just to rule the body, but to police the mind and spirit.[40] Literature may offer a protection against this, or it may

[39] Committing its murders 'in jest', literature might be accused of virtual transgression rendered innocuous by its actual immunity.

[40] What is so affecting in the beast-people's litany of 'the Law' in Wells's novel, is that we hear, not merely a conditioned response, but the jingling of mind-forged manacles that attests to Moreau's partial success in leaving no aspect of their tormented being unregulated by himself. The fact that the wholly-human narrator joins in their ritual, however sceptically, seems to suggest Wells's view that in each of us there is the germ of total compliance, a nascent willingness to sacrifice our quiddities of selfhood on the altar of the project of becoming 'rational' creatures, as defined by someone else persuasive or powerful enough.

not: the 'books' (significantly including *The Man in the Iron Mask*) constantly cited by Tom Sawyer as he lays down the right ways to misbehave are obviously repressive in their effect on Huck and Jim. It seems to Huck, at the end of the book that bears his name, that the only realm for his 'sound heart' lies beyond literature itself: he forswears involvement in any future literary enterprise.

The Scarlet Letter certainly offers a stark contrast between the rough justice of the scaffold and the human complexity of Hester Prynne; yet Hawthorne makes explicit that the law is a constantly evolving process (just as Kafka's machine has become obsolete under a liberalizing administration), and that the carceral society which punishes her turns out to be the community in which Hester chooses to remain (utterly unlike Huck lighting out for the territory).[41] The three scenes on the scaffold are structurally intrinsic to *The Scarlet Letter*, and enforce the point that the rigours of the law are necessary to a fully human life, even if paradoxically they seem life-denying. Clearly much that I have been saying tends toward a sense of the difference between carnivalesque attributes of literature and regulatory functions of law (although a relation is implicit in the former's subversion of the latter), with literature enabling 'frolic' but law conducing to follies of paranoia; but for Hawthorne at least, the choice between maypole and whipping-post was not so simply to be made: 'A' is at once the token of Hester's penal objectification and, as first letter of the alphabet, the starting-point of literacy and of literature itself.

Those more expert in the law than I am have remarked on a tendency towards complacency, in both its theory and its practice, which might helpfully be modified by a salutary application of literature.[42] My point has been to suggest that ignorance and

---

[41] In a recent article, Laura Hanft Korobkin argues that, in spite of the fact that Hawthorne is known to have engaged in considerable antiquarian research for the writing of his novel, *The Scarlet Letter* misrepresents the power of the Puritan magistracy to alter decreed punishments, and departs from historical accuracy in not subjecting Hester to a public whipping (as Fanny Price's father would have approved). He thus chose to soften his depiction of Puritan law in action. See 'The Scarlet Letter of the Law: Hawthorne and Criminal Justice' (1997) 30 *Novel: A Forum on Fiction* 193–217.

[42] Judith Resnik's paper in this book, below 687, for example, alludes to 'Legal culture's self-regard and self-celebration'; James Boyd White criticizes Posner's book for having 'little self-doubt, little sense of shared inquiry' (White, n. 1 above, 2028). Robin West asserts that 'Literature helps us understand others. Literature helps us sympathize with their pain, it helps us share their sorrow, and it

complacency may also colour literature's attitude to law; whether in overstating similarities (literature *as* law), or by overestimating differences, and losing sight of the degree to which law is, as James Boyd White insists, more a site of conversation than a coercive litany requiring unconditional assent. That literature may resent law, and that this resentment may well spring from disappointed rivalry and a defensive sense of powerlessness, might account for the emphasis on its own permissive flexibility, and need not be incompatible with an exaggerated view of its mission to reform the actual, rather than a virtual, world.[43] It may also be that law can be unduly defensive, with regard to literature: 'I am a lawyer and live in Hartford', wrote Wallace Stevens to the editor of the *Dial* in 1922 (asking to be spared the biographical note to accompany publication of his poems in the magazine), '[b]ut such facts are neither gay nor instructive'. Such qualities are perhaps more readily associated with literature than with law; but those whom Stevens designated 'figure[s] of capable imagination' are not necessarily best equipped to be figures of capable legislation.[44]

helps us celebrate their joy. It makes us more moral. It makes us better people' (West n. 33 above, 263). As Hemingway might remark (of West's assertions), it is pretty to think so; but the means by which literature might have these improving consequences are incapable of demonstration—bringing us back to the inefficient moral gearing of Kafka's writing-machine. We would need to confront the problem of why certain fine writers have been rather ghastly people; and we would need to consider other hard cases. If I may be permitted to offer anecdotal evidence, I recall reading some years ago John Mortimer's review of a biography of Lord Chief Justice Goddard, in which he attributed Goddard's failings to a self-certainty that had never exposed itself to the deflations of Dickens's novels. Goddard's daughter (I think) then wrote to the newspaper protesting that she well remembered her father reading Dickens fully and with enjoyment—which leaves one to conclude that in Goddard's case, Dickens's writing hadn't produced the effect Mortimer (or West) envisaged.

43 Both Christine L. Krueger and Jan-Melissa Schramm allude in their contributions to this book, respectively 437 and 417, to the grounds for rivalry between law and literature in nineteenth-century Britain.

44 See *Letters of Wallace Stevens* (Holly Stevens (ed.), London, 1966), 227. A similar note is sounded by Ian Ward in the preface to his (helpful and interesting) book *Law and Literature: Possibilities and Perspectives* (Cambridge, 1995): 'To lawyers like myself, in general, and certainly too often, there seems precious little fun in the law, or in learning about it. Literature, on the other hand, can be fun' (ix). Stevens's phrase comes from his poem 'Mrs Alfred Uruguay' in *The Palm at the End of the Mind*, n. 24 above, 186. I would like in this final note to thank those members of the 1998 colloquium whose suggestions for further reading have taken effect in some earlier notes.

SHAKESPEARE, THE NARRATIVE COMMUNITY AND THE LEGAL IMAGINATION

Ian Ward

The purpose of this essay is to suggest the extent to which a constitution and a constitutional morality is the product of a literary imagination. The first part of the essay will discuss this idea of a literary, or narrative, imagination, and its contemporary affinities with a revived communitarian politics. The second and third parts then discuss two related concepts which lie at the heart of our constitutional theory, and suggest the extent to which the situation within the constitutional imagination is dependent upon a particular literary heritage. In both cases, it will be suggested that Shakespeare both describes, and constitutes, part of this heritage. The first relational conception is that of the common law and the integral nation state, and the second is the role of law in determining the boundaries between distinct spheres of public and private responsibility, which is so central to liberal legalism.

Narrative, Community, Imagination

The interdisciplinary study of law and literature is now well established. Law is a function of text and of language, and is better understood as such. At the same time, literature, meaning novels, poetry, drama, and so forth, can provide a valuable supplement to recognized legal texts, statutes, cases, and commentaries.[1] A legal order or constitution is a product of imagination. So, too, is a piece of literature such as a Shakespearian play. It is this fact which militates against any notion that a constitution is somehow

---

[1] For an introduction to law and literature, see I. Ward, *Law and Literature: Possibilities and Perspectives* (Cambridge, 1995).

set in stone. Just as Shakespeare is 'our contemporary', so too is a constitution. Accordingly, the early modern constitution is not hermetically sealed, and, as a late twentieth-century audience, we approach both it and Shakespeare with a particular 'fore-understanding' of what we think it means, and that 'fore-understanding' is, in large part, fashioned by our current prejudices regarding the nature and purposes of legal and political morality. We bring our own ideas of law to any engagement with Shakespeare's 'politics'. In other words, when we read Shakespeare's constitutional supplement, we do so in the particular context of our own contemporary legal 'prejudices'. Our engagement with Shakespeare, and with the sixteenth and seventeenth centuries, is historical and historicist.[2]

A study of Shakespeare's treatment of constitutional theory will enrich our understanding of constitutionalism today, and it will do so in two senses. In the more immediate sense, we will better appreciate the nature of our current constitution as fashioned to some degree by history. Moreover, the period in which Shakespeare lived and wrote, at the turn of the sixteenth and seventeenth centuries, was critical for the development of the English constitution. It is a particularly rich and formative period in English constitutional history. At the same time, and at a deeper level, through the study of Shakespeare we will better appreciate the historically imaginative nature of a constitution. This is not merely to emphasize the literary quality of any constitution, either early modern or contemporary. It is also to emphasize the potentially empowering facility of language. As we search today for a revived theory of constitutional morality, an understanding of the historical and literary nature of constitutions, as products of interpretation, as active modes of imagining, can both liberate and inspire. Most importantly of all, by demanding our active participation as interpretive actors, such a theory of constitutionalism can reinvest the idea of democracy upon which any revived ideal of constitutional morality must be founded.

---

[2] The idea of 'fore-understandings' and 'prejudices' is central to Hans-Georg Gadamer's theory of hermeneutic understanding. At the same time, an appreciation that interpretation is always an historical task also lay at the root of this thesis. Gadamer's appreciation that the process of reading is always the engagement of text, of the context of text and author, and of the reader and his or her context, is an essential premise for our study of Shakespeare and constitutionalism. See H. Gadamer, *Truth and Method* (London, 1975).

Alistair MacIntyre suggests that the late twentieth century has 'reached' a 'turning point' which demands a reinvigorated sense of political community.[3] Liberalism, and its pretended demarcation between 'private' and 'public' spheres of life has reified the community, and distanced the individual from it. The communitarian counter suggests that constitutions are active, evolving organisms, and a communitarian idea of democracy demands the active participation of all its citizens. Ultimately, it is founded upon the idea of our conversational and dramatic participation. Thus Michael Sandel stresses the need to reinvest an imaginative 'sense' through a narrative understanding of our political selves. The 'political community', he suggests, 'depends on the narratives by which people make sense of their condition and interpret the common life they share; at its best, political deliberation is not only about competing policies but also about competing interpretations of the character of community, of its purposes and ends'. The threat of liberal analytical constitutionalism is one which prescribes a 'fragmented, storyless condition'. The 'loss of the capacity for narrative would amount to the ultimate disempowering of the human subject, for without narrative there is no continuity between present and past, and therefore no responsibility, and therefore no possibility of acting together to govern ourselves'.[4] A democratic community is bound together by a shared historical imagination, and a communitarian politics is one that is founded upon this sense of narrative constitutionalism.

In similar terms, Charles Taylor has sought to re-establish a sense of community on the premise that 'we grasp our lives in a narrative'.[5] A politics of community must be founded on a politics of the self. Such a concentration on identity politics is immediately resonant, not just of the postmodern turn in critical legal studies, but also

---

[3] Adding that the 'barbarians' are no longer 'waiting beyond the frontiers'. They 'have been governing us for quite some time'. See A. MacIntyre, *After Virtue: A Study in Moral Theory* (London, 1985), 263. This conclusion is founded on a substantial body of work which attempts to trace the rise and fall of the idea of community in political thought. See also his *A Short History of Ethics* (London, 1967).

[4] M. Sandel, *Democracy's Discontent: America in Search of a Public Philosophy* (Cambridge, Mass., 1996), 350–1.

[5] C. Taylor, *Sources of the Self: The Making of Modern Identity* (Cambridge, 1989), 47.

of a pervasive movement across disciplines.[6] What distinguishes Taylor's theory of self-identity is the prominent, indeed decisive, role played by literature and the literary imagination. The modern identity crisis is founded on a lack of moral identity, and the retrieval of such an identity is dependent upon relocating a community morality in narrative and interpretive form. We 'learn our languages of moral and spiritual discernment', Taylor tells us, 'by being brought into an ongoing conversation by those who bring us up'. In such terms, we stand in 'conversation' with our 'immediate historic community'. Our identities are constructs of past, present, and future. The reconstructive communitarian vision of politics is, therefore, founded on the reconstitutive potential of literature. To be moved by literature is to be drawn into political sensibilities, to see the fate of others as intrinsically linked with the fate of the self. The self is 'recentred' in literature. We can learn to assert ourselves by describing our own situation in the public sphere, and in doing so we use literature to destroy the pretended barriers which seek to distinguish public from private, and thus divide the self from others.[7]

More recently, Martha Nussbaum has advocated the use of literature as part of the wider responsibility for educating 'world citizens'.[8] The ambition of a liberal education should be one which seeks to liberate the 'mind from the bondage of habit and custom, producing citizens who can function with sensitivity and alertness as citizens of the whole world'. The ability to relate 'stories of people's real diversity and complexity' is essential if this ambition is to be realized. What must be reinvigorated is the 'narrative imagination', which means 'the ability to think what it might be like to be in the shoes of a person different from oneself, to be an intelligent reader of that person's story, and to understand the emotions and wishes and desires that someone so placed might have'. Moreover, the ability to 'identify' with others leads to the ability to make moral judgment, and to engage constructively in the

[6] Jürgen Habermas suggests that modernity is 'obsessed' by questions of identity. Antony Giddens counters that 'high modernity' is defined by its 'identity politics'. For Habermas's comments, see generally *Between Facts and Norms: Contributions to a Discourse Theory of Law and Democracy* (Cambridge, 1996). For Giddens's see A. Giddens, *Modernity and Self-Identity* (Cambridge, 1991).
[7] Taylor, *Sources*, n. 5 above, 25–52.
[8] M. Nussbaum, *Cultivating Humanity: A Classical Defense of Reform in Liberal Education* (Cambridge, Mass., 1997), ix.

processes of civic government. Literature plays a 'vital' political role, by 'cultivating powers of imagination that are essential to citizenship'.[9] The idea of civic responsibility underlines the political affinity which complements Nussbaum's educational vision. A liberal education that is founded on the Socratic ideal of critical questioning and moral judgment can reveal a 'life that is open to the whole world'. It will show that there is

after all more joy in the kind of citizenship that questions than in the kind that simply applauds, more fascination in the study of human beings in all their real variety and complexity than in the zealous pursuit of superficial stereotypes, more genuine love and friendship in the life of questioning and self-government than in submission to authority.

Ultimately, the 'future of democracy' depends upon the need to reinvigorate a sense of political community and civic responsibility through a reawakened political imagination.[10] As she suggested in *Love's Knowledge*, a 'community is formed by author and readers', and in such a way a community can better appreciate the reality that it is bound together by a shared 'ethical interest', even if it admits the contingency of that ethics. A politics that is founded on the idea of community is premised on the binding force of narrative imagination.[11]

Literature, as Iris Murdoch suggests, 'stirs and satisfies our curiosity, it interests us in other people and other scenes, and helps us to be tolerant and generous'. The literary writer, and she cites Shakespeare as a particular example, is an 'inconspicuous' thinker, a philosopher who chooses to philosophize through the media of fiction or poetry. Ultimately, 'literature' helps the 'good citizen' to know what to do. Even if our post-metaphysical world has abandoned ethical absolutes, no one can avoid moral judgments, and so every citizen is engaged in the construction of a political morality in every community.[12] In this sense, art is the only means by

---

[9] Nussbaum, *Humanity*, n. 8 above, 8–11, 85–6.

[10] Nussbaum, *Humanity*, n. 8 above, 84, 94–7.

[11] Nussbaum, *Humanity*, n. 8 above, 48, 142–3, 148–76, suggesting at 166 that the literature 'joins readers with both characters and author (and with one another) in bonds of community'. See also M. Nussbaum, *Love's Knowledge, Essays in Philosophy and Literature* (Oxford, 1990).

[12] I. Murdoch, *Existentialists and Mystics: Writings in Philosophy and Literature* (London, 1997), 3–30, 66–70. In her opinion, Shakespeare's drama reveals a world slowly coming to grips that there are no certainties in life, and the breakdown of civil order is always imminent. See 222.

which the ideal of democracy can be reinvigorated and given meaning in modern society.[13] The ethical engagement is, then, a political engagement, and, by demanding our constant participation, the root of potential democratic renewal. It is here that the 'imagination', as a construct of emotion as well as reason, plays such a pivotal political role. The 'world which we confront is not just a world of facts but a world upon which our imagination has, at any given moment, already worked'. We are constructed, in part, by our historical imagination. Moreover, many of our 'beliefs' are founded in our 'active imagination'. The 'formulation of beliefs about other people often proceeds and must proceed imaginatively and under a direct pressure of will'. We 'have to attend to people, we may have to have faith in them, and here justice and realism may demand the inhibition of certain pictures, the promotion of others'. To be a 'human being' is actively to engage in the political imagination, to make moral judgments, about both self and others.[14] Imagination does not just facilitate moral judgment. The notion of community, founded on the 'love' of others can only make sense if there is a conception of moral good. It does not need to be a rationally determinate 'sense', but communities must be defined by some notion of political morality.[15] The mere absence of metaphysical absolutes does not, then, excuse morality from its political responsibilities, any more than the admission of fundamental political contingency denies the role of morality in binding individuals together in communities. More than ever there is a need to revitalize the 'tired imagination' of political 'practice', and this can only be achieved by a moral philosophy which appreciates its literary constitution.[16]

This relation, the communitarian idea of a narrative reconstitution of political morality, enjoys a clear affinity with the kind of postmodern ethics described by Richard Rorty. Rorty's reconstructed liberal democracy is one constituted by conversationalists, aware that truth is merely their construct. This is the spirit of 'democratic pluralism'. Moreover, the ambition of a postmodern ethics is not just 'democratic pluralism', but a democracy defined by 'justice'. Echoing Plato's original injunction, Rorty's ethics

[13] Murdoch, *Existentialists*, n. 12 above, 228.
[14] Murdoch, *Existentialists*, n. 12 above, 199.
[15] Murdoch, *Existentialists*, n. 12 above, 233.
[16] Murdoch, *Existentialists*, n. 12 above, 184.

defines itself in terms of a congruent justice in the self and the community. The determination of distinct spheres of public and private, of course, preserves the liberal element in his thesis. But the private sphere, the Derridean world of 'private irony', is co-determined by the Deweyan sphere of 'public hope' or 'solidarity'. The two are complementary. The key philosophical switch lies in the conceptual readjustment, from freedom or truth, to freedom and truth. Truth no longer constrains freedom of opinion, but is constructed by it. The marrying of these related dualities, of freedom and truth, and public solidarity and private irony, will realize a liberal utopia which is determined as narrative rather than theoretical. Solidarity becomes a construct of the community of selves, and being created by this community is not a challenge to the autonomy of its constituents.[17] For Rorty, language is lived. It is not something that we can stand outside of, but rather is the medium which constantly dissolves any notion of separately demarcated realms of private and public politics. Accordingly, to 'see one's language, one's conscience, one's morality, and one's hopes as contingent products, as literalizations of what once were accidently produced metaphors, is to adopt a self-identity which suits one for citizenship in an ideally liberal state'.[18] A postmodern political morality respects that deeply pragmatic 'truth' that there is no other truth, other than our narrative conception of our historical and communal identities.

Images of Commonwealth

Shakespeare's elevation to the position of 'national poet' was very much fashioned during the eighteenth and nineteenth centuries. As Jonathan Bate has recently concluded, Shakespeare 'took over from God and King and became the deity of the secular Enlightenment and the guarantor of the new imagined community of the nation-state'.[19] It is a thesis which chimes with Elie Kedourie's suggestion that a distinctive early modern idea of the godly commonwealth and its proto-national determination

[17] R. Rorty, *Contingency, Irony, and Solidarity* (Cambridge, 1989), xiii–vi.
[18] Rorty, *Contingency*, n. 17 above, 50–4, 60–1.
[19] For a discussion, see J. Bate, *The Genius of Shakespeare* (London, 1997), chs. 6–8. In turn, Shakespeare became, not just the 'national poet' of England, but also of Scotland, Germany and America.

provided the intellectual root for an eighteenth-century romanticism. Nationalism was the product of romantic poets, and its residual ideological strength remains a testimony to the power of literature to shape the political imagination.[20] The ideology of commonwealth which shaped modern nationalism is seen in the recourse of nationalists to the idea of a common good.[21] In this way Kant was able to use the idea of the nation state as a building block for the idea of a 'perpetual peace'. Moreover, like the early modern idea of a commonwealth which is founded on the idea of a common law, nationalism is consistently keen to use the presence of a common legal tradition as evidence of a deeper political and cultural affinity.[22] When Sieyès questioned rhetorically 'what is a nation?', the answer was 'a body of associates living under one common law and represented by the same legislature'.[23] The idea of the nation remains intrinsically linked to that of community through the presumed congruence of individual and communal interest, and its expression in law.

The extent to which nationalism and community could be synthesized in order to prescribe a conservative political imagination can be seen in Edmund Burke's *Reflections*, a classic example of a libertarian defence of community, a Counter-Reformation text the intellectual foundations of which are provided by the fictive mythologies of the common law together with the constitutional 'impression' of church and state. The English 'nation', according to Burke, was defined by the 'antient fundamental principles' of its 'government'.[24] The common law defined a distinct English community constituted by individuals who enjoyed a liberty that was 'moral' and 'regulated'. The English 'mind' was thus prescribed in terms of its 'conscious dignity' and 'noble pride' together with a 'generous sense of glory and emulation'. For Burke it was political morality, a constitutional 'spirit' founded in historical texts, and secured by a 'powerful' disposition 'towards antiquity'. Using a consciously jurisprudential metaphor, he suggested

[20] E. Kedourie, *Nationalism* (Oxford, 1996), 56–66. For a general study of the politics of romanticism, see M. Butler, *Romantics, Rebels and Reactionaries* (Oxford, 1981).
[21] E. Hobsbawm, *Nations and Nationalism since 1780* (Cambridge, 1992), 20. [22] See Hobsbawm, *Nations*, n. 21 above, 88.
[23] In Kedourie, *Nationalism*, n. 20 above, 7, 31–2.
[24] E. Burke, *Reflections on the Revolution in France* (Harmondsworth, 1986), 110, 198.

that the common law provided an 'entailed' political 'inheritance' particular to the English national community.[25] In the final analysis it was nationalism alone which could preserve England from the allures of republicanism and 'the wildest democratic ideas of freedom'.[26] Moreover, Englishness was not just described by its imagined constitutional morality. It is a 'partnership not only between those who are living, but between those who are living, those who are dead, and those who are to be born'.[27] Every nation, Burke affirmed, must be defined by a 'particular system of manners' which 'a well-formed mind would be disposed to relish'. Englishmen, Burke affirmed, lived in the past, defined by 'generosity and dignity of thinking of the fourteenth century'. The Englishman does not seek to make political or ethical 'discoveries', but rather cultivates 'inbred sentiments' of affinity and national pride as a bastion against 'smugglers of adulterated metaphysics'.[28]

The origins of the English nation state which Burke revered lay in the godly commonwealth prescribed by late Elizabethan political theory.[29] Elizabeth's famous oration to the troops at Tilbury was couched in terms of a distinctively English national commonwealth. The body of the monarch and the English commonwealth were consciously merged in the popular imagination.[30] The idea of a godly national commonwealth enjoyed considerable intellectual and theological currency. Despite his own reservations about the translation of theological ideas into matters of government, Bacon's *New Atlantis* was an explicitly Christian and godly utopia, governed by an ideal godly prince. Harrington's *Oceana* was defined as 'nothing else but the national conscience'.[31]

---

[25] Burke, *Reflections*, n. 24 above, 117–20, 137.

[26] Burke, *Reflections*, n. 24 above, 140–55.

[27] Burke, *Reflections*, n. 24 above, 194–5.

[28] Burke, *Reflections*, n. 24 above, 172, 181–3, 187.

[29] See C. MacEachern, *The Poetics of English Nationhood* (Cambridge, 1996). Such a suggestion is, of course, controversial. A considerable literature, as she acknowledges, would suggest that a recognizable English nationalism accompanied the intellectual ferment of the English romantics. For a literary account of the more traditional view, see M. Butler, *Romantics, Rebels and Reactionaries: English Literature and its Background 1760–1830* (Oxford, 1981).

[30] See C. Pye, *The Regal Phantasm: Shakespeare and the Politics of Spectacle* (London, 1990), 3–4, 33.

[31] See F. Bacon, *The Advancement of Learning and New Atlantis* (Oxford, 1974) and J. Harrington, *The Commonwealth of Oceana* (Cambridge, 1992), 9, 39–40.

Baxter's *Holy Commonwealth* was also couched in terms of a particular English 'nation' which aspires to reform and to determine itself in terms of its godliness. The 'welfare' of the English 'nation', Baxter suggests, can only be founded on a strengthened relation of church and commonwealth.[32] The church became the symbol of nation and dynasty, and the identity of each merged into the whole of the commonwealth. The ambition of each, in turn, was to elide the fiction and the reality of this commonwealth. The Englishness of episcopalian Protestantism was essential, and the Tudor propagandist placed it at the centre of the political imagination. Aylmer put it bluntly, 'God is English', and England was the 'Israel of old'. As Patrick Collinson has more recently suggested, Protestantism provided the essential narrative sheen of respectability which the 'vulgar Elizabethan nationalism' needed. It described a people 'living, in a sense, in the pages of the Bible'. The puritan divine, William Whateley described an England that was 'God's signet, God's jewel . . . the one only Nation, almost, that doth openly and solely profess the true religion of God'.[33] Accordingly, disobedience represented the rebellion of the political imagination against the image of the English commonwealth. Rebellion against the commonwealth of England, the *Homily Against Disobedience and Wilful Rebellion* impressed, was a sin against the very idea of Englishness. For a subject to rebel against the commonwealth, was not just to rebel against God or a godly prince, but to deny that subject's only political, social and theological identity.[34]

Richard Hooker's *The Laws of Ecclesiastical Polity*, dedicated to portraying the political theology of the Elizabethan settlement in terms of an English godly commonwealth, sought recourse to Aristotle. The need to accommodate and legitimate the idea of a national church, the still relatively new Church of England, demanded a model that would give precedence to the politics, rather than the metaphysics, of good order.[35] Men are 'naturally

---

[32] R. Baxter, *The Holy Commonwealth* (Cambridge, 1994), 160.

[33] P. Collinson, *The Birthpangs of Protestant England* (London, 1988), 7–10.

[34] See Blakemore Evans, *Elizabethan and Jacobean Drama* (London, 1988), 254–7.

[35] For a commentary on the polemical, as opposed to metaphysical, nature of the text, see Arthur McGrade's 'Introduction' to R. Hooker, *The Laws of Ecclesiastical Polity* (Cambridge, 1989), xxi–xxii. See also xxvi, suggesting that the *Laws*, ultimately, portray a 'remarkably republican conception' of the state.

induced to seek communion and fellowship with others', and it is, accordingly, part of man's 'duty no less to love others than themselves'. It is with this premise that Hooker proceeded to make his famous admission that all men live in a 'relation of equality', and which led Locke to triumph him as one of the first democrats.[36] The idea of man's duty to the community is of particular significance, suggesting both a sense of moral responsibility, as well as a distinctly nationalist duty to pursue the 'great good' of the English national community. It is for this reason that the godly Englishman must observe both the common and the civil law.[37] The 'common good' which pervades the *Laws* is very much an Aristotelian one, and it is this concept which binds the whole idea of the godly commonwealth: 'Goodness is seen with the eye of the understanding. And the light of that eye is reason'.[38] Goodness is the ambition of the godly polity, and it, like the very idea of a community, is defined by the historical and natural rationality of the common law. For Hooker, 'the law of the commonweal' is 'the very soul of a politic body, the parts whereof are by law animated, held together, and set on work in such actions as the common good requireth'.[39] In these terms, the Aristotelian model is translated by Hooker into an expressly national one, and it is one, moreover, which is described by the elision of church and state in the form of the Church of England. In constitutional terms Hooker's commonwealth is inclusive, and at the same time, of course, exclusive. Only a godly Englishman can belong to the godly commonwealth described by the common law.[40]

The role of the sovereign was, of course, central to the realization of the ideal political community. Along with the godly commonwealth comes the godly prince, an ideal which enjoyed a considerable authority in early modern political thought. Knox founded the godly commonwealth on the prince who studied to 'promote the glory of God'. Being an emanation of God, the commonwealth must be understood by the godly magistrate as the

---

[36] Hooker, *Laws*, n. 35 above, 79–80.
[37] Hooker, *Laws*, n. 35 above, 85.
[38] Hooker, *Laws*, n. 35 above, 70.
[39] Hooker, *Laws*, n. 35 above, 87–8.
[40] It is this jurisdictional exclusivity which underpins Hooker's dismissal of the Calvinists, and most importantly, Calvinist theories of government, in the Preface to the *Laws* (n. 35 above).

'will of God'.[41] Perhaps most influential amongst contemporaries was Erasmus's *Education of a Christian Prince*, wherein the education of a good and virtuous prince necessarily defined the education of a godly prince. For Erasmus, the foundation of a Christian education lay in a proper 'understanding' of Christ and of the 'spirit' of a godly commonwealth. If the laws of the community are in accord with 'justice and honour' the well-educated prince will necessarily wish to observe them.[42] While adopting a similar approach to the idea of a prince ruling in accordance with reason, Hooker's godly prince was slightly different. The situation of late Tudor England prescribed a monarch who was rather less poetic, and rather more constitutional.[43] The monarch that Hooker defined was godly, precisely because he was constitutionally defined. The king, or queen, of England, as Governor of the Church of England, was defined in terms of a godly commonwealth. Monarch, church and commonwealth were part of a whole, and co-determinative as such. As God's 'lieutenants', moreover, godly princes were bound to rule in accordance with the law of the constitution, so long as it is natural and defined by the rational common good. It is only in such a situation that the godly commonwealth can be in harmony, 'like a harp or melodious instrument'.[44]

Shakespeare addresses Hooker's ideal model on various occasions, but perhaps most immediately in the second Henriad. Classical Shakespearian commentary, such as that provided by Tillyard, writing during the 1940s and with an England desperate to reaffirm its own national identity, suggests that the trilogy described a morality play, with the young Hal proving his worth by resisting the lures of Eastcheap, and then moving on to lead his nation on a glorious crusade in France.[45] Against the traditional view of *Henry V*, cultural materialists and new historicists have

[41] J. Knox, *On Rebellion* (Cambridge, 1994), 23, 29, 83.

[42] D. Erasmus, *The Education of a Christian Prince* (Cambridge, 1997), 13–17, 26, 46, 52, 79. Such a 'creature' will be more 'like a divinity than a mortal, complete with every single virtue'.

[43] For the extent to which Hooker presented a constitutionalized variant of godly magistracy, see MacEachern, *Poetics*, n. 29 above, 17–19.

[44] Hooker, *Laws*, n. 35 above, 133–6, 142, 146–7, 217.

[45] E. Tillyard, *Shakespeare's History Plays* (London, 1962), 269–318. For a critique of Tillyard, see G. Holderness, *Shakespeare Recycled: The Making of Historical Drama* (London, 1992), 21–9.

preferred to suggest that the plays actually describe a polity in the process of breaking apart. The textuality of the play merely emphasizes the extent to which the pretended national unity existed only in the imagination. The play describes the popular consciousness. It does not describe the reality of Shakespeare's England.[46] The thesis certainly chimes with contemporary theories of modernity and nationalism. But, again, it may be that it says more about us than it does Shakespeare.[47]

The genesis of the aspiring godly prince and his godly commonwealth is to be found in the two parts of *Henry IV*. The protestant commonwealth is one which is determined by its concern for a discrete and integral community, and, as such, the role of Eastcheap becomes a central one in the narrative redetermination of the English constitution.[48] Early in Act I of *Part I*, Hal reminds his audience that he is playing a role, and promises that he will 'throw off' his 'loose behaviour', and so

> like bright metal on a sullen ground,
> My reformation, glitt'ring o'er my fault,
> Shall show more goodly, and attract more eyes
> Than that which hath no foil to set it off. (I.ii.203–10)

---

[46] See Holderness, *Shakespeare*, n. 45 above, 229–31, emphasizing that the play in fact reveals the 'conflicts and contradictions of Shakespeare's contemporary society'.

[47] A related thesis, which both emphasizes the slippery nature of theatrical ideality and thus chimes with our present concern with the nature of political imagination, is Stephen Greenblatt's suggestion that Shakespeare uses language in order to describe the illusory nature of Henry's 'self-fashioning'. At the same time as describing his own ascent to ideality, Henry V reveals himself to be a dissimulating and 'conniving hypocrite'. The mere fact that Henry is such a consummate actor reinforces his slipperiness, and, indeed, the potential instability of any politics which depends upon a theatrical authority. Certainly, the theatricality of Henry cannot be doubted. Norman Rabkin observes that the ideal to which Henry must aspire, that of a godly magistrate, necessitated the instability of a multi-textual identity, while Wolfgang Iser has described a prince who can walk through each of the 'plural worlds' of the second Henriad, adjusting his performance to each theatrical context. Henry is the ideal godly prince, precisely because he is the consummate actor. See S. Greenblatt, 'Invisible Bullets: Renaissance Authority and Subversion in *Henry VI* and *Henry V*' in J. Dollimore and A. Sinfield (eds.), *Political Shakespeare: New Essays in Cultural Materialism* (Manchester, 1985), 30. For various related theses, see N. Rabkin, 'Rabbits, Ducks and *Henry V*' (1977) 28 *Shakespeare Quarterly* 279–96 and W. Iser, *Staging Politics: The Lasting Impact of Shakespeare's Politics* (New York, 1993), 162–3.

[48] See variously, C. Barber, *Shakespeare's Festive Comedy* (Princeton, 1959), 192–5; A. Leggatt, *Shakespeare's Political Drama* (London, 1988), 100; and V. Kiernan, *Shakespeare: Citizen and Poet* (London, 1995), 55.

Later, Warwick affirms that

> The Prince but studies his companions
> Like a strange tongue, wherein, to gain the language,
> 'Tis needful that the most immodest word
> Be look'd upon and learnt. (*Henry IV Part II*: IV.iv.67–71)

The putative king's imagination will retain the memory of Eastcheap, and his political morality will be fashioned within its context. As Warwick perceptively notes, the political imagination is fashioned by memory. At the conclusion of the play, Henry advises his audience, and subjects, 'Presume not that I am the thing I was' (V.v.56). Yet, he will always, to some extent, be what he 'was', even if his performance has now changed. He is a new 'thing', a putative godly prince, but he remains the same person, the consummate actor. The evolution from Hal to Henry is that of private citizen to public institution. The 'real' Hal, if such thing can be said to exist, merely passes from one fictive and imaginary form to another, and the fact that he famously takes the crown before his father dies further suggests the illusory nature of his pending reign. He is a usurper like his father, dependent for his future security upon the mortality and weakness of others and the persuasiveness of his own performance.[49]

According to traditional analysis, if *Part I* witnessed Hal overcoming the temptations of Eastcheap, *Part II* sees him learning about Aristotelian justice.[50] Certainly there is a pervasive tension between alternative ideas of justice, the formal justice of the Lord Chief Justice, and the anarchic misrule of Falstaff. Moreover, Hal's theatrical submission to the Lord Chief Justice may indeed be a pivotal moment. Certainly, Tillyard interpreted it to mean that Hal had come to acknowledge his position within the Ancient Constitution.[51] Yet the very theatricality of it, performed by a consummate dissimulator, immediately detracts. If Hal can flirt with anarchy and then turn against it, the same, it is implied, might be the case with regard to formal justice. Hal's commitment

---

[49] See J. Barish, 'The Turning Away of Prince Hal' (1965) 1 *Shakespeare Studies* 12–13.
[50] See S. Hawkins, 'Virtue and Kingship in Shakespeare's *Henry IV*' (1975) 5 *English Literary Renaissance* 316–17.
[51] See Tillyard, *History Plays*, n. 45 above, 270–1, 282–3. See also J. Sisk, 'Prince Hal and the Specialists' (1977) 28 *Shakespeare Quarterly* 524. The actual story of the King's 'submission' was inherited from Elyot's *Boke*.

for 'striking him about Bardolph', a commoner, suggests the Chief Justice's authority and courage (*Henry IV Part II*: I.ii.55–6, V.i.35–8). But Hal is not yet Henry V, and there is no equivalent gesture when he is. Certainly, he reminds the new king that he should observe the law if he wishes to avoid tyranny (V.i.73–101). Likewise, though *Part II* concludes with Henry summoning Parliament and seeking 'noble counsel' in order to settle his commonwealth, there is no guarantee that he will take it, and subsequent events, in *Henry V*, suggest that his primary concern lies not with the constitution of England, but rather with the more martial allures of nationalism (V.ii.134–7, 143).

The fashioning of Hal will be completed at war, as the princely soldier of God. Such a model is immediately presented in the Prologue to *Henry V*. The 'warlike Harry' is about to 'Assume the port of Mars', and unleash 'famine, sword and fire' (Prologue, 5–7).[52] At all times the 'politics' of *Henry V* is cast in imaginary form, and the issues of trust and legitimacy are immediately resolved on these terms. As the Prologue affirms, the play presents a 'kingdom for a stage, princes to act' (Prologue, 3). Kingship, as a form of politics, is a performative and imaginative art. Yet, the pivotal opening scene immediately undercuts the image of the godly commonwealth which is then prescribed by the rest of the play. It opens with two senior clergy plotting to fool Henry into foreign wars in order to protect their finances. The challenge to an ideal commonwealth is the inclination to self-interest. The Archbishop's famous 'honey-bees' speech must be understood in this context. An ideal commonwealth is indeed a figment of the imagination.[53] Moreover, the Archbishop sees in Henry a fellow spirit, a 'true lover of the holy church', someone who one 'would desire' be 'made a prelate', one who can debate effectively in both

---

[52] Hardly the kind of behaviour that was recommended in Erasmus's *Manual*. See R. Battenhouse, '*Henry V* in the Light of Erasmus' (1985) 17 *Shakespeare Studies* 77–88, suggesting that Henry is precisely the antithetical ideal to Erasmus's godly prince.

[53] According to Claire MacEachern, the Archbishop's image affirms the idea of a commonwealth of constituent commonwealths. As such, it emphasizes the extent to which every element is mutually co-dependent. The imaginary force of the commonwealth thus becomes stronger in the participatory sense, but potentially weaker in the countervailing sense that the failure of participation of any element threatens the integrity of the whole. See C. MacEachern, '*Henry V* and the Paradox of the Body Politic' (1994) 45 *Shakespeare Quarterly* 41–2.

'divinity' and 'commonwealth affairs'. Henry, he appreciates, is a true rhetorician, who can 'steal his sweet and honey'd sentences;/So that the art and practic part of life/Must be the mistress to this theoric' (I.i.38–44, 47–52). The long exposition which the Archbishop then presents on the Salic law is not jurisprudentially convincing, and the suspicion remains that Henry himself, already determined upon war, is all too keen to collude with the Archbishop's dubious reasoning. Here, it seems, the lessons of Falstaff's hypocrisy have not been wasted.[54]

Furthermore, when Henry later admits that 'the King is but a man, as I am', it again undercuts the image of godly transcendence that is elsewhere employed in order to justify his own magistracy (*Henry V*: IV.i.100–2). It is a difficult, if critical, compromise. The Elizabethan monarch, as described by the likes of Elyot, had to 'be human, but not too human'.[55] The description clearly echoes the idea of the king's two bodies which described the essential fiction of the medieval monarch, human and spiritual leader, and the textually unstable reality of it. However, as IV.i reveals, under pressure Henry is less certain of God's grace, and equally uncertain of his spiritual capacity as God's magistrate. The idea that the King should exploit his actorly abilities so as to wander about in disguise was a controversial issue in Elizabethan England. It is a role which the Duke in *Measure for Measure* takes to a dangerous and destructive extreme. Strong princes, whose authority is justified by God, should not seek to secure their own confidence by trying, in disguise, to extract assurance from subjects.[56] The fact that Henry then emerges from his ramble musing on the inadequacies of his peasant soldiers, reveals the error of seeking legitimacy in such a way. The very fact that Henry is aware of the performative nature of his kingship, and feels the need to exploit it, again affirms an awareness of its innate ambivalence. Henry the godly prince maintains an ideal image of magistracy, but Henry 'but a man' is acutely aware of its textual ambivalence.

[54] For a discussion of the Salic claim, see G. Smith, 'Shakespeare's *Henry V*: Another Part of the Critical Forest' (1976) 37 *Journal of the History of Ideas* 11 and D. Goy-Blanquet, 'Two Kingdoms for Half-a-Crown' (1991) 44 *Shakespeare Survey* 56.

[55] MacEachern, *Poetics*, n. 29 above, 87–8.

[56] A. Barton, 'The King Disguised: Shakespeare's *Henry V* and the Comical History' in J. Price (ed.), *The Triple Bond* (Philadelphia, 1975), 97–9.

The role of the Chorus in *Henry V* is dedicated to presenting the imaginary, and performative, nature of an ideal narrative commonwealth.[57] Most immediately, it constantly affirms the essential fiction of the king's two bodies, the elision of king and commonwealth, as prescribed by a number of contemporary commentaries such as Elyot's *Boke*. As Montjoy suggests, 'Harry of England' describes the ritual elision of sovereign and nation, and the Chorus seeks to remind us that the war is undertaken, not for Henry's glory but that of England. The Chorus affirms that *Henry V* is not just a play about the reign of Henry, but rather about the shaping of a godly commonwealth. Henry is necessary, but only as an expression of this greater ideal. It is the Chorus which reassures us, on the morning of the battle, that Henry has resolved his doubts, and can thus visit 'all his host/Bids them good morrow with a modest smile,/And calls them brothers, friends and countrymen' (Chorus IV.32–4). Throughout, the play provides a textual foundation for the imaginative recollection of a distinctively English commonwealth and putative nation state. *Henry V* is a history about England, as personified by its king. It is about the *respublica* of England on crusade, an entire nation unified by a common godliness, chosen by God, and so determined.[58]

Claire MacEachern has recently concluded that the play itself 'displays a simultaneous distrust of and a yearning for community'.[59] As the Chorus crucially acknowledges, Henry is the 'mirror of all Christian kings' (Chorus II.6). But it is the reflection described in the audience's imagination which will determine the function of the text in the evolving political morality of its community. Henry is the 'star' of England, a king who now exists only in the collective memory of an imaginative community, and whose fate, and legitimacy, ultimately lies with its textual constitution (Chorus V.6). As Greenblatt concludes, in such a way the play does indeed 'effect a poetics of Elizabethan power', precisely

[57] For a discussion of this innate ambivalence in the Chorus's function, see E. Berry, 'True Things and Mock'ries: Epic and History in *Henry V*' (1979) 78 *Journal of English and German Philology* 3 and G. Walch, '*Henry V* as Working-House of Ideology' (1988) 40 *Shakespeare Survey* 67.

[58] Iser, *Staging Politics*, n. 47 above, 27–9. See also Tillyard, *History Plays*, n. 45 above, 302–3. The crusading image was certainly suggested by the probable source play, *The Famous Victories of Henry the Fifth*.

[59] MacEachern, *Poetics*, n. 29 above, 111.

by making it 'inseperable' from the 'poetics of the theatre'.[60] The meaning of the play cannot be fixed, but its political function, in the prescription of an imaginary ideal, cannot be denied. Certainly, our present sense of community, and particularly the English nation state, cannot be fully appreciated outside *Henry V*. In *Henry V* Shakespeare describes a narrative commonwealth, with all the ambiguities that such a description inheres. England was a textual fiction, a nation state invented by Shakespeare and other late sixteenth-century poets. According to Claire MacEachern, the nation state established in late Elizabethan England was a consciously fictional one, an 'ideal of community' that was forever 'just out of reach'. Indeed, as the pressures to provide a constitutional, as opposed to purely theological or cultural, definition of the English nation state increased, the illusion became ever more apparent, and its efficacy as an illusion correspondingly compromised.[61]

The godly commonwealth described by Hooker existed on paper. The *Laws of Ecclesiastical Polity* were, in the final analysis, a rhetorical feint. Hooker's godly commonwealth was a utopia that everyone could be led to believe in, if and only if its description was sufficiently convincing. In such a way, as a textual fiction, Hooker's commonwealth admits a degree of democratic participation in that it is a community fashioned by the conversation of its participants.[62] Hooker himself appreciated the narrative nature of his constitution, that the common law, which underpinned the commonwealth, was a narrative construction and only legitimate in so far as it captures the political morality of its community as a narrative history; 'we were then alive in our predecessors, and they in their successors do live still'.[63] Aside from *Henry V*, perhaps the most overtly 'patriotic' of Shakespeare's plays is *Henry VIII*. In its final lines, Cranmer makes a famous and prospective appeal to the future Anglican

---

[60] Greenblatt, 'Invisible Bullets', n. 47 above, 41. For similar conclusions, see Iser, *Staging Politics*, n. 47 above, 164–5.

[61] MacEachern, *Poetics*, n. 29 above, 2, 5–6, 7–9. See also 11, emphasizing perceptively that communities only ever exist in the imagination.

[62] J. B. White, *Acts of Hope: Creating Authority in Literature, Law and Politics* (Chicago, 1994), ch. 3.

[63] It is for this reason, he adds, that the common law must enjoy precedence over its immediately textual alternative, the Mosaic law of the scriptures. Hooker, *Laws*, n. 35 above, 93, 107–16.

settlement, the imaginative nature of which is overt. Blessed by 'heaven', the future Elizabeth will make a new nation, and secure the 'happiness of England'. Yet, Cranmer notes, with a degree of foreboding, that the death of the 'unspotted lily' will bring about its own constitutional crisis as much as it will fashion an enduring political image. The 'merry songs of peace' will be subdued by the certain death of a sovereign for whom 'all the world shall mourn' (*Henry VIII*: V.iv.14–62). The presentation of ideal magistracy, and ideal community, was an exercise which, though very necessary, was always riven with an immanent tension.

Public and Private

A determination to legislate for morals is premised on a denial of absolute rights to privacy. It found an extreme form in Francis Bacon's assertion that all law is of importance to the state, and thus no law can ever be denied because it infringes a private space. All private law, accordingly, is public to some degree.[64] Bacon's idea of politics challenges the central tenets of liberal legalism and its assertion of certain core principles of right which can be justified in terms of universal humanism. Over the centuries, one of the most contentious testing-grounds for the liberal thesis, and the Baconian challenge, has been the related areas of privacy, morality, and gender. In more recent times, Lord Devlin has suggested that law has a duty to enforce certain moral standards. Questions of morals, religion, and law are 'inextricably joined', such that 'without the help of Christian teaching the law will fail'.[65] In his analysis of community, and its foundations upon a conception of public good, Devlin revealed an acute awareness of the historical and textual nature of a political morality. Morality is not frozen in time, and neither should be the laws of morality.[66] Our political morality cannot be distinguished from the theological impulses

---

[64] F. Bacon, *The Essays* (London, 1985), 222–5 and *The Advancement of Learning* (Oxford, 1974), 151–2.

[65] Thus, more specifically, criminal law, as an emanation of public law, must assume a public interest defined by a conception of public good, and so in matters relating to sexual conduct there can be no attempted demarcation of a private sphere of morality. For reasons of both law and political theology, sexual relations are a matter of immediate relevance to the public good. See P. Devlin, *The Enforcement of Morals* (Oxford, 1965), 4–6, 23, 25.

[66] Devlin, *Enforcement*, n. 65 above, 115.

which originally established it, and have served to refine it over the centuries. It is, therefore, a morality which is political as well as theological, accepted by Christians and non-Christians alike, the reason why thousands of non-churchgoers still aspire to Christian baptism and marriage ceremonies. A society is always a 'community of ideas', one in which there is a constructively rational political morality, that of the 'right-minded person', and no society can exist without such an historically constructed political morality, and moreover the duty of a judge lies in enforcing the law as determined in the light of such moral principles.[67] The fact that society has the 'right to make a judgement' about certain moral issues is the 'price' of living in communities. A common morality, founded on theological precepts, or indeed any other, fashions a 'common agreement about the way we should go'.[68] There can never be an absolute regime of privacy in modern society, for 'each have rights over the whole', and 'therefore the rights of each must be curtailed so as to ensure as far as possible that the essential needs of each are safeguarded'. Accordingly, Devlin could conclude that one could not 'talk sensibly of a public and private morality'.[69]

According to John Stuart Mill, a society is only entitled to infringe individual freedom in the case of threatened physical harm to another member of the community.[70] In his famous response to Devlin, Herbert Hart reaffirmed Mill's classical defence of private rights. According to Hart, Devlin articulated a revived 'legal moralism' in English society, and a concomitant crisis in liberal ideology in that the return of an eighteenth-century jurisprudential mentality actually challenged the notion of an historical and narrative idea of political morality. Liberal morality, Hart countered, was actually founded on a sphere of absolute privacy. Thus, to attack the existence of this sphere is not to defend a conception of political morality, but rather to assert an alternative, and necessarily imaginary, conception of past morality.[71] A proper historical understanding of political morality must recognize its constructive, and fluid, constitution. Although Devlin

---

[67] Devlin, *Enforcement*, n. 65 above, 9–10, 15, 77–83, 89–94.
[68] Devlin, *Enforcement*, n. 65 above, 120.
[69] Devlin, *Enforcement*, n. 65 above, 12–16, 101.
[70] J. S. Mill, 'On Liberty' (1859) (London, 1985), 68–9.
[71] H. L. A. Hart, *Law, Liberty and Morality* (Oxford, 1968), vii, 4–11, 17–22.

had acknowledged this historicity, according to Hart, by founding his society on one particular moral vision, he had in fact rooted it to some essentially imaginary ideal of a moral-determined community. In reality, rather than there being one rooted morality, there may within a community, be a 'number of mutually tolerant moralities'.[72]

More recently, Ronald Dworkin has attempted to reinvest contemporary 'law and morality' debates with a distinctive philosophical import, while not denying their inevitably political impact. Like Devlin, Dworkin acknowledges that a community is always founded on a particular morality which, in Western society, is a distinct moral theology. It is this which constitutes the political morality which provides principled supports to the constitution.[73] Given the diversity of opinions, a compromise is essential for maintaining the stability of a plural society. However, it need not be a purely political compromise, but can also be a 'principled compromise'. Such a compromise is not fixed, but rather, being the product of constructive rationality within an historical and a textually community, is immanently mutable. There is then no denial that political perceptions of morality change, but such change is limited by the historically described 'principles' which provide a narrative foundation. We cannot locate a moral philosophy, or indeed a political interpretation of it, outside the historical and textual origins of our community. In other words, when we today try to access an understanding of law and sexuality in our society, its moral arguments, and its political interpretations, we do so constrained by the narrative construction of these arguments and interpretations.[74] Our understanding of the morals and the politics of sexuality are constituted, in part at least, by Shakespeare's, just as both Shakespeare's and ours are constituted, in large part perhaps, by the political theology which underpins our present constitutional morality. If Devlin and Hart recognized that the questions of 'law and morality' require an accommodation of public and private interests, Dworkin's critical contribution to the debate is to recognize that such an accommodation can be effected only in terms of a narrative constitution.

---

[72] Hart, *Law*, n. 71 above, 28–9, 38, 63.
[73] See R. Dworkin, *Law's Empire* (Cambridge Mass., 1985).
[74] R. Dworkin, *Life's Dominion: An Argument about Abortion and Euthanasia* (London, 1993), particularly ch. 1.

An alternative approach to questions of law and 'morality' was suggested by Michel Foucault, who argued that such a philosophical discourse is part of a wider hypocrisy which lies at the heart of liberalism; the desire to monitor private sexuality through public discourse. Accordingly, the history of sexuality, from the seventeenth century onwards, should be seen as one defined by a 'rhetoric of allusion and metaphor', the determination of which became a subject of intense and 'volatile' debate. Sex was 'driven out of hiding and constrained to lead a discursive existence'.[75] The discourse of sexuality became a 'disciplinary technology' geared to the subjugation of modern society through the subjugation of the private body.[76] Morality and sexuality are intensely political subjects, because like all 'juridico-discursive' subjects, they are determined by power. The politics of law concentrates on the whole matter of 'governmentality', and a radical critical legal politics recognizes that 'networks of power' are pervasive, channelled through various jurisprudences that seek to control society, some of which may be positive laws, but others of which include moral censure and a variety of similar discourses. Most obvious of such 'micro-centres' of power is the family, an institution which is described as private, but which is a pivotal unit of public authority and control.[77] The 'law' of sexuality, then, is more than just certain positive laws related to sexual 'offences', but also includes texts, such as Shakespeare's, which seek to shape a surrounding moral discourse. In the Foucauldian analysis, sexuality has remained an innately political issue, not just in spite of, but because of liberal political theory. While attempting to delineate a distinct private sphere, liberalism has failed to provide mechanisms to address the implicit disadvantage suffered by those who cannot gain access to the public spheres which can reverse their discrimination.

[75] M. Foucault, *A History of Sexuality* (London, 1990), Vol. I, 7–11, 17, 24–5, 33.

[76] Thus, for example, whereas the discourse of marriage was firmly determined as private, that of sexuality became ever more perceived to be something of public, indeed scientific, interest. Rather than a discourse of sex and morality, there emerged one of sex and rationality, and the pretended justification for the public interest in private matters was redetermined. Science, rather than theology, took to establishing certain imaginary 'truths' of sexuality, prescribing norms of sexual behaviour, conditions of sexual discourse. Foucault, *History*, n. 75 above, 23–4, 40, 57–64, 70–1.   [77] Foucault, *History*, n. 75 above, 93–4, 100.

Whereas liberal jurisprudence has fostered a discourse on sexuality which has been cast in ethical tones, echoing Foucault's analysis, a distinct critical legal feminism has sought to emphasize that such a discourse is irreducibly political. The control of sexuality is a matter simply of politics, of the power relation between gender, rather than any spurious transcendental critique of sexual morality. Thus Catherine Mackinnon attacks the mythologies of liberal rights theory. Law is an irreducibly political institution, dedicated to securing the power and advantage of those who prescribe it, men.[78] Of course, the textual distinction of gender is unavoidable to some degree. Indeed, feminist theory 'writes' an essential textual difference, even as it tries to deny it.[79] As Drucilla Cornell has noted, the politics of gender is something which exists in the relationship between individual, text or context, and audience.[80] Once it is appreciated that any gender identity is textually created in such a way, then we can also appreciate that we are all engaged in the art of fashioning political identities, in and across public and private spheres of life. The transference of jurisprudential debate, from the philosophy of law and morals to the politics of law and gender is itself a testimony to the evolved awareness that the essential intellectual issue is that of identity and its construction. It is, accordingly, for this reason that jurisprudential issues which are framed by demarcated public and private realms are immediately addressed in terms of narrative constitutionalism.

In its attempt both to deny and to accommodate the evolution of a distinct private world, by refining the idea of a godly commonwealth, Tudor government maintained a crucial interest in the politics of the private. The stability of the Tudor dynasty rested on the ability of the organs of government to maintain the image of the English commonwealth, as something which was both public and private, and could be represented in precisely this way. Such an accommodation was, of course, prescribed once again by the peculiar nature of the Anglican settlement. If the fate of the settlement depended upon the mutual support of sovereign, church and community, then the politics of the community

---

[78] See C. MacKinnon, *Towards a Feminist Theory of State* (Cambridge, Mass., 1989) and more recently *Only Words* (London, 1995).

[79] J. Butler, *Gender Trouble: Feminism and the Subversion of Identity* (London, 1990), 1–33.

[80] See for example, D. Cornell, *The Philosophy of the Limit* (London, 1992).

remained of public and constitutional import, even if its constituents' 'rights' were being prescribed in a distinctly 'private' world.[81] The constitutional settlement thus depended in considerable part upon maintaining the illusion of commonwealth upon which the settlement rested. A particular political morality had to be prescribed, one that pertained to individual spirituality and behaviour as well as the collective spirituality of the community. Accordingly, much energy was expended upon the related subjects of sexuality and women. Although the theology of the protestant reformation had prescribed an emerging world of private contemplation and morality, matters of sexuality and gender identity were considered to be of public concern. In this way, of course, such moral questions remained acutely political, and themselves continued to subvert any precipient public–private divide.

The parish church became the theatre of disputation in early modern England. The struggle for the hearts, minds, and morality of the English commonwealth was not purely spiritual, but was also a struggle for the political imagination of what Christopher Hill termed the emerging 'intellectual proletariat'.[82] Ultimately, the fate of the English commonwealth was not decided by kings or even by armies, but was decided in the towns, villages, and parishes, by actors, priests, and gossips. The various political and familial struggles conducted in the myriad of commonwealths of England defined the political morality of Shakespeare's England, and the political imagination was secured by those who could most persuasively portray an ideal of Englishness to which everybody could aspire.[83] The commonwealth, in effect, defined itself, because it, in turn, was defined by a multitude of self-defining constituent commonwealths. In 1620 the moderate puritan Thomas Scot regretted the loss of a magistracy which could be depended upon to administer justice without falling victim to 'faction and partie'. Politics, he mused, was everywhere.[84] As the 'middling sort' took over the provinces, so too they sought to define the political imagination. The reformed English commonwealth was as much a

[81] See J. Dollimore, *Radical Tragedy* (Brighton, 1984), 12–14.
[82] C. Hill, *Society and Puritanism in Pre-Revolutionary England* (London, 1991), 37–9, 57, 82–3.
[83] See L. Stone, *The Causes of the English Civil War* (London, 1977), 95–8.
[84] See R. Ashton, *Reformation and Revolution 1558–1660* (London, 1978), 107.

secularized as a spiritualized polity. The settlement itself denied the possibility of distinct spheres of public and private government and, accordingly, it was no longer a matter of describing the spiritual imagination, but of controlling and defining the political.[85] In 1617, John Drope of Magdalen College, Oxford, preached at Paul's Cross, and his text, taken from Proverbs, was dedicated to dispelling the myth of the ideal godly magistrate as the necessary saviour of the commonwealth. Kings, he urged, 'might steal as well as meaner men'. The commonwealths of England must save themselves. Stratford-upon-Avon was described as a 'little Geneva', where everyone went about discussing politics themselves, swearing, drinking, and listening to whichever preachers they chose. Stratford, it seems, was a commonwealth which had decided to take Drope's advice.[86]

The desire to restore a sense of sexual propriety in the minds of the faithful became a touchstone of the integrity of the reformed English commonwealth, and in doing so also came to represent all the tensions intrinsic to a polity which sought to determine itself in terms of imagined public and private constituencies. According to Luther, man was constantly tested by the allures of the 'flesh'; 'our whole life is nothing but temptation by these three, the flesh, the world, the devil'.[87] The solution to the threat that sexual licentiousness posed to the godly community lay in marriage, a public institution which was necessarily in 'accordance with divine law'.[88] According to the puritan William Perkins, the apex of social order was the institution of marriage, designed, not just for the 'perpetuation of the church', but also for procreation and the 'containment of lust'. The godly commonwealth is defined as one which can adequately constrain the divisive passions of sexuality.[89] For many, the threat of sexual dissolution and moral decay was a matter of controlling women. Sexual instability was particularly associated with female sexual lasciviousness. Helkiah Crooke duly observed that 'females are more wanton and petulent than

[85] See Hill, *Society*, n. 82 above, 88–9, 108–11, 410–24.
[86] See Hill, *Society*, n. 82 above, 42, and Collinson, *Birthpangs*, n. 33 above, 55.
[87] M. Luther, *Selections from his Writings* (J. Dillenberger (ed.), New York, 1962), 145–53, 226, 483.
[88] Luther, *Selections*, n. 87 above, 328–32.
[89] In K. Wrightson, *English Society 1580–1680* (London, 1982), 67.

males we think happeneth because of the impotency of their minds', for 'the imaginations of lustful women are like the imaginations of brute beasts which have no repugnancy or contradiction to restrain them'.[90] It was not lustfulness *per se* which was the problem. It was the threat posed by female sexual aggression towards the stability of the family and the institution of marriage that worried men. As Antony Fletcher has recently observed, it was commonly felt that adultery 'at a social level' was sending 'society as a whole tottering toward dissolution'.[91]

A certain prurient disapproval of overt sexuality was enhanced by the recorded antics of James I's court. The rigorously puritan Lucy Hutchinson denounced the court as a 'nursery of lust and intemperance'.[92] Sir John Harrington recorded that, when in the new king's company, the ladies of the court did 'abandon their sobriety and are seen to roll about in intoxication'.[93] Writing during the interregnum, Richard Baxter took a particular pleasure in suggesting that James and his son were brought down because of their moral improprieties. James's court became representative of something deeply immoral and distinctively un-English. When he was accused of behaving like a 'courtier', a Somerset parson sued for libel. To describe someone as one of James's courtiers was to diminish him in the eyes of his community.[94] A shocked Sir Simonds D'Ewes, like Baxter seeking to make sense of the tumultuous events of the middle decades of the seventeenth century, cited rampant sexual impropriety as the cause of the complementary breakdown of the public commonwealth and private family. The 'holy state of matrimony', he observed, had been 'perfidiously broken and amongst many made but a May-game', and 'even great personages prostituting their bodies to the intent to satisfy and consume their substance in lascivious appetites of all sorts'.[95]

---

[90] In A. Fletcher, *Gender, Sex and Subordination in England 1500–1800* (New Haven, 1995), 71–4.   [91] Fletcher, *Gender*, n. 90 above, 109.

[92] L. Stone, *The Crisis of the Aristocracy 1558–1641* (Oxford, 1967), 188.

[93] Harrington provided a famous description of James's reception masque for the king of Denmark, in which the Queen fell around drunk, whilst 'Hope and Faith were both sick and spewing in the lower hall', Victory was put early to bed, and Peace left to 'most rudely' make 'war with her olive branch'. He had never witnessed 'such lack of good order, discretion, and sobriety as I have now done'. In Blakemore Evans, *Drama*, n. 34 above, 201–2.

[94] See D. Underdown, *Revel, Riot and Rebellion: Popular Politics and Culture in England 1603–1660* (Oxford, 1987), 127.

[95] Stone, *Crisis*, n. 92 above, 299.

Moreover, the infection of sexual decay appeared to have spread throughout the commonwealth. Nashe recorded that the suburbs of London had become 'licensed stews', havens of 'six-penny whoredom'.[96] Court and country, it seemed, were drowning in a sea of sexual impropriety.

Perhaps the most subversive portrayal of sexuality in Shakespeare can be found in *Measure for Measure*, a play which aligns the related questions of sexuality, the public and private spheres of government, and the inherent and defining questions of law and morality. Although Coleridge famously thought the play to be 'horrible', more tragedy than comedy, Hazlitt, in comparison, thought it a wonderfully informing revisionist tract on law and morals.[97] Orthodox twentieth-century interpretations have tended to concentrate upon the idea that the play is indeed a morality tract, refined through a particular Christian, and protestant, prism.[98] Appreciating that any treatment of 'law and morality' questions has deeply constitutional overtones, Donna Hamilton has suggested that the play reveals a deep distrust of the role of the church in a political constitution, and particularly the position of theology in secular laws.[99] A variant of this thesis has concentrated on the extent to which the community's determination to monitor sexual and gender relations betrays the fallacy of the public–private divide which was established as a fulcrum of the kind of image of thrusting protestant community to which Shakespeare's Vienna, and his contemporary London, aspired.[100] Such a thesis, moreover, enjoys a very immediate historical context, with James's proclamations for the destruction of brothels in 1603, and measures the following year for the reform of marriage laws. The setting of *Measure for Measure* is certainly as much London as it is Vienna, and the environs far more Eastcheap than Arden. The problem in Vienna is not just the laxity of its

---

[96] In J. Briggs, *This Stage-Play World* (Oxford, 1997), 38.

[97] See V. Thomas, *The Moral Universe of Shakespeare's Problem Plays* (London, 1991), 173–4.

[98] It is, according to various commentators, a thesis of Christian atonement, the purging and regeneration of communities, the crisis of reformation, even a deep and unsettling scepticism of Christian imagery, bordering on atheism.

[99] D. Hamilton, *Shakespeare and the Politics of Protestant England* (Louisville, 1992), 111–27.

[100] See J. Dollimore, 'Transgression and Surveillance in *Measure for Measure*' in Dollimore and Sinfield, *Political Shakespeare*, n. 47 above, 72–87.

morals, or indeed the laxity of laws, but the problem of insufficient sovereignty, both in the person of the Duke and in office of
magistracy itself.[101] There are public laws for the reformation of
morals and manners, 'strict statutes and most biting laws', but
they have become 'more mock'd than fear'd' such that 'our
decrees,/Dead to infliction, to themselves are dead,/And Liberty
plucks Justice by the nose' (I.iii.19, 27–9). Mistress Overdone's
observation is acute. The pulling down of brothels would indeed
signify more than the application of the law, for it would more
importantly suggest a major reconstitution of the political morality of the community (I.ii.96–7).

There are three magistrates in *Measure for Measure*, and each
presents a distinct approach. Escalus is the least complex, and given
his appreciation of the Aristotelian virtues of moderation and
balance, seems most fit (II.i.37–40). Angelo is a more complex
candidate. Probably, the most obviously puritan magistrate in
Shakespeare, he is also among the least redeeming, using his puritanism in order to create an image of moral superiority, which can
then legitimate his magisterial aspirations. He employs an aesthetics
of magisterial 'terror' in order to impress his fitness for authority
(I.i.19). The hypocrisy makes his attempted rape of Isabella all the
more damning, and his preparedness to corrupt the civil law in the
process all the more alarming (II.iv.174–6). Yet much of his magisterial rhetoric is entirely orthodox, determined that 'We must not
make a scarecrow of the law', aware that the immanent logic of the
law itself, rather than any dubious applications to equity or extrajudicial measures, is the only way to restore an ethic of legal morality
(II.i.1, II.ii.38–41). Although it can be ascribed to his hypocrisy,
Angelo's necessarily cataclysmic fall from power does suggest a
certain ambiguity at the heart of any idealized conception of law
and its presumed ability to monitor private, or public, morality.

The most elusive magistrate is the Duke, and it is he who
needed to present the clearest image, even if it was only an image.
To a certain extent, theatricality is a virtue of government, and the
Duke is certainly amongst Shakespeare's most theatrical of magistrates, as much a stage-manager as he is an actor.[102] Having

[101] See T. Eagleton, *William Shakespeare* (Oxford, 1986), 52–5 and P. Cox,
Shakespeare and the Dramaturgy of Power (Princeton, 1989), 154.
[102] See D. Gless, *Measure for Measure, the Law and the Convent* (Princeton,
1979), 142–76.

resigned his authority to Escalus, he intends to 'Visit both prince and people' in the guise of a priest, in order to better educate himself in the art of government (I.iii.45). King James's recorded propensity for visiting various London institutions, particularly the Merchant's Exchange, in 'disguise', provides an immediate contemporary context.[103] The blurring of public and private roles is immediately destabilizing, while the determination of the Duke to regenerate both his private person and his public office and commonwealth, echoes Prince Hal's similar determination to refashion himself in the image of a godly prince.[104] The abandonment of magisterial responsibilities is a hugely risky venture, and not necessarily becoming of a competent sovereign. Although harmony is finally restored, in the meantime, Claudio could have been executed many times over, Isabella raped, the economy of the commonwealth brought to its knees, and its reluctant subjects forced to accede to a puritan tyranny. The 'old fantastical duke of dark corners', as Lucio describes him, is something of a mixed blessing (IV.iii.156). Indeed, as the Duke himself confesses, it was a risky venture which only hastened the moral degeneracy of his commonwealth, 'Till it o'errun the stew' (V.i.316–17).

It is Isabella, herself an acutely ambivalent figure, part virginal icon, part puritan moralist, who furnishes the reassurance which the Duke and his commonwealth need, and she does so by confirming the constitutional jurisdiction of his prerogative authority. In Act II, scene 2, as a counter to Angelo's legal formalism, Isabella suggests that the common law 'authority' always inheres an equitable prerogative of justice, and in the final scene she affirms the position to the Duke (II.ii.135–60, V.i.67–8). Within the constitutional morality of the common law, there is always room to temper legal form with the particularities of individual justice. Isabella, like Portia in *The Merchant of Venice*, does not go outside the law. She merely reinterprets it in accordance with the Christian principles of justice which are part of its immanent political morality.[105] The

[103]   A number of commentators have suggested the extent to which the Duke might be some sort of model for or of James. See A. Kernan, *Shakespeare, the King's Playwright* (New Haven, 1995), 54.

[104]   C. Lewis, 'Dark Deeds Darkly Answered: Duke Vincentio and Judgment in *Measure for Measure*' (1983) 34 *Shakespeare Quarterly* 280–1.

[105]   For a general discussion of equity in *Measure for Measure*, see M. Winston, 'Craft Against Vice: Morality Play Elements in *Measure for Measure*' (1981) 14 *Shakespeare Studies* 242.

Duke confirms that justice, as prescribed by the Viennese common law, is 'measure for measure', bounded by the immanent rationality of the Aristotelian idea of equity. Government, he affirms, is about harmony, and harmony is about the balancing of interests within the political community, between the public interest of the body politic and the private interests of its constituents (V.i.409).

It is the putative reformation of political morality which underpins the essential ambiguity of the play's approach to questions of law and morality. Pompey bemoans a legal morality which seeks to prohibit prostitution, but which permits usury, whilst such are the financial pressures in Vienna, that brothel-keepers cannot even contemplate observing the law (I.ii.98–103, II.i.250–1, III.ii.6–10). Civil laws can no more defeat the market than they can suppress human inclination. As Pompey asks, with a prescient metaphor, 'Does your worship mean to geld and splay all the youth of the city?' (II.i.227–8). The ravages of the market, as much as the dynamics of human nature, immediately question any community which seeks to define itself in accordance with any imagined morality. Moreover, as is ever the case, the prescription of morality inheres an immediate danger because it seeks to interfere with a pretended realm of private liberty, and such a danger can translate into a crisis of faith in the justice of the entire legal system. Such a crisis characterizes Claudio's shattered illusions in Act I, scene 2, when he rails against the 'demi-gods of Authority', who by seeking to redetermine the 'body public' can be identified with 'tyranny'. The 'body' appears to be a 'horse whereon the governor doth ride/Who, newly in seat, that it might now/He can command, lets it straight feel the spur' (I.ii.148–52). In Claudio's opinion, laws which are no longer justified by the political morality of the community are used in a spurious attempt to legitimate an insecure public authority by the infringement of private liberties. It is a view which is to be eloquently affirmed by Isabella, and indeed grudgingly admitted by Angelo (II.ii.95–6, 101, 109–10, II.iv.174–6).[106] There is, then, a consistent suspicion that the

---

[106] Moreover, there is an added suspicion that Claudio's alleged adultery was anyway rendered lawful by the Viennese common law of 'true contract', itself a legal fiction which enjoyed some authority in contemporary England and which could legitimate pre-marital sex between those contractually committed to marriage (I.ii.134–50). For a discussion of this legal fiction, see J. Birje-Patil, 'Marriage Contracts in *Measure for Measure*' (1969) 5 *Shakespeare Studies*,

enforcement of laws against immorality are merely feints towards a deeper retrenchment of sovereign authority. Reformation of private 'laws' are used in order to refine public government. Lucio, a frequenter of brothels, enjoys an acute appreciation of the 'sanctimonious' hypocrisy of those that seek to condemn him (I.ii.7). 'Grace is grace', he adds, 'despite of all controversy'. The frequenting of brothels does not necessarily signify those whom God has chosen not to save (I.ii.24–5).

At the root of Shakespeare's treatment of questions of sexual morality lay the pervasive problem of the relation between public and private spheres of government, and its essentially theatrical and imaginary foundation. The textuality of plays such as *Measure for Measure* consistently destabilizes received ideas of sexuality, gender, and the public–private distinction which underpins recurring arguments surrounding the vexed questions of law and morality. Sexuality, it seems, is an irreducible dynamic which threatens constant social instability. Literature plays a constitutive role in perpetuating the image of sexuality as a destabilizing force, just as theatrical rituals such as skimmingtons reinforce cultural myths of the shrewish and lascivious woman.[107] When a community senses a danger to its moral propriety, as in *The Merry Wives of Windsor*, it addresses the danger by employing the customary quasi-law of cuckolding. A morality that is at once public and private is preserved by an intensely communal form of law which cannot be identified by any recourse to concepts of liberal legalism. Morality becomes a public issue because it is textually determined, and text is necessarily public. It is striking that the rise of the theatre was seen by many as a complement to the spread of brothels. Both were notoriously cast outside the immediate environs of the city boroughs, and consigned to the suburbs, which in

106–11, K. Wentersdorf, 'The Marriage Contracts in *Measure for Measure*: A Reconsideration' (1979) 32 *Shakespeare Survey* 129–44, and V. Hayne, 'Performing Social Practice: the Example of *Measure for Measure*' (1993) 44 *Shakespeare Quarterly* 3–8.

[107] Skimmingtons could take various forms, but generally involved the ritual humiliation of individuals dressed as cuckolds and placed rear-facing on horseback, and then paraded through the village. They were particularly popular in the west country, but evidence survives of their use well into the seventeenth century in various parts of the country. For examples of their use, see D. Underdown, *A Freeborn People: Politics and the Nation in Seventeenth Century England* (Oxford, 1996), 47–9.

turn became readily associated with the institutions of degeneracy and moral subversion. The theatre, as Shakespeare's contemporaries readily appreciated, determined popular conceptions of morality and gender, and enjoyed a far greater power in so doing than any legal moralism. The constitution of a godly commonwealth was not written in terms of rules or rights, as liberal legalism was to subsequently allege. Rather, it defined and understood itself in terms of a process of writing, a relation between performed magistracy and receptive audience.

IBSEN AND THE ASCRIPTION
OF BLAME IN LAW

John Stanton-Ife

In the name of the criminal law people are fined and imprisoned; in the name of tort law people are held liable to pay damages in compensation. The consequences to those punished or held liable in these ways can be serious and even devastating. Thus, it has always been thought that these legal practices must meet certain ethical conditions if they are to be considered legitimate: it cannot but be a matter of serious moral concern that they cause distress which is sometimes extreme. From the fact that justification is required in these contexts, however, it does not follow that it is clear what shape the justification should take. Since these practices are practices of *blaming* people, the most obvious suggestion is that people should be the subject of blame only over things that are *in their power*.[1] Blame should not be ascribed where the putative defendant was *powerless*, where for example she was unlucky. So there seems to be an important principle at work: 'Ascribe blame only for what is in an agent's power, not for matters that are subject to luck.' Slightly more specifically one might say, 'blame someone only for what they have tried to do' not for what they succeeded or failed to do with the intervention of luck.[2]

But once one starts to look around in the criminal law and in tort law one sees that liability and punishment are not fully allocated on the basis of matters within the agent's control: often pure luck does to some significant extent determine guilt or liability. The tort of negligence, for example, does not hold a person liable merely on proof that she has breached a duty of care, but will also

---

[1] See A. Kenny, *Aristotle on the Perfect Life* (Oxford, 1992), 76.
[2] One could also put this the other way around and say 'praise someone only for what they have tried to do', although in this paper my concern will be only with the negative ascription of blame, not the positive ascription of praise.

require proof that the breach caused the harm complained of. Often, however, the question of whether harm is caused by someone's negligence is not under the control of the negligent person herself. It may be 'up to the world', so to speak, what happens, not up to the person.[3]

At a pivotal moment in Ibsen's late play *The Master Builder* (1892)[4] a scenario emerges that could almost form part of a problem-question for students on a tort law examination paper. The play's central character is a builder—Solness—who is engaged in restoring an old property and adding an extension to it.[5] As he is working on the restoration one day, he notices that there is a crack in the chimney of the house. He checks continually thereafter to see if the crack is still there and always finds that it is. He does not repair it; he does nothing and mentions the crack to nobody: 'a hand seemed to reach out and stop me', he says later when looking back on the tragedy that is to follow. As he was restoring the house a compelling thought came to him that if it were to burn down he would be able to divide the land into building sites and then build according to his own ideas and make his fortune.[6] He even pictured the scene—in his imagination he saw that the house would burn down as he was out with his wife and the two of them would return to find 'the whole of that great wooden box . . . a roaring mass of flames'.[7] And, indeed, the house does subsequently burn down with disastrous consequences. The builder's two infant sons are killed. It is crucially important that the fire does not take place in the way that Solness had anticipated. Investigations into the cause of the fire reveal that it did not begin in the chimney in which he had found the crack: it began in the cupboard in an entirely different part of the house. Now of course if this were a tort problem, Solness could not be held liable: for although he had a duty of care which he appears to have breached, his negligence had not caused the deaths and the damage. For all that had been up to him it might have done, but it in fact did not. The tort of negligence, as it has been recently summarized, 'does not impose a pure duty to try, that is a pure

---

[3] Compare M. Nussbaum, 'Luck and Ethics' in D. Statman (ed.), *Moral Luck* (Albany, New York, 1993), 73, 74.

[4] All citations from this play will come from *Henrik Ibsen: Four Major Plays* (James McFarlane (trans.), Oxford, 1981).   [5] Act II, 319 *et seq.*

[6] Act II, 314.   [7] Act II, 320.

duty not to be negligent. It imposes a hybrid trying/succeeding duty, a duty not to *cause* certain kinds of damage *by* one's negligence'.[8]

On the rather odd hypothesis, then, that Ibsen's scenario is a common law tort problem, we see that blame would not be imposed on Solness solely according to what was under his control. But, of course, it would be silly to entertain the notion that Ibsen had any sort of legal problem in mind when writing *The Master Builder*. However, I will try to show in what follows that Solness's deliberations about the fire and about luck and blame, reveal in Ibsen a concern with the human practice of blame that is also a central problem for law, however different are the contexts of the law and the theatre. The late Ibsen plays in general, as George Steiner has noted, are 'epilogues to previous disaster',[9] they are 'dramas of afterlife engaging vivid shadows such as animate the lower regions of the *Purgatorio*.' He captures their feel aptly by asking us to suppose that Shakespeare had written a play showing Macbeth and Lady Macbeth living out their bleak lives in exile after they had been defeated by their avenging enemies. This paper deals with *The Master Builder* and the disaster to which this late play of Ibsen's is an epilogue is the fire that caused the death of Solness's sons. Just as is true of Dante, much of the epilogue consists in an exploration of how blame should be attached to previous acts and events, though in Ibsen there is no confident religious foundation for the ascription of blame as there is in Dante. If I am right, then, Ibsen shares a central preoccupation of the law with the human practice of blame. But so what? Obviously it would be bizarre to propose that any clear prescriptions for law reform could emerge from reading plays and it would be equally crazy to suggest that works of literature could be improved if their grasp of legal principle were to be made firmer. My belief that Ibsen's work is a fit object of study in the young field of law and literature is that it allows us to examine the practice of blame in the whole context of one life lived with others. It allows attention to the particular, rather than to the usual fare of the law in the general or abstract, and it allows the lawyer to

---

[8] J. Gardner, 'The Purity and Priority of Private Law' (1996) 46 *University of Toronto Law Journal* 459, 489.

[9] G. Steiner, *The Death of Tragedy* (London, 1961), 296. The references to Steiner in the following sentences in the text come from this work, 296–8.

return to the detail that is normally abstracted and generalized away. While offering no new solutions to the age-old question of how blame is to be best allocated to human beings, it helps us to appreciate what is at stake in such practices seen from the perspective of lived human experience. I will try to show that Ibsen's Solness lives out a tension in the idea of blame that also lies at the heart of the law.

The issue of 'moral luck' has already been raised in connection with tort law and the episode of the fire in *The Master Builder*. Bernard Williams in introducing the term intended it to suggest an oxymoron: that there is 'something in our conception of morality . . . that arouses opposition to the idea that moral responsibility or moral merit or moral blame should be subject to luck'.[10] I now say something about the problem as it has been applied in another legal context, the criminal law—where the idea that legal blame should be subject to luck similarly arouses opposition. Luck can come to play a role in the ascription of blame in this criminal context in at least three ways, in relation to a person's 'constitutive luck', 'circumstantial luck', and 'outcome luck'.[11] I address each of these in turn, beginning with 'constitutive luck'.

A person's good or bad constitutive luck is the sort of luck she has in her 'inclinations, capacities and temperament': what sort of a person she is.[12] Ultimately, one cannot control one's temperament, what one is inclined to do or one's capacities to succeed in what one sets out on. Many reflecting long and hard on this have concluded that the very idea of being responsible for one's actions in the sense of a capacity to do otherwise is a deep illusion. One example of this extreme determinist position is in the 'Owenite philosophy' discussed by John Stuart Mill in his essay on 'Utilitarianism'. 'The Owenite' says Mill 'invokes the admitted principle that it is unjust to punish anyone for what he cannot help'. But this leads to the view that it is unjust to punish at all: 'for the criminal did not make his own character; his education

---

[10] B. Williams, 'Postscript' in Statman, n. 3 above, 251. Williams's original article, entitled 'Moral Luck', is also reprinted in Statman, 35.

[11] This three-way division of the concept of luck comes from A. Duff, *Criminal Attempts* (Oxford, 1996), 150. For slightly different terminology see Kenny, n. 1 above, 76 and for a four-way division, see T. Nagel, 'Moral Luck' in Statman, n. 3 above, 60.

[12] Nagel, 'Moral Luck' in Statman, n. 3 above, 60.

and the circumstances which surrounded him, have made him a criminal and for these he is not responsible'.[13] Thus, it is sometimes said that the criminal law should not punish, but should cure or reform.

Mill's statement of the Owenite position also contains within it the second way in which agents are subject to luck: 'circumstantial luck'. This is luck in the kinds of problem and situation a person faces,[14] 'the circumstances which surround' people in Owenite terms. The most striking example of the problem of bad circumstantial luck in the criminal law is in the area of duress. What should a court do if someone accused of murder and terrorist offences shows that he only planted a lethal bomb because he had to do so to avoid the execution of a threat to kill him? In *R*. v. *Howe* the House of Lords affirmed that duress was no defence to murder.[15] As Antony Kenny has put it: 'the Court did not accept the moral principle that one who kills an innocent person out of fear for his own life should be exempted from criminal sanction as a concession to human frailty'.[16] The law, then, might make no concession to the fact that it may have been quite appalling bad luck that put the accused between the devil and the deep blue sea, appalling bad luck that put him in a situation in which his only choice was either to kill innocent people and be sentenced to life imprisonment as a result, or not to kill the innocent but be killed himself.

The third kind of luck important in the criminal law is 'outcome luck'—'luck in the way one's actions and projects turn out'.[17] Possible examples are legion. Outcome luck can be highly significant in cases where 'constructive liability' is imposed in manslaughter; in determining liability and punishment for attempts and completed crimes; and for dangerous driving.[18] Taking manslaughter first, the broad idea of constructive liability has it that 'anyone who decides to transgress the criminal law should be held liable for all the consequences that ensue, even if

[13] J. S. Mill, 'Utilitarianism' in G. Williams (ed.), *John Stuart Mill: On Liberty and Other Essays* (London, 1993), 58.
[14] Nagel, 'Moral Luck' in Statman, n. 3 above, 60.
[15] *R*. v. *Howe* [1987] AC 417.   [16] Kenny, n. 1 above, 83.
[17] Nagel, n. 12 above, 60.
[18] A. Ashworth, 'Taking the Consequences' in S. Shute, J. Gardner and J. Horder (eds.), *Action and Value in Criminal Law* (Oxford, 1993), 107, 124.

they are more serious than expected'.[19] Liability for a more serious offence is 'constructed' out of a lesser degree of fault.[20] Thus
A and B each get into a fight in different places. Each throws a
punch with exactly the same force at his victim but A's victim gets
bruised while B's victim falls awkwardly and dies after his head
hits the pavement. A gets a much less severe punishment than B
due to the fortuitous fall of his victim. A similar problem arises
with attempts—two people each shoot at an intended victim, the
first narrowly missing because her victim moves suddenly, while
the second's shot kills the victim; and with dangerous driving—
two drivers are driving equally dangerously, but a child runs into
the path of one and dies while the other zigzags home on an
empty road.[21] Again, in these cases it is luck and not the state of
the respective wills of the defendants that distinguish their cases
from each other's, it is luck that determines who is a murderer,
who has attempted murder, who has killed a child, and who has
behaved irresponsibly.

Just how the criminal law should respond to these problems of
constitutive, circumstantial and outcome luck is a live issue in
thinking about the criminal law today. Andrew Ashworth's view
is that while someone's bad constitutive and circumstantial luck
should not be a ground for the avoidance of punishment, her bad
outcome luck should be. In his view, what Mill called the 'admitted principle' that 'it is unjust to punish anyone for what he
cannot help' does not stretch as far as the Owenite conclusion that
punishment on the basis of constitutive misfortune is itself unjust,
although it does as far as outcome luck is concerned. As for the
three specific cases of outcome luck mentioned in the last paragraph, it is his view that all of them should turn on the defendant's culpability rather than on the outcome in the particular
case.[22] 'Luck' says Ashworth, 'may be an unavoidable element in
life and in moral judgments, but that does not mean that the criminal law should reflect the vagaries of chance when it has the
opportunity to eliminate them as a basis for censure.'[23] All three
kinds of luck are discernible in *The Master Builder* and this paper

[19] A. Ashworth, *Principles of Criminal Law* (2nd edn, Oxford, 1995), 85.
[20] Ashworth, *Principles of Criminal Law*, n. 19 above, 153.
[21] See generally, Ashworth, 'Taking the Consequences', n. 18 above.
[22] Ashworth, 'Taking the Consequences', n. 18 above, 124.
[23] Ashworth, *Principles of Criminal Law*, n. 19 above, 154.

examines how Ibsen deals with luck in the human practice of ascribing blame. But first some background to the play should be explored.

The primary interest of the play to the lawyer, I have suggested, lies in the interest it shares with the law in the human practice of ascribing blame. At times also the play seems to unfold a little like a trial scene. Notwithstanding the fact that there is no explicit mention of legal concerns—no lawyer figure such as the oppressive Torvald Helmer in *A Doll's House* (1879)[24]—there is a sense that Solness is being tried for offences he has committed. Solness is on trial, we might say, for two offences: causing the death of his two infant sons and for the destruction of his wife's happiness— only it is no ordinary trial, for he himself acts simultaneously as his own accuser, defender, and judge. The doubt that 'nags' him 'day and night', we hear him say, is that rather than being 'completely innocent' he may be entirely 'to blame' for the fire and all its consequences.[25] The second act is largely taken up with the question of his guilt and by the end of it his guilt appears to be established. While there are two offences that Solness accuses himself of, there are further charges that two of his employees would put to him, of destroying their lives as much as that of his own wife. The two employees in question are the dying Knut Brovik, his one time employer and Brovik's son, Ragnar. A further life that only the audience can see destroyed by Solness is that of Kaja Fosli, his secretary and Ragnar's fiancée. Kaja despite her engagement to Ragnar is hopelessly in love with Solness—and this love is to be cruelly exploited.

At the end of the play Solness falls to his death as he tries to defy his own deep fear of heights by hanging a wreath on the top of his newly completed tower. The agent of his death is Hilde Wangel, a young visitor to the house, a character who had already appeared as a boisterous girl in *The Lady from the Sea* (1888).[26] It is she who induces him to climb up the tower in a mad attempt to overcome his vertigo. One way to understand Solness's death is as an execution, as the payment of the debt he has incurred for his guilt. Having found himself guilty of the literal and metaphorical

---

[24] *Ibsen: A Doll's House and Other Plays* (Harmondsworth, 1965).
[25] Act II, 317.
[26] *A Doll's House and Other Plays*, n. 24 above, 233.

deaths of others, the retribution which he had always feared would one day 'come beating on his door' had now, on this understanding, come to exact its price.[27] But Solness's death could also be understood as a triumphant liberation; for it is not clear whether Hilde is his executioner or his liberator. It is possible that Hilde has succeeded in her attempt to 'see him great'; to have him defy the cloying unhappiness and guilt that were oppressing and destroying him. However, I mention the fascinating problem of the third act only to put it to one side. It is the backward-looking aspects of how blame is ascribed that occur in the first two acts that is my concern, but there is a possible forward-looking aspect of the play in the third act; if Hilde is indeed the liberator of Solness, this might qualify the observation that the play is an epilogue to past disaster.

Turning then to Ibsen's treatment of blame in *The Master Builder*, the most striking feature of the play is the constant use of the concept of luck in the deliberations of the characters. The word luck (*lykke*) is explicitly used and often.[28] Both Hilde and Dr Herdal, an early interlocutor of Solness, set in motion his tortured deliberations by commenting on what a lucky man he has been ('Yes indeed, Mr. Solness, you certainly have had all the luck').[29] Furthermore, examples of constitutive luck, circumstantial luck and outcome luck are all to be found in the play. Obviously this is not because Ibsen had any explicit interest in debates about what is now called 'moral luck', but because he was perceiving with some sensitivity something that is a quite general problem about the ascription of blame. We have already seen in some detail the good outcome luck of Solness in the fact that his negligence did not cause the death of his sons. He also had good constitutive luck: he had talent and an iron will; and his circumstantial luck had been excellent. The fire had made his career: exactly as he had foreseen he had divided the land in which the old house had stood into building sites and had built successfully according to his own ideas.

---

[27] Act I, 285.

[28] Nicholas Rescher in his analysis of the varying shades of meaning of the idea of 'luck', 'chance', 'fortune', and other terms points out that the German 'Glück' means not only 'luck' but also 'happiness': 'Moral Luck' in Statman, n. 3 above, 146. Ibsen's Norwegian term 'lykke' similarly means both of these things and so often when the English text speaks of 'happiness' an overtone of 'luck' should also be understood (thus making the emphasis of the play on luck still more pronounced).   [29] Act I, 285.

Ragnar Brovik's circumstantial luck stands in direct contrast to that of Solness. His constitutive luck was good: although not always sure of it himself, it is clear to the audience that Ragnar has enough talent to supplant Solness as the leading builder in the area. In order for that to happen, however, Ragnar needed to be able to set up on his own and such was the standing of Solness in the community that no one would commission any of Ragnar's work without the *imprimatur* of the master; and it was this that Solness had refused to give for years. Similarly, Aline, Solness's wife, had talent but bad circumstantial luck. Her talent, Solness tells Hilde, was to be 'a master builder of souls', but after the death of her sons, she had no outlet for this gift. Speaking of his wife's talent, Solness remarks: 'So building their souls that they might grow straight and fine, noble and beautifully formed, for their full human stature. That was where Aline's talent lay. And look now where it lies. Unused and for ever unusable. No earthly use for anything . . . like a charred heap of ruins.'[30]

Luck intervenes at another crucial point in the play. Old Knut Brovik is dying and in order to die fulfilled he must see that Solness has underwritten some of Ragnar's work, so that he can believe that all his son's and his own waiting have not been in vain. Solness, as mentioned above, had consistently refused to underwrite anything of Ragnar's, but when he finally relents, under the influence of Hilde, it comes just too late, for old Brovik has just died.[31] An hour or two had made the difference between a relatively fulfilled and contented death and a miserable one.

Luck, then, pervades the play but simply noting this does not explain the role that Ibsen takes it to play in the ascription of blame. Are we to be blamed on the basis solely of the will or is the force of luck and fortune so powerful that no sense can be made of blame thus conceived? This is the question I want to examine in some detail. There are many indications in the play that Ibsen is trying to suggest the latter possibility. Solness is sometimes tempted by something akin to what we described as the strong determinist Owenite position, attempting to avoid responsibility on the basis that his luck has made him powerless to act. I now

---

[30] Act II, 317; cf. the lines from Thomas Gray's 'Elegy Written in a Country Churchyard': 'Some mute inglorious Milton here may rest./ Some Cromwell, guiltless of his country's blood.', cited by Nagel in 'Moral Luck' in Statman, n. 3 above, 70.   [31] Act III, 342.

consider whether there is enough evidence for understanding the
play in such a sceptical, deterministic way. One example supporting this reading comes when old Brovik is pleading with Solness to
underwrite some of the work of his son. Solness's response is
intransigent: 'I'm never going to back down! I'll never give way to
anybody! Never of my own free will. Never in this world will I do
that.'[32] In saying this he is assuming that he has the power—the
free will—to do otherwise, but that it is a power that he chooses
not to exercise. Yet almost immediately afterwards he contradicts
himself and is pleading his (constitutive) bad luck in being the
kind of person he is. So, old Brovik asks him, 'that is how you
expect me to die?', to which Solness responds 'half in desperation':
'Don't you understand? There's nothing else I can do! I am what I
am! And I can't change myself'[33]. In the space of four or five lines
Solness has asserted both his free will and his lack of it; both his
ability and his inability to do otherwise. He has implied the
unavailability of constitutive luck as a justification and has then
relied on it.

A second example of Solness pleading his constitutive bad luck
comes in relation to his hoodwinking of his secretary Kaja Fosli.
In order to neutralize the danger to him posed by Ragnar setting
up business on his own, Solness persuades Kaja that he loves her,
so that she would stay, keeping Ragnar there too. He justifies this
to Dr Herdal thus: 'and it's not fair on her, poor thing.
[Vehemently] But there's nothing else I can do! Because if she was
away from me—then away goes Ragnar too'.[34] Solness sees the
unfairness of the situation for Kaja Fosli, but seeks to wriggle out
of the blame for it by asserting that there was nothing else he
could do given the way he was, given the tramlines he was already
set on.

Other evidence might be found that Ibsen is drifting towards
the deterministic view of blame. In fact, such evidence might be
found in one of the most fascinating aspects of the play, Ibsen's
invocation of the imagery of the Nordic trolls. For there is 'troll',
we are told, in Solness and Hilde and the trolls have agency, the
power to cause events to occur. Ibsen adopts the symbolism of the
trolls of Nordic antiquity to embody this power. Sometimes the
trolls are referred to explicitly, as when Solness tells Hilde that it

---

[32] Act I, 273.   [33] Act I, 273.   [34] Act I, 282.

is the troll within us that decides whom we fall in love with, however unsuitable.[35] At other times, they are referred to as 'helpers and servants'. It is the trolls that have seen to it that all of the mysterious events of the play had occurred: it was the 'helpers and servants' who intervened to see to it that the house burned down. As Ibsen's biographer, Michael Meyer points out, he often thought in terms of life as a struggle with the 'trolls within' and the 'trolls without'.[36] One might then find support for the view that Ibsen is suggesting that no coherent idea of blame can survive the onslaughts of luck, in the invocation of the trolls. Perhaps Ibsen's bleak message is this: when humans think of themselves as free agents they are deluded, for it is causal forces beyond their power, trolls, helpers and servants, luck (constitutive and so on) that determine what happens. Perhaps he is darkly implying that humans are not agents; rather they are conduits for the forces of luck?

Before considering whether this is indeed how *The Master Builder* should be read, more should be said about the significance of the trolls, the 'helpers and servants'. For Solness is constantly referring to a dark contra-causal power that he seems to have. He wills something, and the helpers and servants see to it that what he wills comes to pass. But what is this contra-causal power that Solness appears to have? It is a power allowing events to occur simply by virtue of his will. There are a number of examples of this special power. As we have seen, Solness kept Ragnar working for him by means of his hold over Kaja. His means of luring Kaja to him was strange indeed:

Solness: But Ragnar—he was absolutely intent on setting up on his own. There was no arguing with him.
Dr Herdal: Yet he's stayed with you all the same.
Solness: Yes, and I'll tell you why. One day this girl, Kaja Fosli, called in to see them for something. She'd never been here before. And when I saw how completely infatuated with each other these two were, I had an idea: if I could somehow get her into the office here, maybe Ragnar would stay, too.
Dr Herdal: That was a fair assumption.

---

[35] Act II, 325.
[36] M. Meyer, *Ibsen* (London, 1985), 590. Meyer reports that Ibsen once inscribed a copy of *Peer Gynt* with the lines: 'to live is to war with trolls in the heart and soul; to write is to sit in judgment of oneself', 291.

Solness: Yes but I never dropped the slightest hint of this at any time. I just stood and looked at her—wishing with all my soul that I had her here. Then I made one or two pleasant little remarks to her, about one thing and another. Then off she went.

Dr Herdal: Well?

Solness: Well then, the next day, in the evening after old Brovik and Ragnar had gone home, she came back here to me, and acted as though I had come to some arrangement with her.

Dr Herdal: Arrangement? What about?

Solness: About the very thing I'd been wishing for. But about which I had not said a single word.

Dr Herdal: Very odd.[37]

Solness had willed a certain arrangement and it had occurred simply by virtue of his willing it. He had willed that Kaja would come and work for him and she had come, without the use of the usual channels of human communication. Similarly, when Hilde accuses him of having kissed her amorously when a young teenager, after angrily denying it, he speaks as a stage direction dictates 'as though a thought suddenly strikes him':

Or . . . wait a moment! There's more to this than meets the eye, I tell you [Hilde does not move. Solness speaks quietly but emphatically] *I must have willed it . . . wished it . . . desired it. And then . . . mightn't that be the explanation?* [Hilde remains silent. Solness speaks impatiently] All right, damn it . . . so I did do it then![38]

Once he had willed it, there was no longer any question of whether or not he had actually done it. The same was true of the fire. Once Solness had willed it so strongly it was already determined that it was going to occur, through the mediation not of scientific laws, but of Solness's contra-causal power. This might suggest ultimately that one *never* has the power to do otherwise than one does; for one cannot help what one desires and if one has Solness's contra-causal power (his luck) then the trolls will see to it that events happen. On the reading I have been considering, therefore, Ibsen is suggesting something Owenite in flavour—luck crowds out genuine human responsibility.

Despite all of this evidence for an 'Owenite' view of responsibility however—Solness's cries of 'I am what I am'; the invasion of Solness by trolls and helpers and servants—ultimately this

---

[37] Act I, 281.   [38] Act I, 294.

cannot, I think, be a correct reading of the play. I will suggest two reasons for this. First, that such a freedom-denying reading would be impossible to reconcile with the strong impetus for freedom that drives Ibsen elsewhere; and second, that closer attention to the fire episode in *The Master Builder* itself, shows the true role of the helpers and servants to be a more subtle one than that suggested above. Accordingly, a more plausible, freedom-affirming reading will emerge.

As for the first of these, a determinist, Owenite view of blame would be highly surprising coming from Ibsen who had after all championed freedom constantly in his past works. There is the freedom of women in *A Doll's House* and the political freedom of those like Dr Stockman in *An Enemy of the People* (1882) who have uncomfortable truths for established communities.[39] The deterministic reading of the past paragraphs would be an extreme turnaround for the playwright of freedom *par excellence*. Perhaps the strongest indication of the importance of freedom to Ibsen comes in *The Lady from the Sea*. Ellida Wangel 'the Lady from the Sea' had married Dr Wangel and as the play develops we see glimpses of a marriage without joy. It emerges that years earlier Ellida had made a promise to a sailor that they would one day come together for ever. The sailor eventually returns to claim her and she seems unable to resist his allure. Wangel in the meantime at first tries to repel the sailor telling him 'there is no question of choice for my wife. I am here to choose for her and protect her'.[40] Eventually, however, after seeing his wife suffer he shows a sensitivity never shown by Helmer to Nora in *A Doll's House* and he says to her that he will not hold her to her marriage vows: 'I cancel our bargain here and now. You are free to choose your own path. Completely free'.[41] On being given this freedom there is a sea change in Ellida: again in direct contrast to Nora, she decides to stay with her husband. The answer to her suffering was paradoxically to stay exactly where she was in exactly the same circumstances. But they were not really the same circumstances, since the fact that they were now freely chosen had transformed them utterly. Moreover, with her freedom came responsibility. As she says to her husband: 'Now I will come back to you. Now I

---

[39] *Ibsen: An Enemy of the People and Other Plays* (Oxford, 1988).
[40] Note 24 above, Act V, 326.   [41] Act V, 327.

can, because I come to you freely—of my own free will—on my own responsibility.'[42] The condition for the complete change in Ellida was the ability to choose freely and with freedom came responsibility. Freedom is right at the heart of Ibsen's treatment of women. Nora had to abandon her husband and children because the conditions for the free exercise of choice were not available to her, Ellida by contrast could stay with hers once those conditions had been made available to her. Clearly Ibsen is not trying to suggest that Aline Solness's desire to be a 'master builder of souls' made her a lesser woman than Nora who fled the nest, for in Aline's case, there was no suggestion that her desire to nurture was not freely chosen.

In so much else of Ibsen's work, then, it is freedom and with it responsibility that is the guiding value towering over all others. This, however, does not itself establish that in *The Master Builder* he was not concerned to show that human freedom was an illusion, however much of a change it would mark in him. But, in the final analysis, there is enough evidence in the play for concluding that Solness assumes a very different idea of blame and responsibility from the Owenite one displayed in his cries of 'I am what I am'. He does not in the end try to evade responsibility for the consequences of the fire on the basis of the good piece of outcome luck that the fire was not caused by his negligence. The key point is that, while Solness's contra-causal power meant that the fire would occur simply by virtue of his willing it, and while it was the helpers and servants (luck) that saw to it that the house burned, blame for the fire ultimately lies in the *summoning* of the trolls, in the *summoning* of the helpers and servants. Because Solness, unlike old Brovik, had summoned the trolls he must ultimately be responsible, whatever the role of luck. This is the key passage and it has to be cited in some detail for the point to emerge in the context of Solness's contra-causal power:

Solness [confidentially]: Don't you believe too, Hilde, that you find certain people have been singled out, specially chosen, gifted with the power and ability to want something, to desire something, to will something . . . so insistently . . . that they get it in the end? Don't you believe that? . . . One doesn't achieve such great things alone. Oh, no. One has to have . . . helpers and servants . . . if anything's to come of it. But they

---

[42] Act V, 329.

never come of their own accord. One has to summon them, imperiously, inwardly, you understand.

Hilde: Who are these helpers and servants?

Solness: Oh, we can talk about that some other time. Let's keep to the matter of the fire for the present.

Hilde: Don't you think that fire would have occurred anyway—even if you hadn't wished for it?

Solness: If old Knut Brovik had owned the house, it would never have burnt down quite so conveniently for him. I'm quite certain of that. He doesn't know how to call upon these helpers . . . nor upon the servants, either. [Gets up restlessly] You see, Hilde . . . I am actually the one who is to blame for those two little boys having to pay with their lives. And perhaps I'm to blame too for Aline never becoming what she could and should have been. And what she most of all wanted to be.

Hilde: Yes, but if it's only those helpers and servants who . . .?

Solness: Who called on the helpers and servants? I did! And they came and did my bidding. [In rising excitement] That's what people call being lucky. But let me tell you what that sort of luck feels like! It feels as if my breast were a great expanse of raw flesh. And these helpers and servants go flaying off the skin from other people's bodies to patch my wound. Yet the wound never heals . . . never! Oh, if only you knew how it sometimes burns and throbs.[43]

By a long and winding road, then, Solness's agency becomes crucial to his responsibility. *Once he has willed* something, he is powerless to prevent it happening—the helpers and servants will see to that. But he *does* have the power to *summon*, and it is for the *summoning* of the helpers and servants that he must take responsibility. His actions had not caused the fire, but he came to see himself as fully to blame for it because he had summoned his helpers and servants. Ibsen stresses luck in his play not, then, as the earlier reading proposed, to paint an Owenite picture, but in order to re-establish the centrality of the will in ascribing blame.

Despite the omnipresence of the power of luck and fortune in human lives, Ibsen seems to reassert in a very strong form the message of human freedom of *The Lady from the Sea*. Responsibility lies for the will, for the 'summoning'. We may not be able to control luck but we can control what we summon. The view that emerges does not seem far away from the famous lines of Immanuel Kant on the good will:

[43] Act II, 321–2.

The good will is not good because of what it effects or accomplishes or because of its adequacy to achieve some proposed end, it is good only because of its willing, i.e., it is good of itself. And, regarded for itself, it is to be esteemed incomparably higher than anything which could be brought about by it in favour of any inclination or even of the sum total of all inclinations. Even if it should happen that, by a particularly unfortunate fate or by the niggardly provision of a stepmotherly nature, this will should be wholly lacking in power to accomplish its purpose, and if even the greatest effort should not avail it to achieve anything of its end, and if there remained only the good will (not as a mere wish but as the summoning of all the means in our power), it would sparkle like a jewel in its own right, as something that had its full worth in itself. Usefulness or fruitlessness can neither diminish nor augment its worth.[44]

It is probably coincidental that both Kant and Ibsen speak of the 'summoning', of 'all the means in our power', 'of the helpers and servants', but Ibsen shows the same sign in the end as Kant that luck, 'usefulness' and 'fruitlessness' must be cut through and seen as irrelevant to the ascription of blame. At least as Nagel reads him, what Kant says about the good will in the cited passage he would also say of the bad will: 'whether it accomplishes its evil purposes is morally irrelevant', thus placing the earlier discussion of outcome luck squarely under the Kantian principle.[45] This betokens a human desire to avoid moral risk; and this is Solness's desire. It is the same impetus that drives legal writers like Ashworth to try to dispense with outcome luck in the ascription of criminal liability. Whether, as some believe,[46] a view that is more accommodating to 'moral luck', that tries to embrace it to some extent, rather than work towards its elimination, would not be preferable is a fascinating question that will remain a live issue for some time. Here, I have not tried to tackle so difficult a question. In this paper, I have tried, through an understanding of *The Master Builder*, to show a continuity between the problem of the ascription of blame for humans in their ordinary lives and the problem of how the law is to ascribe blame. Solness, whether reasonably or not, in his

---

[44] I. Kant, *Foundations of the Metaphysics of Morals*, first section, third paragraph. The passage is cited and discussed in Nagel, 'Moral Luck', n. 12 above, 57–8.   [45] Nagel, 'Moral Luck' in Statman, n. 3 above, 57–8.
[46] See generally Duff, *Criminal Attempts*, n. 11 above.

deliberations ends up with a view of responsibility that ties it tightly to the will and attempts at the same time to loosen its ties to luck. In doing so, he stands testimony to a human desire for a 'moral' domain insulated from luck, a desire that also tries to assert itself in the law.[47]

[47] I am very grateful to Turid and Anne-Marie Stanton-Ife for discussing Ibsen's plays with me, to my Law and Literature classes of 1996 and 1997 in Belfast for their insight and enthusiasm and to the organizers and participants of the University College London colloquium, June 1998, for all their help.

TESS OF THE D'URBERVILLES AND THE LAW OF PROVOCATION

Melanie Williams

Introduction

It is no surprise to find that the most winning characters in Victorian novels experience little mercy once they carry out a desperate act resulting in the death of another. *Tess of the d'Urbervilles*[1] is just such a case. Tess kills her seducer and her own execution is a foregone conclusion. Victorian law might well have been draconian in its disposition to such crime.[2] In one sense, the novel encourages the reader to accept this: there is no trial, no appeal and the text summarily marks the execution with the fatalistic words ' "Justice" was done, and the President of the Immortals, in Aeschylean phrase, had ended his sport with Tess.'[3] Yet, in another very real sense the novel screams 'injustice!'. In reading *this* message, the lawyer-reader can derive an intriguing and profound lesson for present-day criminal law; that in our obsession with the minutiae of doctrinal propriety we overlook the social construction of victims turned perpetrators and the concomitant complicity of doctrine. This is an issue of central importance to criminal jurisprudence and is most evident in the doctrine of provocation.

Recent academic commentary has focused upon the doctrine's

---

[1] *Tess of the d'Urbervilles* by Thomas Hardy was first published in 1891. All references are to the Penguin Classics edition (Harmondsworth, 1985).

[2] 'I believe it was Andrew Lang who put about the idea that she would not have been hanged. But a curious thing is that a Home Secretary informed me that he would have seen no reason to interfere with her sentence': Thomas Hardy, quoted in Martin Seymour-Smith, *Hardy* (London, 1994), 434. The fate of Tess may also reflect Hardy's memory of a woman, Martha Brown, hanged for killing her husband as a result of his unfaithfulness (Seymour-Smith, *Hardy*, 33).

[3] Hardy, *Tess*, n. 1 above, 489.

allegedly unequal sympathies towards male and female perpetrators: the 'battered woman' responding to provocative behaviour with a 'slow burn' of anger being acknowledged with uncertainty.[4] *Tess of the d'Urbervilles* makes a prescient case not only for this expansion of the doctrine, overcoming the prior partiality of the doctrine and culture for certain 'criminals'; it also demands acknowledgement of the cultural production of *the crime*.

Reviewing the Doctrine: The Ghosts in the Provocation Machine

As with any legal doctrine, the law of provocation has evolved as the product of halting and historically determined conceptual influences and developments in case law. The doctrine can be traced to a period of vastly different cultural experience and values from those which obtain today. In *DPP* v. *Camplin*[5] Lord Diplock, referring back to *R.* v. *Hayward*[6] noted that

> The human infirmity on which the law first took compassion in a violent age when men bore weapons for their own protection when going about their business appears to have been chance medley or a sudden falling out at which both parties had recourse to their weapons and fought on equal terms.

Two aspects of this early model of the provocative encounter have disappeared from modern doctrine.

First, that the law's indulgence in a show of compassion could be linked to the fact of an inherently lawless society—a 'violent age', when it was necessary to bear weapons for one's own protection. It may be presumed that with the advent of more effective legal constraints upon society, this link between social lawlessness and subjective justice became less evident.

The second element of the early model to which reference is no longer made is of a scenario where the parties 'fought on equal terms'. The notion of an essentially 'lawless' community which, while it fails to perform its protective function, will indulge the

---

[4] Articles are many and include A. McColgan, 'In Defence of Battered Women who Kill' (1993) 13 *Oxford Journal of Legal Studies* 508; D. Nicolson, 'Telling Tales: Gender Discrimination, Gender Construction and Battered Women Who Kill' (1995) Vol. III(2) *Feminist Legal Studies* 185; S. Yeo, 'The Role of Gender in the Law of Provocation' (1997) 26(4) *Anglo-American Law Review* 431.   [5] [1978] AC 705 at 713.
[6] (1833) 6 C. & P.157.

impulsive enterprise of its subject and the assumption of some degree of equality between the parties, will be revisited.

Let it be noted at this point, however, that a degree of flexibility attached to the usual requirement of provocation by physical assault, where the accused had suffered the archetypal psychological trauma of encountering either his wife in the act of adultery, or his son being sodomized. (The overtly patriarchal bias is later modified, at least in part, according to *dicta* in *Holmes* v. *DPP*.)[7] A more objective release from the physical assault component was of course achieved in the enactment of s. 3 of the Homicide Act 1957,[8] recognizing that acts and/or words could be provocative. The present law requires first, that the loss of self-control must be a sudden and temporary response to the provocation rendering the accused for the moment not master of his mind. However 'although it is established that a temporary and sudden loss of self-control arising from an act of provocation is essential, it is less clear to what extent previous acts of provocation are admissible'.[9] With regard to phenomena such as 'slow burn' and 'battered woman syndrome', arguably it should be the case that 'a jury might more easily find that there is a sudden loss of self control triggered even by a minor incident if the defendant had endured abuse over a period, on a last-straw basis'.[10] Second, the jury must decide whether the provocation was enough to make a reasonable man respond in the way that the accused responded, but since *DPP* v. *Camplin* the 'reasonable man' has evolved into a multi-dimensional creature who may plead that his susceptibility to the provocation was heightened by possessing 'permanent characteristics' which affected the gravity of the provocation to him. Again, it is not entirely clear whether 'battered woman syndrome' can acquire quite the same pedigree as other 'characteristics'. Nor is it as likely as some other traits to fulfil the erstwhile norm that there be a direct link between the provocative conduct and the characteristic.[11]

---

[7] [1946] AC 588.

[8] See summary 'The genesis of s. 3 Homicide Act 1957' in *Luc Thiet Thuan* v. *R.* [1996] 2 All ER 1033 at 1049.

[9] *Archbold: Criminal Pleading, Evidence and Practice* (P. J. Richardson (ed.), London, 1998), 1467.

[10] *R.* v. *Thornton (No.2)* [1996] 2 All ER 1030 c–d (Lord Taylor CJ).

[11] The issue of 'characteristics' is complex. 'Legitimate' characteristics may be derived from *DPP* v. *Camplin* [1978] AC 705, where examples included 'the fact that the accused was a dwarf, or of a particular colour or ethnic origin, or impotent,

Tess of the d'Urbervilles, 'The Facts' and Three Trial Narratives

Tess of the d'Urbervilles is a pertinent text with which to critique aspects of the doctrine of provocation primarily because it *upbraids* the law: in the case of *Tess*, the execution of justice seems very like the execution of innocence. Despite its fictional context, this reproach appears valid, plausible, and worthy of exploration; and *because* of its fictional context the challenges to doctrine are conceived and conveyed anew. Second, as with novel case law itself, the 'facts' of *Tess* are similar to and different from existing precedents, providing new points of comparison. Aligning the 'facts' of Tess's case with three successive trial narratives allows doctrinal models to be tested against these facts for their degree of 'fit'.

R. v. *DURBEYFIELD*[12]: THE FACTS

A young girl, Tess Durbeyfield, ignorant and innocent of sexual matters, is raped/seduced[13] by Alec d'Urberville, a local member of the *nouveau riche*. She gives birth to an illegitimate child, who subsequently dies. Later she falls in love, and marries Angel Clare,

or suffering from an abscess on the cheek when struck, or undergoing menstruation or menopause. It should be stressed that the relevance of such characteristics depends on whether they would affect the gravity of the provocation'—cited in *Archbold*, n. 9 above, 1468. I use the phrase 'erstwhile norm' because the Privy Council decision in *Luc Thien Thuan* v. *R.* [1996] 2 All ER 1033 has been cited as authority for the proposition that 'it is not necessary in order to establish the defence of provocation for the provocation to have been directed at the relevant characteristic of the defendant' (*per* Lord Goff at 1047). See also Yeo, 'The Role of Gender', n. 4 above, 442. Yet the example given in *Luc Thien Thuan*, 'previous events misled the defendant into believing that an innocent remark by the deceased was so directed when in fact it was not' is an extremely tenuous and therefore potentially unreliable suspension of the link.

[12] Since there is no trial scene in the novel, the case is never referred to by name, however it would have been 'R. v. *Durbeyfield*'. Tess belongs to an impoverished branch of the d'Urberville family; her surname has become debased to Durbeyfield. This clothes a purification, however, for d'Urberville, which with its connotations of Norman urban/town has acquired the pastorally cleansing 'field'. (I would like to thank my daughter Tamzin Williams, for pointing this out.) This beautifully underscores the symbolism in the novel and in Tess's character, whom Hardy was at pains to subtitle 'A Pure Woman'.

[13] Two points in the text of *Tess* suggest that the encounter was closer to the definition of rape: one refers to Tess's ignorance of sexual matters (131), the other to local belief on the matter (140).

a pleasant young man. On their wedding night, he confesses a youthful peccadillo. She in turn feels permitted to disclose her past, but her husband's idealization of her purity means that he cannot accept these facts. He insists that they part. The young woman spends some time in hardship and poverty, but feels unable to appeal to her estranged husband. Destitute, convinced that her husband is lost to her and careless of her fate, she allows the seducer to establish her as his mistress, partly in order to secure aid for her impoverished family. Meanwhile her husband has relented. He returns to see his wife. Desperate to regain the love of her husband, and in an attempt to negate the past, she kills her seducer. Husband and wife are reunited. After a brief period as fugitives, the young woman is captured, tried and hanged for the murder.

Trial—Narrative 1

A contemporaneous narrative gloss of these facts could read as follows:

The accused and the deceased shared a long-established history. While still a young girl, the accused had suffered an assault of the grossest kind at the hands of the deceased. As a result of this assault, her fortunes were sadly affected; she was rejected by her lawful husband and suffered protracted penury. Throughout this time, the deceased pursued her, and eventually she succumbed to his entreaties that she live with him as his mistress. Soon afterwards, her husband returned, it would appear with the intention of effecting a reconciliation. Believing this to be impossible under the circumstances, and taunted by the words of the deceased, the accused stabbed her victim, killing him.

It would not appear that the accused was provoked into committing this murderous act. Although she had long ago suffered grievously at the hands of the deceased, it seems that he treated her thereafter with solicitude. The fact that the accused agreed to live with the deceased as man and wife bears this out. Words were the only provocation offered to the accused on the fateful day. But mere words cannot amount to such provocation that we could say the accused acted impulsively under the influence of 'hot blood'. Nor can it be said that it was necessary to deliver such fateful blows in self-defence—she had not been put in fear for her life by her victim. Thus, it would seem that the accused was entirely in control of her faculties, and the only conclusion to be drawn is that she killed her victim 'in cold blood'.

TRIAL—NARRATIVE 2

A more modern doctrinal gloss might read:

The accused and the deceased shared a long-established history. While still a young girl, the accused had suffered an assault of the grossest kind at the hands of the deceased. As a result of this assault, her fortunes were sadly affected; she was rejected by her lawful husband, and suffered protracted penury. Throughout this time, the deceased pursued her, and eventually she succumbed to his entreaties to live with him as his mistress. Soon afterwards, her husband returned, it would appear with the intention of effecting a reconciliation. Believing that this would be impossible under the circumstances and taunted by the words of the deceased, the accused stabbed her victim, killing him.

It may be that the accused was provoked into committing this murderous act. Words or acts, or both together, may constitute provocative behaviour, which must be judged according to the standard of the reasonable man. In addition, if such words as were spoken by the deceased could be taken to have been provocative, the requisite degree of temporal immediacy—between the provocation and the response—was also present; supporting the view that the accused acted 'in hot blood' rather than with premeditation. However, a further obstacle must be surmounted before the question of provocation can be admitted. Since the *degree* of provocation—words—is disproportionate to the response of fatal assault, the accused must prove that she laboured under some permanent characteristic, and that the provocative words were in some way directed at that very characteristic, so affecting the gravity of the provocation to her.

Now in the accused Tess's case, the provocative words were aimed at the very subject upon which she was most sensitive: her estranged husband. Yet can it be said that this constitutes the type of 'characteristic' formulated above? The kinds of characteristic which could fulfil the model certainly do not guarantee a positive outcome for Tess. Tess did not suffer from a permanent, abnormal characteristic, such as deformity or impotence. Her sensitivity regarding her husband was long standing, but would be unlikely to be classed as 'a permanent characteristic which set the accused apart from the ordinary person in the community'.[14]

If that instant provocation by words is insufficient to afford a defence, what of the wider picture? It could be argued that an incident cannot be regarded in isolation; the accused, Tess, had at a tender age suffered an assault at the hands of the deceased which had damaged her fortunes. On the other hand, aside from this one distant incident, the deceased had, albeit in a somewhat proprietorial manner, treated her with concern. Having killed the deceased the accused stated to her husband: 'I owed it to you, and to myself, Angel. I feared long ago, when I struck him on the mouth with my glove, that I might do it some day for the trap he set for me in my simple youth, and his wrong to you through me.'[15] Although the accused herself refers to the original injury inflicted upon her by the deceased—'the trap he set for me in my simple youth'—as directly related to her action, her later reconciliation with him, and the passage of time, displace the claim that this early fault could still be pleaded as an operating and substantial factor such as to constitute provocation. There had been time for 'a cooling of the blood', and indeed the words 'I owed it to you, and to myself, Angel' suggest not only a complete lack of remorse on the part of the accused, but an element of retribution indicative of premeditation.

TRIAL—NARRATIVE 3

A third and final account of the facts in the case of *R.* v *Durbeyfield* might be along the following lines:

The accused and the deceased shared a long-established history. While still a young girl, the accused had suffered an assault of the grossest kind at the hands of the deceased. As a result of this assault, and despite her best efforts to rebuild her life, the accused suffered what may be termed a 'social death'. Society took little interest in her intrinsic innocence, looking only to the physical

---

[14] *R.* v. *Newell* (1980) 71 Cr. App. R. 331.
[15] Hardy, *Tess*, n. 1 above, 474.

effect of the encounter; the destruction of her virginity rendering her a social outcast. Upon discovery of this fact, the man whom she truly loved, and who seemed to offer her salvation, rejected and abandoned her. Thus, following her social death, the accused became subject to such alienation and privation as to constitute a psychological death. Upon his return, her husband sensed this: 'his original Tess had spiritually ceased to recognize the body before him as hers—allowing it to drift, like a corpse upon the current, in a direction dissociated from its living will.'[16]

The 'reconciliation' with the deceased, her former assailant, is thus explicable: the accused was by this time indifferent to her fate. In addition, the evidence demonstrates that any remaining concern for her own well-being was sacrificed to altruism—she acquiesced in the deceased's offer to protect her destitute family, which was made on condition that she submit to his sexual demands.

The return of her estranged husband triggered a form of reawakening in the accused, bringing the whole series of events, rape, abandonment, and indifference to self into a single cata-clysmic and unified focus. Throughout, the rape had remained central to her destiny, and to the re-ordered logic imposed upon her by social and psychological death: 'I feared . . . that I might do it one day for the trap he set for me in my simple youth, and his wrong to you through me.'[17]

Indeed, this process of re-ordering is such that the act of murder is cleansing and transformative: 'I thought as I ran along that you would be sure to forgive me now that I have done that. It came to me as a shining light that I should get you back that way.'[18] Such fervid investment in the act of killing as a restorative underscores an additional fact: that for one who has already suffered social and psychological death, the prospect of physical, 'legal' (where murder is a capital offence) death is not even a consideration.

It will be apparent to the reader that the first of these trial narratives approximates to the doctrinal position which obtained in law in Hardy's day. Thus Hardy was quite correct in his assessment that the 'trial' of Tess would have been a mere formality; her execution a foregone conclusion. The second narrative approximates to the

---

[16] Hardy, *Tess*, n. 1 above, 467.   [17] Hardy, *Tess*, n. 1 above, 474.
[18] Ibid.

present state of law, and though perhaps less draconian than its fore-bear by no means offers relief—or justice—to the idealized victim, Tess. Yet the kernel of development in the second narrative—derived from modern doctrinal developments—bring this 'trial' a little closer to the possibility of justice championed by the third trial narrative.

This third version of course approximates to Hardy's own version of events. Curiously, criminal law takes little cognizance of the notion of 'former good character'; when dealing with an apparently deliberate act of killing—the mild, abused housewife is as likely as Tess to be classed indiscriminately with the hardened malevolent killer. Yet the hypothetical 'case' put forward in Tess leads one to question and interrogate criminal law's blinkered focus upon factors which, while attempting to create a reliable formula for identifying the truly malevolent killing, is both austere and artificial. Within the notion of 'intention' lies a maelstrom of disordered rationales which disrupt the simple division between intentional and unintentional killing. If Tess has ceased to value her *own* life to the point of indif-ference to her fate, and to capital punishment, becoming mostly a conduit for some process of reparation, little wonder that the life of another may be similarly instrumental. Arguably the almost epiphanic reconstruction of the killing, negating her own and another's life, is akin to the dystopic visionary zeal of the terrorist. Yet while it is clear that terrorist acts—designed as they are to achieve a political objective—reflect an investment by the individual in a minority ideological agenda which the state cannot allow, Tess's dystopic rationale has been forced upon her both by society and by her victim and, unlike the terrorist, her action is endorsed by the 'society' of readers who are privy to her story: Tess has fulfilled an imperative which derives from an unspoken 'natural' law.

Similarly, the division between killing 'in cold blood' and 'in hot blood' perpetuates, rather naively, a medieval mythology of humours both capricious and unscientific. Tess's action can be described neither as 'cold blooded' nor 'hot blooded'. She is best described as devoid of blood—'a corpse upon the current'.[19]

---

[19] The law's reference to 'hot blood' and 'cold blood' is used with full technical gravitas as a ready indication of whether the accused has formed a malicious inten-tion towards the victim. The terminology derives from a medieval and Shakespearean ordering of bodily 'humours'; 'and the heat of blood kindled by ire was never cooled, till the blow was given, *et sic de similibus*': E. Coke, *Institutes of the Laws of England*, Vol. III, 50, quoted in *Russell on Crime* (11th edn, London, 1958).

Narratives of Doctrine, or Indoctrination?

Given that a lawyer, while sympathetic to the disruptive individual injustice experienced by Tess, may conclude that priority must be accorded to the maintenance of legal consistency, there is still room for exploration of how this disruption occurs. For undoubtedly, Tess's narrative pleads the legitimacy of her action.

A similar conclusion may be retrieved from some of the more disturbing modern homicide cases. In case law, however, any attempt to critique freely the dislocation (between the sense that the act of the accused is in some way *legitimate,* and the law's insistence that the intrinsic illegitimacy of a mortal act can only be displaced by demonstrating that the facts conform to doctrine) is subject to two constraints. First, the lawyer will be 'locked in' to the internal logic of that doctrine, and any attempt to extend it in order to accommodate a different viewpoint must honour the existing doctrinal fabric, as demanded by precedent. Second, the very representation of the facts within the fabric of a legal trial or report invokes a subtle process of anaesthesia. Where fiction is free to represent the dimensions of experience and give due recognition to the impact of seemingly trivial incidents, the detached voice of law acknowledges and locates the experience of the accused within a pre-ordained forensic narrative. Thus, even when, in reading a law report the sympathetic reader stumbles upon the more disturbing aspects of the accused's narrative and is disturbed by their poignancy, she is alternatively *seduced* and *harassed* into distancing herself from that reaction. The real-life drama, trauma or tragedy of the accused is recorded or trapped within the *bricolage* of doctrine, like a fly in amber. This effect is enhanced in that the 'objective' narrative voice of law instils the belief that both the recitation of facts, and to a large extent, the legal gloss, comes to the reader unmediated by subjective interference. As Weisberg says of *The Brothers Karamazov*: 'The erroneous conviction of Dmitri is a critique par excellence of the way the law twists reality into a false codified form. Yet, the enormity of the error can only be comprehended in light of the full narration of the events as they occurred.'[20]

In addition, lawyers must employ narrative techniques particular

---

[20] R. Weisberg, *Poethics* (New York, 1992), 230.

to their trade, which choreograph polarized versions of the events. Goodwin identifies one such technique; the constitution of what she terms 'kernel' or key events. Any two opposing lawyers will establish different and competing kernel and satellite events.[21] In addition, both will be locked into the doctrinal drive which insists that those events which *may* be disputed over as forming either kernels or satellites, take precedence over, or efface other elements which do not conform to the doctrinal model; elements which cannot qualify as either kernels or satellites. In present law, for example, similar fact cases to that of Tess would centre upon competing views which either posit a (prosecution) kernel which asserts as central the requirement that reaction to provocation must be immediate, and the (defence) kernel that provocation may be cumulative. Yet it would be illegitimate for either party to suggest either that the provocation might be purely cumulative with no final provocative event inducing the fatal encounter, or that such a final event could be valid currency in the provocation stakes if the constraints of legal doctrine render it arbitrary or trivial.

Goodwin also identifies another narrative device which is pivotal to the relative potency ascribed to events. This is the distinction between 'real' time (the time that the events take to happen) and 'narrational' time: 'As narrators, lawyers strategically manipulate the potential disparity between these types of times to foreground their own choice of kernel events, and to omit details that threaten this kernel status.'[22]

In case law, 'real' time is apparently represented objectively, supported by a chronology of dates and events. Yet as the cumulative events—and provocation—are contained within this chronology, they are necessarily compressed. It may be argued, pragmatically, that an entire and exhaustive narration of each of these events could not be sustained by trial hearings or documentation and to give equal weight to events which may be viewed as largely historical and therefore contextual would be to leave our natural ordering of chronology in disarray. Yet this undoubtedly feeds the assumption that the mere passage of time may dilute or

---

[21] J. Tomasson Goodwin, 'Trial Advocacy Handbooks: Narratology and Opening Statements' (1994) 27 (4) *Mosaic* 215, 223.
[22] Goodwin, 'Trial Advocacy Handbooks', n. 21 above, 224.

eradicate an 'insult' to the accused. This notion of the psyche perhaps borrows from the physiology of the body—mere time may heal the most extensive wound, and then only violent force will succeed in reopening it.

Free to give due cognizance to the subjective experience of such 'kernel' and 'satellite' events, the textual account in *Tess* is very different from the accounts which we have seen in law. Legal orthodoxy would focus upon criminal events—juristic narration would include a detailed 'kernel' inquiry of the circumstances surrounding the killing. A defence might try to claim that the rape/seduction of Tess is also 'kernel', or at the very least 'satellite', while the prosecution would relegate the rape as at most a distant satellite. Interestingly, the text of *Tess* suggests a completely different path. The rape is treated fleetingly; indeed we are reassured that in time Tess 'recovers' from the experience—it is the *social* interdiction which is so damaging. Likewise, the killing is treated fleetingly and with scant detail. Thus two potentially momentous 'legal' events remain tenuous even as 'satellites'.

Which event *is* given 'kernel' treatment in the text, given that a rape and murder can be so readily truncated? One answer is the enforced separation from Angel, which is given a notably 'legalistic' frame. This separation scene occurs approximately halfway through the book—roughly midway between the rape and the killing. The preceding passages and the scene itself minutely record the complex process of alienation between Tess and Angel as the 'social chasm' created by Tess's impurity begins to gape. Angel declares that they must separate—'until I come to you it will be better that you should not try to come to me'; and that this is prescriptive is confirmed by its classification as a *decree*—'The severity of the decree seemed deadly to Tess'. With a profound recognition of the interplay of power, resistance, and submission at such times, the exchange conflates elements of the 'volitional' civil pact and a punitive criminal judgment. Tess submits to Angel's severe decree; although mentally she questions it, she can no longer put her case—'she could contest the point with him no further'. Thereafter, the conditions of the separation are clarified: Tess echoes Angel's terms in true performative style. This culminates in a final conflation of the civil and criminal when simultaneously Tess volunteers her consent to the pact, acknowledges its punitive force (and Angel's arrogation of power as judge) and enters a plea for mercy: 'I agree to the conditions, Angel; because you know best what my punishment ought to be; only—only—don't make it more than I can bear!'[23]

Tess begins a downward spiral which will lead to her eventual destruction. The fictional narrative may achieve what juristic orthodoxies cannot: that such an event is truly 'kernel', and contains psychological and linguistic subtleties indicating a unilateral arrogation of power which may have far-reaching consequences. This arrogation of power, authority and judgment can only take place however because cultural values support the process: in one sense Angel is simply the *creature* of the prevailing but skewed cultural values: the transmitter of the social edict.

(Narrating) the Socio-Legal Nexus

Thus in reconstructing the case of *R.* v. *Durbeyfield*, and in keeping with the realist genre, the fictive narrative is less subject to constraints. First, kernel and satellite events may be arranged purely according to the potency with which they impinge upon the subject. According to this account, the fact of rape, bearing an illegitimate child, even social ignominy may be tolerated with a degree of philosophical acceptance until another event forces the realization that the destruction of Tess's virginity *dictates* her subsequent fate. Angel Clare, Tess's husband, finds the fact distasteful and intolerable; it is a disability which effaces her very identity—'You were one person; now you are another'.[24] However eccentric or uncharitable such a reaction may seem to present eyes, it is clearly quite consistent with former cultural values. Legal doctrine would have some difficulty in encompassing this causal link between the rape and its elevation to the status of an irrevocable event since the elevation is largely dependent upon the chance involvement of a third party.[25] Yet this depiction is faithful to a factor only obliquely recognized by the law—that the potency of a provocation (if we can so regard the rape) is as much shaped by culture and custom. 'Impulsive' 'unpremeditated' behaviour is thus not merely descriptive of a human reaction,

[23] All of these related quotations appear in Hardy, *Tess*, n. 1 above, 324.
[24] Hardy, Tess, n. 1 above, 298.
[25] See *Blackstone's Criminal Practice* (P. Murphy (ed.), London, 1997), 108–9.

refereed by the standard of the reasonable man, it is acculturated, predetermined by a social register of insults.

Hardy's potent critique of legal mores recognizes the interplay between cultural values and legal blind spots. More importantly it exemplifies the fact that when society denies both the crime and the victim, this will *relocate the power of the provocation*. Although such phenomena can be anatomized in fiction, the intimacy of the relationship between social and legal doctrines would, even in modern times, hamper such dispassionate legal inquiry. The novelist's contribution to jurisprudence will almost inevitably be overlooked. Yet ironically, modern developments in the doctrine of provocation indicate a slow advance towards the insights offered by Hardy. Clothing the reasonable man with *characteristics* which make him more vulnerable to the particular provocation may give some recognition to the accused person's entrapment between punitive social values and the peculiar power of the provocation. Recognizing that provocation may have a *cumulative* element brings legal doctrine a little closer to addressing the injustice suffered by Tess.

Natural law theory supposes that laws enacted for the well-being of any society extend and formalize fundamental values originating in 'natural' law. A primary example is the prohibition against any killing which is unjustified according to the value system of the community. Yet *Tess* reminds us that, though we may not be able to locate a response within doctrinal boundaries, as 'self-defence', or classical 'provocation', for example, nevertheless there may be justification for the killing among the community of readers who act as proxies for the temporarily blinkered community of citizens. The fictive model reasserts the primacy of fundamental values.

A mode of narrative disruption is adopted in the fabric of the story of Tess, in order to highlight the interplay between 'social' and 'juristic' values. The text is littered with ironic, and inverted, references to 'natural law'. So, although there is clear recognition that the act of rape is one of violation, which *could*, if *detected*, have invoked criminal sanctions, it is also the fulfilment of a retributive ancestral drive, a retribution supported by Biblical doctrine.[26] And,

---

[26] 'But though to visit the sins of the fathers upon the children may be a morality good enough for divinities, it is scorned by average human nature; and it therefore does not mend the matter': Hardy, *Tess*, n. 1 above, 119.

though such blind retribution would be 'scorned by average human nature', yet in Tess's locality (the world of peasantry) such misfortune would be accepted fatalistically—'it was to be'. Thus any sense of outrage remains unchannelled—no law, secular, natural, or divine is brought to Tess's aid. Yet, it is emphasized to the reader that the event opens an immeasurable social chasm in Tess's life. Tess herself (in common with rape victims through the ages) suffers from feelings of confusion and guilt about her impurity, feelings which remain unsolved by popular religious tenets. On seeing the mutated slogan 'THY, DAMNATION, SLUMBERETH, NOT', Tess trembles asking 'suppose your sin was not of your own seeking?'; and receives the reply 'I cannot split hairs on that burning query'.[27] Tess's husband invokes 'natural' biological law to refute the marriage—that her rapist is Tess's 'husband in nature'. Tess becomes burdened with the fear that this is the case, while Alex (her rapist/seducer) wishes to marry her as 'sanctification for us both'. Thus in a dreadful inversion of the notion of natural law, the laws of nature and divinity are invoked to legitimate the violation of Tess, who later cries 'I shall not cry out. Once victim, always victim—that's the law!'.[28]

Such instances demonstrate the 'skewing' of the concept of law as it is experienced by the subject—'natural' law is cruelly unnatural; effectively severed from the notion of justice—a vision unsayable within any orthodox legal arena.

Sisters in Law

We noted that the second 'trial narrative' reflects the present English law of provocation. The provocation may be partly cumulative but must also have an 'immediate' component, temporally proximate to the response; the accused's susceptibility to a disproportionately mild provocation must be due to a causal link between the provocation and some permanent and odd aspect of his or her personality.

This awkwardly-tailored doctrinal garment is forced about the frame of the accused. If it proves to be ill-fitting, it is confiscated: the fault must lie with the contours of the accused rather than law's measuring skills. Where there is a firm indication of guilt, the

---

[27] Hardy, *Tess*, n. 1 above, 128.   [28] Hardy, *Tess*, n. 1 above, 411.

confiscation justifiably may be outright. On the other hand, there may be subliminal uncertainty as to guilt: the law may suffer residual anxieties about the accused's juridical nakedness. This is unlikely to invoke any major re-drafting of the design; only recourse to a temporary back-buttoned institutional shift, for example the lateral skip to a doctrine such as diminished responsibility.

Thus in the case of *R. v. Ahluwalia*[29] the accused, an Asian woman, had set fire to and killed her husband. She had suffered years of physical and mental abuse at his hands, including the infliction of various injuries which did not abate when she was pregnant. In addition he taunted her with his infidelity. On the night that the accused fatally attacked her husband, an argument took place, during which the deceased demanded money, said he would beat her, stated that he was leaving her (to live with his girlfriend) and threatened to burn her face with a hot iron. Some hours later, in the night, the accused got out of bed. Carefully she poured petrol (which she had bought some days previously with a view to using it on the deceased) into a bucket, carried it to his room, and set fire to him.

From a doctrinal viewpoint, the case presents clear difficulties for the defence. First, although there had been a cumulative provocation, the final encounter was less severe than those recorded previously. In addition, there was a delay of some hours between the final encounter and the response. More damagingly, the accused's purchase of petrol and caustic soda some days before created a clear implication of the formation of intention, of malice aforethought. All of these factors tended to displace any assertion of a sudden and temporary loss of self-control. Finally, it was difficult to identify a characteristic in the accused which would fulfil the doctrinal formula: one which was permanent, setting her apart from the ordinary run of society, and the *focus* of provocative remarks. Indeed at first instance the judge's attempts to make the facts fit the doctrine on this point led to his rather unilluminating direction that 'the defence of provocation was only available to the accused if there had been a sudden and temporary loss of self-control on her part as the result of acts which would have caused a reasonable person *having her characteristics as a married Asian woman* to lose her self-control'.[30]

---

[29] [1992] 4 All ER 889.
[30] *R. v. Ahluwalia* [1992] 4 All ER 889 at 897 (emphasis added).

On appeal, the factual lack of 'fit' with the 'sudden and tem-porary loss of self-control' model was revised by defence counsel in the light of evidence of 'battered woman syndrome'.[31] It was suggested that the syndrome modified reactions to violent treat-ment, so that the response to the final acts or words could be exemplified by a 'slow burn' reaction, rather than an immediate loss of self-control. In addition it was admitted that the syndrome *might* have fulfilled the criteria for a doctrinally 'legitimate' char-acteristic.[32] In the alternative, it was claimed that a more suitable plea might have been that of 'diminished responsibility', a plea which was subsequently accepted at retrial.

Like Tess, Mrs Ahluwalia was a weak candidate for protection by the defence of provocation, even though the second narrative model of the doctrine demonstrates a considerably more progres-sive and liberal design than the first. With such facts might we be justified in feeling a sense of disquiet at a retreat into diminished responsibility doctrine, with its attendant implication of mental instability in an accused who has otherwise functioned as a loving mother and a dutiful wife, just as we experience disquiet at Tess's mandatory execution? This disquiet may spring from many linked aspects; the historical association between the doctrines of provo-cation and self-defence,[33] the hypothesis that the defence of provocation 'functions as a partial justification rather than a partial excuse'.[34] Such justification may arguably involve a present response to a distant wrongdoing which is nevertheless still potent, an appreciation that the margins of doctrine may overlook pertinent factors, such as the previous good character of the accused or her subjection to the mesmeric malevolent power games of her victim, the unknown spectrum in states of mind between the benign and the malicious.[35]

[31] Ibid.

[32] In *R*. v. *Hobson* [1998] 1 Cr. App. R. 31, a retrial was ordered on the basis that it was a matter of significance that 'battered woman syndrome' was not part of the British Classification of Diseases until 1994, two years after the trial of the appellant.   [33] See McColgan, 'In Defence', n. 4 above.

[34] See F. McAuley, 'Anticipating the Past: The Defence of Provocation in Irish Law' (1987) 50 *Modern Law Review* 133.

[35] 'The requirement of loss of self-control seems unnecessarily harnessed to a notion of psychological determinism, which may do descriptive violence to those mental processes which result in such a loss': K. Smith and W. Wilson, 'Impaired Voluntariness and Criminal Responsibility' (1993) 13 *Oxford Journal of Legal Studies* 69.

Tess, we may remember, was subtitled by her creator as a 'pure woman', an assertion meant to be more morally than physically descriptive. Mrs Ahluwalia too tried her hardest to tolerate her invidious position, like Tess modifying her behaviour and her identity to her circumstances. From the anaesthetized account of her story created by law, which characterizes Mrs Ahluwalia as 'the accused', 'the appellant', the one who exhibits perhaps 'premeditation', or 'diminished responsibility'—some narrative details survive, with disturbing echoes between the 'case' of Tess and that of *R. v. Ahluwalia*. Consider two such echoes:

Deepak, if you come back I promise you—I won't touch black coffee again, I won't go town every week, I won't eat green chilli, I ready to leave Chandikah and all my friends, I won't go near Der Goodie Mohan's house again. Even I am not going to attend Bully's wedding, I (will) eat too much or all the time so I can get fat, I won't laugh if you don't like, I won't dye my hair ever, I don't go to my neighbour's house, I won't ask you for any help . . .

(Note from Mrs Ahluwalia to her husband quoted in *R. v. Ahluwalia* [1992] All ER 889 at 892.)

I must cry to you in my trouble—I have no one else . . . I think I must die if you do not come soon, or tell me to come to you . . . Please, please not to be just; only a little kind to me! . . . If you would come I could die in your arms! I would be well content to do that if so be you had forgiven me! . . . If you will send me one little line and say *I am coming soon*, I will bide on, Angel, O so cheerfully! . . . Think how it do hurt my heart not to see you ever, ever! Ah, if I could only make your dear heart ache one little minute of each day as mine does every day and all day long, it might lead you to show pity to your poor lonely one . . . I would be content, ay, glad, to live with you as your servant, if I may not as your wife; so that I could only be near you, and get glimpses of you, and think of you as mine . . .

(Letter from Tess to her husband: *Tess of the d'Urbervilles*, 456.)

But he had a vague consciousness of one thing, though it was not clear to him till later; that his original Tess had spiritually ceased to recognize the body before him as hers—allowing it to drift, like a corpse upon the current, in a direction dissociated from its living will.

(Description of Tess, shortly before her fatal attack on Alec d'Urberville, *Tess of the d'Urbervilles*, 467.)

Other neighbours rushed to the house. They found the door locked and saw the appellant standing at a ground-floor window clutching her son, just staring and looking calm. They shouted to her to get out of the house. She opened a window and said 'I am waiting for my husband' and closed the window again. She was prevailed upon to hand the child out and later emerged herself. She stood staring at the window with a glazed expression.

(Description of Mrs Ahluwalia, immediately after her fatal attack on Mr Ahluwalia, *R. v. Ahluwalia* [1992] All ER 889 at 893.)

Conclusion

The correspondence between these two pairs of quotations reflect a state of depersonalization, a dissociation[36] of self in the wake of intractable emotional brutality. Both women have been failed by society—for them effectively a 'lawless' society in which their entrapment is made absolute by the absence of any conduit for the recognition of their sufferings: the Asian community closed within the concrete isolation that is suburban Crawley meets the universal Victorian community of double standards. While early doctrine may have attended to 'chance medley' where the parties 'met on equal terms' such victims suffer its inverse, a sustained assault in which parity is absent and instant response impossible. It would be tempting to relegate such cases to the less stringent realm of 'diminished responsibility'—indeed a 'dissociative state' may well fulfil the description. Yet there are two objections to such a course. First, it seems anathema to classify them as suffering from such 'abnormality of mind' as 'substantially impaired . . . mental responsibility' when they have in all other respects robustly maintained a mental equilibrium in the face of considerable odds. Second, it rather unfairly sets them on record as 'diminished': as the marked, albeit pathetic creatures of their own decline. The doctrine of provocation at least records, by its very name, the Pyrrhic decline that was *shared*, both by perpetrator and victim.

---

[36] A 'dissociated state' was referred to in *R. v. Thornton (No.2)* [1996] 2 All ER 1023 at 1031. Dissociation is defined in M. Sainsbury and L. Lambeth, *Sainsbury's Key to Psychiatry* (London, 1988), 66 as 'a partial repression wherein a portion of the personality, intolerable to conscious awareness, . . . is split off. . . . Emotions too difficult to bear may be split off and not felt, even though the person remembers the event'.

There is a strong moral foundation to linking the doctrine with the notion of 'partial justification' rather than 'partial excuse': to a very real extent the victim has spurred his own fate. McAuley locates the orthodox position:

Since provocation normally takes the form of an assault by the victim on the offender, the question of gravity can usually be determined objectively, without reference to the defendants personal characteristics. The latter only become relevant when there is no basis on which a purely objective judgement of gravity can be made, in other words, in the relatively rare cases *in which the victim's conduct is prima facie too slight to provide even a partial justification for the defendant's violent outburst.*[37]

McAuley's analysis forms part of a larger discussion upon the moral basis of the defence of provocation. If, as he argues, the defence 'functions as a partial justification . . . a denial that the defendant's actions were entirely wrongful in the first place . . . because of the untoward conduct of his victim',[38] surely it may further be asserted that a 'characteristic' which was *created* by the victim's conduct should have the soundest moral pedigree.

Law's mechanistic vision of provocation, with sudden and temporary loss of self-control as a co-requisite to proximate provocative behaviour brings us no nearer to understanding either the spectrum of moral imperatives between reason and reaction, nor to exploring the nature of the 'numbed core' which the 'hot blood' model assumes. Webster explains that

at the very heart of the historical concept of reason, we find nothing concealed other than the view of human psychology which is central to creationist theory; we find what should perhaps be known as 'beast-angel dualism'. According to this view, the purpose of reason is not to accommodate or understand or explain human nature. It is to control or subjugate the more unruly aspects of it—or even to deny or negate them.[39]

Undoubtedly, a primary purpose of individual and doctrinal 'reason' is, and has been, to control and subjugate the more unruly aspects of human nature. Yet from an initial demand that the instantaneous response be to physical assault, law negotiated a quaint diversion on behalf of the cuckolded husband; the outraged

---

[37] McAuley, 'Anticipating', n. 34 above, at 148 (emphasis added).
[38] McAuley, 'Anticipating', n. 34 above, at 139.
[39] R. Webster, *Why Freud Was Wrong* (London, 1996), 496.

father of the sodomized son. Words alone have become sufficient grounds for provocation, but the ennobled vision of the wronged hero responding 'in hot blood' maintains his spectral presence.

In one modern case, where an outraged father was prevented, by geographical distance, from demonstrating a sudden loss of self-control, there was a glimmer of recognition for a more protracted 'numbed core'. John Dickie Spellacie Baillie,[40] the appellant, who had three teenage sons, was told by his youngest son that he had been threatened by a man who was another son's supplier of drugs. The appellant, armed with a sawn-off shotgun and a cut-throat razor, went to the supplier's house, inflicted injuries with the razor, pursued the supplier from the house, fired the shotgun, and killed him. At first instance, the judge directed the jury on the issue of provocation, stating:

If one takes evidence that this defendant was told by one of his sons of the most recent threat by the deceased, certainly to the sons, what then happens on any view of the evidence is a series of events which in my judgement make it clear that there was time for reflection and time for cooling off, because on any view of the evidence what happens is that he goes to the attic, collects a gun, he brings that down and places it in the car, the car is then driven from his house a distance of some two miles via a petrol filling station to the place where these events occurred and there is then a walking, albeit of a short distance, from a place where the car is to the house. That seems to me to be evidence which takes this case outside the sudden and temporary loss of self control . . .[41]

During the subsequent appeal against conviction for murder, the Court of Appeal confirmed that such an approach was 'too austere' for the purposes of s. 3 of the Homicide Act 1957, which places emphasis very much on the function of the jury as opposed to the judge in determining what constitutes a sudden and temporary loss of self-control. Apart from the inappropriate assessment of the facts as 'taking the case outside' the ambit of the test, reference might also have been made to the judge's recourse to a linguistic device of *decelerated chronology*, in which each physical movement is accorded 'kernel' prominence in order to displace the claim of sudden loss of self-control. Most interesting however was the *rhetorical* support given at appeal by Henry LJ to toleration of

---

[40] R. v. *Baillie (John Dickie Spellacie)* [1995] 2 Cr. App. R. 31.
[41] [1995] 2 Cr. App. R. 31 at 36 C–E.

a less than sudden and less than temporary reaction to provocation. His comments do not merely, as with the Court of Appeal in
R. v. *Ahluwalia*, pay lip-service to the notion of 'delayed reaction',
with an immediately qualifying 'provided that there was at the
time of the killing a sudden and temporary loss of self-control'.
Indeed his remarks depart from purely mechanistic analysis, to
moving rhetoric. Does this signal a departure from merely
hygienic abstractions? Or is the father of drug-addicted sons a
twentieth-century incarnation of his outraged predecessor?
Reasonableness is implicit, with scant recourse to 'characteristics';
the verbal provocation is accorded gravity by reference to its *life-
long implications*; chronology suspends to encompass past,
present and future time:

> We are dealing with threats to sons in their middle to late teens. We are
> dealing with threats by one who is supplying them with narcotics *which
> may lead to the ruin of their lives quite independently of whether the
> actual physical threats are carried out or not. We are dealing with a father
> who, though no stranger to drink, behaved on this evening in a way
> apparently quite inconsistent with anything he had done before* . . .[42]

Might Tess, or Mrs Ahluwalia have deserved full as much judicial
force to be asserted on their behalf?

The three trial narratives derived from the facts of *R.* v.
Durbeyfield reveal law's seductive authentication of its own narrative practices *and* the potential of the doctrine of provocation to
evolve and accommodate revised cultural viewpoints. Formulations
of the doctrine must guard against according an overly improvised
narrative gloss to the incidents, distant and recent, in the perpetrator's history, as well as a random and partial admission of traits to
the exclusive club of 'characteristics'. Particular care should be
taken where social practices may have nurtured the sensitive trait.
The 'characteristic' which determined Tess's future fatal act—like
the 'characteristic' which drove Mrs Ahluwalia at speed towards
the inevitable, tragic conclusion—was culturally determined. Yet
since the law is so intimately both a creator and creation of culture,
doctrinal objectivity is impaired. Hardy postulated in this instance
that it was not the fact of being seduced or raped which scarred
Tess. It was the social construction placed upon her as soiled, as

---

[42] [1995] 2 Cr. App. R. 3l at 38 A–B (emphasis added).

an outcast, as a *thing*. The *thingness* of being 'impure' is neatly evidenced in a Victorian case which has powerful links to the case of Tess. *Moss* v. *Moss*[43] was concerned with determining whether a marriage could be annulled on the basis that the wife was pregnant by another man at the time of marriage: the case was analysed in the language of the law of contract. So what was at issue was whether the mistake about the condition of the bride, or indeed any bride found not to be intact, was a mistake as to her identity, or merely a mistake as to the *quality* of the bride *thing*. This is echoed in *Tess*: 'You were one person, now you are another' says the groom, on discovery of her imperfection. In Ahluwalia, the 'characteristic' first put by the judge as being relevant to the doctrine of provocation is that of being 'a married Asian woman'. This conveys nothing apart from an unhelpful and ghostly stereotype. What *was* relevant was the *thingness* of being a married Asian woman under those circumstances; of being disempowered, isolated, deprived of personhood.

Counsel for Mrs Ahluwalia argued that the condition of battered woman syndrome and the related state of 'learnt helplessness' was a condition which could have constituted a legitimate 'characteristic' for doctrinal purposes. 'Learnt helplessness' certainly describes the state of mind exhibited both by Mrs Ahluwalia and Tess in their letters and behaviour and typifies the alienated state that is dissociation; it is feasible that this state might last for days or weeks and encompass acts of apparent premeditation. Yet there is a danger that, in accommodating this condition within the realm of accepted 'characteristics', the moral force behind such cases will bow to the merely mechanical. For 'learnt helplessness' and 'dissociative states' are at least as relevant to the primitive cold blood–hot blood polarity as to 'characteristics'.[44] Ashworth[45] concludes 'the suddenness test is objectionable in principle because it favours those with quick tempers over those with a slow burning temperament (but no less intensity of emotion), it favours the strong who can retaliate immediately over the weak who dare not, and it often favours men over women'.

---

[43] (1897) PD 459.

[44] Such conditions may inform the polar spectrum, yet remain separate from the morally suspect, instantaneous conditions set apart in *R*. v. *Morhall* [1996] AC 90, affecting the power of self-control.

[45] A. Ashworth, *Principles of Criminal Law* (2nd edn, Oxford, 1995), 268.

One might add that the test also favours mythology over inquiry and rude mechanics over morality. Justice demands that legal doctrine must strive to avoid Hardy's reproach to his time; the preservation of values 'based on nothing more tangible than . . . an arbitrary law of society which had no foundation in Nature'.[46]

---

[46] Hardy, *Tess*, n. 1 above, 353.

FANTASIES OF WOMEN AS LAWMAKERS: EMPOWERMENT OR ENTRAPMENT IN ANGELA CARTER'S *BLOODY CHAMBERS*

Maria Aristodemou

Intertextuality

What is the ontological status of law and of literature? Or, conversely, to follow Lacan's suggestion that 'the real is the impossible',[1] the unimaginable, what is the *imaginary* status of law and of literature? While we can agree that, unlike literature, law deals in the material world of life and death, both law and literature are, in the first instance, signs on a page. Both the legal and literary worlds are constructed by and depend for their definition and existence on words; such words create alternative, fictional worlds which can appear to be inevitable. While much of contemporary literature, however, accepts, delights in, and explores its own constructedness, arbitrariness and artificiality, the writers of law are more concerned to disguise its status as a linguistic artefact. In that sense legal writers are like writers of realist fiction, trying to maintain the illusion of an omniscient narrator, chronological sequence, plot inevitability and causal connection between events. Once such worlds, however, are shown to be not only artificial but also unfair or tyrannical, it is necessary to reveal the ways by which that artificiality is constructed.

The fact that both legal and literary fictions are constituted in language means that it is in language that such artificiality must be

---

[1] 'Since the opposite of the possible is certainly the real, we would be led to define the real as the impossible': *The Four Fundamental Concepts of Psychoanalysis* (Paris, 1973; Harmondsworth, 1979), 167.

examined and uncovered. One of the aspirations, therefore, of law and literature analyses, is that the construction of literary texts may throw light on the construction and fictionality of the so-called real world, including that of the legal world, its values and conventions and of ourselves within it. In that way, what we are accustomed to perceiving as the imaginary, challenges the so-called real and affirms Shelley's view that poets (and for my purposes, poetesses) are the unacknowledged legislators of the world.

A founding assumption of modernist art and literature is the notion of a work of art as the unique expression of an individual's originality and genius. As theorists such as Bakhtin, Julia Kristeva and Umberto Eco have shown, however, the production of meaning is not monologic but dialogic or intertextual. A work of art is not original or unique but is part of existing discourses and texts; such texts, as Bakhtin argued, are constructed like mosaics from other texts with the resulting text resembling a patchwork of previous texts. The elitist, modernist insistence on artistic aura, autonomy, uniqueness, and separation of art from mass culture are closely allied to our notions of ownership and property. However, the author's ability to assign a single meaning to her work is undermined by the role of the reader in interpreting and using such texts. In particular, the death of the author challenges the view of the writer as god whose authority determines the meaning of the text.

Contemporary writers undermine modernist assumptions of artistic autonomy through the use of parody and appropriation of existing representations, stereotypes and conventions. Such texts acknowledge their own situationality and constructedness in language at the same time as they aim to subvert and critique the same conventions. By revealing the artificiality of what we perceive as everyday reality they enable us to see the constructed nature of our values, norms and structures.[2] At the heart of such mimicry/critique is the belief that cultural representations are as unavoidably important as they are political.

Angela Carter was well aware of the political importance of art and impatient with the modernist insistence on the autonomy of

---

[2] See especially P. Waugh, *Metafiction: The Theory and Practice of Self-Conscious Fiction* (London, 1984).

art from politics: 'Fine art that exists for itself alone is art in a final stage of impotence' she admonished.[3] Instead, she brought political concerns to her writing and was keen to make use of art's capacity to envisage new worlds by dismantling old laws and structures and creating new laws in the realm of the imaginary.

Perhaps no genre exemplifies the death of the author, intertextuality and every text's debt to previous writers and texts than the art of fairy tales. The same motifs have been the subject of interested appropriations, imitations and reworkings for hundreds of years from peasants' hearths to the salons of eighteenth-century Paris, to Victorian nursery rooms, to the twentieth-century studios of Walt Disney. That fairy tales should be the subject of such political exercises is not a coincidence: like all literature, fairy tales operate in the realm of ideology, sustaining and promoting their own moral and political messages. Although such messages vary with both audience and tellers, the ubiquity and appeal of fairy tales to children and adults alike make them a powerful source of ideological value systems.

One recent such appropriation is by feminist writers concerned at the patriarchal bias of some of these retellings. By juxtaposing new stories on old texts feminist writers can reveal the oppressive nature of previous stories as well as uncover new voices, new possibilities, and new roles for women within them. The use of prior texts is not, however, a simple matter of appropriation or imitation. All texts and languages, legal or literary, are the carriers of ideas and ideologies and it is the task of the new writer to use and abuse the genre to best suit her new purposes. The problem, however, is whether such musings appease by offering imaginary solutions to real problems.

This issue can only be investigated by interrogating the genre of the fairy tales as a whole before addressing Carter's use of the genre in *The Bloody Chamber*. In this paper I examine the motifs of three well-known tales, 'Bluebeard', 'Little Red Riding Hood', and 'Beauty and the Beast' in sources such as Charles Perrault and Madame de Beaumont[4] before contrasting Carter's interested and interesting appropriation of the same motifs.

---

[3] A. Carter, *The Sadeian Woman* (London, 1979), 13.
[4] These are collected in J. Zipes (ed.), *Beauties, Beasts and Enchantment: Classic French Fairy Tales* (Harmondsworth, 1989).

The Legislative Allure of Fairy Tales

If stories play a part in structuring our world, fairy tales whose ubiquity, longevity, and dissemination is stronger than that of other stories play a crucial role in our understanding of ourselves, anxieties, and dreams. Such tales have an inescapable normative dimension, providing a strong mythology of moral examples for children and adults to follow. For, as Tolkien protested, 'the association of children and fairy-stories is an accident of our domestic history. . . . Children . . . neither like fairy-stories more, nor understand them better than adults do'.[5]

For Bruno Bettelheim, such stories provide a safe place for the resolution of fears and dilemmas involved in the passage from childhood to adulthood.[6] More than easing this passage, however, fairy tales help to cultivate appropriate roles and modes of behaviour for entry into the adult world. In fairy tales there is an abundance of stereotypes of good versus evil, strong versus weak, rich versus poor, man versus woman, and boy versus girl. These binary oppositions help inculcate what behaviour is socially acceptable and will lead to reward in contrast to what is unacceptable and will lead to harm or punishment. Above all, the tales affirmed that there is such a thing as a moral order and that in that other world of the tales goodness is invariably rewarded and evil punished.

For groups outside the dominant ideological and power systems fairy tales also represent what is outside mainstream culture and history. Their lack of elitism, ex-centricity, and malleability offer a way of inscribing oneself in an alternative history and culture. Oral folktales often expressed the hopes and aspirations of a peasant class where paupers became princes and virtuous girls princesses. Through such myths a disadvantaged class faced with poverty and sickness could express their dreams for a different, a happier and more just world.[7] Such reworkings of the myths, developed and adapted with each generation of

---

[5] J. R. R. Tolkien, *Tree and Leaf* (London, 1970), 34.

[6] B. Bettelheim, *The Uses of Enchantment: The Power and Importance of Fairy Tales* (Harmondsworth, 1978).

[7] See the work of Jack Zipes for the view that fairy tales may enable disadvantaged groups to inscribe themselves into history: *Breaking the Magic Spell: Radical Theories of Folk and Fairy Tales* (London, 1979), and *Fairy Tales and the Art of Subversion* (London, 1988).

tellers and listeners, further undermined the bourgeois notion of art as a unique one-off and the modernist distinction between high and low culture and hierarchies between literary genres.

In the nineteenth century, however, the myths of the poor were appropriated and rewritten for the education and entertainment of the bourgeoisie. Although such tales were traditionally told by women, those versions were denigrated by mainstream culture as 'old wives' tales' while the successful dissemination of the versions by Charles Perrault in France and the Grimm brothers in Germany had the effect of concealing rival writings by women. The writings of the *precieuses* in seventeenth-century France was indeed undertaken in direct rebellion to the strictures of the established academies with their emphasis on Greek and Latin classics; their favoured form for expressing their views for the equality of women and the perils of arranged marriages was the fairy tale. As in Carter's collection of fairy stories for Virago, 'the qualities these stories recommend for the survival and prosperity of women are never those of passive subordination' but show 'the richness and diversity with which femininity, in practice, is represented in "unofficial culture" and the richness and diversity of women's response to their predicament—being alive—its strategies, plots and hard work'.[8] Here, female initiative is rewarded rather than punished. However, such versions were forgotten or suppressed in favour of tales that asserted the need for conformity and the danger of female desire. Hence the importance for women writers to wrest the fairy tale back from Perrault and the Brothers Grimm and exploit their possibilities and power.

Carter allies herself with predecessors like the *precieuses* and aims to render the fairy tale once again an instrument of change with women as masters rather than slaves of history-making and law-making. Myth, she thought, 'is more malleable than history' and therefore provides one way of claiming women's fair share of the future by staking their claim to their share of the past.[9] By inscribing women in history, women writers may explore and advocate new perceptions, new structures and new roles for women in society's marital, economic and legal arrangements.

Furthermore, fairy tales are a writing of excess, Carter's own

---

[8]   A. Carter (ed.), *The Virago Book of Fairy Tales* (London, 1990), xiv.
[9]   Carter, *Fairy Tales*, n. 8 above, xvi.

version of Bakhtin's carnivalesque with its irreverence, improprieties, laughter, and resistance to hierarchies and the symbolic; such writing undermines official culture, laws, and conventions by creating an alternative to established values and structures. Dwelling in the realm of fantasy, fairy tales can disrupt classical unities of time and space and subvert the dominant order by intimating the existence of another place, another time, and another law. Fantasy literature in general can threaten cultural stability with disorder and illegality by exploring what lies outside dominant norms and values.[10] By countenancing fragmented, fluid selves and character metamorphoses, it also departs from our culture's reliance on subjects that are unified, whole, and essential and points out the limits of what we are accustomed to seeing as real and inevitable. As Rosemary Jackson argues, fantasy literature dreams of a return to a state of unity in the imaginary, before the intervention of the father, culture, and law. In the world of fantasy there is a dissolution of cultural differentiations between self and other, human and animal, human and god, male and female, day and night, even life and death. In short, fantasy releases signs from their orthodox uses and thereby disrupts a culture's ways of creating and institutionalizing meaning. The liberation of the sign from signifying practices means that women writers in particular can use fantastic literature as a tool with which to subvert the dominant patriarchal order.

Jackson privileges the writing of fantasy as subversion but is there also a danger that such writing may be escapist, filling the hearer with dreams and illusions that prevent them from taking action to improve their lot? Do such explorations provide imaginary appeasement, compensating, in literature, for the lack experienced by writer and reader in everyday life? The fact that such literature has to use the language of the dominant order increases the danger of complicity masquerading as critique.[11]

Legislating Sexual Difference

In nineteenth-century retellings of the tales as in the versions created by Perrault, the Brothers Grimm, and in Victorian nurseries, the

---

[10] R. Jackson, *Fantasy: The Literature of Subversion* (London, 1981).

[11] The notion of 'complicitous critique' as a political strategy in postmodern cultures is developed by L. Hutcheon, *A Poetics of Postmodernism: History, Theory, Fiction* (London, 1988) and *The Politics of Postmodernism* (London, 1989).

moral or didactic aspect of fairy tales became paramount. Writers recognized the legislative allure of fairy tales and rewrote them to accommodate the developing notion of childhood as a time of innocence and education. Such differences were reinforced with Perrault's insistence on attaching a summary of the alleged moral of each tale while the Grimm brothers added Christian expressions and eliminated sexual references from their version of German tales. In short, fairy tales were domesticated and the sexual dimension of human experience denied or suppressed.[12] However, such censorship, aimed at the 'pedagogization of children's sex', is, as Foucault reminds us, a tactic of no more than local significance, leading not only to repression but also to 'a regulated and polymorphous incitement to discourse'.[13] By rejecting 'the repressive hypothesis' Foucault encourages us to examine the incidence, resourcefulness, and polyvalence of power in fields previously regarded as free from its operation.

Fairy tales are one such area, constituting themselves as a field of knowledge with their own legislative effects and moral messages. Such lessons, including what constitutes good and evil, virtue and vice, reward and punishment were not gender neutral but imbued with the values of a patriarchal culture.[14] Sexual difference was inscribed and emphasized with the assignation of separate roles for boys and girls and the use of stereotypical male heroes who are brave, strong, and resourceful and female heroines who are pure, virtuous, docile, and, like Sleeping Beauty, endlessly patient. In stories such as 'Cinderella' and 'Sleeping Beauty' the role model presented to young girls suggested the virtues of patience, selflessness, silence, purity, and docility. Invariably the greatest asset for a girl is beauty for which she is rewarded with a prince, wealth, and marriage. Such girls need not do anything apart from wait, often in a remote tower, to be rescued by a brave

---

[12] M. Cadogan and P. Craig: 'the tendency to emphasise the joys ("the fun") of childhood was part of a deliberate attempt to counter teenage precocity ... girls' writers were by implication in the awkward position of having to deny the nature of adolescence': *You're a Brick, Angela!* (London, 1986), 170.

[13] M. Foucault, *The History of Sexuality, Volume 1: An Introduction* (Paris, 1976; New York, 1978), 104, 34.

[14] See A. Dworkin, *Our Blood: Prophecies and Discourses on Sexual Politics* (London, 1982) and J. Zipes (ed.), *Don't Bet on the Prince: Contemporary Feminist Fairy Tales in North America and England* (London, 1986), especially 185–260.

prince. Fairy tales also re-enact Greek myths warning of the danger of female speech by suggesting that the less a female character speaks the nicer she is.[15] Domesticity is such characters' reward for their beauty, passivity, and uncomplaining helplessness.

In contrast, girls who attempt to take charge of their lives by showing initiative, wit, or resourcefulness are rare among the well-known stories; where they do appear they are denounced as ugly and wicked and their lack of conformity to community expectations is severely punished. Girls are thus led to believe that meekness, suffering, and self-pity will be rewarded and the greatest reward of all is marriage to a rich man. Boys on the other hand are invited to identify with the young prince who rescues the helpless heroine out of her predicament and to admire his courage, perseverance, and thirst for adventure. The same stories provoked competition and suspicion between women (who are all, after all, vying for the attentions of the prince) and between mother and stepdaughter (who are both vying for the attention of the father).

It is such conventions that are interrogated in Angela Carter's playful retellings of familiar folktales. Forever conscious of the immense power of myths, old and new, Angela Carter was concerned to identify, expose and explore them: 'I'm in the demythologising business', she said, that is, investigating how certain ideas, theories, fictions, come to regulate our lives and become invested with a semi-religious coating that prevents us from interrogating them.[16] And what better weapon do we have against such myths, than, *à la* Barthes, to mythify them in their turn and produce other *artificial myths*?[17]

Woman-Born but Man-Made

Writing in the 1970s, Carter was swift to play with Foucault's notions of sex and the body as malleable, material, and constructed in history. For Carter, human nature and the human body are not timelessly natural but constructed and inscribed by

---

[15] M. Warner, *From the Beast to the Blonde: On Fairy Tales and their Tellers* (London, 1994), 387–408.

[16] A. Katsavos, 'An Interview with Angela Carter' (1994) 14(3) *Review of Contemporary Fiction* 11 at 12.

[17] R. Barthes, 'Myth Today' in *Mythologies* (Paris, 1957; London, 1993), 135.

historical and cultural signs so that we cannot speak of a pre-cultural nature (male or female), sex or gender: 'flesh comes to us out of history . . . we may believe we fuck stripped of social artifice; in bed, we even feel we touch the bedrock of human nature itself. But we are deceived. Flesh is not an irreducible human universal'.[18] Such signs are not only fictitious and culturally contingent, they are also dangerous as they are invested with the norms and expectations of a patriarchal society and have been used to confine women to restrictive roles or archetypes.[19] Art and literature is as, if not more, responsible in this respect than law in creating models that reproduce stereotypes of women as Madonnas or whores or, in fairy-tale terms, wicked witches and sleeping beauties.

The notion of the pure virgin and Jung's maternal archetype come in for special denunciation from Carter as 'consolatory nonsenses':

If women allow themselves to be consoled for their culturally determined lack of access to the modes of intellectual debate by the invocation of hypothetical great goddesses they are simply flattering themselves into submission. . . . All the mythic versions of women, from the myth of the redeeming purity of the virgin to that of the healing, reconciling mother, are consolatory nonsenses; and consolatory nonsense seems to be a fair definition of myth anyway . . . mother goddesses are as dangerous as father-gods.[20]

The exaltation of woman's role as mother collapses the feminine into the maternal and female sexuality to reproduction. This threatens women's confinement and exile from history and law-making into a hypothetical world of eternal essences while father is assumed to be the guarantor of autonomy and action within history and law. As in Irigaray's essay 'And One Doesn't Stir Without the Other',[21] the mother must resist the threat of losing her identity in an identification with the daughter while the

---

[18] Carter, *The Sadeian Woman*, n. 3 above, 9.
[19] Carter was insistent on this point: 'The feminine character, and the idea of femininity on which it is modelled, are products of masculine society': *Shaking a Leg* (London, 1997), 110. Also, 'The notion of universality of human experience is a confidence trick and the notion of a universality of female experience is a clever confidence trick.': *The Sadeian Woman*, n. 3 above, 12.
[20] Carter, *The Sadeian Woman*, n. 3 above, 5.
[21] (1981) 7 *Signs* 1.

daughter must achieve autonomy, if necessary, in Carter's view, by destroying the mother.[22]

The confinement of women to stereotypes is illustrated by the Marquis de Sade's twin heroines, the egocentric and aggressive Juliette versus her passive and submissive sister Justine. In psycho-analytic terms the two women conform to Freud's model of female sexuality as either masculine (with the clitoris as substitute penis) or feminine (with the emphasis on vaginal passivity). The striking point of this contrast is not that Juliette is bad and Justine is good but that Juliette is bad and Justine is good *in accordance with definitions laid down by men*.

Carter bravely analyses the two heroines in order to show the pitfalls and limitations of both models. Juliette, guided by Enlightenment reason, attains the 'lonely freedom of the libertine' who has learned that 'to escape slavery, she must embrace tyranny'. She knows that 'in a world governed by God, the King, and the law, that trifold masculine symbolism of authority, it is useless to rebel' and therefore imitates male rules and causes rather than suffers pain. Her self-definition assumes the Cartesian dualism between self and other and espouses an economic theory of sexual pleasure. According to this model 'pleasure consists in the submission of the partner; but that is not enough. The annihilation of the partner is the only sufficient proof of the triumph of the ego'. Juliette's and Eugenie's denial and abuse of the role of the mother aid the project of the demystification of motherhood. But such fear of the mother and adoption of possessive individualism and masculinist reason is not, in the end, seen as a challenge to patriarchal norms. Rather than changing the master's rules, Juliette understands them and uses them to her own advantage; this strategy, however, leaves both the rules and the hierarchies they inscribe intact:

The Sadeian woman . . . subverts only by her own socially conditioned role in the world of god, the king and the law. She does not subvert her society, except incidentally, as a storm trooper of the individual consciousness. She remains in the area of privilege created by her class, just as Sade remains in the philosophic framework of his time.[23]

---

[22] Carter, *The Sadeian Woman*, n. 3 above, 124.
[23] *The Sadeian Woman*, n. 3 above, 133.

If Carter is unhappy with Juliette's 'rationality without human-ism', she is even more impatient with Justine's self-pity, 'unreason of the heart' and 'false logic of feeling'. Justine is the passive victim, the innocent, suffering martyr who, while hoping to be rescued, does nothing to resist oppression; rather than helping herself, she is a party to her own victimization. Such a figure is defined negatively, as the mirror image of a male economy that itself created the myth of female passivity and submissiveness. 'That is why', Carter comments, 'there have been so few notori-ously wicked women in comparison to the number of notoriously wicked men. Our victim's status ensures that we rarely have the opportunity. Virtue is thrust upon us.' Such virtue is celebrated and sustained by a patriarchal culture for its own interests:

To be the object of desire is to be defined in the passive case.
To exist in the passive case is to die in the passive case—that is, to be killed.
This is the moral of the fairy tale about the perfect woman.[24]

Since both the categories and characteristics of Juliette and Justine, masculine and feminine, are not changeless essences, the task of the storyteller is to combat traditional myths about the nature of women and to construct alternative roles.[25] Fairy tales are one site where patriarchal fictions were created and sustained and it is there that Carter begins to inscribe her differences.

Carter Remakes[26]

BLUEBEARD

In Perrault's retelling of this remake of the tale of Psyche and Cupid, death is impliedly an apt punishment for Bluebeard's wife's curiosity and disobedience of her husband's command. As in the tales of Pandora, Eve, and Lot's wife, curiosity in women is seen as threat-ening in a masculine culture that praises the search for knowledge in men but urges women not to look but only to be looked at.

---

24 *The Sadeian Woman*, n. 3 above, 76–7.
25 A. Carter, 'Notes from the Front Line' in M. Wandor (ed.), *On Gender and Writing* (London, 1983), 77.
26 A. Carter, *The Bloody Chamber* (Harmondsworth, 1979); all references in brackets in the text are to this edition.

In Carter's version the protagonist, poor and innocent like de Sade's Justine, is flattered and seduced by the Marquis's attention, sexual knowledge, and wealth. For him she is, as she realizes, a beautiful object, a commodity, a prize, whose poverty and innocence entitles him to legislate and control her. Catching him looking at her in a mirror during their engagement, she sees herself as he sees her, 'with the assessing eye of a connoisseur inspecting horseflesh, or even of a housewife in the market, inspecting cuts on the slab'. He is the 'purchaser' and she is 'his bargain' which he unwraps slowly and deliberately in his own time. However, while this heroine is the object of the male gaze, unlike Justine she retains a sense of her own identity that is separate from her husband's attempt to reduce her to an object of his desire. Her seduction and objectification by his gaze and wealth horrifies and appals her: 'I was aghast to feel myself stirring'.

When the heroine disobeys the Marquis's law by looking into the bloody chamber she attains knowledge, not only of his murdered previous wives but of her own sexuality and independent desire. For this reason she must be punished, that is, pay the price for opening and finding the secret to Pandora's box. Unlike Justine, however, this heroine is no longer innocent and does not surrender to the role of the victim. The instrument for her rescue is not a chivalrous prince, as in previous versions, or her brothers, as in the Grimms' version, but her mother who, through a form of maternal telepathy, realizes her daughter's danger and gallops, gun in hand, to her rescue. This wild mother stuns the monstrous Marquis motionless before 'administering a furious justice by aiming a single irreproachable bullet into his head': 'The puppet-master, open-mouthed, wide-eyed, impotent at the last, saw his dolls break free of their strings, abandon the rituals he had ordained for them since time began and start to live for themselves; the king, aghast, witnesses the revolt of his pawns.' (39)

Although unusual in Carter's work, the appearance of the mother is a significant departure from fairy-tale motifs where the mother is either dead, powerless or, if powerful, a wicked stepmother bent on destroying her daughter. The heroine's admiration of, and positive relation with, her mother is a rare representation of the mother–daughter relationship. Such a relationship, Irigaray's '*dark continent* of the *dark continent*' is 'an extremely explosive kernel in our societies: To think it, to change it, amounts to undermining the patriarchal order'.[27]

Significantly it is the gaze of the mother who, like Medusa, objectifies and annihilates the monstrous patriarch. It is the mother rather than the father who acts to guarantee the law and return the daughter to the symbolic order while the father/lover breaks the law and dismembers its subjects. The symbolic order the protagonist enters is not, however, one ruled by hierarchical or patriarchal expectations. Following the mother's extraordinary feat the protagonist, her mother and her new lover, the blind piano tuner, set up a modest home away from the seductions of the castle. Her relationship with the blind piano tuner is one of accommodation and understanding of each other's needs rather than of antagonism and devourment of one by the other. His blindness ensures that she does not, once again, become the object of the male gaze. Furthermore, the daughter–mother relationship that enables entry into the symbolic and into history is not an essentialized relation of mythical great goddesses but, one that by retaining a sense of humour and self-parody, understands its own identity as performance.

BEAUTY AND THE BEAST

In Freud's view, the daughter's attraction to the father is one of the obstacles to be overcome in the child's successful passage into adulthood. 'Beauty and the Beast' tales enact this incestuous attraction by dramatizing the daughter's love for her father and reluctance to leave him for any one of her many suitors. Her decision to go to the Beast is another act of self-sacrifice as she resolves to die in her father's place. For Bruno Bettelheim the tale depicts the daughter's successful negotiation of the Oedipal complex when she learns to relinquish her attraction for her father in return for a relationship with a stranger member of the opposite sex.[28]

However, in such versions Beauty's progress from father to Beast is not a journey of self-exploration and understanding but

---

[27] *Le Corps-à-Corps avec la mère* 61, 86; quoted in M. Whitford, *Luce Irigaray: Philosophy in the Feminine* (London, 1991), 77.

[28] Bettelheim, n. 6 above, 303–9.

the trading of one patriarch for another. The Beast's transformation into a handsome prince is her reward for obedience and servility to their values and expectations. In Victorian retellings of the tale the focus is, as Carter put it, 'on house training the *id*', that is, instructing young women on how best to conform and survive arranged marriages by suggesting the illusion that inside the Beast there is a handsome prince. For Irigaray, rather than the daughter desiring the father, the father desires the daughter and legislates to protect himself from the consequences of his desire. The focus on the possessiveness of the father rather than the daughter's weakness for the father is also the angle taken by Carter.

In 'The Courtship of Mr Lyon' Beauty is her father's 'pet' who is made an item of bartering in the deals between two men. Beauty herself has not attained an understanding of herself as separate person, feeling herself, in the presence of the Beast as 'Miss Lamb, spotless, sacrificial'. She has dinner with the Beast

because her father wanted her to do so . . . For she knew with a pang of dread, as soon as he spoke, that it would be so and her visit to the Beast must be, on some magically reciprocal scale, the price of her father's good fortune.

Do not think she had no will of her own; only, she was possessed by a sense of obligation to an unusual degree and besides, she would gladly have gone to the ends of the earth for her father, whom she loved dearly (45–6).

The Beast is no better than her father at exploiting Beauty's weak (alias 'good') nature; by exalting Beauty's 'goodness' they confine her in a stereotype of sentimental femininity, deprive her of choices and ensure that such goodness is directed towards serving them rather than herself. Like her father, the Beast is ruthless at extracting Beauty's pity and ultimately love:

'I'm dying Beauty,' he said in a cracked whisper of his former purr. 'Since you left me, I have been sick. I could not go hunting, I found I had not the stomach to kill the gentle beasts, I could not eat. I am sick and I must die; but I shall die happy because you have come to say goodbye to me' (50).

Beauty complies and offers him not only her pity but also her love and her whole self:

'Don't die, Beast! If you'll have me, I'll never leave you.'

Carter is impatient with Beauty's tolerance of her subordinate status in the deals between the two men and spurs her to grow up as a separate person. The tale, she says, is 'an advertisement for moral blackmail: when the Beast says that he is dying because of Beauty, the only morally correct thing for her to have said at that point would be, "Die, then" '.[29] Although this Beauty lacks the initiative to respond in such a way, another Beauty in the next story is wiser in the ways of men and more adept at asserting her independence from both her father and her suitor.

In 'The Tiger's Bride' Beauty, like her mother before her, is again the object of exchange in the relationship between two men. Her father loses everything, including Beauty, in a game of cards with the Beast: 'You must not think my father valued me at less than a king's ransom; but at *no more* than a king's ransom'. This Beauty, however, is aware of her position as object of exchange and instead confronts and renegotiates the terms of the contract:

I was a young girl, a virgin, and therefore men denied me rationality just as they denied it to all those who were not exactly like themselves, in all their unreason . . . I meditated on the nature of my own state, how I had been bought and sold, passed from hand to hand. That clockwork girl who powdered my cheeks for me; had I not been allotted only the same kind of imitative life amongst men that the doll-maker had given her? (63).

Like de Sade's Juliette and unlike Justine she is determined not to remain a victim but to exploit her situation to her own advantage: 'For now my own skin was my sole capital in the world and today I'd make my first investment'.

Beauty divests of her role as the 'cold, white meat of contract' when she confronts and alarms the Beast with her own desire and demand to be his sexual equal. Not only does she refuse to undress for the Beast but she contests and returns his gaze, with the Beast becoming the object of her look and her desire. And rather than Beauty being frightened of the Beast without his mask, she has to reassure the Beast that she will not harm him: 'The tiger will never lie down with the lamb; he acknowledges no pact that is not reciprocal. The lamb must learn to run with the tigers' (64).

In running with rather than away from the tiger, Beauty offers the Beast the possibility of a different relationship between self and other, 'the key to a peaceable kingdom in which his appetite

---

[29] J. Haffenden, *Novelists in Interview* (London, 1985), 83.

need not be my extinction'. The Beast's otherness is not construed as frightening or engulfing but as positive and creative. It is not the Beast who is transformed into a handsome prince when she kisses him but she is transformed into a tiger when he licks off her skin. Stripped of her skin and he of his man's mask, they are free to reinvent themselves outside cultural stereotyping and enjoy a relationship that is reciprocal rather than exploitative. Beauty's transformation from girl to woman and from object of exchange to a subject making her own contracts and laying down her own laws is complete when she dispatches her clockwork twin, a wind-up doll, to her father: 'I will dress her in my own clothes, wind her up, send her back to perform the part of my father's daughter'. Rather than desiring the father, the daughter constructs her own identity independent of his laws and his desires. The Beast is also seen as constructed in a male economy that dictates that men should be predatory and women victims. Confronted with her active rather than passive sexuality the Beast reveals his own wish and ability to be tender, released from having to play the role of the aggressor. The happy denouement is not the result of Beauty's patient inactivity but her discovery of her own animality and independent desire, free of fear and inhibition.

THE COMPANY OF WOLVES

The oral tale that preceded Perrault's retelling of the story of Little Red Riding Hood is no longer well known. In that version, faced with the threat of engulfment, a shrewd and brave Red Riding Hood devises a plan that outwits the wolf and succeeds in saving her own life. In the better-known version by Charles Perrault, Little Red Riding Hood is of course consumed by the wolf, a fit punishment, Perrault implies, for disobeying her mother, straying off the main path and talking to strangers. The Grimms were only slightly more charitable to Little Red Riding Hood by providing a strong man who appears just in time to save her from the trouble she gets herself into. In both cases the young girl is discouraged from being independent and exploring, let alone realizing, her capacities including her awakening sexuality. If she does, it is implied, there will be pain and tears instead of the safety and protection provided by the father-patriarch. At the same time, while the blame is placed on Little Red Riding Hood's rebellion

and thoughtlessness, the wolf is excused from blame for his vora-
cious appetite; as Susan Brownmiller argues, in such tales the
heroine is made to bear the responsibility for rape by implicitly
'asking for it' while the male figure is represented as power,
whether as offender (giving in to female temptation) or protector
(of helpless females).[30]

Unlike the Grimms' version, in Carter's retelling, the sexual
connotations are explicit:

Her breasts have just begun to swell; her hair is like lint, so fair it hardly
makes a shadow on her pale forehead; her cheeks are an emblematic scarlet and white and she has just started her woman's bleeding, the clock
inside her that will strike, henceforward, once a month . . . She does not
know how to shiver. She has her knife and she is afraid of nothing
(113–14).

This Little Red Riding Hood is 'strong-minded', 'wise', and sexually defiant; far from seeing herself as a victim, she is not frightened by the wolf's predatory sexuality and does not flinch when
he threatens to eat her:

The girl burst out laughing; she knew she was nobody's meat. She
laughed at him full in the face, she ripped off his shirt for him and flung it
into the fire, in the fiery wake of her own discarded clothing (118).

This Red Riding Hood is good not because she is patient and innocent but because she is resourceful and brave; as such she is the
active agent in her own sexual development. In turn the wolf is not
terrifying as a masculine economy would dictate; like other beasts
in Carter's tales he suffers from 'atrocious loneliness' and would
love to be less beastly if only [he] knew how'. Faced with the heroine's active sexuality he reveals his own ability to be tender and a
companion rather than an antagonist: 'See! Sweet and sound she
sleeps in granny's bed, between the paws of the tender wolf' (118).

Appropriating the Pornographic Imagination

For commentators like Patricia Duncker what we are witnessing in
this retelling is the ritual disrobing of Little Red Riding Hood as

---

[30] S. Brownmiller, *Against Our Will: Men, Women and Rape* (New York,
1975). Also J. Zipes, *The Trials and Tribulations of Little Red Riding Hood:
Versions of the Tale in Sociocultural Context* (London, 1983).

the willing victim of pornography.[31] As 'the high priestess of postgraduate porn'[32] Carter, like Red Riding Hood, would have
laughed at this interpretation. For the notion of pornography, like
the notion of sexuality, is not intrinsic or immutable, but, like
beauty, lies in the eye of the beholder. Further, pornography relies
on its definition and existence on a supposed 'natural' or 'normal'
sexuality which it supposedly exceeds.[33] Since sexuality is itself
culturally constructed, the boundaries between what is normal
and what is pornographic shift from one generation and from one
culture to the next. No wonder it is so difficult to legislate on
pornography or separate it from eroticism which is, again, in
Carter's words, no more than the pornography of the elite.[34]

Far from seeing pornography as unambiguous violence against
women, Carter instead appropriates the genre and reuses its signs
with a view to empowering her female heroines. She puts forward
the notion of the 'moral pornographer who might use pornography as a critique of current relations between the sexes'[35] and
reveal that sexuality is not timeless or fixed but constructed by
social, economic, and historical circumstances. More controversially, she enlists the help of de Sade in demystifying the concepts
of femininity and motherhood, for separating female sexuality
from reproduction and thus contributing to the emancipation of
women. Although de Sade is seen at the end as in complicity with
the forces of law and state, Carter sees him as putting pornography in the service of women or perhaps allowing it to be invaded
by women.[36]

Western art and literature affirm the myths of patriarchy by
assigning and implicitly prescribing certain roles for men and
others for women. Traditionally, in such pornographic/erotic

---

[31] 'Re-Imagining the Fairy Tales: Angela Carter's *The Bloody Chamber*'
(1984) 10(1) *Literature and History* 3. See also R. Clark, 'Angela Carter's Desire
Machines' (1987) 14 *Women's Studies* 147–61 for the view that the ideological
power of fairy tales cannot be overcome.

[32] *New Socialist* 1987; quoted in M. Makinen, 'Angela Carter's *The Bloody
Chamber* and the Decolonization of Feminine Sexuality' (1992) 42 *Feminist
Review* 2, 3.

[33] See Susan Sontag's reading of pornography as a writing of excess; rather
than a monolithic conception of pornography, Sontag stresses its varying styles:
'The Pornographic Imagination' in S. Sontag, *Styles of Radical Will* (New York,
1969).   [34] *The Sadeian Woman*, n. 3 above, 17.

[35] *The Sadeian Woman*, n. 3 above, 7.

[36] *The Sadeian Woman*, n. 3 above, 37.

representations '*Men act* and *women appear*. Men look at women. Women watch themselves being looked at. This determines not only most relations between men and women but also the relation of women to themselves'.[37] Laura Mulvey's landmark essay 'Visual Pleasure and Narrative Cinema'[38] showed how Hollywood cinema renders women the objects of male desire and the male voyeuristic gaze, thus inscribing gender difference. Fairy tales are no exception, instructing young girls how to make themselves desirable to men while the narrative, textual or cinematic, sees desire from the point of view of the male.[39] The range of roles afforded female heroines in Perrault's retellings is predictably limited and limiting, consistently advising young girls to be beautiful rather than clever, passive rather than active. Here, women heroines do not look but are looked at, serving to confirm, express and reflect male desire and male identity. Conversely women who arrogate to themselves the power of the look are punished for their rebellion and impertinence.

Carter's reply to this scenario is to create heroines who do not subscribe to gender stereotypes and who look and choose, rather than passively allow themselves, to be looked at. This look, as immortalized by one of Carter's screen heroines, Lulu, 'is not so much a "come hither" look as a look that says, to each and every gender, "I'll come to you". (If, that is, she likes the look of you, a big if, in fact).' Like Lulu, Beauty in 'The Tiger's Bride' defies the Beast's right to look at her and instead looks at him back, 'with interest . . . [she] is not presenting herself as an object of contemplation so much as throwing down a gauntlet . . . Essentially, her attitude is one of: "Now show me what *you* can do." '[40]

In a manner that forecast Judith Butler's work on gender as performance, Carter shows that femininity and sexual difference are spectacles created by and conforming to male definitions of women; when women refuse the role of passive victim, the spectacle is revealed for what it is, thus opening the possibility for change and reinvention. Carter creates heroines that delight in the liberating potential of the construction of self in history and who re-create themselves outside the law of the father and the confines

[37] J. Berger, *Ways of Seeing* (Harmondsworth, 1972), 47.
[38] (1975) 16(3) *Screen* 6.
[39] As for example in Jean Cocteau's film 'Beauty and the Beast'.
[40] A. Carter, *Shaking a Leg* (London, 1997), 377.

of the Oedipal complex. Such women stop performing the roles assigned to them by traditional fairy tales, showing that gender roles are 'a kind of persistent impersonation that passes as the real'.[41] Aware of the performative nature of gender, they create and recreate versions of themselves for their own advantage. By being in charge of what the male sees, they elude male scripting and avoid objectification.[42] The men benefit from a similar freedom to remake themselves outside masculinist stereotypes thus showing that the roles ascribed by any culture to beasts, men, and women are not fixed and immutable but open to negotiation.

Such heroines, moreover, undergo changes through the course of the narrative: human nature is not fixed in either men or women so that both men and women may appear, in turn predatory, violent, and aggressive as well as passive, inert, and victims. As Rosaleen's mother says in the film version: 'If there's a beast in men it meets its match in women too.' In the story 'Lady in the House of Love' it is the lady vampire who is the aggressor while the man is an innocent, virgin victim. While in de Sade Juliette and Justine represent unchangeable and continuous essences, in Carter's stories gender roles are relative so that a man may be a lamb and a woman a tiger or may change through the course of the narrative from lamb to tiger and vice versa.

The result is that Carter appropriates the pornographic imagination from an instrument where unequal gender relations are inscribed to a tool through which women can express their difference. Furthermore, her picture of female sexuality is more complex than the dichotomies allowed by de Sade as well as her feminist critics, acknowledging that women, like men can be violent, actively desiring, unruly, dangerous, and polymorphously perverse. Desire for 'this sex which is not one' is not, as Irigaray famously explored, singular or unified, active or passive, but all at once, fluid, ambiguous, and excessive.[43] The subject, male or female, is multiple rather than unitary and open to self-reinventions through

[41] J. Butler, *Gender Trouble* (London, 1990), viii.
[42] P. Palmer, 'From coded mannequin to bird woman: Angela Carter's Magic Flight' in S. Roe (ed.), *Women Reading Women's Writing* (Brighton, 1987) and 'Gender as Performance in the Fictions of Angela Carter and Margaret Atwood' in J. Bristow and T. L. Broughton (eds.), *The Infernal Desires of Angela Carter: Fiction, Femininity, Feminism* (London, 1997).
[43] L. Irigaray, *This Sex Which is not One* (Paris, 1977; Ithaca, 1985).

play and display. Forever changing, it eludes the control of patriarchal scripting (pornographic or otherwise) and of male
economies. By exposing gender roles and categories as the *effects*
of laws and power rather than their cause or origin, Carter
enables us to rethink them for a new, feminist imaginary and a
feminist symbolic order.

Ethics of Alterity

The symbolic order on which previous versions of Beauty and the
Beast rest is unashamedly homosocial: Beauty is the object of
exchange between two men, the guarantor of their promises and
contracts, that is of capitalism itself. Madame de Beaumont's
version illustrates Levi-Strauss's view that 'the total relationship of
exchange which constitutes marriage is not established between a
man and a woman, but between two groups of men and the
woman figures only as one of the objects in the exchange, not as
one of the partners'.[44] However, as Carole Pateman showed, the
notion of the contract in general and the fiction of the social
contract created by liberal theory in particular are in fact patriarchal constructs. The citizen in such exchanges is always male and
women can enter only if they become men. In such contracts
women's relationships with each other are not acknowledged with
the result that, in a male economy, women are forced to play the
role of rivals.[45]

Carter's revisions and reversions of the tales shows us what
would happen if, as Irigaray suggests, commodities like Beauty
'refused to go to the market? What if they maintained another
kind of commerce, among themselves?',[46] laying down their own
rules and their own prices? Such a step need not mean refusing to
take part in exchanges at all, as some of Carter's critics would
prefer, but only taking part as an autonomous subject rather than
an object of the exchange. It does not consist in negotiating the
Oedipal complex and her alleged desire for the father as previous
versions of Beauty and the Beast suggested, but in realizing her
own desire which is equal to but also independent of that of the

---

[44] C. Levi-Strauss, *The Elementary Structures of Kinship* (Boston, 1969),
480–1. [45] C. Pateman, *The Sexual Contract* (Cambridge, 1988).
[46] N. 43 above, at 196.

Beast's. For such new exchanges to take place, however, woman, as Irigaray argues, must attain her own identity distinct from her status as mother and as man's complement. It involves acknowledging woman's differences and relationships with other women, her own genealogies, her own laws, myths, and histories.

Creating a social organization that is based on contiguity and fertility rather than death and sacrifice, as Irigaray argues, involves devising structures and norms that transcend binary oppositions of man and woman as predator or victim, active or passive, submissive or aggressive, conqueror and conquered, rational or feeling. Instead they need to acknowledge the possibility of being one or the other or both at once or changing from one to the other.[47] Such norms resist the dualism between the sexes and rest on reciprocity rather than coercion, mutual communication and recognition rather than antagonism: 'the object of a reciprocal desire which is, in itself both passive object and active subject. Such a partner acts on us as we act on it'.[48]

In relationships where one is consumed by the other, as in de Sade's monsters and in previous retellings of these tales, the result is, in Freud's terms, cultural cannibalism. In the same way that a hungry person tries to satisfy his/her hunger by the possession of an object, the lover hopes to satiate his/her desire by the possession of the love object.[49] Such cannibalism is reinforced by representations in legal and literary fictions that construe woman as man's other rather than acknowledging her identity and difference.

In Irigaray's economy, however, women not only refuse to be man's inferior other, 'dark as the negative of a photograph'[50] or 'dressed meat',[51] but enter society and exchanges in their own space and their own time. Irigaray describes this relationship as an 'amorous exchange', 'acceding to another energy, neither that of the one nor that of the other, but an energy produced together and as a result of the irreducible difference of sex'.[52] In this ethics of

---

[47] *The Sadeian Woman*, n. 3 above, 79.

[48] *The Sadeian Woman*, n. 3 above, 146.

[49] E. Levinas, *Existence and Existents* (Dordrecht, 1988); for an excellent analysis of this point see S. Sandford, 'Writing as a Man; Levinas and the Phenomenology of Eros' (1998) 87 *Radical Philosophy* 6.

[50] A. Carter, *Heroes and Villains* (Harmondsworth, 1981), 137.

[51] A. Carter, *The Passion of New Eve* (London, 1992), 31.

[52] L. Irigaray, 'Questions to Emanuel Levinas' in R. Bernasconi and S. Critchley (eds.), *Rereading Levinas* (Bloomington, 1991), 113.

alterity the relationship between the sexes is not defined by competition and overcoming but by each subject respecting the other's irreducible difference. It is a relationship where, as The Tiger's Bride learns, 'his appetite need not be my extinction'.

A certain degree of cannibalism, of absorbing the other within the self, does of course take place; our own existence and self-definition depend on the existence of the other. As the emotions of anger, jealousy, desire, and above all love, constantly remind us, the boundaries between self and other are fluid. For Derrida infringement of the other is inevitable: 'One eats him regardless and lets oneself be eaten by him . . . The moral question is thus not, nor has it ever been: should one eat or not eat . . . but since *one must* eat in any case . . . how for goodness sake should one eat well?'.[53]

Irigaray's 'j'aime a toi', rather than 'je t'aime', attempts to negotiate this problem by reaching out towards the other as subject rather than assimilating him/her as object. It accepts and benefits from our interconnectedness but tries not to subordinate the other to the self. Possession of the other, it is suggested, is impossible as the other always eludes and exceeds our attempts at incorporation. Successful relationships, therefore, are founded on equality and recognition of the difference of the other, where one does not assimilate the other but allows her/him to grow.[54] This is a relationship of love where each lover confronts the other with admiration and while crossing the boundary between self and other the encounter does not lead to loss of identity but to creativity:

[We] need to reach another dimension, another level of consciousness, a level not of mastery but one that attempts to find spiritual harmony between passivity and activity . . . It would entail . . . becoming capable of giving and receiving, of being active and passive, of having an intention that stays attuned to interactions, that is, of seeking a new economy of existence or being which is neither that of mastery nor that of slavery but rather of exchange without preconstituted object . . . What we would be

---

[53] J. Derrida, *Points . . . Interviews, 1974–94* (Paris, 1992; Stanford, 1995), 282. On this point I am indebted to P. Deutscher's 'Irigaray anxiety: Luce Irigaray and her ethics for improper selves' (1996) 80 *Radical Philosophy* 6.

[54] See also K. Silverman, *Male Subjectivity at the Margins* (New York, 1992) where a similar distinction is made between *idiopathic* identification which cannibalizes the other and *heteropathic* identification which respects the other *as other*.

dealing with, then, is the establishment of another era of civilization, or of culture, in which the exchange of objects, and most particularly of women, would no longer form the basis for the constitution of a cultural order.[55]

Part fantasy, part utopia, such imaginings or imaginaries are nevertheless indispensable for beginning to envisage an alternative form of social organization, that is a new symbolic order.

Authoresses: Collusion or Appeasement?

What is the importance of an aesthetic revolution to political problems and aims? A revolution, moreover, which utilizes the language and genre of the existing system? Can such a strategy avoid the values implicit in that language and that genre? Can mimicry of male language and male discourses avoid being absorbed by male values and male norms? Furthermore, is fantasy an adequate political tool or does it lead writer and reader to forget material circumstances while indulging in a fairyland where all difference and struggle are dissolved and they all lived happily ever after? Is Carter, in other words, creating new consolatory myths of her own?

By choosing to use the genre of the fairy tale Carter is aware that she is treading dangerous ground: 'It is after all very rarely possible for new ideas to find adequate expression in old forms.'[56] Her hope, instead, is that by 'putting new wine in old bottles, the pressure of the new wine may make the old bottles explode'.[57] Fantasy as a subversive instrument of change is also not a panacea for women's politics: while using the power of fantasy to tell new stories, Carter 'kept her feet firmly on the ground'[58] confronting material conditions and contemporary issues on sexuality and social justice; abortion law, access to further education, equal rights, the position of black women. 'I'm a socialist damn it; how can you expect me to be interested in fairies?'[59] At the same time,

---

[55] L. Irigaray, *I Love to You; Sketch of a Possible Felicity in History* (London, 1996), 45.

[56] A. Carter, 'The Language of Sisterhood' in L. Michaels and C. Ricks (eds.), *The State of the Language* (Berkeley, 1980), 228.

[57] 'Notes from the Front Line', n. 25 above, 69.

[58] M. Warner, The *Independent*, 17 February 1992, 25.

[59] M. Harron, The *Guardian*, 25 September 1984, 10.

fantasy enables us to find a space for the articulation of alternative or suppressed stories, interrogating, distorting, and also changing existing stories and beliefs. In this sense fantasy and literature in general are not marginal to mainstream culture but contribute towards what Kristeva termed the semiotic's revolt against the symbolic.[60]

Of course such articulations can only take place from within existing language and existing discourses. Aware of this limitation, Carter adopts a strategy that consists of challenging patriarchy with its own techniques, knowledges, and discourses. This strategy, familiar from Irigaray,[61] consists of borrowing from male discourses, deliberately parodying and exaggerating them, in order to say something new. Like the hysteric, Irigaray argues,

one must assume the feminine role deliberately. Which means already to convert a form of subordination into an affirmation, and thus begin to thwart it . . . To play with mimesis is . . . to try to recover the place of her exploitation by discourse, without allowing herself to be simply reduced to it. It means to resubmit herself to . . . ideas about herself, that are elaborated in/by a masculine logic, but so as to make visible, by an effect of playful repetition, what was supposed to remain invisible: the cover-up of a possible operation of the feminine in language.[62]

Irigaray's engagement with male philosophers is a prime example of intertextuality, flirting with male philosophers, writers, and pornographers, seducing them and imitating them while saying the opposite or something different to what they said.

The problem is, how does one distinguish the person who mimes phallocentric discourse strategically from one who speaks and believes in it? How can one tell the dancer from the dance, the seducer from the seduced?[63] The answer, partly, is that such mimesis is not blind parrotry but ironic parody, moving from imitation of the dominant discourse to creation and celebration of

---

[60] J. Kristeva, *Revolution in Poetic Language* (Paris, 1974; New York, 1984).

[61] 'The option left to me was to have a fling with the philosophers': *This Sex Which is not One*, n. 43 above, 150.

[62] *This Sex Which is not One*, n. 61 above, 76.

[63] P. Palmer 'Gender as Performance', n. 42 above, asks whether the idea of gender as performance is 'a sell-out to society's current obsession with stylizing the body and the erotic', 27. Also in the same volume, C. Britzolakis, 'Angela Carter's Fetishism', wonders whether the emancipation promised by the notions of theatricality and masquerade is more apparent than real.

one's own language and discourses. For such language and such a system is not monolithic or homogeneous but a process. Although Carter's critics worry that it is impossible to escape the sexist ideology of fairy tales, fairy tales and the language they are expressed in are not univocal but polysemic. The result is that linguistic signs, although dominated by certain groups at any one time, can also, through struggle, be the object of appropriation by interested groups including feminists.

Angela Carter's imaginative retellings of traditional fairy tales partake of the freedom available to a parodist when engaging in the task of mimicry combined with critique. While retaining many of the conventions of traditional fairy tales she creatively substitutes new images, characters and plots, subverting old conventions and ideologies at the same time as repeating and borrowing from them. Without destroying the original tales, Angela Carter steals liberally from them reusing the signs for her own very different purposes. Strategic theft is, perhaps the only available option:

Today, there is no area of language exterior to bourgeois ideology; our language comes from it, returns to it, remains locked within it. The only possible answer is neither confrontation nor destruction but only theft: to fragment the old texts of culture, of science, of literature, and to disseminate and disguise the fragments in the same way that we disguise stolen merchandise.[64]

Such parody, as Linda Hutcheon argues, is not nostalgic but ironic and critical, problematizing dominant values and ideologies and laying bare the political nature of all representation.[65]

The reader is also free to construct her own meanings from the available signs; in intertextual texts such as *The Bloody Chamber* such participation is indispensable. The reader's memory of previous texts and representations plays an intrinsic role in the text's engagement in the politics of representation. While such engagement is restricted to readers familiar with the earlier text and has therefore attracted the criticism of elitism, the high currency of fairy tales means that most readers can fruitfully compare and learn from the differences between the two texts. While some readers have found Carter's retellings complicit with patriarchal ideology, the freedom and responsibility for finding alternative

---

[64] I. Hussan, *The Right Promethean Fire: Imagination, Science and Cultural Change* (London, 1980), 17.   [65] N. 11 above.

stories and alternative ideologies rest with the reader's engagement with the text, not the writer's prescriptions.[66]

The result for both writer and reader is to encounter female heroines who do not subscribe to the patriarchal mould but restore the forgotten voices; while they necessarily repeat the original violence, the original trauma, they do so with a different purpose.[67] Here one cannot overestimate the power of irony and humour as tools for subverting earlier texts and cultural orthodoxies. Although humour has the effect of 'blowing up the law, breaking up the truth'[68] it is itself absent from legal discourse, an institution notoriously unable to laugh at itself. Such deconstruction reveals the sexist values implicit in fairy tales at the same time as redefining their ideological position. As Marina Warner puts it, 'Carter snatches out of the jaws of misogyny itself "useful stories" for women. There [she] found Sade a liberating teacher of the male-female status quo and made him illuminate the far reaches of women's polymorphous desires'. The effect is to lift Beauty, Red Riding Hood and Bluebeard's last wife out of the pastel nursery into the labyrinth of female desire.[69]

Of course changes in legal, social, and economic conditions are necessary for achieving women's autonomy; such changes, however, need to be accompanied if not preceded by a transformation in language and representational norms as negative representations of women on the cultural plane contribute to the denigration of women on the political and social plane. Carter represents women and femininity in terms that are not dictated by phallocentric culture and constructs alternative models that respect women's difference. The Marquis de Sade's model of the virtuous victim Justine and of the aggressive Juliette are both shown to be unhelpful. Instead, woman must find her own voice and her own sexuality in order to begin writing/creating herself. The heroines in *The Bloody Chamber* extricate themselves from objects of male desire and male laws, discover their own desires

[66] See M. Makinen, n. 32 above: 'Narrative genres clearly do inscribe ideologies (though that can never fix the readings), but later re-writings that take the genre and adapt it will not necessarily encode the same ideological assumptions'.

[67] See J. Butler, *Excitable Speech: A Politics of the Performative* (London, 1997), especially 37–8.

[68] H. Cixous, 'The Laugh of the Medusa' (1976) 1 *Signs* 875, 888.

[69] M. Warner, *The Second Virago Book of Fairy Tales* (Angela Carter (ed.), London, 1992), x.

and write their own endings to old stories. Following Irigaray's notion of mimesis, they take up the role of lawmakers and recreate themselves independently of male scripting. The fact that these new selves are fashioned on the back of previous well-known texts enables the reader to appreciate the contrast with irony, wit, and humour.

Fantasy, to paraphrase Gillian Beer, may remake the world in the image of (female) desire.[70] Envisaging new imaginary orders is to envisage new laws for what is the symbolic order but another imaginary that has become law?

[70] G. Beer, *The Romance* (London, 1970), 79.

FROM BETTE DAVIS TO MRS WHITEHOUSE: LAW AND LITERATURE— THEORY AND PRACTICE

Michael Thomson

Introduction

'Have you noticed how intellectually diverse Law and Literature has become in recent years?'[1] So begins a recent review by Gary Minda of law and literature scholarship as we approach the new millennium. While Minda enthusiastically, though not unreservedly, celebrates diversity, he fails to engage with the problematic relationship between feminist work and this new discipline.[2] This relationship has been problematic in a number of ways. At an immediate level there has been minimal feminist engagement with this field of scholarship. Indeed, the interaction between feminism and law and literature has been, at best, hesitant, tentative. Far from seeing a marriage of the excluded or marginalized as we might have expected, we have seen a lukewarm encounter, barely an embrace. Why? For some law and literature has been seen as overly textual.[3] Others have contended that the discipline is dominated by male voices.[4] In terms

---

[1] G. Minda, 'Law and Literature at Century's End' (1997) 9 *Cardozo Studies in Law and Literature* 245.

[2] Having said that, he does engage with feminist law and literature work to the degree that he makes the problematic claim that 'feminist theorists' have replaced one inadequate metanarrative with another: Minda, 'At century's end', n. 1 above, 252–3.

[3] See I. Ward, 'Law and Literature: A Feminist Perspective' (1994) 2 *Feminist Legal Studies* 133.

[4] '[W]hen we delved into the newly minted discipline, we found to our dismay that like both "law" and "literature" much of that hyphenated field examines a world in which white men attempt from a place of power to speak as if for us all.' C. Heilbrun and J. Resnik, 'Convergences: Law, Literature and Feminism' (1990) 99 *Yale Law Journal* 1913.

of the latter, we see how this relationship is problematic at another level. While feminists *are* working in this area their voices remain marginalized or excluded. While women authors are seeing their work increasingly the subject of law and literature seminars,[5] feminist academics' work has not been given access to law school seminars in the same way.[6] In this respect women are, as Judith Resnik has written, almost invisible.[7]

Although the exclusion of this work is an important issue I want here to focus on the general feminist failure to engage with this discipline. More specifically I want to concentrate on the lack of engagement with the 'applied' potential of law and literature. Whatever the reason(s) for this failure, it is clear that feminists have not utilized the possibilities created by this new discipline regardless of the obvious, and potentially productive, convergences of ambition.[8] While this may be true, this omission may also be located within a more general academic failure to engage with this work in a creative and applied way. Much of the work done in this area appears contained within unchallenged and unreconstructed paradigms and as traditional as the subjects it seeks to supplement.[9] In response, what I want to do here is to provide a practical example. I illustrate how this area of study may be of use to feminists. In providing this specific example it is hoped that its applicability beyond the feminist academy can be noted.

Despite the fact that feminism has been hesitant in its engagement with law and literature, no such hesitancy has been evident in the way feminist theory and practice has successfully confronted and problematized the disciplines of law and medicine.[10] More pertinently, the interaction of these disciplines has been recognized as an important axis for feminist strategic

---

[5] See E. V. Gemmette, 'Law and Literature: Joining the Class Action' (1995) 19 Valparaiso University Law Review 665, at 686–8, 691.

[6] Gemmette, n. 5 above, 671.

[7] J. Resnik, 'Changing the Topic' (1996) 8 *Cardozo Studies in Law and Literature* 339, at 349.

[8] Ward, n. 3 above, 138.

[9] Resnik, n. 7 above, 348, 352.

[10] See, for example, K. O'Donovan, *Sexual Divisions in Law* (London, 1985); C. Smart, *Feminism and the Power of Law* (London, 1989); P. Foster, *Women and the Health Care Industry: An Unhealthy Relationship?* (Buckingham, 1995); B. Ehrenreich and D. English, *For Her Own Good: 150 Years of the Experts' Advice to Women* (London, 1979).

engagement.[11] In this paper I build upon this work to provide a theoretically-grounded example to justify a more prominent place for law and literature within feminist scholarship. I argue that consideration of the female subject constructed at the axis of law and medicine, through a law and literature lens, has potentially profound implications. More specifically I argue for a rewriting of the doctor who is implicated in the construction of particular female subjectivities both within and outwith law. This paper focuses on the doctor, recognizing him as less fixed, less historically anchored, than the medico-legal Woman he helps to construct, and as such more open to narrative challenge.

The Legal Subject and the (Medico-)Legal Woman

Postmodernism's assertion of the contingency of the (legal) subject has challenged law and legal scholarship. Within this project the subject is read as 'a construction of texts, discourses, and institutions',[12] and as a 'variable and complex function'[13] of these discourses and practices:

The individual subject is rendered inextricable from discourse, a post through which various kinds of messages pass, which leaves her a mere 'nodal point' for the evershifting play of dissonant language games. With the postmodern rejection of all projects claiming to be universal, the unity

---

[11] C. Smart, 'Disruptive Bodies and Unruly Sex: The Regulation of Reproduction and Sexuality in the Nineteenth Century' in C. Smart (ed.), *Regulating Womanhood: Historical Essays on Marriage, Motherhood and Sexuality* (London, 1992), 7; C. Smart, 'Penetrating Women's Bodies: The Problem of Law and Medical Terminology' in P. Abbott and C. Wallace (eds.), *Gender, Power and Sexuality* (Hampshire, 1991), 157; C. Smart, 'The Woman of Legal Discourse' (1992) 1 *Social and Legal Studies* 29; M. Thomson, 'Employing the Body: The Reproductive Body and Employment Exclusion' (1996) 5 *Social and Legal Studies* 243; T. Murphy, 'Bursting Binary Bubbles: Law, Literature, and the Sexed Body' in J. Morison and C. Bell (eds.), *Tall Stories?: Reading Law and Literature* (Aldershot, 1996), 57; E. Fegan, ' "Fathers", Foetuses and Abortion Decision Making: The Reproduction of Maternal Ideology in Canadian Judicial Discourse' (1996) 5 *Social and Legal Studies* 75; M. Thomson, 'Legislating for the Monstrous: Access to Reproductive Services and the Monstrous Feminine' (1997) 6 *Social and Legal Studies* 401.
[12] P. Schlag, 'Normative and Nowhere to Go' (1990) 43 *Stanford Law Review* 167, 173.
[13] M. Foucault, 'What is an Author?' in P. Rabinow (ed.), *The Foucault Reader* (Harmondsworth, 1986), 101, 118.

of the subject is deconstructed and revealed as plural, fragmentary, and contingent.[14]

If, as postmodernism asserts, the (legal) subject is a product of discourse and practice then it becomes possible to challenge the dominant discourse and tell a different *story*, to open up new possibilities. This subversive and transformatory potential has been recognized as one possible role, or justification, for the law and literature enterprise. In some respects this has been part of the project championed by James Boyd White, the founder of the modern law and literature movement.[15] The 'communitarian ethics' White has developed through his work relies on an understanding of community and community values which allows for their transformation through the critical reading of the constitutive texts which produce these communities and their values.[16] Yet as Robin West has persuasively argued, White's reliance on a community's own texts necessarily does violence to those excluded from that textual community: 'If we ground our criticism in our texts, then we will not grant moral entitlement to those "others" our texts objectify. We will not recognize them at all.'[17] Working within a community's existing text does violence not only to the excluded but also to the possibilities of our imagination. This is suggested by Annette Kolodny: 'We read well, and with pleasure, what we already know how to read; and what we know how to read is to a large extent dependent upon what we have already

[14] C. Stychin, 'Identities, Sexualities, and the Postmodern Subject: An Analysis of Artistic Funding by the National Endowment for the Arts' (1994) 12 *Cardozo Arts and Entertainment Journal* 79, at 89–90 (quotations omitted). Importantly, this does not necessarily mean a collapsing of the self, a complete dissolution of agency: '[T]he postmodern deconstruction of subjecthood has revealed the subject not only as socially constructed but also as a product of discourse. This discovery, however, need not mean that the status of the subject is reduced to nothing more than the intersection of various language games . . . Subjects are constructed by discourse, and as subjects we actively and creatively participate in our self definition through discourse. This realization demands that our understanding of subjecthood transcend the binary between liberal, universal conceptions and the poststructuralist dissolution of all notions of a grounded subjectivity. Rather, we must recognize individual activity in 'self' definition and interpretation. (Stychin, 93.)

[15] R. West, 'Communities, Texts and Law: Reflections on the Law and Literature Movement' (1988) 1 *Yale Journal of Law and the Humanities* 129.

[16] J. B. White, 'Is Cultural Criticism Possible?' (1988) 84 *Michigan Law Review* 1373.   [17] West, n. 15 above, at 140.

read (works from which we developed our expectations and our interpretative strategies).'[18]

In response to White's work, and moving us towards the project called for here, West stresses the necessity of the creation of new texts, a creative endeavour which must leave us less bounded:

The criticism of law . . . should be grounded in a different text. It must rest on a claim regarding that which ought to be, not a claim regarding that which is, or how power has been used to date. It must be grounded in the text we didn't write—the text of our natural deeds, our true potential, our utopian ideas.[19]

While recognizing the strategic possibilities of this 'conceptual challenge'[20] we must also recognize that some stories are more open to retelling than others. In other words, some acts of resistance face more *resistance* than others. With this in mind it is worth returning to the specifics of this paper and noting the intense investment in the Woman of law.[21] This (legal) subject is constructed from enduring narratives and discourses which makes the textual work called for by both White and West problematic. Yet recognizing that the legal Woman is very often the 'medical' Woman, and, more importantly, that law quite clearly employs medical knowledge and the figure of the doctor to a significant degree in the construction of this (medico-)legal Woman, it becomes possible to offer an alternative, or rather complementary, strategy for change.

To explain this a little further: gender—which may be conceptualized as a social relation, a structural code—is, like sexuality,

---

[18] A. Kolodny, 'Dancing Through the Minefield' in E. Showalter (ed.), *The New Feminist Criticism: Essays on Women, Literature, and Theory* (New York, 1985), 144, at 155.

[19] R. West, 'Adjudication is not Interpretation: Some Reservations about the Law-as-Literature Movement' (1987) 54 *Tennessee Law Review* 278.

[20] C. Bell, 'Teaching Law as Kafkaesque' in Morison and Bell, n. 11 above, 11 at 30.

[21] Written in this way Woman denotes a recognition of the 'distinction between Woman and women. This is familiar to feminists who have for some centuries argued that the *idea* of Woman (sometimes the *ideal* of Woman) is far removed from real woman.' Smart, 'The Woman of Legal Discourse', n. 11 above, at 35. It is worth adding Smart's qualification that the concept of 'real woman' is itself problematic: 'the claim to an absolute reality located in the body of women against which the excesses of patriarchy can be measured has become less tenable'.

made not given. As this social relation is predicated on the 'conceptual and rigid structural opposition of the two biological sexes',[22] the construction of the sexed body and sexual difference[23] may be understood as *technologies of gender*, that is, as sites at which gender is constructed.[24] Following from this, the construction of the sexed body and sexual difference is central to the construction of gender inequality: 'the bodies of women, whether all too present or disconcertingly absent, have served to ground the devaluation of women by men ... [I]t is the body itself, in whatever physical form it is experienced, which positions women as both morally deficient and existentially disabled'.[25] Or, as Rosalyn Diprose has written:

the central issue in redressing women's social subordination within patri- archal social relations is not so much male control of women's bodies as the way in which women's bodies are socially constituted in relation to men ... [T]he limitations on freedom are primarily due to ways in which women's bodies are constituted and valued in relation to men and in circulating discourses about sexual difference.[26]

Although it may be asserted that Woman is a gendered subject position which legal (and other) discourses bring into being,[27] feminist scholarship has not ignored the degree to which biomed- ical discourse shapes—and perhaps even allows—these constitu- tive discourses. This, as Carol Smart has argued, has its origins in the end of the eighteenth century:

What was witnessed was a polarization of genders in which differences became increasingly fixed and rigid, and at the same time naturalized. Scientific [including medical] discourses were central to this process,

---

[22] T. de Lauretis, *Technologies of Gender: Essays in Theory, Film and Fiction* (London, 1987), 5.

[23] Feher's understanding of the body places the 'sexed' body in context: 'The body . . . is not a reality to be uncovered in a positivistic description of an organ- ism nor is it a transhistorical set of needs and desires to be freed from an equally transhistorical form of repression. This body is instead a reality constantly produced, an effect of techniques promoting specific gestures and postures, sensa- tions and feelings.' From M. Feher, 'Of Bodies and Technologies' in H. Foster (ed.), *Discussions in Contemporary Culture* (Seattle, 1987), 159.

[24] De Lauretis, n. 22 above.

[25] M. Shildrick, *Leaky Bodies and Boundaries: Feminism, Postmodernism and (Bio)ethics* (London, 1997), 14.

[26] R. Diprose, *The Bodies of Women: Ethics, Embodiment and Sexual Difference* (London, 1994), 119–24.

[27] Smart, 'The Woman of Legal Discourse', n. 11 above, 34.

giving new vigour to traditional religious and philosophical beliefs about the inferiority of women. Women became more and more closely associated with their bodies, and their bodies became both overdetermined and pathological. It becomes possible to argue that scientific, medical and later psychoanalytical discourses operated to create the very gender differences we have come to take for granted as natural.[28]

It is this association with the body, the biologically overdetermined, which very often characterizes the Woman of law. Even if it cannot be argued that this Woman is a homogenous or unified subject, there is a continuity in the way she is repeatedly defined by her body.[29] There are, of course, areas where the (medico-)legal Woman is most visible. The legal regulation of abortion or access to reproductive services, for example.[30] Elsewhere in legal discourse, however, it is also possible to unpack law's biomedical association between women and their bodies. Here, as in the more obvious areas of legal regulation just noted, the discourses of law and medicine commingle to produce a subject constantly in need of surveillance and regulation.[31] This may be seen, for example, in areas of employment law[32] and family law.[33]

While being cognizant of the broader productive relationship between biomedicine, sexed bodies and gender noted above, here I intend to focus on one aspect of this relationship. It is the figuring of the doctor, and the doctor/(female)patient relationship that this allows, that I want to argue has strategic possibilities. Although the role of biomedical/sociobiological discourses is well documented I want to address what may be characterized as a particular technology of gender. Recognizing the complex relationship between law, the doctor, and the (medico-)legal Woman, we can start to formulate a new strategy of resistance, a new 'conceptual challenge'. Whereas the (medico-)legal Woman has a problematic

---

[28] Smart, 'The Woman of Legal Discourse', n. 11 above, 36.

[29] For example, white women and women of colour may both at times be constructed in a way which privileges the biological yet with quite different results in terms of the (legal) subject positions which emerge. See, for example, D. E. Roberts, 'Punishing Drug Addicts Who Have Babies: Women of Colour, Equality, and the Right to Privacy' (1991) 104 *Harvard Law Review* 1419.

[30] M. Thomson, *Reproducing Narrative: Reproduction, Gender and Law* (Aldershot, 1998).

[31] Smart, *Regulating Womanhood*, n. 11 above, 7.

[32] See Thomson, 'Employing the Body', n. 11 above.

[33] See, generally, K. O'Donovan, *Family Law Matters* (London, 1993).

permanence—she appears securely anchored in a complex and shifting network of discourses and practices—it becomes possible to consider a rewriting of the doctor whose story, although socially entrenched, seems more open to movement. Importantly, rewriting the doctor has the potential to disrupt the relationship between women/Woman, biomedicine and law, and perhaps to open up the legal Woman to more direct strategies of resistance.

In the next section I consider the construction of the doctor and how this is figured within law. My interest in the doctor is three-fold. First, the doctor is imagined in law as the point at which women interface with scientific, medical, and health technologies. Second, and following from this, how the doctor is figured in legal and other discourses informs the dominant ideal doctor/(female) patient relationship. Finally, and as a corollary to the above, as a subjective presence constructed within legal and other discourses he exists as a focus for resistance. While I recognize that medicine is neither monolithic nor exclusively male, I want to emphasize that the doctor referred to here is very much an ideal type. That is to say, I refer to a model of the doctor which is privileged within the discourses of law, popular culture, and elsewhere. Hence my reference to the doctor exclusively as 'he'.

I turn first to film, a genre which tells and retells powerful myths and stories.[34] In an increasingly visual culture film may be read as an increasingly significant text which, to return to White, helps to constitute our communities, community values, and, I would emphasize, subjectivities. The place of film in law and literature scholarship is strengthened, arguably made a necessity, if we bring together the contemporary importance of this genre with the work of Richard Weisberg: 'We must teach and think about these texts because, here and now, they are the best medium to instruct ourselves and our students about what we do . . . [W]e need this learning in order to practice and . . . in order to understand what our assumptions are and what we do.'[35] Having argued that film has an increasing cultural and political significance I, perhaps perversely, go back to the 1940s to the film *Now Voyager*. This film presents a vivid and useful

[34] See J. Denvir (ed.), *Legal Reelism: Movies as Legal Texts* (Urbana and Chicago, 1996).

[35] R. Weisberg, 'Family Feud: A Response to Robert Weisberg on Law and Literature' (1988) 1 *Yale Journal of Law and the Humanities* 72.

example of the dominant model of the doctor which exists as an important technology of gender. It also illustrates the doctor/(female) patient relationship which follows from this model and acts as a further technology of gender. Turning then to law I consider the degree to which the relationship/technology outlined in the consideration of *Now Voyager* inhabits the legal imagination. In choosing these two texts I recognize their difference and their cultural and historical specificity. What I want to illustrate is a particular model and its persistence: no other argument or claim is made. The choice of story could therefore be seen as arbitrary.

Two Stories

THE FILM

Our literary, televisual, and cinematic worlds are saturated by images of the medical. Our story writers have recognized that we seem to have an insatiable appetite for these narratives. Within the worlds that are created the figure of the doctor is clearly privileged. The 1942 film *Now Voyager* exists as one of Hollywood's first forays into this now recognized mediagenic world. While critics have often approached the film for what it tells us of popular culture's representation of motherhood, I want here to assess the role of Dr Jaquith.[36]

E. Ann Kaplan summarizes the film as '[g]enerically a "woman's melodrama" ', and notes that the 'text asks the spectator to identify with, and to appreciate, the daughter's, Charlotte Vale's, development to maturity and autonomy—her triumphing over her oppressive mother'.[37] Rather than addressing herself to the figure of Dr Jaquith, Kaplan contends that his psychoanalysis is used merely 'as a narrative discourse, as a means for producing character-change and explaining mother–daughter interaction'.[38] Providing a different focus I want here to concentrate not on the

---

[36] For a discussion of this film see L. Jacobs, '*Now Voyager*: Some Problems in Enunciation and Sexual Difference' (1981) 7 *Camera Obscura* 89; M. Plaza, 'The Mother/The Same: The Hatred of the Mother in Psychoanalysis' (1981) 2 *Feminist Issues* 75; E. A. Kaplan, *Motherhood and Representation: The Mother in Popular Culture and Melodrama* (London, 1992), 107.

[37] Kaplan, n. 36 above, 110.   [38] *Ibid*.

analysis but the analyst.[39] *Now Voyager* contains a powerful and enduring narrative which figures the doctor as a normalizing moral presence: he is as Foucault states 'Father and Judge, Family and Law'.[40]

Charlotte's sister-in-law invites the charismatic Dr Jaquith into the cold and matriarchal Boston household. In true Hollywood form he is quick to offer Charlotte (Bette Davis) the promise of a cure for her mental illness and equally quick to blame Mrs Vale for her daughter's ill health. The doctor appears as the only male figure within the house before Charlotte 'recovers'. There is little reference to Mr Vale and Jaquith is clearly placed in the role of the Father, reasserting patriarchy in the family. This is seen not only at the level of his very presence and his interaction with Mrs Vale, but also in Charlotte's dramatic transformation.

When the film begins Charlotte is ambiguously constructed as either a child or an aging spinster. She is clearly positioned outside the parameters of 'normal'/'acceptable' sexuality. Spending her time alone in her bedroom she is desexualized, her hair is severe, her dress is simple. Once removed from the sphere of her mother, brought within the sphere of the Father, Charlotte is transformed, she is allowed to become a woman:

for a short space during the opening sequence, the film touches on deeper psychoanalytic (even Lacanian) levels, showing Mrs Vale as a mother who tries to keep her daughter down with her in the imaginary—who refuses to release her child into the patriarchal Symbolic. In the first scene, Charlotte, although technically adult, barely has access to language, especially when in the presence of her overpowering mother. The psychiatrist's role is to represent the Third Term (the Father, the Law) that has to come between mother and daughter. This achieved, Charlotte is able to separate and to form an adult sexual relationship of her own.[41]

Once Charlotte is removed Mrs Vale correspondingly diminishes in power. She becomes bedridden, feeble, comic and ultimately she

---

[39] While it is significant that Jaquith is a psychoanalyst this does not negate his usefulness as an example of *the doctor*. Although it should be recognized that different medical professionals will be figured differently there are strong recurring narrative themes which connect these subject positions. It is these themes that need to be highlighted if the doctor and the doctor/(female) patient relationship is to be understood and rewritten.

[40] M. Foucault, *Madness and Civilisation: A History of Insanity in the Age of Reason* (London, 1989), 272.

[41] Foucault, *Madness and Civilisation*, n. 40 above, 114.

dies. Interestingly, men, other than Dr Jaquith, only enter the house once Mrs Vale is bedridden and only when Charlotte emerges as a mature sexual actor. Patriarchy has been restored.

The normalizing patriarchal role of the doctor is prevalent throughout the film, although perhaps not so dramatically as in the initial cleaving of Charlotte from the sphere of her mother. Once Charlotte has been brought under the influence of 'the Father, the Law', Jaquith's presence and influence remain apparent. This is perhaps most clearly seen in the manner in which Jaquith regulates Charlotte's first sexual relationship.

It is clear from the start that Jerry—the object of Charlotte's affections—is married, albeit unhappily. We quickly learn of his home life, his manipulative wife and his two daughters. Inevitably, after a period of great happiness, the relationship between Charlotte and Jerry finishes. Charlotte flees Boston for the countryside 'retreat' of Dr Jaquith. Exhausted, perhaps on the verge of another breakdown, Charlotte finds solace and strength not in the (direct) ministerings of Jaquith but in Tina, Jerry's daughter who also happens to be a patient of the doctor. Charlotte gains strength first as Tina's nurse but then also as her *surrogate* mother. Charlotte and Jerry's relationship becomes mediated through Tina. Yet the propriety of this (three-way) relationship is maintained by the doctor. Charlotte's involvement with Tina's case and therefore with Jerry is conditional on the doctor's consent, as he reminds Charlotte 'What the Lord giveth, the Lord taketh away'. Tina becomes the relationship's bond. She becomes their child—so long as the relationship remains sexless.

Dr Jaquith therefore normalizes Charlotte and the relationships that Charlotte has. He standardizes Charlotte's relationship with her mother, and then with the other members of her family. More generally, he reasserts patriarchy in the Vale household principally by allowing Charlotte a sexual identity. Having given Charlotte a sexual identity the doctor ensures that it is confined within appropriate limits. Not only is it heterosexual but it is also confined to the marital/familial. Charlotte is placed in a pseudo-marital relationship and given a *surrogate* child. Yet the relationship is premised on abstinence. Sex would destroy not only the fragile bond between Charlotte, Tina, and Jerry but it would also threaten the *real* (*de jure*) relationship between Jerry and his wife and children. Charlotte has been given sex but it has also been taken away—'What the Lord giveth, the Lord taketh away'.

Now Voyager, like many of the medical tales we have consumed since, suggests a particular model constructed for the doctor in the regulation of gender. This role may be superimposed upon, and understood as an essential part of, the other medical— sociobiological/biomedical—technologies outlined above. In the following section I consider the degree to which this model can be read within legal discourse.

THE WRITTEN WORD

To what extent does the figure of Dr Jaquith inhabit law's imagination? It is possible to uncover a comparable figure at a number of the intersections between law and medicine. We can detail, for example, the role constructed for the doctor under both the Abortion Act 1967[42] and the Human Fertilization and Embryology Act 1990.[43] Consideration of the Parliamentary discourses and the provisions of these statutes reveals a familiar image[44] and role ascribed to the doctor. The doctor is clearly involved in ensuring appropriate sexual/gender behaviour through determining access to the services provided under these Acts. To illustrate, reference can be made to the 'case study' David Steel

[42] S. Sheldon, *Beyond Control: Medical Power and Abortion Law* (London, 1997).

[43] Thomson, 'Legislating for the Monstrous', n. 11 above. In terms of the broader intent of the legislation and the broader context it may be located within see D. Herman and D. Cooper, 'Getting "The Family Right": Legislating Heterosexuality in Britain, 1986–1991' (1991) 10 *Canadian Journal of Family Law* 40.

[44] The debates around the Abortion Act 1967 see the doctor cast as an honourable, expert, and chivalrous man. Typically doctors were referred to as 'professional men' (Jenkins, HC Deb. Vol. 749, col. 967, 1967 (29 June)), 'professional medical gentlemen' (Hobson, HC Deb. Vol. 747, col. 531, 1967 (2 June)), and men who belonged to a 'high and proud profession' (Lyons, HC Deb, Vol. 732, col. 1090, 1966 (22 July)). Being members of such a profession these men practised with 'skill, judgement and knowledge' (Hobson, HC Deb. Vol. 747, col. 1967 (2 June)). '[H]ighly skilled and dedicated' (Mahon, HC Deb. Vol. 750, col. 1352, 1967 (13 July)), they operated within the profession's 'own ethical and medical standards' (Steel, HC Deb. Vol. 747, col. 464, 1967 (2 June)). It was not until the final stages of the debate that David Steel alluded to a 'body of professional men and women'. This was the only time within these debates that the possibility that the doctor may be a woman was explicitly recognized. (HC Deb. Vol. 750, col. 1346, 1967 (13 July)).

presented to the House of Commons in defence of his Medical Termination of Pregnancy Bill in 1967. Steel talks of a request for a termination which a doctor had received from a young woman:

He talked to the girl and put her in touch with people who could help her, her pregnancy is now going through in the normal way. It does not follow that because women desire terminations it will automatically be carried out. If we can manage to get a girl such as that into the hands of the medical profession, the Bill has succeeded in its objective.[45]

Steel made a similar argument during Parliamentary consideration of the abortion law amendments passed under the Human Fertilization and Embryology Act. He asserted that the 1967 legislation had created a legal climate where doctors may see women before they abort and persuade them otherwise.[46] Here the doctor ensures gender-appropriate behaviour—ensuring women don't avoid pregnancy and motherhood. A similar role was also detailed during the Parliamentary consideration of the main provisions of the Human Fertilization and Embryology Act. At one point Lord Mackay warned against an outright prohibition on single women receiving treatment services, arguing that such women would merely go elsewhere:

On the other hand, if the law recognises that in a very small number of cases single women will come forward for treatment, it may be better to encourage them to seek advice. With the child and welfare amendments we have just discussed there is a likelihood that through counselling and discussion with those responsible for licensed treatment they may be discouraged from having children once they have fully considered the implications of the environment into which their children would be born or its future welfare.[47]

It is clear in both instances that the doctor is employed to ensure 'normal' reproduction and 'normal' gender behaviour. He supports a presumption towards childbearing but will only 'assist' this if it is contained within a stable (preferably married) heterosexual union. The familiar mediating and normalizing role outlined here is not confined to legislative construction. This image of the doctor inhabits broader legal discourses. In

---

[45] Steel, HC Deb. Vol. 750, col. 1349, 1967 (13 July).
[46] Steel, HC Deb. Vol. 171, col. 210, 1990 (24 April).
[47] Mackay, HL Deb. Vol. 516, col. 1098, 1990 (6 March).

Whitehouse v. *Jordan*,[48] an action was brought on behalf of Stuart Whitehouse, a severely brain-damaged boy aged 10, against Mr Jordan who, it was claimed, had caused Stuart Whitehouse's injuries as a result of professional negligence in the management of his birth. At the time of the birth Mr Jordan was a senior registrar working for the West Midlands Regional Health Authority. The action against Mr Jordan focused on the use of forceps in the delivery. While the case may be subject to a number of critical readings, of relevance here is the way in which the court responded to and constructed Mr Jordan and Mrs Whitehouse who had brought the action as Stuart's next friend.

Within the judgment Mr Jordan is cast very much as the diligent, gifted, and respectable clinician. He is described as 'very able and promising',[49] 'of near consultant status', and as 'esteemed by his professional colleagues'.[50] He was understood as a young obstetrician of the 'highest skill and repute'.[51] The obstetrical unit he was a member of 'had a high reputation',[52] and was 'held in the highest regard by the medical profession'.[53] Aiding our understanding of Jordan, we learn that when Mrs Whitehouse went into labour at 11.30 p.m. Mr Jordan, although off duty, was in the building working on a research project.[54]

Mrs Whitehouse, on the other hand, is described as: 'a difficult, nervous and at times aggressive patient',[55] as 'anxious and distressed',[56] and as 'intensely . . . tense'.[57] It was noted that: '[s]he was unable, or refused, to agree to vaginal examination during her pregnancy . . . though urged to do so',[58] and that '[s]he was identified clearly as likely to be a difficult case'.[59] The 'instinctive revulsion against her vagina being examined'[60] was held on a number of occasions to be a contributing factor in what subsequently happened.[61] This was implied even though, as Lord Wilberforce recognized, by the time Mr Jordan had arrived Mrs Whitehouse had been given an epidural and he was able to examine her vaginally.[62]

---

48 [1981] 1 All ER 267 (HL).   49 [1980] 1 All ER 650 (CA), 653.
50 [1981] 1 All ER 267, 271.   51 [1980] 1 All ER 650, 662.
52 [1981] 1 All ER 267, 271.   53 [1980] 1 All ER 650, 653.
54 [1980] 1 All ER 650, 656.   55 [1981] 1 All ER 267, 271.
56 *Ibid.*   57 [1981] 1 All ER 267, 273.
58 [1981] 1 All ER 267, 271.   59 *Ibid.*
60 [1980] 1 All ER 650, 653.
61 [1980] 1 All ER 650, 653, also [1981] 1 All ER 267, 271.
62 [1981] 1 All ER 267, 271.

While judicial response to the parties is telling, perhaps more important is the way in which the interaction of Mrs Whitehouse and Mr Jordan is played out in the court. This is seen very clearly in the response to the evidence given by the parties, more particularly in the privileging of the evidence given by Mr Jordan. Mrs Whitehouse asserted before the court that the force with which the trial labour by forceps was attempted was so severe as to lift her hips off the bed. She testified that when the forceps were applied: 'It felt like a deadened electric shock that lifted my hips off the table, up off the bed.'[63] This was denied by Mr Jordan. What is interesting is the extent to which Mrs Whitehouse's evidence was dismissed without real consideration. It was found to be 'more than inexact "in *clinical* detail" '.[64] Mr Jordan's denial was privileged and accepted. This was the case even though the court was to go on to state that direct experience was to be prioritized over other forms of knowledge. However, this seems only to be the direct experience of the doctor not the patient. His subjectivity is clearly given priority over hers. As Lord Wilberforce stated: 'For myself, I would regard Mr Jordan's first hand account of the matter as of *cardinal* importance.'[65]

The court unambiguously constructs Mr Jordan as the rational, competent decision-maker. This is clearly the image required for the doctor to assume a prescriptive and normalizing role. Mr Jordan, like Dr Jaquith, is clearly seen as 'Father and Judge, Family and Law'. His word is Truth, accepted as Law.[66] Mrs Whitehouse on the other hand is given the similarly necessary role of the irrational, aggressive, and difficult woman. The status of Mrs Whitehouse and Mr Jordan is further illustrated in a brief consideration of the court's response to the expert evidence. Whereas Mrs Whitehouse's testimony is summarily dismissed, the consideration of the standard of care maintained during the trial

---

[63] [1981] 1 All ER 267, 273.   [64] *Ibid.* (emphasis added).
[65] *Ibid.* (emphasis added).
[66] This statement may clearly be tied to Sally Sheldon's critique of the *Bolam* test in medical negligence. Sheldon highlights how the standard of care, that is the legal standard, is set by the medical profession. The law is clearly descriptive of medical practice rather than prescriptive, or, as Sheldon forcefully argues, it follows what is accepted practice rather than what is acceptable practice. S. Sheldon, ' "A responsible body of medical men skilled in that particular art . . .": Rethinking the *Bolam* Test' in S. Sheldon and M. Thomson (eds.), *Feminist Perspectives on Health Care Law* (London, 1998), 15.

labour by forceps proceeded on the basis of a report written by
Professor McLaren. What makes this noteworthy is the fact that
Professor McLaren, Mr Jordan's senior, had prepared the report
for the hospital. It had also been made after discussion with Mr
Jordan with the suggestion that if it should be unfavourable it
could be altered.[67] The report had used the word 'disimpacted'
which it was said could suggest that the head of Stuart
Whitehouse had become 'impacted', or stuck, due to excessive
traction by Mr Jordan. The lengthy consideration of the meaning
of 'disimpacted'—and by implication the conduct of Mr Jordan—
therefore had little to do with Mrs Whitehouse's testimony but
was the result of 'friendly fire'. Thus, a 'careless' word by a
supporting colleague (and prior joint defendant) is given greater
credibility and consideration by the court than the claims of the
plaintiff.

A reading of the Abortion Act, the Human Fertilization and
Embryology Act, and *Whitehouse* illustrates how the construction of the doctor detailed in *Now Voyager* may be read as
inhabiting the legal imagination. While Mr Jordan is not
constructed in a directly prescriptive and normalizing role, the
response of the courts to the parties comes from within and reaffirms this model. Sally Sheldon, in her consideration of the case,
further highlights this in noting that it was repeatedly suggested
in court that Mrs Whitehouse's labour was complicated by her
failure to accept the authority of the doctors.[68] More generally
this reading of the texts—celluloid, legislative, judicial—supports
Robin West's contention that '[o]ur legal texts—no less than our
literary texts—reflect and constitute as well as convey our moral
and cultural traditions'.[69] Having argued that the doctor may be
understood as an important axis at which gender is constructed
and regulated, I now move to address the possibilities for challenging this. Reworking the earlier quotation from West, what is
needed is to move beyond a text of how this particular power has
been, and is, used, to a different text—one which perhaps speaks
of 'true potential, . . . utopian ideals', of new realities, truths and
ways of being.[70]

---

67 [1981] 1 All ER 267, 283.   68 Sheldon, n. 66 above, 15.
69 West, n. 15 above, 154.   70 West, n. 19 above, 278.

Dr Kildare, Dr Green . . . Dr Who?

The privileged social discourse of law, with its claim to a universal and authoritative narrative, has been the focus for many resistant discourses. While feminism has made real gains, law has proved resilient, adaptable. As Judith Resnik has noted: 'As women make visible a distinctive array of experiences and then gain power to alter laws and reframe contexts, counter-claims of neutrality and timeless truths attempt to quiet these voices and diminish their power.'[71] Colonizing, and imbricated within, broader social discourses, the (disciplinary) legal association between women and their bodies and, allied to this, the role constructed for the doctor, form important aspects of these counter-claims.[72] Aspects of the emergence and regulation of the new reproductive technologies,[73] employment exclusion policies premised on foetal welfare,[74] and the growth of 'foetal rights' more generally are examples of the way in which medical/scientific discourses reinterpret the female body maintaining a body requiring surveillance and control. Therefore, the degree to which women remain tied to their bodies—or more importantly tied to particular organs, processes, or readings of them—makes (direct) resistance, other than in the most incremental way, a necessary but limited strategy.

Beyond this, there are also the limits of the imagination. The possibility of figuring new possibilities, new relationships, and new realities, is limited to an extent by the degree to which our imaginations are tied to the present and the past. Those who have called for new 'stories' have had to step outside of contemporary structures and conventional history. Luce Irigaray, for example, has called for a reconsideration and reinvigoration of pre-history.[75]

---

[71] Resnik, n. 7 above, 339.

[72] See, for example, R. Siegel, 'Reasoning from the Body: A Historical Perspective on Abortion Regulation and Questions of Equal Protection' (1992) 44 *Stanford Law Review* 261.

[73] C. Smart, ' "There is of course the distinction dictated by nature": Law and the Problem of Paternity' in M. Stanworth (ed.), *Reproductive Technologies: Gender, Motherhood and Medicine* (London, 1987), 98.

[74] Thomson, 'Employing the Body', n. 11 above.

[75] Irigaray interestingly challenges the perception of pre-history as fairy tale or legend. Such a reduction she claims is 'concomitant to repressing and destroying certain cultural dimensions that relate to the economy between the sexes. Such an approach also leads to a partial, reductive, and fruitless conception of History.' L. Irigaray, *Je, tu, nous: Towards a Culture of Difference* (London, 1993), 24.

Marina Warner makes a similar argument in relation to myth.[76] Peter Goodrich's writings regarding the Courts of Love may be understood as one such project within the legal academy.[77] Although we have to search pre-history and myth for stories to retell regarding women, if we choose to rewrite the doctor our task is considerably easier. The history of the modern medical profession is a relatively contemporary and accessible story. It is a lively and intriguing story of competition, money, and status, of class struggle, international power dynamics, and women's bodies. A history within our knowledge, it appears a much more feasible project to reassess this story. We can retell medicine's story focusing on aspects of its occupational project, its desire for social status and fiscal reward, its use of women's bodies.[78] Coupled with this we can look at health-care provision before the emergence of the current model. Importantly, the past is also not so distant that we cannot imagine a different developmental trajectory.

While we can retell medicine's largely ignored history we also need to ask what stories do we need if we are to suggest a different future? The stories that we write must help rewrite the stories law tells about women. To start, it is clear that we need to move beyond a system where the doctor contributes to a discourse which defines and constructs a female body which demands surveillance and control. The doctor needs to be located in a position where he does not exist as a primary site for the construction of a sexual difference which is used as the basis for gender inequality. We need to rewrite the doctor to facilitate a role which

---

[76] 'A myth is a kind of story told in public, which people tell one another; they wear an air of ancient wisdom, but that is part of their seductive charm. Not all antiques are better than a modern design—especially if they're needed in ordinary, daily use. But myth's own secret cunning means that it pretends to present the matter as it is and always must be . . . But, contrary to this understanding, myths aren't writ in stone, they're not fixed, but often, telling the story of the same figures . . . change dramatically both in content and meaning. Myths offer a lens which can be used to see human identity in its social and cultural context—they can lock us up in stock reactions, bigotry and fear, but they're not immutable, and by unpicking them, the stories can lead to others. Myths convey values and expectations, which are always evolving, in the process of being formed, but—this is fortunate—never set so hard they cannot be changed again, and newly told stories can be more helpful than repeating old ones.' M. Warner, *Managing Monsters: Six Myths of Our Time* (London, 1994), 13–14.

[77] P. Goodrich, *The Courts of Love and Other Minor Jurisprudences* (London, 1996).   [78] See Thomson, n. 30 above; also Foster, n. 10 above.

allows greater female autonomy. At present, and as Shildrick writes, the 'clinical encounter is a paradigmatic site for the technologies of the body [and hence the technologies of gender] which both shape and control'.[79]

While we may approach the doctor 'head on', we may also rewrite the doctor through a critical rewriting of biology, and through this the relationship between biology, women, and doctors. Some of Luce Irigaray's work has moved in this direction. One project that she has embarked upon is to reassess the nature of pregnancy and particularly the role of the placenta.[80] Irigaray argues that the placenta performs a complex mediating role which allows two organisms to co-exist peacefully, 'strangely organized and respectful of the life of both'.[81] Taken at its most mundane level this re-imagining of pregnancy moves us beyond the dominant model of pregnancy as conflict and pathology which facilitates a high level of intervention and management.[82] Concomitantly, it allows a more constructive image of pregnancy to emerge.[83]

At a day-to-day level we also need to refigure the doctor so that he does not exist as a point through which the state's interest in the female body is played out. One area we may want to address in order to achieve this is the reassessment of the doctors who inhabit the Abortion Act 1967 and the Human Fertilization and Embryology Act 1990. As an element of feminist strategy it is clear that we need to recognize that the doctor of law, like the Woman of law, is not a unified and homogenous subject. He is going to have to be addressed at the various points he appears in legal (and other) discourses, as is the specific nature of the relationship he has with the Woman of law.

Although I advocate this strategy, a degree of caution is appropriate. Rewriting the doctor is in itself insufficient. What is being

---

[79] Shildrick, n. 25 above, 49.

[80] Although this project is an attempt to challenge the Darwinian and Pavlovian models of social (dis)organization it can be used in the *rewriting* exercise I propose.   [81] Irigaray, n. 75 above, 38.

[82] 'The relative autonomy of the placenta, its regulatory functions ensuring the growth of the one in the body of the other, cannot be reduced either to a mechanism of fusion (an ineffable mixture of the bodies or blood of mother and fetus), or, conversely, to one of aggression (the foetus as foreign body devouring from the inside, a vampire in the maternal body). These descriptions are of imaginary reality and appear quite poor indeed—and obviously extremely culturally determined.' Irigaray, n. 75 above, 38.   [83] Irigaray, n. 75 above, 37–44.

encouraged here is one strategy within a plurality which are needed in this area. The relationship between women and science, and the relationships between different members of the health-care team are two further examples of other possible sites of resistance. A further reason for caution arises if it is recognized that at times women have benefited from their 'alliance' with doctors. The privileging of medical autonomy/clinical judgment has at times been clearly advantageous for women. Making access to abortion and reproductive services a matter of clinical judgment has proved more beneficial for some women than a centrally-determined system would have been. Similarly, such privileging of medical decision-making has acted in women's favour when partners have challenged decisions to terminate.[84]

Conclusions

In this paper I have attempted to provide a practical example to illustrate how the feminist academy, and others, can engage with the potential created by law and literature. In the process I have problematized the figure of the doctor arguing that the doctor is an important site at which gender-appropriate behaviour is prescribed and regulated. Building on this, I have also moved to ask what stories we need. Yet beyond this perhaps this paper is limited. Having set some of the parameters for a 'new doctor', I have failed to answer West's challenge to provide a *different* text, one which responds to how things ought to be. In this respect I have, to some extent, fallen into the common trap of calling for alternative discourses and yet failing to provide such alternatives.[85] Yet every narrative starts from a *story board*, and I have left this one for others.

[84] S. Sheldon, ' "Subject only to the attitude of the surgeon concerned": The Judicial Protection of Medical Discretion' (1996) 5 *Social and Legal Studies* 95.

[85] This criticism is made by, among others, Allen Hutchinson in *Dwelling on the Threshold* (Toronto, 1988), 126.

'HOW CAN YE CRITICISE WHAT'S PLAIN LAW, MAN?': THE LAWYER, THE NOVELIST, AND THE DISCOURSE OF AUTHORITY

Marie Hockenhull Smith

Scott's novel of 1818, *The Heart of Midlothian* centres on historical events in 1736 and draws in the development of Scottish
society within the whole of the long eighteenth century.[1] How
Scott's nineteenth-century representations of eighteenth-century
law relate to what cultural and legal historians would expect to
find is a rich subject in itself. What I wish to examine here is
what those representations communicate about the perennial
matter of the relation between legal agents and the structure of
authority: how far they are incorporated, how much power the
agents embody, and how much they evade. This, which involves
the matter of personal ethical responsibility, is continually problematized by the novel in a way which connects with the concerns
of jurisprudence in postmodernity. To say this is not to perform
an anachronistic re-accenting of the text; as Goodrich *et al.* have
pointed out:

Critical legal studies is not a new phenomenon in jurisprudence, nor is
postmodernity that unusual a category of historical context or crisis.
The pervading postmodern sentiment that 'things are not going well',
that justice has miscarried or law has separated itself from ethics, has
accompanied innumerable distinct cultural movements and styles from

---

[1] Sir Walter Scott, *The Heart of Midlothian* (Claire Lamont (ed.), Oxford,
1982) from which edition all extracts in this paper are taken.

asceticism to pursuit of the millennium, gnosticism to iconoclasm, romanticism to the baroque.[2]

Those who make the familiar identification of Scott with a Tory perspective might baulk at this attribution of a critical legal perspective, but many recent readings concur that Scott rigorously examines the mechanics of law and power.[3] Bruce Beiderwell has suggested that his use of the romance genre can nevertheless dissolve the issues. However, I would argue that Scott's informed, professional representation of the legal system in *The Heart of Midlothian* (*HoM*) resists dilution.

First, a bald summary of the complex plot: the historical Porteous Riots of 1736 provide the context. The imposition of customs outposts on Scotland was one of the most unpopular aspects of Union: stubborn resistance was widespread. The major public execution of Handy Dandy Wilson, a persistent smuggler, opens the narrative; the execution is backed by a great show of state force, but possibly badly organized. Wilson is a hero to a section of the populace because of his selfless role in the escape of his partner George Robertson; the support for him leads to disorder in the scaffold-crowd, and the City Guard under the command of the hated Captain Porteous is provoked into use of excessive force. Sixteen citizens are fatally wounded. Porteous is convicted of murder, but then given a royal respite. The citizens of Edinburgh are unhappy with the political significance of this sequence of events, seeing all their interests little regarded and authority's excesses tolerated by a distant government; an unidentified group incites a mob to storm the prison, the eponymous Heart of Midlothian, abduct Porteous and lynch him. Scott's fiction enters the history through the smuggler George Robertson: he puts him at the centre of the mob, but fictionalizes him as an English gentleman, in flight from the conventions of his father's class and flirting with smuggling for adventure. He enters the Tolbooth prison to avenge Wilson, but also to try to free his lover Effie, waiting to be tried under the Scottish version of the harsh statute of child-murder, which allows a presumption of guilt to

---

[2] C. Douzinas, P. Goodrich, Y. Hachamovitch, *Politics, Postmodernity and Critical Legal Studies* (London, 1994), 2–3.

[3] For example, Bruce Beiderwell, *Power and Punishment in Scott's Novels* (Athens, Ga., 1992), 4.

arise when a woman has not communicated her pregnancy to anyone and the child is found dead or, differentiating it from the English version, is missing. Her illegitimate child has actually been abducted by Meg Murdockson, resentful of George's having seduced her daughter years before. Effie will not consent to be rescued, and is tried. The statute provides that she can rebut the presumption of guilt if she has communicated her pregnancy to someone: for instance, if her sister Jeanie would falsely testify that Effie had revealed her pregnancy to her. Jeanie's conscience will not permit her to do wrong even though right may come of it, and Effie is convicted constructively of murder. Instead, Jeanie saves her from hanging by walking to London and successfully petitioning the Duke of Argyll for a pardon. Jeanie and her family retire to an Arcadian existence on the Duke's estate, while Effie and George disappear into his aristocratic social circles, childless and unhappy, for their sins. Providence catches up with George on a Highland journey when he is pointlessly killed by a wild brigand, his lost son.

The idiosyncratic texture of the novel emanates from its framing device, which attributes the narrative to a convivial conversation between the two sharp and humane lawyers Hardie and Halkit and the aptly-named Dunover, an unfortunate ex-prisoner of the Tolbooth and victim of the legal system. Their reminiscences are supposedly recorded in his 'memorandums' by the fascinated observer Pattieson.

Mr Dunover began to contribute his share to the amusement of the evening . . . Jails, like other places, have their ancient traditions, known only to the inhabitants, and handed down from one set of the melancholy lodgers to the next who occupy their cells. Some of these, which Dunover mentioned, were interesting and served to illustrate the narratives of remarkable trials, which Hardie had at his finger ends, and which his companion was also well-skilled in (*HoM*, 26).

The provenance of the narrative of the novel is thus fictionally from three sides of a legal encounter: observer, practitioner, and subject (of course the first two are also subject in a different way). The terms used establish Dunover's knowledge as the 'Other' of legal discourse: it is 'ancient tradition', 'handed down from one set . . . to the next who occupied their cells', hence like the law it is esoteric and consists of the testimony of generations accreted in the memory. The structure of the fictional narrative recorded as Pattieson's would then be intrinsically internally 'dialogized', from perspectives moving around the protagonists: for instance Scott's account of Effie's trial is shaped from a position of 'outsidedness' that only a detached observer could achieve, with the awareness of objectification that the defendant would feel, and the knowledge and involvement of the lawyer—a kind of narrative cubism. The schematic choice of Pattieson (not a lawyer) as the shaping perspective on a legal story is both a joke and a gesture that expresses an author's inability to keep control over the meaning of what s/he sets down: Pattieson at one point admits he finds a political discussion of 'provosts, bailies, deacons, sets of boroughs' 'most unintelligible' (*HoM*, 24). This fictional manoeuvre makes apparent the real technique of constructing this sort of historical novel, meshing together the different discourses that have represented and addressed the subject matter. The account represents then what Bakhtin terms a heteroglossia, all the many voices brought into dialogue with one another.[4]

The interest is in the plurality of relations (in both senses) which make up the experience of law. The writing makes the reader aware that how things look depends on where the subject stands: a topographical observation is a good analogy: 'the prospect . . . changes at every step, and presents [the objects in view] blended with, or divided from each other, in every possible variety' (*HoM*, 74). It is an aesthetic ordering, but has an 'ethical imperative'.[5] This is not a single story of Law's hegemony and the People, in the way that William Godwin's *Adventures of Caleb Williams* (1794) might be seen to be, but a representation of the law as a knot of narratives running between individual, community, class, and nation; a knot in which the law's hierarchy of retainers, who are responsible for selecting which accounts will dominate, are themselves entangled.

In relating a wide community's experience of law in this way the novel does something different from the way that a public trial explores a defendant's story. There is a pastiche of a full trial

---

[4] '[A] plurality of relations, not just a cacophony of different voices' is how Michael Holquist glosses Bakhtin's term in *Dialogism: Bakhtin and His World* (London, 1990), 88.

[5] Simon Dentith, *Bakhtinian Thought: An Introductory Reader* (London, 1995), 43 describes Bakhtin's use of the idea of 'polyphony'.

within the text, of a defendant the reader knows to be innocent. Its setting within the heteroglossic novel makes apparent the differences between the two genres: the court's exclusion of other discourses, and the rigidity of its conventions create only a fragmentary picture for the jury to assess, and result in a mistaken conviction (*HoM*, 216–39).

The trial of the smugglers Wilson and Robertson, and that of Captain Porteous, are not dramatized within the novel, but interesting comparisons can be made between Scott's representation of their histories and their representation in the authentic trial documents: these were collected and published, together with some other contemporary documents, because of the curiosity raised by the novel.[6] In all three trials, the legal technicalities and the political dilemmas they give rise to are entirely distinct and worthy of separate analysis, but the same general observation is relevant: the comparison with the range of discourses employed by the novel reveals that the trials, despite their valid process, are partial, in the sense of omitting crucial contexts and perspectives; and Scott's plot indicates the misprision of attributing that narrowness only to the disembodied inflexibility of 'the Law'. It is the history of Porteous's employment, crime, and trial and how Scott represents it, which is most interesting here.

The transcript of Porteous's trial for murder shows that the successful prosecution argument individualized blame to such an extent that no party other than Porteous shared in the responsibility, reflecting and confirming the belief of the crowd. Scott constructs a plot which resets Porteous's style of keeping public order within the context which spawned it. The reportage of historical details, and fictional additions and emplotments distribute the individualized blame more widely, leaving an overriding impression that the public authorities complacently made use of, and so were implicated in, Porteous's excesses; that his brutal act was only the most obvious manifestation of misused power. Scott's narration thus brings different discourses into relation with one another within his novel.

The name of Porteous, says Scott's narrator, became 'too memorable from the melancholy circumstances of the day',

---

[6] Charles Kirkpatrick, *Criminal Trials Illustrative of the Tale Entitled 'The Heart of Midlothian'* (Edinburgh, 1818).

'memorable in the traditions of Edinburgh, as well as in the records of criminal jurisprudence' (*HoM*, 33). The comment acknowledges that these are two different genres: the vocabulary of popular tradition will be quite distinct from what legal records privilege. Each form has a different way of reducing the essentials of a story.

A biographical pamphlet contemporary with the 1736 events, published in the 1818 collection, gives one perspective on the popular prejudice. It seems to be driving towards the suggestion that the act of firing on the crowd was an inevitable conclusion to his career: the seeds of it are narrated proleptically in every detail of his life. The writer claims that the young Porteous's 'proneness to commit mischievous and more than childish tricks' made his mother 'positive he would be hanged'; and claims that when his father questioned his vicious career 'he almost put the good old man to death by kicks and blows'.[7] True or not, this establishes a tendency to abuse indulgent mentors that easily extrapolates into betrayal of the good, old magistrates who mistakenly trusted him. In his relationship with his wife he was again violent and abusive: the writer confides 'he did things to her which I am ashamed to write and you would blush to read', because she thwarted his 'adulterous embraces' with her maids. The sexual depravity perhaps connects with one story in circulation that had Porteous sadistically forcing over-small manacles onto Wilson's broad wrists: establishing his tendency to exert himself viciously against someone within his power who challenges his pre-eminence.[8]

The pamphlet describes Porteous's extremity on the day of Wilson's hanging (which Scott borrows from and sets within his own sceptically-framed reportage). It is said that 'his countenance was pale, his eyes rolling and staring, his mouth foaming, his voice broke and confused, his whole gait full of disconcerted and disorderly steps'. This speaks revulsion at Porteous's obsessive fury after his authority has been affronted by the escape of Robertson and the drafting in of the Welsh Fusiliers to help keep order. If this is literal, it damns his employers, the city officers, for trusting public order to this deranged figure: a modern diagnosis would surely see a psychotic condition. However, this pamphlet does not

---

[7] Kirkpatrick, n. 6 above, Preface, xii.
[8] Kirkpatrick, n. 6 above, xix.

cast its net of blame so wide; this image becomes then a rich metonym of the popular idea of Porteus. It is remarkable how many details of disorder are inscribed upon his body in this account: every faculty is out of control. It symbolizes how in the popular view all the lawlessness is transposed onto him: the indiscipline of the other guards, the rioting of the crowd, the negligence of the magistracy are all subsumed by his behaviour. As it is undated, it is difficult to tell whether this is a pre-trial narrative which fed popular outrage, or a post-trial narrative which legitimated the verdict.

The *Caledonian Mercury* of 19 April 1736 gives this account of the events at the Wilson execution. There had been no disturbance till the executioner was cutting Wilson down, when the crowd began to throw stones at the City Guard; then Porteous in an 'unwarrantable and barbarous manner, first discharged his own piece among the spectators, and at the same time ordered his guard to fire in like manner, saying "Fire! and be damned!" without the least orders from the Magistrates who were then attending, and from whom he should have received his orders'. The separation of the magistrates from the event is emphatic; but the fact that 'the narration is attested by T. Crockat, B and Gavin Hamilton, B' reminds us that this is the official version, the Bailies being the municipal councillors from whom the magistrates are drawn.[9]

The transcript of the historical trial on the other hand allows some sense of the voice of Porteous himself.[10] The defence's presentation of him is as the antithesis of the demon of popular imagination: it systematically attempts to ascribe the excess of violence to the guards and the crowd, and the breakdown and confusion to his employers, with Porteous himself the site of order.

His counsel stresses the extraordinary provisions made to police the crowds that day because of the 'reasonable ground to apprehend' a rescue of Wilson. He alleges that the Provost had provided that the City Guard had 'orders to repel force by force, and even to discharge their arms among the mob in case of resistance'. In

[9] Kirkpatrick, n. 6 above, xxvi.
[10] 'Authentic Extract of the Proceedings in the Trial of Captain John Porteous' in Kirkpatrick, n. 6 above, 78–204.

contrast to this aggressive planning, his counsel describes Porteous's 'humble' proposals that the magistrates 'send a procla-mation through the town as a caution to such innocent unwary people as might by curiosity be drawn to the sight of the execu-tion, warning them of their danger, in case any disturbance should happen'. This is Porteous rational, self-possessed, concerned above all for proper organization: with subtle emphasis, his counsel recounts that arming himself is the very last detail he deals with before departure.

His version is that, after requesting instructions from the bailiffs on whether he can cut the body down, he is told to wait 'a quarter hour', but that the crowd attempt to pre-empt that. They attack the guard with heavy stones, the Welsh Fusiliers' surgeon testifying that two soldiers were consequently severely injured; Porteous surmises that the crowd want to try to resuscitate Wilson, or they fear he is dead and want to prevent the body being anatomized. Porteous of course maintains he threatened the crowd only by word and gesture, not with actual violence—he was not the one who brought about the carnage: some witnesses saw the action in this light. The prosecution argues he was heard to shout 'level your pieces and be damned' as the guards fired into the air, meaning to direct them to fire into the crowd.

As well as his 'innocent of the facts' defence, Porteous makes use of an 'innocence of the action' defence: thus maintaining the equivalent of 'I did not do it, but if I did I went too far in obeying orders'. The prosecution are scathing about the inconsistency. The key legal point which the defence want to address is whether the alleged shooting was done when he was *versans in licito* (acting within his licence; engaged in his duty). If so, the defence claim, the punishment should not be capital: 'any excess that for lack of discretion he may have been guilty of cannot be punished poena ordinaria' and recent cases are cited which facilitate taking this pro-enforcer line. This is the point that Scott makes his amateur legal commentator Saddletree reduce to absurdity: Porteous would have been better off if he had fired well before the crowd threw any stones (*HoM*, 47). The defence seem to have made out a strong argument that he was still performing the duty of guarding the scaffold: it had been impressed on Porteous that Wilson was a dangerous criminal who must be properly finished off, and supporters cutting down an apparently dead victim achieved resuscitation often enough for it to be a realistic fear. The prosecution's main rebuttal is that the execution was effectively over before the firing, thus Porteous had no further business there.

The judges must have accepted that the prosecution's interpretation achieved the separation of Porteous's act from any connection with his orders; and, at the same time of course, blamed him alone as an individual monster. Only the briefest of references is made to the defence suggestion that Porteous had authorization to fire: that if there was any such order it would have been illegal, and he would have been 'not at all bound to follow such illegal orders'.

The prosecution point is that the law is best protected by punishing Porteous 'in the most severe manner', 'for an example to others whom it may be necessary for the good of the community to trust'. The interesting thing here is how this has left the integrity and judgment of the city authorities unchallenged, whom for the good of *the law* it was necessary for *the community* to trust.

When Porteous was awarded a respite under the royal prerogative, vast numbers of the local populace felt it to be an offence against justice, and felt justified in carrying out the death sentence themselves. The *Caledonian Mercury* of 23 September 1736 reports the crowds who abduct Porteous chanting to a drum: 'Here! All those who dare avenge innocent blood!'[11] To the authorities, their storming of the Tolbooth was the offence against justice. The *Mercury* expresses that outrage: 'Tuesday night last, a most outrageous and violent insult to the laws and constitution of the nation was made in this city, that perhaps ever happened in any civilised country'.

But that respite, so inexplicable to the people, happens because the two faces of public order cannot be reconciled here. Even in the Pursuer's opening statement it is apparent: the King's Advocate introduces Porteous to the court as 'one of the commanders of the City Guard intended to preserve the peace of the city, and to protect the inhabitants thereof from all violence', employed on that day to prevent danger to the people assembled.[12] This is a form of words which evades the evidence that he was also

---

[11] Appended to Preface in Kirkpatrick, n. 6 above, xxvi.
[12] 'Authentic Extract' in Kirkpatrick, n. 6 above, 78.

employed to protect the city's and state's interests against the violence of the people. Protecting one peace entails violence which breaks the other peace. The conviction ignored the fact that there is an aporia here with Westminster on one side and Edinburgh on the other. As the compiler of the 1818 documents attests, the trial was swiftly followed by an inquiry in the House of Lords on the 'legality and justice' of the sentence.[13] A motion that it was 'erroneous' was suggested, but the legality was accepted and the motion dropped. In the award of respite the Westminster government edges towards imposing their reading, attuned to the defence counsel's warning that: 'the execution of duty will become a very ticklish point . . . few folk will be fond of it if they can possibly live without it . . . [it will] very much discourage any persons from offering their service either to the crown or commonwealth'.

The 1818 compiler informs readers that after the storming of the Tolbooth, the Court of St James reacted by introducing into Parliament a fierce bill designed among other things to punish the city as a whole, and the Lord Provost individually, for failing to prevent the riot and lynching. Its provisions created much offence in Scotland. There have been suggestions that Scott himself was involved in the writing of the preface to this collection.

These contemporary extracts from populist comment, news account and trial record, make it clear that there is a surface agreement between their separate convictions which might endorse the simple view that Porteous was solely to blame. The practice of drawing out the presence of a narrative 'spin' is informed by Scott's emplotment: reading *The Heart of Midlothian* changes the way one reads these historical texts.

In his own novelistic account, Scott draws on and combines such historical texts and incidents in a way that relives the relation between them. Hazlitt's observation comes to mind: 'With reverence be it spoken, he is like the man who having to imitate the squeaking of a pig upon the stage, brought the animal under his coat with him'.[14]

What characterizes the account of the gallows-disturbance in Chapter Three of the novel is its air of not appropriating a

---

[13] Preface in Kirkpatrick, n. 6 above, xxx.

[14] Hazlitt, Extract from 'The Spirit of the Age' in *The New Monthly Magazine*, 1825; reprinted in J. O. Hayden, *Scott: The Critical Heritage* (London, 1970), 87.

perspective on the matter. Everything that is said of Porteous comes as if through a witness's account rather than by imaginative recreation. The narrator disclaims relationship, so that the description of the events of the Wilson execution is to be seen as others' telling, hence such formulations as: Porteous' threats 'were afterwards remembered to his disadvantage'; his jealousy and rage were 'visible to all who saw him on the fatal morning' (*HoM*, 35–9).

The narrator's distance is not completely maintained, since he intrudes a note of scepticism on the story that had most definitively cast Porteous as the very embodiment of state repression: he is said to have personally crushed Wilson's wrists into small manacles; has it not been 'exaggerated by the general prejudice entertained against his memory' (asks the narrator)? The note of responsible caution is a mine: it explodes under the rest of the narrative that previously said 'authentic' and casts up the possibility of partiality in the popular view. Scott is displaying that one should tread carefully with the textuality of historical evidence ('against his *memory*'). Yet the concern to do that makes a contradictory claim that this narrator is relatively trustworthy: because his trust is only given advisedly. Scott seems concerned to communicate that one of the reasons that 'the odium of the whole day's transactions' attaches to Porteous 'and him alone' is the fact that he was the individual who last confronted and contained the irrepressible Wilson: he is his Other, the one associated in the popular mind with extinguishing Wilson's inspiring resistance. Scott's account shows how Wilson was lionized, and how Porteous was proportionately demonized.

The narrator next deals with the matter of the trial, and the ordering of the narration is significant: what he gives first is a firm unshaded account that has a single decided viewpoint:

Captain Porteous *was wrought*, by this *appearance* of insurrection against his authority, into a rage so headlong as made him *forget*, that, the sentence having been *fully executed*, it was his duty not to engage in hostilities with the *misguided* multitude . . .

He commanded the party to give fire, and as several eye-witnesses *concurred* in swearing, he set them the example, by discharging his piece, and shooting a man dead on the spot.

Apparently . . . [he] had begun to doubt the propriety of *his own conduct*, and the reception he met with from the magistrates was such as to make him still more anxious to *gloss it over*. He denied that he had given orders to fire . . . (emphasis added).

The narrator makes it clear what is to be believed. The implication is: *that* was what he did, followed by *this* is only what he claimed. This, as we know from thinking about the trial transcript, is the prosecution's version. Its having priority of place enacts the inviolable nature of the legal verdict: it is now *res judicata*. The defence arguments are held back by Scott because they would theoretically be considered dead and discredited. It is only afterwards that the narrator observes that there was contradictory evidence in the trial which put some/most of the blame elsewhere: the jury are said to have had a 'difficult duty of balancing the positive evidence of many persons . . . with the negative testimony of others', with 'some describing as a formidable riot, what others represented as a trifling disturbance', 'according to their feelings, their predilections, and their opportunities for observation'.[15] This is a mine under the certainty of convictions, a reminder of the textuality of perception.

The arrangement is strange in a literary context, giving the answer before the question, verdict before trial. The effect it creates for the reader is the pattern of a prejudiced trial. We are like a jury who accept the defendant is guilty before we hear his point of view. This shaping connects with the assertion that even before the hanging and the violence, all the positive sentiment for Wilson 'excited a proportionate degree of indignation against Porteous; against whom, as strict, and even violent in the discharge of his unpopular office, the common people had some real and many imagined causes of complaint'. As the narrator says, 'The trial took place before men's tempers had time to cool' (*HoM*, 38).

A look back at the trial documents can bring out two points of comparison to this suggestion of Scott's: Porteous's defence counsel refers to this prejudice, in what must count as one of the earliest complaints against 'trial by the media'. In the Information for the pannel (the defendant is known as the 'pannel' in the Scottish court; the 'information' is his testimony), the defence claims that

---

[15] The trial transcript shows there were forty-four deponents called, very few of whom gave identical evidence. It would have been a complex matter to assess exactly what the consensus was.

the *Caledonian Mercury*'s reporting of the incident had created bias. It had been reported 'as an instance of premeditation and felony forethought' that Porteous had ordered the guards to load with ball and slugshot—but the defence maintain that it was clear that he had received orders to do so and to be prepared to fire them.

But the prejudices against the pannel being once artfully rooted, it was

an easy matter to catch the giddy mob, who are not able to look back and discern the true springs and causes of things: for such is the nature of human passions, that if they are once artfully moved, they will be apt to misguide the understandings, even of persons of observation . . .[16]

It is of course impossible to discover how accurate the evidence was. The following selected detail from a witness's deposition presents a soft target for a claim of distortion: one Murray claims to have heard the defendant say 'Damn them for bougars; why did they not fire even forward and clean the street?' It is appended that he had been 'dull of hearing seven years' and was about twenty yards from the defendant. But there is no reservation about his eyesight and, like many others, he claims to have seen the pannel take a gun off another and fire into the crowd. Quantitatively, there is more that is incriminating than exculpatory.[17]

In his account of the verdict, Scott's narrator does not question whether Porteous was innocent or guilty of the facts, only commenting that 'the verdict of the jury sufficiently shows how the evidence preponderated in their minds' (*HoM*, 39). He also informs the reader that the jury had nevertheless accepted the defence claim that 'the prisoner and his guard had been wounded and beaten, by stones thrown at them by the multitude'. Scott gives nothing on whether this was legally significant, though clearly it was, as the strongest of Porteous's defences rested on his act being to protect the completion of the execution: in the ringing finality of the pronouncement of the death sentence at the end of the chapter, it is as if it had no significance at all. By removing this from the novel's account of the trial, Scott recreates the trial's

---

[16] Kirkpatrick, n. 6 above, 124.
[17] Kirkpatrick, n. 6 above, 153–200.

simple closure, the conviction that this was an entirely straightforward punishment of an individual's violent aberration; the
closure that accorded with the victims' (or their survivors') sense
of justice's priorities.

The process of reading thus recreates that surprise the populace
felt when the Queen stayed the execution, because it comes to
both citizen and reader as a disruption of conviction. On receiving
the news, the crowd utters a 'roar of indignation and disappointed
revenge, similar to that of a tiger from whom his meal has been
rent by his keeper when he was just about to devour it' (*HoM*,
42). The metaphor here introduces the manipulation of mass opinion by two conflicting political-legal authorities, in the Court of St
James's snatching back what the Court of Judiciary threw to
them.

Significantly, it is only now that the substance of the defence
arguments is narrated, representing the effect of the news on the
crowd's memory: it resurrects the version which is technically
discarded. The crowd recalls the pannel's Information:

he had been described by his counsel as the person on whom the magistrates chiefly relied in all emergencies of uncommon difficulty. It was
argued too that his conduct . . . was capable of being attributed to an
imprudent excess of zeal in the execution of his duty. (*HoM*, 41)

Scott makes them a crowd politically aware of the fine point here:

they were conscious . . . that they were no favourites with the rulers of the
period, and that if Captain Porteous's violence was not altogether regarded
as good service, it might certainly be thought, that to visit it with a capital
punishment would render it both delicate and dangerous for future officers, in the same circumstances, to act with effect in repressing tumults.

This is the policy consideration which makes 'the cabinet of St.
James's' see the situation differently from the crowd.

It might be there supposed that upon the *whole matter*, Captain Porteous
was in the exercise of a trust delegated to him by the lawful civil authority
. . . his conduct could be fairly imputed to no other motive than self-
defence in the discharge of his duty. (*HoM*, 41)

Their scepticism and disillusion is apparent here. Because of the
mystique surrounding *res judicata*, the crowd can see this only as
a disruption of truth and an offence against the course of Scottish
justice, particularly unwelcome when emanating from England.

Conversely, the logic behind the government's response is brought out by the narrator detailing the effect of the Porteous verdict on the next soldier called upon to manage public order. He describes Colonel Moyle's reluctance to obey the Provost's command to put down the Tolbooth insurrection because it comes only by word of mouth, having 'the fate of Porteous before his eyes as an example of the severe construction put by a jury on the proceedings of military men acting on their own responsibility' (*HoM*, 62). 'The magistrates, after vain attempts to make themselves heard and obeyed, possessing no means of enforcing their authority, were constrained to abandon the field to the rioters' (*HoM*, 64). The irony for the city authorities is obvious: because they have denied their agency in the first disorder, they find themselves without a means of intervention in the next, and are for that punished by the Westminster government. The subtly ordered dialogic narration has recreated the relation between the different perspectives in order to shed light on the process of their collision.

The account of the crowd's consequent storming of the prison continues to recreate the subjectivity of their voice, which is remarkable in a period where there was particularly strong state anxiety about public disorder. The writing brings out that this is a dialogue between people and state. The epigraph from *The Merchant of Venice*: 'The evil you teach us, we will execute; and it shall go hard but we will better the instruction' (*HoM*, 65) registers the idea that this is a sardonic engagement with the state's discourse of power and punishment. 'Take your own tale home', Robertson says to Porteous (*HoM*, 70). The author's sensitivity to the signification of the gallows informs his shaping of this lynching as the addressees' reply: 'Would ye execute an act of justice as if it were a crime and a cruelty? this sacrifice will lose half its savour if we do not offer it at the very horns of the altar. We will have him die where a murderer should die, on the common gibbet'—thus Robertson's rebuke to an accomplice about to wreak *meaningless* violence on Porteous.

Scott has drawn on contemporary accounts to represent how the popular view of Porteous was constructed: but in these contextualizing descriptions there is no authorial statement that the crowd were wrong to think he was 'the source and origin of their injuries'. However, the plotting of the novel confutes that particular misprision and interrogates other points where the interrelation of the system of power and its agents confuses responsibility.

The repeating pattern of the narrative structure suggests that Scott is implicating another factor for the way authority reacts to the gallows-crowd's minor revolt. Looking at the functions performed in the narrative by the legal hierarchy, it is interesting that Scott the lawyer, far from emplotting law's retainers as being motivated by a desire to achieve justice, conceives each one's objective as only to perform a narrow aspect of government, each one treating whatever constitutes a challenge to that as their antagonist. Schematically it is very bleak: a narrow-minded hierarchy that at every level is ruthless in its repression of the other. It deconstructs the idea of keeping good order as being good government. Lukacs's sense of the novelistic project as 'a degraded search' for 'authentic values in a world itself degraded' seems an appropriate assessment of such a structure.[18]

For example, the characters of those who administer law and order in the city are differentiated, but their drives are the same. Scott's representative anonymous magistrate appears defensive and embattled; whereas Sharpitlaw the procurator fiscal's ongoing fight with the criminal element is more aggressive and egotistical, but both desire only short-term efficiency. Their reliance on Porteous is the clearest indication of their priorities: he was 'a gude servant o' the town . . . though he was an ower free-living man'. The clerk regrets his loss: he 'never had ony fears, or scruples, or doubts, or conscience about ony thing your honours bade him' (*HoM*, 159). In their account of the world, the troublesome scruples of 'your decent sort of men' would stand as their negative opposer.

When the novel's representative judge forgoes a valid opportunity to use his discretion to interpret the Scottish penal statute against child-murder narrowly to avoid convicting an innocent woman, it is the certain rule of law he is upholding. Like the city authorities, he too identifies as the opposer a voicing of support for the other against the law's reading: he is critical of the defending counsel's attempt to

---

[18] Lucien Goldman's paraphrase in his introduction to 'Problems of a Sociology of the Novel' in T. Eagleton and D. Milne (eds.), *Marxist Literary Theory* (Oxford, 1996), 205.

plead his client's case in the teeth of the law . . . He would not follow the prisoner's counsel through the impeachment he had brought against the statute of King William and Queen Mary. He and the jury were sworn to judge according to the laws as they stood . . . when [this law] was found too severe for its purpose, it would doubtless be altered by the wisdom of the legislature (*HoM*, 234).

Scott historicizes this confidence in the editorial notes prepared for the 1830 edition: the 1690 law was not formally altered until 1803, and it had become common practice to circumvent it by extrajudicial, behind-the-scenes evasions. In Scotland the accused woman frequently requested, and was almost always granted, a pre-trial banishment (*HoM*, 528). The counsel has argued that the prosecution should have to prove the occurrence of a live birth before raising the presumption that the defendant has killed her missing child (without improperly relying on her extrajudicial self-incrimination): 'If any of the assize . . . should be of the opinion that this was dealing rather narrowly with the statute, they ought to consider that it was in its nature highly penal, and entitled to no favourable construction' (*HoM*, 233). This was Blackstone's approach to the English statute.[19] Bentham's discussion of Blackstone's third rule of statutory interpretation also offers a succinct guide: 'in the doubt the safest decision was that which was on the mildest side'.[20]

Contemporary theoretical discourse on the development of the law allowed, indeed required, a more active contribution from the judge. This judge seems caught between the demands of the theory and the rhetoric of government. Bakhtin's vocabulary of cultural interaction is helpful in describing his difficulty. Bakhtin's point is that an utterance is both its linguistic matter and a unique context, and so is non-reiterative; even if one repeats a statement exactly, it is actually the second time a different, historically unique utterance—its new context alters its meaning. The judge is mistaken in relying on the words of the statute themselves to reproduce the state's idea of justice (leaving

---

[19] It is 'usual to require presumptive evidence that the child was born alive before the other constrained presumption . . . is admitted to convict the prisoner.' Quoted by R. W. Malcolmson, 'Infanticide in The Eighteenth Century' in J. S. Cockburn (ed.), *Crime in England 1550–1800* (London, 1977), 197.

[20] Jeremy Bentham, *A Comment on the Commentaries and a Fragment on Government* (J. H. Burns and H. L. A. Hart (eds.), London, 1977).

aside for now the question of severity); he has to work with Effie's situation and the words of the statute, not treat its meaning as something already completed. He inevitably makes a new text: his thought of neutrally restating the statute is mistaken, as he simultaneously enacts certain values that are within this situation but outside the language. Bakhtin indicates how each individual is answerable for 'the response generated from the unique place I have in existence': so not only 'The Law' but also the judge is responsible for the judgment.[21]

The name Scott gives to the advocate engaged on Effie's behalf is appropriate for this trial: 'Nichil Novit', with its echo of the 'nihil novit' entry in Scottish trial depositions when a proposed witness has not contributed, wryly suggests this judgment has nothing new to offer.[22]

I would suggest that all the figures in the hierarchy have their own narrative. However, it is clear that they are all logically cognate. These centripetal voices speak with fragments of authoritative discourse, not using their own integrity. Though there are some caricatured moments, the narration does not generally objectify the law's retainers in showing this, but rather represents the risk of reification that their involvement with the rhetoric of power subjects them to: there is a conflict between the dialogic self (fluid, open to the world) and the state's administrative requirements in all these characters, in which the strongest pressure is to capitulate to their function, outlawing polyphony, appreciation of difference.[23] There are many examples: when Sharpitlaw makes a sympathetic-sounding remark to Effie, it is described as being

---

[21] Discussed in Holquist, *Dialogism*, n. 4 above, 59–63.

[22] It occurs, for instance, in the depositions from the Porteous trial. I think this is more pointed than the suggestion attributed to David Marshall in the editorial note in the World's Classics edition, n. 1 above, 550.

[23] Holquist discusses Bakhtin's account of the 'intimate connection between the project of language and the project of selfhood': 'The word Bakhtin uses for "project", (*zadanie*), is another twist on the central distinction between something that is "given" (*dan*) and something that presents itself in the nature of a task, as something that must be "conceived" (*zadan*). The situatedness of the self is a multiple phenomenon: it has been given the task of not being merely given. It must stand out in existence because it is dominated by a "drive to meaning", where meaning is understood as something still in the process of creation, something still bending toward the future as opposed to that which is already completed': Holquist, *Dialogism*, n. 4 above, 23.

dictated partly by natural feeling, of which even he could not divest himself, though accustomed to practise on the passions of others, and keep a most heedful guard over his own, and partly by his wish to introduce the sort of conversation which might best serve his immediate purpose (*HoM*, 169).

On this occasion, which clearly shows the conflict dialogically, the man is ashamed of the functionary:

'You shall see your sister', he began, 'if you'll tell me'—then interrupting himself, he added, in a more hurried tone,—'no d–n it, you shall see your sister whether you tell me anything or no' (*HoM*, 170).

The scenes of the city authorities mulling over their tactics after the killing of Porteous display the distorting and narrowing of judgment created when the self offers too little resistance to the aggressive importunities of the ideology of control. It is naked process without principle: the anxiety that there is yet 'naebody sae muckle as to be put into the Tolbooth *about it*' neglects the convention that guilt generally should precede punishment (emphasis added). Sharpitlaw thinks it would have a 'gude active look' to 'clap into the prison a few blackguards upon suspicion'; 'if ye thought it no strictly just ye could just be easier wi' them the neist time'. The Habeas Corpus-type procedure that prevents this is introduced as only a frustrating inconvenience: the town clerk has to remind his superiors 'they'll run their letters, and be adrift again, before ye ken where ye are' (*HoM*, 160). This scene is of course in a long tradition of policing satire; but in contrast to the Shakespearean type of well-meaning fool inadvertently obstructing then stumbling into justice, they are of the type who are fools because of the way they have naturalized cynicism, advertently obstructing justice and their own humanity. In Bakhtin's terminology, they have a discussion but in distorted monologic voices, unchallenged by any other's dialogic view. It is this dangerous tendency that Scott identifies as characterizing the relationship with Porteous: 'he never had ony fears or scruples, or doubts, or conscience about ony thing your honours bade him'.

However, the reader is put in a position to understand the orientation of their voices. Sharpitlaw gives a glimpse of the sleazy, threatening world that they are responding to: 'Your decent sort of men . . . dinna like to be out at irregular hours, and in a dark cauld night, and they like a clout ower the croun far waur'; this job is far more intractable than sorting out 'a wee bit skulduddery for the benefit of the Kirk-treasurer' (*HoM*, 158).

The comic treatment of the image of the legal counsel is equally bleak. The name of Saddletree's favourite authority, 'Crossmyloof' (dialect: cross-my-palm) reminds us that getting remuneration is the other synecdoche for the legal profession. Each lawyer is a site where the self interacts with the law, contributing a ratio of responsibility and authority to mediate between the received letter and the present need: but here, self-interest wins the contest.

The ratio is unbalanced the other way in Saddletree, though he is a court-groupie rather than a lawyer: Scott presents his unquestioning formalism as an area of concern. Saddletree believes that law has an absolute answer independent of moral dilemmas and political and material conditions. This is a mindset signified by his attempt to disengage himself from his own material base, though his name suggests he is rooted in it; he is contemptuous of his own saddler's trade of 'broggin and elshin through bend-leather', since men like Duncan Forbes[24] 'without muckle greater parts' get to be King's Advocates (*HoM*, 50).

It is his 'supreme deference for all constituted authorities' (*HoM*, 122), and his delight in his power of impressing by exposition of the incontrovertible 'science of jurisprudence' (*HoM*, 55), which make him a ridiculous figure. Arguably, though, he is most satirized because he is an 'amateur of the law' and so unable to inflect the discourse like a professional: yet the author might tactfully insinuate under this cover a mockery of all unthinking formalism, and any failure to challenge law's excesses. 'It's a beautiful point of presumptive murder' (*HoM*, 53), he comments blandly when Effie (his own servant) is charged with child-murder; and during her trial it is his comment on an emotional character-witness (his wife) that provides the *reductio ad absurdum* of the court's inability to look beyond the mechanics of permitted evidence and respond to the indications of innocence in the subjective life before them: 'What signified his bringing a woman here to snotter and snivel and bather their Lordships?' (*HoM*, 227).

---

[24] His Majesty's Advocate in the trial of Porteous.

David Marshall's account accepts him as a trustworthy 'legal expositor', through whom Scott manages to communicate 'not only a sound but admirably succinct account of the law'.[25] Marshall's Saddletree is still cited uncritically in footnotes, yet it is more characterization than exegesis. He is aping the certainties of a particular kind of lawyer: 'How could ye dispute what's plain law, man?' (*HoM*, 122).

Hence in examining the positions taken up by all these members of the legal hierarchy, from the judge to the lay enthusiast, this novel displays a recurrent imbalance in their relation to the law; they rarely bring their humanity into the calculation, or recognize their individual responsibility and so participate in the law's distortion. It is the device of putting a *sceptical* outsider into the hierarchy of law enforcement which most clearly enables a challenge to its own fashion of metanarrative. This is how the character Ratcliffe is deployed.

The probable provenance of the character is revealing: David Hume's *Commentaries* uses the case of one James Ratcliffe, alias Walker, as example of non-violent prison-breaking: he was charged with 'making his escape out of the Tolbooth of Edinburgh, without lawful discharge or liberation'. This character had, as 'seems tacitly admitted in the debate', 'left the gaol when thrown open by the Porteous mob'.[26] Scott makes his fictional Ratcliffe choose to remain in the Tolbooth as Porteous is dragged out. Scott does not suggest his character had any historical existence, but he makes him an experienced escapee like the Ratcliffe Hume mentions, then constructs for him the twist that his familiarity with prisons has metamorphosed into a sense of belonging and he wants an official post in one. His being taken into employment sets up a parallel to the poacher/gamekeeper career of Porteous, and enables Scott to interrogate the system which makes use of such characters. They do not so much cross a boundary as inhabit a tangled intersection.

Ratcliffe's worth as a retainer of the law in the service of the magistrates is his criminal connections and experience:

[25] David Marshall, *Sir Walter Scott and Scott's Law* (Edinburgh, 1932), 126, 130.

[26] David Hume, *Commentaries on the Law of Scotland Respecting Crimes* (Edinburgh, 1797), 404.

It is just sic as Ratcliffe that the town needs in my department; and if sae be that he's disposed to turn his knowledge to the city service, ye'll no find a better man . . . Your decent sort of men . . . can do nae gude ava.

Their delicacy of body and mind hinders them.

They are feared for this, and they are scrupulous about that, and they are na free to tell a lie, though it may be for the benefit of the city. (Sharpitlaw, *HoM*, 158)

The city authorities have no scruples about repeating the mistake they made with Porteous; moreover, their language is interesting for its suppression of any hint of moral involvement in that, or acknowledgement of a causal link between their policy and the public confrontations: 'this scrape of Porteous's'; 'this mischance for the city'; 'a confused mistake': thus Porteous's violence, the trial, the pardon, the lynching are all vaguely conflated, with their own role absent.

Ratcliffe is hired because they anticipate he will be as unscrupulously useful as Porteous. But whereas the Captain never challenged orders, Ratcliffe unexpectedly remains a 'recusant', critical of their investigative methods. He finds it ironic that the 'gude behaviour' which is required of him involves betraying and delivering up whoever Sharpitlaw requires; 'a queer way of beginning the trade of honesty' (*HoM*, 162). He is 'not free' to 'sift' Effie to get information on Robertson: 'It gangs against my conscience.' It seems he is unhappy with the idea of exploiting her vulnerable state and increasing her unhappiness. Ratcliffe's different orientation enables the novel to introduce a non-objectifying view of the oppositional world of law's Other. This cannot be by his figuring the repression of inconvenient communities and the vulnerability of the poor, as he is far from vulnerable, and conceived as strong enough to manipulate the authorities. But he *represents* them almost like a self-appointed delegate, in the sense of being aware of their vulnerability and trying to ensure it is not ill-used. His counter-status is epitomized by the special pass which it is in his power to give: it gives the holder patriarchal protection from being molested by any outlaw: 'Deil ane o' them will touch an acquaintance o' Daddie Ratton's'. It parodies the role patronage plays in the granting of a royal pardon.

Ratcliffe can be seen as the reverse of that problematic functionary who capitulates entirely to law and order. However,

Scott's plotting equally problematizes the radical liberal respons-
iveness of Ratcliffe. There is a point a third of the way through the
book where there is a possibility of a coherent judicial outcome in
the two legal tangles: Sharpitlaw gets information that Robertson
is to meet Effie's sister Jeanie at Muschat's Cairn, the atmospheric
site of a notorious wife-murder; the arrest of Robertson would
give closure to the Porteous affair, and his appearance could lead
to revelations of Effie's innocence. Scott's emplotment prevents it
through Ratcliffe's sympathetic interference on Robertson's
behalf: he aligns himself with the community he is expected to
control.

The scene is a gothic farce: Robertson is ineptly pursued over a
moonlit moor as Madge Wildfire shouts snatches of romantic
ballads to warn and save him; it turns into nightmare for the
entirely blameless Jeanie, as it is she who is seized and molested at
this place that signifies the violent abuse of women (*HoM*, 172–7).
Thus the injudicious liberal subversion of the law which Ratcliffe
represents here eventually impacts on the innocent. Where much
of Scott's representation of the people within the system has
exposed a capitulation to order and form, the deployment of
Ratcliffe suggests that the rebalancing of an over-mechanistic use
of law is not a straightforward matter.

The magistrate Middleburgh, as his name suggests, exists to
signify a more ideal way to profess the law: to attempt to mediate
between legal and popular discourse, the needs of system and
those of the individual. He is the only authority figure who sees
his role as being to relate to law's subjects rather than to oppose:
in seeking to persuade the politically-hostile Deans of the necessity
of Jeanie testifying in Effie's trial, he is working to ensure that
those brought before the law are not shut out by official rituals.
He acknowledges that the rituals do not correspond with the individual's subjective needs, but, as he says to Deans, 'you must use
human means'. He is one minor figure in the middle, whose
efforts are hampered by things beyond his control.

Scott does not follow his *legal* analysis to a conclusion; the
narrative is resolved with the pardon for Effie and the providential
manner in which Robertson's crimes catch up with him. J. P.
Farrell argues that Jeanie's procuring the pardon 'can rehabilitate
the law because she knows the spiritual order that all law must
rest on and the fraught human condition that ineluctably taxes the

law's power of generalisation', but I think this and Robertson's nemesis come across as extrajudicial devices rather than conservative recuperations of the law.[27] Scott may have conceived the writing of the scene where Queen Caroline grants Effie's pardon as an opportunity to flatter the current monarch, as John Sutherland in his biography of Scott suggests.[28] However, Scott's fiction can only effect a rehabilitation of the political relationship between the monarch and such fortunate subjects with access to the chain of patronage; hence the Arcadian aura of unreality in the rest of the novel. The memory of the struggles of other 'melancholy inmates' of the Tolbooth are not obliterated: it is a generic romance closure, leaving the law itself in the midst of its difficulties.

The novel's fundamental characteristic is its resistance to the coercion of subjective lives into objective legal categories; though it is rooted in Scottish/English history of the eighteenth and nineteenth centuries, it is striking how its complex, professional advocate's analysis of the relations between subject and state, Court and Parliament, agent and law, anticipates this problematic of jurisprudence in postmodernity.

The postmodern judge is implicated, he stands in proximity to the litigant who comes before the law and hears his speech or request. Justice returns to ethics when it recognizes the embedded voice of the litigant, when it gives the other in her concrete materiality a locus standi or place of enunciation. The law is necessarily committed to the form of universality and abstract equality; but a just decision must also respect the requests of the contingent, incarnate and concrete other, it must pass through the ethics of alterity in order to respond to its own embeddedness in justice.[29]

[27] J. P. Farrell, *Revolution as Tragedy: The Dilemma of the Moderate from Scott to Arnold* (Ithaca, 1980), 112.
[28] John Sutherland, *The Life of Walter Scott* (Oxford,1995), 209.
[29] C. Douzinas *et al.*, n. 2 above, 24.

THE BIBLE, LAW AND LIBERATION: TOWARDS A POLITICO-LEGAL HERMENEUTICS OF THE SERMON ON THE MOUNT

Fulfilment requires transformation, and transformation entails a certain excess.[1]

*Adam Gearey**

It is only with a proper consideration of the Bible that law and literature can achieve its promised radical insights into the law. Given the confines of this paper, the focus will be on an episode from the New Testament, the Sermon on the Mount in Matthew's Gospel. It will be argued that this is the key passage for a realization of the critical and counter-hegemonic energies of the Bible.

Why a literary reading of the Bible? This assumes, already, a perspective outside faith; but this should be seen not so much as a rejection, but a dialogue. The usefulness of the literary is that it allows the reader to take the position of an interpreter neither completely within nor outside the Christian tradition. It allows a reading that attempts to explain both why the Bible remains a profoundly provocative text, while resisting the dogmatic restraints which come from being wholly within a Christian theological perspective.

This paper hopes to advance an argument that brings together

* This paper is for Robert Cartledge.
[1] Frank Kermode in Robert Alter and Frank Kermode (eds.), *The Literary Guide to the Bible* (London, 1987), 388.

hermeneutics and a politics of strong readings.[2] A strong reading exploits the allegorical nature of a text. The allegorical nature of a text is itself related to the inherently provocative, scandalous, and ambiguous nature of writing. Texts will tend to be allegorized because they demand interpretation, but never entirely mandate the terms of their interpretation: different readers at different times discover new and vital interpretations. The Bible is the allegorical text of the Western tradition. Despite the attempts to present it as a repository of one essential meaning, it tends to generate positions and counter-positions. It will be the contention of this paper that a critical legal theory, an elaboration of a Law, above the law, can be discovered in the text of the Bible. This paper will be a reading of the Sermon as a political allegory, a way of reading that is provoked by the very nature of the narrative of the Law. The interpreter is forced to interpret the Law in a world open to the call of justice whose irreducibility matches the inscrutable demand of the text: 'do something with this book!'

How will law be understood? The focus of this paper will be on Christ's announcement of the New Law, which replaces or supplements the Old Law of Moses. It might be objected that any concern with biblical Law is irrelevant to contemporary jurisprudential concerns. What will be argued, however, is that there is in the very structure of the New Law, an idea of a critical approach to law, a critique that draws on a sense of justice, of higher Law, that is of great relevance to the pressing need to think a justice beyond the positive law.[3]

Already the axe is at the root of the tree.

---

[2] The term is drawn from Harold Bloom's *The Anxiety of Influence* (London, 1975). Strength here is also understood as the power to contend with Oedipal myths and the ossified meanings of the tradition. It also signifies what is to come; Nietzschean overtones not developed by Bloom but haunting the margins of this piece.

[3] The elaboration of this sense of justice owes a great deal to Jacques Derrida and Emmanuel Levinas. In Derrida's reading of Levinas, the law is founded on the absolute demand of a foundation that is very different from the Greek rooting of ethics in the good life whose ends can be determined by reason. Levinas's ethics of alterity make for a different approach to the determination of law and justice in the Western tradition. Levinas provides an understanding of an 'infinite right' whose 'basis' is 'the other'. See Jacques Derrida, 'The Force of Law: The Mystical Foundations of Authority' (1990) *Cardozo Law Review* 11, 958. The basic terms of this problematic relationship are not 'calculated proportion, equitable distribution or distributive justice but rather absolute dissymmetry', an ethics or a law above the law. This is what Derrida terms the 'possibility of justice'. Thinking this

Allegory, 'Postmodernism', and Law and Literature Scholarship

Despite the undeniable centrality of the Bible for the European literary traditions and its organization around narratives of the giving of the Law,[4] the Bible and the problem of allegory have not been a central concern for scholars of law and literature. This could be related to a location of the present scholarship within a certain critical paradigm. Allegory invites the spectre of indeterminacy. For those readings that want to limit the meanings of the text as a necessity for any normative literary ethic,[5] the indeterminate is the ruination of the entire project. As has been argued:

justice means engaging with the determinations of justice in the Western tradition. It means re-reading the canonical texts of the tradition. See *Glas* (University of Nebraska Press, 1986), where Derrida criticizes the Hegelian reading of the Sermon on the Mount. The notion that lies behind the statement that the Law is Love would base justice on a very different foundation. It would rupture the economy of equivalence so that justice would no longer be based on retribution. However, this new notion of justice seems to reinvent the notion of an economy at a different level: 'in fact the simple awareness of doing good is already an inner applause and a kind of economic recompense' (59). The rupture of the economy of justice as exchange seems to be repaired at a higher level in the promise of *Parousia*, of the ultimate judgment 'the promise of a relief that will come to compensate this dissymmetry'. The task is to open this overcoming to a sense of excessive justice without reproducing the negative sense in which it simply repeats the economy of the same.

    [4] One of the great studies of law and narrative in the Bible is Northrop Frye's *The Great Code* (London, 1982). Frye argues that law is central to a dialectical development of biblical narrative. Law features as one of the 'phases of revelation' within an overall schema: 'I see a sequence of seven main phases: creation, revolution or exodus (Israel in Egypt), law, wisdom, prophecy, gospel and apocalypse. Five of these phases have their centre of gravity in The Old Testament and two in the New. Each phase is not an improvement on its predecessor but a wider perspective on it' (106). For further consideration of the intimate link between narrative and law in the Bible, see Bernard S. Jackson, 'The Literary Presentation of Multiculturalism in Early Biblical Law' (1995) 25 *The International Journal for the Semiotics of Law* 181–206. Jackson argues that a narrative form is central to the role that codes of law played in creating and sustaining a sense of Jewish identity. Although this sense of identity is achieved through an act of discriminating self from other, 'us' from 'them', it is not a rigid or monolithic concept as there are a 'plurality of assumed audiences and forms of engagement' (205).

    [5] Richard Weisberg has seen his project in terms of a critique of the legal proclivity to overanalyse, to separate words and the world. A moral reconnection is to be found in the classic literary texts that have offered representations of the law and its failings. Poethics is a critical reading method that attempts to read literary materials as having an inherent ethical force. This approach brings to the law a criterion for 'justice' that is derived from the idea of the well-constructed literary expression: in a 'just' statement of law, form, and content and the 'craftsmanship' of the judgment will bear out its essential truth. Literature can assist the lawyer to

The difficulty with the [new] theology of revelation, as with the 'allegorical interpretation' common among the early Church Fathers, is that secular reason cannot tell the interpreter how far and in what direction to search for a deeper meaning of the words beyond what they say on the surface. Unless such a process is to be wholly indeterminate, there must be some understanding that sets limits on what the text must mean or at least, on what it cannot mean.[6]

Contemporary law and literature scholarship has tended to describe this as the problem of 'postmodernism', which is demonized as a naive celebration of the play of textual meaning, an aberration from a more serious and rigorous approach. It will be argued here, though, that this ignores an entire hermeneutic history, and a problem that will not disappear through simply labelling it 'postmodern'.[7] It could be suggested that postmodernism is an ancient

open to the world of others, an education in empathy and an antidote to the narrowness of a legal training. This project is marked by a pedagogic programme; literature can teach important lessons about justice that are centred on the need to fathom the 'inner world of others', a fathoming that has to be linked to honest self-criticism, an introspection that can be engaged within the reading of literature. See *Poethics and Other Strategies of Law and Literature* (New York, 1984).

For James Boyd White, community is the essential negotiation of competing claims to meaning that are immanent to communication. White argues for an understanding of pluralism, or an other-orientated theory of literary communication. Literature is privileged as it allows an appreciation of the way the world is constructed through words. The notion of 'translation' that White develops as a model for justice has this idea of a community of interpretation at its base. Respect for the other is the central term in the argument that legal language can be improved through developing the insights of literature. Literary language is relational and context-based, predicated on an awareness of the boundaries of any particular discourse and hence must 'acknowledge' the existence of the other. This is contrasted with the 'aggressive' nature of the 'conceptual talk' on which law is based. Legal discourse seeks to map out and define an area through logic and to hold to universal truth claims. See White, *Justice as Translation* (Chicago, 1990).

[6] Thomas Gray, 'The Constitution as Scripture' (1984) 37/1 *Stanford Law Review* 13.

[7] Within legal scholarship, postmodernism can be identified with the work of a number of scholars. Although the term is increasingly problematic, there is a sense in which it describes a movement in thought informed by a critical spirit which rejects the prevalent determinations of law in modernity. In the words of Christopher Stanley, postmodern critique in law 'becomes both an incredulity towards metanarratives and, in the exercise of incredulity, [a placing of] oneself on the "outside" of the established parameters of reason, even if that includes placing morality, rights and justice into a maelstrom of uncertainty so as to re-establish meaning and value': *Law and Urban Excess* (London, 1996), 11. The postmodern direction of the present project could be usefully compared to a genealogical method of research which attempts both the problematization and the reinvention of value mentioned by Stanley. The genealogical method moves away from

condition, and a condition always attached to the interpretation of the Law.

The hermeneutics of the Church Fathers[8] attempted to read the Law in the sacred text as the direct expression of God's message to men. In the Christian tradition this produces a theory of reading which stresses that the scriptures are a record of a historical event. At the same time there is the need to cope with a mystical dimension of the text which does not open to rational or historical readings. The Church Fathers realized that these hidden meanings might destabilize the licensed interpretations of the Church, and always sought to see the figurative level of the text as determined by the literal.[9] Figurative interpretation was,

---

constructions of history which trace a coherent line of development between the present and the past. It is critical of those versions of the past which present the development of institutions as essentially that of the working out of an ideal scheme, where past contradictions are resolved through the inexorable workings of history. Genealogy stresses that history is a series of accidents, that the present is only one of a number of radically contingent possibilities. In contemporary scholarship this genealogical method animates readings of legal history such as Peter Goodrich's *Oedipus Lex* (Berkeley and Los Angeles, 1995). As a study of the institution of the common law, genealogical research is committed to a re-figuring of law's future. Genealogy, 'looks to the plurality of institutional histories and not only to its legitimate forms' (25). It forces a re-thinking of the institution in terms of what it excluded from its history, those failures, or accidents which suggest possible destinies that were not followed. The object of genealogy is fragmentary, it studies the margins of text, the heresies and the mistaken doctrines against which the mainstream defines itself. Within the field of jurisprudence, the essential texts are Costas Douzinas, Ronnie Warrington and Shaun McVeigh, *Postmodern Jurisprudence* (London, 1991) and Costas Douzinas and Ronnie Warrington, *Justice Miscarried* (London, 1994). Although not explicitly genealogical, these texts share a concern with a reinvention of both law and jurisprudence through an opening of law to ethical discourse which positions the other before the self: 'Poststructuralism has pronounced the end of all grand narratives and references, whether of God, truth or form, and has insisted on the death of man as creative author and the centred subject of history and representation. The task of postmodern jurisprudence is to bring out the consequences of this for the legal subject, possessor of abstract rights and duties, and for the legal system of principles, forms and reason. Jurisprudence goes postmodern in order to retain and redraw its old commitment to plural and open forms of reason(s) and communities.' (28)

 [8] It is traditional to divide them into three groups: the Apostolic Fathers, writing in the first and early second centuries; the Apologists of the later second century and the later Alexandrians of *c.* AD 200.

 [9] The writings of the Fathers of the Church show continual lapses into non-licensed methods of interpretation. There is the fear that the allegorizing method of interpretation allows the interpreter too much freedom to make of a text what he will; in other words, allegory dispenses with the sense of the

however, central to the conjunction of the Old and New
Testaments. Jewish scripture had to be read figuratively or allegorically to show that the Bible formed a coherent whole that
related God's involvement with his people. Once this process of
allegorization had been completed, any further development had
to be resisted. As ecclesiastical history can be read as a war
against dissident interpretation and heresy, which eventually split
the Church itself, it could be argued that the struggle to prevent
the text's allegorization was in vain. Approaching biblical
hermeneutics in this way suggests that the early debates about the
Bible's status do not need to be seen as the enshrining of a fixed,
canonical text, but as an anticipation of the post-structuralist
bracketing of a text's meaning.

Thus, an appreciation of the centrality of allegory to scriptural
interpretation is an understanding not only that texts are unstable,
but that interpretation always takes place differently in different
historical contexts. To some extent these concerns animate the
work of Robert Cover, one of the few law and literature scholars
who has written in any detail on the Bible.[10] Cover's insights into
interpretation are based on a consideration of the narratives of

---

law. R. P. C. Hanson, writing of Origen, argues that his allegorical methods of
exegesis 'instead of ensuring that he would in his exegesis maintain close contact
with biblical thought, rendered him deplorably independent of the Bible': *Allegory
and Event* (London, 1959), 76. Indeed Origen's allegorizing is such that 'by
means of it virtually any conclusion could be drawn from the passages of the
Bible'. Also important is Irenaeus, whose work is marked by a similar tendency.
His scriptural hermeneutics constantly fall into allegory. Hanson comments that:
'He denies that prophetic texts can be allegorised to refer to the end of the world
. . . yet, he himself only a few pages previously had interpreted Genesis 27:27 allegorically in an eschatological vein' (114). These problems continue into the
hermeneutic schemas of the later fathers which are normally presented as the resolution of the early textual problems attendant on reading the text of the Law. The
reading models of Aquinas and Augustine may have local differences in ascribing
different levels of interpretation to scripture, but what they have in common is the
distinction between the primary literal truth of the scriptures and a secondary
allegorical level.

[10] The readings which have most explicitly engaged with the Bible in the
American debate draw on Sanford Levinson's essay 'The Constitution in American
Civil Religion' in (1979) *Supreme Court Review* 123. Levinson distinguishes
between two possible ways of interpreting scripture: the 'integrative and the disin-
tegrative'. At root here is a similar distinction between the notion that meanings
are fixed texts and are open to negotiation. Cover's notion of jurisgenesis articulates the tension that exists between these two modes.

Law that run through both Christian and Jewish scriptures.[11] He argues that the sacred text is inherently fissiparous; around its normative pronouncements radically different interpretations proliferate: 'The Torah becomes two, three, many Toroth as there are teachers to teach or students to study.'[12] The important focus of this reading is the concept of jurisgenesis.[13] Jurisgenesis is a way of theorizing the instability of legal meaning within a text. Legal meaning is seen as unificatory only for an 'instant' as differences over the interpretation of central concerns develop within and against this unity. What seems to be implied by jurisgenesis is an attempt to theorize the point of contact between the interpreter, the text and a project in the world. The interpreter reads the texts and interprets them against a horizon of ongoing affairs in a particular time and place. Jurisgenesis could thus address the way that the Christian Bible appropriates Jewish scripture for its own announcement of the law. This insight can be taken further. Although this 'subversive' quality of biblical narrative was deployed by the Christians against the Jews themselves, could their own texts not fall victim to the same process of jurisgenesis? As the consensus which produces any sense of agreement over textual meaning is profoundly unstable, Christian texts are destined to be forever re-interpreted. Rather than following Cover and reading the canon of the Bible as closed, the notion of jurisgenesis could suggest that the text never has a pre-programmed destiny.

The next section of this paper will try and show how this unstable quality of jurisgenesis can be found in the very structure of biblical narrative. Within what is traditionally accepted as the biblical narrative of the Law are counter-narratives, a critical resource which can be used to dramatically refigure the central claims of the New Testament.

---

[11] Robert Cover, 'Nomos and Narrative' (1983) 97/4 *Harvard Law Review* 15. Cover resolutely affirms the narrative base of law in arguing that 'No set of legal institutions or prescriptions exists apart from the narratives that locate it and give it meaning. For every constitution there is an epic, for each decalogue a scripture.' Cover's piece also has a concern with an ethics of the text. His understanding of narrative stresses that all narratives are organized into a moral teleology that attempts to shape the world that it describes. Law is always located in a 'social text', the material world which Cover describes as a nomos.

[12] Cover, n. 11 above, 15–16.   [13] Cover, n. 11 above, 15.

The Narrative of the Law and the Strong Reading

The Christian Bible is a site of contestations over the meaning of the Law; it is a text where readings vie with other readings. It has been organized at a textual level by a figure called typology. Essentially a narrative trope, reading typologically effectively bridges the 'hermeneutic divide'[14] between the Old and New Testaments. Typology allows the scriptures to be organized into a unified whole, a narrative of a 'truth' which works inexorably through history. Events of sacred significance in Jewish scripture are reinterpreted and transfigured into a Christian narrative. The truth of the Jewish scriptures is their fulfilment in the Christian. This is, of course, part of a wider set of claims. Typology operates as an attempt to create a pattern between the scriptures, a pattern which will show that God is working within history, and that the Law is divinely sanctioned. Presently, this typology will be revealed as unstable, incapable of preventing the re-reading of the texts it has itself transformed. Typology remains open to strong readings which will displace the interpretations it has licensed. Before engaging with the failure of typology, it is necessary, first of all, to look in slightly more depth at the operation of this textual figure.

In the Christian Bible, the Old Testament sense of the 'shared crisis' which creates a narrative of 'Israel as a people created by its [own] laws'[15] becomes fulfilled in the New Testament narrative of the giving of the Law, focused now on the New Israel, the revelation of Law through Jesus Christ. It is the providential organization of God's plan which allows 'the Letter of the Old Law [to be seen as] containing or foreshadowing the spirit of the New'.[16] Just as Moses leads the twelve tribes of Israel out of Egypt, Christ calls together the twelve disciples; just as the crossing of the Red Sea is the essential moment in the definition of the Israelites as a separate people chosen by God, Christ's baptism in the waters of the River Jordan is the mark of his status as the Son of God. Most importantly, the revelation of the Law to Moses on Mount Sinai directly foreshadows the

---

[14] James Preus, *From Shadow to Reality* (Cambridge, 1969), 16.
[15] Frye, *The Great Code*, n. 4 above, 118.
[16] Frye, *The Great Code*, n. 4 above, 123.

Sermon on the Mount and Christ's announcement of the New Law.[17]

Beneath these narrative developments of typology is a hermeneutics that interprets any event as belonging in an interpretative grid which reduces the past, present, and the future to an ordained pattern. A particularly informative example would be John 1:1. The opening of John's Gospel is the typological reference to the 'creative word' of God that begins Genesis, but now, the word is linked to Christ. In other words, the future, in typological theory, can only ever be a working out of what has gone before. The New Age will complete the Old Testament promise made to Moses, a key concern for the announcement of the Law and the coming of the Kingdom. Redemption is linked to the bringing of the Law, or, the replacement of the Old Law by the New Law, a gift which represents both a continuation of the past and a juncture, a significant break which establishes a New Israel under the Law of Christ:

And in those days of Noah, so shall also the coming of the Son of man be. For, as in the days before the flood, they were eating and drinking, marrying and giving in marriage, even till the day in which Noah entered the ark, and they knew not till the flood came and took them all away; so also shall the coming of the Son of man be.[18]

In this verse God's work in the Old Testament, his revelation of himself to Noah and to the Patriarchs, becomes a typology for the advent of the Messiah in the New. Christ's crucifixion is interpreted in a similar way: Isaac's sacrifice becomes an antetype for

---

[17] In the Old Testament the dispensation of the Law is the culmination of a series of meetings between God and Moses. The giving of the Law is expressed in the pact which God makes between himself and Israel. In the New Testament Jesus's words in the Sermon on the Mount present him as a new Moses, the setting of the Sermon establishing an explicit link to Mount Sinai in the Old Testament. Central to this schema is the question of the transformation of the Law, perhaps reaching a summation in the Pauline letters, which have at base a contrast between the Old Covenant and the New Covenant. Mosaic Law is seen as an antetype which is fulfilled in the Law announced by Christ. This theme of the overcoming of the law runs through all the Gospels, but is most apparent in the Gospel of Matthew. See Alter and Kermode, *The Literary Guide to the Bible*, n. 1 above, 387–402.

[18] Matthew 24:1–39. All references to Matthew's Gospel are from the King James Version of the Bible.

the crucifixion, the passion and the resurrection. Abraham's willingness to sacrifice Isaac, to destroy what God has given him, is seen as the prefiguring of Christ's death and resurrection which appears to destroy God's gift of his son to the world. The differences between the crucifixion and the sacrifice of Isaac are equally as important; the unfulfilled sacrifice in Genesis becomes fulfilled in the New Testament. It is this 'heightening' that proves the superiority of the New Law.[19] If the New Law is 'written on the heart' it is the crucifixion that proves the truth of the text. To be ready to accept the New Law and follow Christ is to accept the meaning of his sacrifice.[20]

Christian narrative thus seems to work in a time of waiting, anticipating *Parousia* and the final demonstration of majesty. It is this sense of deferral, of having to interpret texts whose truth will only be revealed by some future event, that has given Christian exegesis its keen sense of the need to control the meanings of its central scriptures. Typology is a way of providing licensed interpretations, but its policing of the text can only work if the allegorical dimension of typology is rejected. This task is inherently problematic: the essentially figurative nature of typology means that it is itself a form of allegory. Typology is unstable. There is a cost to the organization of any narrative in typological terms:

It too transforms the Old Testament; in it too the law and the history of Israel lose their national and popular character; but these are replaced by a mystical or ethical system, and the text loses far more its concrete history than in the figural system. (55)

---

[19] Leonhard Goppelt argues in *Typos* (Grand Rapids, 1982), that 'heightening' is essential to the typological sense of narrative. Typology is predicated on a reading of events as not only divinely ordained, but also as making for a type that will be 'greater and more complete' than their antetype. It could be argued that this heightening is what would distinguish typology from repetition; repetition would not carry with it the intensification and fulfilment of the antetype. It might be possible to read this against Derrida's understanding of good and bad repetition in 'Plato's Pharmacy' in Alan Bass (ed.), *Dissemination* (Chicago, 1981).

[20] Critics have argued that this is the defining feature of the Bible. Alter and Kermode in *The Literary Guide to the Bible*, n. 1 above, 385–6, write that 'The endings of all stories are in a certain fashion images of the general end; here is an ending which consciously transforms all that went to the making of it, so that it is rightly bound in one volume with The Old Testament, with its divinely controlled narrative, its *clues*, types and promises.'

Allegory[21] is the literary trope or figure which carries the possibility that the meaning of a text is not fixed, but errant. In keeping with its slippery quality, there are at least two senses to the word. The first sense of allegory is a compound of two Greek words which mean 'to speak other'; allegory is a figure which represents one thing as another. Allegory is also understood as a translation of the Latin *translatere* which developed from the verb to transfer. Allegory, then, has at its core a concern with a carrying over from one context to another. Thus it could be said that allegory is the figure of a reading which seeks to understand a text by relating it to the world. Allegory attempts to negotiate the problematic interface between word and world.

To summarize briefly the arguments of this section of the paper: the very need to create a universal, inclusive narrative of the Law is its undoing. Once typologized, the potential of a text to reinterpret itself is liberated. The Law cannot prevent its reinterpretation. In place of a single narrative there is a plurality of narratives.

What would be the dynamics of a strong reading that allegorized the Christian narrative of the Law?

---

[21] The contemporary scholarly debate on allegory has tended to stress that allegory opens 'closed' texts to a form of interpretation which is resisted as it reveals that meaning is socially and historically constructed rather than immanent to a text. See Christopher Norris, *Paul De Man* (London, 1988). The understanding of allegory in this project will consider allegory in a slightly different way. Rather than see historical interpretation as privileged, the disruptive aspect of allegory will be presented as a response to the inherent indeterminacy of textual meaning. Allegory tends to operate as a trope for re-reading texts, and hence operates against an historical background, but at the same time, allegory can be understood as effectively 'suspending' any form of historical referent in a text. Moreover, the problem of the indeterminacy of meaning and the legal text runs through the Hellenic and Judaic sources for the Christian allegorical tradition. The tension between the need to re-write the law, and to claim authority for this re-writing means that allegory is a figure that remains attached to and disruptive for the Law. See Deborah L. Madsen, *Rereading Allegory* (London, 1995) and Gerald L. Burns, 'The Problem of Figuration in Antiquity' in G. Shapiro and A. Sica (eds.), *Hermeneutics: Questions and Prospects* (Amherst, 1981). The same tension can be found in midrashic or Rabbinic allegory. Like early Greek allegory, Judaic allegory grew up in a time of disjuncture. It was a response to the need to both update and retain the value of tradition. Judaic allegory arose as a form of rabbinical exegesis or midrash on The Torah. Again, the problem was that allegory would destroy the sense of the Law, introducing readings with 'no connection with the ordinance involved at all' and often involving 'a play on words'.

The Sermon on the Mount

The Sermon on the Mount can be read as a political allegory of
the Law; it provokes the reader to compare the claims that are
made about the Law to the world of history. Moreover, it
connects the discourse with other, possibly unlicensed meanings
that nevertheless exist embedded within the text. What follows is
an argument that one possible allegory of the Sermon is to read it
as an ethical critique of the law, a reading of the law that is
informed by a radical sense of social justice. The allegorical nature
of the text is indeed described by the text itself: 'seek and ye shall
find'. One might argue that the sense of this verse is restricted to a
discourse on prayer, but, at the same time, it could be read as
pointing towards a hermeneutics for a reading of the text: what
you look for in this Sermon, you will find. There are other references which can be read as suggesting that this must be connected
with an ethics of action, with a response to the world. As the
conclusion specifies: the point is to hear and to *do*. It might be
possible to counter this claim with an argument that the Sermon
could thus be read to mean anything. Such an objection could in
turn be refuted with an insistence that the Sermon recommends a
particular view of the world, and that this pre-programmes a set
of possibilities in the text. These possibilities have been glimpsed
by different readers.[22] As much as conservative theologians have
tried to interpret it so as to lessen the impact of its radical
demands; the excessiveness of the Sermon has been seized upon by
antinomian and libertarian readers from the Anabaptists to
Christian socialists and radicals.[23]

Scholars have attempted a reading of the Sermon that utilizes
typology to argue that it represents the fulfilment of the Law of

---

[22] One possible reading context for the Sermon is that provided by Liberation
theology. Liberation theology has, on the whole, been uninterested in the law; the
final section of this paper will attempt to link the social and textual interpretative
hermeneutics with ideas of law and action. The overall significance of Liberation
theology was its explicit political engagement with the interpretation of the
Gospels. Borrowed from the Liberation theologians is the need for engagement, the
acknowledgement that interpretation is a political act. However, there is a significant difference: whereas Liberation theology comes from within the Church, this
reading is literary—both outside and within the sustaining context of the Gospel.
The bearing of the literary reading, then, is towards a politics that is informed,
provoked by the Gospels, but not focused on the Church.

[23] See Clarence Bauman, *The Sermon on the Mount* (Macon, Ga., 1985).

Moses, the announcement of a supplement to the Law of the Old Testament. Invariably, such readings lessen the radical impact of the Gospel as an overcoming of the Law. There are a number of typological motifs that run through the Sermon and which have been used to further this reading. Perhaps the most important motif is that of the mountain, references to which frame Jesus's words. The overall function of these typologies is multifaceted, but, very crudely, they function, as explained above, to stress the coherence between the Old and New Testaments and thus the eschatological and teleological location of the Law: 'the most common interpretation of the mountain setting is that it is part of a conscious Matthean attempt to present the Sermon as the Christian Torah and Jesus as the New Moses'.[24] There are certainly some intriguing parallels. The Sermon in Matthew's narrative comes directly after the calling of the disciples in Galilee after the temptation in the desert. There is thus a broad sense of a reference back to Exodus; to the calling together of the twelve tribes of Israel and the wanderings before the Mosaic reception of the Law. As explained previously, this would relate to the wider typological organization of the biblical narrative of the Law. The period of temptation in Matthew, 'forty days and forty nights', is also the period in which Moses 'was in the Mount'.[25] As one cannot be 'too pedantic in the interpretation of symbols'[26] it could be suggested that the Law comes out of ordeal, out of some form of crisis where the Lawgiver has to prove, either through resisting temptation, or a communion with the divine, that they are able to act as the intermediary between God and man. Parallels could also be drawn between the episode of the golden calf, and the repeated trope in Matthew of the failure of faith, the reluctance or inability of the disciples to accept the law of Christ. Some scholars have gone further than this, and seen in the very five-chapter structure of Matthew a deliberate echo of the five books of the Pentateuch.

Reading the allegory of the overcoming of the Law in Matthew means disturbing this typological pattern. The text seems to offer a different story, a narrative of engagement and transformation which is linked to a broader set of 'political' concerns. Matthew's

---

[24] Terence Donaldson, *Jesus on the Mountain* (Sheffield, 1985).
[25] Exodus 24:18.
[26] Donaldson, *Jesus on the Mountain*, n. 24 above, 163.

Gospel opens with a genealogy which is a bestowing of authenticity and also an act of memorialization. This can be read as the foundation of a counter-tradition, a tradition within a tradition; an act that can be linked to the operation of allegory. Allegory has to work on existing material; it is parasitic, a secondary operation on a primary text. As a political strategy it is the recourse of the outsider and the latecomer who is already within a tradition but who claims that canonical texts can be read in a way that is not licensed, and not acceptable to the dominant tradition.

In Matthew, the opening genealogy is a statement of a different memory. To remember is in itself a political act, given the description in the following verses of Herod's massacre of the children of Bethlehem, an attempt to obliterate and eradicate what the text hopes to preserve: the name and memory of Jesus Christ. This concern continues in John the Baptist's heralding of Christ. John the Baptist announces a 'wrath to come',[27] a baptism of fire,[28] an anticipation of an imminent revolution, a profound challenge to the existing spiritual and temporal powers. Again, this can be read as a political allegory; a concern with what is to come, with a disruption and the forging of a new interpretation. This process is intimately connected with the Gospel. As the Gospel of Jesus Christ it is linked to a name and to what that name may come to mean. It could be suggested that the name is the site of transformation, the meeting point of allegory and typology. The genealogy connects the name with what has been, with the legitimization of the past; and yet, as in the provocative words of John the Baptist, there is now a need to prepare for an event which is new, unexpected, and dangerous.

These significations are related to the words 'for my name's sake' and the variations on them that recur throughout Matthew. The stranger and more problematic verses are invariably linked to this trope. An example would be Christ's warning to his disciples that 'brother shall deliver up the brother to death, and the father the child: and the children shall rise up against their parents, and cause them to be put to death.'[29] The metaphors employed here to describe the effects of the Gospel are determined precisely by the

---

[27] Matthew 3:7.
[28] '[H]e shall baptize you with the Holy Ghost and with fire': Matthew 3:11.
[29] Matthew 10:21.

notion of a disruption from within, and also, in the parent/child conceit, with the successor who represents a profoundly radical break with the past, even to the extent that the past is destroyed. Perhaps the most profound statement of the scandal of the Gospel is 'Think not that I am come to send peace on earth: I come not to send peace, but a sword.'[30] Animating this trope are the same notions of separation, of the heralding of a new order. This is a description of interpretative violence of allegory; the strong interpretation which must mandate a new meaning for an old text.

Closely linked with these disruptions is the question of Christ's identity which is raised throughout the Gospel. It is possible to identify a strategy of rupture at work here in the play between the various titles which Jesus either adopts or is described as using. The appellation 'Christ' translates into Greek the Jewish concept of the Messiah, the one who will come and fulfil the promises for a future saviour made in the Old Testament. One can sense in this very idea a typological figure, the coming of one who would restore 'a broken relationship with God'.[31] In the deployment of this term in Matthew's Gospel, however, there is already the sense of a strong reading. As even the most traditional commentaries assert, there is a 'paradox [in the idea] of a Messiah whose role it was to be crucified'.[32] The Matthean use of the term is thus a distortion, a 'paradox' better understandable as a political strategy which appropriates and redefines the meaning of words by using them in alternative contexts. The same typological sense of fulfilment is used to explain the title 'King of the Jews'; and the same ironic disruption of the term is evidenced by the Gospel, especially in Christ's trial and execution. A related distortion can be discovered in the title 'Son of man'. Recent scholarship has described this as a term which in Aramaic or Hebrew had the signification of 'human being'. Distinguishing Jesus's use of the term is the definite article. This particular use might derive from Daniel 7:13–14, but there seems no conclusive evidence that it carries a signification other than every man, or even, it could be argued, comrade or brother.

Possibly the most complex nexus of significations centre on the

---

[30]   Matthew 10:34.
[31]   R. T. France, *Tyndale New Testament Commentary on Matthew* (Leicester, 1985), 42.   [32]   *Ibid.*

title 'Son of God'. The key verse is towards the end of the Gospel: 'And Jesus came and spake unto them, saying, all power is given unto me in heaven and earth.'[33] There are at least two strands of signification which concern both the name and the authority of the Law which animate this verse and which will be pursued for the remainder of this paper. One particularly disturbing line of signification will relate to a silence at critical moments in the Gospel narrative. This silence will be opposed to any typological sense of fulfilment or presence and linked to certain evasions which are provocative of a strong reading. Focused upon first of all though, will be an approach to the 'power' which Christ announces, a power which the Sermon on the Mount relates to an overcoming of the law:

> Think not that I am come to destroy the law, or the prophets: I am not come to destroy, but to fulfil.
> For verily I say to you, Till heaven and earth pass, one jot or tittle shall in no wise pass from the law, till all be fulfilled.[34]

The distinction between destroy and fulfil is effectively a description of the force of allegory. Allegory does not destroy the text it allegorizes, because the text remains; its manifest meaning is, however, changed, transformed or, in the language of the Gospel, fulfilled. These verses describe a strange fulfilment. It is a fulfilment that is still to come, that is, even here, deferred. In this sense it is an acknowledgement that allegory, unlike typology, cannot be completed. Allegory must remain open to the possibility that there may be further allegories, or stronger readings. This approach to the Sermon would hopefully defuse some of the most reactionary readings which seek to interpret the discourse literally and to fix immemorial interpretations. The fundamentalism or legalism of this approach would ignore the allegorical charge of the Gospel.

It has been asserted throughout this piece that the disruptions of allegory demand a hermeneutics which recognizes a double interpretative demand: as much as a text is open to allegory, it must be located, as far as possible, in its historical context. This approach to the Gospel, then, must be alive to both the location of the text as well as its transformation. The call for justice heard in the Sermon must be read in the light of this understanding of the

---

[33] Matthew 28:18.   [34] Matthew 5:17–18.

text and its excess. Commentators have suggested that the background to the Sermon can be traced to Platonic and Aristotelian ideas that were current in the classical world. The overcoming of the law can be linked with equity or justice:

> Justice is above the law and even above the scriptures: according to ancient theology it is a metaphysical entity, a divine quality, and Scripture is its revelatory source: justice must first be recognised through a general interpretation of scripture, so that the individual laws that are also derived from Scripture can be applied in such a way that justice is served.[35]

It has been argued throughout the present essay that reading needs both to respect a text's historical location and update its claims. This passage focuses on the Sermon's central belief in a justice that transcends written rules. Presently this notion of justice will be revised in a way which is hopefully alive both to the Sermon's radical call to faith and to a contemporary revelation of justice as a call to action in the silence of God. For the moment, however, the critique of the law in the Sermon must be developed. The Sermon effectively opposes a law of generosity or compassion to the law understood as the application of the generality of rules to specific cases. The higher Law can be discovered in the beatitudes which open the Sermon. Two are essential: 'Blessed are the poor in spirit: for theirs is the kingdom of heaven' . . . 'Blessed are the meek: for they shall inherit the earth.' How can these enigmatic blessings be interpreted? Exegetical traditions refer to Matthew's redaction of the Q. source and the differences between Matthew's and Luke's renderings of these sayings. The consensus is that these words are encouragements of a particular spirituality. Although this may or may not be an accurate re-creation of the original context of Jesus's words, the point is that they lend themselves to a contemporary interpretation as a call to social justice. They offer themselves as a statement that the kingdom of God is achievable in material terms; that the kingdom of heaven can, in certain ways, be associated with the world of time and action.

This is not simply a statement that the higher Law is a goad to revolutionary action. The allegory of the Law suggests action in and against the law. The Sermon's politics of the law are not simply a

---

[35] Hans Dieter Betz, *The Sermon on the Mount* (Minneapolis, 1995), 179.

revolutionary claim for the overcoming of the law. Just as the entire Gospel works in and against pre-existing scriptures, the praxis of the radical legal interpreter must be to work in and against the law. The Sermon presupposes existing legal structures: the famous saying 'Judge not, that ye be not judged'[36] cannot be read as a 'trashing' of the very idea of legal judgment. Other sections of the Gospel can be used to conform this line of interpretation: the later parable of rendering to Caesar what is Caesar's is an acceptance of the place of state power. However, it would be wrong to turn this into a quietism. The overall message of the Sermon can be given a contemporary purchase by reading it as a statement that positive Law is always more or less illegitimate; there has to be a more profound law that constantly challenges the claims and actions of the state.

How can the understanding of the 'divinity' of justice be appropriated? It is now necessary to return to the silence of God. There are many aspects to this silence. It can be related, first of all, to the disruption of the Old Testament narrative, a refiguring of the idea that the New Testament fulfils the Old, a strategy of narrative rupture. Despite the structure of Matthew, there is a sense in which there are moments when the typological structure could break down; when radical new meanings could emerge in the text. The most profound of these is the tense moment in the narrative when Christ leaves his disciples to pray alone in the garden of Gethsemane. It will be recalled that Christ submits to his arrest as the 'scriptures [must] be fulfilled'.[37] However, despite the need for typological resolution, these words come immediately after a moment of solitary meditation and prayer, when it might be suggested that Christ would rather reject the fulfilment of the book than submit to the predetermined pattern: 'may this cup be taken from me'. This could appear as a frozen moment, a time outside of the manifest meaning of the text. The dramatic return to the action of the narrative with the arrival of Judas is, in its very resolution of the scene, a need to affirm the forward momentum of the narrative, thus to deny any rival interpretation or slippage that these words might imply. Of course, theologians have interpreted this incident as Christ's very human moment of anxiety when he realizes his impending fate. What may still be open to question, however, is the extent to which this anxiety may be their own textual disquiet as the Gospel suggests a Christ who

---

[36] Matthew 7:1.   [37] Matthew 26:54.

would resist the pattern that determines both his fate and his meaning. The political allegory of Matthew would seize upon this moment when Christ appears in rebellion to the will of the father, a revolt against the law in all its forms.[38]

The final and terrifying moment of the Gospel is the silence of the father to Christ's cry on the Cross. At the very climax of the narrative, the very moment when the identity of Christ could be confirmed, there is nothing but human agony in the absence of God. The possible reference to Psalm 22:18 at the moment of death is a further and concluding reversal of typology; the scriptures now move towards a death which cannot be understood in the pattern mandated. Of course, it would be easy to lessen the impact of this narrative detail; to show that it is only through the death on the Cross that the redemption of fallen man can be achieved, that the Old Testament promise had been fulfilled. Again, this would refer to a typology: that of the sacrifice of Isaac. Christ's death is now the realization of the sacrifice; all of history is now redeemed. Another set of references would be to the 'righteous sufferer' of the Psalms.[39] This would reaffirm the conventional interpretation; but the very fact that the text allows a counter-reading, an interpretation so thoroughly opposed to the narrative of the presence of God in history suggests that there is a stubbornness to the Gospel narratives, a resistance to the master discourse of the Christian Church.

What comes out of the silence is again a name; or the name of Jesus Christ. How is the resurrection to be understood as a passing through of the silence, and how can this be related, finally, to the Law? The resurrection is the ultimate mystery; and perhaps the point where even the most radical and materialist accounts of the Gospel stumble. As Myers[40] has commented, the scene of the

---

[38] This should not be confused with Christ's silence before Pilate, which is to do with a contestation of law in its positive and secular forms. For conventional interpreters and commentators this is the drama of spiritual power; Christ's silence testifies to the truth of his authority; here is the King who is despised and rejected by those who cannot, as yet, appreciate that he is the Son of God. At the same time, though, it remains ambiguous. To reply to the demands would be to acknowledge the legitimacy of the trial, and hence of the law. Remaining silent, even to the extent of not replying to the allegations made, is to resist a legal logic. Revolutionaries brought before the courts have occasionally used the show trial as a platform to denounce the hypocrisies and brutalities of the system that is accusing them of being criminals or terrorists.

[39] France, *Commentary*, n. 31 above, 397.

[40] Ched Myers, *Binding the Strongman* (London, 1984).

resurrection is Galilee; its setting is not the next world. Following Belo,[41] he suggests that Christ's own disappearance at the end of the Gospel is the presence of a discipleship practice. However, reading the allegory of Matthew means that rather than the resurrection as body, we could perhaps speak of the resurrection as text. Against Myers, it could be argued that the scene of the resurrection is not strictly Galilee at all; it is the text of the Gospel. The mysteriousness of the resurrection remains as the final symbol of the book:

Go therefore and teach all nations, baptizing them in the name of the Father, and of the Son, and of the Holy Ghost:
Teaching them to observe all things whatsoever I have commanded you: and, lo, I am with you until even the end of the world.[42]

Resurrection throws the reader back to the name of Christ, and what it means to remain in memory of a name. Understanding these final verses, which return to the themes of baptism and the name, is predicated on determining the strange qualities of the 'I' who directly addresses the reader. This 'I' is both the character of Christ in the text and the text itself speaking. Christ as character makes a concrete demand; his 'I' exists only in action, in putting the Gospel into effect. But the 'I' is also the text itself; the shifting polysemic surface. It is not possible to separate Christ from the text of Christ, or, in other words, to follow the name of Christ is to try to do something with the book. In this sense the Gospel circles back to its opening genealogy. In place of the list, of the established order, however, is a welcoming of the future, a space in which what is to come will be remembered. It allows the reader of the text to locate their own genealogy as a follower of Christ. This is effectively to invert the whole principle of both genealogy and typology, as these tropes tend to interpret the future in terms of the past. In other words, the Law of the name of Christ which is announced in the closing apostrophe of the text is what ignites the very possibility of a future that does not simply reproduce the past. It is the allegorical impulse of the text; the in-breaking, the rupture. What comes, comes in a radically unexpected way; it can be anticipated but never understood: the ruination of precedent, of

---

[41]   Ferdinando Belo, *A Political Reading of Mark's Gospel* (London, 1981).
[42]   Matthew 28:19–20.

any conservative or reactionary discourse that would link the Law simply to what had been.

An Ending

Matthew's Gospel allows a reading of itself as an allegory of the overcoming of the law. The name of Christ is part of a wider politics of interpretation that relates back to the trope of allegory. Allegory is a trope that depends upon the notion of the strong interpretation. Unlike the typological tracing of patterns and coherency, allegory tends to replace one nexus of significations with another. What determines the ascendancy of a new allegorical interpretation is, in part, its strength, the extent to which it can mandate a new interpretative code for an existing text. Allegory punctures through any suggestion that there is a teleology; reading allegorically subverts the mandated pattern, plots ruptures. It is not the trope of a reading celebrating pure textuality; rather allegory relates reading and re-reading to the different circumstances of readers and the need to put texts into effect. This would be to accept the slippage between text and world, the possibility of allegory, in the very moment of affirming action. Moreover, allegory celebrates a Messianism, a coming of the end time which is a realization of the coming apocalypse, which is, in the end, the apocalypse of interpretation. Christ heralds the immanence of the kingdom, of the time of judgment. These mysterious terms can be seen as the empty form of allegory, essentially meaningless, or pregnant with signification; they are an invitation to the strong reader to continue the spirit of the allegorical sense of the Gospels.

RIVKA YOSELEWSKA ON THE STAND: THE STRUCTURE OF LEGALITY AND THE CONSTRUCTION OF HEROIC MEMORY AT THE EICHMANN TRIAL

My role is the role of the witness . . . Not to tell, or to tell another story, is . . . to commit perjury[1]

Lawrence Douglas

In the last pages of *Eichmann in Jerusalem*, Hannah Arendt arrogates unto herself the voice of juridical authority, supplying the missing terms of the decision that she believes should have been written by the Jerusalem court.[2] Whatever we may think of this imagined act of judicial usurpation, it highlights Arendt's belief that the Eichmann trial was, in the final analysis, a legal failure. At the heart of her critique lies a strict and formal separation between the legal and the extralegal—specifically, the belief that, as she put it, 'the purpose of a trial is to render justice, and nothing else; even the noblest of ulterior purposes [such as teaching history] . . . can only detract from the law's main business: to weigh the charges brought against the accused, to render judgment, and to mete out due punishment'.[3] As justice requires a

---

[1] Elie Wiesel, 'The Loneliness of God', quoted by Shoshana Felman, 'The Return of the Voice' in Shoshana Felman and Dori Laub (eds.), *Testimony: Crisis of Witnessing in Literature, Psychoanalysis and History* (New York, 1992), 204.

[2] Hannah Arendt, *Eichmann in Jerusalem: A Report on the Banality of Evil* (New York, 1963), 254–6.

[3] Arendt, *Eichmann in Jerusalem*, n. 2 above, 233.

rigid adherence to legal form, Arendt argues that we must be wary of subjecting the trial to extralegal pressures that may distort this form.[4] The danger of using a trial to pursue extralegal, that is, didactic, ends is that it may become a legal farce, a fear that finds expression in Ian Buruma's claim 'when the court of law is used for history lessons, then the risk of show trials cannot be far off'.[5]

Yet to call the Eichmann proceedings a show trial is in important respects to state the obvious. Like Nuremberg, the Eichmann trial was staged as a pedagogic spectacle, an orchestration designed to show the world the truth of astonishing crimes. To do this, the Eichmann trial relied on a representational logic altogether different from the Nuremberg trial. While Nuremberg was organized around the document—conceived as filmic, material, or written artifact—the Eichmann trial was structured around testimony. At Nuremberg, eyewitnesses played a largely supplemental role to the evidence supplied by document; in Jerusalem, the opposite was the case. Although documents were used to establish a tight legal case against the accused, it was the words of the survivors that provided the dramatic focus of the trial and which built a bridge from the accused to the 'world of ashes'.

This was by design. In his personal history of the trial, Israeli Attorney General and lead prosecutor Gideon Hausner argued that though 'efficient and simple', the Nuremberg approach—'a

---

[4] An early critique of this position is presented in Judith Shklar's *Legalism: Law, Morals, and Political Trials* (Cambridge, Mass., 1964), a work that implicitly challenges Arendt's insistence that a trial should never serve an extralegal end. Using the Nuremberg trial as a case study *inter alia*, Shklar questions the prevailing legal orthodoxy that associates legal integrity with the systematic exclusion of all extralegal ends from the criminal trial. Anticipating many of the arguments more recently advanced by votaries of critical legal studies, Shklar argued that law 'is not an answer to politics, neither is it isolated from political purposes and struggles'. *Legalism*, 143. On the contrary, the 'law is a form of political action', (*ibid*) and as such, it is always and necessarily involved in the pursuit of extralegal ends. Yet in contrast to the critical legal scholars, Shklar did not see the intrusion of the extralegal or political as inevitably corrosive of the ideal of liberal justice. Though Shklar counts herself among the critics of the Nuremberg trial, her argument, in contrast to Arendt's, does not rely on any notion of the sanctity and purity of the legal process; on the contrary, she dismisses such a jurisprudential vision as crabbed, offering in its stead an image of the law in which the ends of justice and pedagogy can be entirely compatible. Her position suggests the need for a nuanced examination of the relationship between the legal and the extralegal in each *specific* case in order to discover the points of their agreement and collision.

[5] I. Buruma, *The Wages of Guilt: Memories of War in Germany and Japan* (New York, 1994), 142.

few witnesses and films of concentration camp horror, interspersed with piles of documents'—'failed to reach the hearts of men'.[6] Not only would survivor testimony penetrate the 'citadel of boredom'[7] that in Rebecca West's words came to describe long stretches of the Nuremberg trial, it would also make tangible the 'incomprehensible statistics', and in so doing, 'do justice to the six million personal tragedies'.[8] Survivor testimony was, then, meant to supply the absent voice of the exterminated; as Primo Levi would explain in *The Drowned and the Saved*, because the stories of the dead are lost, survivors 'must speak in their stead, by proxy'.[9]

Yet if Hausner conceived of the trial explicitly in terms of its pedagogic value, he understood pedagogy in normative terms: a trial, in his imagining, does not simply instruct; it 'attracts people's attention, tells a story and conveys a moral'.[10] Viewing the trial as a means of historical tutelage to a younger generation of Israelis, who 'had no real knowledge, and therefore no appreciation, of the way in which their own flesh and blood had perished',[11] Hausner also saw the trial as a means of educating the world at large, 'which had so lightly and happily forgotten the horrors that occurred before its eyes, to such a degree that it even begrudged us the trial of the perpetrator'.[12] Hausner's logic in this latter regard is provocative, as the trial would provide the evidence of the court's very right to conduct the proceedings.

For Hausner, then, justice could not be done simply by condemning the accused. Rather, Hausner treated the Nazis' central crime as both the act of physical annihilation and the more profound attempt to erase memory itself—both of the cultural life of a people and of the crimes of the Final Solution. The very act of creating an opportunity for the public sharing of the narratives of the survivors, the proxies of the dead, was itself a way of doing

[6] Gideon Hausner, *Justice in Jerusalem* (New York, 1966), 291.
[7] Rebecca West, *Train of Powder* (New York, 1955), 3.
[8] Hausner, *Justice in Jerusalem*, n. 6 above, 292.
[9] Primo Levi, *The Drowned and the Saved* (New York, 1988), 84. For a discussion of differences between survivor testimony and the structure of the writings left behind by those who perished see Sara Horowitz, 'Voices of the Killing Ground', in G. H. Hartman (ed.), *Holocaust Remembrance: The Shapes of Memory* (Oxford, 1994), 42–58.
[10] Hausner, *Justice in Jerusalem*, n. 6 above, 292.   [11] *Ibid.*
[12] *Ibid.*

justice. Hausner's reflections on the strategy of the prosecution thus reveal a remarkable reversal of legal priority: instead of testimony serving as a means of proving the state's case, Hausner asks us to imagine the trial as a means for offering public testimonials.

Not surprisingly, Arendt reserves particular contempt for Hausner's use of these testimonies. Not only did Hausner present witnesses whose testimony upset the prosecution's 'futile attempt to proceed according to chronological order',[13] he 'went as far afield as to put witness after witness on the stand who testified to things that, while gruesome and true enough, had no or only the slightest connection with the deeds of the accused'.[14] In so doing, the prosecution implicitly created a new right, which Arendt, paraphrasing a Yad Vashem bulletin, dismissively described as the 'the right of the witnesses to be irrelevant'.[15]

Here again Arendt defined relevance in highly formal terms: any testimony that is not directly or substantially related to clarifying the legal guilt of the accused is, in her mind, irrelevant and without place in a court of law. To say, however, that the Eichmann prosecution simply entertained a more capacious understanding of relevance than Arendt trivializes the challenge that Hausner's prosecution posed to formal understandings of the trial. For the prosecution did more than use a legal instrument, the criminal trial, to pursue extralegal ends. By examining how the prosecution used survivor testimony to construct narratives of heroic memory, I hope to show how the Eichmann trial served to destabilize the very boundary between the legal and the extralegal upon which Arendt's critique of the trial was predicated.

The roles that the Jews played in the Final Solution has, not surprisingly, been an extremely sensitive topic within Holocaust studies. The most nuanced and humane treatments of the subject, such as Primo Levi's concept of the 'gray zone' in *The Drowned and the Saved*, and Zygmunt Bauman's interpretive discussion of

---

[13] Arendt, *Eichmann in Jerusalem*, n. 2 above, 204.
[14] Arendt, *Eichmann in Jerusalem*, n. 2 above, 15.
[15] Arendt, *Eichmann in Jerusalem*, n. 2 above, 205. For a useful discussion of Arendt's critique of the prosecution's use of survivor testimony, see Leora Y. Bilsky, 'When Actor and Spectator Meet in the Courtroom: Reflections on Hannah Arendt's Concept of Judgment' (1996) 8 no. 2 *History and Memory* 137.

the Judenräte in *Modernity and the Holocaust*,[16] discuss the opportunities for dignity and betrayal within a system of radically abrogated choice specifically designed to use victims as instruments of violence (either unwittingly, unavoidably, or sometimes willingly) upon each other. By contrast, Arendt's polemical claim that without the organizational assistance provided by the various Jewish councils, the aims of the Final Solution could never have been realized, became the source of the most vehement critiques of *Eichmann in Jerusalem*.

Arendt's blunt assertion, though lacking empathetic imagination, was hardly novel: such an argument had already been the focus of intense legal and national attention, primarily in Israel. Before the Eichmann proceedings, the most important Holocaust litigation in the young state was the Kasztner trial of 1954, a civil suit involving a libel claim brought by Israel Rezsö Kasztner, a former head of the Hungarian Jewish community and later a press spokesman for the Israeli Ministry of Commerce and Industry, against Malkiel Gruenwald, a marginal political fanatic who, in a newsletter printed and distributed at his own expense, had accused Kasztner of 'paving the way for the murder' of Hungarian Jewry.[17]

The Kasztner case provided a constellation of facts which tested a court's capacity sensitively to situate itself in an impossible history. How, for example, was one to make sense of the fact that Kasztner, as a prominent Jew, was able successfully to negotiate a deal that permitted 1,685 Jews, among them a few dozen members of his family, to escape by a special train to Switzerland? Was this an example of an heroic effort to save a few in the face of otherwise certain destruction, or was this an example of a cowardly willingness to sacrifice the group to save one's kin and self? The trial and appellate courts offered dramatically different

---

[16] Zygmunt Bauman, *Modernity and the Holocaust* (Ithaca, 1992). Also of note are Raul Hilberg's discussion of the Jewish councils in *The Destruction of the European Jews* (Chicago, 1961) (an account that has often been erroneously associated with Arendt's argument—probably because Arendt frequently cites Hilberg's work) and Isiah Trunk's *Judenrat: The Jewish Councils in Eastern Europe under Nazi Occupation* (New York, 1972).

[17] T. Segev, *The Seventh Million: The Israelis and the Holocaust* (transl. Haim Watzman, New York, 1993), 258. For a discussion of the trial and affair, see also Yehuda Bauer, *Jews for Sale?: Nazi-Jewish Negotiations, 1933–45* (New Haven, 1994) and Yechiam Weitz, 'The Herut Movement and the Kasztner Trial' (1994) 8 no. 3 *Holocaust and Genocide Studies* 349.

portraits of Kasztner, who, on 3 March 1957, fell victim to the first political assassination in Israel since the creation of the state.

The Kasztner affair revealed the extreme sensitivity of the topic of Jewish behaviour during the Final Solution within the Jewish and Israeli community, a fact again made clear several years later at the Eichmann trial. Of the numerous disturbances from the spectators that marred the proceedings, a small but significant number were directed not at Eichmann, but at those Jewish witnesses who had served prominently in the Judenräte. These outbursts revealed a tendency to view the survivor as a person who must have behaved venally in order to have lived. As in the medieval ordeal, innocence could be proved only by death.

It is against this backdrop that we must understand Hausner's attempt to use survivor testimony to create narratives of what Lawrence Langer has called 'heroic memory'. By 'heroic memory' Langer names a form of remembrance that attempts 'to salvage from the wreckage of mass murder . . . a tribute to the victory of the human spirit'.[18] The logic of heroic memory, Langer insists, often does violence to the experience of the survivor, as the insistence on the normative relevance of survival often contradicts the radical melancholy of stories that 'resist . . . the organizing impulse of moral theory'.[19]

Yet such was Hausner's organizing impulse. Against the image of the helpless sheep on the one hand and the venal survivor on the other, Hausner used the trial to recast the terms of Holocaust history, forging a collective image of the victims and survivors as a people struggling valiantly to resist their physical, psychic, and religious destruction. In his opening address before the court, Hausner understandably claimed that the controversy regarding 'the proper behaviour of a victim in his relations with the beast of prey' has 'no place in the present trial', and 'we shall leave it to the historian of the Holocaust'.[20] Yet his own declarations notwithstanding, Hausner often laboured not to condemn the accused but to acquit his victims.

---

[18] Lawrence Langer, *Holocaust Testimonies: The Ruins of Memory*, (New Haven, 1991), 165.

[19] Langer, *Holocaust Testimonies*, n. 18 above, 204.

[20] *The Trial of Adolf Eichmann: Record of the Proceedings* ('TAE') 9 vols. (Jerusalem, 1992–6), I, 71.

On the simplest level, this effort explains an emblematic question that Hausner posed to Dr Moshe Beisky, a Tel Aviv magistrate (and later Israeli Supreme Court Justice) originally from Cracow who survived an internment at Plaszow *Judenlager*: '15,000 people stood there—and opposite them hundreds of guards. Why didn't you attack then, why didn't you revolt?'[21] In the words of one journalist, Beisky 'appeared staggered' by Hausner's 'harsh question' and began 'to talk in incomplete sentences, gesturing with both hands'.[22] Yet it was a question that Hausner would pose again and again to witness after witness, and though his tone was at times histrionically aggressive if not directly obnoxious, his intent was clearly to provide the witnesses with an opportunity to explain their (in)action to a sceptical nation and international community.

Hausner's effort to create a narrative of heroic memory also required offering the survivor-witnesses numerous opportunities to describe their various gestures of resistance. Heroes of the Jewish resistance such as Pinchas Zuckerman, Zvia Lubetkin-Zuckerman, and Abba Kovner were called as witnesses. Still other witnesses were encouraged to describe their efforts to keep their religious and personal identities alive. Rivka Kuper, the widow of the leader of the Hebrew underground in Cracow, described lighting candles and singing Sabbath songs in the darkness of a Birkenau block.[23] Liona Neumann, a survivor of the actions in Riga, told the court how she drew strength from studying Hebrew and Zionism with a group of young people in the evening.[24] David Wdowinski, a survivor of the Jewish labour camp in Budzy´n, described how he baked *matzot* on the eve of Passover in 1944 in a camp oven.[25] These stories, however, did more than simply provide poignant examples of people struggling to maintain religious meaning in the face of catastrophe; more importantly, they suggested how a commitment to the Jewish religion, and more specifically, to the politics of Zionism, made possible and supported acts of physical resistance.

By emphasizing the role that piety and Zionism played in helping

---

[21] *TAE* I, 349.
[22] 'Death Camp Survivor Explains Why Jews Did Not Resist', *The Times*, 2 May 1961, 10.
[23] *TAE* I, 432.
[24] *TAE* I, 509.
[25] *TAE* III, 1236.

Jews preserve hope and thereby both resist and survive, the prosecution was able to create a provocative *post hoc* picture of history, in which those who were able to persevere psychically and physically were those who possessed, in embryonic form, precisely those characteristics which are now seen as constituting the core of Israeli national identity. Survival was thus comprehended in a normative framework that affirmed a present ideology of national self-determination.

At times, the very structure of the trial provocatively contrived to support this understanding, such as when the proceedings were interrupted by the sirens observing *Yom Hazikkaron*, the day dedicated to the memory of those who had died in the Israeli war of independence.[26] The transcript captures the complex intrusions of past and present, as the interruption occurred precisely as the court was listening to the excerpt of Eichmann's interrogation in which the accused described his first contact with the technique of gassing:

Eichmann: The captain of the Order Police . . . told me how he had made everything here hermetically sealed, . . . since an engine of a Russian submarine was going to operate here . . .
Presiding Judge: Please stop now. We shall have a two minutes' silence in memory of those who fell in our wars.
[*Silence*]
[*Continues reading the translation*]
. . . and gases of this engine were going to be directed inside and the Jews would be poisoned . . .[27]

The memorializing logic of *Yom Hazikkaron* finds itself, then, provocatively framed by Eichmann's words. The Holocaust, at this moment, is assimilated into the tortured history of the Jewish people at the same time as it emerges as the cataclysm that justifies the present military sacrifices of the Israeli state. Soldiers do battle so that the Jew will never again be mere victim, while the victims are recast as protean soldiers.

The image of the Holocaust victim as fallen soldier was provocatively conjured later in the trial during the testimony of Hulda Campagnano, an Italian survivor (and daughter of a

---

[26] For a discussion of the history and memorializing logic of *Yom Hazikkaron*, see James E. Young, *The Texture of Memory: Holocaust Memorials and Meaning* (New Haven, 1993), 265–72.   [27] *TAE* I, 134.

famous professor of Semitic languages). Following Hausner's lead, Campagnano described the fates of her brother and sister: 'They were both for a certain time in Auschwitz, and they even managed to exchange some words in writing; he would send a note to her, and once she sent a note to him. Afterwards they were separated.'[28] Campagnano never was able to learn what became of her brother. About her sister, however, she explained, 'She was sent to Bergen-Belsen and finally to Theresienstadt, and there she was liberated. She reached this country in 1945. It is from her that I heard many of the details I have just told you. Later she was herself killed by Arabs in the convoy that went up to Mount Scopus in 1948.'[29] On one level, Campagnano's story seems bitterly ironic, since the sister survived the death camps only to die at the hands of Arabs. Yet while Campagnano's story brims with darkness, the irony in this case supports Hausner's larger effort to construct an heroic link between the history of the Holocaust and the reality of the Israeli state. For an organic unity is forged between the past and present, in which the very forces that were once bent on exterminating European Jewry now appear as the military enemies of the fledgling Israeli state. Campagnano's sister appears then not as yet another in an unfathomably large number of victims of the Holocaust; instead, she is recast as a martyr for the young nation. Again, the story supports the deeper claims of heroic memory. Just as survival was enabled by a determined allegiance to the Jewish faith and Zionist commitments, Campagnano's story argues that death was not meaningless: it was a sacrifice for the young state determined to supply security to all Jews.

This brings us to the second sense in which the prosecution constructed heroic memory—that is, by comprehending the act of narrative unburdening as legally potent. Many survivor-witnesses testified that the need to tell what happened supplied a powerful incentive for survival. Leon Wells, a survivor from a small Polish town, declaimed that 'the only idea was that one of us survives and tells the world what happened here'.[30] Dov Freiberg, a survivor of Sobibòr, echoed Wells when he told the court, 'we had to inform the world; somebody had to be sent outside, we had to try and escape'.[31]

---

[28] *TAE* II, 657. [29] *Ibid.* [30] *TAE* I, 374.
[31] *AE* III, 1174.

Similar as their words were, however, one can detect a small but crucial difference in the testimonial imperative of Wells and Freiberg. Wells understood the burden of testimony as a retrospective act of describing and recording a catastrophe that has happened. It is an effort to prevent the extinction of the memory of the *Shoah*. It is the need to silence the taunts which were directed at the inmates by the retreating Nazis: 'And even if some proof should remain and some of you survive, people will say that the events you describe are too monstrous to be believed.'[32] For Freiberg, however, the testimonial imperative is one of prospective warning. As a witness to an ongoing process of extermination, Freiberg believed it necessary to escape in order to tell others and thus organize effective resistance. Freiberg's need to bear witness was linked to a logic of resistance whereas Wells contemplated a far bleaker situation in which resistance has already been rendered futile and testimony serves only to mark the traces of the exterminated.

In the prosecution's construction of heroic memory, Wells' and Freiberg's contrasting motives for bearing witness were complexly conflated. For the prosecution understood the act of bearing witness as more than merely a memorializing performance, an agonizing ritual of tracing absence. Instead, as an act performed in a courtroom in a criminal trial, it was a juridically potent gesture. Such a view erased the fortuitous or accidental from the logic of survival. Because survival was a means of keeping a narrative of atrocity alive, the act of refusing to succumb was endowed with normative prestige. This vision, in turn, offered powerful support for the trial itself. Here, then, we find a more complex variation of the prosecution's challenge to Arendt's legalistic understanding of the trial. Not only was the trial, from the prosecution's perspective, meant to provide an occasion for the public sharing of traumatic narratives, it was, more centrally, an event staged on the behalf of survivors in order to honour an obligation to them. The trial was something owed to the survivors; it was the fulfilment of a pledge implicitly made to them at the moment of their decision to survive. Thus, by turning testimony into legal evidence, the trial transformed the witness from Wells's ancient mariner, a stunned

---

[32] Primo Levi, *The Drowned and the Saved* (Raymond Rosenthal (trans.), New York, 1988), 11–12.

and isolated survivor, into Freiberg's potent resister. Meaning and normative coherence were stamped upon the act of surviving by transforming the narratives of horror into legal evidence. Bleak tales of the Holocaust became tools of legal justice.

Many of the prosecution's witnesses offered implicit support of this provocative logic—illustrative is the testimony of Martin Földi. A Hungarian lawyer, Földi described to the court the selection that took place immediately after his family and he arrived at Auschwitz:

They said to us that the men should stand on the right side with children over the age of 14, and the women on the left with the young boys and girls . . . I stood with my son who was only 12 years old. After we started moving forward, I suddenly came up to a certain man . . . He was dressed in a uniform of the German army, elegant, and he asked me what my profession was. I knew that being lawyer by profession would not be very helpful and, therefore, told him that I was a former officer. He looked at me and asked, 'How old is the boy?' At that moment I could not lie, and told him: 12 years old. And then he said: *'Wo ist die Mutti?'* (And where is your mother?) I answered: 'She went to the left.' Then he said to my son: 'Run after your mother.' . . . I wondered to myself, how would he be able to find his mother there? After all, there were so many women and men, but I caught sight of my wife. How did I recognize her? My little girl was wearing some kind of a red coat. The red spot was a sign that my wife was near there. The red spot was getting smaller and smaller. I walked to the right and never saw them again.[33]

It is, for a number of reasons, a difficult and poignant story. For one familiar with popular-cultural representations of the Holocaust, the image of the receding red coat powerfully antici-pates the device used to dramatic effect by both the novelist Thomas Keneally and the film-maker Steven Spielberg in *Schindler's List*, in the scene in which Schindler tracks the fate of a single girl, dressed in a brightly-coloured coat, during a ghetto action. More provocative, however, is the notion of the lawyer unable to lie to save his son. 'At that moment I could not lie': we are never told *why* he could not lie, though presumably at the time he had absolutely no reason to believe that his veracity would have such tragic consequences. Yet he does not say this. He simply declares that he was disabled from lying, and is unable even to offer an entirely understandable post-factum explanation for his

---

[33] *TAE* III, 968.

fatal veracity. In this sense, Földi once again displayed before the court the very helpless fidelity to the truth that he had demonstrated before the Nazi officer. Yet the very quality that led him to be an inadvertent accomplice in his son's doom now appeared as the single greatest virtue for a witness testifying before a court. Importantly, then, the trial provided Földi with more than the mere opportunity to confess to the terrible consequences of his misplaced veracity. Instead, the trial rectified the normative imbalance of the 'concentrationary universe', in which one's fidelity to the truth could prove catastrophic. By rewarding veracious testimony as probative of the guilt of the accused, the prosecution restored normative coherence to Földi's experience and conferred a degree of closure to his terrible narrative.

The prosecution's position thus found support in the words of many of the witnesses at the Eichmann trial. The testimonies of an equally large group of witnesses, however, often challenged and resisted the prosecution's effort to comprehend the act of bearing legal witness as an act that restores closure and normative coherence to a world disturbed by traumatic memory. At times this resistance manifested itself in the subtle ways that the survivor-witnesses were unable to bring closure to their testimony. Invariably, the Attorney General began each of his examinations by asking the witness to state his or her name and his or her present circumstances; he then immediately shifted to the witness's wartime experiences, beginning with questions about the witness's activities before the coming of the Nazis. This line of questioning quickly turned to the story of atrocity and survival, exploring this material for the bulk of the examination, and then concluding with cursory questions about the witness's liberation. The general form of this examination thus structured these narratives as tales of discrete and radical disruption framed by the bookends of the normal—that is, pre- and post-Holocaust existence. Balance, in this understanding, is incompletely restored first through liberation at the war's end, and now, more completely at the trial that permits the survivor to satisfy the testimonial urge. And by situating the witness first in the present and then moving quickly back to his or her pre-Holocaust experience, these interrogatories insisted on the continuity of self through the episode of disruption. While Hausner remained mindful of the enormous sufferings of the survivors, the narrative form through which this suffering was directed to speak had the consequence of conventionalizing it, and in so doing, containing its deeper, bleaker aspects.

The testimonies of many of the survivor-witnesses, however, resisted these efforts to conventionalize and offer closure. Instructive in this regard was the testimony of Ya'akov Biskowitz, a survivor of Sobibòr. Biskowitz's testimony did not stand out as a particularly important moment in the trial, though it remains memorable in one respect. As a constable in the Israeli police, Biskowitz testified in uniform. The presence of a uniformed man on the stand created the initial impression that Biskowitz would offer testimony regarding matters within his official function, such as the behaviour of the accused during his time in custody. Instead, the uniform served to remind the spectators that the very officials responsible for overseeing the accused numbered among his victims. Against the vision of the police as officials of the state, enjoying a monopoly on means of legitimate violence, we are asked to imagine the present officer as himself once a powerless stateless inmate. The schism between the uniform that denotes power and the story that bespeaks impotence importantly accounts for the discomfiting quality of Biskowitz's testimony. Moreover, in a manner emblematic of much of the testimony at the trial, Biskowitz resisted efforts to offer closure to his narrative by returning to the present. When thanked by the court at the conclusion of his testimony, the witness, dressed in the same khaki uniform of the silent guards who kept watch on the man in the glass booth, was unable to bring himself to leave the stand. 'There was another shocking case which I witnessed', Biskowitz suddenly declared, 'and I should like to describe just this one further incident.'[34] The court politely but firmly declined the officer's invitation, yet Biskowitz's need to circle back to the incomplete story of catastrophe, to resist the effort to conclude his testimony with a tale of liberation, became emblematic of a general pattern in which survivor narratives disturbed the coherent chronologies that the prosecution attempted to secure.

The most provocative clash between the prosecution's normative understanding of survival and the tale of a witness can be found in the testimony of Rivka Yoselewska. First Yoselewska's

---

[34] *TAE* III, 1188.

testimony had to be delayed, as Hausner announced to a shocked courtroom that the witness had suffered a heart attack on the morning she was to take the stand. When she had recovered sufficiently, Yoselewska appeared, in the words of one journalist, 'with a gaunt and tragic face'.[35] A survivor of an *Aktion* conducted on the outskirts of Pinsk, Yoselewska described how she witnessed the killing of her entire family—including her mother, father, grandmother, aunt, cousins, and own daughter—by the *Einsatzkommando*. Horrific in its own right, Yoselewska also told the tale of her own killing, a story made famous in its novelistic treatment in works such as Anatoly Kuznetsov's *Babi Yar* (1967) and D. M. Thomas's *The White Hotel* (1982). She described how immediately after her daughter (dressed in her Sabbath dress) was shot, she herself was shot and flung into the pit of corpses:

I felt nothing . . . I thought I was dead, but that I could feel something even though I was dead . . . I felt I was suffocating, bodies had fallen on me. I felt I was drowning. But still I could not move and felt I was alive and tried to get up. I was choking, I heard shots, and again somebody falling down . . . I had no strength left. But I felt that somehow I was crawling upwards. As I climbed up, people grabbed me, hit me, dragged me downwards, but I pulled myself up with the last bit of strength.[36]

It is a nightmarish narrative whose hallucinatory details and temporal uncertainty find no resolution even after Yoselewska described how she managed to climb out of the pit, a spectral being at once present and yet invisible to those around her: 'Germans came and helped round up the children. They left me alone. I just sat and looked.'[37] Sometime later—it isn't clear when—Yoselewska dragged herself back to the grave which had since been covered with dirt: 'Blood was spouting. Nowadays, when I pass a water fountain I can still see the blood spouting from the grave. The earth rose and heaved. I sat there on the grave and tried to dig my way in with my hands.'[38]

The image of the blood spouting from the grave is astonishing, not least of all because it echoes precisely a story that Eichmann himself had told when describing an *Aktion* he witnessed as a Gestapo observer. Here, then, a story whose details suggest the figurative prose of a biblical tale creates a bizarre link between the

---

[35] The *New York Times*, May 9, 1961, 16.   [36] *TAE* I, 517.
[37] *Ibid*.   [38] *TAE* I, 517–18.

accused and a survivor. Also striking is the image of the survivor as an undead—a person condemned to live, unable, despite her efforts to claw her way back into the grave, to receive the comfort and the companionship of the corpses. For 'three days and three nights', Yoselewska remained sprawled naked on the grave, while Polish peasants, on their way to and from their fields, threw stones at her.[39] After wandering around 'for several weeks', Yoselewska was taken in by a peasant who gave her food; later she joined a group of Jews in the forest and there she lived until the arrival of the Soviets. Absent from her story is any notion of resistance and any idea that her personal survival can be ascribed to anything other than the most inscrutable and, from her perspective, cruel logic. Equally absent is any sense that she was sustained by the prospect of offering testimony or that the act of now bearing witness was one that restores normative or existential order to her life. Indeed, she comprehends her survival as an act of punishment.

The prosecution's response to this narrative followed the pattern that I have noted. The prosecution brought Yoselewska's testimony to a close with a single concluding question: 'And now you are married and you have two children?'[40] Here we must acknowledge how difficult it is to imagine a woman who once tried to claw her way into a mass grave now acting as a mother and wife; yet, the question and her simple response, 'Yes', were meant to return the witness to the present and bring closure to her story on a note of affirmation.

Lest such an affirmation seem too cursory, in its concluding argument before the court, the prosecution returned to Yoselewska's testimony, now transforming the witness into a trope. For Hausner then:

Rivka Yoselewska embodies in her person all that was perpetrated, all that happened to the Jewish people. She was shot. She was already amongst the dead in the funeral pit. Everything drew her downwards, to death. Wounded and wretched, with unbelievable strength she arose out of the grave. Her physical wounds healed, but her heart was torn asunder and broken forever. She found asylum in our country, established her home here and built her life anew. She overcame the evil design. They wanted to kill her, but she lives—they wanted to blot out her memory,

---

[39] *TAE* I, 518.   [40] *Ibid.*

but she has brought forth new children. The dry bones have been given sinews, flesh has grown upon them and they have taken on skin; they have been infused with the spirit of life. Rivka Yoselewska symbolizes the entire Jewish People.[41]

It is a remarkable statement, one that encapsulates the prosecution's understanding of the case. The stunned and disoriented survivor is transformed into both a hero and a symbol; the cruel and inscrutable logic of survival is translated into a morality play about the tenacity of the will; a tale of the desolation of meaning is turned into a story of personal and collective rebirth; and the ruins of memory become the vibrant source of enduring narrative.

But by turning the survivor into a trope of the rebirth of the Jewish people in the state of Israel, the prosecution asks us to imagine the Eichmann trial as itself something more than a tool for adjudging the guilt of the accused or even for memorializing the dead and honouring the experience of the survivors. By identifying the survivor's struggle with the state's fight towards self-determination, Hausner implicitly asks us to see the trial itself as an expression of the very powers of will and memory that made individual survival possible. The prosecution, I have argued, was able to defend this view by recasting the often radical melancholy of survivor narratives into the terms of heroic memory.

More provocatively, however, the dramaturgy of the prosecution at the Eichmann trial challenges the clear distinction between the legal and extralegal, upon which Arendt's critique of the trial was based. For the prosecution, the survivor was imagined as a trope for the rebirth of the Jewish people, and the trial as a trope for new-found efficacy of a reborn nation. Together they served, in the minds of the prosecution, as examples of the reconstruction of a people organized around a new national identity. The unburdening of memory, the sharing of narrative, were means of doing justice, at the same time that doing justice served to preserve the memory of the catastrophe. The experience of juridical potency, the power to give tortured memory the force of legal evidence were not merely examples of what the state could do for survivors. They were indivisible elements in the ongoing project of 'infusing the spirit of life' into a damaged people.

41 *TAE* V, 2004.

THE 'FINAL STRUGGLE': A DISCOURSAL, RHETORICAL, AND SOCIAL ANALYSIS OF TWO CLOSING ARGUMENTS

Jill Tomasson Goodwin

In her book, *Poetic Closure: A Study of How Poems End*, Barbara Herrnstein Smith distinguishes between things that stop or cease—like a ringing telephone or the blowing of the wind—and other things, like music or poetry, that seem to conclude or end. She defines closure, then, in these terms:

We tend to speak of conclusions when a sequence of events has a relatively high degree of structure, when, in other words, we can perceive these events as related to one another by some principle of organization or design that implies the existence of a definite termination point. Under these circumstances, the occurrence of their terminal event is a confirmation of the sequence, and is usually distinctly gratifying. The sense of stable conclusiveness, finality, or 'clinch' which we experience at that point is what is referred to here as closure.[1]

I want to add three more points—or, at least, clarifications—to this definition. First, it seems to me that most 'sequences of events' require a highly structured *medium*; require, that is, a language of some kind to perceive and to represent these sequences, to make them accessible to ourselves and others. Second, the 'principle[s] of organization or design' which make possible a termination point, and which, therefore, lead to a 'distinctly gratifying' experience, have an *effect* upon, and therefore bear consequences for, all agents involved. And third, organization, design, and gratification

---

[1] B. Herrnstein Smith, *Poetic Closure: A Study of How Poems End* (Chicago, 1968), 3.

are never simply, as Herrnstein Smith puts it, 'aspects of our psychological and physiological organization'.[2] They are also, and perhaps mostly, part of our shared, *social* world, the world whose collective and dynamic organization is constantly organizing us— that is, constantly inculcating a desire for, and a need to be gratified by, a particular set of forms whose structures are socially aligned with 'stable conclusiveness, finality or "clinch" '.

In short, then, I want to argue that closure is discursive, rhetorical, and social. Discursive, because closure requires the resources of a highly structured, highly structuring medium by which sequences of events can be represented, perceived, and communicated. Rhetorical, because any discursive representation of events, at the same time, is always, and equally, a selection and a deflection. That is, rhetorical form is motivated—it attempts to make one way of framing our understanding and shaping our responses more likely than another. And social, because this framing of our understanding or shaping of responses through discourse is both prompted by, and is meant to have consequences within, the social domain.

This leads us into a discussion of closing arguments in legal trials. Like all closure, closing arguments require the resources of language to structure events into a recognizably satisfying ending. In the context of the courtroom, closing arguments have a particular set of requirements: as the terminal point of a trial, they must fittingly conclude the continuum that began with the opening statement, bringing together all the disparate elements of evidence, and moulding these into an advocate's theory of the case. These requirements are well expressed by Richard Rieke and Randall Stutman's formulation of 'final struggle'.[3] 'Struggle' highlights the adversarial pitting of the fittedness of one lawyer's closing argument with the other's. 'Final' highlights the last-chance imperative to convince the jury that one theory, distilled in one closing argument, gratifies their need to make a legal decision that meets the social criteria of order and justice.

While accurate, such characterizations as Rieke and Stutman's do not offer us a theorized, close reading of closing arguments,

---

[2] B. Herrnstein Smith, *Poetic Closure: A Study of How Poems End.*

[3] R. D. Rieke and R. D. Stutman, *Communication in Legal Advocacy* (Columbia, SC, 1990), 203.

which to my mind can elucidate how language enacts closure. To offer my own reading, I will briefly outline a theory developed by Glenn Stillar in his book, *Analyzing Everyday Texts: Discourse, Rhetoric, and Social Perspectives* which, as the title suggests, integrates discourse analysis, rhetorical analysis, and social theory.[4] I will then apply this methodology to what I call 'nodes'—intense sites of linguistic and rhetorical activity—found in a pair of closing arguments taken from a recent Canadian criminal trial.[5] And finally, by doing so, I hope to show that in these closing arguments, the defence and prosecuting lawyers exemplify social and socialized courtroom practices.

Methodology: Discoursal, Rhetorical, and Social Analysis

In his book, Glenn Stillar brings together three different, but complementary perspectives on texts as practice, or as symbolic action; namely, the perspectives of discourse, rhetoric, and social theory. Discourse analysis, for example, recognizes that texts, including closing arguments, make and are made up of choices; that is, they select from systems of language resources to make meaning. These choices are organized along three general functions. One is the textual, or organizing function, which enables parts of a text to be linked with other parts to create cohesion, allows some parts to be foregrounded as prominent, and creates coherence in relation to the text's situation of use. The second is the ideational, or representing

---

[4] G. F. Stillar, *Analyzing Everyday Texts: Discourse, Rhetoric, and Social Perspectives* (Thousand Oaks, Calif., 1998).

[5] I have chosen a pair of closing arguments from a fairly recent trial, *Regina* v. *Bardales* (1993) BCSC (unreported) Vancouver Registry 017342. I chose this particular trial for two main reasons: first I wanted readers to have access to the court record of the trial, should they wish to read the full text of the closing arguments. Because an appeal on the judgment of this case was eventually presented before the Supreme Court of Canada, the details of the case are available in *Canadian Criminal Cases: Regina* v. *Bardales* (1996) 107 CCC (3d) 194 (SCC) and can be ordered from the court as a public document. Second, I wished to examine closing arguments which were models of their kind. The British Columbia Court of Appeal comments on the quality of both arguments: all three judges observed that the defence counsel's address to the jury was 'very thorough' ((1995) 101 CCC (3d) 289 (BCCA), 290, 320), and 'detailed and very effective' (294), that both 'counsel performed in a highly competent manner' (330), and that the 'quality of the addresses of counsel' helped the judge formulate his charge to the jury (304).

function, which constructs content through participants, processes, and circumstances. And the third is the interpersonal, or interacting function, which constructs social relations—in our case, between speakers and listeners—through such resources as speech function and attitudinal lexis. These meta-functions are integrated inasmuch as choices made at one level redound, or affect, the other levels.

Moreover, Stillar posits, language resources are rhetorical because, following Kenneth Burke, they represent 'reality' by selecting some events from it and deflecting others; that is, 'every representation is attitudinal and motivated because every representation is the situated . . . practice of . . . agents who necessarily construct "reality" '.[6] As 'practising agents' of the courtroom, the defence and prosecution lawyers in criminal trials construct closing arguments, or 'representations' that reflect particular 'attitudes' towards the person on trial and the crime. By seeking to convince the jury that the accused is either guilty or not guilty, both lawyers necessarily reflect their motives through the language resources they choose. More particularly, these motives can be discerned in the texts by identifying the patterns of selection and combination of various semiotic resources available for making meaning,[7] through the five terms of Burke's pentadic model: act, agent, scene, agency, and purpose.

Finally, Stillar argues, language resources are social, following Pierre Bourdieu, inasmuch as texts are both a product of, and a site for the reproduction of, capital and distinction in social life. For example, each lawyer presents closing arguments within the social context of the courtroom, within a linguistic 'market', if you will, in which the jury appraises the value of their linguistic product, which is itself a product of their linguistic habitus, a set of predisposed linguistic responses.[8] These responses are part of their general habitus, a preconscious 'felt sense' of the best means of persuading the jury of their theory of the case. I will offer now a textual, ideational, and interpersonal analysis of our pair of closing arguments excerpts, and then integrate this discoursal analysis with a rhetorical and social commentary.

[6] Stillar, *Analyzing*, n. 4 above, 64.   [7] *Ibid.*
[8] Stillar, *Analyzing*, n. 4, above, 101.

Text: The Textual Function

The elements of the attempted murder case upon which these closing arguments are based is as follows: at 1.07 a.m. on the night of 26 May 1992, at the corners of Joyce and Church Streets in the city of Vancouver, a man exited a car, threatened one man, Roberto Escobar, and shot another man, Juan Martinez. While both prosecuting and defence lawyers agree on these facts, they disagree on the identity of the shooter: the defence has argued that the witnesses, Escobar and Martinez, are mistaken in their identification of his client, Roger Bardales; the prosecution, that Bardales is the man who committed the crime. I have isolated a small excerpt from each of the closing arguments for analysis, and my choice is based on several considerations. First, because both excerpts belong to sections which have an early place in the closing arguments, they hold a place of structural prominence; second, because both occupy a position of structural prominence within these sections—first place for the defence, last for the prosecutor—they also occupy a second-order position of structural prominence; and third, because both focus on the accused, these excerpts fulfil in particular what Stillar identifies as the textual function: they foreground the 'theme' of the accused as prominent; they use language to link other references to the accused to create 'textual cohesion'; and they create 'coherence' with the text's situation—the trial of the accused.

The defence lawyer, who speaks first to the jury, organizes his twenty-one-page closing argument through enumeration: he provides eight reasons why the jury should have reasonable doubt that Roger Bardales attempted to murder Juan Martinez. After he presents his first reason, which is his strongest evidence—that the assailant had longer hair than Bardales—the defence lawyer argues his second reason: that the testimony of his client could reasonably be true. The first thirty-five lines of this section are the excerpted passage that I will analyse. Because of their schemes of repetition, these lines are ear-catching, logically incremental, and emotionally charged. More particularly, they are striking examples of the language resources of the textual function: they are thematically and cohesively prominent. Let us analyse the thematic information first. In English, the theme of a sentence, or what it is 'about', is marked by its initial position in the sentence.

Stillar quotes M. A. K. Halliday to illustrate the function of the theme:

There is a difference in meaning between *a halfpenny is the smallest English coin*, where halfpenny is Theme ('I'll tell you about a halfpenny'), and *the smallest English coin is a halfpenny*, where the smallest English coin is Theme ('I'll tell you about the smallest English coin'). The difference may be characterized as 'thematic'; the two clauses differ in their choice of theme.[9]

This gloss, 'I'll tell you about', identifies the theme of a sentence: it marks the 'point of departure for the message'.[10] In our thirty-five-line excerpt, the defence has four themes and, of these, three focus on Bardales. In the first sentence of the passage, the lawyer 'tells' the jury 'about' his client—'*Bardales* has testified in this hearing'[11]—and then proceeds for the next thirteen sentences to thematize him, consistently beginning sentences with 'he': '*He* says'; '*He* was cooperative'; '*He* made'; '*He* gave'; '*He* was cooperative'; '*He* admitted'; '*He* admitted'; '*He* didn't try'; '*He* admitted'; '*He* didn't'; '*He* admitted'; '*He* admitted'; '*He* didn't try' (emphasis added).[12] Beyond noting that this kind of repetition is a striking use of anaphora, we need also to note that through consistently repeating 'he', the defence is both structuring the text's flow of information and focusing the jury's attention on his client, and only his client.

The second theme, too, focuses on Bardales, but is much more varied in its choice of grammatical mood. Where the first theme is consistently in the declarative mood, the second is marked by the additive conjunction 'and' and the marked declarative phrase, 'it's true',[13] and uses both the declarative and interrogative moods:

He wasn't taking notes. *Why* would he? *He* didn't think that at some point months down the road he would be drilled about what time he did things and the sequence of events. *He* wasn't taking any notes (emphasis added).[14]

The third and fourth themes are marked by a series of wh- interrogatives—'*What* were you doing last May the 26th?' '*What* time

---

    [9] Stillar, *Analyzing*, n. 4 above, 46–7.   [10] *Ibid.*
    [11] *Regina* v. *Bardales* (1993) BCSC (unreported) Vancouver Registry 017342, 12, l. 11. Although I have used an official transcript of the closing arguments, my copy from the transcriber may depart in pagination and line numbering from the trial transcript.   [12] N. 11 above, 12, ll. 13–27.
    [13] N. 11 above, 12, l. 27.   [14] N. 11 above, 12, ll. 30–4.

did Tony come over?' '*How long* was this phone call with Enrici?' '*What* time did the phone call come in?' (emphasis added)[15]—to illustrate what kinds of questions 'you', the jury, and 'he', Bardales, couldn't answer. Together, three of the themes mark Bardales as the subject of the jury's focus, and the other marks the jury to compare themselves, favourably, with him.

The excerpt from the prosecutor's fifteen-page closing argument is twenty-two lines long, and occurs as the final unit of her first major argument, a six-point objection to the defence lawyer's statements. Beginning with 'My friend said', the prosecutor thematizes the defence's arguments, and links this section of her closing argument, through repetition, with the five previous times she has remarked, 'My friend said'. Rather than attacking Bardales's testimony directly, then, the prosecutor draws attention to the words of his counsel, and by underscoring them, marks them as constructed and strategic: '*My friend said* to you, Mr. Wilson, said, now, when they are stopped their demeanour is very calm and cooperative' (emphasis added).[16]

Having heard this theme five times before, the jury is now ready to question the defence's argument about the demeanour of the accused at the crime scene. To help them, the prosecutor thematizes the accused in the same, unmarked declarative mood that the defence lawyer employed: '*Mr. Bardales* has nothing to be worried about', '*He* doesn't have the car' '*He* doesn't have the gun' (emphasis added).[17] She then thematizes three 'existents'— objects which are said to exist, or in this case, not exist—which grammatically link Bardales to them as the grammatical object, 'him': 'There are *no witnesses*. There is *no one* to implicate him. *No one* to identify him'.[18] Finally, she moves quickly into her third and last theme, which thematizes the jury, and compares, hypothetically, their actions with Bardales's: '*If you thought* that you were being stopped . . . for speeding . . . would you become relieved when the police told you you were being investigated for a shooting?' (emphasis added).[19]

Marking the themes in these two excerpts allows us to compare and contrast what information each lawyer makes prominent: the

[15] N. 11 above, 12, ll. 34–40.
[16] N. 11 above, 35, ll. 30–2.
[17] N. 11 above, 35, ll. 35–6.
[18] N. 11 above, 35, ll. 39–40.
[19] N. 11 above, 35, ll. 44–7.

defence wants the jury to focus solely on Bardales, on 'he', and on the jury, on 'you', but only in relation to answering difficult questions in court. By contrast, the prosecutor wants the jury to focus on three parties: on the defence lawyer, on Bardales, and on themselves, to contrast Bardales's demeanour with their own, had they been him at the scene of the shooting. In short, the lawyers set up rival themes for the jury to adjudicate: the defence, a singular one of Bardales's testimony; the prosecutor, a much more complex one of motivated words (the defence lawyer's) and of duplicitous actions (Bardales's calm demeanour after shooting Martinez).

Cohesion is the other main resource of the textual function, which employs devices to relate parts of one sentence to parts of another over spans of text.[20] Cohesion gives textual unity, as Stillar points out, enabling it to be interpreted as a whole, rather than as a collection of words, and thus is part of the process of meaning-making.[21] Both the defence and prosecutor use cohesive 'reference'—a grammatical subject introduced and used as the reference point for the third-person pronoun—employing 'Bardales' as the participant, and then 'he' to organize their points. Likewise, both use the referent, 'he', repeatedly, employing 'repetition' as a device of 'lexical choice',[22] to underscore the focus and flow of information. In this way, the two excerpts stand out as organizationally similar, knitting their texts together not only by using the same kind of cohesive devices, but also by using the same words.

However, the two excerpts are markedly different in the way that they employ another kind of lexical choice. In particular, they use 'collocation' differently, words which have 'a more than ordinary tendency to co-occur'.[23] For example, the defence lawyer provides cohesion in his first theme by collocating such items as 'sister', 'guy', 'mother', all of which are linked by 'he' (Bardales).[24] And in his second and third themes, the defence provides cohesion by repetition and synonymy of such items as 'forget', 'remember', and 'memory'.[25] By contrast, the prosecutor provides cohesion in her first and second themes by collocating such items as 'gun', 'witness', 'scene', 'shot', 'dead', 'implicate', 'identify', and 'shooting',[26] and in her third, by such items as 'stopped', 'traffic ticket',

---

[20] Stillar, *Analyzing*, n. 4 above, 48.   [21] Stillar, *Analyzing*, n. 4 above, 49.
[22] Stillar, *Analyzing*, n. 4 above, 51.   [23] *Ibid.*
[24] N. 11 above, 12, ll. 20–5.   [25] N. 11 above, 12, ll. 27–45.
[26] N. 11 above, 35, ll. 35–43.

'speeding', 'liquor', 'police', investigated', 'shooting', 'hand-cuffed'.[27] Because collocation serves to set expectations, both lawyers employ it to 'make meaning' about Bardales. Once the defence chooses the 'family' lexicon, the jury thinks of Bardales in terms of family; and likewise, once he chooses the 'memory' lexicon, they link 'remembering' and 'forgetting' with Bardales. By contrast, once the prosecutor chooses a 'crime' lexicon, the jury links the crime and criminal activity with Bardales.

Text: The Ideational Function

While the textual function marks organization, the ideational function marks content, marks how the text represents the world. Several language resources feed this representation: participants and processes, circumstances, time and place, and concept taxonomies. I will define these terms as I work through the analysis.

In our closing argument excerpt, the defence lawyer uses ideational resources to 'represent a particular arrangement of "reality" '.[28] Specifically, he selects details from the testimony and arranges them into a list in which Bardales is the 'processor'—the sentient being who does the 'mentalizing'.[29] Two types of mental processes dominate: mental-verbalization—'he *says*', 'he *made a statement*', 'he *gave*', 'he *disclosed*', and mental-cognitive—'he *admitted*', 'he *didn't try to duck*', 'he *didn't try to back away*'. Equally important, the defence intersperses Bardales's mental 'actions' with another language resource, the 'circumstance' of 'manner'; that is, Bardales 'did' these 'things' in a particular way—'cooperatively':

He *says* it wasn't him. *He was cooperative* with the police when he was stopped fifteen minutes later. *He made a statement* to Bryden. Which is basically the same thing he told you. He *gave*—he *disclosed* his proper address. *He was cooperative*. He *admitted* things here that weren't necessarily in his favour that weren't necessarily calculated to make him look good. He *admitted* that his sister went out with a guy called Fidel. He *didn't try to duck* that issue. He *admitted* that he struck Carlos Escobar

---

[27] N. 11 above, 35, ll. 43–7, 36, ll. 1–2.
[28] Stillar, *Analyzing*, n. 4 above, 28.
[29] Stillar, *Analyzing*, n. 4 above, 23

with a volleyball. He *didn't back away* from that. He *admitted* his mother lived only two or three blocks away from the scene of the shooting. He *didn't try to back away* from any of that (emphasis added).[30]

Arranging reality in this way, the defence lawyer accomplishes several things. First, he signals closure by extracting and summing up Bardales's mental 'actions' from his testimony. Second, by treating Bardales as a *mental* processor, the defence moves him away from being a participant in *action* processes, especially the damning ones of threatening witnesses and shooting victims. And third, he selects and repeats a particular kind of circumstantial manner—'cooperative'—to provide the jury with a positive perspective from which to judge Bardales's actions as part of a continuum of response: he was cooperative at the scene of the crime, and he is still cooperative in the courtroom. The defence then links the past 'time' of Bardales's mental processes—'gave', 'disclosed', 'admitted', 'didn't back away'—to the themes which follow: 'he has forgotten many of the details' and 'you won't remember', 'that's the way human memory works', 'people forget that stuff':[31]

And it's true that he has forgotten many of the details but you must know yourselves that this is consistent with human nature and it's consistent with human memory. He wasn't taking notes. Why would he? He didn't think that at some point months down the road he would be drilled about what time he did things and the sequence of events. He wasn't taking any notes. What were you doing last May the 26th? Even if you keep a diary and it tells you what you did I'll wager that you will just remember the highlights and that's it. You won't remember times unless you have them noted. That's the way memory works.[32]

The defence presents these past mental actions—those Bardales remembers and, as important, those he forgets—in 'before-now' time, but links them both with 'you' and with 'after-now' time, with habitual, eternal time, and an 'ongoing' perspective.[33] This

---

[30] N. 11 above, 12, ll. 13–27.   [31] N. 11 above, 12, ll. 27–45.

[32] N. 11 above, 12, ll. 27–38.

[33] Stillar, *Analyzing*, n. 4 above, 27. Note that I use 'perspective' and 'time' here in a technical sense. Stillar points out that time and perspective are a major part of a text's functioning ideationally to construe experience. 'Time and perspective are semantic relations constructed from the position of the text's point of writing or speaking. Process, participants, and circumstances are construed as being before-now, or after-now in terms of time. Perspective is construed as either ongoing or completed' (27).

linkage helps arrange reality in two ways: it takes the past forgetting—which the jury might judge as lying—and frames it in the
context of future forgetting, locating it in a continuum of mental
processes rather than as a discrete act of dishonesty; and it links
Bardales as mental processor with other mental processors—'you',
the jury, and 'people', placing the forgetting into the realm of an
all-too-human propensity. Finally, over the whole excerpt what
we called 'collocation' in the textual function functions ideationally as 'concept taxonomies', clusters of lexical items that 'help
promote the interests' of the defence's 'perspective'.[34] Specifically,
the defence lawyer uses three lexicons, all of which point to
Bardales's humanity: that Bardales is part of a family ('his sister'
goes out with 'a guy'; 'his mother'); second, that Bardales is an
honest person, 'cooperative', 'admitting', 'not ducking' or 'back-
ing away' from potentially damning evidence; and third, that
Bardales forgets things that aren't important to him, just as we all
do. Selecting these details, and not others, and arranging them in
these particular ways, the defence creates a viewpoint from which
the jury can 'see' and then classify Bardales: in the class of close-
to-family, honest, forgetful people, a regular kind of chap.

To respond, the prosecutor presents a rival arrangement of
reality. She agrees with the defence lawyer's use of circumstantial
manner—that Bardales was 'very calm and cooperative'—but
attacks its motive. To do so, she returns, as did the defence
lawyer, to the scene of the shooting, when Bardales is stopped by
police. But where the defence lawyer makes this scene the departure point for Bardales's continuum of cooperation, the prosecutor
makes it the resting point: the entire excerpt focuses on the *place*
of the crime scene. More particularly, she queries the motive for
Bardales's cooperation through a series of negative verb forms:
'Well at that point Mr. Bardales *has nothing* to be worried about.
He *doesn't have* the car. He *doesn't have* the gun'.[35] The prosecutor constructs 'polarity'—choosing between the positive and negative[36]— for three reasons here: first, her use of the negative verb
form points to Bardales as a 'not-possessor' of the car and gun—
that is, she asserts that he had them before, but he doesn't have

---

[34] Stillar, *Analyzing*, n. 4 above, 31.
[35] N. 11 above, 35, ll. 32–5.
[36] M. A. K. Halliday, *An Introduction to Functional Grammar* (2nd edn, London, 1994), 88.

them now; second, she depicts Bardales as the 'possessor' of 'relational processes'[37] ('he doesn't *have* the gun'; 'he doesn't *have* the car'), two means by which to commit the crime; and third, her ostensible agreement with the defence lawyer is ironic—Bardales is not cooperative by nature, but by criminal premeditation: he can afford to be cooperative because he has rid himself of the incriminating car and gun.

To complete her attack, the prosecutor moves temporally even farther back than the defence lawyer, back to the relevant *time* of the crime. Then she ties Bardales's mental process at the crime scene with the action process of the crime itself: 'And *as far as he's concerned* he *has told* the one witness at the scene to leave which that witness did, and he *has just shot* someone who he can assume is dead' (emphasis added).[38] Here, she uses the mental process 'he's concerned' to point to a consciousness of guilt, guilt for the action processes 'has told the one witness . . . to leave', and 'has just shot someone'. More subtly yet, she uses the present perfect tense ('has told', 'has just shot')—a 'before-now' time and a 'completed' perspective—for two reasons: first, to make the crimes the point of origin for all Bardales's mental processes, including the courtroom admissions; and second, to underscore that the action processes themselves are past completed action, and therefore forensic, and properly adjudicated in a court of law. Having done so, the prosecutor returns to redefine the defence lawyer's meaning of 'cooperative': 'The significance . . . is not that he is nervous, the significance is that he wasn't surprised that they were being stopped in relation to a shooting'.[39] Once again, the prosecutor uses the negative to arrange a rival reality: 'cooperative' now means 'not nervous' and 'not surprised,' two circumstances of manner—nervousness and surprise—which common sense tells the jury are responses of innocent people. Add to this definition the single concept taxonomy over the entire excerpt that promotes the prosecutor's perspective: that Bardales is part of a world where such terms as 'gun', 'witness', 'scene', 'shot', 'dead', 'implicate', 'identify', 'police', 'investigated', and 'handcuffed' are so common that he can appear 'very calm and cooperative'. Selecting these

---

[37] Stillar, *Analyzing*, n. 4 above, 23.
[38] N. 11 above, 35, ll. 35–8.
[39] N. 11 above, 35, ll. 40–3.

details, and arranging them in these particular ways, the prosecutor creates a rival viewpoint from which the jury can see and identify Bardales as a particular kind of person: as one whose cold-bloodedness, actions, and duplicitous demeanour are legally culpable.

Text: The Interpersonal Function

Now we can look at how the organizing and representing functions operate simultaneously with the interpersonal function, the set of language resources that constructs interaction. Interaction is expressed in two ways: one which Stillar calls 'relational', which constructs relations between speakers and listeners; and the other which Stillar calls 'positional', which constructs the speaker's 'wishes, feelings, attitudes, and judgements' about what he or she is discussing.[40] At the end of our pair of closing argument excerpts, both lawyers use relational and positional values to address the issue of Bardales's credibility, a crucial consideration for the jury when the accused takes the stand.

Each lawyer establishes a link between Bardales and Bardales's own words, his testimony, and by extension, to his credibility through the relationships of the courtroom participants: the interaction between the lawyers and the jury, the lawyers and Bardales, and the jury and Bardales. Each of them underscores the adversarial nature of some relationships while promoting the complementarity of others. Take the defence's commentary, for example:

There's two possibilities really to explain his [Bardales's] evidence: one is he is completely enmeshed in a web of lies and deceit necessary to fit the Crown's theory and was lucky enough to escape detection in that deceit. Well, what do you think? You saw him. You heard him. You had a chance to assess him. Does he look like that kind of guy? And then there is a simple explanation, that he is telling the truth.[41]

First, through the speech function of his sentences, the defence lawyer bolsters his own relationship with the jury; that is, his sentence construction assigns interactive roles to both himself and the jury.[42] With the statements, 'there's two possibilities

---

40 Stillar, *Analyzing*, n. 4 above, 32.
41 N. 11 above, 26, ll. 32–41.
42 Stillar, *Analyzing*, n. 4 above, 34.

really to explain', and 'then there is a simple explanation', he assigns himself the roles of legal summarizer and expert. And with the demand, 'Well, what do you think?', he assigns the jury the role of fact-finders, but ones who must seriously question such relationships as the prosecutor's and Bardales's. Second, the defence contrasts his relationship with Bardales against the prosecutor's, simultaneously constructing a positional value towards their respective interpretations of Bardales's credibility. To do so, he marks the prosecutor's theory with 'one' and presents it as both grammatically convoluted ('[Bardales] is completely enmeshed in a web of lies and deceit necessary to fit the Crown's theory and was lucky enough to escape detection in that deceit') and logically impossible (the theory seems, temporally, to have developed before the crime itself). By contrast, he marks his own theory with 'and then', and presents it as both grammatically and logically simple: 'he is telling the truth'.

Simultaneously, the defence attacks the prosecutor's relationship with Bardales through the metaphoric comparison of her as a spider enmeshing victims like Bardales and attacks her theory as a bad 'fit' with the truth, expressing his negative positional evaluation of her strategy with two lexical choices which point to speaker attitude: the adverb of degree in '*completely* enmeshed' and the adverb of manner '*necessary* to fit'. Likewise, the qualitative adjective '*simple* explanation' indicates the defence's favourable positional evaluation of his own relationship with Bardales and his testimony: it is a straightforward one of a defence lawyer defending an honest witness and an innocent man. Finally, the defence invites the jury to consider their own relationship with Bardales through the question: 'Does he look like that kind of guy?'. With the emphasizing adjective '*that*', the defence undermines what he purports is the prosecutor's characterization of Bardales—a liar ('enmeshed in a web of lies') and deceiver ('deceit'), and challenges the jury to use their tactile senses—'you *saw* him', 'you *heard* him', to 'assess' the obviousness of Bardales's credibility.

Not surprisingly, the prosecutor foregrounds different relational and positional values to underscore Bardales's dubious credibility. She highlights only two interactions—hers with the jury and the jury's with Bardales:

I ask you to consider all of Roger Bardales' evidence very carefully. When *you are considering his credibility*, you consider everything he said and decide whether or not he is telling you the truth, based on his evidence, about where he was that night (emphasis added).[43]

The first relational value she establishes is hers with the jury, through her statement, '*I* ask *you*'. Rather than establishing her expertise, as the defence lawyer does, the prosecutor assigns to herself the role of petitioner, deferring and politely asking the jury to take on the more important role of fact finders through her request, 'I *ask* you'. Likewise, she marks their relation with Bardales as one of fact finding by explicitly connecting their fact-finding task with adjudicating his credibility ('when you are considering his credibility'). She marks this relationship, however, not with an attitudinal lexis of challenge, as the defence lawyer does, but, through an adverb of manner, as one of caution and care: 'consider all of Roger Bardales's evidence *very carefully*.' Like the defence lawyer's, the prosecutor's choice of lexis here marks not only her evaluation of Bardales, but sculpts the jury's. More particularly, she reinforces this lexis through the attitudinal function of the mental-cognitive process that she asks of the jury, and which she highlights through textual repetition: '*consider* all . . . evidence', 'when you *are considering* his credibility', 'you *consider* everything he said'. By urging and admonishing them to 'consider', the prosecutor implies that Bardales's evidence needs to be examined critically, and that the jury needs to connect this evidence with Bardales's whereabouts on the night of the shooting. Doing so, the prosecutor transports the jury out of the courtroom to the scene of the crime, and by mentioning it last, marks it as textually important.

Text: Rhetorical Analysis

Until now, I have acknowledged, without underscoring, that in each of the closing arguments, the lawyers have spoken about particular people and events in particular ways to particular ends. The rhetorician, Kenneth Burke, comments on this language practice: 'Even if a given terminology is a *reflection* of reality, by its very nature as a terminology it must be a *selection* of reality; and

---

[43] N. 11 above, 38, ll. 4–9.

to this extent it must function also as a *deflection* of reality'.[44] In other words, the two lawyers construct each of their closing arguments (a collection of related words, 'a given terminology'), which is by definition a particular 'reflection of reality', by selecting from some language resources, and deflecting—or purposely not selecting—from others. In terms of discourse, we have seen the choices both lawyers make from the resources of the textual, ideational, and interpersonal functions. Textually, for example, both lawyers thematize the words of others: the defence selects from the testimony of his client; the prosecution, from the arguments of the defence. Ideationally, both lawyers represent Bardales's actions. But where the defence selects from language resources to underscore that Bardales is a processor of mental processes ('he *disclosed*', 'he *admitted*'), the prosecution selects from language resources to underscore that Bardales is a processor of mental responses ('*as far as he's concerned*') to his criminal actions ('told the one witness to leave', 'shot someone'). And interpersonally, both lawyers represent the interactions of the courtroom participants: the defence focuses on the prosecutor and her adversarial relationship with Bardales; the prosecution, on the testimony of Bardales as it relates to his alleged criminal actions, to his whereabouts on the night of the shooting.

Each lawyer makes these selections based on a set of reasons, which are informed by the exigencies of the courtroom situation. Burke would call this language use, 'motivated', guided by a set of strategies to attain a goal: the defence counsel to have his client be exonerated of the charges; the prosecutor, to convict the accused man. To win their case, each lawyer encourages the jury to judge Bardales in a particular way. The defence wants the jury, through what Burke calls 'identification', to see Bardales as a person like themselves, to construct what is 'real' about Bardales in terms that makes both parties 'consubstantial', or united by similar substance:

A is not identical with his colleague, B. But insofar as their interests are joined, A is *identified* with B. Or he may *identify himself* with B even when their interests are not joined, if he assumes they are, or is persuaded to believe so.[45]

---

[44] K. Burke, *Language as Symbolic Action: Essays on Life, Literature, and Method* (Berkeley and Los Angeles, 1966), 45.

[45] K. Burke, *A Grammar of Motives* (Berkeley and Los Angeles, 1969), 21.

In our case, the defence needs to persuade the jury that their and Bardales's interests are joined in a particular way: that finding Bardales not guilty both serves justice and frees an innocent man. By contrast, the prosecutor wants the jury to believe that their interest and hers are joined in the state's prosecution of people who break the law, and thus to perceive Bardales as a person unlike themselves, to construct what is 'real' about Bardales in terms that make them dissimilar. Once the jury judges him as different, as 'less'—less like themselves, especially less law-abiding—they are more likely to find him guilty.

To persuade the jury, the lawyers foster identification by presenting the terms by which, if accepted, the jury will employ to judge Bardales. In particular, they construct rival terms for Bardales's actions, and especially, to ascribe to him specific motives for his actions. Burke's method, which he calls 'Dramatism', is 'designed to show that the most direct route to the study of human relations and human motives is via a methodological inquiry into cycles or clusters of terms and their functions'.[46] Patterns of selection and combinations of language resources in texts, Burke asserts, can reveal relationships among five terms, all of which are common and socially ascribed: act, agent, scene, agency, and purpose. In our case, the lawyers employ 'some word that names the *act* (names what took place, in thought or deed), and another that names the *scene* (the background of the act, the situation in which it occurred)', as well as 'what person or kind of person (*agent*) performed the act, what means or instruments he used (*agency*), and the *purpose*'.[47] More importantly, each lawyer sets up a relationship between two of these terms, called a 'ratio', which encourages the jury to see one term 'in terms of' the other. So, for example, the defence lawyer might have developed his theory of the case and his closing argument using a scene–act ratio, in which the scene—say, Bardales's troubled childhood, his lack of schooling, his unloving family—all lead him to commit the attempted murder of Juan Martinez, but that the jury should have mercy considering that Bardales is a victim of his past, or 'scene'. Or the prosecutor might have developed another ratio, say, an agency–agent ratio, in which Bardales is the shooter (the agent

[46] K. Burke, *Counter Statement* (3rd edn, Berkeley and Los Angeles, 1968), 445.   [47] Burke, n. 46 above, xv.

who has committed the crime) because his car and gun (the agency or means of the crime) both have traces of Martinez's blood on them. Different terms, put together in different combinations, allow the lawyers to foreground different possibilities, to ascribe different motives to Bardales's actions.

As it happens in our case, both lawyers choose the same ratio, an act–agent ratio. However, each lawyer employs different concepts within the ratio; that is, they represent different *acts* in order to present a very different kind of *agent* to the jury. For the defence, the central act is Bardales's ongoing cooperation throughout the trial. And so the defence develops his closing argument to emphasize the continuum of cooperative acts that Bardales, the agent, has performed, from the time he was stopped by the police to the time he testified in court. By contrast, for the prosecution, the central act is the attempted murder, and so she develops her closing argument to attack, or at least play down, the sincerity of Bardales's cooperation, chiefly by emphasizing his alleged acts on the night of the crime—namely, his shooting of one man and threatening of another.

Both lawyers reinforce this act–agent alignment by grounding, if you will, and foregrounding Bardales, in different, and rival, scenes. Throughout his closing argument, the defence reminds the jury that they have witnessed Bardales and his actions in the scene of the courtroom; throughout hers, the prosecutor, that they must remember what Bardales did at the scene of the crime. This strategy Burke calls the 'principle of consistency'[48] that operates to bind scene, act, and agent:

Using 'scene' in the sense of setting, or background, and 'act' in the sense of action, one could say that 'the scene contains the act.' And using 'agents' in the sense of actors, or acters, one could say that 'the scene contains the agents.' It is a principle of drama that the nature of acts and agents should be consistent with the nature of the scene.[49]

In other words, by 'keeping' Bardales in the scene of the courtroom, the defence encourages the jury to identify Bardales's actions there with the kind of agent he is—cooperative, honest, and therefore, not guilty. And for the prosecutor, the same principle operates: keeping Bardales at the scene of the crime allows her to argue that he, a criminal agent, performs criminal actions.

---

[48] Burke, n. 46 above, 9. [49] Burke, n. 46 above, 3.

Finally, both lawyers use a kind of antimetabole (an a–b/b–a pattern), in which they reverse the act–agent ratio, making it an agent–act ratio. For both, it operates as an effective, though circular, argument: they characterize Bardales as an agent by the acts that he commits, and then argue that because Bardales is this kind of agent, he would, naturally, commit these kinds of acts. While Burke does not discuss this flipping of ratios as a form of reinforcement, he does describe what each ratio does for the other:

The agent is the author of his acts, which are descended from him, being good progeny if he is good, or bad progeny if bad, wise progeny if he is wise, silly progeny if he is silly. And conversely, his acts can make him or remake him in accordance with their nature. They would be his product and/or he would be theirs.[50]

In our case, the defence first posits that Bardales's *acts*—his cooperation in the courtroom—make him a cooperative, honest, and credible defendant; and the prosecutor, that Bardales's acts—his lying at the crime scene—make him a dishonest witness. Then, the defence flips the ratio so that because Bardales is a cooperative *agent* his acts of honesty are good acts, and as good agent, he is innocent of the crime. By contrast, the prosecutor posits that because Bardales is a lying agent his acts of dishonesty are bad acts, and point to his even worse act: that he is lying because he committed attempted murder. Both lawyers encourage the jury to identify with their respective act–agent/agent–act in their respective scene, and which of these the jury chooses will dictate both their perception of Bardales and their judgment of him.

Text: Social Theory

Stillar points out that Burkean rhetorical theory 'understands that rhetorical acts index, construct, and potentially bring about transformations in social relationships and practices'.[51] Certainly, we have seen that 'the rhetorical acts' of the closing arguments employ the metafunctions of language resources to 'construct' ratios about Bardales in such a way as to 'bring about transformations' in the 'social relationship' between Bardales and the jury. By emphasizing identification, the defence lawyer tries to deflect and

---

[50] Burke, n. 46 above, 17.   [51] Stillar, n. 4 above, 92.

diminish the 'fundamental divisions and differences that mark [the] social agents',[52] Bardales and the jury, while the prosecutor tries to foreground and augment these same divisions and differences. In short, both lawyers use language and rhetorical resources to mark and construct the social process of either congregation or segregation, social processes which motivate the jury to judge Bardales as either not guilty or guilty.

To initiate these social—and, ultimately, legally binding—judgments about Bardales, both lawyers utilize a socialized understanding of the courtroom. Stillar points to Pierre Bourdieu's notion of 'habitus' to identify this understanding as a set of 'embodied cultural dispositions that social agents bring to bear in social practice'.[53] Not merely a label for the habits of social agents, 'habitus' is a much more complex notion, having several defining features, all of them socially acquired. First, the habitus is inculcated gradually through learning and training; second, it is structured as part of, and as a reflection of, a particular socialization; third, it is durable because it persists through the life of an individual, operating in a preconscious way; and fourth it is generative and transposable, capable or generating practices in many different fields.[54] For the two lawyers, these dispositions have been inculcated over many years of professional training and practice in law, structured by the economic and social conditions of the university-educated middle class, durable over their professional lifetime, and generative of exact and appropriate responses to many situations in a range of court cases, each with its particular set of facts.

More particularly, both lawyers utilize their habitus to anticipate the jury's own habitus, the socialized practices from their social worlds. Specifically, the lawyers work from what they know are socially acceptable notions of acceptable facts and plausible explanations. These notions work to build up a set of judgments about Bardales, to classify him as a particular kind of social agent. For Bourdieu, classes are 'sets of agents who occupy similar positions in the social space, and hence possess similar kinds and similar qualities of capital, similar life chances, similar dispositions,

---

[52] Stillar, n. 4 above, 93.   [53] Stillar, n. 4 above, 95.
[54] John B. Thompson, 'Editor's Introduction' in Pierre Bourdieu, *Language and Symbolic Power* (Cambridge, 1991), 12–13.

etc.'.[55] Thus, as we have seen, the defence lawyer portrays Bardales as a young man with family connections and friends, a man who cooperates with the police and with the courtroom process—a person that the jury could 'classify' in their own class of social agents. And, as we have seen, the prosecutor portrays Bardales as a young man who uses family and friends to hide the incriminating evidence of guns and cars, whose friends lie for him, and who lies, deceives, and threatens and shoots other people—a person that the jury would classify as not of their own class of social agents.

Finally, in writing and presenting their closing arguments, the defence and prosecuting lawyers exhibit what Bourdieu calls 'linguistic habitus', a subset of dispositions of the habitus, which generates and interprets language practices.[56] Here, both lawyers employ an expert 'felt sense' to match the linguistic product of the closing argument with the demands of a specific social situation— with the particular judge, the particular jury, and the particular details of the case of *Regina* v. *Bardales*. This right felt sense leaves the traces of linguistic and rhetorical choices that we have analysed in the preceding pages: it is a product of the lawyers' more general habitus; it has informed their rival forms of identification and sculpted their choice of ratios; and it has drawn upon, and added to, the metafunctional resources of language. Most importantly, like their habitus, the lawyers' linguistic habitus works at the level of preconscious knowledge, exploited and embodied in inculcated language practices of the law, and not in reflection and conscious choice. In short, the two lawyers demonstrate a facility with rhetorically motivated, fine linguistic choices too subtle and situated to be codified in advice and training.

As social texts, the lawyers' closing arguments demonstrate a 'duality of structure'.[57] First, they are the final product in a sequence of events structured into the formal proceedings that we call a trial. Equally, however, they reproduce in their patterns and principles of argument, expressed through language, the social rightness of the whole legal structure. That is, they provide meaning for

---

[55] Thompson, n. 54 above, 30.

[56] P. Bourdieu, *Language and Symbolic Power* (Cambridge, 1991), 87.

[57] A. Giddens, *The Constitution of Society: Outline of the Theory of Structuration* (Berkeley and Los Angeles, 1984), 94.

us, meaning that points to the legitimacy and efficacy of the meting out of justice, of the fittedness of crime and punishment. This duality of structure, then, allows the lawyers to organize, to represent, and to have their closing arguments interact as symbolic texts in the courtroom, to be both products of, and to reproduce, the legal system in which they, this jury, Roger Bardales, and all of us have a stake.

I have argued, following Herrnstein Smith, that closure is a sequence of events, structured by some principle to signal a terminal point, a point which we experience both as conclusive and distinctly satisfying. Moreover, I have argued that by definition, closure, and by extension, closing argument, is discoursal, rhetorical, and social; that by applying Stillar's methodology to our model excerpts, we see that both the defence and prosecution make choices from the resources of the textual, ideational, and interpersonal functions of discourse; that these choices are rhetorically motivated; and that, finally, these discoursal and rhetorical choices are products of the linguistic habitus of both lawyers, which, in turn, is both the outcome and the medium for the social structures of the law.

The founder of the law and literature movement, James Boyd White, has observed that law students and lawyers are 'culturally embedded figures, partly shaped by the languages and culture they must use, partly shaping them'.[58] As the linguistic products of lawyers, closing arguments, too, I have argued, shape and are shaped by their practitioners' linguistic, rhetorical, and social processes. As such, they can be studied, as White says, so that practitioners can not only 'use these languages [but] understand them and be able to criticize them'.[59]

[58] J. Boyd White, 'Teaching Law and Literature' (1994) 27/4 *Mosaic* 12.
[59] *Ibid.*

CROSSING THE LITERARY MODERNIST DIVIDE AT CENTURY'S END: THE TURN TO TRANSLATION AND THE INVENTION OF IDENTITY IN AMERICA'S STORY OF ORIGINS

Gary Minda

Introduction

James Baldwin, one of America's most famous black writers, was an *outsider* living in Paris for a substantial period of his career. In one of his essays, *Nobody Knows My Name*,[1] Baldwin credits Henry James for having discovered something that has been central to much of Baldwin's writing about America—namely, that '[i]t is a complex fate to be an American'.[2] For Baldwin, the complexity of American identity was rendered even more complex by the fact that he was an American writer living in Paris. Baldwin tells the reader that he [Baldwin] 'left America because [he] doubted [his] ability to survive the fury of the color problem [there]'. As Baldwin then explained:

I wanted to prevent myself from becoming *merely* a Negro; or, even, merely a Negro writer. I wanted to find out in what way the *specialness* of my experience could be made to connect me with other people instead of dividing me from them. (I was as isolated from Negroes as I was from whites, which is what happens when a Negro begins, at bottom, to believe what white people say about him).[3]

For Baldwin, Henry James had a certain literary style and point of view that enabled Baldwin to understand something about his own

---

[1] J. Baldwin, *Nobody Knows My Name* (New York, 1961).
[2] Baldwin, n. 1 above, 17.
[3] *Ibid.*

identity as a black expatriated American. Much later in an interview in 1986, published in *The Henry James Review*, Baldwin observed that he shared with Henry James an understanding about America's central failure—'the failure of America to see through to the reality of others'.[4] This theme, which Baldwin saw in James's novel *The Ambassadors* (1903), was something that Baldwin felt Americans needed to know about if they were ever to understand their selfhood or identity as Americans. Thus, James Baldwin, an outsider living in Europe, came to understand something that lies at the base of the complexity surrounding American identity. To understand who we are, we need to understand the relation we share with the 'other'. Identity, whether of an individual or of a nation, can only be understood in terms of the identity relations of people of a culture. As James Baldwin's fiction teaches, America is a parable for confronting the complex identity relationships that signify American identity.

In this paper I attempt to explain how the failure to see through to the reality of the other is a central literary theme of America's most basic narrative, the story of origins. Failure in America's story of origins is the *failure* of a particular kind of literary translation. America's story of origins is a good story but it is also a story of exclusion and aggression. The structure of this story is organized by a number of narrative plots that signify and thus represent the identity of Americans. America's story of origins necessitates the invention of American identity, and the invention of American identity is the product of a literary translation. The story maintains faith in the myths of America's long-lost past, but it does so by denying the identity of those Americans who have been excluded from the story, and for this reason the story is an example of failure of a particular kind of translation.

Contrary to those who see little consequence flowing from the literary effort,[5] I will use James Boyd White's idea of 'literary

---

[4] See D. Leeming, *James Baldwin: A Biography* (New York, 1994), 254–5.

[5] My effort here is calculated to provide a response to the forms of criticism that Professors Jane B. Baron and Guyora Binder have raised about law and literature. See their contributions to this book at 21 and 63. Baron and Binder share the view that the law and literature categories are reductive and hence flawed. I will attempt to explain how and why the idea of literary translation transcends the categories and distinctions they identify as the problematic categories and aesthetics of law and literature, and how law and literature is offering up a form of cultural and legal criticism that critics such as Baron and Binder should support and engage in their own critical projects.

translation', described in his book, *Justice as Translation: An Essay in Cultural and Legal Criticism*,[6] to explore a different kind of translation, one that promises to bring a renewed focus and interest in cultural criticism and identity construction in law and literature.[7] In order to give White's idea of literary translation critical bite, I argue that the literary translator must bring into the translation the voice of the 'other' so that the reader can get a more complete understanding of the 'other's' identity and culture.[8] Translation can be a powerful literary strategy for engaging cultural and legal criticism, but only if the translator shares the literary commitment of outsiders to discover how identity relations structure the meaning of our most basic literary narratives.

I first examine how identity relates to America's most basic literary narrative, the story of origins. Then I take up the relation between identity and the idea of a 'literary translation' and explain how Professor White's idea of literary translation can be effective for understanding America's story of origins. Finally, I offer accounts of identity in the translations of America's story constructed by literary modernist and literary postmodernist translators.

America's Story of Origins

America's official story is a 'story of origins'.[9] It is the story of the men, documents, and events that we Americans celebrate on the Fourth of July. In Milner Ball's view, the narrative of this story is

---

[6] J. B. White, *Justice As Translation: An Essay in Cultural and Legal Criticism* (Chicago and London, 1985).

[7] This is not to suggest that I agree with everything that White claims about 'justice as translation'. As I will explain, I take issue with the foundationalism of Professor White's idea of a good translator model. Nor do I believe, as Professor White believes, that a 'good translator model' can be discovered in the way a lawyer seeks to understand the language and culture of a client. These are minor disagreements. White's more basic assertions about the nature of language and translation offer, I believe, an effective strategy for giving law and literature initial bite.

[8] The paper will thus explore the potential dangers that the 'turn to translation' may pose for the literary-minded scholar who may make the 'common mistake' that translation, like language, is a 'code' or 'objective medium' for translating the meaning of one language into that of another. White, *Justice as Translation*, n. 6 above, 253.

[9] M. Ball, 'Stories of Origin And Constitutional Possibilities' (1989) 87 *Michigan Law Review* [*Mich. L. Rev.*] 2280.

'anchored' in our most radical document ever written, the Declaration of Independence. The narrative of the Declaration of Independence is a story about resistance to imperialistic power and the failure of one government, England, to extend the full rights of citizenship to the American colonies. In one sense, the Declaration of Independence was necessitated by England's failure to include the colonists within its story of origins.

One could say that the American revolution was a reaction to an English definition of America that associated its citizens with intense opposition to their 'foreign' location. Using John Higham's concept of 'nativism' as 'intense opposition to foreignness',[10] one can see how a form of 'English nativism' constructed an identity of the colonists that denied them the rights of English citizenship. Much later, in nineteenth-century America, a new definition of what it means to be an American was constructed so that Americans could regain equality with the English. As Walter Benn Michaels, a Professor of English and Humanities at the Johns Hopkins University, has noted in his recent book, *Our America: Nativism, Modernism and Pluralism*, Americans replaced class by race and thereby created a new cultural identity that enabled every white man in America to be the equal of an English 'gentleman'.[11]

For most Americans, however, the revolutionary narrative of the Declaration of Independence was more an event than a text, which probably explains why most historians, law professors, and judges do not count the document as being within the authoritative texts they read and purport to follow. For judges and most legal academics, the more important document in our story of origins is the Constitution, which is all about text, and has little to do with real events. The abstract text of the Constitution creates a set of signs that locates the point in time the document was created. Its origins reside within the mystical 'Founding Moment', when 'The People' gave 'Their Consent'. The origins of the 'founding moment' when 'the people' gave 'their consent' establish the key identity relations in constitutional law.[12]

The idea of an American is defined in terms of a long-dead

---

[10]   J. Higham, *Strangers in the Land* (New Brunswick, 1955, reprint 1988), 4.
[11]   W. B. Michaels, *Our America: Nativism, Modernism, and Pluralism* (Durham and London, 1995), 58.
[12]   P. Schlag, 'The Empty Circles of Liberal Justification' (1997) 96 *Mich. L. Rev.* 1, 4.

generation, whose identities become the fundamental ontological identities in America's story. Citizenship, as such, is not the key determinant of American identity; rather what counts is whether one believes he or she shares an inherited connection to America's story of origins. While the precise legal relations of national identity remain flexible to take into account changed circumstances in constitutional law (for example, the abolition of slavery and extension of voting rights to women), the mythology of a universal identity based on the identity of people in America's story of origins continues to be the determining ground for ascertaining what it means to be an American. The identity relations of constitutionalism thus serve to create a frame of reference for understanding the 'Americanism' of people who regard themselves as American.[13]

But constitutional discourse is not the only discourse that operates to construct American identity. To ensure that America remain American, twentieth-century pluralism necessitates the creation of a new cultural identity premised upon the belief that there is a native culture. America's story of origins thus makes sense even if it doesn't include the stories of all Americans because even the claim to be protected by the Constitution no longer determines who can claim to be American; rather what counts is whether one is considered to be part of the cultural identity. We affirm that we are Americans by reference to pluralism, and as a consequence of our relation to pluralism, we deny our culture differences. The commitment to pluralism establishes racial and cultural identity as key 'markers' of Americanism.[14] To insist on one's separate identity and culture, that is to say, to resist cultural assimilation, is to place oneself outside the boundaries of American identity.

Pluralism unites with the key identities of constitutional mythology to define the meaning of Americanism by redefining national identity in terms of a new cultural identity that is America. The 'melting-pot' metaphor of twentieth-century American pluralism, for example, constructs an image of 'melting and [re]forming identities created from the races of European

---

[13] White makes a similar point in observing how the Supreme Court's decisions under the fourth amendment to the US Constitution create 'a judgment [about how] people will be talked about in our public world': *Justice as Translation*, n. 6 above, 180.   [14] White, n. 6 above, 15.

immigrants who came to America and claimed it as their new home'.[15] The metaphor works to define national identity in terms of a uniquely American racial identity constructed from the melting-pot of many different races. The melting-pot metaphor presupposes that the ground of racial and cultural identity are the key determinants of American identity.

There is, however, a nagging problem posed by these stories and narratives about America. The problem is that, as much of James Baldwin's fiction illustrates, the stories and narratives are not the stories or narratives of women, people of colour, native Americans and many others who regard themselves as Americans. Those who are left out of America's stories have all the legal rights and duties of citizenship, but they nonetheless see themselves as outsiders or 'foreigners' in the story.[16] Although they have earned American citizenship and have the right to vote, they experience discrimination as foreigners because they are never regarded as being within the national identity captured by the story of origins. To insist on maintaining their separate culture and identity places them outside the identity relations created by American constitutionalism and pluralist ideology. Insistence on identity difference can have serious consequences for the individual; it can be the cause of alienation and discrimination.

The possibility of revolution signified by the narrative of the Declaration of Independence remains with us because the violence of exclusion creates tension and aggression. The problematic relation between the two texts—the Declaration of Independence and the Constitution—creates instability. One text is a revolutionary manifesto, a cause to take up arms. The other calls for a plan of government, and sets up the justifications for the orderly administration of the state. One text demands that all people be treated equally; the other provides the political explanation for understanding why equality applies only to 'The People' who are the sovereign agents of the government. The potential for conflict between the narratives of these two texts leaves open the possibility for new revolutionary narratives. The narratives that legitimate our legal order thus retain revolutionary force.

---

[15] Michaels, *Our America*, n. 11 above, 60.
[16] See Judith Resnik's remarks in C. Heilbrun and J. Resnik, 'Convergences: Law, Literature, and Feminism' (1990) 99 *Yale Law Journal* [Yale LJ] 1913, 1936.

Modern constitutional scholars are quite aware of this conflict. They insist that we can still find reason for hope and justification in the story of origins. America's story of origins, as Milner Ball tells it, for example, enabled Frederick Douglass to affirm the text of the Constitution as an anti-slavery document, and it allowed Lincoln in his Gettysburg Address of 1863 to declare that the Union has always been dedicated to the 'proposition' of equality. According to Milner Ball, '[t]he methods of both men were means for engaging narrative in the transformation of the legal order, telling stories so that law might include and respect the black people who had been excluded'.[17] In Ball's view, we can discover a good translation of the story, holding out the promise for reconciling our differences in pluralism. The promise of pluralism is that basic documents of the nation can be translated as one harmonized text to justify the pluralist dream of 'one America' for all Americans.

To be sure, the liberal justification of pluralism and much of the legal and political theory of our Constitution is based on a central promise that has never been kept—the promise of reconciling the individual with the interests of the community. The liberal justification seeks to reconcile the individual with the community by a series of narrative strategies based on metaphors of 'melting-pot', 'self-rule', 'self-government', or 'popular sovereignty'. There has always been a certain circularity to the patterns of these narratives. The logic of these narratives creates an 'empty circle'. As Pierre Schlag has explained: 'In the liberal justification, the paramount norm is ruling. It rules us. But, it has been chosen by us. In a fundamental sense the paramount norm is us. We are, in short, ruled by ourselves.'[18]

A similar 'empty circle' is created by the narratives of 'We the People'. Bruce Ackerman's constitutional narratives, for example, always return to the legitimacy of 'We the People'.[19] The identity of 'We the People' is never defined; in fact it remains undefined much in the same way that Oliver Wendell Holmes Jr's construct of a 'reasonable man' has remained undefined for much of this century. The problem with the abstraction 'We the People' is that it merely poses the question: what do you mean by 'We'?

---

[17] Ball, 'Stories of Origin', n. 9 above, 2285.
[18] Schlag, 'The Empty Circles', n. 12 above, 29.
[19] B. Ackerman, *We The People—Foundations*, Vol. 1 (New Haven, 1991).

There is also the question about the agency of these 'people'. As Pierre Schlag has sardonically asked: 'When do these People act? In constitutional conventions? In popular initiatives? In massive street protests?'[20] Another empty circle is posed by the liberal myth of 'consent'. How is it that a small group of white, upper-class European men who drafted the Constitution in 1789 can be said to have given consent for all future generations of Americans?

The problem with liberal narratives that justify America's story of origins is that they all assume that the Constitution is some sort of anti-imperialist hero that is there to defend the individual from evils of imperialism.[21] Defending the Constitution thus becomes a way of defending against imperialistic power. But, as the radical narrative of the Declaration of Independence reminds us, there is no reason to believe that the Constitution will forever be on the side of 'The People'. There are many examples in our history that illustrate the proposition that the Constitution is not always on the side of the people. One need only look to the turn-of-the-century decision of the United States Supreme Court in *Plessy* v. *Ferguson*[22] (upholding the separate-but-equal doctrine that legally sanctioned racial segregation) or the more recent decision of the Court in *Bowers* v. *Hardwick*[23] (the modern-day equivalent of *Plessy* upholding the right of a state to prohibit homosexual practices). These cases give good reasons for understanding how constitutionalism has been used to objectify and hence deny the human identity of unpopular groups of people in society. The possibility that the narratives of constitutionalism would be used to do great violence to certain people, however, is lost in the narratives of pluralism and liberalism that justify the American Constitution.

We are thus left wondering about the reality of what America has become. Between 1890 and 1920 immigration changed the face of America. The identity of America's origins has in fact vanished; America's story of origins describes the identity of a 'vanishing American'.[24] But the truth is that American identity has always remained a matter of much mystery and great controversy. As James Baldwin observed:

---

[20] Schlag, n. 12 above, 15.   [21] Michaels, n. 11 above, 22.
[22] 163 US 537 (1896).   [23] 478 US 186 (1986).
[24] Michaels, *Our America*, n. 11 above, 29–40.

America's history, her aspirations, her peculiar triumphs, her even more peculiar defeats, and her position in the world—yesterday and today—are all so profoundly and stubbornly unique that the very word 'America' remains a new, almost completely undefined and extremely controversial proper noun. No one in the world seems to know exactly what it describes not even we motley millions who call ourselves Americans.[25]

And yet, despite the mystery and controversy surrounding the meaning of the word, Americans remain committed to the idea of cultural identity that is thought to be America.

America's story of origins and the political narratives of pluralism continue to hold sway because the subjects who have access to the narrative, and thus control the narrative's basic canons, have good reasons for believing that the story of origins is good. The story of origins, after all, legitimates identity hierarchy. If you are sitting on the top of the identity pyramid, and see yourself as connected in some mythical way to the founding moment in America's story of origins, the story would seem to be both enduring and desirable indeed. For those at the bottom, however, there is reason to wonder if the story makes any sense at all. Some see failure in the way the story has been translated. For some a new translation is required; hence, the 'turn to translation'.

The Turn to Literary Translation

In the introduction to *Justice as Translation*, James Boyd White quotes Wittgenstein's observation that '[t]o imagine a language means to imagine a form of life'.[26] If we are to imagine the forms of life represented by language of the 'other', we must allow the other's language to be spoken as the other speaks it, and to contemplate the meaning of the words as the other understands them.[27] To look at

---

[25] Baldwin, *Nobody Knows My Name*, n. 1 above, 17.

[26] Baldwin, n. 1 above, ix.

[27] As Richard Weisberg has argued, a 'good translator' must pay more attention to the stories of outsiders and spend less energy on 'bring[ing] about an elegant "translation" of a text that has been ignored': R. Weisberg, *Poethics: And Other Strategies of Law and Literature* (New York, 1992), 249–50. However, this does not mean that White's literary metaphor of *translation* is about bringing out 'elegant translations' of forgotten texts. On the contrary, White's idea of a literary translation offers, as Weisberg's literary interpretations offer, important literary lessons for understanding how to translate the stories of Americans that have been ignored in America's story of origins.

language in this way necessitates not merely translations of the language of the other, but the inclusion of the other's language and culture in the translation.[28] The relevance of literary translation to America's story of origins is that it encourages translators to think about how identity construction works to give meaning to the identity of Americans. To understand why this might be so I need to explain what Professor White means by 'translation'.

White's idea of translation is intended to motivate translators to face a most perplexing and interesting inquiry. Through the process of translation, White contemplates that the 'integration' of the translation will change the translator's understanding of the 'other'. New meanings of both the 'self' and the 'other' are created by thinking about how two fundamental languages and cultures relate to create identity relations. In focusing the literary inquiry on how literary activity of a culture creates meaning about the identity relations of a culture, White encourages us to transcend the categories of 'law' and 'literature' and catch a glimpse at how our language discourses ground both our selfhood and our conception of the other.

Justice as Translation thus provides cultural critics with a literary strategy for bringing law and literature into the debates of contested cultural discourses about America's origins. White's literary objective is neither a form of moral 'sentimentalism',[29] nor is it based on some sort of category hierarchy (literature superior to law, 'law-as-literature' superior to 'law-in-literature', and so forth).[30] The whole point of *Justice as Translation* is to get us to see how our various language discourses keep us from understanding our differences,

---

[28] This, I think, is the point that James Baldwin made clear in his work. See Leeming, *James Baldwin*, n. 4 above. Baldwin believed that literary artists were capable of bringing out the meaning of identity relations, and that we can learn from their work important insights about who we are, and who we might become. As Baldwin observed about Norman Mailer: 'One can never really see into the heart, the mind, the soul of another'; but what we can learn from a writer by reference to his or her literary work. 'For, though it clearly needs to be brought into focus, he [Mailer] has a real vision of ourselves as we are, and it cannot be too often repeated in this country now, that, where is no vision, the people perish.' (Baldwin, *Nobody Knows My Name*, n. 1 above, 190).

[29] Here, I have in mind Professor Guyora Binder's critique of law and literature. See Binder, 'The Law-as-Literature Trope' in this book, 63.

[30] Here, I have in mind Professor Jane B. Baron's critique of law and literature. See Baron, 'The Half-Life of Law and Literature in the U.S.' (1999) 108 *Yale LJ* 1059. See also her contribution to this book, 21.

and how a new form of literary translation might enable us to
catch a glimpse at what keeps official translators of America's
story of origins from acknowledging identity differences.

Why literary translation? Literary translation becomes a way to
reconcile the reality of American identity with the promise of its
story of origins. As Professor White has explained: 'Translation . . .
is . . . the art of facing the impossible, of confronting unbridgeable
discontinuities between texts, between languages, and between
people.'[31] The art of translation is thus intended to provide us
with means for capturing a glimpse of the diverse identities of the
people who inhabit other languages, texts, and cultures. When we
attempt to translate the text of the 'other', we open ourselves to a
most interesting and perplexing inquiry. This inquiry is what
White mysteriously called the 'deep features of our professional
life, at once problematic and liberating, requiring an art of which
we have only the dimmest awareness, but which at the same time
promises a new sense of ourselves and our possibilities'.[32]

By 'literary translation' White means something different from
the way most people understand the word. In its customary understanding, translation is an interpretive practice that converts the
meaning of one language into the meaning of another; for example, the way an interpreter would translate French or German into
English. This common understanding of translation assumes that
language is a 'code' into which messages are encoded or a 'system
of signifiers and signified' that permit one to transport the meaning of one language or text into another. Such an understanding
presumes that language is a 'conduit', and that translation is a
medium for making an interpretation between parallel languages
and cultures.

The whole point of White's idea of a literary translation, however,
is the notion that 'languages (including legal ones) [are] forms of life,
not merely . . . systems or instances of communication'.[33] The idea of
a literary translation is thus intended to be a practice to bring out the
meaning of the 'languages and voices' that can be found in the
worlds we inhabit. A literary translation contemplates the discovery
of new meaning and new identity relations of different languages,
texts, and cultures of human communities. White's idea of literary

---

[31] White, *Justice as Translation*, n. 6 above, 257.
[32] White, n. 6 above, 262.   [33] White, n. 6 above, xiv.

translation is a form of cultural and legal criticism that must be
distinguished from literary criticism. Literary criticism defines meaning by reference to the constitutive power of an interpretative
community;[34] whereas a literary translation seeks to 'bring to
consciousness' the ethical content of the literary practices of the
interpretative community, by confronting the ethics and practices of
another community, so that we might examine how the power of
our community creates the meaning of who we are, as well as the
character and identity of our culture—what White calls the 'stuff of
human life'.[35]

The idea of a 'literary translation' thus allows us to find something missing or hidden in the official narratives about America.
What is missing is the meaning of justice. White's *Justice as
Translation* was in fact written for the purpose of rediscovering
justice in the cultural and legal narratives about the identity relations of Americans. White argues that the different languages and
cultures of the people that constitute America can be translated so
that the justice of identity difference is not only acknowledged but
respected. Translations 'integrate' the differences that separate
people within the 'integration' of the translation.[36]

White's literary effort is aimed at freeing us from a myth about
language and translation, the myth that 'we all live in a common
nonlinguistic world of shapes, objects, animals, colors, ideas,
concepts, and so forth, which different languages happen to label
differently, with different sounds'.[37] White shares James Baldwin's
insight that 'experience is linguistic at every stage', that what we
do and write is a product of who we are, and who we are is a
product of the basic narratives that define the meaning of our
culture and our identity. As Baldwin put it: 'Though we do not
wholly believe it yet, the interior life is a real life, and the intangi-
ble dreams of people have a tangible effect on the world.'[38]

When applied to law, the lessons of literary translations remind us
that judges must remain faithful not just to the texts they interpret,

---

[34] See, e.g., S. Fish, *Is There a Text in this Class?* (Cambridge, Mass., 1980).
[35] White, n. 6 above, 65.
[36] As White explains: 'Translation is . . . a species of . . . "integration": putting
two things together in such a way as to make a third, a new thing with a meaning
of its own': *Justice as Translation*, n. 6 above, 263.
[37] White, n. 6 above, 254.
[38] Baldwin, *Nobody Knows My Name*, n. 1 above, 23.

but also to their responsibility as human agents to keep open the possibility of discovering missing identities lost in law's discourse. When attempting to understand another person, especially a person with a different world view or identity, judges must be open to the possibility that the world view of the other may be a better way to translate (understand) the meaning of some phenomena. As James Baldwin put the point: 'The necessity of Americans to achieve an identity is a historical and a present personal fact, and this is the connection between you and me.'[39]

This is also the meaning of Professor White's idea of justice as translation. Translation leaves open the possibility of discovering something that is new, or perhaps lost, in the legal narratives of America's story of origins. This is, I think, what White means when he says 'There is, then, no "translation," only transformation achieved in a process by which one seeks to attune oneself to another's text and language, to appropriate them yet to respect their difference and autonomy'.[40] White believes that the same is possible with our speech, our discourses—if we let them have their way with our discourses and texts it will work a transformation in meaning, even if a full translation is not possible.

Not all translators are created equal, however; some are better than others. Translation can be a 'wild card' in literary interpretation; it can be like the 'joker' in a deck of cards, designated to be whatever card the player desires. White holds out the model of a 'good translator' as an example of what we should strive to imitate.[41] A good translator is committed to the process of defining a set of intellectual and ethical possibilities from which we can learn about our differences, as people and as professionals. The good translator model does not deny identity differences, she accepts that we speak with different voices and languages. The good translator develops the 'chamber of [her] mind' that enables her to understand identity differences.[42]

Translations are *messy* affairs, as White clearly recognizes. Translations do not always translate the other's language or identity accurately because there is always a cognitive and imaginative process at work that is constantly changing the meaning of the translation to fit the translator's intent. Because the identity of the

---

[39] Baldwin, n. 1 above, 114.
[41] White, n. 6 above, 262.
[40] *Ibid.*
[42] *Ibid.*

translator is a construction of a particular culture, there will always be distortions in the way the translator reads the text of the 'other'. Ideological and psychological motivations will determine actions and desires; the translator will use cognitive tools that narrow the normative field. Metaphors like 'melting-pot' map information from one domain to explain what goes on in a completely different domain. The transference of the metaphor can deny the reality that America is not a melting-pot, that identity differences are real and pervasive in American culture. What we need to know is how to bring the meaning of the identity of the 'other' into the discourse and world of the translator.

Professor White encourages us to think of how translations work between a lawyer and client, and how a good lawyer will move between the languages of the lawyer and the client. But, think for a moment of the legal culture that lawyers and judges inhabit, and think about how that world works to define identity in the law. American legal culture shapes the way judges and lawyers construct not only the narratives of America's story of origins, but the basic identity relations essential to law's discourse. Judges and lawyers take an oath of office; it is their duty to uphold the 'law'. The law they uphold involves a set of cultural practices that motivates them to see the world in a particular way. Legal culture thus motivates judges and lawyers to deny aspects of the reality they translate. Law shapes what judges and lawyers translate by providing them with predetermined tools that are frequently normatively loaded.

Judges and lawyers are also trained to interpret what they see by reference to relevant categories that have an 'in-versus-out' quality. The prototypical categories they use are sometimes defined in terms of identity. The reasonable man standard, used to determine the exercise of due care, motivates judges and lawyers to think in gender terms in the law of negligence. The reasonable man standard, like the convention of using the male form in writing, erases the identity of women from the construction of the negligence standard in the law. Women are presumed to be like men, so when the law refers to the construct of a reasonable man, the signifier of the standard becomes a sign for reinforcing male dominance.

Consider, also, how identity has been constructed under the United States immigration laws. The legal definition of racial identity was at one time a 'taxonomical practice' for determining

American citizenship. As Professor Ian F. Haney Lopéz reminds us in *White by Law*,[43] Congress in 1790 limited naturalization of citizenship to 'white persons'. Hence, for many years, being 'a white person' was a prerequisite for acquiring United States citizenship. Professor Lopéz shows how legal controversies posed by claims of 'whiteness' served to establish in early immigration law an identity meaning of 'white' that was used to determine American citizenship. In determining the category of whiteness in the law, the courts constructed ideas of racial hierarchy that attributed positive characteristics to whites, and negative characteristics to people of colour. The legal decisions constructed an identity meaning of whiteness that reflected the negative image of Afro-Americans and the positive image of whites: 'Blacks [were] constructed as lazy, ignorant, lascivious, and criminal, Whites as industrious, knowledgeable, virtuous, and law abiding.'[44] Professor Lopéz observes that 'judges embraced this identity, in utter disregard of the costs of their actions to immigrants across the country'.[45]

With the passage of the Immigration Act 1924, eligibility for American citizenship was dependent on the number of people living in America in 1927 of the same ethnicity, thus constructing citizenship in terms of ideas of 'national origins'.[46] This Act required a 'racial analysis' to be used in immigration, based on the racial and ethnic composition of the American population. The Act used racial identity for determining eligibility for American citizenship. Citizenship became disconnected from the act of naturalization, and became further connected to the idea of 'racial status'. Citizenship became an inherited racial right, and racial hierarchy of whites became the subtext for determining the qualifications for American citizenship. The Act reinforced the value of 'whiteness' in determining who might qualify as an American. In this way, citizenship and naturalization have maintained the historical connection to the mythology of an American identity

---

[43] I. F. Lopéz, 'White by Law' in R. Delgado (ed.), *Critical Race Theory: The Cutting Edge* (Philadelphia, 1995), 47.
[44] Lopéz, n. 43 above, 548, citing K. L. Crenshaw, 'Reform and retrenchment: Transformation and Legitimation in Antidiscrimination Law' (1988) 101 *Harvard Law Review* 1331, 1373.
[45] Lopéz, 'White by Law', n. 43 above, 549.
[46] J. Higham, *Strangers in the Land* (New Brunswick, 1988), 312–24; W. B. Michaels, *Our America*, n. 11 above, 32.

traceable to the racial identity of a group of people thought to be Americans.[47]

Of course, judges have power to shape the key identity relations used in the law of immigration. They could, if they chose, construct different identity relations in the course of defining the rights and obligations of Americans. But the fact is that they do not. When a judge hears an ethical or policy argument that is not authorized by the text, the judge thinks 'denied' or 'overruled'. When a lawyer interrogates a client, the lawyer coaches the client to see the world in ways that will favour the lawyer's case. When the client is in court, the lawyer translates for the client, and the translation is carefully tailored by the judge so that the translation maintains fidelity to the judge's view of the law. The law 'stacks the cards' of the translation so that the lawyer or the judge always has the power to control the meaning of a translation's integration.

Indeed, because the power of the translator lies hidden in the medium of the translation (namely, within the translator's culture and language; in law itself), the translator is not always fully aware of how she denies identity differences in the course of making a legal translation. One must wonder whether judges or lawyers are able to be 'good translators' since their entire professional being is instrumentally shaped by their deep desire to show fidelity to 'law'. Before we can even begin to talk about what would be a good translator in the legal context, we need first to understand something about the way power is exercised through the legal institutions and conventions of the law.

Law, like all other professions, including literature, exercises a disciplinary power that structures institutional behaviour. The prevailing view of judging is based on the notion that judges make and change law, but that their paramount duty is to decide legal controversies according to the 'law'. Fidelity to law is thus thought to be a constraint on adjudication. The judiciary accordingly translates under a constraint that limits the ability of judges to engage in what White calls the 'art of translation'. For judges, however, translation is not an art; it is a technique for interpreting the meaning of words. The judiciary's power is consequently limited by the canon of judicial responsibility that requires fidelity

---

[47] See Michaels, *Our America*, n. 11 above, 29–33.

to the law's official language and official translations. The power
of the legal canon to construct identity relations in law's discourse
is, of course, not unique to the law. The canon of every discipline
frames how identity constructions are created in the narratives
essential to the discipline's translations. If we are better to understand how the disciplinary power of an institution marginalizes
and ignores the reality of identity differences, we need to begin
looking at the canon. We need, in other words, to redirect our
effort to questions about the canon—the set of traditions that
have decided the 'choice of texts, and have determined who is
given voice, who is read, and who is quoted' and consequently
who is ignored and marginalized in our academic discourses of
law and literature.[48]

Crossing the Literary Modernist Divide

Debate and controversy stimulated by the literary canon has led
some to see *failure* in the effort to translate the texts of law and
literature. Richard Weisberg, for example, has written that he
fears that White's emphasis on translation may commit law and
literature scholars to the world of pure theory and divert energies
away from literary practice altogether.[49] I think, however, that if
one reads White's text closely one can see it as fitting within the
form of translation that Weisberg desires for literary texts. A
'close reading' of *Justice as Translation* reveals that White's notion
of 'justice as translation' is consistent with Richard Weisberg's
effort to uncover the ways in which a literary text limits the
reader's understanding. The literary practice that White describes
is in fact intended to neutralize the ways in which the text
prevents the reader from understanding the ethical meaning of our
languages and texts.[50]

---

[48] C. Heibrun and J. Resnik, 'Convergences', n. 16 above, 1936.

[49] This is a criticism that has been advanced by Richard Weisberg in his book
Poethics, n. 27 above, 13.

[50] Weisberg, however, is right to question the foundationalism of White's
advocacy of a 'good translator model': White, *Justice as Translation*, n. 6 above,
262. The problem with the good translator model (the model which is based on the
idea of a translator that can do the kind of literary translation White imagines) is
that it takes us away from the stories of outsiders who know the experience of
alienation, marginalization, and discrimination at first hand. The problem with the
good translator model is that it commits us to an abstract discourse that finds
inspiration in logic rather than imagination of the translator. Weisberg is right to

The idea of justice as translation is, as White has explained, embedded in '[o]ur deepest obligation and highest hope ... to create a world in which each person is fully recognized, in which each may achieve the realization of his or her capacities for life'.[51] To commit oneself to this idea of translation is to imagine a literary form that resists the modernist's expectation about translation—that is, it resists the idea that 'what is said in one language can be "said" in another', and ... contemplate[s] instead the idea that translation involves a transformative process by which 'one seeks to attune oneself to another's text and language'.[52]

Justice as Translation attempts to describe a literary strategy for giving meaning to people who have a fundamentally different and hence *foreign* linguistic, cultural, political, racial, ethnic identity. White's text inspires us to move across the literary modernist divide and to contemplate a new literary form, which he imagined to be a form of cultural criticism that would place literary activity at the centre of the current debates about the institutional and political arrangements of American society. White's idea of translation is not based on false 'sentimentalism'; rather it represents an effort to bring literary activity in law to a much more serious and high-stakes level, to recover the identities left out of America's basic narratives—cultural, literary, legal, and political.

caution us that if the good translator model is taken too seriously by literary-minded scholars it may 'silence the other' and do little to help 'mold an ethics of law': *Poethics*, n. 27 above, 249–50.

The views raised by Richard Weisberg's reading of White's *Justice as Translation* has given Professor Ian Ward an opportunity to make much of the apparent difference in the literary views of Richard Weisberg and James Boyd White. See I. Ward, *Law and Literature: Possibilities and Perspectives* (Cambridge, 1995), 54–5. Ward sees within Weisberg's criticism of White 'reconstructive ethics of Derridean postmodernist such as Drucilla Cornell' and the 'interpretive responsibility' to remain faithful not to the text, but to the 'fidelity to fellow readers'. I think, however, that Ian Ward's analysis of this is debatable. For one thing, Weisberg is one of the best-known advocates of the view that literary texts provide the reader with universal and foundational ethical 'lessons'; a view that could be associated with a modernist rather than postmodernist perspective. For another, James Boyd White does not disregard the status of readers, as Ward seems to infer from his reading of Weisberg's criticisms of White. As White has explained: 'The text at once creates and constrains a liberty (or a power) in its reader, and in doing so defines for the reader a particular kind of responsibility': *Justice as Translation*, n. 6 above, 269. Indeed, White encourages us to be inventive in our literary translations.

[51] White, *Justice as Translation*, n. 6 above, 269.
[52] White, n. 6 above, 253–4.

In order to do this work we need to think more about how the literary narrative form provides us with a medium for understanding our world. We need, in other words, to understand how literary narratives of identity structure the literary translations of America's story of origins. Translations of different literary narratives about America can give us a new insight into what is behind the complex fate of American identity. One can find different narrative types that seek to define American identity: stories that define identity in terms of notions of 'Our America', and stories that define identity in terms of 'Our Other America'.

'OUR AMERICA'

Walter Benn Michaels's recent book *Our America: Nativism, Modernism, and Pluralism*[53] locates one meaning of 'American' in the structural relation embodied in the texts of early twentieth-century American writers. Michaels shows how the classic American stories of the 1920s, by William Faulkner, Ernest Hemingway, F. Scott Fitzgerald, and others, created a collective narrative that redefined what it means to be an American. The novels of the 1920s have always been regarded as defining the identity of a new American, who came out of the disrupting events of immigration, war, and commerce. Michaels asserts that from these literary narratives we learn of the 'lost' or 'vanishing' American who was reconciled to the identity of the nation in the prior age. He claims that we can learn from these literary texts how Americans constructed a new 'modern' identity for determining what it then meant to be an American.

Novels like Hemingway's *The Sun Also Rises* (1926) and Fitzgerald's *The Great Gatsby* (1925) have always been identified as uniquely American literary texts. Michaels asserts that these texts created a new identity of 'Americanism' that reflected what was going on in American culture. He claims that fictional characters like Jay Gatsby personified the new American identity. Fitzgerald's Gatsby was the self-invented man, who believed in the dream of American success but who was a man 'without a past'.[54] Hemingway's fictional characters in *The Sun Also Rises* become

---

[53] Michaels, *Our America*, n. 11 above.
[54] Michaels, n. 11 above, 26.

examples of American disillusion following the war, and Michaels sees these characters as literary examples of a 'vanishing race'.[55] Michaels finds that Hemingway's characters Robert Cohen and Jake Barnes, expatriates living abroad in Spain, attempt to translate what cannot be translated—the meaning of Americanism in a foreign language and culture.[56]

Michaels thus 'translates' the identity of literary figures in American literature of the 1920s to gain insight into the identity of American culture of that period. Michaels observes that the stories written by American authors during this period offer us a way of understanding how American opposition to foreign immigrants and racial minorities shaped an understanding of national identity based on race. Racial identity, structured by the ideas of racism and 'nativism' (the intense opposition to an internal minority on the grounds of its foreign—un-American—connections) is said to have defined a literary form of modernism. Michaels claims that a particular kind of literary translation, which he calls 'nativist modernism',[57] explains how a new national identity created cultural identity, where race rather than citizenship became the crucial marker for determining who was and who was not an 'American'.

In looking to the way American identity is constructed in American fiction of the 1920s, Michaels discovers how a type of literary translation worked to create a new idea of American identity based on cultural and racial identity. This new identity defined Americanism in terms of a native culture rather than citizenship as such. Michaels discovers how the 'pluralizing of culture' based on the fiction of racial identity enabled American authors such as Hemingway and Fitzgerald to discover a new American identity for the generation of Americans. Racial identity based on 'American nativism' is said to have given rise to what Michaels calls 'American literary modernism'.

Michaels claims that traces of literary modernism can be found not only in literary narratives, but also in the political and legal discourse of the period. Hence he finds that as a result of the passage of the Immigration Act 1924, a 'racial analysis' was required for nationalization of United States citizenship and

---

[55] Michaels, n. 11 above, 12.   [56] Michaels, n. 11 above, 74.
[57] Michaels, n. 11 above, 2.

America thereby committed itself to the nativist goal of keeping some people from *becoming* citizens merely because of their race. He observes how President Calvin Coolidge, in a Fourth of July speech, cited the passage of the Immigration Act 1924 as one of his administration's chief accomplishments in helping 'America . . . remain American'.[58] Michaels also observes how the passage of the Indian Citizenship Act 1887 had the opposite result in assimilating all native Americans as United States citizens. In declaring 'all noncitizen Indians born within the territorial limits of the United States . . . to be citizens of the United States', the Act erased the cultural heritage of native Americans. Michaels notes how the 'Indian Act' served to make real what Zane Grey meant when the hero of his novel, Nophaie, in *The Vanishing American* (1925), is told by an old chief that 'The sun of the Indian's day is setting.'[59]

Here one can see, in Michaels's *Our America,* how translation of American literature might work critically to expose how the modernist's concept of identity is culturally constructed to deny identity differences. I find within Michaels's text a translation that explains how the modernist dream to discover a metanarrative or metatranslation for explaining America's story has worked to exclude the identity of many Americans. For Michaels the term 'nativist modernism' locates literary modernism in a particular conception of *identity* (in his case racial identity). He shows how the idea of racial identity grounds the meaning of what it means to be an American in the literary narratives of the 1920s. For Michaels, nativist modernism becomes a way of translating modernist culture. Here, within Michaels's text we find an explanation for the *failure* of translation of America's story of origins.

The failure in the literary modernist's translation of the American story is that modernists seek to construct identity in terms of a universal identity relation. Literary modernists translate in this way because they, as White recognizes, are committed to the 'reality' of the relations of the signs of the narratives they translate. Literary modernism attempts to create a narrative that imitates what the modernist believes to be the meaning of the 'sign'. The 'materiality of the sign' thus becomes the determining ground for identity construction. Michaels claims that literary modernists look to

---

[58] Michaels, n. 11 above, 32.   [59] Michaels, n. 11 above, 38.

culture as a *technology* for determining the meaning of identity relations. 'Thus, the claim of authenticity for the writer's experience asserts at the same time the primacy of the sign's materiality.'[60]

Michaels observes that literary modernism is constructed out of two potentially opposing accounts of modernism: 'one emphasizing the primacy of experience, the other the primacy of language'.[61] Michaels contends that these two different accounts of modernism work together in the literary works of the 1920s to separate the 'imitation' from the 'real' American. For example, Michaels notes how Hemingway's character, Jake Barnes, in *The Sun Also Rises* remarks that 'There is no Spanish word for bull-fighting'. Michaels observes that Jake's remark is the 'aesthetic of untranslatability'. As Michaels further explains: 'What we call a bullfight cannot properly be translated into Spanish, and what Spaniards call what we call a bullfight is not properly translated by "bullfight." '[62]

Michaels claims that the 'untranslatability' of the word signifies that some words name just one thing, and what the word names is the word's identity. The idea that some words have a unique 'identity' locates the literary modernist's account of American identity. The modernist's commitment to the word achieves what the poet William Carlos Williams once called the commitment to the 'reality of the word' or 'the materiality of letters' thought to be 'real'. According to Williams, the 'reality of the word' is at the 'base' of literary 'modernism'.[63] One might say that literary

---

[60] Michaels, n. 11 above, 73.   [61] *Ibid.*
[62] Michaels, n. 11 above, 74.

[63] Michaels, n. 11 above, 74–5, citing William Carlos Williams, *The Embodiment of Knowledge* (R. Loewinsohn (ed.), New York, 1974). According to Michaels, Williams was a modernist poet committed to the 'materiality of the poem', which is to say, that the 'poem be itself' (Michaels, *Our America*, n. 11 above, 82–3). Professor White's translation of Williams's 'little' poem about the plums left in the icebox finds that the simplicity of the poem is part of its 'excellence'. See White, 'Writing and Reading in Philosophy, Law, and Poetry,' in this book, 1. Williams's effort to 'locate the value of a poem in its identity', is, however, what invites contrasting translations of the meaning of the poem's simple identity. Michaels asserts that Williams's *The Embodiment of Knowledge* sets out a generalized principle that Williams followed in his poetry: that 'every individual, every place, every opportunity of thought is both favored and limited by its emplacement in time and place' (Michaels, *Our America*, n. 11 above, 82, quoting Williams, *The Embodiment of Knowledge* (above), 150). Michaels also notes how Williams applied this principle to his thoughts about America ('America is such a place. The old cultures *cannot*, can never, without our history, our blood or climate, our time of flowering in history—can never be the same as we' (Michaels, *Our America*, n. 11 above, 82).

modernists are committed to the belief that language provides the foundational ground for determining the 'reality' of American identity. The problem with the translations of literary modernist writers is that they essentialize culture as the defining ground for determining American identity. What is left out of the translation of literary modernism are thick descriptions of identity differences and cultural diversity of outsiders in America. The restless quest for the personal meaning of outsiders has since become a crucial feature of the literary narratives of outsiders. Their literary effort is working to bring out the way the 'other America' lives and experiences living in America.

'OUR OTHER AMERICA'

To find examples of literary narratives of outsiders one must look to the works of writers like James Baldwin. Baldwin's *Going to Meet the Man*,[64] for example, provides the translator with stories for understanding how racism affects translations of both its victims and its perpetrators. In the short story, Baldwin views the lynching of a black man from the point of view of a white sheriff who witnessed the lynching as a young child. Baldwin describes how the lynching becomes the source of the sheriff's sexual power over his wife. The lynching becomes a metaphor for the way the sheriff relates to his wife. The sheriff thinks of lynching at the very moment he makes love to his wife. Acting through sexual power, the sheriff whispers to his wife, 'Come on, sugar, I'm going to do you like a nigger, come on sugar, and love me just like you'd love a nigger.'[65] The story reveals how racism can destroy the moral being of its perpetrators by robbing them of any capacity to respect and acknowledge the person of another, let alone the capacity to express and experience the human emotion of love.

A different account of 'outsiderism' is illustrated by one of the most famous of all American 'outsider' novels, Jack Kerouac's 1957 novel of ultimate rootlessness, *On the Road*.[66] The text of this novel was constructed so that the writing would itself be an expression of outsider status. The text of *On the Road* was typed

[64] J. Baldwin, *Going to Meet the Man* (New York, 1948).
[65] Baldwin, n. 1 above, 249. See also Leeming, *James Baldwin*, n. 4 above, 249.
[66] J. Kerouac, *On the Road* (New York, 1957, 1991).

from travel journals during a marathon three-week period sustained by coffee and large quantities of Benzedrine. The original manuscript was, on a single roll of paper, typed as a single-spaced paragraph that was 120 feet long.[67] Kerouac called his non-stop typing technique 'kickwriting'. The sound of rapid typing, impressionistic improvisation, and thick description of everyday occurrences, imitated jazz music of the beat generation. The effort was to create a new narrative form that was as 'hot' and 'hip' as the new music form that was jazz. The 'back-alley music' of jazz became for Kerouac and his friends the music of outsiders. Jazz was 'outsider' music because it was devoted to a new musical canon that celebrated musical translations of the individual performer rather than the conventions of the profession. For Kerouac, the music was a way to express a new literary canon.

What is most striking about *On the Road* is that it is a novel with no central plot other than a road trip that begins and ends in New York. The story becomes a journey in search of Kerouac's own identity which he seeks to locate in the characters of the novel. The characters, though male and white, live the life of the outsider in search of other outsiders. The narrative of the story enables the reader to enter this world of the outsider to feel, taste, and experience without any attempt to censor even its most ugly and disturbing moments.

At the very beginning of the story, Kerouac explains how he has always been drawn to outsiders. One of the main characters in the story, based on one of his bohemian pals, is Neal Cassady: an orphan, car thief, and ladies man, who came to New York to find adventure as a writer. Kerouac, the storyteller, goes on to tell the reader how he had always been drawn to people like Neal. As Kerouac's narrative explains:

[T]he only people for me are the mad ones, the ones who are mad to live, mad to talk, mad to be saved, desirous of everything at the same time, the ones who never yawn or say a commonplace thing, but burn, burn, burn like fabulous yellow roman candles exploding like spiders across the stars and in the middle you see the blue center light pop and everybody goes 'Awww!'[68]

---

[67] See S. Turner, *Jack Kerouac: Angelheaded Hipster* (London, 1996), 119; Ann Charters, 'Introduction' in Kerouac, *On the Road*, n. 66 above, iii–xxix.
[68] Kerouac, *On the Road*, n. 66 above, 5–6.

Can you feel it—the Benzedrine having its way with Kerouac's words, creating an image of the outsider that Kerouac wants to become and discover in his text? Here, one can see the images of the Star Spangled Banner and Fourth of July—'roman candles exploding like spiders across the stars'—used in a very ironic sense to celebrate outsider status in America. One might even say that here we can find within Kerouac's text the effort to bring out a long-lost narrative that has been deeply embedded in America's story of origins. This is not the narrative of the Constitution. It is the revolutionary narrative of the outsider who is proclaiming 'me too, I am an American'. Kerouac's short passage in the novel captures the outsider's quest to discover 'counter-culture' hidden within post-war America.

On the Road is not what we would expect from a 'good translator'. Indeed, it is an example of a very 'bad translator'—'bad' in the way the 'beats' understood the word bad—not serious; playful, naughty, hip, and decidedly 'cool' (that is, non-conventional). The narrative that is created is different from the literary narratives of Hemingway, or even those of Fitzgerald. This is not about discovering some lost identity that was America; it is instead about the discovery of the outsider's voice and text. It is about the discovery of the 'other'.

To be sure, Kerouac's narrative was a text written from the perspective of middle-class males who were, in some fundamental ways, going through a type of mid-life crisis, imitating the 'rites' of youthful rebellion. Kerouac's narrative also leaves out the stories of women and other outsiders. Kerouac's text is even disturbing in that it contains descriptions of relations that some might see as sexist and racist.[69] But Kerouac was writing during a time when sexism and racism were accepted features of 1940s and 1950s America. Kerouac wanted his reader to know about this world, to see it at first hand and to see and understand it without censorship.

---

[69] Ellis Amburn has recently contended that Kerouac was a troubled homophobic homosexual: E. Amburn, *The Hidden Life of Jack Kerouac* (New York, 1998). But see Morris Dickstein, 'Subterranean Kerouac', in the *New York Times Review of Books*, 9 August 1998, 8–9 (arguing that Amburn's book suffers from what Joyce Carol Oates once called 'pathography'—'a reductive emphasis on dysfunction that not only overshadows the subject's achievements but makes them virtually inconceivable').

In a recent issue of the *New Yorker*, Kerouac's journals from the 1950s were published for the first time.[70] In one entry, dated August 1949, Kerouac describes how one night in Denver, Colorado, he was walking in a neighbourhood where Mexicans and blacks lived and passed a group of young black women, one of whom mistook Kerouac for a man named 'Eddy'. Kerouac commented on the sadness of the moment, and wrote in his journal:

I was so sad—in the violet dark, strolling—wishing I could exchange worlds with the happy, true-minded, ecstatic Negroes of America. All this reminded me of Neal and Louanne, who had been children here and nearby. How I yearned to be transformed into an Eddy, a Neal, a jazz musician, a nigger, a construction worker, a softball pitcher, anything in these wild, dark humming streets of Denver night—anything but myself so pale and unhappy, so dim.[71]

I imagine that readers today would be startled by Kerouac's use of the word 'nigger'. Some readers might even conclude that Kerouac was a racist. I want to suggest a different translation. I think Kerouac used the word in the way it is used and understood in the Afro-American community. Kerouac was trying to imagine something that is denied by the way that word works to define the identity of Afro-Americans in the translations of white people. When a white person uses the word 'nigger', it is a signifier of white supremacy and racial hierarchy. Kerouac, I think, deployed the word in his journal to associate it in his thoughts with the way the word is used in Afro-American community not as a signifier of white supremacy, but rather a signifier of affection and racial identity.

Walter Benn Michaels asserts that when a black person insists on writing or speaking 'just like a Nigger', the word is deployed not in its white derogatory sense, but rather as a way to distinguish race identity.[72] I think that the derogatory equivalent of the word 'nigger' in the Afro-American community today would be the white man's word 'negro', a phrase that imitates the way whites

---

[70] J. Kerouac, 'On The Road Again' in the *New Yorker* (22 and 29 June 1998), 46.

[71] Kerouac, 'On The Road Again', n. 70 above, 56.

[72] Michaels, *Our America*, n. 11 above, 89.

categorize black people.[73] Another example of this would be the term 'Oreo'—a derogatory term used in black culture to describe a black person who is 'black on the outside, but white on the inside'. The intra-black usage of the word 'nigger' has overtones of irony, as a mutual put-down and a way of expressing affection. For many blacks, the word 'nigger' establishes a community, just the opposite of its cross-racial usage. It is this sense of community that Kerouac longed for (even if it was a community of outsiders).

I think that Kerouac's journal attempts to capture the sadness he felt for that brief moment on the streets of Denver, wondering what it would be like to take up the identity position of the 'Eddy', the 'other'. In doing so, he expressed feelings of anxiety for a new generation of white Americans who defined their identity in relation to people like Eddy. For Kerouac, the cultural identity of white America in the post-World War II era had become 'pale, unhappy and dim'. By the 1950s, the cultural identity of the American was 'square', and definitely not 'hip'. Kerouac wanted to enter the world of outsiders so that he might experience community with other outsiders.

There is, however, a world of difference separating Kerouac's attempt to experience the subject position of the 'other', and the actual position of the 'other'. Kerouac's novel in a sense can be translated as an attempt by a white American to assume, as a matter of choice, the subject position of an outsider. But there is a real difference between *choosing* to be an outsider, and being *born* the outsider, as James Baldwin understood so well.

Indeed, James Baldwin, who met Kerouac during his prime, actually commented on what he felt about Kerouac's attempt to 'feel' the experience of minorities in America. In reacting to Kerouac's observation about being in Denver and walking in the 'colored section' and 'wishing [he, Kerouac] was a Negro', Baldwin writes in *Nobody Knows My Name*:

Now this is absolute nonsense, of course, objectively considered, and offensive nonsense at that: I would hate to be in Kerouac's shoes if he should ever be mad enough to read this aloud from the stage of Harlem's

---

[73] In James Baldwin's time, I don't think this was even recognized. Baldwin thus frequently used the word 'negro' instead of the word 'black' or 'Afro-American' in his literary accounts of American blacks.

Apollo Theatre. And yet there is real pain in it, and real loss, however thin; and it *is* thin, like soup too long diluted; thin because it does not refer to reality, but to a dream. Compare it, at random, with any old blues:

Backwater blues done caused me
To pack my things and go
'Cause my house fell down
And I can't live there no' mo'.[74]

Baldwin's point was not that only a black person can speak to the experience of being black, but rather that there is a critical difference between the white man's and the black man's subject position. For the black man, 'truth is absolutely naked: if he deludes himself about it, he will die. This is not the way this truth presents itself to white men, who believe the world is theirs and who, albeit unconsciously, expect the world to help them in the achievement of their identity.'[75]

Baldwin goes on to observe that

the anguish which can overtake a white man comes in the middle of his life [an obvious reference to Jack Kerouac], when he must make the almost inconceivable effort to divest himself of everything he has ever expected or believed, when he must take himself apart and put himself together again, walking out of the world, into limbo, or into what certainly looks like limbo.

Baldwin concludes that the type of mid-life crisis that middle-aged white men often experience is not something that a black man can afford, for 'his delusions and defences are either absolutely impenetrable by this time, or he has failed to survive them'.[76]

James Baldwin, like Jack Kerouac, attempted nevertheless to

---

[74] Baldwin, *Nobody Knows My Name*, n. 1 above, 182. The reader should compare this simple 'old blues' poem to William Carlos Williams's little poem about the plums, which Professor White has translated. See n. 63 above. What Baldwin's simple 'old blues' poem reveals is the loss which outsiders deal with in their daily experiences. Williams's poem about the plums left in the icebox, however, expressed the intimate connection between a man and a woman or perhaps the simple poetic expression of an object, as Professor White observes. One poem requires the reader to contemplate the pain of the outsider in America; the other leaves the reader to contemplate the meaning of an object, and its relation to individuals who lack identity.

[75] Baldwin, *Nobody Knows My Name*, n. 1 above, 183.

[76] *Ibid.*

achieve through his literary work the personal experience of the outsider, and in doing so, he was able to achieve a type of power that was a potent tool for opening up post-war American culture. Kerouac's *On the Road* created such power by defining the identity of the American beat generation, and James Baldwin fiction created power by defining of the identity of Afro-American writers. Both writers, in their own ways, helped to define the identity of a new generation of Americans that became a counter-culture of sorts. 'Counter-culture' is the culture of American outsiders; the people who live on the margins of the dominant culture that is America. In the 1950s it was the beat generation; in the 1960s it was the hippies and Yippies, the women's rights and black liberation movements; in the 1980s it was the gay and lesbian liberation movement, and in the 1990s it is multiculturalism and the diversity movement.

The search for the mythical identity that is America requires new translations of our 'other' America in the literary work of outsider writers. James Baldwin observed that outsider artists can gain access to power, but only if they have lived a life where power has worked on them. Baldwin recalls, for example, how Norman Mailer once stated: 'I want to know how power works; how it really works, in detail.' Baldwin's response was: 'Well, I know how power works, it has worked on me, and if I didn't know how power worked, I would be dead.' Baldwin went on to say that all his life he had tried to work out a type of 'literary revenge'. The 'revenge' was to use his literary talents to write novels about America so that he 'would be [able] to achieve a power which outlasts kingdoms'.[77]

A new generation of American outsiders are doing this by creating new narratives of 'literary revenge'. Here, I have in mind the narratives of race by Toni Morrison, Derrick Bell, Patricia Williams and Richard Delgado, and those of gender by Andrea Dworkin, Alice Walker, Margaret Atwood and others. This new breed of literary translator is working to develop a body of literature that provides outsiders in America with a way to regain real power. In hearing their stories about the experience of outsiders, America is forced to rethink the way identity has been constructed in some of our most basic narratives, and, more

[77] *Ibid.*

importantly, how that construction of identity has caused violence to those marginalized by our narratives.

Literary narratives of outsiders have since come to signify a 'crisis' about the narrative form, and we are just now working through the meaning of this crisis. The new narrative forms can be translated, but their meaning requires a new strategy of translating, one that is different from the ones 'we already know'.

Conclusion

The turn to literary translation in law and literature reflects, I believe, a general disenchanted condition with the *ethos* of legal discourse. As the late Robert Cover taught, law has the capacity to inflict acts of violence in the course of administering and enforcing the official narratives of law.[78] And, as White has observed, 'Today we have no slavery, but we do have people suffering greatly, victimized greatly, who in the law and elsewhere are talked about in highly distancing and objectifying ways.'[79] Richard Weisberg's *Poethics* emphasizes a similar concern in admonishing the literary-minded scholar to pay greater 'attention to legal communication and to the plight of those who are the "other" [so that we] may revitalize the ethical component of law'.[80] Hence, although Richard Weisberg and James Boyd White may disagree about whether law-in-literature or law-as-literature offers the most promise for our literary practices, they agree that law and literature must commit itself to understanding the violence of legal discourse.

Commitment to purpose, however, presumes that our literary practices will be successful in bringing out the missing human element in the discourse of law. Before we can even begin to decide what should be done, we need to think more about how the literary form of our narratives and our translations shapes and influences what we do, what we think, and how we translate. To understand the violence of legal discourse we need to study how law ignores the reality of the 'other's' experience and identity. The 'common mistaken notion' that White sees as the idea that 'what

---

[78] R. Cover, 'Violence and the Word' (1986) 95 *Yale LJ* 1601.
[79] White, *Justice as Translation*, n. 6 above, 140.
[80] R. Weisberg, *Poethics*, n. 27 above, 46.

is said' in one language can be 'said in another'[81] is a mistake that has the potential for doing violence to real people. White's effort to conceive of translation as an 'integration' of different languages and cultures and Weisberg's examination of how legal communication can mask the moral horrors such as the Holocaust[82] offer, I believe, literary, ethical, and political strategies for understanding law's violence. To get at the source responsible for legal violence, however, literary practitioners must bring into their practices the voice and narrative of outsiders in America.

As we explore the meaning to be found in the different way translators translate, we can begin to reclaim and discover missing American narratives. As this process of narrative and storytelling unfolds, we Americans are just beginning to construct new translations for understanding what it means to be an American in the twenty-first century. That is, I believe, the most fundamental and most difficult task facing those who are now engaged in the perplexing and most interesting work of translating a text in America. This is where we are today; law and literature at century's end is just coming to acknowledge the full meaning and significance of what it means to translate the meaning of a text. As we approach the end of the century and millennium, law and literature finds itself the subject of many different 'translations'.

The boundaries and foundations of law and literature movement, once defined by the 'law-in-literature' and 'law-as-literature' distinction, have thus become less clear as these different literary perspectives have been shown to be merely different ways to translate a text. And, as Richard Weisberg's remarks make clear, new narrative forms and new identity groups have shifted the debates of law and literature to new theoretical translations.[83] Interlopers within the field have presented the case for rethinking not only old distinctions, but also the very canons and aesthetics of the field as well. These changes are characteristic of larger trends in legal studies that have been associated with modernist and postmodernist phenomena.

---

[81] White, *Justice As Translation*, n. 6 above, 253.
[82] R. Weisberg, *Vichy Law and the Holocaust in France* (New York, 1996).
[83] Richard Weisberg's warnings about the disrupting influences of the diverse new intellectual movements in the academy must be tempered by the realization that law and literature is one of the movements that has brought controversy and debate by questioning the methods, perspectives, and politics of modern jurisprudence. See G. Minda, *Postmodern Legal Movements: Law and Jurisprudence at Century's End* (New York, 1995), 149–66.

The challenge for law and literature is to understand how these changes have affected the narratives and stories that law and literature practitioners seek to translate. Literary forms of modernism and postmodernism can be described and examined. The effort of such work can provide useful information for assessing and interpreting where we are today—the effort might enable us, in other words, to make a better translation of a nation's identity. In this paper I have tried to explain one literary strategy for doing this work. In developing other strategies, we may come to see more clearly what is at stake in the literary practices in which we engage. But in order to do this work we must cross the 'literary modernist divide'[84] and begin thinking about how 'literary translation' relates to cultural criticism and the invention of identity in our most basic narratives used to define nationhood and selfhood.[85]

[84] By 'literary modernist divide' I mean the literary canon and conventions that motivate literary-minded scholars to think of language and translation as a code or system of signifier to signified that can be encoded and interpreted to ascertain the meaning of real or imaginary things. Minda, *Postmodern Legal Movements*, n. 83 above, 238–9. The canon and conventions of literary modernism create an intellectual wall that has prevented modern translators from comprehending how the materiality of the signs they interpret hide meaning, and how translation gives meaning to the identity relations of a culture. Literary modernism is thus a 'divide' that has heretofore prevented the literary translator from thinking more critically about how our linguistic practices produce meaning and how the construction of identity can do great violence to another.

[85] I would like to thank Robert Batey and Rosemary Coombe for their comments and suggestions. This essay was financially supported by Brooklyn Law School's Research Stipend Fund. A special thanks to Dean Joan Wexler for supporting my participation in the law and literature colloquium at University College London.

LAWYERS AND INTROSPECTION

Thomas Morawetz

Introduction

In the United States, the very term 'lawyer' can be one of opprobrium, an epithet laced with disdain and condescension: 'What did you expect? He's a lawyer.' My law students—at least those who are not descended from families of lawyers—often allude ruefully to their families' ambivalence at their choice of career. An implication is that, even if it is not quite like choosing to be a terrorist, it is perhaps more like aspiring to be a politician or a journalist. All these labels have come to serve as a shorthand for compromised and questionable values, for occupations whose work is as likely to stir up trouble and discontent as to make the world a better place.

The cultural understanding of the legal profession is a fertile resource for scholars. In particular, lawyer humour tantalizes sociologists, psychologists, and literary analysts.[1] Most observers have noted a change of tone over the last twenty years. While humour once mocked the obtuseness and pedantry of lawyers, it now comments on their hypocrisy, crassness, and inhumanity. Some lawyers themselves are avid consumers of lawyer humour, and this may be taken to suggest (depending on one's interpretive inclinations) either a healthy capacity to laugh at oneself or an unhealthy masochism.

Law seems to be a paradoxical profession. Positive as well as negative cultural attitudes toward lawyers are expressed in novels, stories, plays, and television shows. In fact, the last fifteen years

---

[1] For an overview, see T. Overton, 'Lawyers, Light Bulbs, and Dead Snakes: The Lawyer Joke as Societal Text' (1995) 42 *UCLA Law Review* [*UCLA L. Rev.*] 1069 and R. Post, 'On the Popular Image of the Lawyer: Reflections in a Dark Glass' (1987) 75 *California Law Review* [*Cal L. Rev.*] 379.

have seen a rebirth of interest in lawyers as the subjects of such fiction. The most obvious way of subdividing this corpus is by using a fault-line that separates works that treat lawyers as soulless objects of disdain and contempt from those that portray them as noble, even heroic.[2]

The paradox that animates the cultural understanding of lawyers is this: the uncompromisingly critical attitude expressed in lawyer humour is made possible and offset by a sense of the importance and dignity of law. We all share an awareness that the legal system and lawyers are the facilitators of public order and values, that they implement justice and rights. Lawyers achieve public order by helping persons secure their ends and resolve conflict to their advantage within their rights. According to this ideal, lawyers are altruistic and selfless, concerned to put the interests of others ahead of their own and use their energies for the well-being of the community rather than themselves. The paradox and bitter irony is that lawyers, seen through the lens of popular imagination, subvert these values by using their power with perfect hypocrisy and selfishness.

In this essay I am concerned *not* primarily with the way lawyers are seen from outside, but with how lawyers see themselves. What are the cognitive and emotional parameters of lawyers' self-understanding in the face of lofty aspirations and public disdain? How much does the public perception affect lawyers' state of mind? Surveys by social scientists suggest that, at least in the United States, dissatisfaction is epidemic among attorneys, especially those new to the profession.[3] There is evidence that the same can be said of lawyers in other Western countries.[4]

Of course, one must be cautious about generalizing about

---

[2] Another fault-line reflects the point of view of the work itself and distinguishes works that look at lawyers behaviouristically or on the outside from those that explore the consciousness and inner life of lawyers. And a third fault-line refers to the author's background. It distinguishes literature written by nonlawyers from that written by attorneys themselves. All three of these fault-lines intersect, yielding richly populated subcategories.

[3] See, for example, *The State of the Legal Profession* (1990), a publication of the American Bar Association, Young Lawyers Division.

[4] To a large extent, the contagion of such attitudes is hardly surprising. The corporate legal cultures in the leading economies of the world have become increasingly interdependent and homogeneous, and the most prominent and visible groups of lawyers belong to that corporate culture. In this context, as in others, the American pattern has arguably been universalized.

lawyers' ambivalent and anxious attitudes towards their work and roles. The backgrounds, circumstances, and psychological profiles of lawyers are infinitely variable. Their dispositions towards their careers are likely to be as diverse as those of any professional group. Moreover, surveys of lawyers who have an international corporate law practice tend to focus on the most visible, prestigious, and stereotyped elements of the profession and may hardly reflect the milieux of most lawyers. It is itself a vexing sociological problem whether and how the circumstances of the profession have really changed in recent decades, and whether they have coalesced in a way that allows us to generalize at all about the attitudes of contemporary lawyers.[5]

Two bodies of writing can be said to suggest such generalizations and to describe and diagnose a crisis in legal professionalism, particularly in the United States. Both reflect, at least tangentially, on the self-perception of lawyers. The first body of writing, widely noted and discussed, is by prominent legal academics. It posits a recent precipitous devolution in professional ideals and practice. The underlying thesis is that ideological, social, economic, and political changes in American society have eroded the ideals of legal professionalism, changing, perhaps irreversibly, the role of lawyers. The most influential of these writings are *The Lost Lawyer* by Anthony Kronman, dean at Yale Law School, and *A Nation under Lawyers* by Mary Ann Glendon, a faculty member at Harvard Law School.[6] Their arguments have not gone unchallenged.

The second body of writing is literary fiction. Several recent American short story writers probe the dissatisfactions and tensions suffered by contemporary lawyers. These themes are immediately relevant to lawyers' self-understanding. The stories examine situations of isolation, alienation, and compromised idealism. Exploring these themes, they echo the empirical findings of psychologists and sociologists.[7]

The arguments of these writers of fiction are not necessarily bound by time and place. They resonate with literary works of

---

[5] The most comprehensive general study of these issues is R. L. Abel, *American Lawyers* (Oxford, 1989).

[6] A. Kronman, *The Lost Lawyer: Failing Ideals of the Legal Profession* (Cambridge, Mass., 1993); M. A. Glendon, *A Nation Under Lawyers: How the Crisis in the Legal Profession Is Transforming American Society* (New York, 1994). [7] See generally *State of Legal Profession*, n. 3 above.

other periods and cultures, reminding us of observations by authors as diverse as Shakespeare, Dickens, and Camus. The clear implication of these fictions is that the compromises lawyers make with idealism and their own consciences are not so much a product of our own time and condition as a pervasive, even essential, characteristic of the lawyers' enterprise.

The diagnoses and prognoses of the legal academics on the one hand and the writers of fiction on the other are radically different. I shall examine the main points of both analyses of the so-called crisis in professionalism and assess their relevance to lawyers' self-understanding.

The Dissolution of Professionalism

Anthony Kronman contends that various trends in the twentieth century have had the cumulative impact of undermining the professional ideals of law. He examines developments in philosophy, law practice, and legal education which have eroded the long-standing ideal of the lawyer-statesman.

THE ECLIPSE OF PRACTICAL WISDOM

Kronman draws heavily on Aristotle's notion of moral development. He observes that for most of Western cultural history, we have entertained and accepted the notion of practical wisdom, a kind of expertise in making moral choices about means and ends. In the public arena of law and politics, practical wisdom in making moral choices draws on such dispositions as fraternity, integrity, compromise, and sympathetic detachment. Kronman argues that the idea of practical wisdom has been eclipsed by moral scepticism in recent thinking and discourse.[8]

Two antithetical cultural developments account for this change. In the early part of the twentieth century, the identification of expertise with scientific training and method undercut the notion of practical wisdom. In the latter part of the twentieth century, an egalitarian kind of scepticism has habitually deconstructed claims of expertise into manifestations of power and control. Both developments need explanation.

---

[8] Kronman, n. 6 above, chs. 1 and 2.

Over more than a century, we have come to favour a quasi-scientific model of expertise in law and in general. Training through apprenticeship in law was displaced long ago by law schools as the standard mode of legal education. The common theme that informs legal pedagogy and legal reform in the twentieth century is formal, quasi-scientific objectification of law. Casebooks and the so-called Socratic method convey to students the notion that the rules of law are to be learned inductively through examining one relevant instance after another.

Between the 1920s and 1950s, traditional areas of common law were formalized. National boards of legal experts compiled comprehensive 'restatements' of law or promulgated model codes, and state legislatures followed suit by modifying and adapting comprehensive statutes. More recently, the 'normal' legal solution for social problems, whether remedies for discrimination or accommodation of problems raised by new technologies, has inevitably been to draft a detailed and comprehensive statute. The legal emulation of science thus included both inductive and deductive methods. Legal pedagogy and judicial reasoning are instances of inductive reasoning. The use of codes, mimicking the civil law, reflects on the other hand a commitment to deductive reasoning.

The commitment of law to a scientific model of rationality can be better understood by taking note of parallel developments in philosophy in the first half of the twentieth century. Immediately after World War I, logical positivism, which equated scientific objectivity with rationality and treated discourse about values as mere expression of preference or emotion, was widely influential. By mid-century, this approach was displaced by a more contextual and relativistic way of understanding various domains of thought, understanding, and practice. Wittgenstein and others drew attention to the variety of our linguistic and conceptual practices, suggesting that moral and legal discourse have their own forms of rationality and coherence.

Renewed attention to the integrity and objectivity of normative thought and discourse, however, did not entail resuscitation of the notion of practical wisdom. Note that it is possible to understand various practices of moral or legal discourse in two different ways, one of them egalitarian, the other not. We can choose to assume that all initiates into the practice are more or less equally endowed with practical wisdom (because practical wisdom consists in finding one's way through the practice). Alternatively, we can choose to believe that practical wisdom is a special gift or achievement that describes only the most skilled persons engaged in the practice. Among late twentieth-century thinkers, the second conviction is likely to seem naive. Critical theory has sensitized us to see claims of expertise and practical wisdom as camouflage for the use of power and advantage by members of privileged classes, races, and genders. By default, we opt for the apparently safer egalitarian assumption and choose to remain dismissive of practical wisdom.

Thus, the scientific impulse and the egalitarian one have conspired against the idea of practical wisdom. The former has seemed to give us a preclusive model for expertise as objectivity, while the latter has made us sceptical of all other claims of expertise.

My account of this process combines my own observations with Kronman's. He stresses that the current vogue of scepticism and anti-rationality can hardly be overestimated. Jurisprudential theories from legal realism to critical theory have all questioned the possibility of making law objective and scientifically rigorous. More importantly they have subverted the ideals not only of scientific rationality but of practical rationality by arguing that the accepted discursive moves of legal decision-makers camouflage power, arbitrary preference, and violence. These insights have further weakened the case for seeing legal expertise as practical wisdom in law.

Kronman goes on to argue that not only legal education but also law practice has progressively drawn away from the idea of practical wisdom.[9] In both domains, the ideals of law practice are confused with technical skills, wiliness in argument, and the ability to find the means to achieve any end. The discourse of professional responsibility is seen not as an attempt to clarify the parameters of professional integrity but rather as a public relations ploy for the legal profession to forestall public censure and a way for lawyers to set ground rules for sorting out the fruits of their collective power. Lawyers too often succeed in achieving their clients' ends to the detriment of the public interest, or they achieve their own (financial) ends to the detriment of their clients.

---

[9] Kronman, n. 6 above, chs. 4 and 5.

Pointedly, Kronman calls his book *The Lost Lawyer*. Lawyers are lost, he implies, not merely in the eyes of onlookers but in their own eyes as well. Avenues for self-justification are closed.

THE RELEVANCE OF PRACTICAL WISDOM

This account of a slice of intellectual history is acute and compelling, even as it is unsurprising and familiar. But one may question its relevance to the common understanding of the professional expertise of lawyers. Even at times when persons have embraced the ideals of practical reasoning and practical wisdom, *claims* to such wisdom on the part of lawyers and others have typically been treated with scepticism. It does not follow from the waning of the concept of practical wisdom that the legal profession as a whole earns more or less respect than in centuries past, nor that it has any more or less power.

What Kronman shows is therefore modest, that with the waning of the notion of practical wisdom in contemporary philosophy, one kind of argument for defending the special qualifications of lawyers has been disabled. But even in a climate that honours and respects practical wisdom, lawyers may by and large have been seen as abusing their claim to be its custodians and practitioners. The opposite is also true. Even in a climate in which this special justification is unavailable, lawyers may play a central role in political and economic events as effectively as ever.

Similarly, the demise of a belief in practical wisdom may have little relevance to understanding lawyers' introspection. It removes one particular way in which lawyers can flatter themselves or appraise themselves positively. But the notion of practical wisdom is an illusory tool for resolving moral and legal dilemmas. There is no reason to think such dilemmas were or even *seemed* more tractable to those who equated legal proficiency with practical wisdom.

As I argue in the next section, the moral parameters of lawyering have, for the most part, hardly changed over the history of the profession. Lawyers troubled by them—by choosing between one's own interest and that of one's client, by having to choose between a client's interest and the public interest, by misgivings about the adversarial process—are likely to find little solace in the mantra of practical wisdom.

Moreover, one can be of two minds about changes in legal education. If the scientific spirit and sceptical doubts have conspired to erode a belief in practical wisdom, the actual available knowledge and sophistication of lawyers have arguably grown over the last century. Under an apprenticeship scheme, the training of lawyers could be hit or miss, dependent on the skills of mentors. In modern times, American lawyers typically complete undergraduate university programmes before law school and spend three years taking law courses in many subjects from many teachers. By contrast with apprenticeship, this educational regime has safeguards that assure at least minimal competence. If competence is not wisdom, it is arguably at least a precondition for it.

During the pre-contemporary period, legal training was restricted. Persons were excluded on the basis of social class, ethnicity, gender, and race. As barriers have fallen away, the profession has arguably become more meritocratic. It is plausible, therefore, that the profession is more open to entry by potentially wise and competent persons than at other times in its history. The actual skills and knowledge of lawyers may, for this reason as well, be higher.

Of course, improved training, wider knowledge and skills, and better demographics all play a complicated and uncertain role in the self-perception of lawyers. Perhaps better training and greater intellectual sophistication have a humbling effect, making lawyers aware how much they do *not* know. Perhaps the same factors make lawyers share a general scepticism towards ascriptions of practical wisdom.

The significance of new styles of lawyering for lawyers' self-conception is also complicated and elusive. If law practice has become more impersonal, more corporate, and less communal, the change can be interpreted in various ways. Nostalgia for the nineteenth-century model of small-town lawyering in bucolic and familial environments can be offset by cynicism about the methods and scruples of old-school lawyers who were not subject to the control of any organized bar, who were often ill-trained, and who may have been at the beck and call of robber barons or bigots. It is clear that lawyers in pre-contemporary periods could not claim to be custodians and purveyors of practical wisdom nor were they likely to see themselves in that light.

THE ROLE OF LAWYERS

Glendon's argument is less concerned than Kronman's with the question of the decline of professional ideals and their impact on lawyers' self-regard. Her argument does, however, complement Kronman's in its concern with the influence lawyers have on the society around them. She decries the fact that 'the American legal profession, at century's close, shows signs of drifting toward a future where there would be no shortage of law and lawyers, but where constitutionalism and craft professionalism would be but ghostly memories, a glittering in the veins of whatever form of government succeeds the republic we did not try hard enough to keep.'[10] Our form of government is jeopardized because we have assimilated and generalized only the worst habits of legalism, adversarial manners that 'exert an unwholesome influence on everyday human relations. Outside the courtroom, few causes are advanced by selective and self-serving presentation of facts and issues, by the artful use of epithet and innuendo, by voiding the slightest concession that the other person might be partly right, or by the strident assertion of rights.'[11]

Glendon argues that these characteristics of advocacy have historically been held in check by procedural controls in institutional contexts. Only in the modern era of anomie have they infected general social relations, contexts where there are no such controls. Thus, the implicit constraints and restraints of our form of government are threatened.

Glendon is hardly alone in arguing that American society has been coarsened. Whether this is so and whether lawyers have played a crucial role are familiar issues in popular sociology. It is generally assumed that we are more contentious and less empathic than we were a few generations ago and that this is a sign that our society is disintegrating. Glendon takes these assumptions as given. But perhaps contentiousness can be understood differently, as a sign that groups that were once suppressed—women, persons of colour, the poor—are asserting their rights and claiming power. Is contentiousness really increasing, or is it simply becoming more public and visible? Perhaps lawyers are not so much the agents of conflict as merely the servants of a process that has other

---

[10] Glendon, n. 6 above, 293. [11] Glendon, n. 6 above, 259.

economic, political, and social roots. Glendon offers her own
opinions, and each of these issues leaves ample room to differ.

Both Kronman and Glendon talk about lawyers while circum-
navigating questions about their psychology. They dwell on skills,
habits, and influences but say little about what it is like to be
inside those skills and habits. This is curiously similar to the
preoccupations and omissions of a typical legal education. Law
schools do little to prepare students for the tensions of introspection. (Clinical programmes, which are available only to relatively
few students, may be an exception.) While law schools are newly
interested in courses on 'lawyering skills' that include case preparation, client interviewing, negotiation, mediation, and informal
advocacy, the emphasis in such courses is interpersonal rather
than intrapersonal. While medical schools, by contrast, increasingly address the most basic psychological strains of practice such
as dealing with the limitations of medicine in the face of the
inevitability of death and the frequent reality of permanent
disability, law schools rarely own up to the psychological strains
of lawyering. To illustrate these strains and their impact of
lawyers' self-perception, we turn to literature rather than law.

Conscience and Consciousness

An old French proverb says that 'no lawyer will ever go to Heaven
so long as there is room for more in Hell'.[12] An English proverb,
equally venerable, says, 'the Devil makes his Christmas pie of
lawyers' tongues'.[13] And, in the eighteenth century, Oliver
Goldsmith observed that 'lawyers are always more ready to get a
man into troubles than out of them'.[14] This suggests that the reputation of lawyers has hardly changed over the centuries. We can
easily find 500-year-old observations that mirror contemporary
lawyer humour.

One may hypothesize that the introspective dimension of
lawyering has also been impervious to change. The reasons for
this may be so obvious and familiar, so banal that the Kronmans
and the Glendons of academia may ignore them as they decon-
struct and lament the contemporary postmodern world. Writers of

---

[12] Bruce Nash *et al.*, *Lawyer's Wit and Wisdom* (Philadelphia, 1995), 48.
[13] Nash, n. 12 above, 48.   [14] Nash, n. 12 above, 47.

fiction, on the other hand, have long been proficient at using time-bound stories to make us think about timeless and pervasive situations.

Those of us who teach about the intersection of law and literature sometimes fall back on a predictable canon. Even if *Billy Budd* and *The Merchant of Venice* are efficient tools for examining law and lawyering, the scrutiny of fresher, less hoary examples is likely to be rewarding. In particular, several contemporary American short story writers have turned the trick of looking at the consciousness and conscience of lawyers in troubling ways.

Early in my course on law and literature, my students read stories by Ward Just ('About Boston'), Cynthia Ozick ('Puttermesser: Her Work History, Her Ancestry, Her Afterlife'), and James Salter ('American Express').[15] Each story takes the point of view of a contemporary American lawyer. Each story is located in its own professional, social, and moral universe. Since I cannot presume familiarity with these works, I will explain how each story supports important lessons.

ISOLATION

All three stories show the isolation of lawyers. The lawyer is a custodian of secrets. As planner, the lawyer must use information from and about clients that must be kept confidential if the lawyer is to do her job and the client is to achieve his ends. This is even more true in advocacy and litigation than in other aspects of practice since the success of the lawyer's litigation strategies often depends on surprise, on doing the unexpected.

Ward Just's story is about a divorce and estates attorney in Boston who has come to know through his clients much about the interplay of old money, new money, and power and whose livelihood depends on his silence and discretion. He has become the passive receptacle and tacit facilitator of others' lives. Perhaps he was predisposed to such discretion. His inspiration for a career in law was the lawyer/friend of his entrepreneurial grandfather. As a child growing up in Chicago, he revered both older men.

[15] Ward Just, 'About Boston', and Cynthia Ozick, 'Puttermesser: Her Work History, Her Ancestry, Her Afterlife' in Jay Wishingrad (ed.), *Legal Fictions: Short Stories about Lawyers and the Law* (Woodstock, NY, 1992); James Salter, 'American Express' in *Dusk and Other Stories* (Berkeley, 1993).

His early ambition to use law to achieve political success in Boston is soon frustrated. He remains, in his own eyes and probably in the eyes of those around him, an interloper and outsider. He is doomed both by the social exclusivity of Boston and, it is implied, by limitations of his own personality. And yet he exists in paradox, as a socially and politically marginal figure who is the influential custodian of the secrets of those in power. He is a success by the standards of his profession while he suffers the alienation of having failed his own aspirations.

VALUE CONFLICT AND LITIGATION

The job of an estates attorney is to implement clients' wishes regardless of motivation or effects. Identification with the ends of clients can be even more troubling when the lawyer is an advocate. To be sure, the adversarial system has much to be said for it. When it works ideally, it is a paradigm of justice in which contending parties have their best case made by trained partisans, and the contest is decided by a disinterested third party. For the practising litigator, however, this idealized model is often remote from reality.

One set of problems is systemic, ways in which the system itself falls short of the ideal. Attorneys vary enormously in skill, diligence, and responsibility. Their efforts in a given case may not be well joined. The cost of litigation is high, making it a risky luxury for most litigants, and also making it a conduit for transferring resources from litigants to lawyers. Lawyers may abuse the system as well as use it. And the ultimate fact-finder, whether judge or jury, may do its job well or badly, honestly or corruptly. Many commentators conclude that the most that can be said for the adversarial system is what Churchill said about democracy, that it is the worst system of decision-making except for all other forms that have been tried.[16]

A second set of problems is of more immediate concern in understanding lawyers' introspection. Even when the system is

---

[16] 'Many forms of government have been tried, and will be tried in this world of sin and woe. No one pretends that democracy is perfect or all-wise. Indeed, it has been said that democracy is the worst form of Government except for all those other forms that have been tried from time to time.' Winston Churchill, speech to House of Commons, 11 November 1947.

working well, the strains and tensions of client representation are psychologically unsettling. For the lawyer, litigation is by design a zero-sum game; her success depends on the adversary's defeat.

Not only must the lawyer usually commit her skills and resources to victory without compromise, but she must do so regardless of her views of the client's ends and moral posture. If it is perhaps rare for a lawyer to represent interests that violate his deepest convictions, it is equally rare for a lawyer's public and private faces to be a perfect fit. Few callings tie success so obviously to pretence and lack of candour.

I shall not go into the familiar arguments by which these dilemmas are rationalized. For many lawyers, a belief in the ultimate justice of the system overrides any misgivings about their role. For others, the idea of role-playing itself has its solace, along with the pretence that, like actors, they can put aside their public face when they wear their private one.

Basic psychology tells us that these demands take a predictable toll. Indeed, the typical circumstances of legal representation approach the criteria that many psychologists would use for pathology. These include working for ends one does not share, using means that one finds morally questionable, allocating one's resources and energy in ways that are demonstrably harmful to some parties or that do not obviously contribute to overall benefit, and having to practise extreme circumspection and guardedness.

Of course, many litigators flourish within these constraints and, in the eyes of themselves, their peers, and the world at large, live honourable lives. The psychological and moral challenges of litigation practice are not inherently disabling but rather define an arena of complex psychological accommodation, one that defies easy understanding. Law in itself is no more a pathological profession, and lawyers in general are no more amoral, than many other callings in the contemporary world.[17]

These constraints have characterized the profession of partisan

---

[17] Some observers find fascinating the chicken-and-egg dilemma of whether the profession attracts persons who are, by nature, comfortable with these constraints or whether legal training shapes—some would say, deforms—lawyers-to-be accordingly. Doubtless both processes play a role. Only some persons are disposed to be lawyers, and only some lawyers are disposed to be litigators. And the training and practice themselves shape actions, beliefs, and attitudes in those disposed to pursue them.

advocacy at least since Plato described and criticized the sophists. Lawyers in ancient cultures, in Elizabethan and Victorian England, and in contemporary world-class cities have all been subject to them. But, as we saw above, discussion of these features within the profession is oddly skewed. They are not ignored, at least in the United States, in our courses and casebooks on professional responsibility. But emphasis is on the public face rather than the private, the interpersonal rather than the intrapersonal. When teachers and scholars discuss these issues, they focus on three concerns: the ways in which ideals of professionalism have failed in contemporary society (as reflected in Kronman and Glendon), the assessment of the success and failures of the adversarial system itself, and the reconception of the lawyer's role to define and bridge the lawyer's obligations to third parties, society at large, and herself. In ignoring the psychological tensions inherent in legal representation, these discussions offer ameliorative prescriptions that seem remote and hard to translate into the mundane opportunities lawyers face.

Works of fiction pick up the slack. They force us to attend to the variety of ways in which individuals adapt. The Salter story I mentioned earlier, 'American Express', is about dehumanization. The two protagonists, who we are told are 'lawyers, sons of lawyers',[18] are one's worst nightmare and, at the same time, agonizingly familiar. They are materialistic, exploitative, cynical, and walled-off against empathy. Salter makes us understand them as paradigms of a certain kind of deformation through law.

Employed 'in the last rank of the armies of the law',[19] Frank and Alan work for three years in the bowels of a large law firm on the infinite complexities of a minor patent infringement case, 'swallowed up by the case with knowledge of little else'.[20] Quitting the firm two months before the case comes to trial, they start their own firm and take the case with them. Courting a disciplinary action, they are in fact not sued and settle the patent case 'for thirty-eight million, a third of it their fee'.[21] Inhabiting a world 'divided . . . into those going up and those coming down',[22] they flourish. Alan marries and divorces; Frank never marries ('I don't trust anyone enough to marry them.'[23]).

[18] Salter, n. 15 above, 29.   [19] Salter, n. 15 above, 28.
[20] Salter, n. 15 above, 34.   [21] Salter, n. 15 above, 35.
[22] *Ibid.*   [23] Salter, n. 15 above, 40.

[Alan] 'What do you want then?'

'This is all right,' Frank said.

Something was missing in him and women had always done anything to find out what it was. They always would. Perhaps it was simpler, Alan thought. Perhaps nothing was missing.[24]

On vacation in Italy, Frank and Alan, on impulse, pick up an Italian schoolgirl. They buy her a fur coat. Frank has sex with her, then offers her sexual favours to Alan, who hesitates and then accepts. 'In his shirt without a tie, [Frank] looked like a rich patient in some hospital.'[25]

The sadness of 'American Express' lies in paradox. Even if 'nothing was missing', Frank is empty. Even if his life is integrated around the conviction that he is among 'those going up' by winning cases, accumulating money, and flaunting independence, that life is hollow. Salter does not ask us to see experience through Frank's eyes because, he implies, there is no seeing there. Frank shuns introspection. His life becomes a ritual of exploitation and self-indulgence for its own sake, not even for the pleasure it yields.

Salter's story can be taken as an indictment of the 1980s, the gilded age of Reaganism. But Alan and Frank are not lawyers by accident. Their opportunism and emotional isolation are, Salter suggests, appropriate to a profession that rewards the prostitution of one's skills and private disengagement from the affective demands of life.

By contrast, Ozick's story acquaints us with a main character who has a rich life of introspection and fantasy and with whom we readily empathize. Puttermesser, a female Jewish attorney, is extravagantly eccentric. Her story is about hierarchy and exclusion in the worlds of law and about the mutual dependence of fantasy and life. Efficient and competent at legal tasks that give little satisfaction, she imagines a life in which she uses law to help victims of persecution and in which her cultural traditions give meaning. The story poses the question, among others, of whether a career in law is a way of achieving moral commitment and meaningful work or whether it provides escape and evasion.

In her imagination, Puttermesser constructs a life that is integrated and satisfying in ways denied by reality. On graduation,

---

[24] *Ibid.*   [25] Salter, n. 15 above, 50.

she enters 'a blueblood Wall Street firm'.[26] 'Hired for her brains and ingratiating (read: immigrant-like) industry, [she] was put into a back office to hunt up all-fours cases for the men up front.'[27] She accepts discrimination as settled differentiation. 'It was right that the Top Rung of law school should earn you the Bottom of the Ladder in the actual world of all fours. The wonderful thing was the fact of the Ladder itself.'[28] Not being one of 'the squash players'[29] groomed for partnership, she eventually leaves for a job in the city bureaucracy in the Department of Receipts and Disbursement. And her farewell lunch is 'an anthropological meal'[30] in which her erstwhile employers 'explored the rites of her tribe. She had not known she was strange to them. They were benevolent because benevolence was theirs to dispense.'[31]

With exquisite irony, Ozick delineates Puttermesser's place in an unforgiving class structure where place is determined by ethnicity and social background. She knows and is resigned to all this, and has little anger. But, in fending off her mother's matchmaking efforts, she says that she is too busy for such trivia because she is working to free Soviet Jews.[32] Puttermesser's other fantasy is that she is carrying forward, through Hebrew lessons, a rich commitment to her cultural heritage.[33] The reality is that she comes from secular Jews, and the relative with whom she imagines herself studying is in fact long dead.

Law and the secular world, Ozick implies, allow us to indulge the fantasies of achievement and self-realization. But the real choices we have as lawyers are not the moral opportunities we thought we would have.[34]

HUBRIS AND PENITENCE

The moral and psychological parameters of lawyering are similar in many Western cultures. Such existential and symbolic fictions

---

[26] Ozick, n. 15 above, 85. [27] *Ibid.*
[28] *Ibid.* [29] Ozick, n. 15 above, 86.
[30] Ozick, n. 15 above, 87. [31] *Ibid.*
[32] Ozick, n. 15 above, 84–5. [33] Ozick, n. 15 above, 92–5.
[34] Ozick's fascination with Puttermesser continues in several other short stories, recently collected as *The Puttermesser Papers* (New York, 1997). In these stories, her wishes and fantasies become reality and become consequential in the world.

as Albert Camus's *The Fall*[35] pose questions about the role and psychology of the attorney. The novel's narrator/protagonist discovers that, as a consummately successful defence attorney, his power allows him to be revered as a tireless defender of the needy and to bask in the awed regard of others. He becomes aware of, and tortured by, the paradox of selfishness clothed in selflessness, and he sees himself, and makes the reader see him, as having no core. He describes himself as having a 'vocation for summits',[36] that is, for distance from others and in the end from his own identity. He takes on the calling of a 'judge-penitent',[37] one who confronts others as a mirror of the moral paradoxes in their own lives. His self-esteem comes from being a facilitator, an achiever of means regardless of ends. His life, as a result, collapses in on itself and comes to be defined only by irony.

The Fall is presented as a series of conversational monologues. The judge-penitent, Jean-Baptiste Clamence, insinuates himself into the company and attention of a stranger, who, as Clamence guesses, is another lawyer. He unfolds his reminiscences, reflections, and confessions over several days. In the end, with his health deteriorating, Clamence hints that his story may possibly be a fiction created to make his interlocutor face his own life.[38] His narrative may be a mirror.

If a main theme of *The Fall* is existential and universal, the importance of claiming and owning one's own life and conscience apart from the regard of others, it is hardly accidental that Clamence is a lawyer compelled to confront other lawyers. Using their training and skills to serve others' ends, lawyers put at risk their own consciences. The exercise of their powers of analysis and persuasion becomes an end in itself. Narcissism is a constant lure. Power and influence as ends define a life without purpose. In the end, hubris leaves room only for all-embracing penitence.

In *The Fall*, as in other contemporary fiction, legal stories ask us to weigh the peculiar accommodations implicit in a life in law. It depicts the special conjunctions of passivity and accomplishment. It examines the predicaments of tying oneself to the ends of others while one objectifies and distances oneself from them, of

---

35 A. Camus, *The Fall* (Justin O'Brien (trans.), New York, 1956).
36 Camus, n. 35 above, 25. 37 Camus, n. 35 above, 138.
38 Camus, n. 35 above, 139–40.

working within a set of practices toward which one often harbours a robust cynicism and scepticism, and finally of defending one's altruism within a role that gives one the power to be consummately selfish. While critics from Plato to today's stand-up comics ridicule and disparage lawyers from outside, some of the best fiction presents the characteristic demands of the profession from inside, as tragedy and possible deformation of human spirit.

Two Models

The so-called crisis in the legal profession can, we have seen, be diagnosed in many ways. We have glimpsed two of them.

Kronman and Glendon agree that philosophical, economic, social, and moral changes in the last half-century or longer have emasculated the ideal of the lawyer-statesman, a model that until recently blessed lawyers with a rationale for their existence. They lament the demise of a golden age in which lawyers could take comfort in their role as custodians of practical wisdom and discretion.

A different approach is to see recent changes as superficial and largely irrelevant to a deep-seated malaise of lawyering. On this account, we may continue to pay lip-service to the ideal of the lawyer-statesman. But the account implies that we have rarely done more than pay lip-service. Lawyers have always been as much needed as they have been despised, and despised for the same reasons that they have been needed. As a result they have had to build buffers against despising themselves, often at psychological cost.

These two explanations of the 'malaise of lawyering' are not necessarily incompatible. One may share the psychological and literary insight that the lawyer's options have always been problematic and argue that the problems are aggravated by present conditions. On this account, the best lawyers in the past were able to transcend the tensions and embody the statesman ideal. Only in the present era has the pyramid been truncated, or to use a different metaphor employed by Kronman, has the ground of self-justification been cut from underneath the best lawyers.

Even if the two explanations can be made compatible, one may have misgivings about nostalgia for an idealized past that is explicit in Kronman and implicit in Glendon. This nostalgia has three questionable dimensions: philosophical, empirical, and psychological.

The philosophical claim is that until recently it was acceptable and desirable to think in terms of shared societal values and moral expertise and to see lawyers as the midwives of such values. Pluralism and egalitarianism have eviscerated these assumptions, and the popular sceptical approach is to see claims about shared values and moral expertise as camouflaging struggles for power. Rather than reject such scepticism, as Kronman does, one might take a middle ground. Doing so has two components. It involves looking critically at lawyers' historical claims to be moral experts and suspecting that such claims have often camouflaged moral conflict, but it also involves entertaining the possibility of still aspiring to such ideals in our era no less than any other.

The empirical and psychological dimensions involve looking at the history of the profession from outside and inside. Can we really say that courts, law schools, and law practice once afforded opportunities and recognition of moral expertise in ways that no longer exist? Or have the gains outweighed the losses, gains in sophistication and cultural awareness, so that law students and lawyers are better prepared and better off than they have ever been? Note that to suggest this is not to say that the contemporary situation is comfortable or satisfactory, but only to question whether it has ever been as the purveyors of nostalgia would have us believe.

Finally, we can question whether the introspective dimension has changed over time. We can identify the tensions and compromises of lawyering which writers of fiction bring to life in specific contexts. Haven't those challenges always defined the nature of the beast as a disconcerting and paradoxical profession?[39]

[39] I wish to thank my research assistants, James Scrimgeour and Kevin Shay, for their astute and helpful suggestions.

TRANSLATION AND JUDICIAL ETHOS: SOME REMARKS ON JAMES BOYD WHITE'S PROPOSAL FOR THE HARMONY OF THE SPHERES

Jeanne Gaakeer

Introduction

The interrelation of law and literature and the way it is given shape by the imaginations of lawyers since the 1970s form an important subject of contemporary legal theory. As early as 1977, J. Allen Smith pointed to the need for a theoretical foundation for this interdisciplinary development now called 'Law and Literature': 'The outcome of all this renewed interest in literature could come to a poor end unless somewhere along the course of its enthusiasm, the movement's leaders adopt theoretical support'.[1] This suggestion has indeed been controversial and stimulating ever since. This is because agreement neither on the need for theory, nor, if at all, on which form of theory, has proved easy to reach. The vitality of the ongoing debate on the topic makes it clear that it is indeed hard to find a middle ground, or rather, that the centre does not hold; it also shows that *Law and Literature* is more than a transitory movement. With its emphasis on law as a human activity of creating meaning, law and literature has redirected the attention to the idea of law as an art, and provided a powerful antidote to what Max Weber in his 'Science as a

---

[1] J. A. Smith, 'Aspects of Law and Literature' (1977) IX *University of Hartford Studies in Literature* 220. The issues dealt with in this paper are presented more extensively in my *Hope Springs Eternal, An Introduction to the Work of James Boyd White* (Amsterdam, 1998).

Vocation' called *Entzauberung*: the disenchantment of the world following the development of science that led twentieth-century scholars to a profound belief in the possibility and transparency of objective knowledge and human progress, with each and every aspect of life calculable and governable. The turn to literature, or, more specifically, the turn to narrative, redirects our attention within legal discourse to a belief in the strength of that essentially human characteristic of the need to tell stories. At the same time it draws attention to the permanent need of interpretation. Thus it epitomizes the link between human beings and their products of law and literature as typically human, social artifacts, the historical explanation of which, I maintain, is '. . . to a large degree arrangement of the discovered facts in patterns which satisfy us because they accord with life as we know it and can imagine it'.[2]

The call for theory for many scholars of Law and Literature is at odds with the very idea of literature. A fine example is James Boyd White's ontological view of narrative. He typifies narrative as 'the deepest need of that part of our nature that marks us as human beings, as the kind of animal that seeks for meaning'.[3] For him, the term theory as a product of reflection should be taken much more in the original meaning of the word, found in classical Greek, where the verb *theorein* means to review a situation and try to learn something from it. In two ways, he shows that interdisciplinary scholarship need not aim at developing a new theory. First, in offering his analyses he tries to stay on the level of the actual performances in language, rather than connecting these to an already existing theoretical framework. Second, he does not eschew offering, and subsequently using, his personal experiences of the congeniality between law and literature. His method is that of exemplary performance.

But what are the consequences of such a position? When the human need to tell one's story and be understood becomes an ontological linchpin, questions of justification of interpretation are driven into the background, if at the same time the cultural situatedness of performances in language becomes the measure of narrative adequacy. Used for a theory of law, does this not easily lead to a form of philosophical idealism, for how can such a view of

---

[2] I. Berlin, 'The concept of scientific history' (1961) *History and Theory* 24.
[3] J. B. White, *Heracles' Bow* (Madison, 1985), 169.

narrative be reconciled with the contingency of its products, especially in law, where authoritative claims are made for the narratives offered?

Ingenium and Ethos

In 1965 White wrote that he deplored the then prevailing lack of professional intimacy between law, history, and literature, fields once common to the legal profession.[4] Since then he has especially emphasized the importance and the consequences of our engagement with language and this emphasis follows from the view that the essence of a lawyer's work lies in the literary process 'of identifying and construing authoritative texts, of translating from another discourse into the law'.[5] All this, for White, involves an 'enterprise of the imagination', or rather, 'the translation of the imagination into reality by the power of language'.[6] Thus he redirects the attention to the idea of law as an art, the success of which depends on the lawyer's *ingenium*, his legal imagination or capacity to see what must be done in a given situation. White's thought on judicial ethos and the concept of translation exemplify the value of the word, which is why it is interesting to pay attention not only to what he discusses but also to what he omits, because this helps illustrate the necessity and the difficulty of the choices we make in law, and the consequences of our professional and societal choices.

White claims that, 'the greatest power of law . . . lies in the way it structures sensibility and vision' and offers the term poetics for law: the art of law is the art of laying bare the contrast between the theoretical rigour of legal concepts with their tendency towards closure, and the openness that the law offers by creating opportunities to speak about the contents and range of its own concepts in the argumentative process made possible by specific procedures.[7] Normatively, the right attitude to one's own language implies finding the right professional stance. This means

---

[4] J. B. White, Review of M. P. Gilmore, *Humanists and Jurists* (1965) 78 *Harvard Law Review* 1713.

[5] J. B. White, 'What Can a Lawyer Learn from Literature' (1989) 102 *Harvard Law Review* 2021.

[6] J. B. White, *The Legal Imagination* (Boston, 1973), 758.

[7] J. B. White, *The Legal Imagination* (abridged edn, Chicago, 1985), xiii.

that, ideally, the lawyer should learn the art of translation. Learning to do this requires an attitude of modesty towards languages other than one's own. This in turn implies an attitude of respect for one's fellow human beings.

Given this starting-point the task of a lawyer is to contribute to the development of a culture of argument, the materials for which are found within one's own culture. This does not imply that the *status quo* of the culture is indisputable; it means that any change deemed necessary must be made from within. The most important condition for a lawyer's participation in a specific legal culture is not that this culture is free of injustice, for that would be quite unrealistic. It is the possibility of discussing justice that a legal culture should guarantee. The language of law must translate the unpolished stories of life into arguments about justice. The possibility of constituting community in any form depends on this. The question then becomes: what are the methodological elements of the process and how much attention is being paid or can be paid at all to the frayed edges of law's fabric, especially when one is averse to theoretical propositions?

If, as White claims, law becomes 'an art of persuasion that creates the object of its persuasion, for it constitutes both the community and the culture it commends', and if the fundamental uncertainty inherent in the dynamic process of continuous changes in language and culture can only be faced by means of a constitutive rhetoric that takes as its starting-point the contingency of both, we cannot escape the question in what way, if at all, this idea of 'working with and within language' can be a means of justification for the choices made in claiming meaning and constituting community and, at the same time, offer a vehicle for textual and cultural criticism.[8] How can performances in language, especially legal interpretations or judicial language performances, be criticized, if both author and reader are products of contingent culture?

---

[8] White, n. 3 above, 35. Epistemologically, constitutive rhetoric proposes and offers a paradigm shift, that is to say a return from a positivist theory of knowledge based on rational thought and empirical proof to a revival of the Aristotelean tradition in which arguing from the probable shows, as well as it affirms, the performative nature of language to the extent that the probable is shown, in an actual performance, to work as a means of persuasion; that is why it can function as a means to bring about social cohesion within an audience.

White offers a thesis with respect to a writer's ethos and its relation to both text and reader to answer this type of question. He claims that, 'a writer always gives himself a character in what he writes; it shows in the tone of voice he adopts, in the signals he gives the reader as to how to take that tone of voice, in the attitude he invites his reader to have towards the world or towards people or ideas within it, in the straightforwardness or trickiness with which he addresses his reader—his honesty or falseness—and in the way he treats the materials of his language and culture'.[9] All texts thus have an ethical dimension: ethical in the sense that the author's ethos reveals itself in the text, and ethical in the relation constituted between text and reader. Here lies the key for the criticism of legal language performances.

Interpretation as a Form of Translation

Not surprisingly, White offers us an analogy when he sets out to specify the ways in which the language of law establishes relations with and between its readers. He proposes a new metaphor for law, 'justice as translation', central to which is the acknowledgement of both the necessity of a process of mediation between languages, between people, and the impossibility of total identity.

Key words, designating a method of mediation and interpretation, are integration, composition, and translation. Integration, then, is 'a kind of composition, and that in a literal, and literary, sense: a putting together of two things to make out of them a third, a new whole, with a meaning of its own'.[10] Applied to the field of interdisciplinary work, especially in law and literature, this idea of integration implies that interdisciplinary work should not come to a stop at a mere exchange of findings between disciplines, but should rather aim at articulating the specificity of our acting with languages, both legal and literary, so that the foundations of both disciplines can be understood in their mutual connection. It makes it clear that from a methodological point of view, integration aims at resisting closure and wants to keep open the multiplicity of meaning characteristic of the literary approach.

Integration, or translation, is also 'a model of law and justice,

[9] J. B. White, *When Words Lose Their Meaning* (Chicago, 1984), 15.
[10] J. B. White, *Justice as Translation* (Chicago, 1990), 4.

for these two are at their heart also ways of establishing right relations, both between one person and another and between a mind
and the languages it confronts'.[11] White does not give a concise
definition, for that would mean reducing translation to a label and
that would be contrary to what a literary approach entails. In law,
translation means that constituting the right relations is a creative
act of interpretation aimed at establishing a new situation in the
world. It is an act of translating authoritative texts of the past into
the present. An attitude of respect for the original text is called
for, and that is, of course, complicated by the fact that only at the
very moment of translation do we fix the original meaning of the
text, that is to say the meaning we think is current; that act, too, is
based on the assumption that this meaning is available to us in a
more or less uncontaminated form.

Now any translation or interpretation causes modification of
the original in more than one way. First, it is obvious that a reduction of meaning takes place whenever the translator chooses the
meaning he will use from the range of possibilities offered by the
original. Translation thus is also a process of loss of those meanings the translator might have chosen, but did not. Second, there is
the idea of meaning as culture specific, a point forcefully brought
home by White's example: 'The German "Wald" is different from
the English "forest", or the American "woods", not only linguisti-
cally but physically: the trees are different'.[12] Translation, then, as
'the art of many-voicedness' is the art of accepting and handling
residue and loss. And the same goes for interpretation.[13] The standard for judging any interpretive performance is 'its coherence, [to
be tested] by the kinds of fidelity it establishes with the original,
and by the ethical and cultural meaning it performs as a gesture of
its own'.[14]

For the expression of the idea of interpreting and translating
judicial opinions, White turns to a powerful image from
Coleridge's *Biographia Literaria*, that of 'complexity controlled or
contraries comprehended'. Redefined for law: 'The idea of
"comprehending contraries" is if anything even more plainly

---

[11] White, n. 10 above, 230.
[12] White, n. 10 above, 235. Lawrence Lessig calls this 'the transformed significance' of a selected term. See L. Lessig, 'Fidelity in Translation' (1993) 71 *Texas
Law Review* 1202.   [13] White, n. 10 above, 27.
[14] White, n. 10 above, 256.

essential to the judicial opinion, for the very idea of the legal hearing and of legal argument (of which the judicial opinion is intended to be a resolution) is that it works by opposition'.[15] Judicial opinions should be judged, then, for the way in which they have incorporated the contradictory positions by clearly showing that both sides of a case have been carefully weighed. As White forcefully puts it: 'The law thus serves as the language into which other languages, and stories told in them, are translated and in that way comprised into a single order'.[16] Should we not ask then whether this single order of law differs or aims to differ in status from other forms of discourse? White explains that law in the form of the judicial opinion is 'structurally multivocal, a system of translation that is open, *in principle at least*, in all directions'.[17] In principle, there's the rub. Is White's text self-referential? Does he exemplify in his own texts his proposals for law and interdisciplinary legal scholarship?

Mimesis or Metaphor: The Vices of Economic Discourse

The discussion about the contrast between Law and Economics and Law and Literature forms an interesting starting-point to clarify this issue. It is a clear example of opposing views of language and world which also illustrates the misunderstanding on the part of some of White's critics. White, for example, finds in the economic thought dominant in the Chicago school of Law and Economics the Hobbesian vice of calculability and governability of human life associated with the idea of neutrality of language and concepts, and questions the way in which the language of economics gets qualified.[18]

---

[15] White, n. 3 above, 114, 116. [16] White, n. 3 above, 240.
[17] White, n. 3 above, 241 (emphasis added).
[18] At the basis of this direction in economic thought lies Richard Posner's 'wealth maximization' principle; see also L. A. Kornhauser, 'The Great Image of Authority' (1984) 36 *Stanford Law Review* 349, J. B. White, 'Economics and Law: Two Cultures in Tension' (1986) 54 *Tennessee Law Review* 161, and White, n. 10 above, ch. 3. The language theme is also transposed to the subject of conceptual thought. 'Concept' for White is a problematic term because the underlying premise of the way in which it is used is once again the quality of neutrality which implies transparency of the semantic load of a concept in a language and, following this, unproblematic translation of a concept into another language. That would be an imperialistic view in that it is based on the supposition that the 'conceptual world . . . is supposed to exist on a plane above and beyond language, which disappears when its task is done' . . . 'At the practical level there is an implicit claim that our own language [i.e. of concepts] is or can be a metalanguage, in which all propositions can be uttered, all truths stated', and, furthermore, because '. . . conceptual

He calls his reader's attention to the single-voicedness of economic reasoning, with wealth-maximization as the key word, and calculation and risk assessment as the core of economic activity which is essentially the process of exchange; exchange then being the method of determining value: the price for which things are sold. The prevailing idea that economic theory does quite rightly reflect life as we know it, which means that it is both descriptive and prescriptive, is a view on the conceptual language of theory as a filing system which, precisely because it is a unified discourse that insists that the answers it gives are the right ones, is unable to pay any attention to political and cultural influences, to the ideological aspect of any discourse that can leave things unsaid.[19]

In other words, given its underlying premise of methodological individualism and of the closed texture of economic concepts, it fails to appreciate the exuberances and deficiencies of any translation, of any discourse; it cannot account for the possibility that the whole might be different from the sum of its parts. Those championing the market model, because the market is said to maximize the wealth of its participants and because it rests on the idea of voluntary participation making freedom and autonomy characteristic of the system, regard the promotion of efficiency as the theory's main contribution. Politically, the value of the promotion of efficiency has a nefarious influence, so White claims, precisely because it reduces freedom to mere non-interference by the government, whereas political freedom should be constitutive of community.[20] When questions crucial to legal discourse, of value,

talk assumes that the speaker "has" a concept, indeed must have a concept in order to speak, as if the function of language is to express something that exists on an altogether different plane, in a languageless place called mind' (White, n. 10 above, 31, 36).

[19] It means, for example, that the language of economics is unable to find a mode to discuss the intrinsic aspects of preferences, in the sense that value judgments about the perceived rightness or wrongness of preferences are impossible. See also R. West, 'Taking Preferences Seriously' (1990) 69 *Tulane Law Review* 659, who claims that the economic judge is an efficient judge who proves and consolidates in her decisions the very presuppositions about language and life which economic theory espouses, disregarding all others.

[20] White follows the late Isaiah Berlin's distinction between 'freedom from' and 'freedom to' in 'Two Concepts of Liberty' (in I. Berlin, *Four Essays on Liberty* (Oxford, 1969)). For White the predominance of the idea of voluntary participation and methodological individualism leads to a 'dollar democracy' in which 'one dollar, one vote' triumphs over 'one man, one vote'. This type of economic discourse refuses to acknowledge that '... the human will is often an engine of

equality, reciprocity, and participation, are left unasked, the result is that the translation of the discourses of law and economics into 'law and economics', as a movement, cannot be successfully accomplished.

The mimetic world-view abhorred by White as the norm for any discipline is embraced by Richard Posner who has launched the attack on law and literature. Posner divorces law from legal theory.[21] For him, methods of interpretation derived from other disciplines may prove fruitful for legal analysis, but for a lawyer it is useful to study another discipline only when this discipline uses law 'in some organic sense' and this is indeed the case with economics, but not with literature.[22] Literature can only be of service to law in the form of its methods of interpretation borrowed from literary theory, because of the trivial fact that legal texts do indeed need some form of interpretation. To the proof of this premise Posner has dedicated a study entitled *Law and Literature: A Misunderstood Relation* which essentially deals with only one question, that of objectivity in interpretation, and thus, in law.

In dismissing a 'new critical' view on interpretation for law, he shows the political nature of his preference, to put it in economic terms; political especially in the light of the economic view on the unproblematic nature of revealed preferences: a text of law should be read as a command, from author to interpreter, and the main characteristic of a command is that it aims to convey determinate meaning.[23] For literary analyses New Criticism is an acceptable

destruction' and in its pretension of neutrality with respect to values it is at odds with law as a value-oriented discourse. What is necessary is '. . . education, and this primarily an education into an understanding of the limited and dependent place the human being has in the world—limited in its own comprehension, even of itself, and dependent, both upon nature and upon others, for everything of value' (White, n. 10 above, 74). It is perfectly clear that for him the value of the word is not economically determinable. See also for a similar argument, J. B. White, 'How Should we Talk about Corporations?' (1985) 94 *Yale Law Journal* 1416, and 'Meaning in the Life of the Lawyer' (1996) 26 *Cumberland Law Review* 763.

21 'Law is subject matter rather than technique. Legal analysis is the application to the law of analytic methods that have their source elsewhere', R. A. Posner, 'Law and Literature: A Relation Reargued' (1986) 72 *Virginia Law Review* 1359.

22 Posner, n. 21 above, 1360.

23 R. A. Posner, *Law and Literature: A Misunderstood Relation* (Cambridge, Mass., 1988), 240. The revised and enlarged edition, entitled *Law and Literature* (Cambridge, Mass. and London), was published in 1998. See also A. Julius, 'Let's Kill all the Lawyers' in the *Times Literary Supplement*, 8 May 1998, 27, for a review of this revised edition.

method. For law it is not, since that would lead to unbridled delegation of power to a judge. Power and its restriction, together with a Hobbesian fear of uncertainty, are Posner's central themes. Posner's own legal intentionalism, however, gets him into trouble, and quickly too.[24] The reason for this is that the questions we ask ourselves and our texts, be they historical or not, in our contemporary context can never be transported to the situation in which the original legislator found himself. Our questions can simply never be his; it is a hermeneutic mirage to think they can.

It comes as no surprise that Posner is a critic of White's idea of translation. Posner distinguishes an 'Interpretation as translation school', and criticizes it, not unexpectedly, if we look at his language theory, for the way in which the exuberances and deficiencies are to be accepted as an integral part of any translation or interpretation. For Posner, White's view is highly exaggerated: 'Some sentences can be translated into another language without any loss of meaning: instructions for assembling a kitchen table, for example'.[25] But that argument is beside the point in more than one way. Not only does anyone who has ever bought a cheap do-it-yourself kit know that Posner's optimistic view is immediately falsified by actual practice. What is more, now that the context of this remark does not give rise to the idea that he meant this to be taken facetiously, it is quite obvious that he has totally misunderstood that White offers translation as a mode of thought to try to do justice to the complexity of human relations and to solve a variety of problems encountered in law, and not as a mere conveyance of meaning, or 'equivalence in different languages', as Posner has it.[26] The misunderstanding can also be explained by

---

[24] When he claims: 'A legal intentionalist holds that what you are trying to do in reading a statute or the Constitution is to figure out from the words, the structure, the background, and any other available information how the legislators whose votes were necessary for enactment would probably have answered your question of statutory interpretation if it had occurred to them', he offers a hypothesis that is unworkable even when modified to a call for judicial interpretation that 'that is most likely to advance the common enterprise of governance' (Posner, n. 23 above, 218, 253). For a similar argument about language as a neutral vehicle for transferring meaning, see R. A. Posner, 'Remarks on Law and Literature' (1992) *Loyola University Law Journal (Chi.)* 181.

[25] R. A. Posner, *Overcoming Law* (Cambridge, Mass., 1995), 493. The argument is repeated in the revised and enlarged edition of *Law and Literature* (Posner, n. 23 above).

[26] Posner, n. 25 above, 496.

Posner's rejection of the metaphor as a mode of thought for law: the Posnerian poet uses metaphor and other stylistic devices 'to create arresting images', whereas in the discursive, analytical prose of law 'the appearance of continuity of legal doctrine' is what matters.[27] If the metaphor can at all fulfil a cognitive function by showing us things in an unexpected manner, it is a model 'of an undisciplined and misleading character', since the truth value of the metaphor is at bottom totally irrelevant, and so is its performative aspect.[28] That is a view that is in stark contrast to White's, now that Posner subordinates metaphor and narrative to 'real' science. Thus, in speaking of 'interpretation as translation', he brings translation together with a subject he consequently described as fruitless for law and that settles the case for Law and Literature, and for White.[29]

The Harmony of the Spheres

What does the model of translation mean for a mutually illuminating interpretation and consequently integration of disciplines? Is White's translation of law and other disciplines true to the spirit of his own metaphor? Because his approach advocates looking at the things law is analogous to, he claims that we should not speak of 'law *and* sociology or history or economics or literature, but

---

[27] Posner, n. 23 above, 3.

[28] Posner, n. 25 above, 523–4.

[29] Posner's hermeneutics favour a literal reading of fiction, too, as his debate with Robin West on Franz Kafka's novels shows. See R. West, 'Authority, Autonomy, and Choice' (1986) 99 *Harvard Law Review* 384, and R. A. Posner, 'The Ethical Significance of Free Choice' (1986) 99 *Harvard Law Review* 1449. Not unexpectedly, given the faith that law and economics, despite its often vehement protestations to the contrary, puts in its own models as representations of reality. Language then easily becomes the neutral vehicle for the communication of information in which 'facts' are entities in the world that can be transmitted by means of words; those encoded thoughts that are our perceptions of these very same facts. It is precisely this economic *adequatio rei et intellectus* that law and literature opposes in its view that literature most often shows us that what we thought was reality, was, 'in fact', illusion, and that literature in showing us alternative realities can thus warn lawyers against attributing too much importance to what they think are facts, yet are no more than mere products of our points of view. The idea, in short, that literature teaches us to leave behind the mimetic theory of law and economics, and be receptive to the view that what we think of as reality, might only be the metaphor that has proved to be victorious.

law *as* each of these'.[30] Translation of disciplines should not be regarded as a mechanical act, but as something to be done time and again with the materials available, which is why the outcome of the process of translation cannot be anticipated with total certainty from the very start. This leads to the conclusion that a movement like Law and Literature cannot be expected to give us practical directions for the solution to specific cases, or to take the place of law's practice, generally. Interdisciplinary work should rather show us cultures and modes of thought which we can incorporate in legal discourse, or, contrariwise, try successfully to resist.

Now, in *Justice as Translation*, an almost casual, yet destructive, remark can be found about the place of economics. It shows the problems White encounters when he tries to reconcile the language of law with that of other disciplines, while at the same time he is convinced that law should have a special position in the whole debate: 'Economics should not be abolished, but neither should it be allowed, as some want it to be, to take over the law; and in all forms those who use it should seek not the kind of exclusivity the language seems to call for but integration with, *and subordination to*, other forms of discourse'.[31] The dominance of the language of law is confirmed more specifically in 'Imagining the Law' when White says that the law as a system of discourse should have a 'translation' type of relation with other disciplines precisely because 'each of these other discourses is translated into law'. 'This is itself an activity calling for the highest sort of art, by which the law must maintain its character as a meeting ground for other systems of speech.' Put differently, 'law is a language into which other languages must continually be translated'.[32] This thought is not wholly new, for, as we saw, earlier White suggested that 'The law thus serves as the language into which other

---

[30] White, n. 3 above, 43. White has recently offered some observations on legal education, in order to call to a halt the current deprofessionalization in law. At the same time he has affirmed, yet also reformulated, his views on the position of law with respect to interdisciplinary movements. Law, then, is to be taught, 'Not without economics, or politics, or psychology, or history, for all have much to contribute to legal thought and debate; but not *as* any of these things', i.e. if this 'as' would be taken to mean identity (White, 'Meaning', n. 20 above, 767).

[31] White, n. 10 above, 48 (emphasis added).

[32] J. B. White, 'Imagining the Law' in A. Sarat (ed.), *The Rhetoric of Law* (Ann Arbor, 1994), 38, 55.

languages, and stories told in them, are translated and in that way comprised into a single order'.[33] Recently, White has taken his argument one step further. In explicitly opting for the humanities, he considers the possibility that some languages may never be translated successfully, thus adding an element of limitation to his original concept of translation in accepting the possibility of non-translatability of discourses, of intransigent positions.[34]

What are we to think of this when he also claims that ultimately there is 'no "superdiscourse" that can control all the others'?[35] Following this absence of a superdiscourse, the necessity to defend one's own position as well as possible, in the hope that others will respond favourably, goes together with the claim that the meaning proposed by this very discourse of defence is potentially the very superdiscourse that aims to assume precedence above other discourses. For White the claim of law as part of the humanities, offered throughout his work with the Nietzschean credo 'here is my way; what is yours?', is relativistic in that it rests on the notion that other positions are possible, yet also claims to be itself the most valuable approach. In the end, despite the fact that 'the insistence upon the adequacy of a single language is a kind of tyranny', his interdisciplinary hermeneutics offer law as both objective and product of integration, as *ordo ordinans*, the ordering order for communal life.[36]

---

[33] White, n. 3 above, 240. See also the text accompanying n. 16 above.

[34] J. B. White, *Acts of Hope* (Ann Arbor, 1994), 123: 'There are similar incompatibilities among our own discourses today, especially I think between the ways of using language and the mind characteristic of the humanities and the forms of language and thought cast in the model made by natural science—those of economists, public choice theorists, and analytic philosophers. ... The gap between these two modes of expression cannot, so far as I know, be bridged by the use of any other language. The choice of language ends up being the choice of result, since what is most deeply at issue is how we should think and talk and who we should therefore be'.

[35] White, n. 34 above, 123.

[36] White, n. 10 above, 264. Both White's view on interdisciplinarity and the controversy between Posner and White make clear that the debate on law's autonomy still rages. The fear of scholars who see law's autonomy threatened by influences from other disciplines, some more welcome than others, is closely bound with an instrumentalist view of law and interdisciplinary legal scholarship. The result of such interdisciplinary legal scholarship is that law is once more fenced off. Those who like White point to the interrelations between law and another discipline at a foundational level have no need to do so. For them law's autonomy was never endangered in the first place.

'HOW CAN WE KNOW THE DANCER FROM THE DANCE?'[37]

What does this mean for the form of life that is law? The proposal for interpretive harmony within law starts from the premise that the judge is the translator whose text is to be studied for the form and content of his discourse of constitutive rhetoric. White then turns to the conversational process of the law offered in the opinions of the Supreme Court justices, and claims that the function of the judicial ethos is to emphasize the relational aspect of law:

> For me the really important question to ask about a court that decides a difficult case is not whether it reached the result I happen to prefer but whether it establishes an appropriate character for itself and an appropriate set of relations with its own intellectual inheritance and the people in the case. *The central idea of justice, on this view, is a matter, not of rules, distributions, or correctives but a matter of relations.*[38]

In order to measure the judge's success as far as his acknowledgement and reconciliation of the pressures at work in the process of judicial construction are concerned, we should look upon a judicial opinion as if it were a poem, because both are metaphors, ways of 'saying one thing and meaning another, saying one thing in terms of another'.[39] To this is added a far-reaching claim with respect to the relation between form and content of a text, based on the central question of a writer's ethos and the community proposed by the text:

> If we address these questions well, good answers will emerge to the secondary questions too, for implicit in any tolerable response to them are standards of justice—attitudes towards ourselves and others—that will inform what we say and do far better than any *a priori* theory or empirical science could do. *If we can get our voice and sense of audience and language right, everything else we care about, or, should care about, will follow. Such at least is my hope.*[40]

Precisely because words are not neutral vehicles for the transference of meaning, but rather proposals for a form of life in the

---

[37] W. B. Yeats, 'Among School Children' (1927).
[38] White, n. 9 above, 283 (emphasis added).
[39] White, n. 6 above, 773, referring to Robert Frost's view on poetry.
[40] White, n. 3 above, 107–8 (emphasis added).

Wittgensteinian sense, any language performance is a proposal for a relation between author and reader, between the text at hand and other texts. If these preconditions of the investigation of the ethos put forward in a text are met, the questions of substantive justice can also be answered.

How are we to judge the judicial opinion if this is the thesis? Especially when the idea of tradition as interpretive authority is acknowledged.[41] My thesis would be that White's proposal for an interpretive strategy for law is a specific form of translation. On the one hand, the text should be probed for the judicial ethos it shows. On the other, this should be done in light of the tradition in which the text is produced. A clear example, I think, of this attempt at balancing the two can be seen in White's comparison of the opinions of justices Harlan and Douglas in *United States* v. *White*.[42] Unlike Douglas, Harlan holds up his own performance for the reader to test. The reason White suggests for the fact that Douglas stops short of the text itself is the *sola scriptura* tradition of Protestantism which finds in Scripture the exclusive source and, consequently, in law regards the text of the Constitution as sole source of knowledge.[43] Harlan, then, follows what Sanford Levinson has called the catholic approach of textual exegesis with its emphasis on tradition and authority.[44] White does not explicitly word the contrast in these terms, but his distinct preference for Harlan makes it likely that he favours the catholic approach, at

[41] When White speaks of the tension between 'the individual mind and the cultural inheritance, or what Eliot called "tradition and the individual talent" ', he also uses it to evoke the moral connotation of law as inheritance, namely that of our duty to treat the materials of our legal past respectfully, such that our treatment may actually improve them for future generations (White, n. 3 above, 119).

[42] 401 US 745 (1971).

[43] White, n. 10 above, 172: 'To compare for a moment legal with biblical interpretation, one is reminded of those Protestants—among whom Douglas was in fact raised—who focused like all Protestants upon the sacred text rather than the tradition, but who read the text with an eye not to its letter but to its spirit'. See also J. B. White, 'Judging the Judges: Three Opinions' (1990) 92 *West Virginia Law Review* 697.

[44] White refers to Levinson's *Constitutional Faith* (1988). It should be noted, however, that already in his article 'The Constitution in American Civil Religion' (1979) *The Supreme Court Review* 123, Sanford Levinson compared the Constitution with a sacred text and the Supreme Court with the highest religious authority. See also T. C. Grey, 'The Constitution as Scripture' (1984) 37 *Stanford Law Review* 1 who distinguishes between (protestant) 'textualists' and (catholic) 'supplementers' and also mentions the 'rejectionists' who deem the choice between 'text' and 'text plus something else' absurd.

least for law.[45] Yet emphasis on the judicial opinion as a poem to be read for the ethos proposed can itself be thought of as *sola scriptura*. Thus translation of *sola scriptura* and the catholic approach can be looked upon as an attractive middle way between the two. To put it in comparable terminology, translation in this form is the Anglican *via media* of legal interpretation.

But there is a danger inherent in the idea of 'comprehending contraries'. In its focus on the actual textual performance, on the contradictory views which the judicial opinion aims to reconcile, this model leaves little or no room for the question of the possible exclusion of voices in a text. Even though a judge's responsibility lies in establishing relations that facilitate 'a conversation in which democracy begins', a metaphor inspired by John Dewey's well-known phrase 'Democracy begins in conversation'. A possible reproach might be: how about the voices of those we do not hear in the text, or, more generally, the authors of texts left undiscussed? Those law and literature scholars, White among them, who show a preference for the Western canon for the development of their literary-legal jurisprudence have to face this type of attack, launched especially by feminist legal theory. What about the tales from the unexpected?[46] White's defence against the charge of a form of high-culture blindness inherent in his choice of canonical texts, such as Jane Austen's *Emma* (1816), is that a truly great text, literary or legal, sometimes offers room to those excluded in the very act of refusing to talk about or with them: 'The denial of standing . . . the denial of a cause of action—all these are speech

---

[45] In his own works, too, there is a shift away from a dominant *sola scriptura* of the ideal reader in *When Words Lose Their Meaning* to the emphasis on tradition in the form of precedents in *Justice as Translation* and on the expression and function of authority in literature and law in *Acts of Hope*. But see J. B. White, *This Book of Starres* (Ann Arbor, 1994), 19–20: 'Attention was focused on the text, *where I still think it belongs*', which makes it likely that for literary analyses *sola scriptura* has not lost its attraction for White yet.

[46] And there is also the tension between this idea of democracy and White's choice for the judicial opinion as representative genre of legal text and as a form of life since rhetorically speaking the judicial opinion is a bounded textual form with strictly defined actors and an audience that is always in part involved in the process of its creation, with the judge's as the unifying voice. After all, to paraphrase Marianne Moore's definition of poems, we should keep in mind that law and judicial opinions are 'imaginary gardens with real people in them'. What is more, given the relatively small number of cases decided by the Supreme Court (approx. 80 per year), the constitutive ethos of lower courts may well be more important when it comes to constituting community.

acts that incorporate for the moment what they will exclude'.[47]
Yet, this refutation seems rather an easy way to get out of the
controversy, and it does not have any consequence, evidently
because of the predominance of the modernist subject's contingent
choice, in this case, from the Western canon. Do the ideas of intellectual integration and translation escape conformity with the
high-culture norm or are they a thinly veiled attempt at elitism?[48]
They can be saved if we differentiate, as Richard Rorty suggests
we should do, between an essentialist and a functionalist approach
to the canon. The former takes 'canonical status as an indication
of the presence of a link to eternal truth', whereas the latter,
which I am convinced White espouses, points to the canon '. . . to
offer suggestions to the young about where they might find excitement and hope'.[49]

Narrative and Subjectivity

The problematic aspect of all this is the very unity of form and
content promoted as an essential criterion for textual exegesis in
combination with the *via media* translation of tradition and
textual performance. It can, for instance, be seen in the treatment of Justice Brandeis, White's persona in the text, when
Brandeis's opinion in *Olmstead* v. *United States* is offered as
exemplary for judicial excellence, and the 'is' and the 'ought'
coincide.[50] Brandeis has indeed been able to get his voice and
sense of audience right. His ethos is indeed adequate, which is
why his decision about substantive questions, too, is appropriate. The distinction between 'is' and 'ought', fact and value, does
not find support in our actual experience of the combination of

[47] White, n. 3 above, 121. See also White, n. 10 above, 223: 'To think about
the law as a conversational process does not mean that we have to focus our attention only on those who directly participate in it; indeed, this kind of thinking
provides a way of talking about those who are left out or objectified, and a way of
criticizing law on that basis'.

[48] See S. S. Heinzelman, 'Hard Cases, Easy Cases and Weird Cases: Canon
Formation in Law and Literature' (1988) 21 *Mosaic* 59, and 'Another Version of
"Sweetness and Light": White on Cultural and Legal Criticism' (1992) 17 *Law and
Social Inquiry* 259.

[49] R. Rorty, 'The inspirational value of great works of literature' (1996) 16
Raritan 15. For White's view on the canon, see n. 34 above, 310.

[50] 277 US 438, 1928. The central question in *Olmstead* was whether wire-
tapping without probable cause or a warrant violates fourth amendment rights.

narrative and moral act, as White claims in *Heracles' Bow*: 'It is
from the "is", from the story told in a certain way, that we get
our most important "oughts": our sense that a particular story is
incomplete without a certain ending, which we can supply'.[51]
The constitution of justice thus coincides with the argumentative
process of law in its ideal form. What is more, by trying to
understand these texts and learn from the way in which they
affect us, we can translate the experience, and we can try to
mediate the experiential and the critical. That is White's claim
for law with respect to precedent illustrated in his Brandeis
analysis.[52] For a constitution in Brandeis's eyes is not only made
by its framers, but also by its interpreters who help bring the
text into the present through readings of the development of its
meaning in the form of precedents. There are no external,
universal criteria to escape to, only the formation of critical
judgment in and through this process. We develop our critical
standards literally from commonplace to principle, by agreeing
on certain points and taking them as guidelines for future
action.[53] That is the answer to the accusation that this is a form
of relativism that neglects to give critical purchase to its own
practices. Yet, the problem of how to account for subjective,
because human, imposition remains. A view of law in which the
normative predominance of actual performances and the contingency of cultural criticism as well as an aversion to theorizing
are the prominent features runs the risk of evading, as Lawrence
Joseph claims it should not, the question '. . . how to incorporate
subjectivity and objectivity of decisionmaking texts into a theory

[51] White, n. 3 above, 175.

[52] This resembles what D. R. Schwartz has called humanistic formalism:
'Indeed, does not an ethical reader understand a moral responsibility to try to
recreate the text as it was written for its original audience, as well as to define what
the text means to us now' (D. R. Schwartz, 'The Ethics of Reading' (1988) *Novel*
217).

[53] This is in contrast to Stanley Fish's ultimately sceptical view that interpretation is primarily an interpretive community's business and that there is no way in
which to determine which interpretation is valid, since interpretive communities
are not stable, and deciding who is a member is itself an interpretive act. In 'The
Judicial Opinion and the Poem' (1984) 82 *Michigan Law Review* 1685, White
explicitly calls his way of reading and criticizing 'profoundly *antitheoretical*'
(emphasis in original). See also J. B. White, 'Response to *Judging Religion* by
Winnifred Fallers Sullivan' (1998) 81 *Marquette Law Review* 511: 'What we need
is not more theory, but more experience, both practical and imaginative.'

of adjudicative law'.[54] There is a modernist emphasis on subjectivity in White's work in his claim that there are no certain foundations. Yet he offers a clear and consistent method to be followed. The recognition of the inevitability of subjectivity following from the fact that interpretation is a form of construction is not carried to its theoretical conclusion. For his analyses of literary texts this is less of a problem, aimed as they are at a discussion of the ways in which authority is constituted *in* the text. The effect of authoritative legal claims on people's lives *outside* the text is of course a different matter.

Conclusion

Things can hardly be otherwise if we think of law as a man-made artefact and of ourselves as 'the whole race . . . a poet that writes down the eccentric propositions of its fate', and, subsequently, we accept the cultural contingency of our critical and interpretive acts.[55] Despite its possible drawbacks, looking upon the judicial opinion as a poem and as a form of life, in my opinion offers a valuable contribution to legal theory that, precisely because of its literary character, illuminates aspects that usually remain hidden in a conceptually oriented theory. Nevertheless, a number of epistemological questions cannot be answered and the result is something of a paradox, especially now that White does not always allow in his own, normative text the many-voicedness he constantly advocates. In that sense it often lacks a self-referential character when the norm is not itself exemplified in the text. Now this might well be considered a serious flaw in the whole argument, but I would propose a more positive, constructive reading. White's text is emblematic of one of law's largest problems: the privileged discourse of law in which the principle of balancing and translating, or rather, of equality generally, is at once descriptive and prescriptive does indeed constitute a form of community, as

---

[54] L. Joseph, 'Theories of Poetry, Theories of Law' (1993) 46 *Vanderbilt Law Review* 1251. Joseph credits Robin West for having been the first to recognize (in her 'Adjudication is not Interpretation' (1987) 54 *Tennessee Law Review* 203) that the subjective element of legal interpretation conflicts with the institutional side of law.

[55] Wallace Stevens, 'Men Made Out Of Words' in *The Collected Poems* (New York, 1947).

much as this dominant metaphor conceals the fact that not everybody has his share in the community, or, worse perhaps, that not everybody will (even) want to belong to the community proposed by law. The normative aspect of 'equality under law', precisely because this concept is made an absolute for law, throws questions of substantive inequalities between people into the background, smoothing out the possibility that the community constituted by law may actually be smaller than the ideal would have us believe. If justice is indeed the constitution of a social world, we should ask ourselves how law can serve as a phenomenon that in our contemporary quest for justice may form the social fabric between people or groups with often conflicting interests. Though inadvertently perhaps, White's own attempt at offering a mode of thought and criticism for law, and culture in general, can help us realize just that.

That lesson is valuable too for lawyers in the European Union, although at first glance it is not at all obvious that White's literary-legal methodology offers possibilities for analysing judicial decisions in legal systems different from the American.[56] Yet, my thesis would be that constitutive rhetoric and translation do hold as an approach for the criticism of a certain type of European court. Since criticism of the judicial ethos informs us about the form proposed for the community in which a specific decision will be influential, it will be informative not only for Western European lawyers but also for those interested in comparative law to follow White's proposals and read decisions of the Court of Justice of the European Communities or the European Court of Human Rights as proposals for the shape and contents of the European Community at the supranational level. There are a number of reasons for doing this. First of all, the equitable function of these courts may provide remedies in individual cases, if

---

[56] Think, for example, of how differently judicial decisions are made and published in civil law countries. Or, when it comes to the subject of community, of the differences between a constitutional monarchy and a federal state. In legal systems without a written constitution, or, as is the case in the Dutch system, with a constitutional prohibition on judicial review, and with the secrecy of the judge's chambers, which means that judges do not disclose their deliberations, it hardly seems possible to undertake a Whitean type of legal analysis. The importance of the figure of the lawgiver for the development of Western European law and legal systems, and the lack of a culture of judicial opinion writing complicate such an attempt even more.

state legislation should remain unclear or even silent on the legal issue involved. These courts can instruct or advise national legislative bodies on the legislative direction to be taken in order to ensure coherence in a specific field of law in all Member States at the European level. Second, certain cultural differences and differences in national legislation in various fields may prove to be obstacles that must be overcome in the European context, if a minimum basis for a truly European community is to be determined—allowing, of course, for local variety within reasonable range.[57] When a national court refers to the Court of Justice of the European Communities for a preliminary ruling under one of the articles of the EC Treaty, it asks a question on a point of Community law, the answer to which will not only be normative for the national court in question, but for the European Community at large. And exactly because decisions of these supranational courts are proposals for the European Community, the concept of judicial ethos becomes even more relevant when a decision in a specific case is experienced not only as a legal mistake in the technical sense, but as one that is morally doubtful.[58] Those interested in comparative law and legal theory might benefit from such an approach, even more so when US Supreme Court as well as Community decisions on related subjects are analysed. Simultaneous research into historical cross-sections of a field of law, both nationally and internationally, will prove most interesting for purposes of comparative law.[59] There lies one of the practical values of a literary approach to law generally, and White's proposal for achieving harmony by means of a literary-legal jurisprudence, specifically.

---

[57] Think, for example, of the different interpretations of the term 'family life' under the articles 8 and 12 of the European Convention for the Protection of Human Rights, including a variety of human relations, not merely the marriage bond, and compare these to more conservative definitions of family as found in the Irish Constitution.

[58] A recent example of a controversial judicial ethos is the opinion of Advocate-General Tesauro in Case C–450/93 *Kalanke* v. *Freie Hansestadt Bremen* [1996] All ER (EC) 66 on the subject of equal treatment of men and women, and the meaning of formal and substantive equality.

[59] Compare, for example, Justice Thomas's opinion in *Adarand Constructors* v. *Federico Pena* (115 S. Ct. 2097, 12 June 1995) on the concepts of equal treatment and equality to Tesauro's in *Kalanke*, n. 58 above.

THE SOVEREIGN SELF: IDENTITY AND RESPONSIBILITY IN VICTORIAN ENGLAND

Simon Petch

'A society without a sovereign is a phrase without a meaning'.[1] Thus Fitzjames Stephen suggests the centrality of the term 'sovereign' to the social discourses of Victorian England. And by offering a metaphor instead of a definition, Stephen's phrase also suggests some difficulty in defining the term. Both the centrality and the difficulty are traceable to the opening sentence of Bentham's *Principles of Morals and Legislation* (1781): 'Nature has placed mankind under the governance of two sovereign masters, *pain* and *pleasure*.'[2] Bentham had said in *A Fragment on Government* (1776) that '*pain* and *pleasure* at least, are words which a man has no need, we may hope, to go to a Lawyer to know the meaning of'.[3] But 'sovereign' is a different matter, for as both adjective and noun, and together with its abstract derivative 'sovereignty', it is a key term in the English legal vocabulary, and hence the most powerful (if least discussed) word in Bentham's opening sentence. In *The Province of Jurisprudence Determined* (1832), John Austin extends Bentham's analysis of 'sovereignty'. To Austin a law is a command of a sovereign enforced by a sanction, but the harder Austin tries to locate the legal sovereign as a 'determinate and common superior' in the politics of the British

---

[1] James Fitzjames Stephen, 'Sovereignty', *Horae Sabbaticae*, second series (London, 1892), 61.
[2] Jeremy Bentham, *Introduction to the Principles of Morals and Legislation* (repr. New York, 1988), 1.
[3] Jeremy Bentham, *A Fragment on Government* (repr. Cambridge, 1988), 28.

Constitution, the more he finds the sovereign power diffused through a series of institutions: 'speaking accurately, the members of the commons' house are merely trustees for the body by which they are elected and appointed: and, consequently, the sovereignty always resides in the king and peers, with the electoral body of the commons.'[4] Fifty years later Albert Venn Dicey, in his magisterial study of the law of the constitution, took issue with Austin on this point: 'Nothing is more certain than that no English judge ever conceded, or under the present constitution can concede, that Parliament is in any legal sense a "trustee" for the electors. Of such a feigned "trust" the Courts know nothing.'[5] Austin, to Dicey's palpable irritation, has confused the legal sense of the word 'sovereignty' with its political sense; but it is less a matter of confusion than of slippage (Dicey concedes that 'the two significations' are 'intimately connected together').[6] For to establish the political signification of 'sovereignty', Austin has to perplex its legal sense by compounding it with the additional legal concept of 'trust' and its correlative notions of delegation and representation; and his syntax, normally so precise, is destabilized by his prepositions 'in' and 'with'. Unable to restrict 'sovereignty' to a purely legal meaning, Austin is equally unable to restrain its figurative force. While his model of legal relationship is '*the relation of sovereign and subject*, or *the relation of sovereignty and subjection*'[7] (emphasis added), 'sovereignty' is elusive of clear definition, and this very instability declares the concept available as a source of metaphorical power.

The 'sovereign' of Bentham's sentence blends public and private by fusing political with psychological meaning, and the force of the many metaphors of government that dominate the opening paragraph of *The Principles of Morals and Legislation* establishes that subjection to 'the standard of right and wrong' is a matter of subjectivity. Sovereignty became a metaphor for the investigation of selfhood in Victorian England. In Tennyson's first great classical poem, 'Oenone' (originally published in 1832, the same year as

    [4] John Austin, *The Province of Jurisprudence Determined* (W. E. Rumble (ed.), Cambridge, 1995), 194.
    [5] Albert Venn Dicey, *Introduction to the Study of the Law of the Constitution* (London, 1885; 3rd edn, London, 1889), 71.
    [6] Dicey, n. 5 above, 70.
    [7] Austin, *The Province of Jurisprudence Determined*, n. 4 above, 166.

Austin's *The Province of Jurisprudence Determined*), Paris has to choose or judge between the offerings of the Olympian goddesses Herè, Pallas, and Aphrodite. Pallas, the poem's authority figure, offers him the wisdom of an internalized sovereign principle: ' "Self-reverence, self-knowledge, self-control,/These three alone lead life to sovereign power." '[8] Such wisdom is a fusion of law and morality, a chance to 'live by law' and 'to follow right',[9] a sovereign principle which is the necessary condition of liberty. But Aphrodite makes a better offer—'The fairest and most loving wife in Greece'—that Paris is unable to refuse; and his rejection of the self-sovereignty offered by Pallas is not only the betrayal of his marriage to Oenone (for the 'most loving wife in Greece' is Helen) but also the first rift in the foundations of Troy. The poem, which opens with a glimpse of Ilion's columned citadel, and which concludes with Cassandra's prophecy of the sacking of the city, blends public and private by establishing a strong connection between Paris's rejection of self-sovereignty and the collapse into anarchy of a great civilization. Tennyson hated utilitarianism, but his poem unwittingly draws on Bentham in its fusion of public and private sovereignty. In the process of the transformation of English domestic political culture by the extension of the franchise during the nineteenth century, the concept of sovereignty was internalized in such a way as to inform the language of the self: 'self-government', to John Stuart Mill, means 'the government of each by himself';[10] and 'On Liberty' (1859) is grounded in the belief that 'Over himself, over his own body and mind, the individual is sovereign.'[11] When John Henry Newman claimed, in *Apologia Pro Vita Sua* (1864), that 'religious men would rather be in error with the sanction of their conscience, than be right with the mere judgment of their reason',[12] his use of 'sanction', like the uses of 'sovereign' cited above, draws force from Austin's definition of law as the command of a sovereign power enforced by a sanction. Newman realized that the charge levelled at him by

---

[8] Tennyson, 'Oenone', ll. 142–3, in *Tennyson: A Selected Edition* (C. Ricks (ed.), Harlow, 1989), 43. The poem was extensively revised between 1832 and its next appearance in 1842: the later version is cited here.

[9] Tennyson, 'Oenone', n. 8 above, ll. 145, 147.

[10] J. S. Mill, *On Liberty* in *On Liberty and Other Writings* (S. Collini (ed.), Cambridge, 1989), 8.   [11] Mill, n. 10 above, 13.

[12] John Henry Newman, Note on 'Lying and Equivocation,' in *Apologia Pro Vita Sua* (David J. DeLaura (ed.), New York, 1968), 267.

Henry Kingsley went beyond the stated issue of Untruthfulness to the comprehensive question of self-sovereignty, 'that living intelligence, by which I write and argue, and act',[13] and he tendered his conscience as evidence to counter what he called 'the articles of impeachment'[14] against him. Because of the *Apologia*, Newman's conscience became the most publicly harrowed or racked conscience in Victorian England, and his example acknowledged conscience as the authoritative principle of self-sovereignty throughout Victorian spiritual and moral discourse. In 1875 the *London Quarterly Review* carried an unsigned article entitled 'Conscience' which surveyed several books on Christian and moral philosophy.[15] The review is cast as an inquiry into the nature of the conscience, and in critiquing several contemporary theories of conscience it explains conscience by an analogy between 'internal self-government' and the necessary 'regulation of social conduct'.[16] The blending of legal language with epistemological process enables the writer to formulate a central distinction, that conscience is not a moral law but a constitutional law of the mind through which the mind knows its own allegiance to what is right and good: 'In other words, *conscience is that law of the mind which gives (or contains within itself) "the consciousness of obligation," in all our moral activities, to be loyal to truth, righteousness, and goodness*'[17] (emphasis added).

Such internalized precepts and principles of constitutional self-sovereignty are at the heart of Victorian religious and moral discourse, and are most visible when such discourses intersect with the law. The judgment of the Privy Council in the case of *Gorham v. Bishop of Exeter*, handed down in March 1850, held that, in the framing of the Thirty-Nine Articles of faith, the Church 'could not have intended to include in the Articles an authoritative statement of all Christian doctrine', and that some points had been left 'to the private judgment of pious and conscientious persons'.[18] The Privy Council's upholding of a Minister's right to such private

---

[13] Newman, 'Lying and Equivocation', n. 12 above, 11.

[14] Newman, 'Lying and Equivocation', n. 12 above, 10.

[15] 'Conscience' (1875) 44 *London Quarterly Review* 91–103.

[16] 'Conscience', n. 15 above, 92.

[17] 'Conscience', n. 15 above, 100.

[18] E. F. Moore, *The Case of the Rev. G. C. Gorham against the Bishop of Exeter* (London, 1852), 463; see also 471.

judgment ratified the individual conscience as a valid principle of sovereignty in matters of scriptural interpretation. The issue was furiously revived ten years later by the publication of *Essays and Reviews*, a collection of essays by liberal-minded theologians. Samuel Wilberforce, bishop of Oxford, took bitter exception to 'THE idea of the whole volume . . . this power of each man of settling what is and what is not true in the Inspired Record . . . Thus "conscience", aided by "private judgment", that is to say, every man's own private conviction of what befits God and what befits himself, is for every man to override the Bible.'[19] When the matter came before the Court of Arches (two of the writers were sitting clergymen who had been prosecuted by their bishops), Fitzjames Stephen (in his defence of one of the writers) hailed the Gorham judgment as 'the Magna Charter of the clergy of the Church of England'.[20] The Privy Council was bound by the *Gorham* precedent, and its judgment (in 1864) on the *Essays and Reviews* case consolidated the authority of the conscience as a principle of private judgment.[21]

Having suggested the pervasiveness and the flexibility of the concept of sovereignty in Victorian moral discourses, and having established the individual conscience as the regulating authority of self-sovereignty, I shall examine three areas in which the concept of self-sovereignty can be focused and interrogated through the interaction of law and literature. These are: insanity, contract, and the status of women.

Insanity

Insanity is a constitutional crisis in the sovereignty of the self, and the two landmark cases in the evolution of the law governing the insanity defence in the first half of the nineteenth century involved assault on the sovereign power of the state. In 1800 James Hadfield attempted to shoot George III, but was acquitted of high

---

[19] Samuel Wilberforce, 'Essays and Reviews' (1861) 109 *Quarterly Review* 255–6.

[20] James Fitzjames Stephen, *Defence of the Rev. Rowland Williams, D. D. in the Arches' Court of Canterbury* (London, 1862), 4.

[21] See George C. Brodrick and William H. Fremantle (eds.), *A Collection of the Judgments of the Privy Council in Ecclesiastical Cases Relating to Doctrine and Discipline* (London, 1865), 280–9.

treason, 'he being under the influence of insanity at the time the act was committed'.[22] In 1843 Daniel McNaughtan, in attempting to assassinate the prime minister Sir Robert Peel, mistakenly killed his private secretary, and was tried for murder. In the light of the medical evidence submitted, which suggested that McNaughtan was suffering severe delusions of persecution, the judge directed the jury to find him not guilty on the ground of insanity. The Lord Chancellor then led the House of Lords in formulating a set of questions which the judges, appearing together, were to answer. The main response to the question of legal insanity was formulated by Chief Justice Tindall as follows: 'To establish a defence on the ground of insanity, it must be clearly proved, that, at the time of the committing of the act, the party accused was labouring under such a defect of reason, from disease of the mind, as not to know the nature and quality of the act he was doing, or, if he did know it, that he did not know he was doing what was wrong.'[23] Against this cognitive test of right and wrong some doctors—and, as the century progressed, an increasing number of lawyers—maintained that insanity was a matter of volition, and that some impulses were irresistible.[24] This claim was focused on the concept of moral insanity, a term which entered the medical vocabulary in the 1830s in the work of James Prichard. Prichard described the state of moral insanity as a 'modification of insanity', in which an

---

[22] The jurors in Hadfield's case, cited by Richard Moran, 'The Modern Foundation for the Insanity Defense: The Cases of James Hadfield (1800) and Daniel McNaughtan (1843)' in Richard Moran (ed.), *The Insanity Defense* (1985) 477 *The Annals of the American Academy of Political and Social Science* 35. Moran's spelling of McNaughtan has been adopted in this paper, but variant spellings are also cited.

[23] Moran, *The Insanity Defense*, n. 22 above, 41. For contemporary comment on the McNaughtan case and the subsequent ruling, see George Harris, 'The Plea of Insanity in Criminal Cases' (1843) 29 *British and Foreign Review*; unsigned notice, 'Trial of Daniel M'Naughten, the Bar of the Central Criminal Court, and the Plea of Insanity' (1843) 27 *Fraser's Magazine*; and J. A. Roebuck, 'The Plea of Insanity' (1843) 39 *Westminster Review*.

[24] In 1863 Fitzjames Stephen maintained that the proven existence of irresistible impulse 'would disprove malice', and claimed that in such cases 'the person accused is entitled to be acquitted, because the act was not voluntary and was not properly his act'; see James Fitzjames Stephen, *A General View of the Criminal Law of England* (London, 1863), 95. Twenty years later Stephen went further and, arguing for a broad interpretation of the McNaughtan ruling, concluded that the law should acknowledge mental diseases which destroy the power of self-control: see James Fitzjames Stephen, 'Relation of Madness to Crime', ch. xix of *History of the Criminal Law of England*, 3 vols. (London, 1883), II, 124–86.

individual's 'temper and disposition are found to have undergone a change; to be not what they were previously . . . he has become an altered man'.[25] Prichard designates the primary symptom of moral insanity as a change in character: all his examples show people acting radically out of character. In a contemporary report of the McNaughtan trial, the term was explained as follows:

This moral insanity . . . consists in the total deprivation of some portion of the moral nature, producing an irresistible propensity to some kind of evil, without at all affecting the understanding, so that the unhappy victim is often fully conscious at the same time of the enormity of his inclination, and of his total inability to restrain it. Nay, one portion of the moral nature is sometimes in arms against the other, so that the uncontrollable appetite of murder, and the most intense horror of the crime, shall be present in the same individual.[26]

The writer anticipates by more than forty years the 'divided ecstasy of mind' with which Henry Jekyll responds to the murder of Sir Danvers Carew by Edward Hyde: 'no man morally sane could have been guilty of that crime', says Jekyll;

I set out through the lamplit streets, in the same divided ecstasy of mind, gloating on my crime, light-headedly devising others in the future, and yet still hastening and still harkening in my wake for the steps of the avenger. Hyde had a song upon his lips as he compounded the draught, and as he drank it, pledged the dead man. The pangs of transformation had not done tearing him, before Henry Jekyll, with streaming tears of gratitude and remorse, had fallen upon his knees and lifted his clasped hands to God.[27]

In the legal consideration of insanity, civil competence was as much an issue as criminal responsibility,[28] and Stevenson exploits the idea of civil competence to chart the continuity between Jekyll and Hyde. Jekyll's will is the first warning to the lawyer Utterson

[25] James Cowles Prichard, *On the Different Forms of Insanity in Relation to Jurisprudence* (London, 1842), 33–4. Prichard is here quoting his own *Treatise on Insanity* (London, 1833).

[26] J. S. S., review of R. M. Bousfield and R. Merrett, *Report of the 'Trial of Daniel M'Naughton'* (1843) 29 *The Law Magazine* 393–4.

[27] Robert Louis Stevenson, *The Strange Case of Dr Jekyll and Mr Hyde* (1886) in *Dr Jekyll and Mr Hyde* and *Weir of Hermiston* (Emma Letley (ed.), Oxford, 1987), 69–70.

[28] On the implications for civil law of the McNaughtan ruling, see Serjeant Ballantine, *Some Experiences of a Barrister's Life* (London, 1882), 197–8.

that all is not well with his friend. The will makes provision that in the case of Jekyll's death all his possessions are to pass into the hands of his 'friend and benefactor' Edward Hyde, and also that in the case of Jekyll's disappearance or unexplained absence for more than three months, 'the said Edward Hyde should step into the said Henry Jekyll's shoes without further delay'.[29] Jekyll, DCL, LLD, has written his will according to the principles of civil law which amount, in Henry Sumner Maine's words in *Ancient Law: Its Connection with the Early History of Society and its Relation to Modern Ideas* (1861), to an 'elimination . . . of the fact of death'.[30] In this 'theory of a man's posthumous existence in the person of his heir', legal personality descends on the heir or co-heirs, in whom the identity of the dead man is continued.[31] In drafting his will, Jekyll—who is 'co-heir with [Hyde] to death'[32]—has taken care that Hyde shall inherit none of his cares or obligations, of which he has therefore divested himself. He makes Utterson promise to 'get [Hyde] his rights for him',[33] so that according to the will, Hyde gets the better half of Jekyll's legal personality; for rather than finding himself instantly clothed with Jekyll's 'entire legal person',[34] he has Jekyll's rights unencumbered with any obligations. Utterson thinks the will 'madness';[35] more precisely, it indicates defective self-sovereignty. In fact, it is the legal ratification of mutual identity, of which the hand in which it is written furnishes the first substantial evidence.[36]

The horror of the story is the protagonists' collaboration on the self-sovereignty they conspire to destroy. Jekyll and Hyde have a common memory, and the only control on their relationship is Jekyll's conscience; but Jekyll's conscience is undone by 'the animal within me licking the chops of memory'.[37] As he says helplessly

[29] Stevenson, *Dr Jekyll and Mr Hyde*, n. 27 above, 14.

[30] Henry Sumner Maine, *Ancient Law: Its Connection with the Early History of Society and its Relation to Modern Ideas* (repr. New York, 1986), 157. Stevenson graduated in law at Edinburgh University in 1875.

[31] Maine, *Ancient Law*, n. 30 above, 151.

[32] Stevenson, *Dr Jekyll and Mr Hyde*, n. 27 above, 74.

[33] Stevenson, *Dr Jekyll and Mr Hyde*, n. 27 above, 23.

[34] Maine, *Ancient Law*, n. 30 above, 150.

[35] Stevenson, *Dr Jekyll and Mr Hyde*, n. 27 above, 14.

[36] Stevenson, *Dr Jekyll and Mr Hyde*, n. 27 above, 34.

[37] Stevenson, *Dr Jekyll and Mr Hyde*, n. 27 above, 71.

'the situation was apart from ordinary laws, and insidiously relaxed the grasp of conscience.'[38] The result is a radically subversive investigation of what Austin calls 'the relation of sovereignty and subjection', and by the end of Stevenson's tale not only memory and conscience, but also volition,[39] are in disarray. Jekyll anticipates even further fragmentation of the self, hazarding the guess 'that man will be ultimately known for a mere polity of multifarious, incongruous and independent denizens.'[40] The language of civil order here storms 'the very fortress of identity'[41] from within: a denizen is an alien with the right of residence. In the theory of moral identity here advanced, self-alienation is the human condition, and we are all denizens rather than citizens; each of us is Edward Hyde.

Contract

The public policy of sanctity and liberty of contract that obtained in Victorian England, in which the sanctity of contract depends on liberty, and liberty depends on competent understanding, was canonically formulated by Sir George Jessel in 1875: 'if there is one thing more than another which public policy requires, it is that men of full age and competent understanding shall have the utmost liberty of contracting and that their contracts, when entered into freely and voluntarily, shall be held sacred and shall be enforced by Courts of Justice.'[42] The policy was soundly based in contract theory. To Maine contract is the essence of substantive law, because it expresses 'the complete reciprocity and indissoluble connection of rights and duties';[43] it is a chain of law between the contracting parties. It is also the mark of ethical advancement: in Maine's most celebrated formulation, 'the movement of the progressive societies has hitherto been a movement *from Status to Contract*'.[44] And in the will theory, which dominated nineteenth-century thought on

---

[38] Stevenson, *Dr Jekyll and Mr Hyde*, n. 27 above, 66.
[39] David Dudley Field had designated the will as 'the executive department of the mind' in 'Emotional Insanity' (1873) 2 *Law Magazine and Review (New Series)* 791.   [40] Stevenson, *Dr Jekyll and Mr Hyde*, n. 27 above, 61.
[41] Stevenson, *Dr Jekyll and Mr Hyde*, n. 27 above, 62.
[42] *Printing and Numerical Registering Co.* v. *Sampson* (1875); cited by P. S. Atiyah in *An Introduction to the Law of Contract* (Oxford, 1961), 3.
[43] Maine, *Ancient Law*, n. 30 above, 290.
[44] Maine, *Ancient Law*, n. 30 above, 141.

contract,[45] a contract is a cross-positing of wills. This theory is based on the sovereignty of the self, for only the self that respects the sovereignty of others as well as its own can realize this principle of association based on individual free will. In contract people exchange 'bits of themselves'[46] with no loss of their individual sovereignty; for a contract is a relationship of equal or equivalent sovereignty.

The commercial prosperity of a country [said Balfour Browne] depends not only on the excellence of the production but also upon the honesty of distribution; and distribution is carried on through or by means of that relation between men, which we call Contract . . . for contract is founded on obligation, and obligation upon moral trustworthiness.[47]

The ideal of contract celebrated here as a principle of commercial relationship and social cohesion ignores the reality of commercial behaviour in the world of *laissez-faire* capitalism. The nexus of wills advocated by Balfour Browne, and the nexus of rights and duties celebrated by Maine, are equally pre-empted by the nexus of cash-payment lamented by Carlyle.[48] In Dickens's *Our Mutual Friend* (1865), the barrister Eugene Wrayburn complains of ' "people's breaking promises and contracts and bargains of all sorts" ',[49] and this process drives the action of the novel. Dickens's analysis of his commercial culture is the inversion of Maine's world; it is Modern Law, from which the principle of reciprocity is absent. As people barter and exchange 'bits of themselves', their fragmented selves spin out of control and thrash around in the social economy of a post-contractual world—a world, that is, in which contract no longer functions as a principle of social discipline.

Silas Wegg wishes to acquire the bone of his amputated leg from Mr Venus, an articulator of bones, who bought it 'in open

[45] Atiyah, n. 42 above, 3; and James Gordley, *The Philosophical Origins of Modern Contract Doctrine* (Oxford, 1991), 161–2.

[46] J. H. Balfour Browne, 'Contract' (1873) 2 *Law Magazine and Review (New Series)* 403. (This paper was the first part of a two-part article on contract; the second part is also in this issue. Balfour Browne, a poet and essayist as well as a lawyer, was best known for *The Medical Jurisprudence of Insanity*, London, 1871.) [47] Balfour Browne, 'Contract', n. 46 above, 402.

[48] Thomas Carlyle, 'Chartism' (1840), in *Thomas Carlyle: Selected Writings* (Alan Shelston (ed.), Harmondsworth, 1971), 199.

[49] Charles Dickens, *Our Mutual Friend* (New York, 1994), 238.

contract'[50] from a hospital porter. As they dispute the legality of this transaction, the leg becomes a synecdoche for Wegg's self-sovereignty: he wants to get it back 'to collect myself',[51] and in their conversations it merits the personal pronouns of 'you' and 'I'. Near the beginning of this extended, and darkly comic discussion of contract and individual coherence, a boy comes into the shop to buy a stuffed canary.[52] Venus includes some teeth in the three-pennyworth of change he gives the boy, whom he promptly calls back, for he has intended no deception. But bits of human beings—bones, teeth—are circulating in the economy, in which they are equivalent to cash. What Venus calls 'open contract' is simply the law of the market; and it prevails over anything else.

In *Our Mutual Friend* individuals lose their sovereignty as they become unwitting parties to contracts which deprive them of the power of volition. While consent is the essence of contract, it is also the intractable problem that makes pure contract impossible, for the very elusiveness of linguistic formulation renders consent the point of stress around which contracts collapse. When Pollock and Anson wrote their treatises on contract in the 1870s[53] they acknowledged this problem in the difficulty which they faced in defining consent. The issue is straightforward enough; in Anson's words: 'Every expression of a common intention arrived at by two or more parties is ultimately reducible to question and answer.'[54] But the chronological gap between question and answer signifies a rhetorical fissure in the strongest and surest of agreements. The point of stipulation in Roman law, in which the promisee phrased the promises which the promisor was to repeat,[55] was to work the model of question and answer into fusion by closing the gap between proposal and acceptance as far as language is able to close it. The gap is overtly acknowledged by Anson and Pollock in their discussions of the leading case of *Adams v. Lindsell* (1817),[56]

---

[50] *Our Mutual Friend*, n. 49 above, 297.
[51] *Our Mutual Friend*, n. 49 above, 82.
[52] *Our Mutual Friend*, n. 49 above, 81.
[53] Frederick Pollock, *Principles of Contract at Law and in Equity* (London, 1876); Sir William Anson, *Principles of the English Law of Contract* (Oxford, 1879).
[54] Anson, *Principles of the English Law of Contract*, n. 53 above, 11.
[55] Maine, *Ancient Law*, n. 30 above, 273.
[56] Pollock, *Principles of Contract*, n. 53 above, 13–14; Anson, *Principles of the English Law of Contract*, n. 53 above, 20–1.

which turned on the issue of the time delay involved in making a
contract through the mail. In *Adams* v. *Lindsell* temporal delay
figures a hermeneutic gap which, although it can be papered over
by a legal fiction, subverts the moving idea behind all contract,
'that the two minds were at one at the same moment of time'.[57]
One senses Anson's exasperation with the issue of consent when,
in his seventh edition, he turns dramatically to metaphor:
'Acceptance is to Offer what a lighted match is to a train of
gunpowder.'[58] His figure vividly expresses the intensity of his
desire for the absolute fusion of offer and acceptance, but a fuse is
not a figure of fusion, and Anson's image turns contract into a
gunpowder plot which threatens all sovereignty. Contract, as
revealed by a careful reading of Pollock or Anson, is inevitably the
locus of competing stories and competing meanings. This is also
the case in *Our Mutual Friend*: as individuals cede 'bits of themselves' to others without their own conscious consent, the
contracts in which they are involved slip out of their control.

In *Our Mutual Friend*, the principles of contract are parodically
inverted in the blackmail of Bradley Headstone by Rogue
Riderhood, for the sovereignty of the will is eroded without
consent. Riderhood has seen Headstone's attempted murder of
Eugene Wrayburn, and has also witnessed Headstone's attempt to
implicate Riderhood by impersonating him. Riderhood drives a
hard bargain for the 'settlement' to which he wishes to bring
Headstone: he wants him to sell his furniture, pawn his clothes, to
clean out Miss Peecher who adores him and who (as Riderhood
realizes) will sell herself up to get Headstone out of trouble.[59]
Riderhood's word for this, 'settlement', is a configuration of
contract and blackmail, and the process it represents has been
initiated by Headstone's impersonation of Riderhood in an
attempt to throw guilt onto to him. In theory, the impulse to
contract was the intention to enter into legal relations.
Headstone's impersonation of Riderhood has constituted an intention on his part to enter into illegal (and covert) relations; and
Riderhood now completes the contract by enforcing the illegal
power to compel specific performance of whatever conditions he

---

[57] Anson, *Principles of the English Law of Contract*, n. 53 above, 19.
[58] Anson, *Principles of the English Law of Contract* (7th edn, Oxford, 1893),
27.   [59] Dickens, *Our Mutual Friend*, n. 49 above, 798–9.

cares to name. The contract is piecemeal, consent is unwitting and circumstantial, and the anti-legal chain which binds Headstone and Riderhood carries them to a mutual death. Headstone impersonates Riderhood who then owns Headstone: like Jekyll and Hyde, they have become a continuous but dual personality in which self-sovereignty is as impossible to locate as the 'moment of time' in which (in Anson's phrase) the 'two minds were at one'. Maine's *vinculum juris* is here recast as a ring of mutual self-involvement. When the bodies are found together 'under the ooze and scum of one of the rotting gates', Riderhood is girdled with the 'iron ring' of Headstone's obsessive grasp; 'and the rivets of the iron ring held tight'.[60]

This novel's relentless analysis of contract is focused, in the presentation of the Lammle marriage, on gender relationships. Each party believes that they are marrying a person of property, and both are deceived. The honeymoon couple's mutual undeception takes place on the beach at Shanklin, and in a hinterland of legal discourse, in a chapter entitled 'A Marriage Contract'.[61] Their conversation is at once a dispute, a confession, and a claiming of rights, and its discursive model is contract; for it is cast as question and answer, and it leads to a mutual agreement to work together in their joint interests in furtherance of any scheme that will bring them money. This is the true marriage contract, as an acknowledgment of the pretences that led to the marriage becomes the basis of another pretence, that marriage is a business partnership. Yet it is also a true marriage, governed by the doctrine of coverture, for Sophronia has no choice other than to take on the identity of her husband by becoming a fortune-hunter too. As the contract is formed, Alfred questions from a position of strength, and she answers from a position of weakness. She is passionate, humiliated, and contemptuous, but she is also powerless, while he is diabolical, and possessed of a 'repressive power'. The dynamics of their partnership are chilling because of the disparity of their positions, which is ratified by the new contract even as it is drawn up.

In *The Subjection of Women* (1869) Mill pointed out that the marriage laws were not in accordance with the laws of contract:

---

[60] *Our Mutual Friend*, n. 49 above, 802.
[61] *Our Mutual Friend*, n. 49 above, 114–27.

'If the law dealt with other contracts as it does with marriage, it would ordain that one partner should administer the common business as if it was his private concern', and 'that the others should have only delegated powers'.[62] Fitzjames Stephen, arguing against Mill, regarded marriage as 'a contract between a stronger and a weaker person involving subordination for certain purposes on the part of the weaker to the stronger'.[63] The language of contract inevitably shaped discussion of the marital relation, but in *Our Mutual Friend* the implications of the Lammle marriage contract point beyond that marriage to the generally subservient status of a woman in 'the relation of sovereign and subject'.

Women

In October 1867 *St Paul's Magazine* carried a paper by its editor, Anthony Trollope, 'On Sovereignty'.[64] This essay in comparative law measures the relative efficacy of three kinds of sovereign, the 'autocratic sovereign' of France, the 'elected temporary sovereign' of the United States, and the 'constitutional sovereign' of England. Written in the wake of the second Reform Bill, and so under the pressure of democracy, the essay justifies the constitutional sovereignty of Britain by equating sovereignty with democracy. Trollope's argument is that sovereignty in a constitutional monarchy hinges on the paradox of an hereditary monarch without political power. The monarch's choice of those who have the exercise of political power is subject to control, which renders possible the construction of a sovereignty that is fully compatible with democracy. The gendered fallacy of this argument, as Mill would demonstrate in *The Subjection of Women*, lay in the fact that women were excluded from all levels of democratic activity. With the sole exception of royalty, 'the disabilities of women are the only case . . . in which laws and institutions take persons at their birth, and ordain that they shall never in their lives be able to compete for certain things.' But the exception proves the rule, for

---

[62] J. S. Mill, *The Subjection of Women* (London, 1869), *On Liberty and Other Writings* (S. Collini (ed.), Cambridge, 1989), 155–6.

[63] James Fitzjames Stephen, *Liberty, Equality, Fraternity* (2nd edn, London, 1874), in *Liberty, Equality, Fraternity And Three Brief Essays* (Chicago, 1991), 195.

[64] Anthony Trollope, 'On Sovereignty' (1867) 1 *St Paul's Magazine* 76.

the 'high social function' of monarchy is circumscribed by constitutional conditions which 'prevent the person to whom it ostensibly belongs from really performing it', and the responsible
minister, the prime minister, obtains his post 'by a competition
from which no full-grown member of the male sex is legally
excluded'.[65] Trollope's point about the hinge on which democratic
sovereignty turns in a constitutional monarchy is here inverted
and exposed as an example of gender politics which ensures that
the sovereign power is a male prerogative, whatever the sex of the
nominal sovereign.

Neither Trollope nor Mill mentions Queen Victoria, but in the
context of their arguments she is both a living anomaly and a self-
evident paradox: a female sovereign denied sovereignty by her sex,
because the legally sovereign self in Victorian England was male
and masculine. The problematic status of the Queen was an obvious figure for women's disempowerment in English constitutional
sovereignty, and is beautifully focused in a conversation between
two working-class women in Elizabeth Gaskell's *Mary Barton*
(1848), Mrs Wilson and Aunt Alice.[66] Their discussion of the
domestic difficulties faced by married women working in factories
is complicated by their awareness of a female monarch who is also
a wife. In their misunderstanding of constitutional process—when
the Queen makes the laws, she must obey Prince Albert, who
wouldn't want his wife to be away from home—sovereignty and
gender are at odds. Comedy controls the uncomfortable questions,
but behind the comedy the domestic issue of the Queen's necessary obedience of Prince Albert is both complicated by, and
continuous with, the constitutional issue of who makes the laws.
This cultural situation in which women were denied sovereignty
inspired three main responses. The first, for which the most
prominent spokesperson was Mill, was that women should get the
vote. There was plenty of opposition to this, and much of it was
grounded in the argument that the practical effect of extending the
franchise to married women 'would be to give each married man
two votes in every election . . . If, on the other hand, the wife gave
an independent, conscientious vote, think of the consequences at

[65] Mill, *The Subjection of Women*, n. 62 above, 136–7.
[66] Elizabeth Gaskell, *Mary Barton: A Tale of Manchester Life* (Harmondsworth, 1970), 165–6.

the domestic hearth!'[67] Trollope, in his presentation of the assertive Winifred Hurtle in *The Way We Live Now* (1875), offers a variation on Mill's position—a conservative variation, because Trollope's idea of an independent woman is uncomplicated by the question of suffrage. The novel grounds the self-sovereignty it accords Mrs Hurtle in the economic independence sanctioned by the laws regulating women's property in the United States. These laws, according to one of the Americans in the novel, ' "are just the reverse of what the greediness of man has established here. The wife there can claim her share of her husband's property, but hers is exclusively her own." '[68] Mrs Hurtle devotes her considerable energy to defending the fortune she inherited from her mother, but her independence goes beyond the matter of property. In Oregon she shot a man who was about to rape her, an act of summary justice for which she was not tried as 'the world of Oregon had considered that the circumstances justified the deed';[69] and she once stood, armed, before her bedroom door to prevent her drunken husband from entering. Later, in Kansas, she successfully sued for divorce the husband who had abandoned her, on the grounds of drunkenness and cruelty (which she would not have been able to do in England). Her acts of violence are metaphors for her independence and assertiveness, which (she tells an Englishman) are not necessary in ' "this soft civilisation of yours" '.[70] Winifred Hurtle's conduct of herself is validated by her country's legal system, of which it is the consequence. A strong contrast to all the English women in the novel, she is also a serious touchstone for female independence.

The second response to the denial of female sovereignty is found in writings by women; for it is, in Mill's phrase, in 'a literature of their own'[71] that women most powerfully employ a language of their own to establish a sovereignty of their own; and they invariably do this by trying to position themselves outside the law. It is as if the only way for a woman to preserve her self-sovereignty is by contracting out of social arrangements, and a significant index of female self-sovereignty in Victorian literature is a

---

67 C. N. Cresswell, *Woman and her Work in the World* (London, 1876), 90.
68 Anthony Trollope, *The Way We Live Now*, 2 vols. (Oxford, 1982), II, 454.
69 Trollope, *The Way We Live Now*, n. 68 above, I, 243.
70 Trollope, *The Way We Live Now*, n. 68 above, I, 445.
71 Mill, *The Subjection of Women*, n. 62 above, 187.

woman's rejection of what is legally hers to inherit. In George Eliot's *Felix Holt* (1866) Esther Lyon turns her back on the Transome estate, and in *Middlemarch* (1871) Dorothea Casaubon rejects her husband's will because of its mean-spirited codicil. Dorothea has £700 settled on her at her marriage to Casaubon, but stands to inherit much more under the terms of his will that are not acceptable to her. After Casaubon's death Dorothea's father opposes her marriage to Will Ladislaw, and threatens to break the entail on his estate so that any son of their marriage will not inherit it. Reconciliation is eventually effected by the strength of the sororal relationship of Dorothea and Celia in resisting the patriarchal power of disposition and dispensation. But here the resistance has a conventional resolution, in the re-establishment of the conservative social contract represented by primogeniture, and resistance to the will is rewarded by the continuance of the entail. In *Aurora Leigh* (1856) Elizabeth Barrett Browning offers a more radical solution. Due to a clause inserted in the entail a century ago to exclude offspring by a foreign wife, Aurora is an 'undowered orphan'.[72] To remedy this situation Romney Leigh's father asked Aurora's father for her hand for her cousin Romney, on whom the entail then descended, wishing to settle the estate on them both. Aurora Leigh rejects Romney's offer of marriage, for her claim to the estate would be restored only through his sovereignty. In Aurora's words Romney Leigh is 'self-tied/By a contract', and his reduction of love to a 'simple law-clause' would compromise her own self-sovereignty.[73]

The third response to women's lack of sovereignty can be seen in writing by men which accords women a degree of self-sovereignty by constructing them as figures of equity. Throughout Victorian literature, as written by men, the relationship of women to legal institutions is analogous to the supplemental relationship of equity to the common law. As equity mitigated the rigour of the common law so, in the economies of justice that obtain in Victorian literature, figures of equity (of fairness and conscience) are both female and feminine. The prototype here is Portia in Shakespeare's *The Merchant of Venice*, and her descendants in the

---

[72] Elizabeth Barrett Browning, *Aurora Leigh*, 2 vols. (New York, 1996), II, 606.
[73] Barrett Browning, *Aurora Leigh*, n. 72 above, II, 779–80, 785.

great Victorian texts with legal subject-matter are Esther
Summerson in *Bleak House* (1853) and Pompilia in Browning's
The Ring and the Book (1868–9). The interrogative voices of
these young women promote alternative principles of value in
worlds dominated by the malpractices of the English High Court
of Chancery or by the cynically competing jurisdictions of Rome
and Tuscany. Esther Summerson is the exemplification of
Matthew Bagnet's belief that 'the noun-substantive, Goodness, [is]
of the feminine gender'.[74] In Victorian culture generally,
conscience is gendered feminine in both positive and negative
ways. The central figure in Holman Hunt's 'The Awakening
Conscience' is a young woman represented at a crucial moment of
moral self-awareness, from which her male companion is
excluded.[75] And John Henry Newman, to his many inveterate
enemies, was 'wanting in virility';[76] his logic betrayed 'a characteristically feminine mind, poetic, impressible, receptive, and reproductive, rather than original and commanding';[77] and his faith,
which was 'merely and absolutely the response of the conscience
to authority', was evidence of a conscience 'ill-lighted or
perverted' by his feminine disposition.[78]

The complex configuration of contradictions outlined in this
paper suggests a fundamental illogicality in Victorian thinking
about the sovereignty of the self. The key to self-sovereignty is the
feminine principle of conscience, but the sovereign self is masculine: the exercise of self-sovereignty in a woman's 'conscientious
vote' is unthinkable. The apparently neutral terms of sovereignty
and conscience acquire rhetorical force through the gendered
inflection of social discourses, which declare the conceptual and
rhetorical bases of self-sovereignty at odds with each other.
Therefore, while Austin relies on 'a generic and commodious
meaning'[79] for sovereignty, the stress implicit in the term, as
suggested by its difficulty of definition, is activated in several

---

[74]   Charles Dickens, *Bleak House* (New York, 1977), 587.

[75]   Hunt's painting is discussed by Frederick Denison Maurice, *The
Conscience: Lectures on Casuistry* (London, 1868; 3rd edn, London, 1883),
103–4.

[76]   J. H. Rigg, 'Cardinal Newman' (1890) 15 *London Quarterly Review (New
Series)* 212.

[77]   Rigg, 'Cardinal Newman', n. 76 above, 229.

[78]   Rigg, 'Cardinal Newman', n. 76 above, 216, 231.

[79]   Austin, *The Province of Jurisprudence Determined*, n. 4 above, 189n.

discursive areas, both internal (in the case of insanity) and external (in the case of contract). But in the relation of gender and identity such stress is accented to a point at which 'the relation of sovereignty and subjection' disintegrates under the pressure of its own self-contradiction.[80]

[80] This paper is dedicated to the memory of Colin Pedley (1934–98), of St Edward's School, Oxford, and Oxford Brookes University. Scholar, teacher, friend: 'No work begun shall ever pause for death'.

IS LITERATURE MORE ETHICAL THAN LAW? FITZJAMES STEPHEN AND LITERARY RESPONSES TO THE ADVENT OF FULL LEGAL REPRESENTATION FOR FELONS

Jan-Melissa Schramm

There comes a moment towards the end of Anthony Trollope's *Orley Farm* (1862) when the leading defence lawyer Thomas Furnival awaits the jury's verdict on a charge of perjury which his client, Lady Mason, was alleged to have committed over twenty years ago. Although convinced of her guilt, he has defended her with positive and personal assertions of her innocence and she is duly acquitted. The reader, privy to Lady Mason's explicit confession of culpability, knows this to be an inaccurate verdict generated at least in part by the rhetorical excesses of counsel. Trollope comments:

And yet as [Furnival] sat down he knew that she had been guilty! To his ear her guilt had never been confessed; but yet he knew that it was so, and, knowing that, he had been able to speak as though her innocence were a thing of course. . . . And more than this, stranger than this, worse than this—when the legal world knew—as the legal world soon did know—that all this had been so, the legal world found no fault with Mr Furnival, conceiving that he had done his duty by his client in a manner becoming an English barrister and an English gentleman.[1]

---

[1] Anthony Trollope, *Orley Farm* (London, 1993), 660–1. Other references to this edition are included in the text.

Trollope invokes the assumption that truth-telling is a quality of gentility in order to suggest with gentle irony that the professional standards of the Victorian English Bar fell below those which would be expected of a gentleman in ordinary social interaction. As he states earlier in the same novel, 'no amount of eloquence will make an English lawyer think that loyalty to truth should come before loyalty to his client' (147). Trollope's representation of Furnival's plight in *Orley Farm*—the ethical dilemma of defending a client whom he believes to be guilty—has been described as an exaggeration, like much of the commentary on the law in Charles Dickens's work, designed to serve the author's own polemical purposes. It is certainly true that some Victorian authors were intent on disparaging and misrepresenting the activities of the criminal Bar in order to define more clearly their own nascent professional responsibilities. But Trollope's fiction—like that of Dickens, George Eliot, and Elizabeth Gaskell—also accurately reflects much of the debate about the licence of counsel, the efficacy of professional self-regulation, and the development of ethical standards which preoccupied the Bar during the 1830s and 1840s. Throughout this period, fictional authors accused members of the Bar of acting as accessories after the fact to secure what Trollope memorably phrased as 'the manumission of murderers' (*Orley Farm*, 86). In this essay I explore literary responses to the growth of the professional criminal Bar and suggest why the advent of full legal representation for felons activated such intense analysis of the ethical agendas of law and literature.

Public Opinion and the Power of the Press

Allegations against the Bar in the periodical presses and daily papers were to reach their peak in the 1840s, with fictional representation of the rhetorical excesses of the Bar continuing for a further twenty years as authors responded to, and experimented with, the example set by their storytelling counterparts in courts of law. But in a sense, the conditions for the conflict were established several decades earlier, and in 1824—three years after Parliament began to debate the extension of full legal representation to those accused of felony—we see a timely awareness of the factors which were to determine the parameters of subsequent debate.

On 24 October 1823, William Weare was murdered in a secluded country lane near Watford. His gambling associate, John Thurtell, was linked to the crime by circumstantial evidence and the subsequent confessions of his two accomplices. Within days of the crime, the site was besieged with tourists and voyeurs:

The neighbourhood of Elstree was on Monday crowded with persons of all ranks, viewing the cottage of Probart, and the surrounding premises—the pond in the garden—the spot in the lane in which the murder was committed—the hole in the hedge through which the corpse was pushed—the half-finished grave—the pond in which the body was ultimately found—all in their turn became objects of intense observation.— Mr Clutterbuck, the Magistrate, was on the spot, with his clerk, making a ground plan of the place. Various anecdotes were in circulation of the 'doings at the cottage', and of the loose characters by whom it was visited; and from all that passed, it would seem that a feeling of terror had been produced on the minds of the neighbours towards its occasional inmates.[2]

Two aspects of this account are noteworthy—the confusion of professional and opportunistic inspection, and the melodramatic narrative created by the repetition of each site of forensic significance, 'the pond in the garden . . . the half-finished grave'. Each stage of the investigative proceedings was extensively reported in the papers prior to the trial, including confessional statements made by the accomplices which attributed responsibility to Thurtell. Although criminal ballads and broadsheets accompanied the spectacle of the scaffold in the eighteenth century—and hence literary treatment of crime was not without precedent—Eric R. Watson has called Thurtell's case the first 'trial by newspaper'.[3] It generated vigorous debate regarding the public's right to hear and assess all the evidence (admissible or otherwise) before judicial proceedings were concluded.

At the Hertford Winter Assizes of 1823, Thurtell's counsel, Andrews and Chitty, sought an adjournment of proceedings for a period of one month to enable the prejudicial publicity to settle,

---

[2] The *Examiner*, 9 November 1823. Thurtell's case is included in the Notable English Trials Series; see Eric R. Watson (ed.), *The Trial of Thurtell and Hunt* (Edinburgh and London, 1920).

[3] Watson, 'Preface' in *The Trial of Thurtell and Hunt*, n. 2 above, vii. On literary responses to the trial of Thurtell, see Albert Borowitz, *The Thurtell-Hunt Murder Case* (London, 1987), ch. 18.

and Park J., referring with distaste to the 'pruriency for news among people of the present day', granted the application.[4] In defence of journalistic activity, the *Examiner* stated that 'the press is the great organ of knowledge' which disseminates information to the public and to the prisoner who would otherwise be kept in the dark regarding the evidence to be adduced against him: 'The law (blessings on it) never contemplated that he should know the evidence to be brought forward against him'—an inequity which the *Examiner* considered as on a par with the denial of counsel to those accused of felony.[5] The press appealed to publicity as one of the fundamental safeguards of procedural fairness in the administration of the common law, but despite the value of this tradition the scene was set for competition between the courts and other arenas of representation.

When the trial opened on 6 January 1824, Thurtell (who was required to make his own address to the jury) spoke of the damage he had sustained as a consequence of the adverse pre-trial publicity; the public had heard an alternative narrative of his guilt, including rumours which a court of law, with its more stringent rules of evidence, may have declared inadmissible or irrelevant. The jury, however, was not persuaded by his oration and he was convicted and executed, thus inaugurating a mythology of infamy which was to fascinate and repel authors and journalists for the next thirty years. As Thomas De Quincey pointed out in his essay 'On Murder Considered as One of the Fine Arts' (1827), the recent spate of murders had created an assumption that '[d]esign, . . ., grouping, light and shade, poetry, sentiment, are now deemed indispensable to attempts of this nature';[6] although Thurtell's style was dismissed as being 'as harsh as Albert Durer, and as coarse as Fuseli',[7] the coverage of his trial represented crime as a transgressive act which implicated both law and literature in the generation of effect and catharsis. The Newgate novel, with its controversial representations of criminality, could be excluded from the critical canon with comparative ease, but, as Joel Black observes, 'the age of realism rationalized the criminal subject of literature *as Reason*

---

[4] The *Examiner*, 7 December 1823.
[5] The *Examiner*, 21 December 1823.
[6] Thomas de Quincy [*sic*], *On Murder Considered as One of the Fine Arts, and On War: Two Essays by Thomas de Quincy* [*sic*] (London, 1980), 3.
[7] De Quincey, n. 6 above, 30.

in the figure of the detective; this is what Foucault called "the appropriation of the criminal in acceptable forms" '.[8] To a certain extent, authors and lawyers were to mediate to the public the 'acceptable' face of transgression—that of inquiry and investigation—but they were also to be tainted with suggestions of vicarious guilt.

Shortly after Thurtell's execution, Walter Scott suggested that '[his] tale seems to interest the public as long as that of Waterloo, showing that a bloody murther will do the business of the newspapers when a bloody battle is not to be heard'[9] and, writing in the *Edinburgh Review* in 1824, Lord Denman made a similar point; trials were analysed in the press with renewed vigour in times of peace.[10] Adopting Bentham's criticisms of the exclusionary rules of evidence in English courts at the time, Denman too praised publicity, properly directed, as an essential safeguard of English legal practice: '[J]udges . . . should be hourly taught to feel that *there is* a tribunal to which an appeal constantly lies against their decisions,—the tribunal of public opinion.'[11] An audience, with a taste for forensic inquiry, and informed by the press, was thus being taught to monitor the just administration of the criminal law. A nexus had been established which, with the enactment of the Prisoners' Counsel Act in 1836, was shortly to bring authors and criminal barristers into close competition.

The Prisoners' Counsel Act and the Extension of Full Legal Representation to those Accused of Felony

Unlike prisoners charged with misdemeanours or, since 1696, with high treason, prisoners charged with felony before 1836 were unable to secure the benefits of full legal representation to deal

---

[8] Joel Black, *The Aesthetics of Murder: A Study in Romantic Literature and Contemporary Culture* (Baltimore, 1991), 46.

[9] *The Letters of Sir Walter Scott 1823–1825* (H. Grierson (ed.), London, 1935), 160, cited in Borowitz, n. 3 above, 254–5.

[10] [Thomas Denman], 'Law of Evidence—Criminal Procedure—Publicity' (1824) *Edinburgh Review* no. lxxix, 169–207, at 171. This article is unsigned, but it is attributed to Denman by *The Wellesley Index to Victorian Periodicals* (Walter Houghton *et al.* (eds.), Toronto, 1966–89, 5 vols.), I, 465.

[11] [Denman], n. 10 above, 170.

with the merits of their case.[12] The conception of evidence as that which is 'evident', and of facts as 'speaking for themselves', had underpinned the theory of the criminal trial current in the eighteenth century. It supported Sergeant William Hawkins's famous belief that 'every one of Common Understanding may as properly speak to a Matter of Fact, as if he were the best Lawyer; . . . it requires no manner of skill to make a plain and honest Defence'.[13] The legal historian John Langbein has called this the 'accused speaks' theory of the criminal trial in which 'the testimonial and defensive functions [of the prisoner's role] were inextricably merged'.[14] Langbein reports that defence counsel began to appear in the first half of the eighteenth century, although their numbers were not 'quantitatively significant' until the 1780s[15] and restrictions were to remain upon the extent to which counsel could fully represent a prisoner for a further fifty years. During this time, a lawyer could assist a client in the preparation of his statement outside the courtroom; in court, he could cross-examine a witness on the client's behalf, but he could not assume the right to tell the client's story and he could not address the jury in an opening or closing speech. Any defence a prisoner made to the charges against him had to be personally constructed and presented.

In 1821, a bill to extend representation to those accused of felony came before the House of Commons, but reform was rejected repeatedly because of concerns that the introduction of defence counsel would (in the words of the Attorney-General, John Copley in 1826):

convert the court into an arena, where opposing advocates might meet in professional conflict, and where, instead of endeavouring to elicit the truth by a reference to plain facts, or the real merits of the case, the time

---

[12] On eighteenth- and nineteenth-century criminal trial procedure, see John H. Langbein, 'The Criminal Trial before the Lawyers' (1978) 45 *University of Chicago Law Review* 263; Langbein, 'Shaping the Eighteenth-Century Criminal Trial: A View from the Ryder Sources' (1983) 50 *University of Chicago Law Review* 1; J. M. Beattie, *Crime and the Courts in England 1660–1800* (Oxford, 1986), and Beattie 'Scales of Justice: Defense Counsel and the English Criminal Trial in the Eighteenth and Nineteenth Centuries' (1991) 9 *Law and History Review* 221.

[13] William Hawkins, *A Treatise of the Pleas of the Crown* (2nd edn, London, 1724), Book II, 400.

[14] John H. Langbein, 'The Historical Origins of the Privilege Against Self-Incrimination at Common Law' (1993–4) 93 *Michigan Law Review* 1047, 1048.

[15] Langbein, 'Privilege Against Self-Incrimination', n. 14 above, 1048.

of the public would be wasted by contests between the counsel on either side, animated, as they would be, by all the excitement, zeal, and pertinacity, which such contests usually inspired.[16]

However, the bill, known as the Prisoners' Counsel Bill—finally came into force in October 1836 when confidence in the unadorned reality of empirical fact had been increasingly replaced by a widespread acknowledgement that facts of innocence or guilt do not 'speak for themselves'—an acknowledgement which opened the way for acts of both legal and fictional advocacy. But the Bar was under intense scrutiny—could it be trusted to put truth ahead of rhetoric?

On 5 May 1840, Lord William Russell, uncle of the Prime Minister, was murdered, and his valet, Francois Courvoisier, was charged with the crime. Courvoisier asserted his innocence and retained as his counsel, a famous Irish barrister called Charles Phillips who had practised in London since 1821. Phillips was known for a bombastic rhetorical style—Thurtell had borrowed from a collection of his speeches in the construction of his own defence[17]—and by the time he defended Courvoisier, Phillips had already come to the attention of the young Charles Dickens, who may have used him as a model for the plaintiff's counsel in the famous trial of *Bardell* v. *Pickwick* in *The Posthumous Papers of the Pickwick Club* (1837).[18] When he took on the defence of Courvoisier in 1840, Phillips initially believed his client's protestations of innocence. While the trial was still part heard, however, Courvoisier made significant admissions of his guilt. Controversially, Phillips continued to employ all the strategies of defence which he would have used had his client been innocent; he tried to implicate other servants in the crime, he accused the police of planting evidence of guilt in Courvoisier's rooms, he attacked the credibility of female witnesses for the prosecution, and he employed incisive religious rhetoric in his address to the jury. Courvoisier was convicted and the trial became a *cause célèbre* when Phillips's conduct was published in the press.

---

[16] Parliamentary Debates (London, 1826), vol. 15, col. 599, 25 April 1826. On the history and implementation of the Prisoners' Counsel Act, see David Cairns, *Advocacy and the Making of the Adversarial Criminal Trial 1800–1865* (Oxford, 1998). [17] Borowitz, n. 3 above, 166, 171.
[18] See William Holdsworth, *Charles Dickens as a Legal Historian* (New Haven, 1929), 68.

The indignation of the influential *Examiner* and its editor Albany Fonblanque knew no bounds. Its editorials called Phillips's line of defence the 'lie' of defence and argued that he had greatly exceeded the bounds of adversarial licence in the service of his client:

Whether all this accords or not with professional morality, it is not for us to decide; but, if it does, the public will probably be disposed to think that the profession should change its name from the profession of the Law to the profession of the Lie.

We should like to know the breadth of the distinction between an accomplice after the fact and an advocate who makes the most unscrupulous endeavours to procure the acquittal of a man whom he knows to be an assassin.[19]

Immediately after the trial, two letters signed by 'Manlius' appeared in the *Morning Chronicle* under the heading 'The License of Counsel' which some critics attribute, on strong evidence, to Dickens.[20] The first letter (?21 June 1840) accused Phillips of impugning the morality of advocacy and called for the restriction of adversarial licence. This elicited a prompt response (23 June 1840) from a lawyer of the Middle Temple (according to the legal historian David Cairns, possibly even Phillips himself) who stressed counsel's obligation to 'exert, to the utmost of his power, all his talents and abilities to procure his [client's] acquittal'.[21] He should use 'every means in his power' to do so, but if he cannot do that he must at least ensure that his client is 'legally convicted':[22]

It is therefore his bounden duty to point out to the jury any contradictions, inaccuracies, or omissions that may appear to him in the evidence produced by the prosecutors; and if, through any maudlin sentimentality, or through any fear of inculpating others, he should neglect to do so, he would be guilty of a gross violation of duty, and would deserve to have his gown stripped off his back.[23]

Dickens responded angrily. In his second letter dated 26 June, he conceded the importance of an independent Bar and he 'recognise[d]

---

[19] The *Examiner*, 28 June 1840. For the text of Phillips's speech in the *Courvoisier* case, see Cairns, n. 16 above, 186–200.

[20] *The Letters of Charles Dickens*, 8 vols. (Madeline House and Graham Storey *et al.* (eds.), Oxford, 1965–89), II, 86.

[21] *Letters*, n. 20 above, II, 491; and see Cairns, n. 16 above, 133.

[22] *Letters*, n. 20 above, II, 491.

[23] *Letters*, n. 20 above, II, 492.

the right of any counsel to take a brief from any man, however great his crime, and, keeping within due bounds, to do his best to save him'; what he denied was the 'right to defeat the ends of truth and justice by wantonly scattering aspersions upon innocent people'.[24] Dickens was present at the execution of Courvoisier on 6 July, and as he later wrote in a letter to the *Daily News*, he had 'a particular detestation of that murderer; not only for the cruel deed he had done, but for his slow and subtle treachery, and for his wicked defence'.[25]

The Press at War with the Bar

For the rest of the 1840s, the Bar wrestled with the ethics of Phillips's conduct and in subsequent analysis of the duties of counsel, two positions emerged. The first was the one adopted by Phillips which was modelled on Lord Brougham's defence of Queen Caroline in 1820, and which argued that an advocate must use 'all expedient means . . . to protect [his] client at all hazards and costs to all others'. The other position was modelled on Lord Langdale's speech in *Hutchinson* v. *Stephens*, and stressed that an advocate's zeal should be qualified by 'considerations affecting the general interests of justice'.[26] The press was strongly critical of the former position, but the harsh images of the law generated by press reports and by authors of fictional works during this time were not disinterested; literary attacks on one of the country's most venerable professions were a check on the morality of the Bar but they were also a means of exploring the writers' conceptions of their own professional responsibilities.

Hence it is no surprise that criticism of the Bar was particularly intense during the so-called 'Bar-Press War' which erupted in 1845 when the Oxford and Western Circuits prohibited their members from reporting for the newspapers, in an attempt to

---

[24] *Letters*, n. 20 above, II, 91.
[25] 28 February 1846. Reproduced in *Selected Letters of Charles Dickens* (David Paroissien (ed.), Basingstoke, 1985), 220.
[26] *Hutchinson* v. *Stephens* (1837) 1 Keen 659 at 668. For a summary of the various positions, see the debate in the *Examiner* following the executions of Frederick and Maria Manning, 24 November 1849, and Cairns, n. 16 above, ch. 6. See also Bege Bowers Neel, 'Lawyers on Trial: Attitudes Towards the Lawyers' Use and Abuse of Rhetoric in Nineteenth-Century England' (unpub. doctoral thesis, University of Tennessee, 1984).

prevent favouritism or personal antagonism from influencing the selection of reported cases. The press chose to interpret this edict as a suggestion that reporting itself was a disreputable activity, and the howls of outrage from the *Examiner* reflect in turn the offended honour of the press as a consequence of this perceived snub.[27] Countering the tendency of the Bar to conceive of its past in terms of the adventurous exploits of 'great men',[28] journals such as *Punch* and the *Examiner* created a satirical mythology of the Bar's own malefactors in order to justify a ruthless attack on the profession's amorality; the rhetorical excesses of counsel in a number of notorious cases—Brougham's defence of Queen Caroline, Chitty's tearful assistance of Thurtell, Phillips's apparent duplicity on behalf of Courvoisier, and Sir Fitzroy Kelly's sentimental defence of the poisoner John Tawell—were rehearsed again and again as examples of the untrustworthiness of the Bar:

If an honest man is to be bullied in a witness-box, the barrister is instructed to bully him. If a murderer is to be rescued from the gallows, the barrister blubbers over him, as in TAWELL's case, or accuses a wrong person, as in COURVOISIER's case. If a naughty woman is to be screened, a barrister will bring Heaven itself into court, and call Providence to witness that she is pure and spotless, as a certain great advocate and schoolmaster abroad did for a certain lamented QUEEN CAROLINE . . . See all these things, O Press! Send your commissioners in the train of these spotless men of law—and have your say . . . Don't fail to point out their eminent merits. Hold up their respectability to public admiration.[29]

A leading article in the *Examiner* quoted this article from *Punch* with approval, observing that '[i]n a dictionary in the year 3000 may appear, under the head of Lawyers corruptly so called, but properly Liars, a class of men who indiscriminately advocated right or wrong for hire'.[30] On a less satirical note, however, it questioned whether the Bar was capable of effective self-regulation on real issues of moral application; addressing the cases instanced by *Punch*, it asked whether these excesses were attended with any 'practical effect':

---

[27] 'The Bar and the Press' the *Examiner*, 16 August 1845.
[28] See Raymond Cocks, *Foundations of the Modern Bar* (London, 1983), 27–9.
[29] 'War between the Press and the Bar: Mr Punch to the Gentlemen of the Press' (1845) 9 *Punch*, 64–5. Richard Altick attributes this passage to William Thackeray; see *Punch: The Lively Youth of a British Institution, 1841–1851* (Columbus, 1997), 503.   [30] The *Examiner*, 16 August 1845.

Were the advocates expelled the circuit, or disbarred, as having compromised the dignity of the profession? Did their brethren shun them? Was any mark of discountenance put upon them? On the very first opportunity, one [Phillips] was raised to the Bench in the Court of Bankruptcy; the other [Kelly] to the Solicitor-Generalship, whence he will pass to one of the highest seats in judicature.[31]

Recognizing the 'rare talents' of the editor of the *Examiner*, the *Law Magazine* chose to respond to this article on behalf of the legal profession.[32] It objected to the journalistic recital of the law's misdemeanours, when '[p]etty instances of professional misconduct are . . . hawked from paper to paper to swell the chorus of the cry',[33] and it argued instead that the Bar already had an unwritten rule of conduct applicable to such cases as that of *Courvoisier*:

[I]t is the established rule of the Bar not to defend cases which they know to be unjust: that it is the ordinary practice to hold what are termed 'watching briefs' in such cases, when the duty of counsel is merely that of taking care that his client has fair play, and that the evidence against him is legally sufficient, without any attempt to resist the verdict; and that even when this is not the case, and the evidence leaves no reasonable doubt on which side the verdict ought to be, no respectable advocate perseveres in the struggle. Every assize witnesses many such cases, and such is perfectly well known to be the rule of the profession. That instances occur of its infraction we are far from denying; but it is also notorious that the individuals who earn an unenviable and precarious income by setting this rule at defiance are alike under the ban of the Bench and the Bar, constantly checked and censured by the former, and held very lightly in esteem by the latter. The noisy obtrusiveness of such men attracts notice, whilst the quiet surrender of bad cases creates none. And hence it is that the false estimate of the practice of the great body of the Bar mainly arises.[34]

The *Examiner* remained unpersuaded, however; in response to this article, it reiterated that the barristers who had reported for the newspapers after the prohibition were expelled from the circuit messes, whilst those who worked for the 'manumission of murderers' (in Trollope's phrase) were elevated to the Bench.[35]

---

31 The *Examiner*, 16 August 1845.
32 'The Newspapers Against the Bar' *Law Magazine* 3 (1845), 165–87, 166.
33 'The Newspapers Against the Bar', n. 32 above, 185.
34 'The Newspapers Against the Bar', n. 32 above, 186.
35 The *Examiner*, 15 November 1845.

The dispute was only ended when the London QCs ruled that legal reporting was not a disreputable activity for its members to undertake.[36]

By the end of the 1840s, the opinion of the legal profession had settled in favour of some limits to the exercise of adversarial licence; Sergeant Thomas Noon Talfourd, the dramatist and close friend of Dickens, entered the fray with an article in the *Law Magazine* which stressed that the zeal of counsel must cease 'when his cause conflicts with the higher requisites of religion, of morality, or of patriotism',[37] and Lord Langdale's approach was approved by William Forsyth in his book on the duties of an advocate, entitled *Hortensius* (1849).[38] In his Preface to the Cheap Edition of *Pickwick Papers* in 1847, Dickens expressed satisfaction at these developments, but it was short-lived, however, as a fresh scandal of advocacy was soon to attract his attention.

The Literary Response

In November 1849, the trial and subsequent execution of Frederick and Maria Manning for murder reactivated debate about the licence of counsel and Phillips's conduct in the *Courvoisier* case. Their execution, which Dickens attended, coincided with Phillips's first public explanation of his proceedings in the earlier trial. Phillip Collins records the traditional belief that Maria Manning provided Dickens with the model for the representation of Hortense,[39] the Frenchwoman who murders Tulkinghorn in *Bleak House* (1853). I believe that he may also have taken her name from *Hortensius*, Forsyth's study of the duties of advocates, and this suggests that Dickens's fear of the immorality of advocacy also contributed to the genesis of *Bleak House*.

We see this clearly in the cameo plot in which George

---

[36] See Neel, n. 26 above, 64.

[37] [Thomas Noon Talfourd], 'On the Principle of Advocacy as Developed in the Practice of the Bar' *Law Magazine* 4 (1846) 1, 21. The article is unsigned, but Cairns explains how it represents the culmination of ideas which Talfourd developed throughout his career: Cairns, n. 16 above, 146–9.

[38] William Forsyth, *Hortensius: An Historical Essay on the Office and Duties of an Advocate* (2nd edn, London, 1874), 385.

[39] Phillip Collins, *Dickens and Crime* (3rd edn, Basingstoke, 1962, repr. 1994), 235, 280, 344.

Rouncewell finds himself wrongfully suspected of the murder which Hortense has committed. Rejecting the assistance of lawyers as unethical and obsessed with technicalities, George elects to conduct his own defence:

'I should have got a lawyer, and he would have said (as I have often read in the newspapers), "my client says nothing, my client reserves his defence—my client this, that, and t'other". Well, 'tis not the custom of that breed to go straight, according to my opinion, or to think that other men do. Say, I am innocent, and I get a lawyer. He would be as likely to believe me guilty as not; perhaps more. What would he do, whether or not? Act as if I was;—shut my mouth up, tell me not to commit myself, keep circumstances back, chop the evidence small, quibble, and get me off perhaps!'[40]

Instead, George wants his innocence established on substantive grounds—'I must come off clear and full or not at all' (ch. 52, 706)—and he is content to acknowledge the veracity of facts which may appear unfavourable to his case. True innocence should be established despite the manipulation of evidence by the prosecution:

'[W]hen I hear stated against me what is true, I say it's true; and when they tell me, "whatever you say will be used," I tell them I don't mind that; I mean it to be used. If they can't make me innocent out of the whole truth, they are not likely to do it out of anything less, or anything else. And if they are, it's worth nothing to me'. (ch. 52, 706–7)

This is precisely the procedural dilemma which confronted practitioners with the implementation of the Prisoners' Counsel Act. Once the choice was made to enjoy the benefit of legal representation, an accused felon was unable to speak for himself. In the months after the Act was passed, it was established that the court could not hear the representations of both counsel and the accused. There was some uncertainty as the bench came to terms with the consequences of the Act,[41] but the basic rule was that 'if

---

[40] Charles Dickens, *Bleak House* (Oxford, 1948, repr. 1978), ch. 52, 706. Other references to this edition are included in the text.

[41] Zelman Cowen discusses judicial confusion on this point and notes that Baron Alderson allowed both counsel and accused to make representations to the court in *R. v. Dyer* (1844) 1 Cox CC 113. However, this practice seems to have been the exception rather than the rule, at least until the 1880s when the position changed: see Cowen and P. B. Carter, *Essays on the Law of Evidence* (Oxford, 1956), 205–18.

the prisoner's counsel has addressed the jury, the prisoner himself will not be allowed to address the jury also'; as Coleridge J. told the accused in *R. v. Boucher* (1837) 8 Car. & P. 141, 'Prisoner, your counsel has spoken for you. I cannot hear you both'. In procedural terms, there was a further complication; as Coleridge J. explained in *R. v. Beard* (1837) 8 Car. & P. 142, 'the counsel for a prisoner cannot be allowed to state the prisoner's story, unless he is able to confirm it by evidence':

I cannot permit a prisoner's counsel to tell the jury anything which he is not in a position to prove. If the prisoner does not employ counsel, he is at liberty to make a statement for himself and tell his own story; which is to have such weight with the jury, as all circumstances considered it is entitled to, but if he employs counsel, he must submit to the rules which have been established with respect to the conducting of cases by counsel. (142)

As Cairns has noted, this could lead to severe injustice and the exclusion of the only relevant exculpatory material in a prisoner's defence; as he was not allowed to give evidence on oath prior to 1898, he was not in a position to 'prove' facts of innocence which lay within his knowledge only.[42] For example, in the case of *R. v. Malings* (1838) 8 Car. & P. 242, the accused's defence to a charge of assault was that he had acted in self-defence; no one else was present at the time, the prisoner was not able to give his version of events on oath and thus the counsel's defence could not be founded upon his client's instructions as to innocence. In these exceptional circumstances, the presiding judge, Baron Alderson, allowed the accused to state the material facts for his counsel to comment upon:

It is true that the prisoner's statement may often defeat the defence intended by his counsel; but if so, the ends of justice will be furthered. Besides, it is often the genuine defence of the party, and not a mere imaginary case invented by the ingenuity of counsel. (243)

However, this ruling was not allowed to create a precedent, as Baron Gurney observed in *R. v. Walking* (1838) 8 Car. & P. 243, and Coleridge J.'s conception of the prisoner's role in his own defence was again asserted by Patteson J. in *R. v. Rider* (1838) 8 Car. & P. 539:

---

[42] Cairns, n. 16 above, 118–19.

The general rule certainly ought to be, that a prisoner defended by counsel should be entirely in the hands of his counsel, and that rule should not be infringed on, except in very special cases indeed. If the prisoner were allowed to make a statement, and stated as a fact anything which could not be proved by evidence, the jury should dismiss that statement from their minds; but if what the prisoner states is merely a comment on what is already in evidence, his counsel can do that much better than he can. (540)

Thus the role of the accused as 'testimonial resource' (in Langbein's phrase) is increasingly closed off to the courts, and in its place, counsel is restricted to commentary on the material already in evidence, which cannot include the prisoner's narrative as he is precluded from giving his evidence on oath.

Langbein describes this development as a move from the 'old "accused speaks" theory' of the criminal trial to 'the newer "testing the prosecution" theory', which only became possible with the emergence of the professional criminal Bar and the division of the testimonial and defensive functions of responding to a criminal charge.[43] The testimonial aspect of a prisoner's defence was subordinated to a lawyer's claims of technical expertise which could establish innocence on non-substantive grounds. For George in *Bleak House*, as for Felix in George Eliot's *Felix Holt* (1866), integrity is equated with a rejection of legal representation and a preference for straightforward narratives of innocence. The preference for an 'accused speaks' model of the trial is to be found time and time again in Victorian fiction; just as the reader has access to evidence of Pickwick's and George's innocence in the form of testimonial declarations, so too Eliot confirms Silas's innocence in *Silas Marner* (1861), Felix's lack of criminal intent in *Felix Holt* and Hetty's probable guilt in *Adam Bede* (1858) by providing the reader with confessional confirmation of their various states of criminal responsibility. Similarly Elizabeth Gaskell ensures that the reader has access to evidence of Jem Wilson's substantive innocence prior to his trial for murder in *Mary Barton* (1848) and Trollope ensures that Lady Mason confesses to the reader if not the court. All are reluctant to follow the law by abandoning the view of the accused as a 'testimonial resource'; they insist instead that discovery of truth is dependent upon the parties telling their stories in their own words, a paradigm of idealistic and arguably

[43] Langbein, 'Privilege Against Self-Incrimination', n. 14 above, 1048.

naive epistemology which harks back to Sergeant Hawkins's belief in the ease with which an innocent man may construct a 'plain and honest defence'.

Like Fielding, Dickens adopted a prosecutorial stance in much of his social criticism. For example, we see in his response to the trial and execution of the poisoner William Palmer (1856) an acceptance—shared, for once, by the *Examiner* as well as the legal profession—that crimes committed in secret may be detected by the law without recourse to the felon's story; where the prosecution succeeds in discharging the burden of proof the accused cannot hide behind his silence.[44] That Dickens in his fiction undertakes the defence of the unjustly accused is an interesting inversion of his critical concerns, but George and Pickwick are in good company among other fictional protagonists such as Tom Jones, Caleb Williams, Waverley, Jem Wilson, Felix Holt, and even perhaps Browning's Pompilia. The business of the eighteenth- or nineteenth-century author is also, it seems, to secure the prisoner's acquittal, and it is the similarities of their tasks as well as the different methods employed to produce such acquittals which generated law and literature's combative approach to the delimitation of their discourses.[45]

The extent to which literature can act as a moral commentary on the excesses of the law—to act as a higher court of public appeal—is dependent on the extent to which fiction is itself committed to realist representation and the amelioration of injustice. It was the great jurist James Fitzjames Stephen who was most articulate in his defence of the morality of advocacy and he questioned the right of the authors to shape public opinion about the administration of justice when they had no concomitant responsibility to present evidence fairly or dispassionately. Stephen claimed that newspaper reports and the efforts of modern novelists in turn generated the very opprobrium in which the legal profession was held. In his famous article on 'The License of Modern Novelists' which appeared in the

---

[44] See for example, 'The Demeanour of Murderers' *Household Words*, 14 June 1856, and the *Examiner*, 21 June 1856. On the evidence in Palmer's case see *Criminal Court Session Papers* 44 (London, 1855–6), 5–225. A full account of the trial is contained in the Notable English Trials series: see George H. Knott (ed.), *The Trial of William Palmer* (Edinburgh and London, 1912).

[45] See Alexander Welsh, *Strong Representations: Narrative and Circumstantial Evidence in England* (Baltimore, 1992), chs. 1–2.

Edinburgh Review in 1857 and which clearly mirrors Dickens's attacks on 'The License of Counsel' in the 1840s, Stephen is troubled by an author's lack of public accountability. In the case of Charles Reade's *It is Never too Late to Mend* (1853) (which included an attack on a badly run Midlands prison), he charges the author with libel for exaggerating the criminality of the acts on which the narrative is based. Stephen is disturbed by the possibility that literature may serve as a 'high commission . . . to try offences which elude the repression of the law, and to denounce with hyperbolical violence actions which may not have been committed at all, or which have been committed from very different motives'.[46] In a later article entitled 'The Morality of Advocacy', Stephen cites the murder trial in *Mary Barton* as an example of the unrealistic excesses which novelists attribute to contemporary court proceedings: 'To judge from the representations given by popular writers, it would appear to be the common opinion that such practices are regarded, both by the bench and by the bar, as triumphs of ingenuity.'[47] He stresses that, in actuality, improper behaviour by advocates is subject to the internal regulation of the profession; there is no such check on the morality of fictional authors. Dickens and Stephen are essentially wrangling about the *locus* of authority to speak (should an advocate identify himself completely with his brief, should a realistic novelist confine himself to well-documented facts?) and these are primarily questions about the ethical treatment of evidence.

Stephen was somewhat insensitive to the imaginative nature of the creative act, but his observations on the capacity of the Bar for effective self-regulation carried considerable weight. In his analysis of the development of professional legal ethics, Anthony Thornton notes that the Bar had no written Code of Conduct until 1980; '[t]his remarkable lack of any written code of conduct over a period of six centuries is explained by the tightly-knit nature of the profession'.[48] But the Victorian era was a time of tremendous

[46] James Fitzjames Stephen, 'The License of Modern Novelists' (1857) *Edinburgh Review* 106 124, 156. This article is unsigned, but it is attributed to Stephen by *The Wellesley Periodical Index*, n. 10 above, I, 506.

[47] Stephen, 'The Morality of Advocacy' (1861) *Cornhill Magazine* 3 447, 453. This article is unsigned, but it is attributed to Stephen by *The Wellesley Periodical Index*, n. 10 above, I, 328.

[48] Anthony Thornton, 'The Professional Responsibility and Ethics of the English Bar' in Ross Cranston (ed.), *Legal Ethics and Professional Responsibility* (Oxford, 1995) 53, 55.

professional as well as substantive change; legal historians such as Raymond Cocks and Daniel Duman have seen the history of the Bar in the nineteenth century in terms of a decline in the cohesion and authority of the Circuit Messes, and an eventual move towards more formalized standards of ethical conduct.[49] The General Council of the Bar was established in 1894 and it was given 'the right to determine the code of professional etiquette, while reserving for the benchers of each Inn the sole responsibility for the enforcement of discipline'.[50] Annex H of the current edition of the *Code of Conduct of the Bar of England and Wales* (1990) now sets out the procedure which a barrister should follow in the event that his/her lay client confesses to the crime with which he is charged but then insists that his representative proceed to take the matter to a fully defended hearing:

13.1 In considering the duty of counsel retained to defend a person charged with an offence who confesses to his counsel that he did commit the offence charged, it is essential to bear the following points clearly in mind:

    (a) that every punishable crime is a breach of common or statute law committed by a person of sound mind and understanding;

    (b) that the issue in a criminal trial is always whether the defendant is guilty of the offence charged, never whether he is innocent;

    (c) that the burden of proof rests on the prosecution.

13.2 It follows that the mere fact that a person charged with a crime has confessed to his counsel that he did commit the offence charged is no bar to that barrister appearing or continuing to appear in his defence, nor indeed does such a confession release the barrister from his imperative duty to do all that he honourably can for his client.

13.3 Such a confession, however, imposes very strict limitations on the conduct of the defence. A barrister must not assert as true that which he knows to be false. He must not connive at, much less attempt to substantiate, a fraud.

13.4 While, therefore, it would be right to take any objections to the competency of the court, to the form of the indictment, to the admissibility of any evidence or to the evidence admitted, it would be wrong to suggest that some other person had committed the offence charged, or to call any evidence which the barrister must know to be false having regard

---

[49] See Cocks, *Foundations of the Modern Bar*, n. 28 above, and Daniel Duman, 'Pathway to Professionalism: The English Bar in the Eighteenth and Nineteenth Centuries' *Journal of Social History* 13 (1980) no. 4, 615.

[50] Duman, n. 48 above, 624.

to the confession, such, for instance, as evidence in support of an alibi. In other words, a barrister must not (whether by calling the defendant or otherwise) set up an affirmative case inconsistent with the confession made to him.

Yet, as Thornton concedes, this area of practice is often misunderstood by the general public who seem to remain concerned by the extent of adversarial licence;[51] a perception persists that criminal barristers are deceitful in defending on a regular basis those whom they 'know' to be guilty. This is despite a number of developments in the interim; unsworn statements by represented accused seem to have been more widely accepted in the 1880s and the enactment of the Criminal Evidence Act in 1898 enabled the accused to tell his story on oath in his own words if he chose to do so, a development designed both to eradicate 'sham defences' which bore no relation to the merits of the case in hand and to facilitate the construction of a genuine defence where the accused was innocent.[52] The figure of the lawyer no longer appropriates the prisoner's story and simultaneously excludes his voice from the courtroom. But it is perhaps a testament to the power of the indignant satire of *Punch* and the *Examiner*, the trenchant criticism of Dickens, and the imaginative intensity of the great Victorian realist narratives that public anxieties about the ethics of advocacy are still shaped by the controversies which arose when lawyers first assumed the prisoner's right to speak.

[51] Thornton, n. 47 above, 83, footnote 78.
[52] See n. 41 above and also Christopher Allen, *The Law of Evidence in Victorian England* (Cambridge, 1997), 144–80.

VICTORIAN NARRATIVE JURISPRUDENCE

Christine L. Krueger

Advocacy by legal scholars on behalf of narrative in legal reasoning might strike students of Victorian social problem literature as urging us 'back to the future'. On the one hand, we may be heartened that members of one of the professions which discredited literary authors as sources of political insight are promoting the value of storytelling in deciding court cases and deliberating public policy. Their vision of public discourse recalls the cultural conditions of the last century, when men of letters, if not women, might also be men of law, and when overtly political literature commanded sufficient public attention on social questions to be considered pernicious by some jurists, like Sir James Fitzjames Stephen. Once again, the voice of Shelley is heard in the land: 'poets are the unacknowledged legislators of the world'. If esteemed law school professors like Robert Weisberg say so, perhaps it is, after all, true.[1] On the other hand, as much as we may be drawn to this heady blend of imagination and social activism—a combination which probably attracted many of us to our field of study and might promise to return literature from its exile on the margins of hedonistic consumerism—it is difficult to ignore the objections raised by literary historical scholarship on the rise of print culture, the professionalization of authorship, and, above all, the intimate connections between aesthetics and the bourgeois social order. In his *Lectures on the Relation Between Law and Public Opinion in England*, the Victorian A. V. Dicey cautioned fellow lawyers that 'historical research . . . tends to quench the confident enthusiasm necessary for carrying out even the most well approved and the most beneficial among

---

[1] Robert Weisberg, 'Proclaiming Trials as Narratives: Premises and Pretenses' in Peter Brooks and Paul Gewirtz (eds.), *Law's Stories* (New Haven, 1996), 83.

democratic innovations'.[2] In this paper, I hope to provide some encouragement to literary historians to contribute to the narrative jurisprudence project, and incentives to lawyers to engage in literary history as they have, *pace* Dicey, the history of law.

The question addressed in this essay is: what can literary history contribute to contemporary narrative jurisprudence? Despite the fact that narrative jurisprudence critiques legal formalism, and does so in part on historicist grounds, its own understanding of narrative is typically formalist rather than historicist, identifying particular structural features, such as coherency, concrete detail, metaphor, or point of view, as those elements of narrative which are of epistemological significance. As Kathryn Abrams, a leading narrative legal scholar, argues, stories possessing these qualities make epistemological claims rivalling, or superseding, those based on statistical significance or logical deduction.[3] I will argue that the goals of narrative jurisprudence are better served, the significance of narrative evidence made more clear, and therefore its defence more robust, if its advocates attend to their place in an historical process of social formation carried out by fusing aesthetics and rationalism. I will elaborate this general claim, and discuss several specific implications for narrative jurisprudence aimed at bringing its epistemology of narrative more closely in line with its ethical claims. Realistic narrative, a mode of aesthetic representation privileged in narrative jurisprudence, will illustrate the import of an analysis of the history of literary forms. Looking at realistic narrative—especially the novel—as a method of cultural signification evolving out of a need to address the epistemological and ethical problems posed by a bourgeois social order clarifies some of the more vexing issues in narrative jurisprudence. These include the relationship of experiential evidence to normative judgments, of private to public decision-making, of socially and economically positioned speakers to discursive forms, and of emotional to rational forms of argument. Before turning to these questions, however, I wish to summarize both the peculiar relevance of Victorian literary history to narrative jurisprudence and the special difficulties it raises.

---

[2] A. V. Dicey, *Lectures on the Relation Between Law and Public Opinion in England* (London, 1905, 2nd edn, 1914, repr. 1962), 461.

[3] Kathryn Abrams, 'Hearing the Call of Stories' (1991) 79 *California Law Review* 976.

It is not only the public role envisioned for literature by narrative legal scholars that attracts the attention of Victorianists, but the specific texts to which they appeal. Although narrative legal scholars regularly discuss other texts, notably, Plato's dialogues, *The Merchant of Venice*, and *Measure for Measure*, Victorian novels, too, seem to have special attractions. Indeed, the novels of Fitzjames Stephen's particular nemesis, Charles Dickens, have proven uniquely congenial. Leading law and literature scholar Richard Weisberg devotes an entire chapter to Dickens's lawyers in his influential study *Poethics*, where he claims that 'fiction about law continues to uncover better than any other medium the private lives of lawyers . . . and compels us to recognize that lawyers' private lives directly affect their public performances'.[4] Along with other Victorians, including Henry James and Olive Schreiner, Dickens has also been cited by philosophers promoting literature's public role; both Richard Rorty and Martha Nussbaum use Dickens to illustrate how the imagination and emotions assist in just decision-making. Rorty names Dickens among the authors whose novels provide 'the details about kinds of suffering being endured by people to whom we had previously not attended', a reason why the novel is among 'the principal vehicles of moral change and progress'.[5] Dickens's *Hard Times* (1854) figures prominently in Martha Nussbaum's book *Poetic Justice*, where she writes: 'I defend the literary imagination precisely because it seems to me an essential ingredient of an ethical stance that asks us to concern ourselves with the good of other people whose lives are distant from our own'.[6]

Not only are acknowledged poets of interest to narrative jurisprudence, but so are 'outsiders'—women, workers, people of colour—the very groups whose stories began to enter into public discourse in significant numbers in the nineteenth century.[7] Whereas

[4] Richard Weisberg, *Poethics and Other Strategies of Law and Literature* (New York, 1992), 35.
[5] Richard Rorty, *Contingency, Irony, and Solidarity* (Cambridge, 1989), xvi.
[6] Martha C. Nussbaum, *Poetic Justice: The Literary Imagination and Public Life* (Boston, 1995), xvi.
[7] Examples of feminist narrative scholarship include Kathryn Abrams, 'The Narrative and the Normative in Legal Scholarship' in Susan Sage-Heinzelman and Zipporah Batshaw Wiseman (eds.), *Representing Women: Law, Literature, and Feminism* (Durham, 1994), 44–56; Carolyn Heilbrun and Judith Resnik, 'Convergences: Law, Literature, and Feminism' (1990) 99 *Yale Law Journal*

Richard Weisberg and James Boyd White (like Rorty and Nussbaum) turn to canonical texts to educate the legal imagination, another group of narrative jurisprudence advocates, such as Kathryn Abrams and Richard Delgado, privileges the stories of historically disenfranchised authors. For these feminist and critical race theorists, narrative jurisprudence must encompass storytelling generally if it genuinely seeks knowledge of 'people to whom we had previously not attended', for their stories may not be recognizable as 'literary' at all. Once again, historians of Victorian culture find themselves on familiar ground, since our domain has comprehended not only Arnold and Tennyson, but Dickens and Trollope ('popular' authors in their day), George Eliot and Elizabeth Barrett Browning, William Cobbett and Ellen Johnston (the 'Factory Girl' poet), as well as the texts of so-called popular culture, from *Reynolds's Newspaper* (for the working classes) to melodramas like *Black-eyed Susan* (1829). Narrative jurisprudence appears committed to Victorian politico-aesthetic projects, such as that set out by Thomas Carlyle, who urged his reform-minded contemporaries to inquire into working men's beliefs. To the question 'What is just?', 'The words they promulgate are notable by way of answer', he wrote in *Chartism* (1840), 'their actions are still more notable. Chartism with its spikes, Swing with its tinderbox, speak a loud though inarticulate language'. Familiar with Victorian versions of such arguments, we are sympathetic to the claim that outsiders' stories enable typically privileged decision-makers to empathize with subjects whose constraints and needs are unfamiliar.

1913–56; Judith Resnik, 'Feminism and the Language of Judging' (1990) 22 *Arizona State Law Journal* 31–8; and Martha Minow, *Not Only For Myself: Identity, Politics, and the Law* (New York, 1997). For examples of critical race theorists see Derrick Bell, *Faces at the Bottom of the Well: The Permanence of Racism* (New York, 1992), Patricia J. Williams, *The Alchemy of Race and Rights* (Cambridge, Mass., 1991), and Richard Delgado and Jean Stefancic, *Failed Revolutions: Social Reform and the Limits of the Legal Imagination* (Boulder, 1994). For discussions of nineteenth-century working-class writers, see R. K. Webb, *The British Working Class Reader, 1790–1848: Literacy and Social Tension* (London, 1955), and Martha Vicinus, *The Industrial Muse: A Study of Nineteenth Century British Working-Class Literature* (London, 1974). Women writers of nineteenth-century social discourse are discussed in Joseph Kestner, *Protest and Reform: The British Social Narrative by Women, 1827–1867* (Madison, Wis., 1985), Judith Lowder Newton, *Women, Power, and Subversion: Social Strategies in British Fiction, 1778–1860* (Athens, Ga., 1981), and Christine L. Krueger, *The Reader's Repentance: Women Writers, Women Preachers and Nineteenth-Century Social Discourse* (Chicago, 1992).

What is more, Carlyle's formulation seems related to one of the leading metaphors of the law and literature movement, coined by James Boyd White: 'justice as translation'.[8] The activity of legal interpretation, to which White's metaphor refers, may be the complement of a process wherein professionals are enjoined to translate into legally potent language the 'inarticulate' words of the disenfranchised. This was the rationale of much Victorian social problem literature aimed at reforming laws governing business practices, factory conditions, and gender relations. Carlyle congratulated Elizabeth Gaskell for achieving precisely this kind of translation in her novel of Manchester factory conditions, *Mary Barton* (1848), calling the novel 'a real contribution (about the first real one) towards developing a huge subject, which has lain dumb too long, and really ought to speak for itself, and tell us its meaning a little, if there be any voice in it at all'.[9] In this, as in other respects, narrative jurisprudence participates in debates about representation that reach back to the earliest theories of representative democracy and the interrelated issues of discursive and aesthetic representation. It is hardly for trivial reasons, then, that Victorian writers were interested in the law, or that contemporary narrative legal scholars so often recur to them.

What has not been adequately recognized are the profound features of this involvement. For, even where they adduce early modern, or ancient stories, narrative legal scholars—*as well as their critics*—are reading those texts through the history of the political and ethical functions of the aesthetic. Both James Boyd White and Richard A. Posner, like S. T. Coleridge and Jeremy Bentham before them, operate within a paradigm of a just society wherein the aesthetic has come to play a new role in producing theories of representation, rights, and above all, moral good. Narrative jurisprudence can exploit the dialectical relationship between aesthetics and rationalism whereby these concepts are formed, as I shall argue below, but only by attending to its functions within the history of modern social formations, by uncovering the archaeology of its own problematics.

[8] James Boyd White, *Justice as Translation: An Essay in Cultural and Legal Studies* (Chicago, 1990).

[9] Thomas Carlyle to Elizabeth Cleghorn Gaskell, 8 November 1848, John Rylands, MS 730/14, quoted in Jenny Uglow, *Elizabeth Gaskell: A Habit of Stories* (London, 1993), 217.

To take one brief example, Seyla Benhabib has posited against liberal universalism, with its abstract agent and exclusionary rules of evidence (the so-called 'reasonable person' operating behind the Rawlsian 'veil of ignorance') a paradoxical general *and* concrete 'other', whose specificity, embodiedness, and embeddedness can be represented through a life story on which, she maintains, normative judgments can be based.[10] Her dispute with Rawls may be construed as a methodological one, namely, how best to achieve justice for all members of a diverse society. With the general concrete 'other', Benhabib hopes to finesse the apparent incongruity of particularistic, experiential evidence and abstraction, which the techniques of nineteenth-century literary realism were uniquely designed to negotiate. Catherine Gallagher has noted, for example, the paradoxical relationship between George Eliot's early theories of literary representation and 'liberal, even Utilitarian, theories of value and political representation'. She characterizes George Eliot's 'project in the literary realm as identical to James Mill's project in the political realm to represent as many of the metonymic relationships of the social world as possible'.[11] Whereas in the political realm, descriptive representation promised to convert a numerical aggregate of individuals into political value, in the literary, realism aimed at building up meaning out of the accumulation of facts. Kathryn Abrams identifies this problematic gap between the particular and the normative as the objection most often posed against narrative jurisprudence.[12] For historians of literary realism, these objections raise the spectre of a thorough-going, and potentially devastating, critique.

The hermeneutics of suspicion have caused literary critics to retreat from celebratory claims to more cautious, if not downright cynical, positions about the politics of literary representation. Realistic literature figures prominently in arguments promoting the benefits of storytelling in law, but it does not resemble many

[10] Seyla Benhabib uses the term 'concrete subject' in developing a communicative ethic of need interpretations in 'The Generalized and the Concrete Other' in Seyla Benhabib and Drucilla Cornell (eds.), *Feminism as Critique: On the Politics of Gender* (Minneapolis, 1988), 91–5.

[11] Catherine Gallagher, *The Industrial Reformation of English Fiction: Social Discourse and Narrative Form, 1832–1867* (Chicago, 1985), 223–4.

[12] Abrams, n. 3 above, 978. For an example of these objections to narrative jurisprudence see Richard A. Posner, *Overcoming Law* (Cambridge, Mass., 1995), ch. 18, esp. 381–2.

literary critics' historicized version of realism as a set of conventions particularly suited to patriarchal bourgeois goals in a phase of liberalism and capitalism.[13] Familiar texts like *Hard Times* seem foreign when we encounter them in arguments extolling their power to effect sympathetic identification because we have been alerted to their rationalizations of bourgeois hegemony in the guise of advocacy for the disenfranchised. It should be noted here as well that autobiography, central to the project of outsider narrative jurisprudence, likewise carries with it an ethically ambiguous history. Aware of the constructed nature of this popular genre, not to mention the coercive features of confession, we must hesitate before claims that outsiders should be invited to share their life-stories in courts of law.[14] Ruling-class interest in the stories of the disenfranchised has gone hand in hand with a desire to possess those stories, or as Judith R. Walkowitz terms it (speaking of Victorian social investigators, like Henry Mayhew) to achieve 'intrapsychic incorporation'.[15] These assertions regarding the historical complicity in oppressive practices of the very narrative genres to which narrative jurisprudence typically appeals contain the basis for post-structuralist legal theorists' critiques of narrative jurisprudence, and as such, they must be addressed.[16]

Even if we were to set aside the worries generated by these post-structuralist accounts of language and power, however, literary history presents another set of challenges. These issue from several decades of scholarship on the history of literacy, print

[13] Examples of such criticism must begin with Ian Watt, *The Rise of the Novel* (Harmondsworth, 1957), wherein Watt tied 'formal realism' to the rise of the middle class. Watt's materialist analysis has been refined by, among others, Gallagher, n. 11 above; John Bender, *Imagining the Penitentiary: Fiction and the Architecture of the Mind in Eighteenth-Century England* (Chicago, 1987); Nancy Armstrong, *Desire and Domestic Fiction: A Political History of the Novel* (Oxford, 1987); and D. A. Miller, *The Novel and The Police* (Berkeley, 1988). See also the essays in Nancy Armstrong and Leonard Tennenhouse (eds.), *The Violence of Representation: Literature and the History of Violence* (London, 1989).

[14] Peter Brooks, 'Storytelling Without Fear? Confession in Law and Literature' in Brooks and Gewirtz, n. 1 above, 114–34.

[15] Judith R. Walkowitz, *City of Dreadful Delight: Narratives of Sexual Danger in Late-Victorian London* (London, 1992), 20.

[16] See, for example, Costas Douzinas and Ronnie Warrington, with Shaun McVeigh, *Postmodern Jurisprudence: The Law of Text in the Texts of Law* (London, 1991). For evidence of the growing scepticism regarding the political viability of narrative by two leading advocates of narrative jurisprudence, see Richard Delgado and Jean Stefancic, n. 7 above.

culture, and the economics of authorship, which complicate story-telling as evidence of experience and literature as a progressive form of representation.[17] Were our freedom of expression guaranteed absolutely, constrained neither by censorship nor an unequal distribution of linguistic capital, our freedom of publication is not. The mass-marketing of literature, which arises in the nineteenth century and persists into our own, implicates all published texts in the processes of commodification and market competition. These works, in turn, shape storytelling practices generally, as, for example, the representations of outsiders—the working class—mass-marketed in realistic fiction, such as Dickens's, occluded authentic working-class autobiographies and forced working-class writers to narrate their lives in conformity with realistic narrative conventions.[18] In nineteenth-century America, slave narratives, which were published to raise money for the abolition movement, were edited to conform with European standards of autobiography.[19] The professionalization of authorship which followed upon commodification could also homogenize: in the eighteenth

[17] The classic works on this subject remain Robert Altick, *The English Common Reader: A Social History of the Mass Reading Public 1800–1900* (Chicago, 1957), and Webb, n. 7 above. Analysis of print culture in the nineteenth century has taken diverse tacks. For example, John Sutherland discusses examples of editorial, publishing, and marketing influences on narratives in *Victorian Fiction: Writers, Publishers, Readers* (London, 1995). In two books, *Modes of Production of Victorian Novels* (Chicago, 1986) and *Literary Capital and the Late Victorian Novel* (Madison, Wis., 1993), N. N. Feltes traces the transformation of the British publishing industry from a petty commodity to a capitalist mode of production. Peter Brooks connects narrative desire with capitalist consumerism in *Reading for the Plot: Design and Intention in Narrative* (Cambridge, Mass., 1992). John Guillory has contextualized the whole question of canon formation as a literary critical crisis within the history of literature curricula in *Cultural Capital: The Problem of Literary Canon Formation* (Chicago, 1993).

[18] For a discussion of this phenomenon see Regenia Gagnier, *Subjectivities: A History of Self-Representation in Britain, 1832–1920* (Oxford, 1991), 138–70. Regarding the mass-marketing of middle-class authored fictions representing the working class, Judith R. Walkowitz remarks: 'Thanks to these literary outpourings, the middle-class reading public became emotionally invested in a set of representations about the poor that cast poor Londoners as central characters in narratives that divested them of any agency or ability to extricate themselves from their situation', n. 15 above, 30.

[19] See, for example, John Sekora, 'Is the Slave Narrative a Species of Autobiography?' in James Olney (ed.), *Studies in Autobiography* (Oxford, 1988), 99–111, and William L. Andrews, 'The Representation of Slavery and the Rise of Afro-American Literary Realism, 1865–1920' in Deborah E. McDowell and Arnold Rampersad (eds.), *Slavery and the Literary Imagination* (Baltimore, 1989), 62–6.

century, women made up two-thirds of the publishing novelists; by the 1840s, their numbers had declined to 20 per cent.[20] Such phenomena remind us that we do not live in an oral culture where storytelling might exist in an autonomous realm free of the discourses of class, race, and gender, which are themselves features of a history of material conditions.

At this point, advocates of narrative jurisprudence might be inclined to heed Dicey's advice, concluding that historical research can have only a corrosive effect on legal reform efforts. Perhaps literary historians have grown too pessimistic, projecting our own cultural irrelevancy onto our subject matter. But, as Martha Nussbaum has remarked, if the literary discipline fails to contribute towards 'shaping the private and public life of our culture, telling us how to imagine and think about ourselves', we 'capitulate to the values [and] modes of rationality . . . set by other disciplines'.[21]

What then can literary history contribute to narrative jurisprudence? We might begin by historicizing narrative jurisprudence itself, locating it within an ongoing relationship between ethics and aesthetics, reason and sentiment, which makes nineteenth-century literary and legal practices peculiarly germane. Kathryn Abrams associates the turn to narrative with the postmodern critiques of objectivity in the history of science and philosophy, replacing objective proofs with strategies of persuasion.[22] But it could be argued that the rational and aesthetic, scientific and sentimental, are not in fact antagonist categories, but mutually dependent ones. The case for narrative jurisprudence is strengthened by this historical account of the aesthetic. Rather than viewing the aesthetic as a transhistorical ideal, literary history invites us to attend to the changing meaning of the aesthetic, particularly in its dialectical relationship with the rational, with the result that aesthetic reasoning can be shown to play a central role in the formation of the modern democratic state.

Nineteenth-century cultural conditions throw into relief the connections between legal and literary representation, enabling us to understand contemporary narrative jurisprudence not as an

---

[20] Terry Lovell, *Consuming Fiction* (London, 1987), 42–3.
[21] Martha C. Nussbaum, *Love's Knowledge: Essays on Philosophy and Literature* (Oxford, 1990), 192.   [22] Abrams, n. 3 above, 1014–15.

upstart or marginal movement, but one integrally involved in articulating and legitimating a view of the state wherein order would be produced not through abject obedience to awful power but through sympathy and sensibility—fundamentally aesthetic faculties. As William Roscoe put the problem in 1819, '[t]he question would no longer be, whether stripes and bloodshed can prevail against guilt and ignorance, but whether sympathy, prudence, and compassion, have lost their influence on the moral feelings of mankind.'[23] Citing Roscoe, the legal historian Randall McGowan claims that nineteenth-century legal reform was directly related to aestheticization; the promulgation of 'an ideal of social union founded upon subjective feelings' wherein 'sympathetic bonds were expected to produce a social order far more smoothly regulated than that of any preceding civilization'.[24] On this view, public opinion, and eventually representational democracy, would necessarily take on new significance, since laws could be legitimated only in terms of their general benefit.

Importantly, in such a construction of social order, rationalism and aestheticism are linked. Terry Eagleton, among others, has demonstrated this union in the moral philosophy of Adam Smith, Shaftesbury, and Hume, each of whom construes the aesthetic as a mode of cognition by which sensation, desire, and particularity are captured for middle-class ideology, not only making the social order appear rational, but rational precisely because it seems to fit our individual sensibilities. For them, '[t]he ultimate binary force of the bourgeois social order, in contrast to the coercion apparatus of absolutism, will be habits, pieties, sentiments, and affections'. However, 'if a new social order is to be constructed on the basis of virtue, custom and opinion', Eagleton observes, 'then a radical rationalism must first of all dismantle the political structures of the present, submitting their mindless prejudices and traditionalist privileges to disinterested critique'. In Eagleton's view these processes gave rise not only to Benthamite Utilitarianism, but Burkean sentimentality, and, it could be claimed, the rhetorical strategies of realistic fiction and Romantic poetry. We need only recall the importance of publicity in Bentham's legal reforms to

---

[23] William Roscoe, *Observations on Penal Jurisprudence* (London, 1819), no page.

[24] Randall McGowen, 'Punishing Violence, Sentencing Crime' in Armstrong and Tennenhouse, n. 13 above, 142.

appreciate that the rationalist tradition as much as the sentimental contributed to the ethical and political functions of narrative in Victorian literary history.[25] Indeed, literary history records a tradition of Benthamite social fiction, including William Godwin's *Caleb Williams* (1794), Edward Bulwer Lytton's *Paul Clifford* (1830), and Harriet Martineau's *Illustrations of Political Economy* (1832–5). And though it may strike us as strange, no less a legal historian than Maine attributed the principal ideas in Dickens's *Hard Times* to Bentham.[26]

While both Eagleton and McGowan are analysing a phenomenon of 'high culture', perhaps the most remarkable result of the integration of rational and aesthetic reasoning is the burgeoning popular legal culture of the nineteenth century. Lawrence M. Friedman, discussing contemporary America, uses the term 'popular legal culture' to refer to 'the mind-set of the people who interact with legal institutions—lay people, bankers, merchants, policemen, women who want a divorce, and so on'.[27] Popular legal culture is arguably coincident with legal culture itself, but the peculiar features of modern popular legal culture evolve with the bourgeois state, wherein the literary and legal, the rational and aesthetic, are wholly intertwined. In the nineteenth century, to an unprecedented degree, a wide range of lay people spoke back to the law and represented the law to itself in the form of published documents—pamphlets, ballads, melodramas, novels—which came to be called public opinion. The Queen Caroline affair, the Tichborne Claimant movement, or the Armstrong case arising out of 'The Maiden Tribute of Modern Babylon' are only a few of the most celebrated examples of a new mass popular legal culture, in which arises what Dror Wahrman has called 'the metapolitical jurisdiction of "public opinion" '.[28] That

---

25   Terry Eagleton, *The Ideology of the Aesthetic* (Oxford, 1990), 20, 26.

26   Patrick Brantlinger notes Sir Henry Sumner Maine, *Popular Government*, in his discussion of Benthamite fiction in *The Spirit of Reform: British Literature and Politics, 1832–1867* (Cambridge, Mass., 1977), 35–59.

27   Lawrence M. Friedman, 'Law, Lawyers, and Popular Culture' (1989) 98 *Yale Law Journal* 1584.

28   Dror Wahrman, 'Public Opinion, Violence and the Limits of Constitutional Politics' in James Vernon (ed.), *Re-reading the Constitution: New Narratives in the Political History of England's Long Nineteenth Century* (Cambridge, 1996), 113–14. Wahrman traces the rise of a trans-class discourse of public opinion to the sentiment aroused on behalf of Queen Caroline when George IV brought an adultery suit against her in 1820. In the case of the Tichborne claimant, one Arthur Orton claimed to be the long lost Sir Roger Tichborne. Working-class people

new jurisdiction results from, among other things, engagements between the legal and literary.

More importantly, it reveals the dialectic relationship between lawyers and lay people mediated through narratives. If the law had ever been an autonomous institution, as Coke had imagined, it certainly ceased to be under these conditions. If anything, the more centralized the legal system became, the more new economic and social practices and new technologies conspired to reinstate the personal engagement that had characterized local justice. What is more, the evidence of an evolving literate popular legal culture demonstrates the fallacy of a category of subjects incapable of legal agency. Douglas Hay's analysis of malicious prosecutions brought by the poor against their masters in the eighteenth and nineteenth centuries is relevant to popular legal culture generally. Hay claims that only 'naive sociology, or uncritical jurisprudence, or unimaginative history' denies legal agency to all but a ruling elite. Speaking of the poor and middling ranks who went to law, Hay concludes, 'when they could, they used [the law], or at least what parts of it they knew and could afford . . . [a]nd when they succeeded in those purposes, parts of the law, its rhetoric, its instruments, acquired a legitimacy they otherwise would not have had'.[29]

Hay's remark reminds us that when lay people become legal actors they both shape, and are shaped by, legal culture. As the popular literature produced on the Queen Caroline affair, or by members of the Tichborne movement makes clear, lay people not only sought to influence the law, but revealed the degree to which they perceived their own experiences, especially family life, in legal terms. Indeed, as Martha Vicinus has argued, the very literary

figured prominently in the popular support for Orton, who was nonetheless exposed in two celebrated trials between 1871 and 1874. The Tichborne cause grew into a full-scale media event, with a Tichborne newspaper, pamphlets, and the founding of the Magna Charta Association to defend Orton's claim. For a detailed discussion of this case see Rowan McWilliam, 'Radicalism and Popular Culture: The Tichborne Case and the Politics of "Fair Play" ' in E. F. Biagini and A. J. Reid (eds.), *Currents of Radicalism* (Cambridge, 1991), 44–64. Judith R. Walkowitz treats W. T. Stead's 'Maiden Tribute of Modern Babylon' and the Armstrong case, n. 15 above, 121–34.

[29] Douglas Hay, 'Prosecution and Power: Malicious Prosecution in the English Courts, 1750–1850' in Douglas Hay and Francis Snyder (eds.), *Policing and Prosecution in Britain, 1750–1850* (Oxford, 1989), 394.

forms imposed on working-class writers who wished to engage public opinion required them to 'struggle to create and sustain a distinctive literature in the face of bourgeois economic and cultural control'.[30] The dialectics of popular legal culture— lawyers with lay people, literature with law—involved all its participants in one another's belief systems and discourses. A dramatic illustration of popular legal culture as a 'metapolitical jurisdiction' in its own right is offered by the suit brought in 1885 against W. T. Stead, and four other defendants, by the mother of Eliza Armstrong. In order to pressure Parliament to pass the Criminal Law Amendment Act with provisions aimed at shutting down the child prostitution trade, Stead set out to expose the trade by purchasing Eliza Armstrong from her mother and publishing an account of the transaction. 'The Maiden Tribute of Modern Babylon', which appeared in the *Pall Mall Gazette*, not only caused a public outcry (a crowd estimated at 250,000 protested in Hyde Park) and forced Parliament's hand, but also prompted Mrs Armstrong, who had become the target of her working-class neighbours' outrage, to have Stead charged with abduction. Eliza testified against him, and Stead served three months in Holloway Prison. As Judith R. Walkowitz remarks, '[m]ost authors of political fictions did not expect to be pursued by their own characters into the law courts and confronted with opposing versions of the story'.[31] Perhaps this is the origin of 'justice as translation', not as an interpretive model, but as a cultural dynamic.

This effort to historicize narrative jurisprudence is hardly exhaustive, but it does suggest an important principle. Because the categories of the aesthetic and rational, the literary and legal, professional and lay legal actors, are dialectically related, it is surely the case that narrative should not be construed as a uniquely effective tool for attaining social justice by virtue of its purely oppositional stance towards the law. Rather, it is one mode among many in which conflicting interests can be negotiated. To illustrate this point, I will return now to realistic fiction as a genre privileged in narrative jurisprudence, and then consider two examples of its complicated political strategies, Charles Reade's *Hard Cash* (1863) and Elizabeth Gaskell's *Lois the Witch* (1859).

[30] Vicinus, n. 7 above, 2.   [31] Walkowitz, n. 15 above, 106.

Narrative would play a crucial role in making mass democracy in the course of the nineteenth century by providing what Patrick Joyce has termed 'political subjectivities which created agency and legitimacy'.[32] Noting that 'the "contractual" and "institutional" capacity of literary genres implicitly attributes to them an explanatory function that is both epistemological and social', Michael McKeon asserts that '[g]enres provide a conceptual framework for the mediation (if not the "solution") of intractable problems, a method for rendering such problems intelligible'.[33] For twentieth-century narrative jurisprudence, as for the first theorists of representational democracy within bourgeois capitalism, those intractable problems centre on representation itself and its functions of mediating between facts and values, dominant and subordinate social groups, social constructions and the world outside of words. Speaking of realistic novelists, George Levine describes a quest similar to that of lawyers:

Realists take upon themselves a special role as mediator, and assume self-consciously a moral burden that takes a special form: their responsibility is to a reality that increasingly seems 'unnameable' . . . but it is also to an audience that requires to be weaned or freed from the misnaming literatures past and current. The quest for the world beyond words is deeply moral, suggesting the need to reorganize experience and reinvest it with value for a new audience reading from a new base of economic power.[34]

One could look to many sources, published and unpublished, for evidence of Victorian narrative jurisprudence attempting this task. Not only social problem fiction, but political journalism, court reports, trial transcripts and depositions bear signs of generic literary conventions, including along with realism, melodrama, sentimental and domestic romance, and sensation fiction. This material reveals the reciprocity between rationalistic and aesthetic forms of representation. That is, stories appealing to the emotions and imagination according to recognizable literary patterns abound in court records and spark rationalistic objections from those against whom they are used. For example, judges are recorded to have

---

[32] Patrick Joyce, 'The Constitution and the Narrative of Victorian Politics' in Vernon (ed.), n. 28 above, 187–8.

[33] Michael McKeon, *The Origins of the English Novel, 1600–1740* (Baltimore, 1987), 20.

[34] George Levine, *The Realistic Imagination: English Fiction from Frankenstein to Lady Chatterly's Lover* (Chicago, 1981), 12.

wept at the melodramatic stories of seduced and abandoned girls who were forced to murder the babies they could not afford to feed, and medical men, determined to stem a perceived flood of infanticides, were scandalized at the courts' chivalric susceptibilities and imperviousness to empirical medical evidence.[35] Dickens himself appears to have been gullible when it came to such storytelling. Candidates for admission to Urania House for magdalens soon learned that its benefactor Mr Dickens was sympathetic towards women who told a good tale of wronged honour and piteous victimization along the lines of such popular melodramas as *Black-eyed Susan* (1829) or novels like Scott's *The Heart of Midlothian* (1818).[36] Conversely, authors of social problem fiction, although they borrowed heavily from romance and melodrama, also made appeals to empirical evidence, including eyewitness accounts, but especially Parliamentary Blue Books (first sold to the public in 1836) and surveys undertaken by charities. Arguably it was precisely the availability of such empirical data that enabled women to author politically significant narratives. As Joseph Kestner remarks, '[f]iction "founded on fact" provided middle-class women not only with "something to do", for which Florence Nightingale pleaded in *Cassandra*, but with something important to do ... Writing social fiction allowed women, although not enfranchised, to participate in the legislative process'.[37] A politically diverse group of women turned fact into fiction, including Elizabeth Gaskell, Charlotte Elizabeth Tonna, Frances Trollope, and Elizabeth Stone. What is more, those life-stories published by women to protest their treatment before the law, such as Caroline Norton's *Letter to the Queen on Lord Cranworth's Marriage and Divorce Bill* (1854) or Rosina Bulwer Lytton's *Blighted Life* (1880), steeped rational argument and factual evidence in those literary conventions which made stories persuasive, both sentimental and rationalistic.

This picture of Victorian narrative jurisprudence includes a

---

[35] Christine L. Krueger, 'Literary Defenses and Medical Prosecutions: Representing Infanticide in Nineteenth-Century Britain' (1997) 40 *Victorian Studies* 271–94.

[36] For a discussion of the narratives of applicants to London charitable institutions for fallen women, see Anna Clark, *Women's Silence, Men's Violence: Sexual Assault in England 1770–1845* (London, 1987), 77–89.

[37] Kestner, n. 7 above, 13.

decision-making elite prone to aestheticism and sentimentality and disenfranchised storytellers who resort to narrative in order to get a hearing for their empirically verifiable claims. How is it that we have come to see storytelling and legal reasoning as mutually exclusive, so much so that a whole movement now devotes itself to reconnecting them? And, remembering the circumstances under which they were once joined, why—if they are separated—should we desire their reunion?

The origins of their separation as a legal principle are generally located in Benthamite legal positivism. Although the degree of Bentham's influence on nineteenth-century jurisprudence has been questioned by Philip Schofield and others, his views on fiction and evidence nevertheless offer a useful perspective on Victorian narrative jurisprudence.[38] As Bentham saw it, law was shot through with fictions designed to disguise the 'sinister interests' of a ruling elite. He complained bitterly of the pernicious legal fiction that judges merely proclaimed the common law rather than made law through their interpretations. Judicial interpretation meant for Bentham that judges were *de facto* legislators—unelected and largely unaccountable. Perhaps judges were the unacknowledged poets of the world. For Bentham, developing a science of law had gone hand in hand with legislative and legal reform. Placing substantive law on a scientific footing meant replacing legislation that served 'sinister interests' with laws that promoted the greatest happiness of the greatest number. Codification of the common law and rational rules of evidence could hold jurists in check.

Influenced by Bentham, thinkers from William Godwin to Sir James Fitzjames Stephen registered alarm at the influence print culture had on public opinion and the new threat this posed to legal and political processes. As early as the 1790s, the explosion of political journals, ranging from Tory to Radical, was shattering the myth of a unified society and the possibility of public discourse founded on shared interests. Godwin, who in *Political Justice* (1793) had welcomed the democratizing power of print

---

[38] Sir Henry Sumner Maine may be the original source of the claim for Bentham's influence on English law (*Ancient Law*, London, 1930, 90). Sir William Holdsworth concurred in *A History of English Law* (London, 1922–66), Vol. 13, 42. Recent scholarship has questioned Bentham's impact: see, e.g., Philip Schofield, 'Jeremy Bentham and Nineteenth-Century English Jurisprudence' (1991) 12 *Journal of Legal History* 61–2.

culture, in his novel *Caleb Williams* (1794) represented the infection of that culture by the same sinister interests that democracy hoped to root out.[39] A generation later, Sir James Fitzjames Stephen was expending a fair measure of his remarkable energy on literary criticism bemoaning the pernicious effect of novels on public debate.

Stephen put his faith in rules of evidence to protect the law from this new product of consumer capitalism. Rules of evidence in law were meant to produce the 'reasonable man' out of individual judges and jury men by dictating a reasoning process that would ensure just decisions by which others could live. Troubling that procedural solution in the Victorian period was, among other things, a growing suspicion that the reasonable man might not be a universally competent decision-maker after all, but lacked the capacity to judge the motives and actions of women. Illustrative is Harriet Taylor Mill's complaint in *The Enfranchisement of Women* (1851) that women were never tried by a jury of their peers. Men, having legislated women's inferior status, were thereby incompetent to judge them. Thus was the disunity of political interests revealed and produced by mass print culture and the promulgation of theories of representative democracy made an epistemological problem.

The daunting problem of negotiating among alternative realities was a leading concern of realistic fiction. Charles Reade, trained barrister-turned-novelist and social reformer, expressed this view when he commented on a woman's conviction for murder, 'it is the misfortune of women that few men, except one or two writers of fiction, can put themselves in a woman's place, and so qualify themselves to judge her . . .'[40] Unlike many of his contemporaries, including Thomas Carlyle and George Eliot, Reade did not see literary representation as a substitute for legal representation. He argued that equal treatment under the law could be achieved if the rules of evidence were applied impartially to women, if juries considered evidence relevant to women's motives and actions as they routinely did for men. The author of

[39] Garrett A. Sullivan, Jr, ' "A Story to Be Hastily Gobbled Up": *Caleb Williams* and Print Culture' (1993) 32 *Studies in Romanticism* 332.

[40] Charles Reade, *Readiana: Comments on Current Events* (London, 1883), 260.

fiction, expert at taking the experience of others, part of that world hitherto beyond words, and through fiction, bringing it into representation and thereby valuation, should be the ideal legal reasoner.

In his own social problem fiction, Reade pursued Bentham's goal of exposing the 'sinister motives' of legislators and jurists. He believed that they could be checked through publicity. 'In England', Reade remarked, ' "Justice" is the daughter of "Publicity" '.[41] Public trials, therefore, were the surest guarantee of social justice and novels were forums for trying cases in the court of public opinion. *Hard Cash*, Reade's 1863 novel attacking the lunacy laws, is a prime example of the sort of story meant to elicit sympathy for a disenfranchised subject. The novel fictionalizes an actual legal case involving a young man named Fletcher, who had escaped from the asylum where his family had incarcerated him for what Reade discovered were financial motives. Reade's agitation on Fletcher's behalf led to a Chancery lunacy inquiry, which resulted in the restoration of Fletcher's rights and property.

Just as public trials were the surest guarantee of justice, novels were legitimate courts of public opinion. For example, in *Hard Cash*, at the peak of his protagonist's frustration in the lunatic asylum, Reade addresses the reader:

Chained sane amongst the mad; on his wedding-day; expecting with tied hands the sinister acts of the soul-murderers who had the power to make their lie truth! We can paint the body writhing vainly against its unjust bonds; but who can paint the loathing, agonized, soul in a mental situation so ghastly? For my part I feel it in my heart of hearts; but am impotent to convey it to others; impotent, impotent.

Pray think of it yourselves, men and women, if you have not *sworn* never to think over a novel. Think of it for your own sakes; Alfred's turn to-day, it may be yours tomorrow.[42]

Like a barrister summing up before a jury, Reade asks his readers—men and women—to make a sympathetic identification with the protagonist's plight, and to attach their self-interest to his. Declaring his impotence to paint the particulars of Alfred's mental state, the limitations of his powers of representation, Reade

---

[41] Reade, n. 40 above, 116.
[42] Charles Reade, *Hard Cash*, 2 vols. (London, 1863), II, 289.

enjoins his readers to accept his character's situation as paradigmatic, filling in the details of his suffering from their own imaginations.

Sir James Fitzjames Stephen included Reade among the novelists of whom he complained in the pages of the *Saturday Review*
that their sensationalistic and polemical renderings of contemporary issues rendered productive political discussion impossible.
Still, while Stephen appears never to have changed his mind
regarding Dickens, he recommended *Hard Cash* to his wife for its
'realism'.[43] Arguably, what satisfied Stephen about *Hard Cash*
was not its coherent plotting, nor its concrete detail, but the accuracy Reade brought to his account of court proceedings. One
might also speculate that, unlike Reade's famous novels of prison
life, this novel featured a normative legal actor—a propertied
male—who has been wrongfully deprived of the autonomy,
agency, and powers of self-representation that attach to his status.
What is more, although statute law is blamed for this injustice,
Reade presents the courts as the champions of civil rights and
common sense. It may not be surprising, then, that Stephen—a
propertied male soon to become a jurist himself—found *Hard
Cash* congenial, though we may wonder what his wife made of it.

We know what Rosina Bulwer Lytton—the novelist, wife of
Edward Bulwer Lytton, and daughter of the feminist Anna
Wheeler—thought of *Hard Cash* and Reade's involvement in the
Fletcher case. She had been wrongfully incarcerated in a lunatic
asylum by her husband, and released thanks to a public outcry
raised by her friends. In the wake of *Hard Cash*, she sent Reade a
lengthy account of her own ordeal in the hope that he would enlist
public support for her in her battles with Bulwer over money and
access to their son. In that account, not published until 1880 after
Bulwer's death, Rosina blamed her troubles on a conspiracy of
jurists, doctors, and novelists—headed by the Queen, whom she
described as 'our little selfish, sensuous, inane and carnal Queen'.[44]
According to Rosina, Charles Dickens, editor of the periodical in
which *Hard Cash* was serialized, friend of Bulwer and Dr John
Connoly (who had signed Rosina's lunacy certificate), was 'a

---

[43] K. J. M. Smith, *James Fitzjames Stephen: Portrait of a Victorian Rationalist*
(Cambridge, 1988), 16–18, 47.

[44] Rosina Bulwer Lytton, *A Blighted Life*, with an Introduction by Marie
Mulvey Roberts, (Bristol, 1994), 42.

patent humbug'. 'Whenever the literary element enters', she complained, 'their *comeraderie* [*sic*], expediency, clap-trap, treachery, moral cowardice and concrete meanness are sure to follow'.[45] As far as Rosina Bulwer Lytton was concerned, fiction writing alone did nothing to qualify a man to sympathize with the persecuted. Indeed, the writer of *Hard Times* had himself threatened his own wife with incarceration in a lunatic asylum. Before Reade could do anything on Rosina Bulwer Lytton's behalf, part of her story was leaked and published. Because Bulwer had earlier demanded that his wife sign an agreement to publish no further accounts of their troubles, he threatened to sue. She was defeated. She published a retraction and moved to the Continent.

In this instance of Victorian narrative jurisprudence, the sort of sympathetic identification for which stories are valued appears to have been as much constrained by gender as was the law. Although Rosina Bulwer Lytton owed her freedom from the asylum to the *Daily Telegraph* and her vocal friends, her husband's legal status enabled him to silence her. John Sutherland has argued that Reade's principal effort on Rosina's behalf was *Hard Cash* itself. Dickens mysteriously delayed its publication in *All the Year Round* from 1862 to 1863, perhaps when he discovered the novel's subject matter and realized the insult to Bulwer, Connoly, and himself.[46] Nonetheless, *Hard Cash* makes its case on behalf of the decidedly insider propertied male.

Victorian feminist narrative jurisprudence is preoccupied with women's silence before the law. Time and again, female novelists use trial scenes not for vindication, as Reade did, but to dramatize the fact that no matter how realistic—that is, coherent, detailed, concrete—a story women tell, they are subject to *ad feminam* attacks. They are, *ipso facto*, not credible witnesses.[47] What should be remembered, however, is that many of these writers are aware of gender as a cultural discourse, as potent a force in literature as in law. What is more, while literature constitutes for some women writers a peculiarly feminine mode of representation, others recognize that it is a domain allowed to them precisely because of its inferior political and epistemological status. In such

---

[45] Lytton, n. 44 above, 4.   [46] Sutherland, n. 17 above, 55–86.

[47] Christine L. Krueger, 'Witnessing Women: Trial Testimony in Novels by Tonna, Gaskell and Eliot' in Heinzelman and Wiseman, n. 7 above, 337–55.

writers one finds storytelling used to agitate for non-fictional, empirical modes of representation.

Elizabeth Gaskell, who, in her first social problem novel *Mary Barton* (1848), had announced her plan to speak for the dumb masses of the labouring poor, seems to have developed a more sophisticated sense of storytelling politics through her own encounters with the public controversy which met her three social problem novels.[48] This is evident in her story about what is surely women's most traumatic encounter with the law historically, namely, the witch trials. Gaskell's 1859 story *Lois the Witch*, set in Salem during the 1691–2 trials, focuses on the danger of public sentiment informed by storytelling, and its power to override legal processes to the detriment of 'outsiders'. Gaskell incorporates the rich historiography of witchcraft in this tale of a young orphaned English woman sent to live with her Salem relatives, including the Romantic tendency to aestheticize witchcraft. She advocates storytelling not, however, as an explanatory technique where rational analysis has failed, but as a prompt to the empirical imagination.

Running throughout *Lois the Witch* are incidents of storytelling and interpretation. One story told is of an attack on Marblehead by French pirates, who took a woman prisoner. Despite the woman's cries for help, no one attempted a rescue and she died. During the crisis, an old blind and deaf woman stood up and pronounced a curse on the people of Marblehead and their descendants for their cowardly abandonment of the woman. According to the story, the people still hear the woman's cries in the marsh 'Lord Jesu! have mercy on me! Save me from the power of man O Lord Jesu!'[49] The audience for this story offer several examples of politically dangerous interpretations. Two young girls find in the woman's plight and the idea of a curse a thrilling sensation. A church elder responds to the story by attempting to erase both gender and injustice from the account, and treats it as an example of Satan's efforts to test the people of Marblehead. His displacement prompts a direct contradiction from the Widow Smith, an old woman who enjoys an authority unusual for women of her community, the narrator tells us: because of her goodness

---

[48] See Uglow, n. 9 above, 216–18.
[49] Elizabeth Gaskell, *Lois the Witch* in Angus Easson (ed.), *Cousin Phillis and Other Tales* (Oxford, 1981), 113.

of heart, she is 'allowed a liberty of speech which was tacitly denied to many, under penalty of being esteemed ungodly if they infringed certain conventional limits'.[50] 'It was no vision', she retorts; 'they were real living men who went ashore, men who broke down branches and left their footmarks on the ground'.[51] The Widow Smith cites forensic details—the broken branches and the footprints—as evidence that a real crime has taken place against a real woman. In so far as the people of Marblehead are cursed, it is in the commitment of storytellers—in this instance, female witnesses and female storytellers—to recalling precisely what happened. The power of his story lies in its reference to empirical facts.

For Gaskell, there is comfort—or at least some hope—in hard facts. Before dismissing her as a naive positivist, it is worth understanding what she means by this term. When Lois first arrives in Boston, exhausted, lonely, and fearful, the captain of her ship attempts to cheer her by 'talk[ing] on about the hard facts, connected with the life that lay before her ... and perhaps', the narrator comments, 'Lois was more brightened by this style of conversation, and the new ideas it presented to her, than she would have been by the tenderest woman's sympathy'.[52] Later, Captain Holderness counters a story Lois has heard about Satan's forces in the wilderness with an objective account of the battles among the French, English, and Indians and their causes. Unlike the story of Satanic forces, his story resists explanation where evidence is lacking. Such a story made up of 'hard facts' in Gaskell's sense, is valuable because it warns us of present danger but it does not mythologize the danger and thereby rob us of an effective agency. By contrast, storytelling that claims extraordinary empathic powers—the ability to read others' minds— conceals sinister motives and fuels the fanaticism and hatred that leads to Lois' execution as a witch. As Gaskell presents it, for motives far more complex and unrepresentable than misogyny, the citizens of Salem abandoned the rules of a just society. Empathy, to be meaningful, is the effect, not the cause of an ethical principle—for Gaskell, a 'hard fact'. Therefore, the rhetoric of her storytelling is put in the service of a defence of the rule of law. 'Hard

---

[50] Gaskell, n. 49 above, 111–12.   [51] Gaskell, n. 49 above, 114.
[52] Gaskell, n. 49 above, 108.

facts' point us outside the story to what remains unrepresented and, perhaps, unintelligible.

Gaskell's position arises out of realism itself, which gestures to a world outside itself by marking the artificiality of its own coherent form. Whereas Drucilla Cornell, or Roberto Unger, sees the aesthetic in the moment of social commitment, Elizabeth Gaskell, herself disenfranchised and a spokeswoman for the downtrodden, sees an encounter with brute embodied experience as the foundation of commitment and fears the aestheticization of cruelty, power, and fanaticism.[53] She interrupts her story, as George Levine puts it speaking of realism generally, 'to avoid the inevitable conventionality of language in pursuit of the unattainable unmediated reality'.[54] By so doing, Levine continues, '[t]he realistic novel persistently drives us itself to question not only the nature of artificially imposed social relations, but the nature of nature, and the nature of the novel'.[55]

Two conclusions for narrative jurisprudence might be drawn. The first is that information becomes intelligible, narratable, readable as a story because, in Bernard Jackson's phrase, it can be placed within a 'framework of existing social knowledge'.[56] If narrative jurisprudence seeks to transform that framework, what it might consider valuing about storytelling is neither its coherence, nor an artful postmodern incoherence, but how stories gesture outside themselves towards what they cannot accommodate. Practically speaking, what are the details that resist coherence and aestheticization? I give you as an example the suicide note of Eliza Clark, entered into evidence by Eliza Gorman, at her niece's trial for the murder of her children at the Central Criminal Court on 15 May 1846. Clark had been discovered preparing to jump off of Battersea bridge, from which she had just thrown her three children. The note was addressed to Clark's husband:

---

[53] See, for example, Drucilla Cornell, 'Toward a Modern/Postmodern Reconstruction of Ethics' (1985) 133 *University of Pennsylvania Law Review* 291–380, and Roberto Mangabeira Unger, *Knowledge and Politics* (New York, 1976), 232.

[54] Levine, n. 34 above, 8.

[55] Levine, n. 34 above, 21.

[56] Bernard S. Jackson, 'Narrative Theories and Legal Discourse' in Christopher Nash (ed.), *Narrative in Culture: the Uses of Storytelling in the Sciences, Philosophy, and Literature* (London, 1990), 30.

Now my *Jemmy*, you need not give me any more of your threats, because I do not need them, and I hope the next wife you get, you will know how to use *them*, and not act a brute to them as you have to me, and bid me good-bye in the morning, and come home at night and knock my head through the panel of the door, and break my rest the whole night, and swear in the morning that he would come home drunk and kill me, and I would rather prefer seeing my children go before me, and then I shall know that they did not starve. And if you go to Battersea bridge you will find the children there.[57]

Clark was declared not guilty by reason of insanity. Her story was not suppressed; nor did it fail to elicit sympathy; categorizing it as insanity meant that it just didn't bring about any meaningful change.

My second conclusion is that, despite the exclusionary rules of evidence drawn up in the course of the nineteenth century, Victorian narrative jurisprudence may have succeeded too well in the court of public opinion.[58] Our culture is not lacking in narrative representations soliciting sympathy for the Eliza Clarks among us. But public opinion shaped by mass-marketed sentiments does not necessarily produce the public will to change those material conditions. And conditions still exist wherein Eliza Clark's decision might strike some of us as rational. Locating narrative jurisprudence in its Victorian history highlights, as Cythia V. Ward puts it, 'a serious underlying political problem that is largely masked by vague endorsements of empathic understanding'.[59] What we lack in public decision-making, perhaps as opposed to courts of law, is not stories that help us to empathize; if anything, those have become even more commodified in the age of mass-media agony shows, while voter participation in the United States is nearing an all-time low. Rather, we lack interest in analyses of material conditions and the will to change those conditions. By the time Eliza Clark appears in Central Criminal Court, hard facts have overtaken any narrative on which the law could act.

---

[57] *Central Criminal Court Minutes of Evidence*, Vol. XXIV (London, 1846), 28.

[58] For a recent discussion, see C. J. W. Allen, *The Law of Evidence in Victorian England* (Cambridge, 1997).

[59] Cynthia V. Ward, 'A Kinder, Gentler Liberalism? Visions of Empathy in Feminist and Communitarian Literature' (1994) 61 *University of Chicago Law Review* 954.

What literary history might contribute to narrative jurisprudence, finally, is an incentive for negotiating with its critics, particularly those in the law and economics movement. While it is doubtless galling that the discussion of law and literature seems preoccupied with such texts as Richard Posner's *Law and Literature*, it might also be argued that the continuing engagement between the two late twentieth-century manifestations of the aesthetic-rationalistic dialectic has produced some salutary revisions, including on Judge Posner's part.[60] In Martha Nussbaum's view, imagination is a supplement to rule-based reasoning, and, I would add, other forms of knowing, namely analysis of empirical data and logical deduction.[61] When one of the founders of the law and literature movement, Richard Weisberg, turns to the holocaust, he reminds us of the enduring importance of 'hard facts'.[62] Maintaining the negotiations between the world of words and the world of things that was the hallmark of both Victorian literary realism and liberal democratic theory. Rather than demonize empiricism as the enemy of narrative, we might do well to remember our common goals and encourage a popular legal culture which engages the public imagination in representations of the full scope of human experience. Without this continued negotiation, narrative jurisprudence would signal a current crisis in democratic justice, as it may have done for the Victorians.[63]

[60] In *Overcoming Law*, n. 12 above, Richard A. Posner writes, 'Emotion can clarify as well as fog understanding. If, for example, an advocate's appeal to the emotions induces in the judge or juror an empathetic understanding of a victim's or an accused wrongdoer's motives, drives, and beliefs, the appeal may enable the tribunal to form a more accurate impression of essential facts and so render a more just judgment' (511).

[61] Nussbaum, n. 6 above, xvi. Nussbaum dedicates this book to her 'intellectual adversary', Richard A. Posner, 'who was in many ways [the first Rosenthal] lecture's Mr Gradgrind' (xi).

[62] See, for example, Weisberg, n. 4 above, 143–87, and *Vichy Law and Holocaust France* (New York, 1996).

[63] I am grateful to Rowan McWilliam and George Justice for their advice on this essay and to Maria Keaton for her valuable research assistance.

'BORN PIOUS, LITERARY, AND LEGAL'[1] LORD COLERIDGE'S CRITICISMS IN LAW AND LITERATURE

Ray Geary

Introduction

Any consideration of the career of Lord Chief Justice Coleridge invokes a mystery. Why, despite all his achievements, was that career not deemed to have been a success? His obituary in *The Times*[2] offered only a grudging appreciation of his accomplishments. When his friends referred to him they constantly felt the need to apologize on his behalf, and one summary of his career opined that, 'posterity will probably with difficulty understand his importance in his own day'.[3] In fact on any consideration of his achievements alone the opposite view is more aptly the case. As a lawyer Coleridge was one of the most prominent barristers of his day; he was an important liberal politician, he held high political office as Solicitor-General and then Attorney-General, and he occupied the position of Lord Chief Justice of England. He was involved in many of the leading cases of his day, either as counsel or judge, and in the latter capacity delivered judgments that are still leading authorities today. In addition, he was prominent in the Victorian literary world, having early in his career written literary reviews of some of the most influential authors of his day, and later maintaining close connections with many of the leading

---

[1] *Vanity Fair*, 5 March 1887.
[2] 'Death of Lord Coleridge', *The Times*, 15 June 1894, 10.
[3] V. Gibbs (ed.), *The Complete Peerage*, 14 vols. (London, 1913), III, 372.

literary figures, as well as speaking and writing on literature. Such prominence in both the literary and legal worlds would normally have been expected to attract a due recognition of his talents. His accomplishments and honours were listed, but they were not granted an unqualified appreciation, and that view has permeated down to the present day. What was it that raised the suspicions of his contemporaries and still clouds our appreciation of him today?

In this paper it is argued that the mystery can be resolved by an understanding of his temperament as it was reflected in his literary and legal style, and that this can be achieved through an analysis of his literary criticisms and legal judgments. Coleridge's personality, training and experience all inclined him towards adopting the style of the advocate, an adversarial position, in whatever endeavour he undertook. While this brought him conspicuous success as a barrister, it was inappropriate in his roles as a critic and judge. Allied to this was an imperious nature that prevented Coleridge being able to perceive the hostility and hurt that this style evoked, and also an instinctive resentment on his part at any suggestion of his probity being called into question. The offence that Coleridge caused was through a matter of style, however, rather than through personal malice. Moreover, this was unappreciated by those who had been offended by his condemnations, apart from those who knew him well. The result was a mutual incomprehension by Coleridge and those whom he had offended.

Although other lawyers and critics were crossing the legal and literary boundaries at a less exalted level, Coleridge was unique as a Lord Chief Justice in having been so involved in literature, and as a literary critic in assuming so high a judicial office. By comparing his literary criticisms with his legal judgments and summations his style becomes manifest, stark in the case of the criticisms, and more subdued in the case of the judgments. The style of the literary criticism helps to illuminate his later legal judgments and summations, and equally the latter help to mitigate the harshness of the criticisms. They were written at totally different times and in different contexts, but taken together they form a clearer image of Coleridge as a man and as a judge. In addition they provide an example of the interconnectedness of the Victorian legal and literary worlds, and also illustrate the remarkable odyssey that Coleridge undertook as regards his religious convictions, the results of which are still resonant today. In order to illustrate this, this paper first outlines his career, and then examines Coleridge's contributions to literary criticism and his judicial utterances respectively, particularly as they reflect the changes in his religious persuasions.

Lord Coleridge

John Duke Coleridge was born in 1820, the great nephew of Samuel Taylor Coleridge, and the son of Sir John Taylor Coleridge. His father was himself a distinguished judge and had contributed literary criticisms to the *British Critic* and the *Quarterly Review*, and had acted as editor of the *Quarterly Review*. Sir John Coleridge had also edited Blackstone's *Commentaries*[4] and written a biography of John Keble,[5] who was a close friend and godfather to the younger Coleridge, and one of the leaders, along with E. B. Pusey and John Henry Newman, of the Oxford, or Tractarian, Movement. This was the attempt to bring about a revival of the High Church ideals of the late seventeenth century to the modern Anglican Church, but which was to result in the conversion of a considerable number of Anglicans to the Roman Catholic Church, including Newman and Coleridge's brother, Henry. Like his father, Coleridge attended Eton and Oxford University. It was at Oxford that he began to develop friendships that were to have a lasting significance for him. Among his contemporaries were the poets A. H. Clough and Matthew Arnold, and it was at Oxford that Coleridge first came under the influence of John Henry Newman. That influence was to have a profound effect on his religious beliefs and to determine the content of much of his literary criticism.

Coleridge graduated from Oxford in 1842 and was called to the Bar in 1846. Although he was facilitated by his father's reputation and connections, his earnings at the Bar were not sufficient for his needs, particularly as he had married in 1846. His father had previously recorded that he had written his own reviews, 'more for profit than anything else'.[6] Coleridge adopted a similar strategy and began to write for a number of periodicals, but

---

[4] Sir W. Blackstone, *Commentaries on the Laws of England*, 4 vols. (16th edn, London, 1825).

[5] Sir J. Coleridge, *A Memoir of the Rev John Keble* (London, 1869; 4th edn, London, 1874).

[6] E. Coleridge, *Life and Correspondence of John Duke Lord Coleridge, Lord Chief Justice of England*, 2 vols. (London, 1904), I, 13.

particularly for the High Church newspapers the *Christian Remembrancer* and the *Guardian*.[7]

At the same time his career as a barrister was slowly prospering and he was gaining a reputation as an advocate, a strong physical presence being allied to a powerful oratory style that appealed to the Victorian appreciation of a style that combined literary taste with sentimental rhetoric, strong reasoning, and pathos. In 1853 he had unsuccessfully defended George Sparks on a charge of murder and in attempting to save his client from the gallows had concluded his speech by reciting extensively from *Othello*.[8] The first case to bring him to national prominence, however, occurred in 1857, when he appeared for the prosecution in the case of Thomas Pooley,[9] who was charged with blasphemy, before Sir John Coleridge. Pooley was convicted but later found to be insane and pardoned, but in the interim John Stuart Mill had used the case to illustrate in his essay 'On Liberty' how public opinion could still be suppressed by the rigours of the criminal law.[10] In a review of 'On Liberty' in *Fraser's Magazine* Henry Buckle launched a sustained attack on the conduct of Sir John Coleridge and, by implication, his son. The accusation was that they had colluded to secure the conviction of a poor, demented man of a crime that, had it been committed by someone in a higher social position, would have escaped censure.[11] John Duke Coleridge responded with a strident letter to *Fraser's Magazine*, but what appears to have rankled so strongly with Coleridge was not that his understanding of the law was being criticized, but that his standing as a gentleman and his probity as a barrister were being questioned. Coleridge wrote, 'It is hard that a gentleman should have to touch such dirty stuff as this ... But Mr Buckle will perhaps understand me when I say that, besides not knowing me, he does not comprehend the common feelings of a gentleman, nor the first principles which actuate the high profession to which it is my pride and honour to belong'.[12] He was a man very conscious

---

7 Coleridge, *Life*, n. 6 above, I, 205.
8 Coleridge, *Life*, n. 6 above, I, 200. The Sparks case was not reported.
9 R. v. *Pooley* (1857) 8 State Tr. NS 1089.
10 J. S. Mill, 'On Liberty' (London, 1859; Harmondsworth, 1974), 90.
11 H. Buckle, 'Mill on Liberty' (1859) *Fraser's Magazine* 533.
12 Lord Coleridge, 'Mr Buckle and Sir John Coleridge' (1859) *Fraser's Magazine* 638.

of his own position, demanding of himself and expecting others to display the same probity. As his biographer found, 'He set up for himself, and placed before others, a higher standard than a difficult temper, an impetuous temperament, could always reach'.[13] The controversy that resulted from the Pooley case did not prevent Coleridge from consolidating his position as a barrister and he continued to appear in a series of widely publicized cases. These included the libel cases of *Hunter* v. *Sharpe*[14] and *Risk Allah Bey* v. *Whitehurst*,[15] and 'the convent case' of *Saurin* v. *Starr*, which his father considered 'placed him on the very pinnacle of reputation as an advocate, both for thought and comprehensive grasp, and for language and manner'.[16]

The most public case in which he appeared was, however, that of the Tichborne claimant that lasted for 102 days between 1871 and 1872 (the case was not reported). Coleridge appeared for the trustees of the Tichborne estate, who alleged that the apparent heir to the estate was an imposter. His cross-examination of the claimant lasted twenty-two days and he then proceeded to open the case for the defendants with a speech lasting twenty-three days. During the course of this speech George Eliot, with whom Coleridge was acquainted, attended the trial and commented:

We have been to hear Coleridge addressing the jury on the Tichborne trial—a very interesting occasion to me. He is a marvellous speaker among Englishmen, has an exquisitely melodious voice, perfect gesture, and a power of keeping the thread of his syntax to the end of his sentences, which make him delightful to follow . . . The digest of the evidence which Coleridge gives, is one of the best illustrations of the value or valuelessness of testimony that could be given.[17]

That case confirmed Coleridge's pre-eminent position as a barrister, and the phrase that he had constantly employed 'Would you be surprised to hear?' became widely quoted. He had also widened his endeavours, having entered Parliament as the Liberal Member for Exeter in 1865. From this point he remained a loyal follower of Gladstone and his loyalty was rewarded with the Liberal election victory of 1868, when he was made Solicitor-General and

---

[13] Coleridge, *Life*, n. 6 above, II, 397. [14] (1866) 15 LT 421.
[15] (1868) 18 LT 615. [16] Coleridge, *Life*, n. 6 above, II, 145.
[17] G. S. Haight (ed.), *The George Eliot Letters*, 7 vols. (New Haven, 1955), V, 243.

then Attorney-General in 1871. In 1873 Coleridge was appointed Chief Justice of the Common Pleas and the following year raised to the Peerage as Baron Coleridge of Ottery St Mary. He became Lord Chief Justice of England in 1880.

To that position he brought fixed opinions on matters other than those relating to the law. He had a strong aversion to the aristocracy, 'for anything is better than the public and private debasement which an aristocracy inflicts upon a nation'.[18] Similarly, he detested vivisection and was prominent in the campaign against the practice, claiming in an article: 'that even if it be admitted to be a means of gaining scientific knowledge, such knowledge is unlawful knowledge if it is pursued by means which are immoral; and that a disregard of all proportion between means and ends often makes both alike unlawful and indefensible'.[19] This is also a clear example of the deontological stance normally adopted by Coleridge in both his literary criticisms and in at least some of his legal judgments. A utilitarian approach was not one that he could countenance.

Coleridge achieved his most conspicuous success as an advocate. His years as Lord Chief Justice were clouded by criticisms of some of his judgments (even though in some areas of the law he made a significant and lasting contribution) and by personal embarrassment. In 1886 he suffered the indignity of having to appear as a defendant in a libel action brought by his son-in-law in the very court over which he presided as Lord Chief Justice.[20]

During his final years Coleridge continued to sit as Lord Chief Justice, despite poor health, and to cultivate the acquaintanceship of literary figures. Thomas Hardy records attending a dinner in 1892 where,

They were all men of law but myself—mostly judges. Their stories, so old and boring to one another, were all new to me, and I was delighted. Hawkins told me his experiences in the Tichborne case ... Lord Coleridge (the cross-examiner in the same case, with his famous, 'Would you be surprised to hear?') was also anecdotic.[21]

[18] C. Yarnall, *Forty Years of Friendship* (London, 1911), 53.
[19] Lord Coleridge, 'The Nineteenth Century Defenders of Vivisection' (1882) *Fortnightly Review* 231.
[20] *The Times*, 17 to 26 November 1886.
[21] F. Hardy, *The Life of Thomas Hardy*, 2 vols. (London, 1933), II, 14.

Henry James was another acquaintence,[22] and it was towards such acquaintences, and to literature, that Coleridge increasingly turned in his later years before dying in 1894, still occupying the position of Lord Chief Justice.

The Literary Critic

Coleridge's period as a literary critic extended from 1849, when he became responsible for the literary department of the *Guardian*, until 1856. This period coincided with his early years as a barrister, and in both professions he was attempting to hone the adversarial skills of the advocate. In his reviews Coleridge did not consider his role to be that of the dispassionate critic, but rather that of the aroused advocate. When he perceived moral or religious contagion his role was to highlight it in the strongest possible terms and to minimize any merits that the work under consideration might appear to possess. It was not for him to consider the case of the author, unless it was to be raised only to be demolished, just as it was not his role to concede the strengths of the case of the opposing counsel in court.

For example, in a review of *Yeast* by Charles Kingsley in 1851, Coleridge found some avenues for praise. He admitted 'the great artistic power of the writer', 'eloquent and imaginative expressions', and 'real pains to master the causes of our social evils', but he then continued:

Even as a literary work, 'Yeast' is very unsatisfactory . . . But a far graver than any literary error is the general tone of the writing on moral and religious subjects . . . Above all, we are utterly at issue with him in an opinion which is implied throughout the volume, that a certain amount of youthful profligacy does no real and permanent harm to the character: perhaps strengthens it for a useful and even religious life; and that the existence of the passions is a proof that they are to be gratified.[23]

Kingsley indignantly replied with a letter to the *Guardian*, declaring that the review had consisted of calumnies, tendentious argument and a total misrepresentation of his true position. It concluded each point with the words, *Mentiris impudentissime*.[24]

---

[22] L. Edel, *Henry James—Letters*, 4 vols. (London, 1980), III, 258.
[23] The *Guardian*, 7 May 1851, 332.
[24] F. E. Kingsley, *Charles Kingsley: His Letters and Memories of his Life* (London, 1877; 4th edn, London, 1877), 283.

Coleridge responded in the same manner as he had with Buckle; his probity had been called into question and he indignantly replied, 'I should be very glad to think that I was mistaken on this matter, but the author's calling me a liar fails to convince me'.[25]

When he came to review Charlotte Brontë's *Villette* in 1853 she was still writing under the pseudonym of Currer Bell, despite the success of her previous novels, *Jane Eyre* (1847) and *Shirley* (1849). Again, Coleridge found the position adopted on religious and moral questions to be objectionable, considering that, 'These faults—and faults like these, moral as well as artistic—at present prevent Currer Bell from attaining to that excellence which her powers might enable her to reach; and from the perusal of these volumes we fear that she is by no means on the road towards correcting them'.[26] For Coleridge the fact that the author's religious position did not accord with his own, which was still that of a convinced Tractarian, was sufficient to nullify the entire work.

Brontë's response was more mellow than that of Kingsley, since she considered that, 'Surely the poor *"Guardian"* critic has a right to lisp his opinion that Currer Bell's female characters do not realize his notion of ladyhood'.[27] She correctly considered that she had been a victim of the 'Puseyites',[28] as 'Currer Bell's remarks on Romanism have drawn down on him the condign displeasure of the High Church party, which displeasure has been unequivocally expressed through their principal organs—the *Guardian* . . . and the *Christian Remembrancer*'.[29]

It is only when he considers that there is no case to answer that Coleridge's acerbic tone disappears and he assumes a more muted tone, although when he does resort to this the result is portentous and lacklustre. This can be seen in Coleridge's review of the works of Charlotte Yonge, including her *Heir of Redclyffe* (1853), where he says of that novel that, ' "And when I rose I found myself in prayer" would be no unfitting sentence for the frame of mind in which most readers of any religious feeling will close this striking book'.[30] Such sentiments may have suited a Victorian audience, but

[25] Coleridge, *Life*, n. 6 above, I, 214.

[26] M. Allott, *The Brontës: The Critical Heritage* (London, 1974), 194.

[27] T. J. Wise and J. A. Symington, *The Brontës*, 4 vols. (Oxford, 1932), IV, 50.

[28] Wise and Symington, *The Brontës*, n. 27 above, IV, 58.

[29] C. Shorter, *The Brontës: Life and Letters*, 2 vols. (London, 1908), II, 315.

[30] Lord Coleridge, 'Miss Yonge's Novels' (1853) *Christian Remembrancer* 47.

they also enfeeble Coleridge's style. The strength of that style lies in the vehemence with which Coleridge castigated the supposed faults of what were, to him, his literary opponents. Without the opportunity of adopting an adversarial stance his reviews lose all power and interest, a situation that was to repeat itself in different circumstances when he became Lord Chief Justice. Before then, however, Coleridge was to demonstrate his natural style most markedly when he considered the works of two of the most significant stylists of the nineteenth century, Matthew Arnold and John Ruskin.

When Matthew Arnold published his *Poems* in 1853, the first volume to bear his name, he included a preface in which he set out his theory of poetry. Coleridge utterly repudiated his theory, considering it fallacious and arguing that,

As a general rule, it is a great mistake for a poet to commit himself to a theory of poetry. To theorise on poetry is not his vocation, and it is seldom that he has the intellectual qualities requisite for the work . . . it is the critic, not the artist, who is properly thus employed.[31]

He went on to provide a detailed criticism of what he perceived as being the faults of the preface. Other critics were also criticizing the preface, but, 'Of all the attacks on the preface the longest, and most thoroughgoing was the unaccountably vicious review by John Duke Coleridge'.[32] The ferocity of Coleridge can be accounted for by the fact that it was his habitual style, the style that he adopted as an advocate, rather than one motivated by personal animosity.

In terms of the poems themselves, Coleridge offered some unqualified praise, but he also had the tendency constantly to concede the merits that he perceived in them, only to modify the praise with a qualification: that they displayed taste and ability, but were imitative of other, greater, poets, including Milton, Wordsworth, and Tennyson; the wide learning and classical scholarship that they demonstrated inevitably led to obfuscation and affectation. There were, however, two graver charges contained within Coleridge's general criticisms. One related specifically to the poem 'Sohrab and Rustum', and one related to the collection as a whole.

---

[31] Lord Coleridge, 'Arnold's Poems' (1854) *Christian Remembrancer* 316.
[32] S. Coulling, *Matthew Arnold and His Critics* (Athens, Ohio, 1974), 48.

The specific charge was one of plagiarism, in which he alleged that the poem could have been derivative of an unacknowledged translation.[33] Arnold responded by adding a long note to 'Sohrab and Rustum' for the 1854 edition of his *Poems*. Here he repudiated the charge of plagiarism and set out precisely where he had obtained the material for the poem, before adding: 'It would have been more charitable, perhaps, had the reviewer, before making this good-natured suggestion, ascertained, by reference to M. Mohl's work, how far it was confirmed by the fact'.[34]

The second charge was not levelled against Arnold personally, but as an author who did not accord Christianity its rightful reverence within the scheme of his poetry:

The art that has no relevancy to actual life, that passes by God's truth and the facts of man's nature as if they had no existence, the art that does not seek to ennoble and purify and help us in our life-long struggle with sin and evil, however beautiful, however outwardly serene and majestic, is false, and poor, and contemptible.[35]

Arnold's answer was to write: 'My love to J.D.C., and tell him that the limited circulation of the "*Christian Remembrancer*" makes the unquestionable viciousness of his article of little importance. I am sure he will be gratified to think that it is so'.[36] Coleridge and Arnold were to remain life-long friends and Coleridge regretted the attack that he had launched on his friend. He later wrote of Arnold, 'Once his poems were reviewed by an intimate friend in a spirit which the reviewer soon bitterly repented; but though Matthew Arnold discovered his critic, and could not but dislike the criticism, it never interposed even the thinnest cloud between the friends'.[37] Coleridge was also to declare that, 'Mr Matthew Arnold is the most distinguished Englishman living'.[38]

John Ruskin also attracted Coleridge's ire at this time, with volumes III and IV of 'Modern Painters' being reviewed in the *Guardian* in 1856. Both reviews were hostile, the reason for which

---

[33] Coleridge, 'Arnold's Poems', n. 31 above, 321.
[34] M. Allott (ed.), *The Poems of Matthew Arnold* (2nd edn, London, 1979), 679.
[35] Coleridge, 'Arnold's Poems', n. 31 above, 331.
[36] G. Russell, *Letters of Matthew Arnold*, 2 vols. (London, 1895), I, 35.
[37] Lord Coleridge, 'Matthew Arnold' (1889) *The New Review* 122.
[38] Anon, 'Genius and Versatility' (1883) 49 *Macmillan's Magazine* 87.

was explained by Coleridge in correspondence with his friend, Ellis Yarnall. He began by expressing his admiration for Ruskin and for what he has previously done, and then proceeded to argue that Ruskin's style had become 'reckless and arrogant', that his judgment and his intellect were not equal to his instinct. Further, he maintained that the merits of the earlier volumes were being diminished by repetition and declining power. The most telling phrase is that, 'I was at Oxford with him, and I know what sort of a scholar he was'.[39]

Those reviews in 1856 effectively ended Coleridge's period as a literary critic, as the law began to demand more of his time and professional advancement eased his financial worries. In 1855 he had been appointed recorder of Portsmouth and in 1861 he became a QC. Looking back at his career he later admitted that the major faults that could be attributed to his reviews were that they, 'might be much better done and in a better temper'. His biographer considered that:

He was over-sensitive, and when he believed the principles which he held sacred were at stake and, less pardonably, when he smarted from real or imaginary wrongs done to himself, 'he shot out his arrows, even bitter words' . . . he was easily moved to wrath, and to speak and write words which could not be recalled, which were, sometimes, unjust, and always indiscreet.[40]

This fault was compounded by the style and language that he adopted in his reviews, in so far as they become that of the advocate advancing his case in a court of law; adversarial, carping, overemphasizing the strengths of his own position and diminishing or ignoring those of his opponent, the subject of the review.

As Lord Chief Justice, however, Coleridge was to arouse displeasure for both similar and different reasons. His style remained broadly similar, but there had been a significant change in his religious outlook. When he had written his literary criticisms Coleridge had done so in the certainty of his beliefs in the tenets of the High Church. But by 1861 he was writing, 'I get no help from Anglicanism for all my deepest and strongest needs',[41] and his biographer was describing him in 1870 as being 'an

[39] Yarnall, *Forty*, n. 18 above, 4.
[40] Coleridge, *Life*, n. 6 above, II, 398–9.
[41] Coleridge, *Life*, n. 6 above, I, 264.

advanced Broad Churchman'.[42] By 1880, when he became Lord
Chief Justice, Coleridge had completed his religious odyssey and it
was from a radically different religious perspective that his judgments and summations were enunciated.

Lord Chief Justice

Coleridge's judicial reputation steadily declined towards the end
of his life and it was later remarked that, 'His principal failing,
perhaps, was a tendency, more marked in later years, to let things
slide, to take no great trouble, and to find more pleasure in his
favourite authors than in the reports and the business of his
Court'.[43] His initial years in office, however, appear to have been
marked by a thoroughness that was later lacking in his judgments.
In 1883 he delivered the judgment in *Bradlaugh* v. *Newdegate*, a
case involving an action for the old tort of maintenance that arose
from Bradlaugh having sat and voted as an MP, despite not
having taken and subscribed the oath as he was required to do
under the Parliamentary Oaths Act 1866. This Bradlaugh was
unable to do because, as an atheist, he refused to take the oath on
the Bible. Coleridge found in favour of Bradlaugh and in the
process delivered a lucid exposition on the law of maintenance. As
he had 'no kind of sympathy'[44] with the opinions of Bradlaugh,
the restraint of the language of the judgment is notable for the
balance that it achieves and the tolerance that it displays towards
views that were inimical to his own. It also demonstrates that
Coleridge could be an exemplary expositor of the law when he felt
sufficiently interested to do so.

Two weeks earlier Bradlaugh had appeared before Coleridge on
a charge of blasphemous libel because he had allowed a publication, the *Freethinker*, to be published and sold from his premises
and it was alleged that that publication had contained blasphemous libels.[45] Bradlaugh was acquitted, but the publisher and editor
of the *Freethinker* subsequently appeared before Coleridge on the
same charge in the case of *R.* v. *Ramsey and Foote*.[46] This trial
has been described by the literary critic Joss Marsh as being, 'The

---

[42] Coleridge, *Life*, n. 6 above, II, 112.   [43] *The Times*, n. 2 above, 10.
[44] (1883) 11 QBD 1 at 14.
[45] *R.* v. *Bradlaugh and Others* (1883) 15 Cox CC 217.
[46] (1883) 15 Cox CC 231.

most "celebrated" blasphemy trial for over forty years—in terms of law and abiding consequences, of the whole century, indeed of modern times'.[47]

Foote and Ramsey did not deny that they had been responsible for the publication of the relevant numbers of the *Freethinker*, but argued that the material to which objections had been raised was not blasphemous. It was simply a denial of the truth of Christianity and of the Scriptures, and ridicule of the Hebrew idea of God. In this, they contended, they were going no further than other writers, including Charles Darwin, Thomas Huxley, John Stuart Mill and Matthew Arnold, and attempted to show this by reading extracts from their works. Foote argued that, 'Matthew Arnold . . . was in no fear of prosecution; it was the poorer and humbler Freethinkers who were to be made the scapegoats of refined and highly-cultivated agnostics'.[48] Coleridge considered that:

Now, as to this, let me say that, as I understand it, it is, and I believe always has been, the law; and at all events I now lay it down as law, that, if the decencies of controversy are observed, even the fundamentals of religion may be attacked without the writer being guilty of blasphemy. But no one can fail to see the difference between the works of the writers who have been quoted and the language used in the publications now before us.[49]

As a result of this case, as Lord Scarman stated in *R. v. Lemon*, 'Lord Coleridge CJ finally dispelled any further possibility of a mere denial of the truth of the Christian religion being treated as a blasphemous libel'.[50] The position established by Coleridge in this case was a remarkable one given the views that he had expressed in his literary criticisms. It had important ramifications for religion, literature, and the intellectual culture of the time. No longer was religion to be afforded special protection through the blasphemy laws. Religious faith was to be a matter of opinion as long as the 'decencies of controversy' were observed. Marsh has argued that, 'The gains in this for "serious" literature were clear. The Coleridge ruling signaled the change of climate that made possible a wave of agnostic and atheist confessional fictions and memoirs, from the 1880s through the fin de siècle'.[51]

---

[47] J. Marsh, *Word Crimes* (Chicago, 1998), 144.
[48] *The Times*, 25 April 1883, 6.   [49] (1883) 15 Cox CC 231 at 238.
[50] [1979] 1 All ER 898 at 924.   [51] Marsh, *Word*, n. 47 above, 201.

In a wider context it was also legitimating and embracing many of the scientific and philosophical developments of the Victorian era. As Huxley's biographer, Desmond, has argued, Coleridge

was an FRS, inducted into the Royal Society by Huxley himself; more, he was a friend who relished Huxley's complimentary books. Through this suave old boy, high society was throwing a protective cloak around its agnostic elite. It was redrawing the red line, redefining the class divide. It was permitting its aristocrats of intellect to question Christianity, while threatening rougher working-class attacks.[52]

It has also been suggested that the 1892 dinner that Coleridge attended with Thomas Hardy, referred to above, may have been an occasion when Coleridge's possible anecdotes on Ramsey and Foote, and also Pooley, may have influenced Hardy as he was contemplating the composition of *Jude the Obscure* (1895).[53]

That, though, was not the only occasion when Coleridge may have influenced developments in literature. His judgment in *R. v. Dudley and Stephens* almost certainly influenced Joseph Conrad when he was composing his short story 'Falk' (1903),[54] and H. G. Wells may have used the events of the case in depicting the threat of shipwreck cannibalism in *The Island of Doctor Moreau* (1896).[55] The case itself had involved Dudley and Stephens being adrift at sea with Richard Parker, a boy of 17, following a shipwreck. After twenty days of extreme deprivation Parker, who was the weakest of them, was murdered and the survivors fed on his body for four days until they were rescued. They openly admitted what they had done but considered that they had been compelled to do so through necessity. Dudley and Stephens were charged with murder and after various machinations the case eventually came before Coleridge.[56]

The controversies of the case, however, had already been twice previewed. In 1846 the Arctic explorer Sir John Franklin and his expedition had disappeared seeking a Northwest Passage.

---

[52] A. Desmond, *Huxley* (Harmondsworth, 1998), 526.

[53] Marsh, *Word*, n. 47 above, 297.

[54] A. Boyer, 'Crime, Cannibalism and Joseph Conrad' (1986) 20 *Loyola of Los Angeles Law Review* 9.

[55] H. G. Wells, *The Island of Doctor Moreau* (1896) (Jefferson, North Carolina, 1996), 63.

[56] A. W. B. Simpson, *Cannibalism and the Common Law* (Chicago, 1984; Harmondsworth, 1986).

Eventually the remains of the party were found in 1854, and it was alleged that they had been driven to cannibalism before they died. A fierce debate then ensued in England as to whether English gentlemen could ever resort to such an 'unspeakable' act,[57] and Coleridge was both aware of this debate and an admirer of Franklin.[58] Equally, he may previously have encountered Richard Parker. In 1838 Edgar Allan Poe had published *The Narrative of Arthur Gordon Pym*, a work that Coleridge may have been aware of. In 1857 he had written to Yarnall: 'I have also been reading with attention a great deal of the works of Poe, one of your most original and remarkable writers'.[59] Poe's story recounts how, following a shipwreck, the survivors are compelled by necessity to draw lots and then murder and eat one of their companions; the victim's name was Richard Parker.[60]

In *R. v. Dudley and Stephens*, Coleridge delivered the judgment on behalf of the court. He proceeded to enunciate on the legal authorities on the question of necessity, citing Matthew Hale as clear authority that in England hunger is no justification for larceny, and, 'If, therefore, Lord Hale is clear—as he is—that extreme necessity of hunger does not justify larceny, what would he have said to the doctrine that it justified murder?'[61] What Coleridge omitted to quote is that Hale then proceeded to say that one of the reasons for this position was that nobody should starve in England because necessities could be supplied through collections for the poor and through the power of the civil magistrate. Hale then went on to acknowledge that, 'By the Rhodian Law, and the common maritime custom, if the common provision for the ship's company fail, the master may under certain temperaments break open the private chests of the mariners or passengers, and make a distribution of that particular and private provision for the preservation of the ship's company'.[62]

After disposing of the legal authorities, Coleridge went on to dispose of any pernicious attractions that necessity may have had by invoking particular images and symbols:

[57] G. Beer, *Open Fields* (Oxford, 1996), 46.
[58] Coleridge, *Life*, n. 6 above, I, 294.
[59] Yarnall, *Forty*, n. 18 above, 32.
[60] E. A. Poe, *Arthur Gordon Pym* (Oxford, 1994), 94.
[61] (1884) 14 QBD 273 at 283.
[62] M. Hale, *The History of the Pleas of the Crown*, 2 vols. (London, 1736), I, 55.

The duty, in case of shipwreck, of a captain to his crew, of the crew to the passengers, of soldiers to women and children, as in the noble case of the '*Birkenhead*'; these duties impose on men the moral necessity, not of the preservation, but of the sacrifice of their lives for others, from which in no country, least of all, it is to be hoped, in England, will men ever shrink, as indeed, they have not shrunk . . . it is enough in a Christian country to remind ourselves of the Great Example whom we profess to follow . . . In this case the weakest, the youngest, the most unresisting, was chosen. Was it more necessary to kill him than one of the grown men? The answer must be 'No'—

He concluded,

'So spake the Fiend, and with necessity,
The tyrant's plea, excused his devilish deeds'.[63]

Dudley and Stephens were found guilty of murder and sentenced to death, a sentence that was later commuted to six months' imprisonment.

Coleridge was capable of providing a clear exposition on the law when he considered it to be necessary, as in *Bradlaugh* v. *Newdegate*, but a more common tendency was to advocate a particular stance at the expense of any countervailing arguments. In *Dudley and Stephens* he advocated a deontological position and in *Ramsey and Foote* a viewpoint that reflected his own religious odyssey. The result is that while both are still authoritative judgments, they have also both been criticized. *Ramsey and Foote* was criticized at the time by Stephen,[64] and *Dudley and Stephens* more recently by Glazebrook[65] and Smith.[66]

In his later years, however, this tendency began to disappear, especially as he was also debilitated by ill health. He no longer felt the commitment of the advocate for a particular cause in the cases before him, and his judgments and summations consequently suffered. As he had once lost the stimulating force of his religion, so he began to lose the stimulus of the law and the adversarial use in which he could employ it. In 1887 *Vanity Fair* described him as,

---

[63]   (1884) 14 QBD 273 at 287.

[64]   J. F. Stephen, 'Blasphemy and Blasphemous Libel' (1884) *Fortnightly Review* 289.

[65]   P. R. Glazebrook, 'The Necessity Plea in English Criminal Law' (1972) 30 *Cambridge Law Journal* 87.

[66]   J. C. Smith, *Justification and Excuse in the Criminal Law* (London, 1989).

born pious, literary, and legal . . . Lord Coleridge is a very moral man. He throws off without an effort the most beautiful moral platitudes. In cases which require hard, sound law, he is less admirable; but his morality is superior to, and compensatory for, all shortcomings in this respect . . .[67]

Conclusion

When Coleridge died in 1894, he did so surrounded by the trappings of his office and the honours that had accrued to him, but with his reputation diminished. In his final years he had no longer felt the motivation of the advocate for the cases being argued before him, nor the energy to deal with the intricacies of the law that they required. The result was that he appeared to be lacklustre and pious. All that had been left of his former success as an advocate was the theatricality that was inherent in that role and, it was alleged, his court became a matter of theatre. The enemies that Coleridge had made because of his style and temperament throughout a long career could take their revenge. The strengths that Coleridge had portrayed were slighted and his faults emphasized. Even his friends had to qualify their appreciation of him. Grant-Duff was to write:

In jury cases his quickness in apprehending facts and his lucidity in arranging them were very remarkable indeed. He was not one of the most learned of lawyers, but he was a great deal more learned than many people believed him to be, and as an ecclesiastical lawyer had perhaps few or no superiors. His fault—a natural fault in one who had been so successful as an advocate—was that of being too apt to take one side. He allowed, also, certain political or class prepossessions to interfere somewhat with the even course of justice.[68]

Coleridge's ultimate failure was due to the very factors that had brought him outstanding success as an advocate. The style and temperament that had brought him that success were inappropriate when he was Lord Chief Justice, and when even his enthusiasm for advocacy waned there was nothing else left. While his literary pronouncements have become a matter of literary footnotes, however, his legal pronouncements still retain authority

---

[67] *Vanity Fair*, n. 1 above.
[68] Sir M. E. Grant Duff, 'Coleridge, John Duke Coleridge', in *Encyclopaedia Britannica* (10th edn, London, 1902), XXVII, 135.

despite the dimming of his reputation as Lord Chief Justice. The reason is that, as Bentham observed, 'The deference that is due to the determination of former judgments is due, not to their wisdom, but to their authority: not in compliment to dead men's vanity, but in concern for the welfare of the living'.[69]

But Coleridge's literary criticisms are still relevant today, for a number of reasons. They provide an important illustration of the Victorian legal and literary worlds that Coleridge inhabited so prominently. They provide a stark example of his style that can be used to obtain a clearer reading of his more subdued judgments and directions to juries. They also highlight the position that Coleridge maintained on religion in the 1840s. That position can then be compared to the stance that he upheld as Lord Chief Justice in the 1880s, emphasizing the distance that he had had to travel to come to his summing up in *Ramsey and Foote*. Finally, they demonstrate the intensity with which he regarded literature and consequently help to clarify our image of Coleridge as an individual.

In 1846 there had been three major influences on his life: religion, law, and literature. By the end of his life the motivating influences of religion and law had waned, and only literature remained. A year before his death he wrote of what could be obtained from literary works: 'They are the best of companions, in sickness, in misfortune, in sorrow, in sleepless nights and days of pain, you will find your recollection of great and wholesome literature a constant solace and refreshment'.[70]

For Coleridge that was almost literally true. His biographer recounts how more than thirty years after the Franklin controversy and the alleged cannibalism, 'Lord Coleridge was one of the guests at a literary breakfast, when the conversation turned on this "unspeakable" controversy. It was interrupted by Coleridge gravely asking his host for—"another slice of Shakespeare"!'.[71]

---

[69] J. H. Burns and H. L. A. Hart (eds.), *A Comment on the Commentaries and A Fragment of Government* (London, 1977), 196.

[70] Lord Coleridge, 'Education and Instruction' (1893) 64 *The Contemporary Review* 837.

[71] Coleridge, *Life*, n. 6 above, I, 295.

DEFAMATION AND FICTION

Eric Barendt

Introduction

The application of defamation (or libel)[1] law to fiction is one aspect of the law *of* literature. Recently, a prominent English writer on law and literature has implied it is a minor issue, hardly worthy of attention even in a book as comprehensive in its treatment of the field as Richard Posner's *Law and Literature*.[2] Certainly, it seems of little interest to most members of the law and literature movement, concerned as they are with larger questions of the interpretation of legal and literary texts and of the treatment in literature of legal issues. Libel lawyers too pay little attention to the topic. Admittedly, there were a number of US law review articles in the 1980s, but there have been few of note in the last ten years. Nor have I found any academic study of this topic in English legal literature.[3]

Without doubt the impact of libel law on fiction is less significant than it is on political commentary, the investigation of financial scandal, and the publicity given to the attributes of pop stars and other celebrities. In practice, book publishers, for instance, are very worried that the publication of a biography or book on current affairs will give rise to a libel action; they are much less concerned whether a similar risk will arise on the publication of a novel.[4]

---

[1] The terms 'defamation' and 'libel' law are used interchangeably in this essay. The distinction between the two types of defamation—slander and libel—is irrelevant in the context of actions for defamation by fiction; the action is for libel, whether the allegations are made in a novel or in the course of a television drama-documentary.

[2] See the review by Anthony Julius, *Times Literary Supplement*, 8 May 1998 of the second edition of R. A. Posner, *Law and Literature* (Harvard, 1998).

[3] However, D. Hooper, *Public Scandal, Odium and Contempt* (London, 1984), an entertaining survey of leading defamation cases, devotes one chapter to the impact of libel law on literature.

[4] See E. Barendt, L. Lustgarten, K. Norrie, and H. Stephenson, *Libel and the Media* (Oxford, 1997), 130–1.

Nevertheless, there are libel risks attached to the publication of fiction. Publishers frequently refer novels to libel lawyers for them to read before publication. Moreover, two of the best-known English libel cases, discussed below, arguably concerned defamation by fiction. (Interestingly, however, neither of them involved a novel or short story. It is worth pointing out that the problems discussed in this essay may arise in the context of films and television and radio programmes, such as soaps and 'dramadocs',[5] as well as in the context of novels and short stories.) The legal risks are nicely illustrated by a recent libel settlement.[6] A name, Alex Wilbraham, was chosen at random from the New York telephone directory for a character in a novel about schooldays in Eton; this fictional Wilbraham was described as a homosexual drug user. In fact, there was a real Alex Wilbraham who had been at Eton at much the same time as the author, though apparently neither remembered the other. The publisher was required to pay Wilbraham substantial (undisclosed) damages to settle his libel claim.

The same issues arise in the United States and other jurisdictions. In one controversial case, the California Court of Appeal upheld an award of damages against the author and publisher of a novel, *Touching* (by Gwen Mitchell (1971)), which had depicted a marathon nude group therapy session conducted by a 'Dr Simon Herford'.[7] The plaintiff Paul Bindrim, a clinical psychologist with a group therapy practice, claimed successfully that the book referred to him, though it was wholly inaccurate in its description of his therapy sessions. Three witnesses testified that they thought the therapist Herford in the book was the plaintiff; that was enough to persuade the appellate court that reasonable readers could identify the plaintiff with the fictional character. There was no defence to the plaintiff's action, as the allegations could not be justified. (The difficulties of mounting a defence in these circumstances is discussed later in this essay.)

---

[5] D. Paget, *No Other Way to Tell It* (Manchester, 1998) draws a distinction between dramadocs and docudrama. The former term refers to the dramatic reconstruction of real events and protagonists—equivalent perhaps to literary faction— while the latter genre involves wholly invented events and protagonists to illustrate social phenomena and trends.

[6] Barendt *et al.*, *Libel and the Media*, n. 4 above, 132.

[7] *Bindrim* v. *Mitchell*, 92 Cal. App. 3d 61, 155 Cal. Reptr. 29, *cert. denied*, 444 US 984 (1979).

The impact of defamation law on novels and other works of fiction is, therefore, far from negligible. Whether the law is satisfactory in this area should certainly engage the attention of libel lawyers. Members of the law and literature movement should also pay attention to it. For a start, it is unlikely that the movement will be taken seriously by lawyers unless it does concern itself with matters of practical law and law reform. Moreover, quite apart from that point, it should surely be of interest that libel law is generally unconcerned with the intentions of the author and the publisher. Its approach is to ask how reasonable, or ordinary, readers, would understand the allegations: would such readers regard them as defamatory of the plaintiff? The common law is not guilty of the authorial intention fallacy, that is, the outmoded literary theory that the meaning of a work of fiction is best discovered by asking what the author intended. Instead, as we will see, the jury decides whether the allegations refer to the plaintiff and whether they are defamatory of her. Now there are some difficulties to this approach, which will be explored later in this essay. But at least the common law gives a community of readers—the jury—the decisive voice in interpreting the work of fiction. That should interest members of the law and literature movement.

The Legal Problem

A libel must refer to the plaintiff, or, to use the quaint language of the law reports, the plaintiff 'must prove a publication of and concerning him of libellous matter'.[8] This requirement rarely presents difficulties when the allegations are made, say, in a news report about a politician or other plaintiff; it is clear that the allegations are made about her, since the report will almost invariably state her name, and perhaps provide other identifying details, such as age and address. In contrast, a novel, or other work of fiction, generally refers to the personality, attributes, and conduct of a fictitious character whose name, as in the *Wilbraham* case, may have been taken from a telephone directory, or may just have been made up. Normally, of course, the names of the characters in a novel or other work of fiction are inevitably the same as those of some (or one or two) people in real life, but their background,

---

[8] *Sadgrove* v. *Holt* [1901] 2 KB 1, 4 *per* A. L. Smith MR.

physique, personality, and behaviour will not be similarly identical to those of any living individual. But the author, whatever his intentions, may be liable at common law for the wrong of civil libel, if ordinary readers would reasonably understand the allegations as referring to the plaintiff who may have an identical or similar name to that of the fictional character.

This principle was established for English law in the well-known case, *Hulton* v. *Jones*.[9] The plaintiff, Artemus Jones, a barrister practising on the Welsh circuit, sued in libel for the implications arising from a comic sketch in the *Sunday Chronicle*. The sketch described a Peckham churchwarden with the name of Artemus Jones enjoying himself at a motor rally in Dieppe 'with a woman who is not his wife, who must be, you know—the other thing!'. The plaintiff called his father, and four other witnesses from north Wales, who testified that they thought the sketch referred to him, while the newspaper argued that the name was made up. The House of Lords, upholding the decision of the majority of the Court of Appeal, ruled that it is immaterial whether the defendant intended to refer to the plaintiff or was even aware of his existence. A newspaper must take the risk that ordinary reasonable readers would consider the sketch referred to the Welsh barrister with the same name as that of the character in the sketch. It is even immaterial whether the newspaper was negligent in this respect, just as it is immaterial whether it was careless with regard to the truth of the allegations. In short, at common law, the publisher of fiction is strictly liable for the inadvertent defamation of a plaintiff who, in the view of ordinary readers, is identifiable as the character in the novel, film, or dramadoc. In fact, the House of Lords did not need to formulate the strict liability rule to impose liability in this case; the real Artemus Jones had, it seemed, contributed articles for the newspaper for some six or seven years up to 1901, so there is some evidence it was having a joke at his expense!

The question of identification also arose in *Youssoupoff* v. *MGM Pictures Ltd*,[10] though it is more famous for the ruling that it is defamatory to allege that a woman has been seduced or

---

[9] [1910] AC 20, affirming the decision of the Court of Appeal: [1909] 2 KB 444.

[10] *Youssoupoff* v. *MGM Pictures Ltd* (1934) 50 TLR 581 (CA).

raped. The film, *Rasputin, the Mad Monk*, represented that a Princess Natasha, a minor character, had been ravished by Rasputin. Princess Irina Youssoupoff, whose husband had participated in the killing of Rasputin, claimed that reasonable viewers, at least those who knew her, would understand that the Princess Natasha of the film was really her. Evidence was given on both sides of the question: some people said that on watching the film they thought that the character Princess Natasha depicted the plaintiff, while others testified that they did not think the film related to the plaintiff. The jury agreed with the former view, and awarded Princess Irina £25,000 damages.

One further English case should be mentioned at this stage, though it did not involve a novel or, in the strictest sense, a work of fiction at all.[11] An article in the *Sun* tabloid newspaper wrongly stated that a kennel girl, who was helping the police with inquiries into dog-doping, had been kidnapped by members of the dog-doping gang and kept in a house in Finchley. In fact, she was staying at her own choice with the plaintiff in his flat about three miles from the Finchley area; she was seen with him in public, on some occasions in a state of distress. Six people testified in the course of the plaintiff's libel action that, after reading the article, they thought he might have been involved in the dog-doping and kidnapping. Two of them had telephoned the plaintiff to draw his attention to the piece. On the other hand, one witness thought the story was 'rubbish', though he was also of the view that it did refer to the plaintiff. The majority of the House of Lords in *Morgan* v. *Odhams Press Ltd* held that there was enough evidence for the jury to conclude, as it did, that reasonable readers, knowing the circumstances, would consider it defamatory of the plaintiff. It did not matter that some of the witnesses did not think the allegations were true; it was enough that they thought they referred to the plaintiff. Moreover, it was immaterial that a careful reader would not have thought that the allegations referred to the plaintiff, because, for instance, the article had stated that the girl was kept in Finchley, when in fact he lived in Cricklewood. As Lord Morris put it, '[t]he average reader does not read a sensational article with cautious and critical analytical care'.[12] He

---

[11] *Morgan* v. *Odhams Press Ltd* [1971] 1 WLR 1239.
[12] *Morgan*, n. 11 above, 1254.

pointed out that the plaintiff in *Hulton* v. *Jones* had succeeded, although a careful reader could not possibly have believed that the sketch about a churchwarden living in Peckham referred to the Welsh barrister, Artemus Jones, who was not a churchwarden and was not resident in Peckham.

These cases lay a potential minefield for authors, publishers, and the producers of television dramadocs. To summarize their effect, it is for the plaintiff in a libel action to show that the defamatory allegations are made with reference to her, a requirement that in the United States is referred to as 'colloquium'. Witnesses may be called to give evidence that they considered the fictional person, perhaps portrayed in the novel as of criminal character, was really the plaintiff. Judges direct juries to consider how an ordinary, reasonable reader will interpret the novel, not how it would be understood by a careful reader who reads a text with attention to detail. The author's intention is immaterial; a disclaimer stating that characters in the novel are not to be identified with living persons has no legal effect. Nor does it matter, according to the *Morgan* case, whether ordinary readers would believe the allegations made of the plaintiff; it is enough that they would consider that they refer to her. (We will see later that some American cases appear to take a different view on this last point.)

The central difficulty is this. Once the issue of colloquium has been determined in the plaintiff's favour, the case is over. For the author of fiction has no defence. He cannot argue that the allegations are true, so that the libel is justified. (Equally, he cannot succeed with a fair comment defence, since comment, at common law, must be based on substantially true facts.) Of course, a novelist describes the personality of the fictional character truthfully; indeed, that in a sense is inevitable, although of course 'untrue' remarks may be made by one character in a novel about another. But a novelist cannot argue that the allegations are justified with regard to the plaintiff, when his work by its very nature describes events that did not occur and (usually) persons who do not exist or who have never existed. Admittedly, one type of fiction, that known as 'faction', does in a sense describe the behaviour of real (living) people, but it ascribes fantastic conduct to them in order, the author would claim, to offer some deeper insight into their psyche or cultural significance. A notorious example is Robert Coover's novel, *The Public Burning* (1976), which depicts

President Richard Nixon's attempt to seduce Ethel Rosenberg while she was in prison, and his own victimization by a public act of sodomy.[13] But the courts would have little time for any argument that defamatory allegations which are factually inaccurate may take advantage of the defence of justification, because they serve some 'higher' artistic or literary truth.

As has been pointed out by American commentators, the legal position is in a sense rather paradoxical.[14] On the one hand, the plaintiff argues that reasonable readers (or viewers) associate the character in the novel (or film) with her, because they share some characteristics—the identity of an unusual name in *Hulton* v. *Jones*, involvement with leading personalities during the Russian Revolution in the *Youssoupoff* case. On the other hand, once the requirement of identification, or colloquium, is satisfied, it would then be said, if the issue does arise, that the plaintiff in real life did not do the criminal or other bad things attributed to the character in the novel. This is easy for the plaintiff, since obviously she did not in fact do the precise things which the writer purported to describe in the work of fiction. Thus, in the *Bindrim* case,[15] it was impossible for the defendants to argue that the plaintiff did conduct therapy sessions of the type ascribed to the fictional psychologist, Dr Herford. Understandably, the position has been criticized; the plaintiff highlights the resemblances between herself and the fictional character, but obviously does not bring out those respects in which there is no resemblance. If they were given equal weight, the jury might well be much less likely to find colloquium, that is, that the libel refers to the plaintiff.

The libel difficulties faced by writers of fiction are not alleviated in the United States by the constitutional principle formulated in *New York Times* v. *Sullivan*.[16] Under this principle, as developed in subsequent rulings of the Supreme Court, a public official or public figure plaintiff cannot succeed in an action for defamation unless she can prove that the defendant knew that the libellous allegations were untrue, or was reckless with regard to their

[13] See I. Silver, 'Libel, the "Higher Truths of Art", and the First Amendment' (1978) 126 *University of Pennsylvania Law Review* [*U. Pa. L. Rev.*] 1065, 1067–70.

[14] H. Kalven, 'The New York Times Case: A Note on the "Central Meaning of the First Amendment" ' [1964] *Supreme Court Review* 191, 199.

[15] N. 7 above.   [16] 376 US 254 (1964).

accuracy. It is incompatible with the First Amendment to ask the author to prove the truth of the allegations, as is required by the common law of justification and fair comment. The principle has substantially liberalized the freedom of journalists in the United States to report and comment on matters of political and social interest. But it is of no help at all to the writers of fiction. '[F]iction, by its very nature, embodies an intention to falsify.'[17] As a result creative writers are less well protected under the first amendment than, say, working journalists and commentators on politics, financial, and social affairs. The author of a *roman-à-clef* novel, such as J. Klein's *Primary Colors* (1996), may be liable in defamation for depicting the apparently fictional figure as, say, sexually promiscuous, when a more precise allegation of a similar nature against a named politician or other public figure would be covered by the *New York Times* rule.[18]

Of course, there may be good reasons against extending (or more accurately reformulating) the constitutional principle to cover the writers of fiction. Fred Schauer has argued that the justifications for the *New York Times* rule—the need for uninhibited criticism of politicians, the fear that government may use the libel laws to suppress discussion—do not apply to fiction. Fiction is important, but less important to national debate than news reporting and political analysis.[19] Moreover, political speech has generally received a fuller measure of protection under the First Amendment than other types of expression, such as commercial advertising and erotic or pornographic material.

I am not, however, concerned with the merits of these contentions. Arguments as to how far the writers of fiction should be protected against the risks of libel actions should not be determined solely by reference to the principles of First Amendment jurisprudence, which in any case are of only comparative interest in England and other jurisdictions. Authors can make a powerful case that libel law affects their capacity to write challenging fiction, and that the law should be reformulated in the interests of

[17] F. Schauer, 'Liars, Novelists, and the Law of Defamation' 51 *Brooklyn Law Review* 233, 236. This volume of the *Brooklyn Law Review* publishes several articles written for a symposium, Defamation in Fiction.

[18] See R. Smolla, 'Let the Author Beware: The Rejuvenation of the American Law of Libel' (1983) 132 *U. Pa. Law Rev.* 1, 42–7.

[19] Schauer, n. 17 above, 253–8.

literary and artistic freedom. Commentators on libel law in the United States have usually supported this case; some of them have advocated a degree of immunity from libel actions for the writers and publishers of fiction.

The Case for Reform

Defamation law, it is said, poses unreasonable risks for authors and publishers of novels, and for that matter the writers and producers of television programmes and films. They may be sued by someone who happens to have the same name as the subject of a novel or looks like a character in a dramadoc or a soap. But novelists cannot help drawing on people they have known in real life, however much they may attempt to disguise the identity of acquaintances they remember; alternatively, they may subconsciously bring up characteristics of people they have met fleetingly in sketching features of their characters. As the authors of a US law review article put it:[20]

[T]he nature of the writing process virtually guarantees similarities between real people and fictional characters. Writers consciously draw upon the people and places that populate their novels. Additionally, the unconscious mind, with its storehouse of impressions, generates fiction based on fact. By chance, authors conjure out of their imaginations characters that closely resemble actual people they have never met, seen, or even heard about.

On this perspective, it is more or less inevitable that writers will occasionally incur liability in defamation.

The position is even more serious for the writers of 'faction' which deliberately involves real people, treating them as characters in a myth or engaging in fantasy about their behaviour or aspirations. In these cases there is no difficulty of identification. Moreover, as already pointed out, the courts will not accept the argument that the author is stating a higher truth when he involves a real person in a fantastic episode.[21] The law is concerned with factual truth, not the higher truths of art and literature. Television dramadocs which reconstruct historical

---

[20] D. Rosen and C. L. Babcock, 'Of and Concerning Real People and Writers of Fiction' (1981) 7 *Communications/Entertainments Law Journal* 221, 233.

[21] See Silver, n. 13 above.

events and which make defamatory allegations about a participant in those events are particularly risky.[22] These risks may
even deter the writing of innovative types of fiction and the
production of dramadocs.[23] Even if reasonable readers or viewers may interpret allegations as defamatory of the plaintiff, why,
it has been argued, should authors be responsible for these reactions? Arguably, that undermines the independence of readers
and viewers.[24]

Various solutions have been advocated to deal with these difficulties. Vivian Wilson has suggested that for works classified as
'fiction', there should be no liability for libel unless there is
convincing evidence that the writer's intention was to defame the
plaintiff.[25] Some commentators take the similar view that there
should only be liability for what have been described as 'sham'
cases,[26] where the writer uses the device of fiction deliberately to
defame a real person against whom he bears a grudge. Others
would reformulate the *New York Times* principle, to allow the
imposition of liability only on proof that the defendant has reck-
lessly, or perhaps carelessly, failed to do all that he could to
prevent readers identifying the character in the novel or drama
with the plaintiff, a real person whom the defendant consciously
used as the basis for the character ('failed disguise' cases). The
authors of one leading article, Marc Franklin and Robert Trager,
would require writers, or publishers on their behalf, at least to
check directories to avoid the use of the name of a real person (or
firm or company) for a character portrayed by the novel in an
unfavourable light.[27] This practice, known as 'negative checking',

---

[22] *American Broadcasting Paramount Theatres v. Simpson*, 126 SE 2d 873
(1962), holding a television company liable for 'defamacast' [*sic*] at the suit of one
of the two prison officers who guarded Al Capone inside the car taking him from
Atlanta to Alcatraz, when the programme suggested one of the officers had
accepted a bribe to enable Capone to escape.

[23] Rosen and Babcock, n. 20 above, 245.

[24] Rosen and Babcock, n. 20 above, 246–7.

[25] V. D. Wilson, 'The Libel and the Art of Fiction' (1981) 44 *Law and
Contemporary Problems* 27.

[26] The term is used by M. A. Franklin and R. Trager, 'Literature and Libel'
(1982) 4 *Comm/Ent LJ* 205, 223. Rosen and Babcock, n. 20 above, would confine
liability to these cases. A classic 'sham' case is *Corrigan* v. *Bobbs-Merrill Co.*, 126
NE 260 (1920), where the author vilified the plaintiff under the barely fictitious
name, Cornigan, to get at a judge.

[27] Franklin and Trager, n. 26 above, 229–30.

is common practice among major British broadcasters such as the BBC, though not with book publishers.[28]

There is a little support for a more radical solution: absolute immunity from defamation liability for the writers and publishers of fiction.[29] The best argument for this position is that adoption of any of the alternative reforms summarized in the previous paragraph would fail to remove the chilling effect of libel laws. It is difficult, or at least expensive, for publishers to take every conceivable precaution, such as negative checking of available directories and comprehensive questioning of authors about the sources of their characters. There is evidence that some fiction works are not published for these reasons.[30] This amounts to a significant loss in any liberal society which prizes creative writing and artistic endeavour.

One difficulty with some of these solutions is that they require the court to determine what is a work of 'fiction'. Otherwise the same immunity from defamation liability could be claimed by journalists who engage in inaccurate or dishonest factual reporting. Distorted accounts in newspapers could be presented as 'fiction' and so entitled to its immunity. That would be wrong, since the public expects, and is entitled to expect, factual accuracy, rather than fiction from the news media. (I will come back to this particular point later in the essay.) Further, there will be nice questions whether novelistic journalism[31] and television dramadocs would qualify as fiction for the purposes of any special rules. Although courts in the United States are accustomed to categorizing both written and pictorial material for the purposes of the First Amendment,[32] the difficulties in drawing the line appropriately constitute a strong argument against any special protection for 'fiction' from defamation suits.

---

[28] Barendt *et al.*, *Libel and the Media*, n. 4 above, 114–15, 132.

[29] H. Stam, 'Defamation in Fiction: The Case for Absolute First Amendment Protection' (1980) 29 *American University Law Rev.* 571, a much cited student note. [30] Stam, n. 29 above, 581–2.

[31] Truman Capote's *In Cold Blood* is a famous example of this genre. Arguably, the sketch in *Hulton* v. *Jones* also belongs to it. Certainly, counsel for the plaintiff argued in the House of Lords that the case did not concern fiction in the true sense, but a newspaper which purported to deal in facts.

[32] They have resolved questions such as whether pornographic material is 'obscene', and whether professional advertising should be treated as 'commercial' rather than 'political' speech.

A Critique of the Conventional Wisdom

Although the solutions put forward by American legal scholars vary, most of them agree that fiction deserves significantly greater protection from the threat of defamation actions than the law presently provides. As already noted, Fred Schauer is a notable exception to this community of opinion; he contends that fiction is less worthy of protection under the First Amendment than investigative journalism and political comment. In this essay, however, I do not want to carry on the debate about the proper scope of the First Amendment. Rather, it seems to me that the case made by the reformers may be answered by drawing attention to three aspects of libel law. The first of these points may meet their anxieties to some extent, while the others suggest that in two fundamental respects the approach of the common law to libel claims arising from fiction may in the final analysis be quite sensible.

One general point may be made before I come to these three more specific ones. Much American writing in this area assumes, as it must against the backdrop of the First Amendment to the US Constitution, the priority of freedom of speech over the right of the individual to protect her reputation. The point, put shortly, is that the former freedom is protected by the Constitution and the latter is not. In contrast, English law assumes that it must accommodate or balance two interests, which in principle are of broadly equal weight.[33] Indeed, there is a strong argument that in some major respects English libel law is skewed in favour of the right to reputation to the prejudice of freedom of speech and of the press. The presumption of falsity and the strict liability of the defendant, formulated in *Hulton* v. *Jones*,[34] exemplify this bias. There is, it should be said, a powerful case for re-examination of fundamental principles of English libel law, including the rule that there may be liability for unintentional defamation of someone of whose existence the publisher was unaware. That case, however, is really for the wholesale reform of the law of libel, rather than, as in much of the American literature mentioned in this essay, for the special treatment of fiction in this context. It is possible to favour radical

---

[33] It is a nice question, outside the scope of this essay, whether this will remain the case after incorporation of the European Human Rights Convention into UK law by the Human Rights Act 1998.   [34] N. 9 above.

reform, and yet be sceptical of the case for sectional reform
(discussed below).

1. THE TREATMENT OF INCREDIBLE ALLEGATIONS

One unattractive feature of libel law, highlighted for English law
by the *Morgan* case,[35] is that the plaintiff may succeed in her
action, even though members of the public to whom the allegations were published did not believe them. This consequence flows
from the rule that damages are presumed in the case of libel (if not
generally in slander). The plaintiff's feelings may be hurt, even if
nobody believes what is written about her.[36] This principle
produces particularly harsh results in fiction cases. In these cases,
as pointed out earlier,[37] a plaintiff may argue that passages in the
novel refer to her, even though in the nature of things the allegations cannot be true and it is unlikely that they will be believed by
people who know her. In other words, she may recover for allegations which may well be fantastic or incredible, or for allegations
which nobody takes seriously.

Some American courts have taken a different tack. In the first
place, there are cases where the court finds the allegations to be so
incredible that no reasonable jury would identify the character
with the plaintiff.[38] On the other hand, it should be conceded,
more often courts have taken the approach that as long as reasonable readers believe the allegations refer to the plaintiff, it does not
matter whether they also believe in their truth. In the *Bindrim*
case, for instance, the California Court of Appeal was solely
concerned with the question whether reasonable readers might
consider that the fictional Dr Herford and the plaintiff were in
effect the same person; no attention was given to the question
whether they would believe that the plaintiff had used obscene
language, as the novel alleged. But it has been decided by a federal
appellate court that a plaintiff cannot sue on fantastic or incredible allegations, even when they clearly referred to the plaintiff. In

---

[35] N. 11 above.
[36] N. 11 above, 1246 *per* Lord Reid.
[37] Page 481 above.
[38] See in particular *Wheeler* v. *Dell Publishing Co.*, 300 F 2d 372 (7th Cir.
1962), where the Circuit Court ruled that the representation of the character in the
novel was so unsavoury that no reasonable reader would identify her with the
plaintiff.

Pring v. *Penthouse International Ltd*,[39] the court reversed a libel judgment in favour of a Miss Wyoming who had sued for a spoof of the Miss America contest, crediting her with performing fellatio with her coach on national television, causing him to levitate. There was no doubt here that the fanciful allegations referred to Charlene, a Miss Wyoming, but that was not decisive of the libel case. The court considered that reasonable readers would understand the allegations were fantasy; they did not amount to credible assertions of fact.

Consistent adoption of this approach would almost certainly reduce the difficulties faced by writers of fiction. In particular, they should minimize the risks of liability arising from a work of faction, in particular where it satirizes or ridicules a named or identifiable public figure. Indeed, perhaps libel actions should only be sustainable when they are based on allegations of fact, rather than of expression of opinion or caricatures? That is broadly the position which the US Supreme Court has adopted in recent cases.[40] Juries should be asked to determine whether the defamatory statements made *credible* allegations about attributes or conduct of the plaintiff, not merely whether reasonable readers would consider that they referred to her. A libel action should only succeed if reasonable readers would believe the allegations; if they would not, the defendant should at most be liable for the tort of intentional (or reckless) infliction of mental distress to the plaintiff.

2. THE CONFUSION OF FACT AND FICTION

One argument for exculpating writers of fiction from defamation liability is that readers can, or at least should be able to, distinguish works of fiction from factual reporting, and that, therefore, they are most unlikely to identify characters in the former with real people whom they know or know of. But many people, it

---

[39]   695 F. 2d 438 (10th Cir., 1982).
[40]   See *Hustler Magazine* v. *Falwell*, 485 US 46 (1988), and *Milkovich* v. *Loraine Journal Co.*, 497 US 1 (1990). The former case strictly involved an action for the tort of deliberate infliction of emotional distress, resulting from publication of a nasty caricature, but the jury dismissed a libel action, specifically finding that the spoof advertisement, suggesting the plaintiff had his first sexual experience with his mother, made no credible assertion of fact.

appears, do find it difficult to distinguish fact and fiction. Their confusion can assume different forms. In the first place, real people such as the late Diana, Princess of Wales, and other celebrities are surrounded by myth; they are credited with attitudes and attributes without any strong evidence that they really had them. Second, the viewers of soaps, and the readers of popular romantic fiction, experience the lives of their characters as emotionally real.[41] Many members of the public protest, when characters in television soaps are prematurely killed off or they are unjustly imprisoned.[42] Of course, to treat the characters in soaps as if they are real people is not the same as identifying them with actual people in the real world. Moreover, the phenomenon is almost certainly much more marked with television soaps than it is with fiction. But against this background it would hardly be astonishing if readers (and viewers) do sometimes confuse characters in fiction with contemporaries in the real world. If a character in a political novel, featuring parliamentary debates and cabinet meetings, were described as a tall man with grey hair and the air of kindly bank manager, would it be surprising if readers thought he was a thin disguise for John Major?

Writers and publishers should surely be aware of this confusion. Indeed, though it would require some research to substantiate this proposition, I expect that many writers of popular fiction capitalize on it. Nor would this be only a recent phenomenon. It was often believed that the characters in Trollope's Palliser novels were based on contemporary politicians such as Russell, Derby, Gladstone, Disraeli, and John Bright.[43] Disraeli himself was one of the earliest writers of *romans-à-clef*, subsequently publishing keys with which readers could identify the characters in his novels. Whether authors do exploit the popular confusion of real and fictional characters, or are merely aware of it, they should not altogether escape responsibility for it. At least they should try to disguise their characters, in order, so far as possible, to reduce the

[41] S. Livingstone, *Making Sense of Television: the Psychology of Audience Interpretation* (Oxford, 1990) is a study of this phenomenon.

[42] In the spring of 1998, questions were even asked in Parliament and the Party leaders issued statements, expressing their concern for the fate of Deirdre Barlow, a character in *Coronation Street* 'unjustly' convicted of fraud.

[43] Trollope himself disclaimed this, writing in *An Autobiography* (London, 1883) that his fictional politicians were 'more or less portraits, not of living men, but of living political characters'.

risk that readers may think that they are really reading the inside
story of, say, a political or social scandal in the guise of fiction.
This is particularly true of authors such as Jeffrey Archer, Michael
Dobbs, and Edwina Currie whose position gives them access to
'inside' political information; it is understandable if readers tend
to associate characters in their novels with those of their actual
contemporaries.

3. JURIES AND READER RESPONSE

In England and in the United States the issue of identification of
the plaintiff (or colloquium), as well as the more commonly
disputed question whether the allegations bear a defamatory
meaning, are matters for the jury. The role of the jury in libel
cases, particularly with regard to the assessment of damages, has
been controversial in the last decade or so in England, though the
courts have often referred to this role as of constitutional importance.[44] It dates back to Fox's Libel Act 1792 when the jury was
first given the responsibility of determining whether a publication
amounted to a seditious libel on the government.

Judges are reluctant, perhaps too reluctant, to withdraw questions from a libel jury, on the ground, say, that the words cannot
bear a particular meaning or that they could not be considered
defamatory. One explanation for this reluctance is that it is more
sensible for issues of meaning to be left to the jury because they
are better placed than the judge to determine how an article or
programme would be regarded by the reasonable or ordinary
reader or viewer. As the *Morgan* case indicated,[45] the test is not
how the material would be read by a particularly careful reader,
but how it would be understood by an ordinary, sensible reader
who might skim through it. Further, as emphasized throughout
this essay, the author's intentions are wholly immaterial; it does
not matter that he did not intend to defame the plaintiff, nor even
whether he had heard of the plaintiff.

In this context, it is possible to regard the jury as a community of
readers, invited to determine how reasonable readers (or viewers)

---

[44] See, e.g. Scrutton LJ in *Youssoupoff* v. *MGM Pictures Ltd* (1934) 50 TLR
581, 584, and Beldam LJ in *Kiam* v. *Neil (No. 2)* [1996] EMLR 493, 507.
[45] N. 11 above.

would respond to the novel, dramadoc, or other material. Albeit totally unconsciously, the law has perhaps adopted the tenets of the 'reader response' theorists who argue that the significance of a work of literature is not captured by asking questions about the intentions of the author and who do not insist that a text bears a single, plain, and right meaning. A literary work bears within reason the meaning which a community of readers puts on it. Ordinary readers of a novel by Jeffrey Archer, Edwina Currie, or Jilly Cooper may find meanings which would not be placed on the text by a literary critic, let alone by the author. Equally, they may determine, quite contrary to the author's intentions, that ordinary readers would think that one of the characters is really the plaintiff.

The results in some cases may be unexpected, though it is hard to feel much sympathy with the defendants in *Hulton* v. *Jones*, or for that matter with those in the *Youssoupoff* case or even in the Californian case, *Bindrim*. All of them were reckless, or at the least careless, in failing to appreciate the consequences of their publications. Moreover, authors, producers, and publishers should be aware that readers and viewers frequently confuse fact and fiction; their confusion may particularly be understandable when a novel is written by a practising (or just retired) politician or a dramadoc presents a sensational 'account' of a recent controversial event.

There is, however, one aspect of the law in practice which does cause me unease. Both plaintiff and defendant, as in the *Youssoupoff* case, may call witnesses on the question of identification. In the nature of things, it is far easier for the plaintiff to produce friends who read the novel or saw the television programme and thought the allegations referred to her, than it is for the defendant to call witnesses who saw no connection.[46] Juries may be persuaded that reasonable readers would identify the plaintiff with the character on the evidence of a handful of witnesses, when the majority of readers did not make any connection. Indeed,

---

[46] In *Longmore* v. *BBC*, 15 Dec. 1981 (unreported), a firm of solicitors practising in Hertford obtained damages after disparaging remarks in a radio play set in the Birmingham area about a fictitious firm of solicitors with a similar name. The judge was particularly impressed by the evidence of a woman who had known the plaintiff for 20 years and heard the play while she was ironing (I am grateful to David Hooper for sending me the transcript).

some libel actions in England appear to have been prompted by friends of the plaintiff who had suggested to her an identity with a fictional character, which otherwise might have totally escaped her.[47] In many cases, therefore, there is likely to be an imbalance of testimony in favour of the plaintiff on what may be the only significant issue in the case. It is hard to know how this could be corrected, unless the extreme step was taken to rule out evidence on the question altogether.

Conclusion

Libel law does, therefore, cause problems for the writers and publishers of fiction. But it also causes problems for all writers and branches of the media. The solution to these difficulties is to reform fundamental aspects of defamation law, in particular, its strict liability, the presumption of damage in libel actions, and perhaps the presumption of falsity. Radical reform would remove some of burdens and costs attached to the publication of novels and the production of television dramadocs.

I am less impressed by the case made for special rules to protect the authors of fiction, still less the argument that their work is of such value that absolute immunity is justified. Quite apart from the difficulty of defining what is 'fiction' for the purpose of any special rules, it is not clear to me why authors in 'sham' cases should enjoy immunity; I also see no reason why liability should not be imposed on reckless and negligent authors and publishers of fiction, where *mutatis mutandis* it would be imposed on similarly irresponsible journalists. Finally, I think writers can hardly complain if their work is interpreted by a jury—a community of readers—to have libelled the plaintiff. They may legitimately complain about the law of libel, but that is another matter.[48]

[47] See some of the cases discussed by Hooper, n. 3 above, ch. 9.

[48] I am grateful to Beth Johnston, Yale University, for helping me with the research for this essay, and for comments from Professor David Anderson, University of Texas and David Hooper, Biddle and Co.

ART CRIMES

Anthony Julius

Introduction

'When Benvenuto Cellini crucified a living man to study the play of muscles in his death agony', remarked Oscar Wilde, 'a pope was right to grant him absolution. What is the death of a vague individual if it enables an immortal work to blossom and to create, in Keats's words, an eternal source of ecstasy?'[1] Few would concur with such a statement, and if pressed to explain why, some such principle as 'aesthetic ends do not justify criminal means' would probably be offered. This principle seems intuitively right and hardly demands amplification, let alone more formal defence. But let me take Wilde seriously, which entails treating his observation as a provocation rather than as a proposition demanding immediate, unqualified assent.

Cellini's offence was, of course, indefensible. If it was preparatory, say, to creating his great statue *Perseus*, reckoned to be one of the glories of Florentine art,[2] then it would have been better if that statue had never existed. (Arguably, indeed, it ought to be melted down, in an act of reparative iconoclasm; at the very least, should we not refrain from exhibiting the result of Cellini's findings, just as we refrain from exploiting the medical findings of the Nazi doctors at Auschwitz?) Walter Benjamin's aphorism, that every work of civilization is also a work of barbarism has, in such a context, a more literal truth than ordinarily acknowledged.[3]

But must art always subordinate itself to law (it is the illegality of Cellini's act, rather than its immorality, that interests me here)? The example of Cellini is too unproblematical in its extreme

---

[1] Quoted in Martin Jay, 'The Aesthetic Alibi' in *Cultural Semantics* (Amherst, 1998), 113.

[2] Harold Osborne, *The Oxford Companion to Art* (Oxford, 1970), 212.

[3] Walter Benjamin, 'Theses on the Philosophy of History' in *Illuminations* (London, 1973), 258.

wickedness; a general response to this question must address more taxing, less obvious instances. Cellini's case is easy to decide, and easy cases make bad jurisprudence.

Art can be, very often is, offensive. And when it offends, it does so against one or more of the following regimes: it violates the law; it violates morality; it violates social sentiment. Art does this, and artists do too. When the British sculptor Anthony-Noel Kelly, for example, took body parts in order to create sculptures, he succeeded in violating all three regimes (*R v. Anthony-Noel Kelly* [1998] 3 All ER 741). He committed an offence under the Anatomy Act 1984; he betrayed his colleagues ('a gross breach of trust', according to the trial judge);[4] he failed to show proper respect for the dead (once used, the parts were buried in a hole in the ground, without even a container). Following his conviction, he handed over the casts to the Royal College of Surgeons, the owners of the stolen heads, torsoes, and limbs. While he had limited aesthetic success, another criminal artist, Harald Nägeli (known, because of his prolific graffiti art as the 'sprayer of Zurich'), was both pursued, arrested, convicted, and jailed, and yet also was sponsored, collected, and defended by artists and art institutions. In 1987, a Heidelberg town employee charged with cleaning the fronts of buildings destroyed 'by mistake' two of Nägeli's sprayed drawings because (it was reported) 'he had not noticed that they were works of art'.[5]

The contingent nature of art's relation to law, morality, and social sentiment, and the positive delight that art takes in the ethically transgressive, are two, albeit contradictory, commonplaces of aesthetics.[6] They are also, however, a continuing affront to received, non-philosophical opinion (which generally still expects art to be lawful, educative, benign). Contrast, for example, the public responses to, and the art world's defences of, the Royal Academy's 1997 'Sensation' exhibition. The public recoiled, while

---

[4] Kathryn Knight, 'Sculptor jailed for theft of body parts', *The Times*, 4 April 1998, 5.

[5] Dario Gamboni, *The Destruction of Art: Iconoclasm and Vandalism since the French Revolution* (London, 1997), 328.

[6] See Anthony Julius, *T. S. Eliot, Anti-Semitism and Literary Form* (Cambridge, 1995), 119–20; and Joss Marsh, *Word Crimes: Blasphemy, Culture, and Literature in Nineteenth-Century England* (Chicago, 1998), 12: 'The will to transgression and the urge to avoid it may be integral elements in all literary production'.

attending in record numbers (but, in the main, as if visiting a freak show); the curator celebrated as 'trangressive' the art on display.[7] The two sides may be taken to have agreed on the affront, while disagreeing on its value. Art alarms as it pleases. Just when we wish to celebrate it, it troubles us. It bites the hands that applaud it.

But art can also be, often is, uplifting. Not in the cheap, Biedermeier,[8] sense of offering easy pleasures, but rigorous, exacting, clarifying, engaging, challenging—a bracing alternative to, in Hardy's phrase, 'smugger things'.[9] Crimes against art works are thus assaults not just on private property but also on certain collective values and goods, that is, the pleasure that we all take in art, the way it enhances our lives, its implicit celebration of the power and gifts of the imagination. Such crimes therefore cause particular dismay (hence our horror at certain acts of iconoclasm). Art works both explain the world to us and make us at home in it; to destroy an art work is an unusual act of dispossession, leaving desolate not just its owner but a much wider circle of admirers. It is destruction, of course, but it is also desecration.[10]

So if art offends, it is also offended against, and when offended against, the offence is against us too. Sometimes, the same art work both inflicts and suffers injury (sometimes the second, in consequence of the first). How, then, may we define art crimes (by 'art' I include literature; by 'crime' I include torts)? There are three kinds: (1) crimes against art works; (2) crimes committed in the creation of art works; (3) art works which are also crimes. The purpose of

---

[7] 'Artists must continue the conquest of new territory and new taboos': Norman Rosenthal, 'The Blood Must Continue to Flow' in *Sensation* (London, 1997): cf. Lawrence Durrell on Henry Miller, 'he had been forced to outrage the sensibilities of his contemporaries, to force the steel locks of the tabu . . . the art and the outrage march hand in hand': Henry Miller, Lawrence Durrell, and Alfred Perlès, *Art and Outrage* (London, 1973), 8, 54.

[8] 'Biedermeier' is the term given to German and Austrian art in the period 1815–48, which was solid, philistine, sentimental, familiar, accessible (see Osborne, n. 2 above). Arthur Danto contrasts Biedermeier art with the art of the avant-garde, as two ideal types, the one comfortable, the other quite the reverse, an art that 'will never become something that pleases the eye or enlivens the spirit': 'Why does art need to be explained? Hegel, Biedermeier, and the intractably avant-garde', introduction to Linda Weintraub, *Art on the Edge and Over* (Litchfield, 1996), 12–16.

[9] 'To a Lady Offended by a Book of the Writer's', *The Complete Poems* (London, 1976), 65.

[10] David Freedberg, *Iconoclasts and their Motives* (Maarssen, 1995), 7, 35–6.

this essay is to outline these three kinds of art crime. Law and aesthetics offer rival accounts of art; classifying art crimes is a good way of probing the most contentious aspects of this rivalry, one which arises in part because law and aesthetics each has something to say about art, and in part because law seeks to regulate art.

Of course, writing of 'law' and 'aesthetics' as if each was univocal elides the competing voices, speaking up for different interests, which comprise both. Take copyright law, for example. Itself compromised by its unstable compromise of the claims of its various constituencies (authors, readers, publishers, and others), it is also in conflict with legally sanctioned principles of freedom of speech.[11] Aesthetic doctrines, however ostensibly general, usually privilege one kind of art work, and argue for the revaluation of other art works. Purporting to describe all art, they restrict their definitions, discriminating as they describe, their embrace, however wide, inevitably also exclusionary.

The aesthetics of the artist, of the philosopher, and the art work itself, should also be distinguished. The *spontaneous* aesthetics of the artist amounts to no more than the claim that what he has produced is art and is of aesthetic value. He wants his work to be protected, but not otherwise interfered with. The *theoretical* aesthetics of the philosopher has more general pretensions. It engages with law usually only to the extent of debating the relation between art and morality. (Of course, the artist's aesthetic is not wholly particular, nor the philosopher's wholly general, because just as the former's commitment to his own work entails a commitment to other, like work, so the latter's commitment to art in general shrinks down to a commitment to certain art forms over others. The artist cannot ignore other work without falling into inconsistency; the philosopher cannot embrace all work without lapsing into vacuity. Thus E. M. Forster comes to the defence of D. H. Lawrence at the *Lady Chatterley* trial (*R* v. *Penguin Books Limited* [1961] Crim. L.R. 176),[12] and Aristotle derives his theory of tragedy from Sophocles and Euripides.)[13] And there is

---

[11] Fiona Macmillan Patfield, 'Towards a Reconciliation of Free Speech and Copyright' in *The Yearbook of Media and Entertainment Law 1996* (Oxford, 1996), 199–233.

[12] C. H. Rolph, *The Trial of Lady Chatterley* (London, 1961), 112–13.

[13] Stephen Halliwell, 'Aristotle's Poetics' in *The Cambridge History of Literary Criticism—Volume 1: Classical Criticism* (Cambridge, 1993), 169–74.

the *implicit* aesthetics of the art work itself, that is to say, it indicates by implication both the class of art work to which it belongs and the kind of interpretation which makes most sense of it as an art work. Flaubert had something of this in mind, I suspect, when he observed that every work of art has its special poetics by which it is made and subsists.[14]

It follows from this that when I write below of 'law' or 'aesthetics' I simplify.

Art crimes (1)

One means by which art crimes of the first kind may be classified is by distinguishing between those crimes committed against art works which have regard to the works' aesthetic properties or status, and those which do not. Collateral damage during military bombardment, and assaults on statues of unpopular politicians, are instances of the second; burning books, and paint thrown at pictures that are contrary to the offender's notion of what counts as 'art', are familiar instances of the first. Theories of iconoclasm, for example, often depend on just such a distinction; they make the intention of the offender paramount.

A better classification, however, divides art crimes into two complementary groups: offences of reproduction and offences of destruction. This approach pays less attention to the offender's intention, more to the effect on the art work of his crime. It also acknowledges the family resemblances both between the first and the third kinds of art crimes, and between art crimes of the first kind and certain lawful artistic practices. Thus:

(1) *Offences of reproduction* are at the terminal point of a passage which begins with an original work, and then passes through pastiche, then plagiarism, then breach of copyright, misattribution of authorship and passing off, and forgery.

(2) *Offences of destruction* are at the terminal point of a passage which begins with an original work, and then passes through

---

[14] 'Chaque oeuvre d'art a sa poétique spéciale en vertu de la quelle elle est fait et elle subsiste': quoted in René Wellek, *A History of Modern Criticism 1750–1950: The Later Nineteenth Century* (Cambridge, 1983), 12. That is, so to speak, the ontological aspect of the art work's implicit aesthetics. Elsewhere, Flaubert addressed the hermeneutic aspect: 'Chaque oeuvre à faire a sa poétique en soi, *qu'il faut trouver*' (at 478).

adaptations, then parody, then breach of moral rights, trespass, suppression or other breach of speech rights,[15] and criminal damage.

The first passage concludes with mere copying, the second, with mere erasure. The one replicates, the other extinguishes. The first is an attack upon a work's uniqueness, the other on its existence, but both thereby attack its economic value. These passages move through forms of derivative art, or 'literature in the second degree' (Genette),[16] and then leave art's boundaries altogether in a descent through civil wrongs towards criminality. In each case the destination is jail. What begins in the studio or the study ends in a prison cell and we may thus imagine two kinds of solitariness: the isolation of creativity, the isolation of iniquity.

We may further imagine a boundary dividing the artist from the criminal, art from crime, instances of the supererogatorily good from instances of quotidian evil, originating from the parasitic (whether duplicative or destructive). Cross this boundary and one ceases to be an artist and becomes merely an offender. The boundary is the means both by which art is protected and true artists distinguished from bogus ones. Positing such a boundary, however, immediately raises two questions. First, is a *wholly* original work possible? To which the answer is: no, but no matter. Second, how porous is the boundary? To which the answer is: so porous as to render it practically useless. It is a juridical boundary to which artists are, in the main, indifferent.

Offences of reproduction do not tend to injure the art work itself, while offences of destruction self-evidently may do. Unlawful copying of a poem does not harm the poem; on the contrary, it may enhance its reputation by making it more generally available. Vandalizing a picture, by contrast, takes it out of circulation. This helps make the point that art works do not in themselves have rights. While the crime itself may be committed against the art work, the rights violated by this act are the artist's, or the work's owner, or some other third party. This is not, of

[15] In the United States, of course, artists may rely on powerful first amendment rights. 'Visual speech', according to the authors of an American art law textbook, enjoys 'constitutional protections virtually on a par with that of pure speech': Ralph E. Lerner and Judith Bresler, *Art Law* (2nd edn, New York, 1998), 668; see also 676–80.

[16] Gérard Genette, *Literature in the Second Degree* (Lincoln, 1997).

course, to deny that damaged art works have a certain pathos: during the First World War, such works were exhibited in Paris as 'Assassinated Art'; during the Second World War, Italians faked evidence of damage to art by the Allies, and characterized the Liberation campaign as a war against art.[17] However, it is artists, and not their works, that suffer persecution.[18]

While there may indeed be objections to the ordering of the sequences, and their composition, and while other arrangements could be defended (and certainly imagined), the essential point, that the law exists to protect art, artist, and collector (though by no means with equal commitment), and must therefore adjudicate on certain critical aesthetic questions—specifically, determining what is art and what is non-art—holds good. Law claims to be art's friend, even though the protection it offers is often deficient (consider the case of the Parthenon marbles).[19]

Offences of Reproduction

Pastiche is to be distinguished from plagiarism. Pastiche is open homage; plagiarism is secret indebtedness. Pastiche is a literary exercise ('I will now compose in the style of . . .'), a test of technique, a study in virtuoso ventriloquism, sometimes a fusty academicism, sometimes a commentary on the imitated work,[20] sometimes a display of mimetic talent,[21] related in certain respects to the 'art' of translation. Plagiarism is akin to that, but almost invariably (though not always) written or composed under the sign of fraud. It practises a deception; the skills it requires are

---

[17] Gamboni, n. 5 above, 43.   [18] Gamboni, n. 5 above, 46–7.

[19] Illegally obtained, the Greek claim for their return is unenforceable: see Christopher Hitchens, *The Elgin Marbles* (London, 1998).

[20] A pastiche, Genette observes (quoting Proust), may thus be 'criticism in action' (Genette, n. 16 above, 8).

[21] As in the *Chasse Spirituelle* affair. On 19 May 1949 *Le Mercure de France* put on sale a slim volume entitled *La Chasse Spirituelle*, attributed to Rimbaud. In fact, it was written by two actors who wanted to prove their competence in the Rimbaud idiom, a competence that had been challenged by experts a few months earlier (the actors had put on a dramatized version of *A Season in Hell*). They took in a number of Rimbaud specialists, for a while. Indeed, these specialists refused to accept that they had been duped, and insisted against the evidence of the actors' own manuscript that their work was truly Rimbaud's. For a fuller account of the 'affaire', see Genette, n. 16 above, 158–61.

*those of the confidence trickster. (Of course, pastiche is not itself
always honest: when accompanied by a false signature, it is the art
of the forger.)*

Art, however, muddies these distinctions. Consider, for example, the cento and the collage. The cento, a poem made up of lines
or verses by other writers, and the collage, in which photographs,
news cuttings, and all kinds of objects are arranged and pasted on
the painting ground, are examples of art forms which both appropriate *and* originate. That is to say, in their constituent parts, they
merely do the former, while in the specific combinations which
they effect, they do the latter.[22] Each is an independent composition, and not a mere digest or abridgement. There are, of course,
differences between the two, in part attributable to the differences
in medium. While the cento reproduces, the collage lifts; in the
one case, the source remains, in the other, it is transferred onto the
new work. The cento is duplicative; the collage is substitutive.

Plagiarism is not just another word for copyright infringement,
though there is considerable overlap in meaning. Acknowledged
but unpermitted copying infringes without plagiarizing; unacknowledged copying of works out of copyright plagiarizes without
infringing. A distinction should also be made between, on the one
hand, plagiarism and copyright infringement, and on the other,
the related, statutory tort known as misattribution of authorship
(s. 84 of the Copyright, Designs and Patents Act 1988—hereafter
CDPA). A person has the right not to have a literary, dramatic,
musical or artistic work falsely attributed to him as author. (The
eighteenth-century poet Chatterton was guilty of an unusual kind
of misattribution, one to a fictional person of his own creation.)[23]

The s. 84 wrong is both the converse of copyright infringement
and an instance of it. It is the *converse*, because while a copyright
infringee complains that the infringer has stolen his work, a s. 84
plaintiff complains that someone else's work has been attributed to

---

[22] For the cento, see Margaret A. Rose, *Parody: Ancient, Modern, and Post-
Modern* (Cambridge, 1993), 78, and the entries in Alex Preminger (ed.), *The
Princeton Encyclopedia of Poetry and Poetics* (New Jersey, 1974); J. A. Cuddon, *A
Dictionary of Literary Terms* (London, 1977); for collage, see Osborne, n. 2 above.

[23] And his motives? An early biographer speculated: 'he may have had a secret
pleasure in hearing the poems, which he brought forward as Rowley's, so highly
appreciated by the world, the consciousness that those works were the production
of his own muse, must have filled him with exultation': John Dix, *The Life of
Thomas Chatterton* (London, 1837), 51.

him. The infringee has something taken away from him which he wants to keep (or control); the s. 84 plaintiff has something given to him, which he wishes to repudiate. It is an *instance* of infringement, because an author's name is part of his work. His work gives his name brand value. Memoirists, for example, realize themselves in their work; they are their own literary creations. So both the s. 84 tortfeasor and the infringer always claim the credit for something that's not their own—either a name or a work (or part of a work).

(There is an important economic aspect to this worth noting here. A novel written by a well-known author will attract greater sales than the same novel written by a tyro; the well-known author has an economic interest in maintaining his literary reputation. Section 84 protects that interest.)

In contrast with the s. 84 tortfeasor, both the forger and the plagiarist pass off a copy as an original. In each case this deception entails the adopting of the work of another as one's own. And the commercial intention is often the same: to profit by a fraud. Although they may be characterized by their common absence of originality, five distinctions may be drawn between them which, when taken together, define the two offences.

(1) While the forger conceals his own identity, the plagiarist advertises it. The forger puts the true artist's signature in place of his own; the plagiarist does not. The plagiarist is the forger, but transformed by conceit. He wants the credit for the work, not just the profit. The forger will imitate a style, creating a new instance of it, and then pass it off as the work of the style's originator. Forgery thus elides the distinction between pastiche and plagiarism. It is a crooked homage. The plagiarist seeks to pass off someone else's work as his own; the forger seeks to pass off his own work as someone else's.

(2) Forgery is principally a crime of fine art; plagiarism tends to be a crime of literature. Forgery is usually, but not always, a visual offence; plagiarism is invariably a verbal one. It's difficult to plagiarize a painting (but not impossible—the patenting by the Neo-Dadaist Yves Klein of his colour IKB—'International Klein Blue'—would make the unlicensed copying of, say, his painting *IKB 79* an offence of this kind);

---

[24] Shakespeare is a notable exception: see S. Schoenbaum, *Shakespeare's Lives* (Oxford, 1991), *passim*.

forgeries of literary works are relatively uncommon.[24] Literary fraudsters tend to want recognition; art fraudsters are more interested in the money.

(3) The economics of forgery and plagiarism are different. Forgery will be more profitable than plagiarism when greater value attaches to the author's name than to his work. So this is the choice that presents itself to the literary villain: do I make more money plagiarizing a Dick Francis novel, or writing my own novel and passing it off as Francis's? My name plus his work, or my work plus his name? Within the literary market, plagiarism is not a serious problem—or only a serious problem when taken seriously (see below)—and forgery even less so. By contrast, in the art market, forgery is a huge problem: one expert 'fake-buster' has estimated that 40 per cent of art works currently in circulation are fakes.[25]

(4) A plagiarist will admix his own work with the plagiarized work; the forger's work by contrast is both all his own work and wholly the work of the forged artist. A good forger must have qualities of empathy and humility; the plagiarist needs neither—just brazenness. A good forger may be an artist of considerable imitative skills;[26] there is no such species of artist as the 'good plagiarist'. The art forger, David Stein, jailed for his forgeries, was allowed when incarcerated to continue to paint in the style of (other) artists, so long as the works bore his own signature. In 1970, a New York gallery advertised the exhibition of almost seventy Stein paintings with the notice 'Forgeries by Stein'.[27] This blurs the distinction that the law makes between art and non-art: forgeries are mere 'simulated' art, and forgers are guilty of (in the language of the New York statute) 'criminal simulation'.[28]

(5) Forgery and plagiarism raise distinct questions about aesthetic value. Plagiarism challenges: isn't *all* literature derivative? Forgery challenges: why do we value a picture less when we discover its true provenance? Ask each question of the other, and the answer is obvious. Plainly, forgeries are derivative in a

[25] Jonathan Jones, 'Forgery's Great Renaissance', *Guardian*, 25 April 1998.
[26] Eric Hebborn, *Confessions of a Master Forger* (London, 1997).
[27] Lerner and Bresler, n. 15 above, 206.
[28] Lerner and Bresler, n. 15 above, 215.

distinct, uninteresting way; equally plainly, plagiarisms, when discovered, devalue the plagiarizing work as a whole (we can get the same—indeed, already have it—elsewhere).

Offences of Destruction

Just as pastiches are lawful imitations, and thus at the starting-point of certain practices that become unlawfully duplicative, so adaptations are variations which open a series of possible interventions in an art work that conclude with its destruction. (One should distinguish adaptations from performances. Performances of a piece of music are not variations on it, but constitute it. The piece of music is the score plus a performance of it.) Variations may comprise the re-ordering, supplementation, or deformation, of the work.[29]

Adaptations of certain kinds may breach copyright: translations, the converting of dramatic works into non-dramatic works (and vice versa), and pictorial versions of a copyrighted work's 'story or action' may all be infringements (s. 21 CDPA). They are different from the art work copied, but they are also duplicative of it and thus fall foul of the law.

One kind of adaptation is parody; its relation to the parodied work has been characterized as repetition with critical difference.[30] The satirist attacks the man, the parodist attacks his work;[31] in this sense, as Nabokov put it, while satire is a lesson, parody is a game.[32] Pastiche and parody each subordinate themselves to the copied work, but while the first does so in love, the second does so the better to attack. Each offers a tribute, the first in praise, the second in dispraise. Parody can also have readers rather than authors as its target. This is often the case when the parody is of a fashionable literary movement or school, teasing the public for the esteem in which the movement or school is held (as in the Ern Malley, and the Sokal, affairs).[33] But here the work only *becomes* a

---

[29] See Nelson Goodman and Catherine Z. Elgin, *Reconceptions in Philosophy & Other Arts & Sciences* (London, 1988), ch. 4.

[30] Linda Hutcheon, *A Theory of Parody* (London, 1985), 6.

[31] For a careful account of the multiple differences between parody and satire, see Rose, n. 22 above, 80–6.   [32] Quoted: Hutcheon, n. 30 above, at 78.

[33] Michael Heyward, *The Ern Malley Affair* (London, 1993); Alan Sokal and Jean Bricmont, *Intellectual Impostures* (London, 1998). This is the least interesting aspect of parody, the conservative ridiculing of artistic fashion's extremes (see Hutcheon, n. 30 above, 11, 77). For another example of a parody-hoax (or rather, what was first a hoax, and then a parody) see Martin Gardner, *The Night is Large*

parody when its author's deception of his audience comes to an end (he is rumbled, or unmasks himself); until then, it is a hoax. In this limited sense, parody may be described as a context-specific form.[34]

The distinction between parody and hoax can have considerable legal significance. In 1997, the politician and diarist Alan Clark sued the London *Evening Standard* over diaries published by the newspaper and purportedly written by him but actually written by Peter Bradshaw. He said that readers were encouraged to believe that the diaries were his own (and therefore a s. 84 breach); the newspaper responded that they were obvious parodies. Clark won. The judge insisted that his judgment was 'no bar to publication of parodies'.[35] This must be right: parodies do not need to be published under the name of the parodied author to be effective, and (evidently) *should* not be, if they are to be lawful. Max Hastings, the *Evening Standard*'s editor, both made this point, and missed its significance, when he disclosed that Bradshaw was reluctant to write the diaries 'because he likes to write best in his own style *under his own name*' (emphasis added).[36] The reason Bradshaw (and his newspaper) got into trouble is because his work was closer to a hoax than a parody (that is to say, not quite either): however unintentionally, readers were led to believe that Clark was the author, not Bradshaw himself.

Parody can also be, indeed often is, plagiarism—but of a licensed kind. Parody requires readers to have the parodied work in mind to order to appreciate the joke; they must not be encouraged to believe that they are reading that work. Parodies lead readers to regard the parodied work in a new (and critical) light.[37]

(London, 1996), 480. Gardner is writing about an earlier book of his, *The Whys of a Philosophical Scrivener*: 'In the book's chapter on aesthetics, I played a dirty trick on readers. I quoted what I said was a poem by William Carlos Williams and asked readers to compare it with a parody I had written of Williams's style. Actually, the parody was an authentic quote from one of Williams's poems, and what I said was by Williams was my parody. Naturally George Groth [a reviewer] was too dense to be aware of this sneaky switch.'

[34] See Rose, n. 22 above, 69–70, and Hutcheon, n. 30 above, 38–9.
[35] *Clark* v. *Associated Newspapers Ltd* [1998] 1 All ER 959, at 972.
[36] Peter Bradshaw, *Not Alan Clark's Diaries* (London, 1998), x.
[37] Parody 'is an intuitive kind of literary criticism, shorthand for what "serious" critics must write out at length. It is Method acting, since a successful parodist must live himself, imaginatively, into his parodee. It is jujitsu, using the impetus of the opponent to defeat him': Dwight Macdonald, *Parodies: An Anthology from Chaucer to Beerbohm—and After* (New York, 1985), xiii.

If the parodies themselves are read as further instances of the kind of work they parody, this point is lost. Therefore if a parody merely plagiarizes, it fails as parody and becomes a candidate for infringement proceedings, a heavy punishment indeed for an aesthetic failure.

Intermediate between parody and physical injury to art works is the relocating of site-specific art works and the withdrawal from exhibition of other art works. (Sometimes, relocation leads to withdrawal, which in turn leads to destruction: when Richard Serra's site-specific sculpture *Tilted Arc* was removed from its location in Federal Plaza, Manhattan, a new location could not be found and so it was dismantled and warehoused.)[38] These are offences of destruction because they confound the work's *reason* for existence—to be viewed, or to be viewed in a particular place—even if they do not confound its *actual* existence. 'To remove the piece', insisted Serra, 'is to destroy the piece.'[39]

Just as we need to distinguish between the literary offence of plagiarism and the legal offence of copyright infringement, so we need to distinguish between iconoclasm and criminal damage. (The two discourses—the political-aesthetic and the juridical—overlap but are not identical here.) Acts of criminal damage are not always iconoclastic; iconoclasts do not always damage the works of art that they attack. Iconoclasm is both enjoined and prohibited; in certain contexts it is a term of praise, in others, of opprobrium. Iconoclasts attack false idols; and there is a relation between modern art and destruction.[40] Iconoclasts are thus truth-tellers and innovators. But also: iconoclasm is stigmatized (often correctly) as brutish, ignorant, mere vandalism; in the power it often attributes to mere images, it is also archaic. It is thus one thing, and its opposite. The iconoclast can be an artist or an enemy of art; sometimes, he can be both, and sometimes neither (as with the destruction of Stalin statuary in Eastern Europe).

The major cultural moments of iconoclasm are considered to be Byzantium, the Reformation, the French Revolution, and the Nazi persecution of 'degenerate art'.[41] (To which I would add flag dese-cration in the United States in the last thirty or so years. For

---

[38] See Clara Weyergraf-Serra and Martha Buskirk (eds.), *The Destruction of 'Tilted Arc': Documents* (Cambridge, Mass., 1991).
[39] Quoted by Gamboni, n. 5 above, at 320.
[40] Gamboni, n. 5 above, 9.
[41] Gamboni, n. 5 above, 10.

example, during the period of protests against the war in Vietnam, a New York artist exhibited a United States flag stuffed into the shape of a six-foot human form hanging by the neck from a yellow noose—a perfect instance of iconoclastic art.)[42] Banning or privileging art works are here the result of a particular struggle: between Catholics and Protestants, royalists and revolutionaries, Nazis and modernists. Iconoclasm is thus often political in motivation; portraits of sovereigns, for example, will attract both reverence and hostility. Destroy the picture; unseat the monarch. During the French Revolution desecrating images contributed to the de-legitimization of the King. It made it easier to kill him.[43]

Iconoclasm can be creative or it can be destructive; sometimes it can be both. The iconoclast may wish to substitute his own work for the work he damages, on occasions by adding to the damaged work (in which case, the 'new' work constitutes a kind of palimpsest). Iconoclasm directed at one art form can stimulate practitioners of other art forms: Reformation iconoclasm had precisely this impact on English poetry of the period.[44] If iconoclasm is a legitimate form of expression, as well as the means by which the expression of others is attacked, it is both the object, and an instrument, of censorship. Any legal system which denies the autonomy of art, and thereby seeks to bring it under a regime in which it may be called to account, is at least potentially iconoclastic. Just as art may be iconoclastic, then, so also may law.

Are art and law in a different kind of complicity too? Art is often implicated in crime, which leads to choices being made between prosecution and appreciation (unless it is possible to do both).

Art crimes (2)

By placing the crime in front of the art work, art crimes of the *second* kind reverse the narrative order of the *first*. In the *first* kind, an existing art work is copied or damaged; in the *second* kind, a crime precedes the art work. For example: a poet 'borrows' a boat in order to contemplate a late night scene, a

---

[42] Lerner and Bresler, n. 15 above, 707–8.
[43] Gamboni, n. 5 above, 31.
[44] See Ernest B. Gilman, *Iconoclasm and Poetry in the English Reformation* (Chicago, 1986).

sculptor misappropriates body parts, and a poem or a sculpture is the result.

In Book I of *The Prelude* Wordsworth tells the story of a row on a lake, late at night, on holiday from school:

> One evening . . .
> I went alone into a shepherd's boat,
> A skiff that to a willow tree was tied
> Within a rocky cave, its usual home.
>
> . . .
>
> No sooner had I sight of this small skiff,
> Discovered thus by unexpected chance,
> Than I unloosed her tether and embarked.
>
> . . .
>
>   It was an act of stealth
> And troubled pleasure . . .[45]

The taking of the boat, that is. Still, he pushed on, and he writes with a restrained wonder about the experience of that evening. It was thrilling, and then it became terrifying, as he fancied the cliff that loomed over him a 'living thing'. At this point, he turned back, leaving 'my bark' (note the possessive—felonious—pronoun) 'in her mooring place'. During the days that followed, his 'brain/Worked with a dim and undetermined sense/Of unknown modes of being'. Lacking the perspective, he was unable to reflect on what had happened; he was instead possessed by intimations of 'huge and mighty forms, that do not live/Like living men'. They 'moved', he says, 'slowly through the mind/By day, and were a trouble to my dreams.'

The 'troubled' of the passage concerning the boat is thus picked up later on. The word, in one form, is used to describe the poet's response to his own unlawful act, and then, in another form, to describe the animating effect of the evening's experiences on his imagination. The hint is that the unlawful act was a necessary, initiating step toward the ultimate end, the poem which is *The Prelude* itself. Without the boat, the trip would have been impossible, or at any rate, that trip on that occasion.

Wordsworth's 'case' is an example of the second kind of art crime. Two points can now be made about it. First, the relation it establishes between crime and art work is a contingent one (one

---

[45] William Wordsworth, *The Prelude: A Parallel Text* (London, 1975), 54–6.

can imagine circumstances in which this passage in the poem could have been written without the prior unlawful act). Second, whatever the precise nature of its relation to that prior act, the art work has an existence independent of the crime which contributed to its creation. The crime is part of the work's pre-history, that is, the history of its creation. It is *not* part of its ontology, its mode of existence. The crime is not, that is, constitutive of the art work.

It is this double dislocation of art work from crime which allows prosecutors to insist in art crime cases of this second kind that their prosecutions have 'nothing to do with' art. This was precisely the claim of the prosecutor in the *Kelly* case (discussed below).

Art crimes (3)

Art crimes of the *third* kind may be distinguished from the *second* kind by virtue of the fact that they make just such a prosecutor's claim difficult. This is because here the art work *is* the crime. These art crimes abandon the narrative structure of the *first* and *second* kinds. The crime is the art, the art, the crime. They are crimes of art.

Admit art crimes of this third kind and the jurisprudence of art becomes (in part, at least) a criminology. The following are examples of such art crimes: literary works indebted in certain proscribed ways to earlier literary works; certain kinds of iconoclastic art; parodies that amount to derogatory treatment of the art works they parody; graffiti; pornography. It follows that certain entire art forms, and not just particular art works, have a relation with crime which is enabling and creative. Transgression, of one kind or another, is essential to their composition. In its efforts to protect art in general, law will often outlaw particular instances of art, for example, works which contain a high degree of borrowed material.

I should distinguish between two different types of art crimes of the third kind. There are art works which are criminal in consequence of their relation to other art works, and there are those other art works which are unlawful for some other reason. The best examples of the first form are plagiarizing works, parodies, and certain (other) kinds of iconoclastic art. These are all crimes *of* art which are also crimes *against* art—art preying upon art.

Good examples of the second are graffiti, pornography, blasphem-ing literature, satires, defamatory novels,[46] and art works censored for their political content.

The first form is the more interesting because here the law finds itself in the paradoxical position of proscribing one kind of art in order to defend another kind. Let me term the one form 'strong art crimes' and the other form, 'weak art crimes'. (Of course, certain art works can offend in both ways: blasphemous or porno-graphic parodies, for example.)[47]

The distinction derives from two different arguments between law and art. With strong art crimes, law tends to say: this is not art, and art to respond: yes, it is. With weak art crimes, law tends to say, it doesn't matter whether this is art, and art to respond: yes, it does.[48]

Take the contrasting cases of plagiarizing works and blasphe-mous works. With the former, an action for infringement may be met with the defence: this work borrows creatively, and though it may be derivative, it is original too. That is to say, it is a new art work, and not merely a replica of an existing one. With the latter, a prosecution for blasphemy may be met with the defence that the work's aesthetic status or merit entitles it to special protection.[49]

Law thus either refuses the work the status of art (strong art

---

[46] On some of the legal issues, see Eric Barendt, 'Defamation and Fiction', in this book; for some elaborated examples of 'literature as revenge,' see Louise DeSalvo, *Conceived with Malice* (New York, 1994).

[47] See Marsh, n. 6 above, 23–4.

[48] The distinction is not absolute. Even though the sex film archivist and histo-rian David Flint is used as a source by the British and American Film Institutes, 'that doesn't matter to the police', he has explained, 'because they don't consider [his archive material] to be legitimate films . . . As far as they're concerned, *they're not real films, they're just criminal acts.*' (*Guardian*, 10 July 1998, *Friday Review*, 7, my italics). Likewise, consider Republican Senator Jesse Helms on Andres Serrano: 'I cannot go into detail about the crudeness and depravity of [his] art . . . I will not even acknowledge that it is art. I do not even acknowledge that [he] was an artist. I think he was a jerk' quoted in Ronald K. L. Collins and David M. Skover, *The Death of Discourse* (Boulder, Colorado, 1996), 176. Laurie Adams has written well about 'the absurd confrontation between art and the law when the law tries to establish that something is or is not art: *Art on Trial* (New York, 1976), 220.

[49] The argument will usually fail. In William Hone's 1817 trial in London, he defended his blasphemous parodies by reference to their substantial literary pedi-gree. The trial judge would have none of it: 'if the publication be profane, it ought not to be tolerated'. The trial was, Marsh comments, 'a moment of separation between literature and the subliterary' (see Marsh, n. 6 above, 36).

crimes) or is indifferent to its status as art (weak art crimes). Art may find itself either with the plaintiff or on both sides of the contest (strong art crimes) or on the side of the defence (weak art crimes).[50]

Strong Art Crimes

In certain plagiarism cases, and in certain 'moral rights' cases (on which more below), there is only *one* art work, and it is the victim. These cases concern works that merely replicate other works, and actions destructive of works, and they constitute art crimes of the first kind, *simpliciter*. (When merely the unacknowledged recycling of existing work, plagiarism is solely an economic, that is non-aesthetic, assault on art.) In other plagiarism and moral rights cases, however, there are *two* art works, one is the victim, and the other, the aggressor. It is these cases that constitute strong art crimes. Works of 'appropriation art'—say, Sherry Levine's rephotographed photographs by Edward Weston or her facsimiles of Mondrian's watercolours[51]—are good examples of what I have in mind here, but Shakespeare's work is the paradigm instance of the strong art crime. Were Shakespeare (and the authors of his 'sources') to be writing today, he could be prosecuted for copyright infringement.

I should first put the crime in its correct legal context. Copyright law is a settlement of two opposing principles. The first principle, expressed as a proposition, can be put thus: literary works are the property of their authors until alienated by them, and should be treated no differently from other forms of private property. And this is the second principle: literary works are written out of other literary works (writers in creative dialogue with their forebears), and are thus common property, part of the cityscape of the public domain. The first principle may be defended by a combination of arguments about the nature of

---

[50] For a good account of some recent art controversies (including, where relevant, the litigation) in the United States, see Steven C. Dubin, *Arresting Images: Impolitic Art and Uncivil Actions* (London, 1992).

[51] Robert Atkins, *Artspeak* (New York, 1990), 42. He describes her as an 'appropriator', and defines appropriation itself as 'the practice of creating a new work by taking a pre-existing image from another context . . . and combining that appropriated image with new ones. *Or, a well-known art work may be represented as the appropriator's own*' (emphasis added).

private property and the nature of literary creativity. While the second principle may likewise be defended by a comparable combination, the tendency has been to emphasize the specifically literary arguments: there has been little support for arguments that would circumscribe—or, more radically, deny—the claims of private property in general.

These principles are, each one of them, persuasive and coherent. Copyright law, by contrast, is neither. Diminished by its embrace of both principles, faithful to neither, it leaves its constituencies—authors, publishers, and readers—dissatisfied. If it is to be defended, it has to be on policy grounds. It represents a settlement, not a deduction. It is derived not from an examination of the question: what is the nature of literary creativity? but rather: how should the claim of the author to perpetual copyright and the claim of the public to instant and unrestricted access be balanced? There is thus no place in its final formulations for the triumphant declaration, *quod erat demonstrandum*!

One consequence of this is that copyright law is unstable and subject to revision. It is always going to be open to the objection that it gives undue weight to one or other competing interest. And in this passage from principle to interest, which is a decline in theoretical standing, the potential rationality of copyright law is sacrificed. Because copyright law is thus a *politically* rather than an *intellectually* contested terrain, not grounded in one principle but in a plurality of incompatible principles, it tends not to attract the attention of jurists (compare contract law or criminal law). This is because it is in a mess and thus hardly conducive to jurisprudential inquiry—other than of a deconstructive kind in which its various incoherences are held up to critical scrutiny.[52]

The history of copyright is thus the history of a struggle, each Act and reported case a battle won or lost by one side or the other. Authors complain that their interests are inadequately protected; audiences complain that their access to authors' work is unduly fettered. Authors both need, and are mistrustful, of their audiences. The relationship between authors and audiences is thus one of unhappy mutual dependence. Intellectual property law

[52] See, for example, Fiona Macmillan Patfield, 'Legal policy and the limits of literary copyright' in Patrick Parrinder and Warren Cherniak (eds.), *Textual Monopolies: Literary Copyright and the Public Domain* (London, 1997).

intervenes to institutionalize that unhappiness. Authors want to be read, but they also want to be paid for what they write. And carry on getting paid. They want to control the terms on which their works are enjoyed, and they can't do this without the assistance of the State. The State helps—some would say, too much, others still argue, too little. Those who argue for the most extensive private rights are called maximalists; those who argue against those rights we might term minimalists. Not all authors are themselves maximalists; not all maximalists are authors—many, indeed, are entrepreneurs wishing to exploit the property rights assigned to them *by* authors. Authors, in fact, face both ways. They want both to exploit the work of other authors and to protect their own: 'We earn our money out of the stupid law but we hate it because we know that's a jive. What else can we do?'[53]

The law is in particular disarray at present. Not only does intellectual property law fail satisfactorily to resolve the competing claims made on it by authors and audiences, it has also failed to keep abreast of their activities. It doesn't protect them; it doesn't altogether comprehend what they're doing. Intellectual property law no longer encompasses the field. It is thus *both* incoherent *and* incomplete, inadequate in two distinct senses. The 1911 Act did not address film; the 1956 Act did not address video. And the 1988 Act? It's adrift in cyberspace. Technology is outstripping the legal categories designed to contain it. And this is the only hope for the minimalists—that technology will simply make impossible the legal regulation of access to information.

And yet: what do these complexities have to do with the case of literary theft? A writes a poem; B copies it down and then claims it as his own: where's the difficulty? B is discredited; it's a scandal of reputation. And limited to that. The institution of literature itself is hardly implicated in the scandal. But what then of the paradoxical truth that novels, plays, and poems, can be *both* original *and* derivative: original *because* derivative, even. If we reject plagiarism do we also reject literature itself? It would be odd if we had to conclude that aspect of the institution of literature which most undermines it is yet also fundamental to its existence. Can plagiarism be *both* its poison *and* its nourishment?

It is usual to think of literary invention as taking place in the

---

[53] Kathy Acker, *Hannibal Lecter, My Father* (New York, 1991), 12.

middle reaches of two extremes. At one end, we may imagine total originality, the impossible work written in new language addressing subjects never before addressed; at the other end, total derivativeness, the scandalous work, a mere transcription of an already existing literary work. Close to the one end, typically, we locate writers of genius, and we might put Shakespeare closest to that extreme of originality. At the other, ignominious, end, we place the cheats, the tricksters—thieves of the labour of others.

But what if Shakespeare himself were a plagiarist? Can a writer be, so to speak, at both ends of the spectrum at the same time? Both original and derivative? Both a creator and a thief? If the answer is 'yes', then, at the very least, we need to rethink our understanding of literary merit. The 'greatest' just might *not* equal 'the most original'.

Of course, if Shakespeare's appropriations were adaptations, then it might be easier. But many are not: he just took whole passages and transcribed them. Does this make him a lesser playwright? Only if we could imagine someone else doing everything that he did but without taking those lines and plots from others. If we cannot imagine such an author, however, then we are on the brink of suggesting that the thefts were a necessary part of the creation. The truth is that most writers both steal and create; some of the more interesting ones create by stealing. It thus might be said that while a plagiarist most certainly is a writer with a bad name, a writer with a *good* name is merely an *undetected* plagiarist. Under today's literary regime, he's lucky, but under other, earlier regimes, he'd be considered unlettered or mad.

But surely—the protest runs—plagiarism can no more be excused than any other kind of unpermitted appropriation. To hold otherwise is to sanction two wrongs: the depriving of one author of the benefit of his work, the conferring on another author of an undeserved reputation. The first is unjustly impoverished; the second, unjustly enriched. Indeed, if authors had no property rights in their work (or were unable to enforce those rights) they would not be able to secure royalties, and the amount of writing would drop, perhaps to zero, as they turned away from writing towards other, more profitable pursuits. The law of copyright, which protects authors from plagiarists, thus ensures the continuity of literature itself.

Or so it could be argued. But such an argument would not

survive an encounter with the massive counter-example of Shakespeare, whose work suggests, as Richard Posner has conceded, that any copyright law, however narrow, inhibits literary creativity.[54] Emerson confronted just this argument in his essay on Shakespeare. Great men, he wrote, are more distinguished by range and extent than by originality. No great man is original. The greatest genius is the most indebted man. Genius, indeed, consists in not being original at all, but rather in being wholly *receptive.* Shakespeare owed debts in all directions. He knew that tradition supplies a better fable than any invention can. In his times, our own petulant demand for originality was not so much pressed. The great poet comes to value his memory equally with his invention. He doesn't much mind from where his thoughts have been derived: from whatever source, they are equally welcome. It has come to be, Emerson rather scandalously proposes, practically a rule in literature that a man having once shown himself capable of original writing is thenceforth entitled to steal from the writings of others at his discretion. And then, pursuing his paradox to its terminal point, Emerson declares: Shakespeare is unique.[55] Harold Bloom, a great Emersonian, holds likewise when he remarks that Shakespeare understood that literature and plagiarism were scarcely to be distinguished. Plagiarism, Bloom insists, is a legal distinction, not a literary one.[56]

Artists and writers themselves are divided on the subject of plagiarism. They defend themselves, while tending to acknowledge, in qualified terms, its general unavoidability. They certainly don't like it when their own work is ripped off; Albrecht Durer's inscription on a woodcut is representative: 'Woe to you! You thieves and imitators of other people's labour and talents. Beware

[54] 'The more extensive is copyright protection, the more inhibited is the literary imagination. This is not a good reason for abolishing copyright, but it is a reason possibly for narrowing it, and more clearly for not broadening it': Richard Posner, *Law and Literature* (2nd edn, Cambridge, Mass., 1998), 403.

[55] Ralph Waldo Emerson, *Emerson's Literary Criticism* (Lincoln, 1995), 162–79.

[56] 'It shocks me increasingly to observe the vanishing of Freud's originalities in the presence of Shakespeare, but it would not have shocked Shakespeare, who understood that literature and plagiarism were scarcely to be distinguished. Plagiarism is a legal distinction, not a literary one, just as the sacred and the secular form a political and religious distinction and are not literary categories at all': Harold Bloom, *The Western Canon* (London, 1994), 74–5.

of laying your audacious hand on this artwork.'[57] They don't like it when they are accused of ripping off the work of others; Paul Celan, for example, was devastated by the charge, and even years afterwards, a friend recalled that he would 'burst into sobs at the memory of a defamation he'd suffered'.[58] One plagiarized poet holds responsible 'the contemporary intellectual climate' for making plagiarism acceptable.[59] He has a point: plagiarism has been defended (and defined) as 'contextual free play' or 'inter-art traffic',[60] and the most creative plagiarist in the English language this century, T. S. Eliot—a man who plagiarized Emerson when making his own defence of plagiarism—declared: immature poets imitate; mature poets *steal*.[61] Freed of its slightly Raskolnikovian amorality—my literary superiority licenses my literary crimes—this has become a commonplace of a certain kind of avant-gardist aesthetics:

Plagiarism is the conscious manipulation of pre-existing elements in the creation of 'aesthetic' works. Plagiarism is inherent in all 'artistic' activity, since both pictorial and literary 'arts' function with an inherited language, even when their practitioners aim at overthrowing this received syntax (as happened with modernism and post-modernism).

---

[57] Lerner and Bresler, n. 15 above, 205. In the argot of graffiti writers, 'biting' means appropriating the style of another writer, and is very much deprecated: 'writers employ the notion . . . in much the same way that conventional art worlds negotiate and utilize more formal notions of forgery or copyright violation': Jeff Ferrell, *Crimes of Style* (Boston, 1996), 87.

[58] Françoise Meltzer, *Hot Property* (Chicago, 1994), 65.

[59] 'Some of my theory-minded colleagues . . . argu[e] that my insistence on ownership is a denial of the communal nature of art . . . While I doubt that Jones [the plagiariser] thought in these terms when he was copying down my work, I do believe he benefited from the contemporary intellectual climate . . . In fact, had he underpinned his activities with theory, he might have found vigorous defenders among literary theorists': Neil Bowers, *Words for the Taking: The Hunt for a Plagiarist* (New York, 1997), 123.

[60] See Hutcheon, n. 30 above, 5, 8.

[61] T. S. Eliot, *Selected Essays* (London, 1951), 206 (emphasis added). (For a discussion of this passage, see Julius, n. 6 above, pp. 130–2.) But there are limits to the extent to which writers will celebrate their own plagiarisms. The novelist Alasdair Gray, for example, makes a joke of his plagiarisms toward the end of his novel *Lanark*, but only once he has established it as a major and indisputably original work of fiction (London, 1985, 485). And Kathy Acker, as a second example, begins an interview by confessing 'if I had to be totally honest I would say that what I'm doing is breach of copyright', but then goes on to distinguish her practices from mere plagiarism, 'I had changed words, I had changed intentionality': Acker, n. 53 above, 11–13.

At the beginning of the twentieth-century, the way in which pre-existing elements were used in 'artistic' productions underwent a quantitative leap with the discovery of collage. This development was pre-figured in the 'writings' of Isidore Ducasse (1846–70), who is better known by his pen name Lautreamont.

In his Poems, Ducasse wrote: 'Plagiarism is necessary. Progress implies it.' This maxim summarises the use to which plagiarism has been put ever since. Two, or more, divergent elements are brought together to create new meanings. The resulting sum is greater than the individual parts. Plagiarism enriches human language.[62]

Though this statement is perhaps best regarded as a literary 'heresy' (in the sense defined by Eliot, that is, an attempt to simplify the truth by reducing it to the limits of our ordinary understanding),[63] there is no doubt that plagiarism is indispensable to art, and chief among art crimes.

Let me now turn to parody. According to the eighteenth-century rhetorician, Dumarsais, parody 'distorts in a mocking manner verses that were composed by someone else with a different goal in mind'.[64] The French *Code de la propriété intellectuelle*, for example, protects this kind of disrespectful handling of another's work from infringement actions,[65] while in the United States parody is regarded as 'fair dealing' with the parodied work and thus not an infringement.[66] The courts are thus willing to find that parodies do not infringe copyright, and to regard parodies as new works derived from the works that they parody.[67] Likewise, trademark appropriation for the purposes of parody tends not to be regarded as infringement.[68] However, as one would expect, law and aesthetics diverge in their characterizations of parody. For example: French law treats parody, pastiche, and caricature as synonymous, relating the first to musical works, the second to

[62] Stewart Home, *Neoism, Plagiarism and Praxis* (Edinburgh, 1995), 51.

[63] T. S. Eliot, *The Idea of a Christian Society and Other Writings* (London, 1982), 74.   [64] Quoted by Genette, n. 16 above, 16.

[65] 'Art L. 122–5.—Lorsque l'oeuvre a été divulgée, l'auteur ne peut interdire: . . . 4. La parodie, le pastiche et la caricature, comte tenu des lois du genre.'

[66] *Campbell* v. *Acuff-Rose Music, Inc.,* 510 US 569, 114 S. Ct. 1164 (1994). But contrast the position in England, where 'such cases have usually been dealt with by asking whether an infringement has in fact occurred, rather than by considering the fair-dealing exemption [under s. 30 of the CDPA]' (Patfield, 'Towards a Reconciliation', n. 11 above, 229).

[67] *Joy Music* v. *Sunday Pictorial Newspapers (1920) Ltd* [1960] 1 All ER 709.

[68] Lerner and Bresler, n. 15 above, 712–18.

literary works, and the third to works of art;[69] in one case, a distinction was drawn between parodies that were humorous and those which were spiteful, these latter parodies being unlawful; in another case, 'parody' and 'burlesque' were taken to be synonymous.[70]

If parody is safe from infringement charges, what of the integrity right of the author of the parodied work (see s. 80 CDPA—the so-called moral right to object to the derogatory treatment of one's work)? Most moral rights cases concern entirely non-aesthetic mutilations or distortions—the cropping of pictures, the dismantling of sculptures, and a recent example, the anthologising of a poem with a word missing from its first line.[71] But parodies may also be 'distortions or mutilations of the work, or ... otherwise prejudicial to the honour or reputation of the author' (in the phrasing of s. 80). By defending the copyright or trademark case, do parodists thereby expose themselves to the moral rights case? If they do, then the lawyer's distinction between the 'take-off' and the 'rip-off'[72]—the parodic first is permitted, the replicative second is not—ceases to offer the promise of an escape, and instead threatens two different routes, so to speak, to jail. Parody is an acknowledged literary genre; s. 80 might also make it, in certain instances at least, an unlawful one.[73]

---

[69] Claude Colombet, *Propriété littéraire et artistique et droits voisins* (Paris, 1992), 167.

[70] *Joy Music*, n. 67 above.

[71] The poet Ruth Fainlight reported, in a letter to the *Times Literary Supplement*, that Penguin had published her poem 'Handbag' in an anthology omitting a word from its first line: 'My mother's old bag' instead of 'My mother's old leather handbag', thereby 'weakening the line, disrupt[ing] the metre as well as the pattern of assonance and alliteration through the entire poem'. This is a plain case of breach of s. 80. ('Publish and be Damned', *Times Literary Supplement*, 12 June 1998). Although she did not sue—or even threaten legal action—she could have done so, and Penguin would have had no defence.

[72] *Clark v. Associated Newspapers Ltd* [1998] 1 All ER 959, at 968.

[73] However, if parodies *can* escape infringement claims, they will probably also be able to evade that it will also escape moral rights claims (often thrown in by authors just as a make-weight). The Asterix litigation in Germany is a good, recent example of how parodies fare in combined infringement/moral rights cases (the case is reported at [1995] 7 European Intellectual Property Review D-198). The defendant was the publisher of a comic book entitled 'ALCOLIX—the parody'. The owners of the exclusive licence in the Asterix series and characters sued, alleging both infringement and breach of moral rights (because the Asterix characters were associated by the parody with alcohol abuse and cruelty). The owners lost in the Federal Supreme Court. The parodist's creative effort was

Weak Art Crimes (and the Aesthetic Alibi)

Works of graffiti, especially when they take the form of unlicensed murals, are good examples of weak art crimes because while they are unlawful,[74] they do not offend against other works of art or, if they do, do so only contingently. Indeed, graffiti is invariably found in urban landscapes conspicuous for their lack of aesthetic quality (which is why graffiti is not iconoclastic). Blasphemous art works are another good example of such crimes because, as with graffiti, it is in the nature of their offence to strike against a non-aesthetic interest. Graffiti is an assault on property rights, blasphemy, an assault on ecclesiastical rights, such rights in each case sanctioned by the State. And as a final example, consider the literary satire, which is often defamatory of its target.

In prosecutions/civil actions in respect of such art crimes, artist-defendants invariably wish to argue that the criminal/tortious nature of their art work is trumped either by its artistic status and/or its artistic value. These are two versions—relating to ontology and value—of a defence which has been termed 'the aesthetic alibi'.

According to Martin Jay the alibi is deployed to make otherwise objectionable conduct acceptable when part of an aesthetic project. It transforms the proscribed into the permitted: 'what would be libellous or offensive in everyday life is granted a special dispensation, if it is understood to take place within the protective shield of an aesthetic frame'. We even, he adds, 'invent new categories like "performance art" to permit behaviour that without its protection

acknowledged. Though the parody necessarily contained adoptions, it achieved the appropriate interior distance from the parodied work by arguing with it. The question of infringement would be determined by applying the perspective of the reader who both knows the old, protected work and has the intellectual understanding demanded by the new work. This provides the working space needed for sophisticated art forms and artistic freedoms, guaranteed by art. 5(3) of the German Constitution. 'Art', it declares, is 'free'.

[74] Under New York's Penal Code, graffiti is defined as the 'etching, painting, covering, drawing upon or otherwise placing of a mark upon public or private property with intent to damage such property' (Lerner and Bresler, n. 15 above, 711). For an examination of the 'criminal art' of graffiti, see Susan Stewart, *Crimes of Writing* (Durham, 1994), ch. 7. And for a similarly enthusiastic account—celebrating its 'creative lawbreaking'—see Jeff Ferrell, n. 57 above, 29. According to Ferrell, graffiti 'threatens not only the legal boundaries of private property and public space, but the political and aesthetic boundaries of legitimate—even legitimately "alternative"—art' (41).

would in all likelihood threaten the perpetrator with immediate incarceration in a mental institution, if not a jail.'[75] Artists themselves are alive to this, as are the defenders of practices the aesthetic status of which is contested, such as graffiti.[76] While 'this culture is horridly moralistic', Kathy Acker observes, 'under the aegis of art, you're allowed to actually deal with matters of sexuality and other matters of plain old freedom.' But, she adds, this 'keeps the artist from fighting'.[77] The aesthetic alibi protects the artist, but at the price of neutralizing her. Still, fall on the wrong side of the line, and one is a criminal; from the perspective of a writer convicted of blasphemy for his parodies of Scripture, the alibi 'turns a literary difference into a criminal offence'. If it is not literature it is a crime. Put more positively, 'literariness' thus 'grants rights', as Jess Marsh has noted in her work on the nineteenth-century blasphemy trials.

In the rigour of its division between 'art' and 'non-art' the aesthetic alibi is thus a very specific variation on the general freedom of speech defence. In the United States, art has the protection of the first amendment precisely because it is regarded as having communicative power on a par with that of the written or spoken word.[78] That is to say, art is protected because it is *like* (certain kinds of) non-art—social commentary, political propaganda, and so on. It is symbolic speech. By contrast, the aesthetic alibi pleads that art is to be protected because it is *un*like anything else, it is always and only its special self. First amendment champions of art find safety for it as merely one kind of speech among other, protected kinds; aesthetic alibi advocates conversely find safety for art in its isolation from all other kinds of speech.

[75] Jay, n. 1 above, 111.

[76] '. . . campaigners . . . employ the derivative phrase "graffiti vandalism" to describe all forms of graffiti, whether murals, throw-ups, or tags. The effect, of course, is to lock graffiti into the context of vandalism, to tie it to activities like window smashing and cemetery desecration, *and to deny graffiti any special status as creative or artistic activity*' (Ferrell, n. 57 above, 138, my italics).

[77] Acker, n. 53 above, 16.

[78] Lerner and Bresler, n. 15 above, 677. In the recent case of *Nelson* v. *Streeter*, 16 F.3d 145 [7th Cir. 1994], the court declared: 'It has been clear since long before 1988 that government officials are not permitted to burn books that offend them, and we do not see any difference between burning an offensive book and burning an offensive painting' (quoted: Lerner and Bresler, n. 15 above, 694). An artist had painted a satirical picture of the then recently deceased mayor of Chicago, Harold Washington.

There is of course a striking difference between the legal and the aesthetic breadth of the aesthetic alibi. In English law, for example, it is only available[79] in obscenity cases—the 'public good' defence in s. 4 of the Obscene Publications Act 1959[80]— while in aesthetics, it tends to be advanced against attacks on art from all quarters. (I simplify: certain works of art—parodies and satire—might also benefit from the aesthetic alibi, in the guise this time of the fair-dealing exemption in s. 30 CDPA, and thus be protected from infringement actions;[81] conversely, there are theories of art which do not shrink from anticipating the suppressing of works which fail to meet certain moral criteria—think of Tolstoy's *What is Art?*, for example).[82] But while obscene works thus enjoy a certain measure of protection, they also suffer a greater degree of exposure than other kinds of art work. This is

[79] It is therefore not available, for example, in race hatred cases: see ss. 18–22 Public Order Act (although s. 20, which concerns public performances of plays, does require 'the performance as a whole' to be taken into account. In any event, it is not impossible that certain productions, say, of *The Merchant of Venice* could risk prosecution). In general, the position varies from jurisdiction to jurisdiction. In California, for example, where any unauthorized use of a deceased person's name, photograph or likeness for commercial purposes is actionable, there is a specific exception where such use is in connection with 'single and original works of fine art' (CAL. CIV. CODE para. 990 [West 1982 & Supp. 1997]; cited in Lerner and Bresler, n. 15 above, 753).

[80] Available, that is, after a fashion. The aesthetic merit of the work is one only of a number of possible grounds for this defence: 'A person shall not be convicted of an offence . . . if it is proved that publication of the article in question is justified as being for the public good on the ground that it is in the interests of science, literature, art or learning, or of other objects of general concern.' Indeed, publication of an obscene work wholly without aesthetic merit might nonetheless be 'in the interests of literature': see Geoffrey Robertson, *Obscenity* (London, 1979), 170; see also Eric Barendt, *Freedom of Speech* (Oxford, 1987), 269–72. Compare, in any event, the current position in the U.S., as expressed by the Supreme Court; 'At a minimum, prurient, patently offensive depiction or description of sexual conduct must have serious literary, artistic, political or scientific value to merit First Amendment protection' (*Miller* v. *California*, 413 US 15, 93 S. Ct. 2607 [1973]; cited by Lerner and Bresler, n. 15 above, 728).

[81] 'The use of copyright material in artistic works does not seem to be covered by any of the fair-dealing exemptions, unless it amounts to criticism, or possibly parody or satire . . . As at least some art may be considered to be appropriation of pre-existing work for purposes such as subversion or re-invention, this may be regarded as having a chilling effect on artistic free speech' (Patfield, 'Towards a Reconciliation', n. 11 above, 230).

[82] 'Not only should . . . no sacrifices be offered up to what among us is called art, but on the contrary the efforts of those who wish to live rightly should be directed to the destruction of this art, for it is one of the most cruel of the evils that harass our section of humanity': *What is Art?* (London, 1994), 197.

because there is (in English law, at least) a public policy defence to copyright infringement where the plagiarized work is obscene, blasphemous, or otherwise immoral.[83] An obscene work thus may escape suppression only to suffer unhindered copying. Allowing for this rather unusual case, while law thus grants art certain privileges and protections, excepting it from certain penalties (or taxes—think of the US Customs case regarding the Brancusi *Bird in Space*),[84] and safeguarding it from certain dangers, it does not confer on art wholesale immunities. Art is by no means above the law.

Prosecutors/plaintiffs respond to the aesthetic alibi by: (i) denying that the contested work has artistic status, as in breach of copyright cases which assume that an art work which is not original is not an art work at all; or (ii) conceding the contested work's status, but denying its merit, as in pornography cases; or (iii) conceding both its status and its merit, but denying that either is relevant as a defence, as in hate speech cases and moral rights cases.

What the law refuses to recognize as art (or of sufficient artistic merit) may nonetheless be accepted within the art community as art (even, art of a high order). Law may therefore find itself making distinctions between art works refused by art itself, protecting some, prohibiting others. Sometimes, law will first prohibit and then protect—as in the case of Baudelaire's *Les fleurs du mal*, where a French Court of Appeal in 1949 reversed an 1857 decision condemning six poems for obscenity.[85]

The *Kelly* case is a good, recent example of the limitations of the aesthetic alibi in a juridical context. The prosecutor in the case

---

[83] In the case of *Glyn* v. *Weston Feature Films* [1916] 1 Ch. 261, the defendant film company was able to adapt Elinor Glyn's novel, *Three Weeks*, without infringing her copyright (see Patfield, 'Towards a Reconciliation', n. 11 above, 225, 232). Note also: 'so closely connected had the two crimes of blasphemy and obscenity become . . . that concepts which grew up around the one crime could shift with slippery ease to the other. Hence the arc of connection between the 1840 Moxon-Shelley trial for blasphemy and D. H. Lawrence's posthumous arraignment for obscenity' (Marsh, n. 6 above, 209).

[84] The importer of the Brancusi work successfully argued—against Customs opposition—that it was a work of art and thus exempt from duty: see Laurie Adams, *Art on Trial* (New York, 1976), ch. 2, and Gamboni, n. 5 above, 325–6.

[85] E. S. Burt, ' "An Immoderate Taste for Truth": Censoring History in Baudelaire's "Les bijoux" ' in Robert C. Post (ed.), *Censorship and Silencing: Practices of Cultural Regulation* (Los Angeles, 1998), 111.

insisted on the opening day of the trial that the case was not about art, nor was it even about outraging public decency.[86] It was just, he said, about theft. He was wrong, of course; the theft was the least of it. Still, his misstatement was a strategic one. To admit art into the courtroom would have raised a difficult question. Should the use to which the defendant put the body parts be a defence? Does the aesthetic end justify the criminal means (the aesthetic alibi)?

As a defendant, Mr Kelly was of little interest. He had his defences under the Anatomy Act 1984, though they failed to get him acquitted. It was only as an artist—or someone who claims the privileges and status of the artist—that he was intriguing. And indeed he insisted that he was an artist. After a period of silence, he defended himself in a series of press interviews: 'I have never made money from this. This is about art.'[87]

The Anatomy Act discriminates in favour of medical research and against the use by artists of cadavers. It recognizes as legitimate a person's wish for his or her body to be used for anatomical examination. Yet if any person, during his last illness and in the presence of two witnesses, expressed the wish that his body be left to Mr Kelly, or any other artist, the Act would not permit it. This seems objectionable for at least two reasons.

First, why shouldn't a person be free—public health considerations allowing—to dispose of his own body as he wishes? If he chooses to perpetuate his existence as a work of art, then why not? Who wouldn't prefer to gaze out at respectful gallery audiences, if the only alternative was gazing up at gagging (or bored) first-year medical students?

Second, the Act's prejudice against art and in favour of science exhibits a disregard for the claims of art, and artistic endeavour, typical of our culture. The Act is philistine. It only permits anatomical examinations when undertaken in the course of teaching, studying, or researching into, morphology. If Leonardo da Vinci were alive and working in England today, he too might therefore be at risk of prosecution under the Anatomy Act. Indeed, Mr Kelly has been compared to da Vinci, and praised as 'a

---

[86] Kathy Marks, 'Artist stole dozens of heads, limbs, and torsos, court is told', The *Independent*, 24 March 1998, 1.

[87] Quoted: Catherine Pepinster, 'I am not a monster. I am an artist', The *Independent on Sunday*, 13 April 1997, 3.

serious medical artist of considerable talent'.[88] The human body has been an object of artists' attention since murals decorated our first dwelling places. If we want art, rather than kitsch, we have to let our artists take risks—with their subjects, as well as with our sensibilities.

For the moralists, the Kelly case presented no special difficulty. Respect for the dead is a necessary piety: if we cannot respect the dead, what prospect is there for teaching respect for the living? The violence done to corpses is often an aspect of the horror of war. Atrocities of the kind depicted by Goya in his great documentary work, *The Disasters of War*, are always and only occasions for deep dismay. They do not—or should not—be regarded as providing interesting opportunities for a certain kind of 'shock art'. They are degraded when they are treated merely as the means to some greater (though ultimately dubious) aesthetic end. As in war, so in peace. Bodies should indeed be left in peace. They should not be permitted to become the playthings of artists (or anyone else).

This sense that the dead have rights which artists may not violate is a powerful one, perhaps amounting to a taboo, and should not lightly be dismissed. It explains the widespread revulsion expressed by visitors to the exhibitions of artist Sue Fox's photographs of dead bodies in a Manchester morgue. It explains the equally widespread disgust generated by the Chapman brothers' three-dimensional version of Goya's *Great Deeds Against the Dead* shown in the recent Royal Academy 'Sensation' exhibition. And it explains the readiness of the jury to convict the artist who exhibited a sculpture of a mannequin's head wearing foetal earrings.[89] There is the sense that these art works violate their subjects, that they prey upon the dead, exploiting them in their passivity, their vulnerability.

Conclusion

Artists will always force the boundaries of what is held to be art; it follows that they will also force the boundaries of what is

---

[88] Melvyn Howe, 'Body-snatch man wanted to be a Da Vinci', *Belfast Newsletter*, 25 March 1998, 5.

[89] Stephen White, 'Drawn and hung—or decently quartered?', *The Times*, 12 August 1997, 33.

lawful. Just as aesthetics lags behind art, so law lags behind aesthetics. This does not mean that there is not an aesthetics implicit in law. Quite to the contrary. It is the existence of such an implicit aesthetics that both produces and then validates law's proscriptions. Graffiti, for example, is a crime which is (as Ferrell has argued) constructed out of the clash of alternative aesthetics;[90] and though forgery likewise is a crime, it is not a 'natural' one, because it derives from historically specific notions of writing and authorship.[91] Art law itself is predicated on categories of private property (including the author's own intellectual property)[92] and originality which artists, and thereafter theories of art, are bound to challenge. Indeed, little of what is termed 'art law' is worthy of the name. Art law (in this jurisdiction at least) does not so much protect freedom of artistic expression as property interests in art (including the author's). Certainly, when the two collide, the former is usually the loser.

This leads, from the perspective of artists, to a certain disrespect for law, a qualified antinomianism: law has no place in art, because there should be no constraints on the imagination. (Artists usually make an exception of copyright infringement, because it does not appear to involve the inhibiting of artistic expression, only its parasitic replication.) They would like a special 'first amendment' right, one which prohibits any abridgement of freedom of artistic expression, and which is both stronger and narrower than the more general laws protecting speech. Stronger, because the special right would trump other rights (not to be defamed, for example); narrower, because it would relate only to art works. It is the sheer clumsiness of legal interventions in art that most exasperates its champions. Take, for example, the art critic Hilton Kramer's dismay at the New York flag desecration trial: 'Suddenly, complicated questions of aesthetic intention and artistic realization—questions that require a certain specialized intelligence and taste even to be properly phrased, let alone answered—were cast into an alien legalistic

---

[90] Ferrell, n. 57 above, 160.
[91] Stewart, n. 74 above, 27.
[92] 'ACKER: I sell copyright, that's how I make my living. LOTRINGER: You sell copyright? ACKER: That's how writers make their money. Absolutely precisely. The work isn't the property, it's the copyright': Acker, n. 53 above, 12.

vocabulary that precluded the very possibility of a serious answer.'[93]

From the perspective of moralists, however, artists deserve no greater licence than any other citizen. Art—or rather, artistic status—excuses nothing. As prosecuting counsel in the *Madame Bovary* trial put it: 'Art without rules is no longer art: it is like a woman ready to take all her clothes off. Obliging art simply to respect the rules of public decency is not to enslave it but to honour it.'[94] The aesthetic alibi, to advocates of such a position, is already too strong; it should be withdrawn altogether. And for a person such as Catherine MacKinnon, for example, so far from art providing a saving qualification to the pornographic, it colludes with pornography, reinforcing what is most objectionable about such representations of women: 'if a woman is subjected, why should it matter that the work has other value? Perhaps what redeems a work's value among men enhances its injury to women. Existing standards of literature, art . . . are, in feminist light, remarkably consonant with pornography's mode, meaning, and message.'[95] Moralists are not—or need not be (MacKinnon is a possible exception)—Platonists. They do not mistrust art; they merely hold that it should not have any special privileges. Art is a form of private property; as such it should be protected. Art is liable to offend against laws of decency, or whatever; when it does, it should be prohibited. And (a different point), if art's protection is to be secured by excluding certain of its instances from law's ambit, so be it. If art's inoffensiveness is to be secured by suppressing some of its instances, then so be it again.

These two positions, the artist's and the moralist's, cannot, I think, be reconciled. And there is no third position available to harmonize the contrary perspectives. We remain in the realm of discretion and contention: should this or that work be prosecuted? should this or that defendant be able to plead the aesthetic status

[93] Quoted in Adams, n. 84 above, 162. Of course, as far as the prosecutor was concerned, 'no exception [to the flag mutilation law] had been intended for sculpture' (149). The New York flag desecration case is *People* v. *Radich*, 270 N.Y.S. 2d 680, *United States ex rel. Radich* v. *Criminal Court of the City of N.Y.*, 459 F.2d 745 (2nd Cir. 1972).

[94] Quoted in Nicholas Harrison, *Circles of Censorship: Censorship and its Metaphors in French History, Literature, and Theory* (Oxford, 1995), 49.

[95] Catherine A. MacKinnon, *Towards a Feminist Theory of the State* (Cambridge, Mass., 1989), 202.

of his work as a defence? should the class of offences in which the aesthetic alibi is a defence be extended, and if so, which offences (or torts) should be added?[96] These questions remain inescapable; no grand synthesis will eliminate them. Law and art will remain in tension; the best that law and art (by which I include literature) studies can do is to describe the various aspects of their conflict.

[96] Libel is an obvious candidate: see Barendt, n. 80 above, and also Posner, n. 54 above, 382–9.

READING BLASPHEMY: THE NECESSITY FOR LITERARY ANALYSIS IN LEGAL SCHOLARSHIP

Anthony Bradney

Introduction

The familiar distinction taken in law and literature is between 'law *in* literature', and 'law *as* literature'. Essentially, 'law *as* literature' examines the possible relevance of literary texts, particularly those which present themselves as telling a legal story, as texts appropriate for study by legal scholars ... 'Law *as* literature', on the other hand, seeks to apply the techniques of literary criticism to legal texts.[1]

For such work very large claims can be made. Both forms of law and literature have the potential to bring powerful new insights into fundamental and far-reaching aspects of legal scholarship. This essay, however, is concerned with a third form of 'law and literature': the use of literary analysis when investigating both the content and efficacy of individual legal rules. The essay will argue that, in some areas of law, by ignoring literary analysis, as has hitherto largely been the case, legal scholars have done substantial damage to the quality of their work. Unlike the first two forms of law and literature the scope for this type of law and literature is relatively limited. It applies only to those instances where literary works are themselves the subject of legal rules. However, within the areas where this type of law and literature can be used its use is vital; a failure to use it distorts and damages all other forms of argument.

In order to demonstrate the necessity for the use by legal

---

[1] I. Ward, *Law and Literature* (Cambridge, 1995), 3.

scholars of this form of law and literature the law of blasphemy
will be used as an illustrative example. It is only an illustrative
example and there is nothing of importance in the choice of the
example. Other areas of law which also deal with literary works,
such as the law of obscenity or the law of intellectual property,
might, with equal advantage, have been chosen.

The Traditional Approach to the Analysis of the Law of Blasphemy

Feldman's *Civil Liberties and Human Rights in England and
Wales*, probably the leading and certainly the most exhaustive
account of civil liberties in England and Wales, devotes thirteen
pages to the law of blasphemy.[2] These pages draw, in their analysis, upon primary legal material, cases and statutes, secondary
legal material such as academic commentaries and official reports
by bodies such as the Law Commission, and secondary academic
material looking at legal history, history more widely, and philosophical work. There is little reference at any point in the pages to
literary material. The titles of some works which have been the
subject of blasphemy actions are noted but none of the usual
details about place of publication, date of publication and
publisher are given. The titles are noted as an object but the
contents of the works in question never become part of Feldman's
argument about the law of blasphemy. In contrast, in the case of
material which Feldman does use as part of his argument the usual
details of publication are given. The content of the books and
poems which have been the subject of prosecution are either not
described at all or are described in the briefest form. For example,
Kirkup's poem 'The Love That Dares to Speak its Name', subject
of prosecution in *Whitehouse* v. *Lemon*, is described as a poem
containing 'suggestions that Jesus had contemplated or enjoyed
homosexual acts with the apostles'.[3] This perfunctory reference to
two lines out of the eleven verses of Kirkup's poem stands in
contrast to the detailed use that Feldman makes of other types of
material. Feldman does observe that the 'literary forms' are different from other forms of writing, 'using rhetorical devices such as

---

[2] D. Feldman, *Civil Liberties and Human Rights* (Oxford, 1993), 685–98.
[3] [1979] 2 WLR 281; Feldman, n. 2 above, 693.

metaphor rather than reason to deliver their message'.[4] However, Feldman chooses not to use literary scholarship to sustain and expand upon this observation nor does he develop this remark in his analysis.

Feldman's approach to the law of blasphemy follows the traditional pattern of legal scholarship where that object which is the subject of a blasphemy action, the poem or novel, is silent when it comes either to the doctrinal analysis of the outcome of the action or to the philosophical and policy-orientated analysis of the appropriateness of the action.

It is now a common-place to note that legal scholarship has long since abandoned the simple and simplistic examination of law through pure doctrinal method.[5] Present-day legal scholars draw upon a wide range of techniques. Concepts, arguments, and data are readily taken from the social sciences as well as from some areas of the humanities such as history or philosophy.[6] However, to date, notwithstanding the 'law and literature' movement, the field of literary analysis has not been something to which legal scholars have looked for assistance. 'Law and literature' has had its own area of work but that has not permeated substantive or established areas of legal scholarship in the way that, for example, sociology, economics, and philosophy increasingly has. Feldman's work would have looked strange if he had failed to draw upon, for example, philosophical material but is unremarkable in not drawing upon literary material. What loss, if any, is there in this failure to look to literature and literary analysis when considering this area of law?

Rushdie's *The Satanic Verses*: Literary Analysis and the Desirability of a Blasphemy Law

The publication of *The Satanic Verses* and the subsequent failure of an attempt to prosecute the publishers for blasphemy in *R. v. Chief Metropolitan Magistrate, ex parte Choudhury* has reopened

---

⁴ Feldman, n. 2 above, 693.
⁵ See, for example, A. Bradney, 'Law as a Parasitic Discipline' (1998) 25 *Journal of Law and Society* 71, 71–3.
⁶ B. Hepple, 'The Renewal of the Liberal Law Degree' (1996) 55 *Cambridge Law Journal* 470, 485.

the debate about the viability of the present law of blasphemy.[7] What is now at issue is the proper place for a law of blasphemy in a society that is, or wants to be, multiracial, multicultural and multireligious.

The list of Muslim complaints about *The Satanic Verses* is long and varied. Since the United Kingdom Muslim community is divided both ethnically and in its precise understanding of Islam, not all complaints find equal resonance in all parts of the community. Qureshi and Khan, in their contribution to the debate about *The Satanic Verses*, list the principal Muslim complaints as being:

(1) insult of Divine revelation;
(2) insult to historical personalities of Islam;
(3) insult to Muslim women from the household of the Prophet;
(4) insult to the Prophet of Islam.[8]

To this initial list should be added complaints about the language of the novel. Thus, for example, Deedat spends eight of the twenty-four pages of his pamphlet on *The Satanic Verses* counting, describing and criticizing Rushdie's use of words such as 'fuck', 'fucking' and 'bastard' in the novel while in Akhtar's more sophisticated critique of *The Satanic Verses* one of his criticisms of the novel is that it is 'at times gratuitously obscene'.[9] There have also been complaints about the tone of the novel. Kabbani has written that the objections to *The Satanic Verses* arose because it was 'read by Muslims not as a serious critique but as frivolous mockery'.[10] In a similar fashion Akhtar unfavourably compares Rushdie's 'unprincipled prose' in *The Satanic Verses* with Mahfuz's 'reverent scepticism about Islamic conviction' in his novel *The Children of the Man of the Mountain*.[11] As important as the specific complaints about the content of *The Satanic Verses* is the fact that Muslim critics argue that Western, non-Muslim readers of *The Satanic Verses* bring to it only a partial vision. Such readers, it is said, cannot understand the nuances of references to

---

[7] S. Rushdie, *The Satanic Verses* (London, 1988); *R. v. Chief Metropolitan Magistrate, exp. Choudhury* [1991] 1 All ER 306.

[8] S. Qureshi and J. Khan, *The Politics of Satanic Verses: Unmasking Western Attitudes* (Leicester, 1989), 1–2.

[9] A. Deedat, *How Rushdie Fooled the West* (Birmingham, s. d.); S. Akhtar, *Be Careful with Muhammad!: The Salman Rushdie Affair* (London, 1989), 25.

[10] R. Kabbani, *Letter to Christendom* (London, 1989, 66).

[11] Ahktar, n. 9 above, 31, 30.

moments in Islamic history or facets of Muslim culture and therefore cannot understand the impact that Rushdie's handling of
these matters would have on Muslims.[12]

The sum of Muslim complaints about *The Satanic Verses* is the
call for a law of blasphemy that would protect them from the
offence occasioned by its publication.[13] Reading *The Satanic
Verses* provides a ready response to all of the above. First, *The
Satanic Verses* is not about Islam.

[A]t the centre of the novel is a group of characters most of whom are
British Muslims, or not particularly religious persons of Muslim background, struggling with just the sort of problems that have arisen to
surround the book, problems of hybridization and ghettoization, of
reconciling the old and the new.[14]

The novel begins with, focuses on, and ends with these characters, not with Islam nor with characters or events derived from
Islam. It never directly deals with Islam. It is a novel obsessed with
'the teeming reality of the society—Indian and immigrant—that is
Rushdie's principal subject'.[15] It is a novel about people who

have suffered the same kind of disease: one of detachment, of being
unable to connect ourselves to things, events, feelings. Most people define
themselves by their work, or where they come from, or suchlike; we have
lived too far inside our heads. It makes actuality damn hard to handle.[16]

And, finally, it is also a secular response to the question: how
do historical, revealed religions arise?

Two of the nine sections of the book, 'Mahound' and 'Return
to Jahilia', those complained of, look at the rise of a new religion.
In these sections there is no direct reference to Islam, Islamic
culture, or Islamic history. However, the characters and events
described are clearly drawn from versions of Islamic culture and
history. This is a necessary process. 'Nothing comes from nothing
. . . no story comes from nowhere; new stories are born from old'

---

[12] See, for example, Z. Sardar and M. Wyn Davies, *Distorted Imaginations:
Lessons from the Rushdie Affair* (London, 1990), ch. 6.
[13] See, for example, *The Muslim Manifesto* (London, 1991), 9.
[14] S. Rushdie, *Imaginary Homelands* (London, 1991), 394.
[15] P. Engblom, 'A Multitude of Voices: Carnivalization and Dialogicality on
the Novels of Salman Rushdie' in D. Fletcher (ed.), *Reading Rushdie: Perspectives
on the Fiction of Salman Rushdie* (Amsterdam, 1994), 296.
[16] S. Rushdie, *The Satanic Verses* (n. 7 above, 490).

as Rushdie remarks in a later novel, *Haroun and the Sea of Stories*.[17] If Rushdie is to communicate he must draw upon images which are known to his readers. If he is to tell *his* story he must recast those images. The recasting is as important, perhaps more important, than the source of the imagery. In the recasting Rushdie can create the story he wants. The recasting is radical, being both of character, history, and language. In *Shame*, Rushdie had written 'I, too, like all migrants, am a fantasist, I build imaginary countries and impose them on ones that exist.'[18] This is also part of the structure and argument of *The Satanic Verses*.

None of the above is to argue that the roots of the images in *The Satanic Verses* are unimportant. The novel should, in important senses, be read as the work of a Muslim dissident and as a Muslim book.[19] Nevertheless, one cannot understand the recast images, or hear the newly wrought language, if one only partially reads the novel; if one looks at some sections or some passages but not at the whole. Passages about Jahilia must be read in the context of the book as a whole. Meddeb argues that Islam will, in the long term, see *The Satanic Verses* as a part of its own necessary transformation and 'Islam will erect a statute to Rushdie'.[20] This, unlikely as it now seems, may be one effect of the novel. Nevertheless, Brennan is wrong in asserting that '*The Satanic Verses* poses as a revelation of a refurbished Islam based on the flawed humanity of the Prophet' not because this is an illegitimate reading of parts of the book but because those parts are not the whole of the book.[21] Part of the reason why it is not an insult to Islam is that it is not simply or directly about Islam.

Language as well as history must be warped if it is to serve Rushdie's purpose. For Indian novelists, whether writing in India or as part of the Indian diaspora, '[t]he telling has not been easy. One has to convey in a language that is not one's own the spirit that is one's own.'[22] In *The Satanic Verses*, as in his earlier novels,

---

[17] S. Rushdie, *Haroun and the Sea of Stories* (London, 1990), 86.

[18] S. Rushdie, *Shame* (London, 1983), 87.

[19] See S. Jalal Al-Azm, 'The Importance of Being Earnest' and S. Suleri, 'Contraband Histories: Salman Rushdie and the Embodiment of Blasphemy' in Fletcher, *Reading Rushdie*, n. 15 above, 255, 222.

[20] A. Meddeb, 'Waiting for Another Community' in *For Rushdie: Essays by Arab and Muslim Writers in Defense of Free Speech* (New York, 1994), 223.

[21] T. Brennan, *Salman Rushdie and the Third World* (London, 1989), 146.

[22] R. Rao, *Kanthapura* (Delhi, 1989), v.

Rushdie seeks to shape language so that it is true both to his characters and his politics. Thus, for example, Rushdie's use of the term 'Mahound', the medieval, pejorative, European name for Muhammad, for the character to whom the new religion is revealed, is a deliberate attempt to recapture a name rather than a gratuitous insult to the historical figure of Muhammad. 'To turn insults into strengths, whigs, tories, Blacks all chose to wear with pride the names they were given with scorn; likewise, our mountain-climbing, prophet-motivated solitary is to be the medieval baby-frightener, the devil's synonym: Mahound'.[23] 'Reclaim the metaphor' as he writes elsewhere.[24]

Critics have been divided about the success of Rushdie's attempt to decolonize the English language. Whilst Parameswaran has written that 'Rushdie's experimentation with language is one of his most remarkable achievements' Jussawalla, for example, has argued of *Midnight's Children*, '[t]he message is lost in the stylistic mire'.[25] However, whether the language is successful or not, to see it as being anything other than carefully considered is to ignore the content of the novel.

Many of the Muslim critiques of *The Satanic Verses* noted above suggest or imply a casualness or triviality in the novel. Such arguments cannot be sustained in the light of the writing. There is nothing 'gratuitous' about *The Satanic Verses*. It is intricate and deliberate in its form and ambitious in its use of language but, in a sense, there is nothing new in it when it is compared with Rushdie's earlier work.

Much of Rushdie's work has been concerned with the subjective, the individual, and the personal; with the way in which we make up our own worlds. In *Midnight's Children* Rushdie had written '[e]ven a baby is faced with the problem of defining itself'.[26] In *The Satanic Verses* he goes on to observe that '[a] man who sets out to make himself up is taking on the Creator's role, according to one way of seeing things; he's unnatural, a blasphemer'.[27] In making

---

[23] Rushdie, *The Satanic Verses*, n. 7 above, 93.
[24] Rushdie, *The Satanic Verses*, n. 7 above, 186.
[25] U. Parameswaran, *The Perforated Sheet: Essays on Salman Rushdie's Art* (New Delhi, 1988), 16; F. Jussawalla, *Family Quarrels: Toward a Criticism of Indian Writing in English* (New York, 1985), 18.
[26] S. Rushdie, *Midnight's Children* (London, 1981), 129.
[27] Rushdie, *The Satanic Verses*, n. 7 above, 49.

ourselves up poets, writers, have a particular place. 'A poet's work
. . . To name the unnameable, to point at frauds, to take sides,
start arguments, shape the world and stop it from going to
sleep.'[28]

This role creates an opposition to religions. In *The Satanic
Verses* Salman the Persian, a poet, acts as scribe to Mahound,
taking down his revelations. Gradually he begins to substitute
some of his words for those dictated to him. As Salman the
Persian says, '[i]ts [*sic*] his Word against mine'.[29] Rushdie's
metaphor reveals his consciousness of the necessary blasphemy
that there is in the secular attempt to understand the world.

In considering how one make one's self up Rushdie is distrust-
ful of final judgments. 'Anyone ever tries to tell you how this most
beautiful and most evil of planets is somehow homogeneous,
composed only of reconcilable elements, that it all *adds up*, you
get on the 'phone to the straitjacket tailor.'[30]

There is here an opposition to Islam but it is an opposition of
ideas not an opposition of insults; an opposition based on the
belief that 'The natural inheritance of everyone who is capable of
spiritual life is an unsubdued forest where the wolf howls and the
obscene bird of the night chatters.'[31]

One final point needs to be noted. *The Satanic Verses* is a
novel. It is a novel which draws upon the largely Western experience of novel writing. Whilst it does make some use of Muslim
images it also makes heavy use, sometimes acknowledged, sometimes not, of images and tropes drawn from Western writing.
Thus, for example, the epigraph to the novel is taken from Daniel
Defoe and on the first page of the novel Gibreel Farishta recites
Brecht's line, 'I tell you, you must die, I tell you, I tell you'.[32]
Equally the novel draws upon Hindu mythology and there are
detailed references to the Bombay film industry.[33] While it is true
that, as Muslim critics have suggested, a lack of knowledge of
Islam and Muslim culture will lead to a misreading of *The Satanic*

[28] Rushdie, *The Satanic Verses*, n. 7 above, 97.
[29] Rushdie, *The Satanic Verses*, n. 7 above, 368.
[30] Rushdie, *The Satanic Verses*, n. 7 above, 295.
[31] Rushdie, *The Satanic Verses*, n. 7 above, 397.
[32] Rushdie, *The Satanic Verses*, n. 7 above, 3.
[33] C. Cundy, *Salman Rushdie* (London, 1996), 3; S. Aravamudan, 'Being
God's Postman is No Fun, Yaar' in Fletcher, *Reading Rushdie*, n. 15 above, 190–4.

Verses it is also true, for the same reasons, that a lack of knowledge of Western literature will also lead to a misreading.

In his essay 'In Good Faith' Rushdie has written:

> *The Satanic Verses* is, I profoundly hope, a work of radical dissent and questioning and reimagining. It is not, however, the book it has been made out to be, that book containing 'nothing but filth and insults and abuse' that has brought people out on to the streets across the world. That book simply does not exist.[34]

The Satanic Verses is not an insult nor can what it contains be said to be insults if every passage is read in the context of the whole. It is, among other things, a secular reaction to the notion of revealed religion; a reaction which does not accept revealed religion on the terms that such religions set themselves. Reading and analysing the novel suggests that the Muslim case for reform of the blasphemy law is based upon a reading of the novel which may be honest but is certainly partial and possibly perverse. The novel sets out an alternative case to that of revealed religions and in doing so challenges such religions in a fundamental manner. If such a work is to be seen as being an insult, if such a work is to be encompassed in the law of blasphemy, then everybody who brings a secular understanding to Islam is little more than a living insult, a walking blasphemy.

Blasphemy as Argument: The Poetry of Siegfried Sassoon

In 1976 *Gay News* published a poem by James Kirkup entitled 'The Love That Dares to Speak Its Name'. In 1977, because of that act of publication, *Gay News* and its editor Denis Lemon were convicted of blasphemy.[35] Since that date reading the poem has not been a criminal offence; any further act of publication, however, has.[36]

'The Love That Dares to Speak Its Name' is sixty-six lines long and is divided into eleven verses. Much of the first eight verses is concerned with a detailed description of an act of sexual intercourse

---

[34] Rushdie, *Imaginary Homelands*, n. 14 above, 395.
[35] *R. v. Lemon* [1979] AC 617.
[36] In practice the poem has been republished many times since its successful prosecution: see N. Walter, *Blasphemy: Ancient and Modern* (London, 1990), 73–4.

between a centurion and the dead body of Christ. Within these eleven verses there is one verse devoted to conjecture, which, in the internal context of the poem seems metaphorical in form, about Christ's sexual relations before his death with a range of figures including the disciples, Pontius Pilate, John the Baptist, and Paul. The final three verses are largely a meditation on the analogy between acts of male homosexual intercourse and their aftermath and the Christian understanding of the process of crucifixion and resurrection.

There is a long tradition of blasphemy in English poetry. In order to read Kirkup's poem it is useful to begin with some of the First World War poetry of Siegfried Sassoon. A number of Sassoon's best-known poems are part of that tradition of blasphemy, counterposing Christian theology, the Christian church, and the sufferings of soldiers in the front line during the First World War. In 'The Redeemer', a poem set at night in the trenches, Sassoon first describes the misery of preparing for an attack and then a soldier seen in the light of a flare.

> . . . He stood before me there;
> I say that He was Christ; stiff in the glare,
> And leaning forward from His burdening task,
> Both arms supporting it; His eyes on mine
> Stared from the woeful head that seemed a mask
> Of mortal pain in Hell's unholy shine.

The poem then expands both on the pain of the soldiers and the fact that they are, nevertheless, 'not uncontent to die' for those still at home. Finally it returns to a soldier preparing for the next day's actions.

> He faced me, reeling in his weariness,
> Shouldering his load of planks, so hard to bear.
> I say that He was Christ, who wrought to bless
> All groping things with freedom bright as air,
> And with His mercy washed and made them fair.
> Then the flame sank, and all grew black as pitch,
> While we began to struggle along the ditch;
> And someone flung his burden in the muck,
> Mumbling: 'Oh Christ Almighty, now I'm stuck!'

The first reference to Christ in the poem is the simple, though for most at the time blasphemous, acknowledgement, of Christ in the common soldier. The second repeats this image and then over-paints it with the blasphemous slang which precisely, both literally and metaphorically, describes the position of the private soldier in the trenches at the time of the poem.

In 'They' Sassoon switches from Christian theology to the Christian church as incarnated in the British trenches during the war. A Bishop preaches the just war to the soldiers:

> ... 'When the boys come back
> 'They will not be the same; for they'll have fought
> 'In a just cause: they lead the last attack
> 'On Anti-Christ; their comrades' blood has bought
> 'New right to breed an honourable race,
> 'They have challenged Death and dared him face to face.'

Sassoon's portrait of the soldier's response is even simpler than the picture and more direct than the one he had drawn in 'The Redeemer'.

> 'We're none of us the same!' the boys reply.
> 'For George lost both his legs; and Bill's stone blind;
> 'Poor Jim's shot through the lungs and like to die;
> 'And Bert's gone syphilitic; you'll not find
> 'A chap who's served that hasn't found *some* change.'
> And the Bishop said: 'The ways of God are strange!'

The war had begun with a number of attempts to link Christian theology and the British war effort. In October 1914 the popular poet Alice Meynell had published a poem in *The Times* which ended with the lines

> The soldier dying dies upon a kiss,
> The very kiss of Christ.[37]

In the following month a booklet of messages from British religious leaders asking for volunteers to join the armed services was published. The booklet included messages from both the Archbishop of Canterbury and the Archbishop of York.[38] This Christian teaching was seen by Sassoon as pompous and irrelevant in the light of the prosaic but continual cruelties that were the reality of the soldiers' lives.

Finally, and most directly, in a third poem, 'Stand-to: Good

---

[37] *The Times*, 10 October 1914.   [38] *The Times*, 20 November 1914.

Friday Morning', Sassoon queries the power of the Christian message of final salvation for those fighting in the trenches of France.

> I'd been on duty from two and till four.
> I went and stared at the dug-out door.
> Down in the frowst I heard them snore.
> 'Stand to!' Somebody grunted and swore.
> Dawn was misty; the skies were still;
> Larks were singing, discordant, shrill;
> *They* seemed happy; but *I* felt ill.
> Deep in the water I splashed my way
> Up to the trench to our bogged front line.
> Rain had fallen the whole damned night.
> 'O Jesus, send me a wound to-day,
> And I'll believe in Your bread and wine,
> And get my bloody old sins washed white!'

In this poem the juxtaposition of Good Friday in the title and the message of the last three lines lends a particular fierceness to the blasphemy. Here also it is not just one Christian church, not just one institution, that is on trial but the whole Christian religion and in that trial the religion is, in a theological sense, blasphemously convicted.

These poems are not the only examples of blasphemy in the work of Sassoon during this period of his work. In her critical account of Sassoon, Moorcroft Wilson says, for example, of an unpublished poem, 'Christ and the Soldier', written at much the same time, 'The ironic play between the suffering and wounds of Christ and those of the soldiers at the Front, together with blasphemous and irreverent phrases . . . probably ensured that, even if Sassoon has decided to allow publication, it would not have been easy.'[39]

Of the three poems quoted above one, 'Stand-to', was prosecuted for blasphemy when it was published in New Zealand. The jury was instructed by the trial judge to consider 'whether, it is necessary, in order that there be every freedom for the expression of thought, that language of this sort should be indulged in' and that 'we have not yet reached the stage of what was termed

---

[39] J. Moorcroft Wilson, *Siegfried Sassoon: The Making of a War Poet; A Biography 1886–1918* (London, 1998), 284.

"growing toleration" to allow whatever abominable or filthy language may have been used in the trenches to be published in a printed book in order that people may have a true account of the life that went on there'.[40]

The jury failed to convict though it did add a rider to its verdict asking that 'similar publications of such literature should be discouraged'.[41] The theological, if not the legal, extent of the blasphemy nevertheless remains plain.

Sassoon's poems are arguments. *The Satanic Verses* avoids direct confrontation with Islam, preferring a more general argument about revealed religion. Sassoon's poems are, on the contrary, direct challenges both to a particular, official theological outlook, that the Allies were fighting a holy war, that was common at the time of the First World War and to the Christian message in the context of the experience of soldiers in the trenches. A later reading of poetry can sometimes forget the outrage caused by the poems when they were first read. Wordsworth's 'I wandered lonely as a cloud' is now commonly misread as a chocolate-box nature scene.[42] On publication it was taken by some as evidence that Wordsworth was 'an egoistic manufacturer of metaphysical importance with trivial themes' and caused much offence.[43] Similarly, we can understate the power of Sassoon's poems at the time of their publication. They are, or they contain, in a religious sense, blasphemies. And that, at a time when religion was more public and more dominant in the United Kingdom, is precisely and centrally the point of them.

Kirkup's poem, like Sassoon's early work, is undoubtedly, from some theological viewpoints, a blasphemy. '[T]he thrust of the poem was to attribute sin to Christ; and the prosecution . . . can be interpreted as a heresy trial. One of the great theological quarrels of all time, the so-called Arian heresy, was concerned with the question of whether Christ could sin.'[44]

Kirkup wrote of his poem, 'I wanted to portray strong, deep

---

[40] *The King* v. *Glover* [1922] Gazette Law Reports 185 at 186 and 187.
[41] *The King* v. *Glover* [1922] Gazette Law Reports 185 at 188.
[42] For a more complex reading see F. Pottle, 'The Eye and the Object in the Poetry of Wordsworth' in G. Dunklin (ed.), *Wordsworth: Centenary Studies Presented at Cornell and Princeton Universities* (Princeton, 1951).
[43] H. Pearson (ed.), *The Swan of Litchfield: A Selection from the Correspondence of Anna Seward* (London, 1936), 301.
[44] Clifford Longley in *The Times*, 18 July 1977.

emotion and intense passion (in both senses of the word), to present a human earthly and imperfect Christ symbolising my own outcast state, and that of all outcasts in our society.'[45]

As in the case of Sassoon, Kirkup had a particular theological argument that he wanted to put in poetical form. It seems doubtful that Kirkup's poem was read in this sense by the trial jury; that it was seen as a theological dissertation about who was included in the Christian message. Indeed, it seems doubtful that the poem was in fact read, in any meaningful sense, by the jury; that there was anything more than eyes crossing words. Expert evidence on the literary interpretation or the theological significance of the poem was not allowed. Alan King-Hamilton, the trial judge, considered these matters to be 'simple'.[46] *Pace* King-Hamilton's view, twelve randomly chosen people are unlikely to have had the necessary expertise to read any poetry with any accuracy, let alone poetry with the challenging subject matter that Kirkup had chosen. Reading 'new mint[ed] . . . speech' is not an ordinary matter and an ordinary reading is not likely to be a reading of the poetry.[47] Eyes may have scanned paper, words may have been understood in isolation, but the whole is unlikely ever to have been seen. As a result, the conviction has meant that the argument of the poem, and among other things the poem is exactly an argument, is thus lost from sight.

Even the briefest consideration of British history shows that its literature has long been part of the process of schism, generation, revaluation, renewal and continuation that is its history of religion.[48] Now, as a result of *Whitehouse* v. *Lemon*, 'The Love That Dares to Speak its Name' is a hidden part of that history.

Literary Analysis and the *Actus Reus* of Blasphemy

The previous two sections of this essay have argued that consideration of the literary nature of works prosecuted, or presented for

---

[45] Walter, *Blasphemy Ancient and Modern*, n. 36 above, 72.

[46] G. Robertson, *Obscenity* (London, 1979), 240; A. King-Hamilton, *And Nothing But the Truth* (London, 1982), 176.

[47] E. Pound, 'The Wisdom of Poetry' in E. Pound, *Selected Prose: 1909–1965* (London, 1973), 331.

[48] Nor is this just true for the United Kingdom. See, for example, in relation to Islam, Meddeb, 'Waiting for Another Community', n. 20 above.

prosecution, under a blasphemy law adds to and alters the nature
of arguments about the philosophical status and social efficacy of
such a law. I now turn to consider whether, in the light of their
nature, literary works can ever appropriately, in a doctrinal sense,
be the subject of prosecution.

The mental element, the *mens rea*, of blasphemy is now relatively clear, the offence is one of strict liability where there is only
the need to show that publication took place, not that there was
any awareness of the blasphemous nature of that which was
published. The nature of that which makes something blasphemous, the *actus reus*, is more obscure.[49] Most analysis of the *actus
reus* begins with Lord Parker in *Bowman* v. *Secular Society Ltd*.
In order for there to be blasphemy at common law 'there must be
an element of vilification, ridicule, or irreverence as would be
likely to exasperate the feelings of others'.[50]

Precisely what this *dictum* might mean has long been the
subject for debate. The Law Commission in their Working Paper
on blasphemy and related areas of law on blasphemy concluded
that '. . . it is hardly an exaggeration to say that whether or not a
publication is a blasphemous libel can only be judged *ex post
facto*'.[51] However, the fact that there need only be 'an element'
within the work in question which might be seen as 'vilification,
ridicule or irreverence', while understandable because a requirement that the whole work should be seen as 'vilification, ridicule
or irreverence' and should be seen only as that, would put an
impossible probative and evidentiary burden on the prosecution,
seems to suggest that the blasphemous content of the whole work
need only be relatively slight. 'An element' may be a small part or
may be only one among many things in a work. On this test it will
be relatively easy to show that a poem, play, or novel is blasphemous even though it may only be blasphemous in part and its
blasphemy may only be a part of it. However, our understanding
of the *actus reus* of blasphemy has to take account of the fact that
it has long been recognized that merely denying any truth of
Christianity as understood by the Church of England is not, of
itself, committing the crime of blasphemy. According to Lord

---

[49] For the *mens rea* see *Whitehouse* v. *Lemon* [1979] 2 WLR 281.
[50] *Bowman* v. *Secular Society Ltd* [1917] AC 406, 446.
[51] *Offences Against Religion and Public Worship*, Law Commission Working
Paper No. 79 (London, 1981), para. 6.1.

Coleridge, as long as comment stays within the bounds of the 'decencies of controversy' and there is no 'wilful intent to pervert, insult or mislead others' and 'no wilful misrepresentations or wilful sophistry, calculated to mislead the ignorant and unwary' there can be no criminal blasphemy.[52]

Reconciling Lord Parker's statement with that of Lord Coleridge is not easy. It seems not merely plausible but likely that believers will be as much exasperated by the content of denial as by its tone and indeed may be more exasperated by denial that is rendered in a seemingly cogent, rational form than by, for example, a random epithet. Moreover, many forms of denying the Christian message must, by their very nature, contain an element of seeming irreverence because the denial is based upon suggestions about the psychological frailty or philosophical and historical credulity of believers and because the denial results in a doubt about either the good faith of believers or their intellectual reliability. Put shortly, some forms of aetheism may involve believing that Christians are people of good will who are misguided but, in respects other than their religious faith, are good citizens. Other forms of aetheism will involve the propositions that believers are wilfully incapable of understanding either themselves or the world around them and, because of that bad faith, make judgments about the world which result in untold harm. The latter view, which has characterized much atheistic literature, cannot, it seems, be put with reverence.

The Law Commission's abandonment of any attempt to define the *actus reus* of blasphemy must make for caution in this area. The pronouncements upon which writers concerned with the doctrine of the law of blasphemy ponder are too antique and too slight to bear the burden of very much analysis. Yet the need, inherent in the modern law of blasphemy, to allow some freedom of comment about matters of religion, while still putting a boundary around that comment, indicates that steps towards a resolution of the problem of the *actus reus* might be made by suggesting that, although the *mens rea* of the crime is one of no *mens rea* at all—the crime is one of strict liability and the only question is did the accused publish the matter in question—the *actus reus* does contain a question of intent. 'To vilify' or 'to ridicule' are purposeful activities. To do them you

---

[52] R. v. *Ramsey and Foote* (1883) 15 Cox CC 231 at 238 and 236.

need to intend what they mean even if you do not understand the terms themselves. You can vilify without being able to define 'vilify' but you cannot vilify without intending what is meant by vilification. More intriguingly, the person who wholly rejects religion, including even the *bona fides* of those who say they are believers, is the person who is least capable of 'irreverence'. They cannot act in an irreverent manner because they do not believe in the possibility of reverence, at least in relation to religion. They are best described as 'areverent'. As Rushdie writes in *The Satanic Verses*, '[w]here there is no belief, there is no blasphemy'.[53] On this test, distinguishing between those who have involved themselves in the *actus reus* of blasphemy and those who have not will be, in an evidentiary sense, very difficult but, in probative terms, will involve a very plain philosophical distinction. Those who set out to describe the world as they see it and to describe it as clearly and sincerely as they can, whether they do that simply in order to state their vision or whether they do it in order to convert others to that vision, cannot be said to be setting out to vilify or to ridicule and cannot be said to be being irreverent. They are simply setting out the world as they see it.

The requirement of a subjective element in the act of blasphemy, albeit not a requirement that there be a subjective intent to blaspheme, might seem unnecessary and even counter to the social policy that lies behind the law. To the believer there may seem to be no distinction between the pronouncements of those who seek to state the world as they see it and those who, making exactly the same pronouncements, do so because they seek to vilify, ridicule or to be irreverent. Both exasperate the feelings of the believer. But the law of blasphemy is addressed to both believers and non-believers and a requirement of intent in the *actus reus* of the blasphemy may capture the policy needs of both groups allowing both to express themselves where they intend no harm to the other.

If the above approach is taken to the law of blasphemy then one consequence is that, at a stroke, literature, or some readings of literature, or some readings of some forms of literature, are taken outside the scope of the criminal law of blasphemy. Brodsky, for example, has written that 'poetry is . . . the most concise, the most condensed way of conveying human

[53] Rushdie, *The Satanic Verses*, n. 7 above, 380.

experience'.[54] He has also asserted that 'a poem offers you a sample of complete, not slanted, human intelligence at work'.[55] If this is poetry how could a poem ever meet the test for the *actus reus* of blasphemy described above? A complete sample of human experience says 'this is the world for the poet; this is the world of the poet'. It does not set out to vilify or ridicule because it is importantly about the poet not about anybody else. Similarly, if writers have voices which are 'fully and undisguisably their own, who, to borrow William Gass's image, *sign every word they write*' how can their work ever simply vilify or ridicule?[56] In vilification or ridicule there is not the element of the deeply personal appraisal that is referred to here. Vilification and ridicule are banal. Nothing in them signs every word of their content. If writers are 'strong poets', 'major figures with the persistence to wrestle with their strong precursors, even to death', how can they in that writing commit the criminal law of blasphemy as described above?[57] Works which wrench the reader to the author's way of seeing the world do not admit of the vision of others. They do not vilify or ridicule others because they are not about how others see the world, they are about how the author sees the world. Strong claims for literature are made in different ways and about different forms and about different writers. Those who make such claims, if correct, take their charges outside the law of blasphemy.[58]

To take such a view as the above is to take literature, not writing, outside the realms of the law of blasphemy. Poetry will not be capable of being blasphemous, verse might be and doggerel certainly would be. Most writers are not 'strong poets'; most do not have a clear personal voice.

---

[54] J. Brodsky, *On Grief and Reason* (London, 1996), 100.
[55] Brodsky, n. 54 above, 206.
[56] S. Rushdie, 'Is Nothing Sacred?' in S. Rushdie, *Imaginary Homelands* (London, 1992), 415, 425–6.
[57] H. Bloom, *The Anxiety of Influence* (London, 1973), 5.
[58] Another argument that has some similarity with the above in taking literature out of the purview of the law of blasphemy is to say that the misreadings of those who saw *The Satanic Verses* and 'The Love That Dares to Speak its Name' as blasphemous in law are not merely illustrative, individual misreadings but that, rather, to see criminal blasphemy in literature will always, because of literature's inherent complexity, involve reading only part of the work in question.

The Law of Blasphemy and *Literary* Analysis

An argument for reading the works which are the subject of potential prosecution is not necessarily an argument for the literary analysis of those works. Indeed, some writers have issued cautions about the use of literary analysis.

The proper mission of the Law and Literature movement is to read literature, not as ('wannabe') literary critics, but as lawyers seeking to pursue the legal themes of power, authority, order, adjudication, penalty, justice and so on which occupy us all.[59]

Others have counselled that law and literature should be seen as being 'fun'.[60]

To some extent the first argument is a familiar one. Those who have used 'non-legal' material in the examination of law have long debated the merits of various levels and forms of engagement with that material.[61] Nor are such debates limited to the proper manner in which law can appropriate the work of another discipline. Other disciplines have the same debates. In literature, for example, Ricks has criticized not the use of philosophy in the analysis of literature but the fact that literary theorists have, in his view, begun to adjudicate on debates in philosophy.[62] For Ricks, literary critics should remain literary critics whatever materials they choose to use; for Morison and Bell, and for others, lawyers should remain lawyers. The second argument seems to carry us along in a different direction, asking us to remember an essential difference in the nature of the material, the literature, we are now engaging with and not, in our handling of it, damage or neglect this nature.

Plainly the texts, the poems, the plays, and the novels, are the most important matter in work of the kind described in this

[59] J. Morison and C. Bell, 'Introduction' in J. Morison and C. Bell (eds)., *Tall Stories? Reading Law and Literature* (Aldershot, 1996), 1–2.

[60] C. Bell, 'Teaching Law as Kafkaesque' in Morison and Bell, n. 59 above, 31.

[61] See, for example, P. Thomas (ed.), *Socio-Legal Studies* (Aldershot, 1997) in general, and in particular, A. Bradshaw, 'Sense and Sensibility: Debates and Developments In Socio-Legal Research Methods' and P. Fitzpatrick, 'Distant Relations: The New Constructionism In Critical and Socio-Legal Studies' in that volume.

[62] C. Ricks, 'Literary Principles as Against Theory' in C. Ricks, *Essays in Appreciation* (Oxford, 1996), 312–13.

essay. That point is central to this essay. The texts are primary material. They contain arguments and, arguably, a different kind of argument to that found in the more traditional, non-legal material with which those in law schools have become familiar over the last two decades. What is vital, and what has not yet happened, is an engagement with that material. Moreover, the engagement in this essay has, implicitly, followed the tradition of Richards, Empson, and Leavis in emphasizing a personal reading of the text.[63] The reading is a personal one though not one that is simply subjective. The reading is driven by the material in the text and takes the form of saying about the text, 'this is so, isn't it', though, unlike Leavis, one would have to acknowledge, at the very least, the difficulty of disentangling cultural baggage in achieving that reading of the text. To attempt such a reading is indeed 'fun', but fun in the Platonic sense that contemplation is the supreme form of human good, not in the sense that this reading is any easier or any less important than other work done by legal scholars. The commentaries, the secondary material, being something that can teach us more about the primary material, are part of the attempt at the reading of the text. The secondary material is usually less 'fun', or, perhaps more accurately, less graceful than the primary material but to treat literature as 'fun' comes very close to treating it less seriously than other kinds of material. If we accept that 'literature *is* a dictionary of meaning, a compendium of meanings for this or that human lot, for this or that experience. It is the dictionary of the language in which life speaks to man'[64] then we should conclude that literature should be treated with the same care as anything else we use. And that means considering what other people have had to say about the works we are looking at and ensuring that our work has the usual patina of scholarship. Thus what this essay argues for is not just a consideration of literature but also literary analysis.

In seeking to engage with literary analysis as well as with the texts that are in issue the danger is that, as with other use of

[63] Although any such reading with a 'Leavisite basis . . . [has to] problematise the concepts that that school of criticism takes for granted': F. Azim, *The Colonial Rise of the Novel* (London, 1993), 4.
[64] Brodsky, n. 54 above, 33.

'non-legal' materials, literary analysis is used badly; that the historical arguments are bad history, the philosophical arguments are bad philosophy and the literary criticism is bad literary criticism. This is a serious danger but the only remedy for this ill is the process of criticism leading to validation or falsification that follows publication. Moreover, to lock ourselves into a position of functioning as 'lawyers', even when we use 'non-legal' materials, is to stultify and freeze debate. We need to be alive to the possibility that what 'law and literature' might do is to convince us that 'the legal themes' which 'occupy us all' are in fact the wrong themes or that they do not exhaust the possibilities of discussion. We are not bound by a pattern of self-perpetuating professional fields and should not forget Steiner's caustic comment that 'cows have fields'.[65]

Conclusion

The aims of this essay are modest. It seeks to do no more than establish that there is material within literature which is worthy of consideration within the law school and which has not yet had that consideration. Whether the individual points put in this essay receive assent is neither here nor there. To accept that they have been made and that they cannot either be ignored or answered by reference to the usual materials would be sufficient for the purposes of the essay. Blasphemy is not central to this essay; law and literature is. The essay could as readily have treated areas of law other than blasphemy.

Borges in his well-known short story *Pierre Menard, Author of the Quixote* describes a writer who sets out to rewrite certain chapters of Cervantes' *Don Quixote*, initially by seeking, '[t]o know Spanish well, to re-embrace the Catholic faith, to fight against Moors and Turks, to forget European history between 1602 And 1918, and to *be* Miguel de Cervantes' and later, having rejected this method as being too easy, 'to continue being Pierre Menard and to arrive at *Don Quixote* through the experiences of Pierre Menard'.[66] Sarlo, in her study of Borges, writes of this story, '[w]ith Menard's method, original writings do not exist and

---

[65] G. Steiner, *Errata* (London, 1997), 155.
[66] Jorge Luis Borges, *Fictions* (London, 1965), 46.

intellectual property is called into question'.[67] As such the story provides a fundamental challenge to the notion that is the foundation of the law of intellectual property.

Literature offers legal scholarship a fertile field for reflection. Whether law will take that offer up remains in doubt.

[67] B. Sarlo, *Jorge Luis Borges: A Writer on the Edge* (London, 1993), 32.

CAPTURING CHILDHOOD: THE INDIAN CHILD IN THE EUROPEAN IMAGINATION

One may scan work after work on history, society, and morality and find little reference to the fact that all people start as children and that all peoples begin in their nurseries . . . [T]ribes and nations, in many intuitive ways, use child training to the end of gaining their particular form of mature human identity, their unique version of integrity . . .

Erik Erikson, *Childhood and Society*[1]

The historical image of the Indians is pretty well set, we are the bad guys who burned the wagon trains and images are the white man's game.

Vine Deloria Jr, *Custer Died for Your Sins*[2]

Anne McGillivray

The child of Rousseau's noble savage was also his untutored Emile.[3] Residential schooling, a tutorial regime for Indian childhood, was installed by Canada in the late nineteenth century. The schools were to eradicate Indian culture by pressing the child into Christian citizenship, in the larger moral commodification of childhood in which children were culturally severable

[1] E. Erikson, *Childhood and Society* (Boston, 1963), 16.
[2] V. Deloria, *Custer Died for Your Sins: An Indian Manifesto* (New York, 1969), 272.
[3] J.-J. Rousseau, *Emile* (1762; republished in translation, London, 1974). Rousseau imaged a new childhood, innocent, even divine. Innocence being unsustainable and bookish education corrupting, *Emile* promoted a tutored mediation of childhood experience. His 'noble savage', developed in other works, set the Romantic image of the Indian. See Gowanlock's deconstruction, text accompanying n. 73 below.

and transformable.[4] Assimilation did not succeed. Many children
were abused sexually and physically. Canada apologized in 1997
and by 1998, 1,200 former pupils had filed lawsuits.[5] One First
Nation, seizing a central issue, is suing Canada and three
Christian denominations for cultural destruction through residential schooling.[6] State interference in the lives of perishing or
dangerous children was justified by failed parenting. 'Being
Indian' came to mean inheriting a failed culture. What images
shaped and justified these transformative efforts? How was Indian
childhood seen in the Eurocolonial imagination?

From first contact, Indians were objects of the European gaze.[7]
Columbus took captives to Europe as proof of discovery. By
1501, Indians had been exhibited to promote colonial ventures,
satisfy public curiosity and make money.[8] Images of a young
Inuit woman and her 7-year-old daughter exhibited at Antwerp
in 1557 were circulated throughout Europe in broadsheets calling upon tropes of the naked anthrophagous Wild Man. Inuit
displayed in London by Frobisher included Arnaq ('woman') and
her infant Nutaaq ('a new thing'), taken in 1577. All captives
died within a few weeks, the baby last despite employment of a
wet nurse.[9] The exhibits inspired Trinculo's speech in *The
Tempest*, on meeting Caliban:

What have we here? a man or a fish? dead or alive? A fish: he smells like
a fish . . . Were I in England . . . and had but this fish painted, not a holiday fool there but would give a piece of silver: there would this monster

---

[4] A. McGillivray, 'Introduction: Governing Childhood'; 'Therapies of
Freedom: The Colonization of Aboriginal Childhood' in McGillivray (ed.),
Governing Childhood (Aldershot, 1997). 'Indian' is used here as the historic
designation of North American First Nations. The preferred term is 'Aboriginal'
which includes the Innu, registered Indians, Métis and others of First Nations
descent.

[5] 'Residential schools devastated Indian society, lawsuit claims', *Toronto Star*,
23 June 1998. A healing fund of $350 million was established by Indian Affairs.

[6] Key First Nation alleges that schools promised in the 'numbered Treaties'
would recognize Indian society and let it flourish but instead undermined elders'
influence, prevented cultural transmission and contributed to deplorable social
conditions ('Residential', n. above.)

[7] See O. P. Dickason, *The Myth of the Savage and the Beginnings of French
Colonialism in the Americas* (Edmonton, 1997).

[8] C. F. Feest, 'Editor's Postscript' in Feest (ed.), *Indians and Europe: An
Interdisciplinary Collection of Essays* (Aachen, 1987).

[9] W. C. Sturtevant and D. B. Quinn, 'This New Prey: Eskimos in Europe in
1567, 1576, and 1577' in Feest, n. 8 above, 61.

make a man; any strange beast there makes a man: when they will not give a doit to relieve a lame beggar, they will lay out ten to see a dead Indian.[10]

Shakespeare drew Caliban, anagram of 'cannibal', from reports of enslaved Carib Indians, extinct by 1640.

Like the infant Nutaaq peering from his mother's hood, early images of Indian childhood are interstitial, encoded in a variety of texts. A rich source is the captivity accounts which set the image of the Indian in the popular mind and fictioned the politics of extermination across four centuries. The concern is not 'truth' but images produced in the multiple causes of truth. For Foucault,

The possibility exists for fiction to function in truth, for a fictional discourse to induce effects of truth, and for bringing it about that a true discourse engenders or 'manufactures' something that does not as yet exist, that is, 'fictions' it. One 'fictions' history on the basis of a political reality that makes it true, one 'fictions' a politics not yet in existence on the basis of a historical truth.[11]

Travellers' tales of foreign spaces and spaces of the soul, captivity accounts fiction nineteenth-century politics of cultural extermination and the extermination of Indian childhood.

Reading Captivity

Indian captivity predates European contact. The Jesuit Lafitau describes the taking of captives and their award to lodges which have lost a family member.[12] The captive might be adopted (a girl might replace a boy or a youth an infant) or ransomed or killed, if the lodge is poor or the captive unfit due to age, weakness or character.

---

[10] W. Shakespeare, *The Tempest*, II. ii. 24 *et seq.*

[11] M. Foucault, 'The Will to Know: The History of Sexuality' in C. Gordon (ed.), *Power/Knowledge: Selected Interviews and Other Writings 1972–1977* (New York, 1980), 193.

[12] J. F. Lafitau, *Customs of the American Indians Compared with the Customs of Primitive Times* (originally published as *Moeurs des sauvages ameriquains, compares aux moeurs des premiers temps*, Paris, 1724), (W. N. Fenton and E. L. Moore (eds., and trans.), Toronto, 1974), 155. A missionary to New France Iroquois from 1712 to 1717, Lafitau exemplifies the scholarly trend of comparing Old and New World paganism and advanced a primitivism informing Rousseau's later construct of the noble savage. Lafitau's respect for New World cultures was unprecedented. The work received wide popular readership in its day. An English translation awaited the 1974 Champlain Society edition.

Death is certain if the lodge has lost 'many warriors or other persons . . . even a child at the breast for whom mourning is still recent'.[13] Torture includes ingenious use of coals, knives, heated axeheads and torches, partial flaying and beating, periodic revival with food and rest, not ceasing until death. 'The Jesuits, by furnishing the presents necessary for saving them, have saved many of these unfortunate victims whom they have retrieved from these barbarians' fires.'[14] Capturing Eurocolonials became an important tactic in New World European warfare.

As an archetypal initiation into the heroic, a Jungian journey from Separation to Transformation to Return, captivity gripped the popular imagination.[15] Three of four best-sellers from 1680 to 1729 were captivity accounts, one the first work attributed to an American woman, Mary Rowlandson, captured in Massachusetts in 1676.[16] The fourth, also an Everyman's redemptive journey of the soul, was Bunyan's *The Pilgrim's Progress* (1678). Historical streams are traceable—discovery, trials of the spirit, propaganda for imperialist expansion, tales told 'behind the frontier' to enhance Eurocolonial heritage, artistic imagination 'beyond the frontier'.[17] Earlier accounts inform subsequent ones, tropes are readily exchanged and accounts are mediated (often ghost-written or 'as told to'), making divisions between fact and fiction, observation and hearsay, anticipation and experience, fluid. (Women took care to say they had not been ravished, for example, but ravishment became a trope of captivity.) Accounts reject primitivist Romantic views of the noble savage, reflected in Longfellow's *Hiawatha* (1855).[18] Anti-primitivism is most apparent in post-1850 'Indian-hater' stories, forerunner of the Western. Here the Indian symbolizes everything hostile to the settler, justifying vendetta in

---

[13] Lafitau, n. 12 above, 172.   [14] Lafitau, n. 12 above, 155.

[15] R. VanDerBeets, *The Indian Captivity Narrative: An American Genre* (Lanham, Md., 1984).

[16] M. Rowlandson, *A True History of the Capture and Restoration of Mrs. Mary Rowlandson, A Minister's Wife in New England. Wherein is set forth, The Cruel and Inhuman Usage she underwent amongst the* Heathens *for Eleven Weeks time: and her Deliverance from them* (Boston, London, 1682).

[17] J. Levernier and H. Cohen (eds.), *The Indians and Their Captives* (Westport, London, 1977), Introduction. About 2,000 accounts purportedly based on fact and published prior to 1880 are collected in the Newberry Library, republished by Garland Books.

[18] S. Sullivan, 'The Literary Debate over "the Indian" in the Nineteenth Century' (1985) 9 *American Indian Culture and Research Journal* 13–31.

late-frontier settlement. Two thousand Eurocolonials left accounts of captivity. 'Countless' never returned.[19] Captivity is 'a massive historical reality' shaping national character, feeding artistic imagination and defining Eurocolonial culture.[20]

This reality lies in 'the rich narrative and imaginal activity that has taken place around the topos of captivity'.[21] Captivity is 'an ultimate boundary situation where human existence, identity, and cultural meaning are called into question', new relations of power are installed and cultural markers are stripped through deprivation and ritual degradation. The body is 'a painful register of the shattered or porous boundaries of inside and outside, self and other, past and present . . . whose integrity is ever in danger of being violated by being pricked, slashed, gashed, crushed, clubbed, scratched, scalped, bitten, burned, penetrated, painted, scarred and tattooed'.[22] Returned captives, often taking bicultural roles as traders and guides, retained inscriptions in speech and gait, subverting Enlightenment distinctions between savagery and civilization, self and Other. Assimilation was the ultimate subversion.[23]

With the construction of childhood as a distinct life estate, captivity accounts were directed at children. Gray and Bowen, Publishers, announced in 1830 'a series of works for Youth' designed 'to supply the children of the United States, an entertaining abstract of the most popular books of travels . . . written in a style of great simplicity . . . divested of anything which ought not to be exhibited to the youthful mind.' Chapters include 'How the Indians set people on fire', 'How the Indian chief poisoned many people', and 'How the Indian beat 2 squaws for quarrelling'. The 'youthful mind' was used to strong stuff. In the post-1850 focus on the moral child, Protestant presses published captivity tales for children. An 1854 Presbyterian publication, *The Captives of Abb's Valley*, tells of how the young captive's faith melts his captors' hearts, their cruelty changes to kindness and they convert to Christianity.[24] Indian-ness is problematized. In *Regina, the*

[19] Levernier and Cohen, n. 17 above.

[20] VanDerBeets, n. 15 above, 50.

[21] G. L. Ebersole, *Captured by Texts: Puritan to Postmodern Images of Indian Captivity* (Richmond, Va., 1995). All quotations in this paragraph are from this source.   [22] Ebersole, n. 21 above, 7.

[23] Ebersole, n. 21 above, 4.

[24] J. M. Brown, *The Captives of Abb's Valley: A Legend of Frontier Life* (Philadelphia, 1854, repr. Garland, 1965), 5.

German Captive (1856), the Reverend Weiser writes, 'The American Indians are fast passing away, and our children should know something about their cruelties, and thus see why God has permitted them to be banished from their native land.'[25] In *The Child Captives* (1870), Margaret Hosmer declares her

earnest desire to represent Indian life as it truly is, not totally without humanity and even tenderness of instinct, but sadly and bitterly benighted. In truth, without Christianizing influences, they are beset by evils in example and association of far too black and degrading a nature to be mentioned in a book like this.[26]

The child captive is hard-working, obedient, honest, pure, faithful in prayer and Bible study. The savage is dying and for good reason. Savage children lack 'the charm, intellect, and moral aptitude of their white counterparts; moreover their education and even their forms of play are declared to be such that the limited potential the Indian children begin with is never developed', writes the anonymous author of Miss Coleson's captivity (1864).[27] 'In sum, Indians are found to be closer in nature to animals than to civilized human beings, since their sense of hearing, sight and smell, are much more acute than those of white people, and enables them to distinguish objects at an incredible distance.' In captivity lessons for children, the able, terrifying Indian child and her loving parents are lost, as is the challenge to the dichotomy of red and white, savagery and civilization—the 'white Indian'.

Childhood in Captivity

Taking for his text the inscription of spiritual warfare on captive bodies, 'a Book of some Consequences', Cotton Mather instructs his 1698 congregation in the tropes of captivity.[28]

---

[25] R. Weiser, *Regina the German Captive; or, True Piety Among the Lowly* (1856; repr. Garland, 1969), 6–7.

[26] M. Hosmer, *The Child Captives* (1870, repr. Garland, 1983), 229–30.

[27] Anon., *Miss Coleson's Narrative of Her Captivity Among the Sioux Indians!* (1864, repr. Garland, 1979), 36–8. All quotations in this paragraph are from this source.

[28] C. Mather, *Humiliations Follow'd with Deliverances* (1697) in *Magnalia Christi Americana* (1702, repr. *The Ecclesiastical History of New England*, repr. Garland 3), 220–1. All quotations in this paragraph are from this source.

Let the Daughters of our Zion think with themselves, what it would be, for fierce Indians to break into their houses, and brain their Husbands and their Children before their Eyes, and Lead them away a Long Journey into the Woods; and if they began to fail and faint in the Journey, then for a Tawny Salvage to come with Hell fire in his Eyes, and cut 'em down with his Hatchet; or, if they could miraculously hold out, then for some Filthy and ugly Squaw's to become their insolent Mistresses, and insolently to abuse 'em at their pleasure a thousand inexpressible ways; and, if they had any of their Sucking Infants with them, then to see those Tender Infants handled at such a rate, that they should beg of the Tygres, to dispatch 'em out of hand.

Mather's audience included Hannah Dustan, 'an *Example*, full of Encouragement unto those humiliations'. Dustan escaped with her maid and a boy by killing ten Indians, including children, in their sleep and returned to take their scalps for bounty. Mather details the torture of captured children and admonishes the children in his audience, 'Oh! See that you become Serious, Pious, Orderly Children; Obedient unto your Parents, Conscientious to keep the Lords Day, and afraid of committing any Wickedness.' Goodness averts Indian captivity and a worse captivity by sin.

Mather's 'captivity by sin' is assimilation into Indian life. No Indian had been assimilated into European culture in eighteenth-century British North America but countless Eurocolonials became 'Indian'. Benjamin Franklin writes in 1753,

When an Indian Child has been brought up among us, taught our language and habituated to our Customs, yet if he goes to see his relations and makes one Indian Ramble with them, there is no perswading him ever to return, and that this is not natural merely as Indians, but as men, is plain from this, that when white persons of either sex have been taken prisoners young by the Indians, and lived a while among them, tho' ransomed by their Friends, and treated with all imagineable tenderness to prevail with them to stay among the English, yet in a short Time they become disgusted with our manner of life, and the care and pains that are necessary to support it, and take the first good Opportunity of escaping again into the Woods, from whence there is no reclaiming them.[29]

In his 1782 *Letters from an American Farmer*, Crevecoeur offers a different theory. Captured children became 'so perfectly Indianized' that their parents did not know them or 'ran to their

---

[29] B. Franklin, *The Papers of Benjamin Franklin* (New Haven, 1961).

adopted parents for protection against the effusions of love their unhappy real parents lavished upon them!'.[30] Indian life

cannot be, therefore, so bad as we generally conceive it to be and there must be in the Indians' social bond something singularly captivating, and far superior to anything to be boasted of among us; for thousands of Europeans are Indians, as we have no examples of even one of these Aborigines having from choice become European!

John Hunter, adopted as a small child in Missouri in 1801, observed

three or four white children, apparently of my own age, while travelling among the different tribes. They appeared, like myself, to have been at first forced to assume the Indian's character, and habits; but time and a conformity to custom had nationalized them, and they seemed as happy and content as Indians as though they had descended directly from the Indians and were in possession of their patrimony . . . It is a remarkable fact, that white people when brought up in the company of Indians, became unalterably attached to their customs, and seldom afterwards abandon them.[31]

Snelling writes in 1830, 'A very short residence among the aborigines learns them to despise the refinement and artificial wants of civilized society, and spurn the restraints legally and conventionally established to bind men to each other'.[32] 'The wild, independent habits of the wilderness are at first pleasing from novelty, and soon become riveted by custom. An Indian wife, and a family of half breed children complete the change'. Half-breed children are physically 'an improvement on the Indian and the white' but 'in manners and morals . . . on a par with the Indians.' The assimilated child becomes a 'squaw man' whose children join the ranks of the dispossessed and corrupting white.[33]

---

[30] M. G. St J. de Crevecoeur, *Letters from an American Farmer* (London, 1782, repr. New York, 1926). All quotations in this paragraph are from this source.

[31] J. D. Hunter, *Memoirs of a Captivity Among the Indians of North America, From Childhood to the Age of Nineteen* (London, 1823).

[32] Quoted, Ebersole, n. 21 above, 203–4.

[33] 'I had also met some, whose parents, either on the side of the father or mother, had been white: they sustained the character of brave warriors; but in general no cast, differing from that of the tribe, is held in repute or estimation.' Hunter, n. 31 above. The Métis projected another vision; see R. Smandych and A. McGillivray, 'Images of Aboriginal Childhood: Contested Governance in the Canadian West to 1850' in R. Halpern and M. Daunton (eds.), *The British Encounter with Indigenous Peoples* (London, 1998).

The attraction of 'wild, independent habits' brought many to the New World and cannot explain assimilation. Why some assimilated and others did not was investigated by Norman Heard.[34] Women over 50 and married men were usually killed outright. Young women were most likely to resist unless they married and bore children. Length of captivity was not a controlling factor. The younger the captive, the greater the likelihood of assimilation, with the cut-off at the age of about 12. The major factor is treatment, with variation widest between eastern and western Indian Nations. Eastern Nations, wealthy and settled, held adoption ceremonies soon after capture but other Nations, troubled by loss of labour, land, gatherings, and game, might blame captives, use them for hard labour or trade them from band to band. When the child meets with kindness and sees the alien culture in a new light, assimilation begins. Brutal treatment, Heard concludes, delays but does not prevent assimilation. Such treatment, Ackerknecht suggests, selected for 'white Indians' who were the physical and intellectual equals of their captors.[35]

Central is maternal affection. Despite agonizing separation, Jemima Howe writes of the 'fondness' of her boys' Indian mothers (below). Canadian explorer Pierre-Esprit Radisson, captured by Mohawk in 1651 at 16, writes lovingly of his adoptive mother.[36] David Boyd, taken by Pennsylvania Delaware at the age of 13 in 1799, tells his white grandchildren of his affection for his Indian mother.[37] John Hunter, taken in infancy in 1801, writes of his

painful loss. The squaw who had adopted me among her children, and who had treated me with great tenderness and affection, was accidentally drowned . . . I sincerely and deeply felt the bereavement; and cannot, even at this late day, reflect on her maternal conduct to me . . . without the association of feelings to which, in other respects, I am a stranger. She

[34] N. J. Heard, *White Into Red: A Study of the Assimilation of White Persons Captured by Indians* (Metuchen, NJ, 1973).

[35] E. H. Ackerknecht, ' "White Indians": Psychological and Physiological Peculiarities of White Children Abducted and Reared by North American Indians' (1944), XV *Bulletin of the History of Medicine* 15. The 'deep attachment' of assimilated children is 'evidence in favor of the Indians' and 'shows that in its downfall and persecution this culture still retained values which could make it worthwhile even for white people to stay within its orbit'.

[36] P. E. Radisson, *The Explorations of Pierre Esprit Radisson* (Minneapolis, 1961). [37] Heard, n. 34 above, 60.

was indeed a mother to me . . . I have no hope of seeing happier days
than I experienced in this early period of my life . . .[38]

John Tanner, taken at 6 in 1786, was devoted to his Ottawa
mother.[39] This is reflected in other accounts. Children at yearly
showings of captives under war treaty terms displayed preference
for Indian parents, as Franklin and Crevecoeur observe. The
Reverend John Williams, son-in-law of Cotton Mather, travelled
to Quebec to ransom his daughter Eunice and other Puritans.
Eunice refused to return; 'she is there still; and she has forgotten
to speak English.'[40] He refused the condition imposed by Jesuits
that he convert to Catholicism and returned empty-handed.[41] '*All
means were used to seduce poor souls.*' Frances Slocum, 'lost sister
of the Wyoming', 5 years old on capture by Miami in
Pennsylvania in 1778, concealed her identity for fifty years in fear
that her relatives would find her. When her brothers tracked her
down in 1837, she said, 'I am an old tree . . . I was a sapling when
they took me away. It is all gone past.'[42] She would not return. As
Ackerknecht observes, 'It is remarkable with how deep a love and
devotion they all speak of . . . the *gentle Indian mothers*.'[43]

'The Indian women', Lafitau writes, 'love their children

---

[38] Hunter, n. 31 above, 26–7. Hunter's credentials were blackened by
Governor Lewis Cass who termed him a bold imposter as he 'elevates the Indian
character far above its true standard, depresses that of the frontier settler far
below' and 'whines' about Indian land purchase and whiskey sales to Indians. L.
Cass, *North American Review* (1826), 53–119. Cass himself massively profited
from Indian land sales; see Ackerknecht, n. 35 above.

[39] E. James, *A Narrative of the Captivity and Adventures of John Tanner
During 30 Years of Residence Among the Indians of the Interior of North
America* (London, 1830). Tanner's credentials were blackened by ethnologist
Henry Schoolcraft, whose brother Tanner allegedly killed; see Ackerknecht, n. 35
above.

[40] C. Johnson, *An Unredeemed Captive* (Holyoke, Mass., 1897).

[41] J. Williams, *The Redeemed Captive Returning to Zion, a* FAITHFUL HISTORY
*of Remarkable Occurences in the Captivity and Deliverance of Mr. John Williams
of Deerfield, Rev. . . .* (Boston, 1795). Williams (58) records the Jesuitical
complaint that 'they could do nothing with the grown [Indian] persons there; and
they hindered the children's compliance. Whereupon the Jesuits counselled the
Macquas to sell all the grown persons from the fort; a strategem to seduce poor
children.'

[42] J. F. Meginness, *Biography of Francis Slocum* (Williamsburg, Pa., 1891),
196.

[43] Ackerknecht, n. 35 above, 34. They '*found a kind of unity of thought and
action and a kind of social cohesion* which deeply appealed to them, and which
they did not find with the whites.'

extremely passionately and, although they do not give them signs of their affection by such warm caresses as the Europeans, their tenderness is no less real, solid and lasting.'[44] They 'are careful not to give their children to others to be nursed. They would think that they were cheating themselves out of the affection due a mother and they are much surprised to see that there are nations in the world where such a practice [wetnursing] is accepted and sanctioned.' Should the mother die, 'nurses are found in their family and what seems still more astonishing, old grandmothers who have long passed the age to bear children and yet still have milk, take the mother's place.' Should the child die, a captured child might take its place.

Dividing Childhood

Child captives were divided from mothers, one another, even from life. Canadian-born Fanny Kelly,[45] taken by Sioux on the Missouri Trail in 1872, writes, 'The whites once captured and brought to the village were divided up among the natives to see who would own them. But, since my daughter had been killed in the attack, I was given an Indian child to replace my little girl.'[46] Kelly writes of children earlier captured, 'I was deeply pained to see their pale, pinched features, as they cried for food there was none to be had, and they are sometimes cruelly treated by the larger Indian children on account of their unfortunate birth.' Mrs Swarton writes,

The eldest of my Sons they kill'd, about two Months after I was taken, and the rest scatter'd from me. I was now left a Widow, and as bereav'd of my Children; though, I had them alive, yet it was very seldom that I could see 'em, and I had not Liberty to discourse with 'em without danger either of my own Life or theirs . . .[47]

Dividing captives among families and villages was 'not done out of cruelty but rather to hasten reconciliation of this change', writes John Hunter.[48]

Captivity ripped children from mothers yet gave them to other

---

[44] Lafitau, n. 12 above, 356.
[45] F. Kelly, *Narrative of My Captivity Among the Sioux Indians* (Hartford, Toronto, 1872).   [46] Kelly, n. 45 above, 97.
[47] Mather, n. 28 above, 32.   [48] Hunter, n. 31 above, 5.

mothers. Accounts stress maternal desolation. Jemima Howe, taken with her children at Fort Drummer in 1756, writes, 'Of no avail were the cries of this tender mother—a mother so desolated by the loss of her children, who were thus torn from her fond embraces and removed many hundred miles from each other, into the utmost recess of Canada.'[49] She nursed her infant but

ordered to return my poor child to those of them, who still claimed it as their property. The babe clung to my bosom with all its might; but I was obliged to pluck it thence, and deliver it, shrieking and screaming, enough to penetrate a heart of stone, into the hands of those unfeeling wretches whose tender mercies may be termed cruel.[50]

She caught up with the infant a month later.

I had preserved my milk, in hopes of seeing my beloved child again. And here I found it, it is true, but . . . greatly emaciated and almost starved . . . I took it in my arms, put its face to mine, and it instantly bit me with such violence, that it seemed as if I must have parted with a piece of my cheek.

Howe was told her boys were dead. She envisioned their 'naked carcasses . . . hanged upon the limbs of the trees' but was 'relieved from those horrid imaginations; for as I was walking one day upon the ice, observing a smoke at some distance upon the land, it must proceed, thought I from the fire of some Indian hut, and who knows but some one of my poor children may be there.' She found Caleb 'in tolerable health and circumstances, under the protection of a fond Indian mother'. Told where Squire lived,

I beheld, as I drew nigh my little son without the camp; but he looked, thought I, like a starved and mangy puppy, that had been wallowing in the ashes. My little boy appeared to be very fond of his new mother, kept as near me as possible while I staid, and when I told him I must go, he fell as though he had been knocked down with a club . . . I departed, you may well suppose, with a heavy load at my heart.

With the help of Indian women, Howe travelled to Quebec and was ransomed by a French officer as an indentured servant. She had arranged for her daughters to enter convents to prevent

---

[49] J. Howe, *A Genuine and Correct Account of the Captivity, Sufferings & Deliverance of Mrs. Jemima Howe, of Hinsdale, in New Hampshire . . . Interspersed with an Exact Account of the Brutal Manners, Horrid Customs, and Monstrous Barbarities of the Savages of America* (1792; repr. London, 1815), 76.
[50] Howe, n. 49 above, 9–12.

Indian marriage. After the 1760 Quebec conquest, she returned to find daughter one married to a French officer; the other, a novice, returned only under much pressure.

When the story is told from the child's perspective, the picture brightens. Mrs Lytle and three children were captured in 1780 in the Allegheny Valley.[51] The infant was killed. The story features 9-year-old Eleanor. Imagining 'the horrors with which the rumours of the times had invested a captivity among the Indians—perhaps even a torturing death—the poor children could no longer restrain their grief, but gave vent to sobs and lamentations . . .' A kindly Indian, Seneca Chief Big-White-Man (himself an assimilated captive[52]) soothes them. He presents Eleanor to his mother. 'My mother—I bring you a child to supply the place of my brother, who was killed by the Lenape six moons ago. She shall dwell in my lodge, and be to me a sister.' Eleanor became 'the adopted child of the tribe' and could not be ransomed.

Nothing could exceed the consideration and affection with which she was treated, not only by himself, but by his mother, the *Old Queen*. All their stock of brooches and wampum was employed in the decoration of her person . . . no efforts were spared to promote her happiness, and to render her forgetful of her former home and kindred . . .

She was reunited with her white mother in 1783. The Chief, seeing the affection between them, said 'She shall go. The mother shall have her child again.'

The Jesuit Bressani, in his 60s, was taken in 1644 by Iroquois. After torture (below), he was

given, with all the usual ceremonies to an old woman to replace her grandfather, formerly killed by Hurons, but instead of having me burnt as all desire, and had already been resolved, she redeemed me from their hands at the expense of some beads, which the French call porcelaine.

[51] J. Kinzie, *Wau-bun, the 'Early Day' in the North-west* (New York, 1856), 268. Eleanor married Chicago's first citizen and Kinzie married her son, Michilimakinac Indian agent. Accounts 'behind the frontier' divest captivity from much of its horror. Captivity tropes are mocked in her account of two Lytle children who ran away. When the girl tired, the boy said ' "Then Maggie, I must kill you, for I cannot let you be killed by the Indians." The idea of the little boy that he could save his sister from savage barbarity by taking her life himself, shows what tales of horror the children of the early settlers were familiar with.'

[52] According to Ackerknecht, n. 35 above.

The savages themselves were extremely surprised by this result, so contrary was it to their intentions . . .[53]

The Iroquois hate 'the black-robed Jesuits' and fear their spiritual power. The 'old woman' perhaps sympathized with his willing spirit or knew his ransomed value.

Children might be killed. 'Braining' babies is first represented in the 1698 Mather account of Hannah Dustan, lying-in after the birth of her eighth child. When Indians raided the homestead, in Nathaniel Hawthorne's retelling, 'the poor babe set up a feeble wail; it was its death cry. In an instant, an Indian seized it by the heels, swung it in the air, dashed out its brains against the trunk of the nearest tree, and threw the little corpse at the mother's feet.' Elizabeth Hanson, taken in New England, writes that her youngest child 'continued shrieking and crying very much, and the Indians, to ease themselves of the noise, and to prevent the danger of a discovery that might arise from it, immediately, before my face, knocked his brains out.'[54] John Tanner tells of a girl killed with a tomahawk because of her incessant crying, a lesson to other child captives.[55] Radisson (cited above) writes of an Iroquois who 'took the child, set foot on his head, taking his legs in his hands, wrought the head by often turning from off the body. Another soldier took the other child from his mother's breast, that was not yet quite dead, by the feet and knocks his head against the trunk of a tree . . . This is the cruelest thing in nature.' Captives 'were executed, some for not being able to serve, and the children for hindering their mothers to work, so they reckon [it] a trouble to let them live. Oh, wicked and barbarous humanity!'

Radisson describes the triage of captives, of whom he was one, following his attempted escape.

My father, taking his place, lights his pipe and smokes as the rest. They held great silence during this. They bring prisoners: to wit, seven women and two men, more [than] ten children from the age of three to twelve years. They placed them all by me, who as yet had my arms tied, the others all at liberty, being not tied, which put me into some despair lest I pay for

---

[53] F. G. Bressani, *Relations abregées de quelques missions des pères de la Compagnie de Jesus dans la Nouvelle France* (repr. Montreal, 1852).

[54] E. Hanson, *God's Mercy Surmounting Man's Cruelty, Exemplified in the Captivity and Surprising Deliverance of Elizabeth Hanson, Wife of John Hanson* (1724; 3rd edn, Stanford NY, 1803). [55] James, n. 39 above, 4.

all . . . killed two children with hatchets, and a woman of fifty years old, and the rest threw out of the cottage (saving only myself) at full liberty.

The Captor's Child

For Lafitau, Indian childhood is a perfect biosocial fit, teaching skills suited to a harsh physical environment and to complex societies with all the attributes of European civilization—religion, politics, government, marriage and family, education, warfare, trade, games, medicine, rites of mourning. Children are not punished.

The mothers . . . let them do everything that they like when they are very young, under the pretext that they are not yet at the age of reason and that, when they reach those years, they will follow the light and correct themselves, a bad principle which favours vicious habits which they cannot shake off. [56]

But, although 'no-one would dare strike and punish them . . . the children are docile enough, they have sufficient deference for the members of their lodge, and respect for the elders from whom one scarcely ever sees them emancipated; a thing which indicates that in methods of bringing up children, gentleness is often more efficacious than punishments, especially violent ones.' The degradation of corporal punishment might provoke the child's suicide; Indians are 'so sensitive, that, for a little too bitter a reproach, it is not unusual to see them poison themselves with water hemlock and do away with themselves'.

Colonel James Smith, captured and adopted at 18 by the Delaware and Canasatauga in 1755, recorded his captivity to improve Eurocolonial tactics of war. 'They have their children under tolerable command; seldom ever whip them, and their common mode of chastising is by ducking them in cold water; therefore their children are more obedient in the winter season than they are in the summer, though they are then not so often ducked.'[57] Assimilated captive John Hunter writes,

[56] Lafitau, n. 12 above, 361. 'The worst punishment given them when they are still little is to throw water in their faces or to threaten them with it; when they grow older, the mothers satisfy themselves with pointing out to them their duties, which they are not always of a mind to obey.'
[57] J. Smith, *An Account of the Remarkable Occurrences in the Life and Travels of James Smith During his Captivity with the Indians* (1799; repr. Cincinnati, 1870; Garland, 1955), 254.

Children are instructed in regard and reverence of age. The young are always silent in the presence of the aged, and counsel which, from an equal or middle aged person would not be listened to, would, on coming from an old man be regarded as oracular, and most scrupulously followed . . . education of youth is derived from imitating their superiors . . . or from experience derived from a more extended observation and intercourse . . .[58]

Elizabeth Hanson was given an Indian *pabulum* for her starving baby.

By this time, what with fatigue of spirits, hard labor, mean diet, and often want of natural rest, I was brought so low, that my milk was dried up, my babe very poor and weak, just skin and bones. An Indian woman perceiving my uneasiness about my child, began some discourse with me, in which she advised me to take the kernels of walnuts, clean them and beat them with a little water, which I did, and advised me to add to this water a little of the finest of Indian corn meal, and boil it a little together. I did so, and it became palatable, and was very nourishing to the babe, so that she began to thrive and look well . . . I found that on this kind of diet the Indians did often nurse their infants.[59]

The baby's health provoked a tortuous practical joke, her 'master' pretending the baby was being fattened for him to eat.

Fathers and communities played important roles. Jemima Howe writes that after delivery, husbands

take to their beds to nurse the child instead of the mother, and to be attended upon like lying-in women . . . When a child dies suddenly, its death is always imputed to the intemperance of the father. Either he has drank too much chica, or ate too much swine's flesh and honey, or he has rode too violently on horseback, or crossed a river in a cold wind . . . [Indians] adopt the practise of rigorous fastings, and even of painful penances . . . to appease the malignant deities, and to hinder them from hurting their children, by such penances voluntarily undertaken.[60]

Alexander Henry, captured in 1809, describes the death of a Huron child fatally burned by falling into a boiling kettle of maple syrup.[61] A feast 'made to the Great Spirit and Master of Life, that he may be pleased to save and heal the child' was held until the child's death.

---

[58] Hunter, n. 31 above, 206–7.   [59] Hanson, n. 54 above.
[60] Howe, n. 49 above, 11–14.
[61] A. Henry, *Narrative of the Captivity of Alexander Henry, Esq., Who in the Time of Pontiacs War, Fell into the Hands of the Huron Indians* (New York, 1809; Garland, 1955), 319.

To preserve the body from the wolves it was placed upon a scaffold, where it remained till we went to the lake, on the border of which was the burial ground of the family . . . on the bark was laid the body of the child, accompanied with an axe, a pair of snow shoes, a small kettle . . .

Taught by precept and example, Indian children were trained in torture and, Lafitau writes,

prepare for this event from the tenderest age. People have seen children press their two bare arms against each other, putting burning coals between them, challenging each other as to who would hold out with most firmness and win the contest in endurance. I have myself seen a child of five to six years whose body had been burned by a sad accident when boiling water was poured over him, who, every time that they dressed his wounds, sang his death song with unbelievable courage even though he was enduring bitter pain.

One child trained himself to escape from capture but won only with his hands behind his back. '[W]e find more examples of this intrepid courage among those whom we treat as barbarians, than among the civilized nations to whom the arts and all that serves to polish and humanize them, give an abundance and gentleness of life which serves only to render them cowardly and soft.'[62]

Indian children participated in torture. Sarah Gerish writes that

young Indians, both male and female, are as much to be dreaded by captives as those of maturer years, and in many cases much more so; for unlike civilized people, they have no restraints upon their mischievous and savage propensities, which they indulge in cruelties surpassing any examples here related. They often vie with each other in attempting excessive acts of torture.[63]

Radisson's torturers left the bound captives with

one little band of hell who stayed about us for to learn the trade of barbary. Those little devils, seeing themselves all alone, contrived inventions of wickedness. This is nothing strange, seeing that they are [so] brought up and suck the cruelty from their mother's breast . . . the little ones do exercise themselves about such cruelties. They deck [the open

---

[62] Lafitau, n. 12 above, 158.
[63] S. Gerish, *Narrative of the Captivity and Sufferings of Miss Sarah Gerish, who was Taken at the Sacking of Dover, in the Year 1689, By the Indians, as Communicated to the Reverend Cotton Mather* (1698; Garland, 1955), 69.

wounds of] the bodies all over with hard straw, putting in the end of this stray thorns . . .[64]

Mothers begin the training.

A woman came there with her boy, enticed him to cut off one of my fingers with a flint stone. The boy was not four years old. This takes my finger and begins to work, but in vain because he had not the strength to break my fingers [and] his mother made him suck the very blood that runned from my finger.[65]

The Jesuit Bressani records his torture by Indian youth. 'We . . . were then left at the mercy of the youth, who made us come down from the scaffold where we had been about two hours, to make us dance in their fashion, and because I did not succeed, nor was indeed able, these young people beat me, pricked me, plucked out my hair, my beard etc.'[66]

Running the gauntlet is detailed by Colonel James Smith.[67] David Boyd, taken at 13 in 1799, repeatedly ran a gauntlet of 'vindictive squaws and young savage rogues armed with sticks, stones or whatever suited their purpose best, each desirous of touching up the young paleface boy.'[68] The Chief tells him that besting a youth in a fight will end the gauntlet.

There was one boy who was particularly ingenious in the cruelties he bestowed . . . [David] sprang upon his tormentor; they had a rough and tumble wrestle, but at last the pale face found himself on top and he redressed his wrongs as only an infuriated boy could . . . [The other boys] dropped their weapons and patted him on the back saying, 'Make fine Indian'.

'But, whatever reproach of barbarism is to be brought against the Indians in relation to the enemies who fall into their hands, they should, on the other hand, be done this justice that, among themselves, they spare each other more than Europeans do', Lafitau writes.[69] Duelling, and failure to mourn and retaliate for fellows murdered by enemies, shock Indian sensibilities. 'They have offered themselves to avenge Frenchmen who did not seem moved by the massacre of their brothers and fellow citizens, assassinated by other Indian tribes. When their proposals received no answer, they were scandalized.'

[64] Radisson, n. 36 above, 19.   [65] Radisson, n. 36 above, 18–21.
[66] Bressani, n. 53 above, 26–7.   [67] Smith, n. 57 above, 212.
[68] Heard, n. 34 above, 60.   [69] Lafitau, n. 12 above, 163.

Despite attempts to reify the Indian as a unitary phenomenon, captivity accounts reveal layered discourses and actors who refuse stereotypes of good or evil, savagery or nobility. Captives are helped and protected by Indians. Not all whites are good; not all Indians are bad. Mary Rowlandson describes her subversion from a despiser of those ruled by appetite to a captive of appetite stealing meat from the starving infant of another captive mother.[70]

I had quickly eaten up mine, but the child could not bite it, it was so tough and sinewy, but lay sucking, gnawing, chewing and slabbering of it in the mouth and hand, then I took it of the Child and eat it myself, and it was savoury to my taste. Then I may say as Job, chapter vi., 7. *The things that my soul refused to touch are as my sorrowful meat.*

Captivity in the Canadian West

Captivity accounts were a cornerstone of United States imperialist expansionism and Indian wars. Canada won its West by treaty and intended the humanitarian treatment of First Nations. Did captivity accounts influence Canadian Indian policy? Accounts were popular among Canadian colonial readers as elsewhere, rattling good tales and a primary source of information (however skewed) about Indians. Post-1870 Indian policy in the new Canadian West found support in three Canadian captivities which cemented public opinion of Indians and 'Half-breeds'. The Canadianized 1872 edition of the account of Ontario-born Fanny Kelly, taken by Sioux on the Missouri Trail, ran to six printings. Kelly becomes 'Queen of the Sioux' and footnotes stress the benevolence of Canadian Indian policy compared with United States wrongs. Canadians are asked to find it unimaginable that this could happen in Canada. It did, in 1885. Theresa Gowanlock and Theresa Delaney, white women widowed and captured by Cree at Frog Lake, Saskatchewan West, published their accounts in *Two Months in the Camp of Big Bear*, referencing captivity tropes of threatened ravishment, heinous Indians, squaws and squalor.[71]

White women were iconic in Western settlement. In discourses

---

[70] Rowlandson, n. 16 above.
[71] S. Carter, *Capturing Women: The Manipulation of Cultural Imagery in the Canadian West* (Montreal, 1997).

of their civilizing virtues, Indian women and their virtues disappear.[72] The Theresas ignore the shared captivity of women of Indian ancestry and Gowanlock writes disparagingly of Indian women and children.

In travelling, the Indians ride, and their squaws walk and do all the work, and they pack their dogs and have 'travores' on their horses, upon which they tied their little children, and then all would move off together; dogs howling, and babies crying, and Indians beating their wives, and carts tumbling over the banks of the trail, and children falling . . .[73]

She assumes a baby in a papoose carrier to be dead. The Indian wife of the Frog Lake Indian agent was widowed and captured with the Theresas; her daughter is a 'dear little thing' with 'no one to care for her' although 'squaws also carried her around on their backs with nothing but a thin print dress on and in her bare feet. How I did feel for her, she was such a bright little girl, her father when alive took care of her. It was very hard to see her going around like any of the Indian children.'[74] Chapter 14 is titled 'Indian Boys' ('Just here a word about Indian Boys would not be amiss' but it is not clear why). 'An Indian boy is a live, wild, and untamed being . . . full of mischief and cruelty to those he hates, and passably kind to those he likes. I never saw in their character anything that could be called love' nor did they laugh unless cruelty aroused 'the little fragment of humour.' Boys vied 'as to who would get the most and the prettiest' flowers for the captives each day but the 'general behaviour of Indian boys was nevertheless most intolerable to us white people . . . Like father, like son; the virtues of young Indians were extremely few.'

'The Indians are not only vicious, treacherous and superstitious, but they are childlike and simple', Chapter 11 begins. They are the

noble 'red man', the happy murderer of defenceless settlers, the despoilers of happy homes, the polluters of poor women and children. They did all that, and yet they are called the noble 'red man.' It might sound musical in the ears of the poet to write of the virtues of that race, but I consider it

---

[72] Carter, n. 71 above.
[73] T. Gowanlock and T. Delaney, *Two Months in the Camp of Big Bear: The Life and Adventures of Theresa Gowanlock and Theresa Delaney* (Parkdale, Ont., 1885), 36.   [74] Gowanlock, n. 73 above, 37.

a perversion of the real facts . . . unless they were *noble* murderers, *noble* cowards, *noble* thieves.[75]

Theresa Delaney, wife of an Indian Affairs superintendent and resident in Frog Lake for three years, takes an official protectivist line. Indians in her tired poetic account are as children, sweet, savage, curious and eager to learn, misled by bad whites and 'mixed breeds'. The Theresas parted ways as soon as possible, their accounts differing in tone but united in supporting state governance of Indians. The accounts for the most part reject Métis and Indian claims and reinforce government benevolence. The failed Riel rebellion, of which Frog Lake was part, made all of half-Indian ancestry suspect and the massacre by renegade Cree led to repressive measures against Plains Indian leadership.

Childhood is now poised at the centre of racial purity. Two later Canadian 'captivities' foregrounded white girlhood. A girl 'with not a drop of Indian blood in her veins' was spotted among Alberta Blackfoot by Frederick Villiers of the London *Graphic* on a viceregal journey in 1889.[76] This 'flaxen-haired captive', 'The Waif of the Plains', skyrocketed to fame. The New York *World* sent agents into the dark Canadian West to find her, as it sent Stanley to Africa in search of Livingstone twenty years before. Canada must rescue her from 'the horrible fate that is surely in store for her . . . even if it brings every Indian in the North-west Territories about their ears', the *Macleod Gazette* writes and a reader responds that it 'makes ones blood boil!' and 'here is a white girl in the hands of a savage tribe, under England's own rule, liable to the most degrading life, and nothing has been done to save her!'.[77] But she is 'Papoose After All', 'The Supposed Captive White Girl Turns Out to Be a Half-Breed', 'Her Mother a Squaw', 1890 *World* headlines blared.[78] A 'Canadian white girl' in South Dakota, supposedly captured in Manitoba by Sitting Bull, was claimed by the Turtons of Cannington Manor in 1892. They had lost an 8-year-old girl to the bush and convinced officials that Anatanwin, a 15-year-old 'white' Lakota-speaking child, was 'our Gertie' dyed with walnut and tall for her years.[79] Although neighbours were doubtful, the US press remained true,

---

[75] Gowanlock, n. 73 above, 43.
[76] Carter, n.71 above.
[77] Carter, n.71 above, 139.
[78] Carter, n. 71 above, 140.
[79] Carter, n. 71 above, 149–57.

opining that she was 'a thousandfold better off in a good American [*sic*] home'. Anatanwin's aunt, who cared for her since her mother's death, signed papers on condition that the child visit every three months and decide at age 18 'for herself, without any undue influence, and determine of her own free will, whether she elects to remain with the said Turtons or return to her relatives at Cheyenne River Agency'. Anatanwin did not return. Perhaps she did not know she had a choice.

With the end of Riel's rebellion and the foregrounding of white women's normalizing regime in the Canadian West, there remained the problem of sad or bad Indian mothers now placed on reserves, whose gentleness is ineptitude and whose children must be taken into white spaces to be saved.

Capturing Indian Childhood

The imaginal is not without effect. The conflicts of ethos depicted in captivity accounts generated powerful images which helped justify the extinction of 'Indian-ness' through the colonization of childhood.[80] Three hundred years after Mather's sermon, the metanarrative of Indian childhood in Canada is one of wholesale capture of children for a remaking in which the 'Indian' in the child must be killed to 'save' the child. Agonies of the Indian child captured in white spaces—the residential school, the child welfare system—is documented in hundreds, perhaps thousands, of reports and autohistorical accounts. The metanarrative of captivity, in which the Eurocolonial child is forced into Indian spaces, is inverted.

Extermination or assimilation, death of body or culture, were the choices available to the nineteenth-century policymaker. Extermination was precluded by British-Canadian humanitarianism. The rising interest in the governance of childhood confirmed the premise of mission thinking, that the Indian child might be salvaged if removed from the degrading influence of her parent culture. That Indian culture was dying was not debated. 'Annihilation is not a cheerful word', Joseph Dixon writes in 1913, 'but it is coined from the alphabet of Indian life and heralds the infinite pathos of a vanishing race. We are at the end

---

[80] McGillivray, 'Therapies', n. 4 above.

of historical origins. The impression is profound.'[81] Chief White Horse confirms the impression.

The first lesson I got while riding on the iron horse was to see the coaches filled with white people, and when I went in they all looked at me as though I was a great curiosity to them. When I first saw the white people I felt backward . . . but I finally felt more at ease, for I thought, I am going to die anyway.[82]

Extinction is inscribed on the land. 'I looked out of the window, saw a country over which I had once hunted, and the thought of the buffalo came back to me, and I cried in my heart.' Recording the 'noble, though vanishing race' is the task of 'students, explorers, artists, poets, men of letters, genius, generosity and industry' who must 'make known to future generations what manner of men and women were those whom we have displaced and despoiled . . . the yesterdays of this imperial and imperious race'.[83]

The Other, in this ethnographic imagination, cannot write. Her image must be arranged, its meaning assigned. The authors give 'impressions' of Indian everyday life. 'The Indian child rules the family. They are rarely, if ever, corrected. No Indian mother was ever known to strike her child. If they want anything they cry until they get it—and they know how to cry. In play they are as mirthful and boisterous as any white child.'[84] The photograph, 'Little Friends', shows a nude baby amid puppies. 'The Flower of the Wigwam', an apprehensive girl in a blanket, shadows a text explaining, 'The Indian is averse to being photographed, for he feels that every picture made of himself by so much shortens his life [that] his soul will be that much smaller in the future world.' The authors led him to 'pull in twain the veil of his superstitious and unexplained reserve and give to the world what the world so much craves to know—what the Indian thinks and feels.'[85] The craving is safe by 1913, when what the Indian thinks or feels is irrelevent to state policy. Indian childhood, stripped of more troubling aspects, is both tourist attraction and centre of aggressive civilization.

---

[81] J. K. Dixon, *The Vanishing Race: The Last Great Indian Council, a record in picture and story of the last great Indian council . . . their speeches and folklore tales—their solemn farewell and* THE INDIAN'S STORY OF THE CUSTER FIGHT (New York, 1914).   [82] Dixon, n. 81 above, 210.

[83] Dixon, n. 81 above, 5.   [84] Dixon, n. 81 above, 32–3.

[85] Dixon, n. 81 above, 8–9.

The 1842 Canadian Bagot Commission recommended farm boarding schools for Indian children away from parental interference. Residential schooling was approved by Upper Canada Chiefs in 1846.[86] Nicholas Davin investigated United States 'aggressive civilization', the removal of Plains youth 'from the tribal way of life' for industrial schooling, in 1879. His Indian Affairs *Report on Industrial Schools for Indians and Half-breeds*[87] reflects the Bagot conclusion that schooling works best when farm-based and church-run. Beginning in the 1880s in fulfilment of Treaty obligations, the system expanded throughout the Canadian West. Despite Davin's emphasis on 'Half-breeds' as civilizing mediators, Métis children had no formal place in the schools. Eighty schools were built and some 100,000 children attended.[88] Children aged 3 to 14 were taken from families, shorn (a sign of mourning leading children to wonder who had died), separated by age and gender, renamed and placed under a discipline supported by corporal punishment. The curriculum consisted of morning classes with field or house work for the rest of the day. In the early years children were punished for speaking their native tongue. By 1905, a third or more had died of tuberculosis. Child welfare policy after World War II unwittingly continued the politics of cultural extermination. Early warnings by child welfare societies and Aboriginal organizations were not heard.

Replacing a complex ecosocial structure with a 'civilizing' regime had the opposite effect in the erosion of the cultural mythos by which Indians governed themselves. The result is a carceral archipelago[89] stretching from reserve and residential school to out-group fostering and adoption, young offender facilities and prisons, poverty and racism. The capture of Eurocolonial children pales beside the capture of Indian children by

---

[86] J. R. Miller, *Shingwauk's Vision: a History of Native Residential Schools* (Toronto, 1996); McGillivray, 'Therapies', n. 4 above.

[87] N. Davin, *Report on the Working of Industrial Schools for the Education of Indians and Mixed-bloods in the United States, and on the Advisability of Establishing Similar Institutions in the North-West Territories of the Dominion* (Ottawa, 1879).

[88] A. Armitage, *Comparing the Policy of Aboriginal Assimilation: Australia, Canada, and New Zealand* (Vancouver, 1995) 107. In 1936, enrolment in the schools stood at 42 per cent of Indian children in Manitoba, 77 per cent in Saskatchewan and 98 per cent in Alberta, compared with 3 per cent in Quebec and 36 per cent in Ontario.

[89] M. Foucault, *Discipline and Punish: The Birth of the Prison* (A. Sheridan (trans.), New York, 1977).

Eurocolonial institutions. Missionary Harriet Caswell writes in 1892 that, if the record of assimilated captives were placed beside the record of Indian wrongs, 'it maybe doubted, whether the comparison would not be so greatly in favor of the Indians so far as humanity is concerned, notwithstanding all that has been said and written of the cruelty of savages'.[90]

The predictive power of images and the fictioning of a future politics is seen in Caliban's speech to his adoptive father Prospero. The stages of Eurocolonial Indian policy—discovery, flattery and firewater, exploitation and conquest, adoption and rejection, removal to the 'hard rock' of the reserve, the bitter politics of reclamation—are set out.

> This island's mine, by Sycorax my mother,
> Which thou takest from me.
> When thou camest first,
> Thou stroked me and madest much of me, wouldst give me
> Waters with berries in't, and teach me how
> To name the bigger light, and how the less,
> That burn by day and night; and then I loved thee
> And show'd thee all the qualities o' the isle,
> The fresh springs, brine-pits, barren place and fertile.
> Cursed be I that did so! All the charms
> Of Sycorax, toads, beetles, bats light on you!
> For I am all the subjects that you have,
> Which first was mine own king; and here you sty me
> In this hard rock whiles you do keep from me
> The rest o' the island.[91]

Abjuring his 'rough magic', Prospero returns to Europe and leaves his adoptive son Caliban to his island, a choice which cannot now be made however fervent the politics. Banished for his designs on Miranda, Caliban has long since married the magician's daughter.[92]

---

[90] Ackerknecht, n. 35 above, 35.

[91] *The Tempest*, Act I. ii. 331 *et seq.* Caliban repents his folly, Act V. i. 95 *et seq.* 'Prospero: "You'd be king of the isle, sirrah?" ... Caliban: "Ay, that I will, and I'll be wise hereafter/And seek for grace. What a thrice-double ass/Was I, to take this drunkard for a god/And worship this dull fool!" Prospero: "Go to; away!" ' 'Strangely enough it is the part of Caliban which has attracted the attention of some of the greater actors [who here] displayed great ingenuity in their attempts to delineate Shakespeare's "savage and deformed slave." ' H. Graig (ed.), *The Complete Works of Shakespeare* (Chicago, 1961).

[92] I am grateful to Brian Hogeveen, Dawana St Germaine and Pièrrette Hébert who provided able research assistance.

LEGALIZING VIOLENCE: FANON, ROMANCE, COLONIAL LAW

Gary Boire

Law and Order among Barbarians

In his 'Critique of Violence,' written in the early 1920s, Walter Benjamin remarks that 'all violence *as a means* is either lawmaking or lawpreserving' (my emphasis).[1] He cautions, however, that this 'lawpreserving violence, in its duration, indirectly weakens the lawmaking violence represented by it, through the suppression of hostile counter-violence'.[2] In more ways than one Benjamin's concept of a paradoxical violence—*law-making*, *law-preserving*, yet *law-destroying*—inflects Frantz Fanon's psychoanalytical deconstructions of imperial power and, by extension, that power's embodiment within colonial law.

Although Fanon never launched an extended study devoted exclusively to law *per se*, he did evolve throughout his oeuvre an extraordinarily contoured investigation into how a pervasive legal violence functions ambivalently in a colonial setting. In works ranging from early essays in '*L'Esprit*' and '*El Moudjahid*' in the 1950s (and later collected in *Toward the African Revolution* in 1964), to *Black Skin, White Masks* (1952) and *Studies in a Dying Colonialism* (1959), to his posthumously published masterpiece, *The Wretched of the Earth* (1961) (particularly chapter 1: 'Concerning Violence'), the trope of colonial law and its various mechanisms recurs in all of its ulcerating ambivalence and niggling multiplicity. Certainly Fanon sees Franco-Algerian law as forceful coercion, yet he simultaneously explores *how* it functions as a

---

[1] W. Benjamin, 'Critique of Violence' in P. Demetz (ed.), *Walter Benjamin Reflections: Essays, Aphorisms, Autobiographical Writings* (New York, 1978), 287. [2] Benjamin, 'Critique', n. 1 above, 300.

necessary 'scene' of imperial exorcism, colonial interpellation, and post-colonial resistance.[3]

If this sounds enigmatic and elusive it is because colonial law is, for Fanon, a multivalent phenomenon: a material force, a form of representation, a multidimensional constitutive discourse, a system that forms colonial subjects and subjectivities, not to mention a site of resistant struggle. Whatever else it might be, and however else it might function, colonial law is, for Fanon, primarily a violent 'textualizing' field of opposing, yet overlapping, forces. On one hand, there are the multiple social and political forces of the imperium embodied within law and designed to (re)configure the colonized subject; on the other hand, there are the combative forces of colonial resistance directed against (and often from within) the law itself that seek recuperation and compensation. For Fanon, the law is anything but an ass; it is, on the contrary, one of—if not the—principal technology of power in the modern world. As Stephan Feuchtwang so succinctly puts it, '[colonial] occupation was a re-creation, as new, of an ideal of government. The ideal repeated in the colony was that which the discourses on population, police, laws and wealth had developed along with an idea of humanity'.[4]

Now, in the late 1990s, it is hardly original to note that Fanon identifies colonial law with imperial violence. The entire host of current Fanonian scholars—Lewis R. Gordon, Henry Louis Gates, Jr, Gayatri Spivak, Husein Bulhan, Tsenay Serequeberhan, Ato Sekyi-Otu, Benita Perry, Neil Lazarus, Homi Bhabha, and Gwen Bergner, to name only a few—accepts the equation as given.[5] As

---

[3] F. Fanon, *Black Skin, White Masks* (Charles Lam Markmann (trans.), New York, 1967), (originally published as *Peau noire, masques blancs* (Paris, 1952); *Studies in a Dying Colonialism* (Haakon Chevalier (trans.), intro. Adolfo Gilly, New York, 1965, (originally published as *L'An cinq de la révolution Algérienne* (Paris, 1959); *The Wretched of the Earth* (Constance Farrington (trans.), pref. Jean-Paul Sartre, Harmondsworth, 1983, (originally published as *Les damnés de la terre* (Paris, 1961); *Toward the African Revolution* (Haakon Chevalier (trans.), New York, 1967), (originally published as *Pour la révolution Africaine* (Paris, 1964).

[4] Stephan Feuchtwang, 'Fanonian Spaces' (1987) 1 *New Formations* 125.

[5] L. R. Gordon, T. Denean Sharpley-Whiting and Renée T. White (eds.), *Fanon: A Critical reader* (Oxford, 1996); Henry Louis Gates, Jr, 'Critical Fanonism' (1991) 17 *Critical Inquiry* 233; Gayatri Spivak, 'Can the Subaltern Speak?' in B. Ashcroft, G. Griffiths and H. Tiffin (eds.), *The Post-Colonial Studies Reader* (London, 1995), 24–8; H. Bulhan, *Frantz Fanon and the Psychology of Oppression* (New York, 1985); T. Serequeberhan, *The Hermeneutics of African*

Fanon himself remarks in his famous letter of resignation from the psychiatric hospital in Blida-Joinville in 1956:

If psychiatry is the medical technique that aims to enable man no longer to be a stranger to his environment, I owe it to myself to affirm that the Arab, permanently an alien in his own country, lives in a state of absolute depersonalisation. What is the status of Algeria? A systematised de-humanisation. It was an absurd gamble to undertake, at whatever cost, to bring into existence a certain number of values, when the lawlessness, the inequality, the multi-daily murder of man were raised to the status of legislative principles. (*Toward the African Revolution*, 53)

What makes Fanon crucial to our understanding of both imperial power and colonial law is not, however, this kind of uncompromising protest against the material violence of imperialism, but rather his investigations into *how* and *why* this violence operates as a constitutive—yet paradoxical—legal force: *how* and *why* this violence both creates and seeks to preserve an interpellative legal system of civil society and social subjectivity. But a system that also undermines itself through the initiation of a furious counter-violence within the colonized subject. What Fanon elucidates, in effect, is a law that legalizes violence, but also a violence that legalizes itself *while* creating the foundation of its own demise.

In the following discussion I investigate some of the principal contours involved in this constitutive violence; to do so I consider how Fanon conceptualizes the imposition of French law in Algeria, first, as a so-called civilizing force and, second, as a Eurocentric language. More precisely, a language that narrates a peculiar family romance, an Oedipal scheme of subject formation within the colonial family. Finally, I mention how this language is translated by guerrilla resistance into a combative vocabulary, a form of ambivalent counter-violence directed

Philosophy (New York, 1994); A. Sekyi-Otu, *Fanon's Dialectic of Experience* (Cambridge, Mass. and London, 1996); Benita Parry, 'Problems in Current Theories of Colonial Discourse' in B. Ashcroft, G. Griffiths and H. Tiffin (eds.), *The Post-Colonial Studies Reader* (London, 1995), 41; N. Lazarus, *Resistance in Postcolonial African Fiction* (New Haven and London, 1990); H. K. Bhabha, *The Location of Culture* (London, 1994), 40–84; Gwen Bergner, 'Who Is That Masked Woman? or, The Role of Gender in Fanon's *Black Skin, White Masks*' (1995) 110 *Publications of the Modern Language Association* 75.

against (and from within) the alien language of European desire.[6]

In *Disappointments and Illusions of French Colonialism*, first published in 1957, Fanon explicitly identifies the imposition of French law with the Eurocentric ideal of the *mission civilisatrice*. 'Colonial expeditions', he argues, conform to given and known patterns and one of these is 'the necessity to establish law and order among barbarians' (57). Fanon is unequivocal on this point: European law, whatever its stated intentions, inevitably attempts to erase native societies and cultures while superimposing itself upon them. As he protests in *The Wretched of the Earth* (1961), 'cultural obliteration is made possible by the negation of national reality, by new legal relations introduced by the occupying power' (190).[7]

Fanon speaks here with substantial historical accuracy, for as Allen Christelow has shown, from the moment of their military arrival in Algiers in 1830 French authorities meticulously sought to undermine the range and scope of Islamic law, reaching a frenzied apogee in the mid-1880s with the campaign to abolish Muslim courts altogether.[8] Moreover, as David S. Powers has observed, French authorities initially enacted a series of legislative

---

[6] The language of law inflects even Fanon's own expression as early as 1956. In a speech to the First Congress of Negro Writers and Artists in Paris he argues that colonial power functions most effectively through an aggressive stultification of the local culture. As he develops the image of impotence Fanon inexorably introduces a decidedly *legal* language, more precisely the image of a kangaroo court: 'The setting up of the colonial system does not of itself bring about the death of the native culture. Historic observation reveals, on the contrary, that the aim sought is rather a continued agony than a total disappearance of the pre-existing culture. This culture, once living and open to the future, becomes closed, fixed in the colonial status, caught in the yoke of oppression. Both present and mummified, it *testifies* against its members. It defines them in fact *without appeal*' (*Toward the African Revolution*, n. 3 above, 34; my emphases).

[7] In his discussion of the 1947 Madagascan rebellion, moreover, Fanon shares with a philosopher like Benjamin (and writers and filmakers like Ngugi wa Thiong'o, Chinua Achebe, Euzhan Palcy, Neil Jordan, and Jim Sheridan) the unblinking perception that colonial law (and its mechanisms) can be, and often is, used *instrumentally* by governing authorities: 'Colonialism, in order to reach its ends, used the traditional methods: frequent arrests, racist propaganda between tribes, and the creation of a party out of the unorganized elements of the *lumpenproletariat*. This party, with the name of the Disinherited Madagascans, gave the colonial authorities by its distinctively provocative actions the legal excuse to maintain order' (*The Wretched of the Earth*, n. 3 above, 91).

[8] A. Christelow, *Muslim Law Courts and the French Colonial State in Algeria* (Princeton, New Jersey, 1985), 233–43.

decrees intended to replace Islamic jurisprudence with its French alternative. Powers cites a number of the more prominent of these impositions: French public law replaced Muslim laws regulating the role of the state in 1830; in 1844 French property law began to replace Muslim laws controlling ownership of land (this especially was designed to favour colonial possession); by 1859 French penal law had replaced Muslim laws regulating the punishment of crimes; and by 1873 the only area of Islamic law that remained under the control of Muslim judges was that of personal status— marriage, divorce, and inheritance.[9] As Powers remarks, this last concession was 'a deliberate move designed to highlight the social difference between colonizer and colonized; the intention was to withhold civil rights from the natives'. Or, as Fanon might remark, to negate completely any vestige of a 'national reality'. But this process of cultural obliteration followed a more contorted pathway than mere bureaucratic enactments would suggest. It involved, in fact, more a form of aggressive hybridization than irresistible force. For many French civil and political authorities 'the law was not obliged to be neutral or objective'. Instead, as Powers has shown in his study of Muslim family endowments, the law was regarded as 'the natural tool of colonial policy'.[10] Add to this the fact that the unilateral replacement of a jurisprudence (like the translation of a text) is no easy matter. However rigorous the attempt at erasure, however superimposed one system is over another, traces of the repressed inexorably remain and uncannily resurface. And in French Algeria this was especially true in the case of legal 'category' itself.

One of the principal difficulties faced by colonial legists in what Fanon describes as 'new legal relations' was the problem of 'category'—in this case, the intrinsic incompatibility of European and Islamic divisions and categories of law. As Powers points out, in French jurisprudence 'all legal subjects fall into one of three distinct categories: persons, property, and obligations. In Islamic jurisprudence . . . the category to which a particular subject belongs is of little or no concern; questions pertaining to personal status therefore appear in virtually every chapter of an Islamic legal text'.[11]

---

[9] David S. Powers, 'Orientalism, Colonialism, and Legal History: The Attack on Muslim Family Endowments in Algeria and India' (1989) 31 *Comparative Studies in Society and History* 539. [10] Powers, n. 9 above, 543.
[11] Powers, n. 9 above, 541.

On one hand, French authorities were faced with a thorny, though relatively straightforward bureaucratic problem: the collision of two different systems of law. On the other hand, this inherent incommensurability of the two systems initiated an intriguing theoretical conundrum, one that raised for Fanon (and continues to raise for post-colonialists) discomfiting issues of alternative subjectivities, legalized racist violence, as well as pervasive cultural angst.

If Islamic law allowed issues of 'personal status' to appear throughout its various categories, then European legists faced what they perceived as the spectre of a nomadic Islamic subject, a subject that would thwart any attempt to establish European legal categories as the social norm. More specifically, they faced the impossibility of fixing native personal status as separate from issues of colonial private property and colonial social obligations. Eurocentric legal categorization, in other words, confronted the threatening metaphor that had always and already perplexed the Orientalist fields of cultural and anthropological production. Edward Said's nomadic 'other subject'—transgressing and permeating the various discrete categories of Eurocentric law (and indeed categories of knowledge, control and ontology)—emerged as the ultimate embodiment of a paradoxical counter-violence: a symbol of desymbolization that threatened to destroy the very notion of legal category itself.[12]

In one sense, then, the many different Orientalist knowledges that clustered around the pluralistic, nomadic, and threatening native subject were called upon to provide the metaphoric bases for so-called 'necessary' revisions in legal doctrine. And, indeed, these revised doctrines—outlined in detail by Christelow and Powers—subsequently functioned as the legal foundation to corroborate the still-burgeoning fields of Orientalist studies. The intersection of laws and literatures, of legal doctrines and Orientalist studies, centred on this 'othered' native subject; and this criminalized native body, in turn, as Fanon (and many others following him) argues, in both its materiality and its anarchic counter-European symbolic capability, haunted (and continues to

---

[12] E. Said, *Orientalism* (Harmondsworth, 1987). On this topic of 'desymbolization' I am greatly indebted to René Girard's fascinating essay, 'The Plague in Literature and Myth' in R. Girard, *'To Double Business Bound': Essays on Literature, Mimesis, and Anthropology* (Baltimore and London, 1978), 136–54.

haunt) the Eurocentric imaginary throughout the colonial and post-colonial periods.

A material case in point that illustrates this conundrum was France's institution in 1955 of the controversial *Loi-Cadre*. Faced with increased Front de liberation nationale bombings throughout Algeria, yet harried at home by a National Assembly averse to yet more colonial entanglements, the Overseas Ministry of Gaston Deferre had the delicate task of reasserting imperial domination while pacifying uneasy compatriots both at home and abroad. Deferre's political manoeuvring amounted to a spectacular (and Jesuitical) sleight of legal hand. On 3 April 1955 France declared in Algeria an *état d'urgence* instead of the more extreme *état de siege* and Law No. 55–385 went into effect throughout the colony.[13] Whereas the latter declaration would have imposed martial law and military control on the colony (thus risking massive alienation in both Algeria and the French National Assembly), the former allowed the curtailment of civil liberties without removing control from civil authorities (thus increasing the violent control of colonial holdings). According to Haakon Chevalier, Fanon's translator, the *Loi-Cadre* amounted to an 'outline law in which are laid down broad lines within the limits of which the government will be authorized to take executive measures' (*Toward the African Revolution*, 104). But, as Rita Maran more pointedly observes, the decision amounted principally to 'protection of the state by the state'. That is: the Special Powers Law removed virtually all restrictions on police power and gave the government the right to institute 'any exceptional measure required by the circumstances with a view to the re-establishment of order, the protection of persons'. Since the authorities knew of the routine practice of torture by the police in Algeria (a fact extensively corroborated by Fanon himself), both the government in Paris and the Governor-General in Algeria 'could have predicted the accelerated use of torture when the Special Powers Law went into effect'.[14]

For Fanon the *Loi-Cadre* constituted a complex cluster of technologies designed to violently create and preserve legal control, yet paradoxically destined to inspire its own disintegration. Certainly he recognizes the *Loi-Cadre* as a desperate political measure and

---

[13] R. Maran, *Torture: The Role of Ideology in the French-Algerian War* (New York, 1989).　　　[14] Maran, n. 13 above, 40.

describes it in *Toward the African Revolution* variously as an invented 'new formula' (104), a 'caricature' (116), and a 'parody of liberal policy' (129). He also acknowledges its capability to initiate and disguise state-sanctioned violence and, in a curious echo of Benjamin, he touches on the strategic nature of torture within the colonial setting: 'Torture is inherent in the whole colonialist configuration' (64); 'Torture is an expression and a means of the occupant–occupied relationship' (66–7); and 'The police agent who tortures an Algerian infringes no law. His act fits into the framework of the colonialist institution' (71). In a stunning counter-discursive manoeuvre Fanon finally projects these individualized examples of legalized violence against a vast geographical backdrop and, while predicting its demise, describes the *Loi-Cadre* as a type of national torture as well as a technical means of preservation: 'the old *Loi-Cadre* which was meant to break Africa up into fragments is relegated to the museum of history, along with other attempts by colonialism to maintain itself' (139).

Torture, of course, had been explicitly forbidden by the European Convention on Human Rights in 1950 and was, as Maran has shown, 'at all times a violation of international law as well as of French domestic law'.[15] What Fanon here elucidates, in effect, is a law which, in its violence, mirrors that which it forbids in its 'othered' natives, a law that enacts that which it most fears yet most desires in its horror, its abjection, over the criminalized native body. The *Loi-Cadre*, in other words, illuminates for Fanon the paradoxical nature of imperial legality: law that is simultaneously 'law' yet transgression, simultaneously a language that speaks civil and moral order yet a 'white noise' that undoes both, a classificatory discourse that both establishes and disestablishes differential categories. Imperial law embodied in the example of the *Loi-Cadre*, in other words, is a form of violence that legalizes, a form of legality that imposes violence.

As Fanon remarks of this paradox,

The existence of an armed struggle shows that the people are decided to trust to violent methods only. He of whom *they* have never stopped saying that the only language he understands is that of force, decides to give utterance by force. In fact, as always, the settler has shown him the way he should take if he is to become free. The argument the native

---

15 Maran, n. 13 above, 42.

chooses has been furnished by the settler, and by an ironic turning of the tables it is the native who now affirms that the colonialist understands nothing but force. (*The Wretched of the Earth*, 66)

As René Girard reminds us, 'the efforts to stifle violence with violence achieve[s] no more, ultimately, than an increase in the level of violence. Counterviolence turns out to be the same as violence'.[16] Or, as Feuchtwang has observed in his remarkable commentary on Fanon, 'What Fanon describes is a violent organization, eventually of rival sovereignties claiming the same space and the same central authority for government. The rivalry is composed out of the same European discourses of sovereignty'.[17]

The concept of differentiating category, in other words, collapses; the criminalized native-other is finally revealed, not as some *thing* that exists 'out there', defined as transgressive for and by a disinterested colonial authority. The process of criminalizing subjected peoples, rather, is shown to involve a state of cognitive dissonance wherein the colonizing power attempts to 'fix', make static, in the painted statue of the colonized subject, an image, a representation which unconsciously contains disavowed aspects of the colonizing social imaginary itself. What we have, in effect, is a psycho-social process of political exorcism and the result, as Peter Stallybrass and Allon White rightly argue, is 'a mobile, conflictual fusion of power, fear and desire in the construction of subjectivity: a psychological dependence upon precisely those Others which are being rigorously opposed and excluded at the social level'.[18]

The Language of Force

Central to understanding the spectral power of this epistemic violence is Fanon's realization that the many mechanisms of colonial law act within the *socius* as a type of regulatory language, an interpellative system of representations which the colonized subject is manipulated to internalize. Colonial law assumes the

---

[16] Girard, n. 12 above, 139. [17] Feutchwang, n. 4 above, 128.
[18] P. Stallybrass and A. White, *The Politics and Poetics of Experience* (London, 1986), 5. See also Bhabha, n. 5 above, 44: 'The representative figure of [colonial delirium] . . . is the image of post-Enlightenment man tethered to, not confronted by, his dark reflection, the shadow of colonized man, that splits his presence, distorts his outline, breaches his boundaries, repeats his action at a distance, disturbs and divides the very time of his being.'

role of *Logos*, what Fanon explicitly calls in *Studies in a Dying Colonialism* (1959), a 'language' that 'puts order into the original anarchy of the colonized country' (91). Two years later, in *The Wretched of the Earth*, Fanon further develops this suggestively 'lingual' vocabulary to describe how the colonial police and military 'speak' the will of authority: 'It is obvious that agents of government *speak the language of pure force* . . . [they are] the bringer of violence into the home and *into the mind of the native*' (29; emphasis added).[19]

Like Michel Foucault, Fanon recognizes that colonial legal mechanisms regiment the criminalized colonial body and, as one of many social discourses, inscribe that body within a network of various social and political systems.[20] In Fanon's suggestive image of lingual violence traumatically *entering* the mind of the native, moreover, we have, in addition to the tortuous image of oral rape, the seeds of a concept that Pierre Bourdieu would later describe as the 'habitus'.[21] What Loic Wacquant so succinctly glosses as 'a system of lasting and transposable dispositions to perceive, ratiocinate, evaluate and act which is the *incorporated* product of socialisation, [a system] which then tends to perpetuate these conditions by functioning as the principle of the generation and structuration of practices and representations'.[22] For Fanon this unbearable circularity leads only to delirium, to the madness that contaminates

[19] Compare *Studies in a Dying Colonialism* (n. 3 above) where Fanon presents a curiously gendered terminology of internalization and resistance: '[The Algerian woman] must . . . confront the essentially hostile world of the occupier and the mobilized, vigilant, and efficient police forces. Each time she ventures into the European city, the Algerian woman must achieve a victory over herself, over her childish fears. She must consider the image of the occupier lodged somewhere in her mind and in her body, remodel it, initiate the essential work of eroding it, make it inessential, remove something of the shame that is attached to it, devalidate it' (52). Consider also 'Decolonization and Independence' (1958): 'French colonialism will not be legitimized by the Algerian people. No spectacular undertaking will make us forget the legalized racism, the illiteracy, the flunkeyism generated and maintained in the very depth of the consciousness of our people' (*Toward the African Revolution*, n. 3 above, 101).
[20] See especially the section, 'Docile Bodies' in M. Foucault, *Discipline and Punish: The Birth of the Prison* (Alan Sheridan (trans.), New York, 1979), 135, (originally published as *Surveiller et punir; naissance de la prison* (Paris, 1975).
[21] Pierre Bourdieu (R. Terdiman trans.), 'The Force of Law: Towards a Sociology of the Juridical Field' (1987) 38 *The Hastings Law Journal* 814.
[22] Loic J. D. Wacquant, 'Symbolic Violence and the Making of the French Agriculturalist: An Enquiry into Pierre Bourdieu's Sociology' (1987) 23 *The Australian and New Zealand Journal of Sociology* 76.

the entire spectrum of the colonial worlds. This neurosis, what Benita Parry has called the 'autocolonisation of the native', has, in turn, profound implications, not only for the role of colonial law, but for the formation of all identities within the colonial setting.[23]

Consider at this point Fanon's numerous formulations of the family as a microcosmic political structure, one integrally bound up with the laws of the larger society. Normally, as Fanon suggests, a subject moves from microcosm to macrocosm as an expected rite of passage—but in the case of the colonial subject this tethering of domestic and social is fraught with destructive complications. This insight is most apparent early on in *Black Skin, White Masks* (1952), a text described by Gwen Bergner as a classic study in 'raced masculine subject formation'.[24] Here Fanon argues that 'white law' is a critical element in the construction of an alienated black subjectivity. In chapter 6, 'The Negro and Psychopathology', he elaborates how the microcosmic heterosexual white European family replicates the (phallocentric) national narrative of the imperial power. This family, in effect, acts as the first step in creating a happy and well-adjusted (white) masculine citizenry; according to Fanon,

There are close connections between the structure of the family and the structure of the nation. Militarization and the centralization of authority automatically entail a resurgence of the authority of the father. In Europe and in every country characterized as civilized or civilizing, the family is a miniature of the nation. As the child emerges from the shadow of his parents, he finds himself once more among the same laws, the same principles, the same values. A normal child that has grown up in a normal family will be a normal man. (141–2)[25]

Later, in *Studies in a Dying Colonialism*, Fanon reiterates this dialogical relationship between the family and the nation state:

---

[23] Parry, n. 5 above, 41.   [24] Bergner, n. 5 above, 80.

[25] Fanon continued to anticipate the insights of later theorists such as Althusser (on interpellation), Bourdieu (on the *habitus*), and Foucault (on internalization)—that the internalization of colonial values by local cultures can be (and is) used as a powerful state apparatus: a technology or discipline of control. See, for example, his 1956 speech to The First Congress of Negro Writers and Artists: 'For a time it looked as though racism had disappeared. This soul-soothing, unreal impression was simply the consequence of the evolution of forms of exploitation. Psychologists spoke of a prejudice having become unconscious. The truth is that the rigor of the system made the daily affirmation of superiority superfluous' (*Toward the African Revolution*, n. 3 above, 37).

'under normal conditions, an interaction must exist between the family and society at large. The home is the basis of the truth of society, but society authenticates and legitimizes the family' (66).

The male subject, apparently, smoothly transitions through an in-between conduit connecting patriarchal law and paternalistic state law, reconciles himself with both his 'original' biological father and the latter's social echo, and in a flourishing finale to Freud's family romance, takes his powerful place within the male social imaginary—a new member, as it were, in the old club of men. Both Fanon's abrasive masculinist bias and his sense of a totalized, homogeneous 'nation' not only underscore his use of the male and nation state here (and often throughout his work) as the social norm, but indirectly (and importantly) reveals Fanon *himself* as one of those black native *colonisés*. A subject who has himself internalized colonial hierarchies of gender difference and Eurocentric conceptions of national borders.[26] And it is precisely here, in the case of the male colonized subject, that the transition from the 'Law of the Father' to the 'Law of the Fatherland' is at first an abrupt, then a continuing process of subject disfiguration. That in-between space connecting home and state functions, not as a healthy conduit, but as a diseased agonistic space of alienation and resistance—a scene of traumatic subject disintegration. For as Fanon remarks, 'the colonial structure is the very negation of this reciprocal justification' (*Studies in a Dying Colonialism*, 66).

---

[26] Fanon goes some way towards addressing his own masculinist biases in 'Algeria Unveiled', chapter 1 of *Studies in a Dying Colonialism* (n. 3 above). In a fascinating discussion of militant Algerian women, Fanon explores how these women deploy the *haïk*, or facial and bodily veil, as an object of political resistance—and as a means of concealing weapons such as grenades and guns. Fanon also addresses the need for the liberation of women from traditional familial structures, most notably from the absolute power of the family patriarch. The chapter concludes with a flourish of revolutionary rhetoric: 'Side by side with us, our sisters do their part in further breaking down the enemy system and in liquidating the old mystifications once and for all' (67). Yet despite this ringing call to equal arms, there remains throughout Fanon's later works an obvious ambivalence about, and suppression of, women in virtually all discussions having to do with subject formation. The old mystifications unfortunately seem not to have been liquidated and resurface strongly in *The Wretched of the Earth* (n. 3 above). Fanon's masculinist foundation is a well-known target of his critics—an aspect that not only lends itself to gender critique, but which also reflects the extent to which Fanon himself was interpellated by the gender biases of the colonial powers he was exploring. See Bergner, n. 5 above, for a fascinating exploration of these contradictions and gender blindspots.

Within Fanon's Oedipal scheme the *colonisé* must then choose (itself a questionable freedom) between family or nation but either 'choice' is a recipe for psychological catastrophe. The choice of family 'means' a choice of savagery and transgression over civilization and law—and therefore an alienating definition of oneself (and one's culture) as barbaric. It is also a choice that implicitly undermines the legitimacy of the colonized domestic sphere; this, by implication, de-powers both the colonial father and the domestic self, both of whom are continually 'othered' by the state. The choice of nation and its laws, conversely, 'means' a rejection of one's always and already inferior self for a position in which one will always and already remain inferior to, and under threat by, the social patriarchy. In this condition, for Fanon, the colonized male seems unconsciously to opt for infantilization—a state of powerless expectation and dependence. This state in which the native must continually mimic that which is unattainable becomes a breeding ground for a furious yet ambivalent counter-violence. For within the Law of the Fatherland the male native may react against, yet always remain (ideally, for the state) the object of, the patriarchal imperial gaze, a gaze that has its ultimate effect when internalized by the object itself.

In a language strongly proleptic of current sexual abuse narratives (and uncannily reminiscent of Fanon's fragmentary imagery associated with the *Loi-Cadre*) Fanon powerfully registers the 'splitting' effects on the colonized consciousness by this colonial gaze (which is itself split along what Terry Goldie has described as an axis of fear and temptation.[27] In his famous example of undergoing the look of a frightened white French child, Fanon describes himself being seen in terms of a traumatizing stereotype:

I subjected myself to an objective examination, I discovered my blackness, my ethnic characteristics; and I was battered down by tom-toms, cannibalism, intellectual deficiency, fetishism, racial defects, slave ships . . . What else could it be for me but an amputation, an excision, a hemorrhage that spattered my whole body with black blood? (*Black Skin, White Masks*, 112)

As Bergner has convincingly argued, Fanon's conception here is remarkably similar to Freudian and Lacanian accounts of gendered subject formation—yet it is a conception containing a curious substitution.

[27] T. Goldie, *Fear and Temptation: The Image of the Indigene in Canadian, Australian, and New Zealand Literatures* (Kingston, Ontario, 1989).

For Freud 'pivotal moments of seeing trigger a "recognition" of sexual difference: sightings of female genitals "convince" the child of woman's castration, and primal scenes ... also "prove" woman's lack'.[28] Here, in Fanon, Freud's female child is replaced by the native male adult. Within the gaze of the Fatherland the colonial male subject—like his female Freudian counterpart—sees himself certainly as an object, but in this case a feminized male object, an object of lack, both fragmented and fetishized. In a twist of Freudian subject formation, Fanon has the colonized man of colour seeing himself being seen as an object defined into what Homi Bhabha has described as the static stereotype.[29]

In the final analysis colonial law functions for Fanon as a system of classification, a taxonomy, a regulator, if not creator of identity. Within white colonial law the alienated black native continually reads his own inferior status; the law functions, certainly as a narrative of disenfranchisement, but also as a never-to-be resolved patriarchal narrative—a contaminated family romance that disallows the male native a healthy transition to individuated subjectivity. In this sense, colonial law continually repeats the 'original' moment of alienation, that 'initiatory' instance when the native first sees himself as 'other' to a white norm. Colonial law, like a bad dream, 'works', as the superego of the nation, a component of the *socius* that continually either represses (that is, mystifies) or re-registers in a different key the original trauma of being 'othered'.[30] Colonial law remains without doubt the ultimate mystification of authoritarian power, a

---

28 Bergner, n. 5 above, 78.

29 Bhabha addresses these notions of 'fixity', 'constructivity', and 'repetition' in his discussion of stereotyping: 'An important feature of colonial discourse is its dependence on the concept of "fixity" in the ideological construction of otherness. Fixity, as the sign of cultural/historical/racial difference in the discourse of colonialism, is a paradoxical mode of representation: it connotes rigidity and an unchanging order as well as disorder, degeneracy and daemonic repetition. Likewise the stereotype, which is its major discursive strategy, is a form of knowledge and identification that vacillates between what is always "in place", already known, and something that must be anxiously repeated': Bhabha, n. 5 above, 66.

30 See J. Laplanche and J. B. Pontalis who are cited by Bhabha in *his* representation of the imperial *Entstellung* as a process of displacement, distortion, dislocation, and repetition. According to Laplanche and Pontalis, in the overall effect of the dream-work 'latent thoughts are transformed into a manifest formation in which they are not easily recognizable. They are not only transposed, as it were, into another key, but they are also distorted in such a fashion that only an effort of interpretation can reconstitute them' (cited in Bhabha, n. 5 above, 264).

power that victimizes, albeit in differing degrees, all members of the *socius*.

But such power, *pace* Gayatri Spivak, is hardly irresistible;[31] on the contrary, authoritarian power produces in its own workings what Walter Benjamin had earlier described as a 'counterviolence'—a dialogical resistance that is both material and discursive. Together these activities form an opposition that disrupts while interrogating the very foundations of colonial power, for as Benita Parry remarks of Spivak, 'discourses of representation should not be confused with material realities'.[32] Similarly, for Fanon, the subaltern *can* speak and is heard—but only in the ambivalent language of combat; and it is to this concluding topic that I now wish to turn.

A Family Romance

Throughout his various studies of the Franco-Algerian war Fanon describes in considerable detail the kinds of outlawed material actions deployed by the FLN. He lists, for example, guerilla tactics such as smuggling weapons, medicines, and radio batteries, political assassinations, terrorist bombings—even the illegal use of the *haïk* (veil) by militant Algerian women (*Studies in a Dying Colonialism*, 35 *et seq.*). Similarly, discursive agitation takes various illegal forms and includes the broadcast of pirate radio stations, the circulation of anti-government leaflets, as well as public broadsheets and secretly produced journals such as *El Moudjahid*. Given that colonialism for Fanon is nothing short of legalized violence—'violence in its natural state'—it will 'only yield when confronted with greater violence' (*The Wretched of the Earth*, 48). But counter-violence, as Benjamin and Girard have shown, is hardly a straightforward process—a mere magnetic reaction between opposing poles. Fanon is equally contoured: for his revolutionary counter-violence is certainly bound up with the transgression of colonial law, but also—and more importantly—with the transgression of the internalized and psychologically disfiguring versions of those laws. This latter type of violation results in a personal language of revolutionary combat, but it is a language characterized by an extraordinary, and at times contradictory, ambivalence.

[31] Spivak, n. 5 above.   [32] Parry, n. 5 above, 37.

What makes Fanon's discussion of colonial law so challenging is, not so much his examination of *how* this law initiates and continues an interpellative process of alienation, but rather his *ambivalent* exploration of *how* an anti-colonial combative discourse might constitute an effective resistance to such interpellative attempts. In *Studies in a Dying Colonialism*, for example, he again deploys the metaphor of the family, the domestic microcosm of legal and social structures, but—and this is the critical ambivalence—in the seven-year period since *Black Skin, White Masks* (quoted above), Fanon's representation of the native family has changed radically by 1959. No longer a univocal representation of alienated consciousness, the colonial family now (sometimes) takes on the semblance of an alienating presence itself. The representation of the colonial family (especially the colonial father) ceases to be a unitary image of 'good', but instead now pendulates between overlapping and at times contradictory values. Sometimes victim, sometimes victimizer, Fanon's colonial family now functions, on the one hand, as a static representation of de-powered colonized subjectivity; yet on the other hand, it simultaneously replicates oppressive colonial processes of interpellation.

Fanon presents his entire drama of resistance in Oedipal terminology, wherein the native male subject must necessarily transgress both social patriarchal law as well as domestic paternal 'law' in order to achieve political and personal freedom. As Fanon argues in solid Freudian fashion, authentic freedom involves the transcendence of infantile desires and the resolution of unconscious conflicts; whether or not these aims are fulfilled in Fanon's anti-colonial struggle is a moot point:

For a long time, political action in a colonised country is a legal action that is carried on within the parliamentary framework. After a certain period, when official and peaceful channels are exhausted, the militant hardens his position. The political party passes over to direct action, and the problems that the son faces are problems of life and death for the country. In a parallel way, his attitude toward his father and other members of his family frees itself of everything that proves unnecessary and detrimental to the revolutionary situation. The person is born, assumes his autonomy, and becomes the creator of his own values. The old, stultifying attachment to the father melts in the sun of the Revolution. (*Studies in a Dying Colonialism*, 101)

In this revolutionary scenario Fanon clearly conflates two separate processes of liberation: the personal Oedipal phase of the male subject seamlessly blends with the revolutionary political transformation of the nation. Earlier, in *Black Skin, White Masks*, Fanon had posited two contradictory systems of law co-existing zeugmatically in the mind of the male subject—the law of the colonial father which stood in conflict with the law of the colonial state.[33] This zeugmatic constellation was then posited as one of the prime causes of the native's 'neurotic orientation' (*Black Skin, White Masks*, 60). Now, however, in 1959, Fanon superimposes social law onto paternal power: both codes then intriguingly conflate to form a unified prohibition directed against the 'birth' of the revolutionary son. The Algerian father, once the embodiment of familial security and absolute (pre-colonial) authority, is now completely absorbed by colonialism. De-powered, amputated by colonial authorities, the father is used instrumentally by them: he is now both Oedipal nightmare and colonialist obstacle to the son's revolutionary desire. And at this point only the violence of revolutionary action erases this double inscription; as Fanon remarks aphoristically (and punningly in translation), 'the old, stultifying attachment to the father melts in the sun of the Revolution' (*Studies in a Dying Colonialism*, 101).[34]

Political freedom (and colonial subject formation), it would appear, seem to involve a necessary counter-violence or, more precisely, an irrevocable Oedipal desire that leads to a complete amputation of paternal and social laws. Yet it is at this point—the

[33] In an unpublished essay, 'From Asymptote to Zeugma', Alan Lawson (University of Queensland, delivered to the Commonwealth in Canada Conference, Wilfrid Laurier University, Waterloo, Ontario, Canada, 6 November 1997), offers a fascinating gloss on this kind of simultaneity that can exist between two contradictory laws; in his search for an appropriate *post-colonial* figure of speech to express the settler dilemma of existing in two worlds at once, he argues: 'Some classical rhetoricians distinguish between syllepsis in which the "yoking" is fully grammatical and zeugma in which it is not or not quite . . . Indeed, the lack of fit is quite useful. Zeugma, syllepsis, puns are tropes of collocation, of awkward proximity . . . They're about things that are relatable but not commensurable. That might be a way of re-thinking the new post-colonial relations of land-ownership . . . this might be a way to read the co-existence of two incommensurable, politically-unequal laws, or epistemologies.' I am grateful to Alan Lawson for the opportunity to read his manuscript and to quote from it in this discussion.

[34] Compare the following comment made by Fanon in a 1955 essay in *L'Esprit*: 'The downfall of France [in World War II], for the West Indian, was in a sense the murder of the father' (1967: 22).

point of the most extreme breakage—that Fanon unreflectively shifts registers when he simultaneously tries to do (at least) three things at once.

First, he quite clearly insists on the necessity of paternal over-throw and in 'The Algerian Family', chapter 3 of *Studies in a Dying Colonialism*, deploys an intriguing mix of languages suggestive of both Oedipal parricide and revolutionary jurispru-dence:

Several Algerian families have experienced those atrocious tragedies in which the son, present at a meeting that had to decide the fate of his father who was a traitor to his fatherland, had no other choice but to support the majority and accept the most irrevocable judgements. (105)

Yet one page earlier in the same text (and this is my second point), Fanon works equally hard to recuperate the colonial father, to ensure, almost nostalgically, the continuation of the *pre*-colonial family structure when he contradictorily insists that '*at no time* do we find a really painful clash' between father and son (104; emphasis added). Added to this contradiction Fanon then medi-ates a third option when he simultaneously installs the colonial father as a follower of the son, and recreates the son as a quasi-Wordsworthian 'father to the man' (and to the new post-colonial nation). As Fanon himself remarks within a few pages of the execution scene cited above,

The young Algerian would feel called upon to defend his position, to justify his line of behavior before his father. He would firmly condemn and reject the father's counsels of prudence. *But he would not reject and ban the father.* What he would try to do, on the contrary, would be to convert the family . . . The old paternal assurance, already shaken, would collapse once and for all . . . [the father] would then discover that the only way to do it was to join his son. It was during this period that the father buried the old values and decided to follow along on the new path. (103)

In one sense Fanon describes what seems to be a muddled version of Freud's Oedipal struggle for power. The vocabularies of over-throw, recuperation, burial, and regeneration—all these represen-tations suggest Fanon's own difficulties in articulating what Freud described as the son's *real* desire—and that is the desire to break the law of the father (here over-imposed by the Law of the Fatherland) in order to become the father, to 'convert' the family to his own paternal authority. But Fanon's pendulations between recuperation and rejection reflect more than a theoretical blindspot. His contradictions, I want to argue, function most powerfully (and poignantly) as a critique of colonial modes of representation—particularly the law—and how these modes have performed a double inscription of configuration and disfiguration.

Consider again, for example, the Algerian father. Once the embodiment of absolute authority and the principal role-player in the pre-colonial male child's subject formation, he becomes within orientalizing colonial representations a combination of (a) an embodiment of savagery whom colonial law must restrain in order to maintain moral and social order; (b) an outdated and anti-feminist despot whose supposed authoritarianism is superseded by a more civilized, 'liberating' Western law; (c) a potential obstacle to colonial interpellation of the son; yet also (d) a potential collaborator with the colonial enterprise of interpellation. The Algerian father, in other words, becomes, within colonialist representations, a fragmented figure, one who contains contradictory coexisting traces, echoes, of power within powerlessness, law within lawlessness (and vice versa), civility within savagery. Fanon's revolutionary son then has but little choice to respond contradictorily to such an anatomized figure. Faced with such a paradoxical patriarch, it is only within the folds of paradox that the language of combat might make itself heard. What Fanon's apparent contradictions *do*, then, is to re-perform textually the kinds of contradictory positions imposed upon colonial masculinity by colonial power—itself a hopelessly ambivalent construction of avowals and disavowals. In a word, faced with a colonial violence which is itself split and splitting, the revolutionary son (and author) has little choice but to replicate in his counter-violence the textualizing structurations/representations that have shattered native identities.

Having abrogated the role of parental overseer (and in the process infantilized the colonial nation), colonial authorities must, by necessity, face rebellion by those offspring seeking their own political and personal freedoms. In this sense Fanon's Oedipalization of revolutionary struggle is simply one of his many attempts to evolve a political theory based on psychoanalytical principles (Bergner (footnote 5) *passim*). But such a reading trivializes the desperately *political* nature of his own representational ambivalence. Consider the following.

Homi Bhabha argues in his brilliant gloss on Fanon that post-Enlightenment thought conceived the civil state as 'the ultimate expression of the innate ethical and rational bent of the human mind; the social instinct is the progressive destiny of human nature, the necessary transition from Nature to Culture'.[35] This Utopian construction depends, moreover, on what Bhabha calls the 'direct access from individual interests to social authority [Fanon's transition from family to nation, which] is objectified in the representative structure of a General Will—Law or Culture—where Psyche and Society mirror each other, transparently translating their difference, without loss, into a historical totality'.[36]

But, as I have argued above, within the asylum of the colonial worlds there is no direct transition or access, no General Will, no transparent mirroring where a mythified citizenry might read its own shared interests in a communal Law. Instead, colonial citizens, as they move from family to nation, read a contaminated, ambivalent script where, as Bhabha argues, the 'collaborations of political and psychic violence *within* civil virtue, alienation within identity, drive Fanon to describe the splitting of the colonial space of consciousness and society as marked by a 'Manichaean delirium'.[37] And indeed, throughout 'Colonial War and Mental Disorders', chapter 5 of *The Wretched of the Earth*, Fanon cites various case studies of mental aberrations as material illustrations of this delirium wherein the identities formed through colonial governance emerge as fragmented, split, characterized either by an outwardly directed aggression or an inwardly destructive self-hatred.

Within *this* state of affairs the language and force of law become both a hybridized space and process: a site of struggle to be sure, but also a procedure, a manoeuvre by which the state might continually create and re-create its citizenry in its own image. For the settler, this violent law is the last bastion of order and ordering: a form of necessary force, a form of categorizing representation that discloses the alien nature of the native character. For the native, and for Fanon, colonial law, this legalizing violence, is a brutal categorizing force that functions both materially and psychologically. It is a force that constructs the native to

---

[35] Bhabha, n. 5 above, 43.   [36] *Ibid.*
[37] *Ibid.*

be both the totalized projected embodiment of disavowed internal presences and an ambivalent palimpsest of broken emotions, thoughts, and feelings. Caught within these impossible representations of colonial law, the criminalized native is dragged into white discourse (and white history) as the dark other, that nightmare figure 'tethered' (to use Bhabha's word) to the delirious, the hysterical, the traumatizing, the lawmaking Eurocentric self. Together and apart, both are folded by, and into, the weave of law, Fanon's principal metaphor of colonial violence and, by implication, colonial desire.[38]

[38] The author gratefully acknowledges that financial support for this research was received from a grant partly funded by Wilfrid Laurier University Operating funds, and partly by the SSHRCC General Research Grant awarded to Wilfrid Laurier University.

GOVERNING BODIES, TEMPERING TONGUES: ELIZABETH BARTON AND TUDOR TREASON

The miracle was this: the maid . . . was brought hither and laid before the image of our Lady . . . [where] her face was wonderfully disfigured, her tongue hanging out and her eyes were in a manner plucked out and laid upon her cheeks, and so greatly disordered. Then there was heard a voice speaking within her belly . . . her lips not greatly moving . . . [she spoke about] the joys of heaven in a voice so sweetly and so heavenly that every man was ravished.[1]

If the subject is produced in speech through a set of foreclosures, then this founding and formative limitation sets the scene for the agency of the subject . . . [but not] the sovereign subject.[2]

Mary Polito

In the fall of 1533, Elizabeth Barton, a nun and well-known mystic and prophet, was brought to the tower of London for interrogation about certain prophecies of political significance. In particular, she had prophesied that the king's divorce and remarriage to Anne Boleyn would be his doom, that one month after such an event, the king (Henry VIII) would be king no more. The month safely come and gone, the king sought a case of high treason against her under the Treason Statute of 1352. A body of prestigious clerics and men of law assembled in Star Chamber and dutifully questioned Barton, who apparently confessed herself a

---

[1] Thomas Cranmer, *The Remains of Thomas Cranmer, D. D. Archbishop of Canterbury*, Vol. I (Oxford, 1933), 80.
[2] J. Butler, *Excitable Speech* (New York, 1997), 139.

fraud at this time. Despite her confession, having studied the evidence and debated the question of whether her activities were indictable, as 'compassing or imagining' the death of the king, the council concluded (undutifully) that there was no firm case, that her prophecies did not constitute evidence of a secret conspiracy against the king or his family, especially allowing that she had spoken them to the king in person the year before.

The king, his ministers, and these judges did agree on one thing: that it would be in the interest of national security to launch a tour in which Barton would reiterate her confession in every corner of the realm. For the first such event, workmen erected a large wooden platform and bleachers for spectators at St Paul's Cross. On Sunday 23 November, Barton and nine men associated with her were brought to this stage where an audience of over 2,000 heard Bishop John Salcot preach a lengthy sermon narrating the government's version of the nun's history. Edward Hall relates that as Salcott preached, he held up to view the many documents circulating about Barton and gestured to the principals who each ritualistically delivered 'with their [own] handes . . . to the preacher . . . appoynted, a bil declaryng their subtile, craftie and supersticious doynges'.[3] The king did not give up on the treason charge however; he brought a bill of attainder against Barton and the others in January 1534; on 20 April, Barton and five men were dragged on a hurdle from the Tower to Tyburn and hanged. She alone was then decapitated.

The uptake of Barton's case was that immediate actions were taken by the king and his ministers aimed at strengthening both the juridical arm and the rhetorical reach of the Reformation. Legislation was written that categorized certain speech acts and certain silences as actionable, even as newly designed rituals of statecraft were conscripted to the service of the crown. One key piece of legislation in this regard was the Act of Succession, the document that declared the princess Elizabeth and any future siblings to be the rightful heirs to the throne. To foreclose on dissent, the Act called for a national exercise by which every

---

[3] E. Hall, *Hall's Chronicle; Containing the History of England during the Reign of Henry the Fourth to the End of the Reign of Henry the Eighth, in which are particularly described the manners and customs of those periods* (1548) (New York, 1965), 807. While the performance was repeated in Canterbury on 7 December, the national tour did not materialize.

subject in the realm would swear a 'corporal oath' declaring their allegiance to the Act in their every thought, word, and deed. Failure to swear the oath would be judged high treason. Certainly oaths of fealty were not new, and there was also the precedent of oaths sworn by conquered Frenchmen in Henry's earlier campaigns in France. Historians agree, however, that the oath sworn by every English subject in 1534 was novel in kind and scope, 'the first employment . . . of a spiritual instrument of commitment as a political test'[4] and 'in scale . . . entirely new'.[5] It was more than a test, however. As an illocutionary speech act (that category of act that J. L. Austin defines as achieving an institutional effect in the moment of its utterance[6]) it signalled the government's attempt to collapse speech into conduct, to turn speaking into doing for political purposes. As the Act announced: '[all the king's subjects] shall truly firmly and constantly, without fraud or guile, observe fulfil maintain defend and keep to their cunning wit and uttermost powers, the whole effect and contents of this present act'.[7] It is surely no coincidence that on the day of Barton's execution, the citizens of London were so sworn.

At the same time, the king's legislators were put to work drafting a new treason statute. As the propagandist Richard Morison put it, 'The Maid died, and a handful of monks with her; and in dying gave occasion for the making of a most valuable law'.[8] The new statute instituted treasonous words as well as treasonous silences as a capital offence, the term 'misprision' of treason sliding semantically between words unspoken (the failure to report on the treasonous intentions or acts of others) and words spoken (words against the king, that are assumed to be conduct, to constitute a threat to his well-being or that of his family). The preamble to the Act begins with a justification of the king's divorce and a declaration that the king is legislating only 'For the discharge of

---

[4] G. Elton, *Policy and Police: The Enforcement of the Reformation in the Age of Thomas Cromwell* (Cambridge, 1972), 222.

[5] S. J. Gunn, *Early Tudor Government* (New York, 1995), 181.

[6] J. L. Austin, *How to Do Things with Words* (2nd edn, Cambridge, Mass., 1962), 98–101.

[7] G. Elton (ed.), *The Tudor Constitution: Documents and Commentary* (Cambridge, 1962), 10.

[8] R. Morison, *Apomaxis Calumniarum* (1537) quoted in A. Neame, *The Holy Maid of Kent: The Life of Elizabeth Barton, 1506–1534* (London, 1971), 347.

hys conscience and for the welthe and sueritie of this hys Realme'
and that this law has been brought forward '[t]o prevent the catastrophe of giving to[o] greate a scope of unreasonable lybertie . . .
to al cankarde and traytrous hartes willers and wurkars of the
same'.[9] The law must police the secret space where all hearts and
wills dwell and to achieve this purpose, the Act therefore declares
that:

If any person or personnes after the fyrste daye of February nexte
comynge do malicyiously wyshe will or desyre by wordes or writinge, or
by crafte ymagen invent practyse or attempte, any bodely harme . . . or
schlaunderously & malyciously publishe & pronounce, by expresse
writinge or wordes, that the Kynge . . . be heretyke scismatike Tiraunt
ynfidell or Usurper of the Crowne . . . they shalbe adjuged traytours . . .
[and every such offence] ajuged hyge Treason.[10]

My contention is that the cluster of events which transpired
around the case of Elizabeth Barton allows us to observe the emergence of the conditions within which the early modern juridical
subject was to be rendered a thinking, speaking, and acting being.
Indeed thinking and speaking are brought under the jurisdiction of
the state in novel ways as the consciousness and the conscience of
the legal subject are conscripted to the cause of strengthening the
state through a repertoire of individualizing practices.

Individualizing practices are a particular tool in the transcoding
of pastoral care from the church to the state: the intimate, and
daily care of individualized bodies and souls. The scope of such
governance is to intervene in every facet of each citizen's life: to
'conduct the conduct' of every thought, word and deed; such
'pastoral technology' Michel Foucault argues 'profoundly
disrupted the structures of ancient society' in the sixteenth
century,[11] as 'power of the pastoral type . . . suddenly spread out
into the whole social body . . . [finding] support in a multitude of
institutions'.[12] Such governmentality employs 'tactics rather than

---

[9] *Statutes at Large, from the First Year of King Richard III to the Thirty-first
Year of King Henry VIII, inclusive. Vol. IV* (London, 1763), 446.
[10] To further the scope of the secular, the Act also proscribes appeals to benefit of clergy and to sanctuary in the case of treason.
[11] M. Foucault, 'Omnes et Singulatim: Towards a Criticism of Political
Reason' in S. M. McMurrin (ed.), *The Tanner Lectures on Human Value*, 2 vols.
(Cambridge, 1981), II, 231.
[12] M. Foucault, 'The Subject and Power' (1982) 8 *Critical Inquiry* 781.

laws, and even uses laws themselves as tactics',[13] just as the oath follows the Act as a means to secure an internalized truth through externalized bodily acts before witnesses. These processes thus force individuals back on themselves, newly constrained by their own identities. One's 'intention' becomes a privileged practice of individuation where the reward is a conviction that the self is a territorialized site of secret refuge.

The problematics of such governance are fervently addressed in various genres of writing in this period. For example, Christopher St German's popular dialogue *Doctor and Student* (1532) is a self-help book offering a guide to exercising one's civil conscience. Thomas Elyot's *The Boke Named the Governor* (1531) aims at producing a class of self-regulating bureaucrats with a large personal investment in the strength of the government. We find as well a striking representation of the pastoral figure of the 'good shepherd' sovereign in the speech made to Parliament in November 1530 by Thomas More, as reported by the chronicler Edward Hall. This benevolent pastor, More suggests, 'not alonely kepeth and attendeth well his shepe, but all so forseeth & provideth for althyng, which either may be hurtful or noysome to his floke, or may preserve and defend the same agaynst all peryles that may chaunce to come'.[14] As for that bad sheep, the recently fallen Cardinal Wolsey, he should not have imagined that the shepherd/king was unaware of his every move, indeed his every thought 'for his graces sight was so quike and penetrable, that he saw him, ye and saw through him, both with in and without so that all thing to him was open'.[15]

The intention of the government to secure that area 'within' the subject to the service of its own interests is also evidenced in a report from an investigator who, in 1534, was carrying out inquiries to aid in Thomas Cromwell's grand administrative reckoning that would produce the *Valor Ecclesiasticus* (1535). From Syon Abbey, where Barton had often visited, Thomas Bedyll reports that the 'conversion' of the nuns to the 'kynges title' of head of the church had been accomplished. This notion of conversion betrays the ruler's desire for an intimate relation with each of his subjects' souls and selves. This monarch in fact desires and needs 'sovereign

---

[13] M. Foucault, 'Governmentality' in Graham Burchell, Colin Gordon and Peter Miller (eds.), *The Foucault Effect: Studies in Governmentality* (Chicago, 1991), 87. [14] *Hall's Chronicle*, n. 3 above, 764.
[15] *Ibid.*

subjects' (created in his own image) who are in some sense freely
and willfully converted to the cult of the state. The sovereign subject
is thus a subject of this particular brand of sovereign. And just as
the king's words as such 'do something' in the instance of their
uttering, so is the subject's word deemed to be an action that is both
felicitous and culpable. The institution of state jurisdiction over
speech acts, Judith Butler argues, is a constitutive element of the
founding of the 'sovereign' nation state of modernity. '[T]he juridi-
calization of history', Butler concludes, 'is achieved precisely
through the search for subjects to prosecute who might be held
accountable and, hence, temporarily resolve the problem of a fundamentally unprosecutable history'.[16] Barton and a careful selection of
her followers are made to suffer the consequences of the religious
and political history that had produced the discourse within which
they were able to speak against the actions of the government.

Clearly, the gentle, pastoral, personal, and highly intrusive
monarch is simultaneously an increasingly absolutist monarch, a
monarch whose power is centred in his own person. Treason
itself, as John Bellamy has observed, was increasingly seen as a
crime, not against the realm as it had been in feudal England, but
against the ruler's own person, after the Roman fashion.[17]
Executions increased, novel tortures were devised and terror had
its clear and present place. Sovereign power enacted its revenge on
transgressive subjects before witnesses in a liturgy and a theatre of
punishment. Yet this is clearly a self-conscious regime that is
concerned with more than rule by law; such governance is
concerned with the problematics of rule, with 'men and things':
'government is the right disposition of things'.[18]

The Act of Succession, the Oath of Succession, the Treason Act
of 1534, and the monarchy that underwrote them, are complex
and productive forces in the world. This legislation proscribes traitorous action, while at the same time hailing subjects with a
tendency for dissension even as new categories of traitorous action
are produced. Thus we see how such power is not only, or even
primarily, negative, a process that 'excludes', 'represses', 'censors',
'abstracts', 'masks', 'conceals'; rather it is productive, 'it produces

---

[16] Butler, *Excitable Speech*, n. 2 above, 50.
[17] See John Bellamy, *The Law of Treason in England in the Later Middle Ages*
(Cambridge, 1970).
[18] Foucault, 'Governmentality', n. 13 above, 93.

reality; it produces domains of objects and rituals of truth'.[19] In the Commissioners' reports of the swearing and the trials of those who refused to swear and were charged with treason, we witness the production of 'knowable man (soul, individuality, consciousness, conduct, whatever it is called), as the object effect of this domination-observation'.[20] The oath, with its regulation of the swearing hands, moving lips and 'cunning wits' of every subject in England clearly aims to call these subjects into the service of policing their own convictions and measuring them against their knowledge of those words they have sworn before the king's deputies. Conversely, the Treason Act aims to proscribe against lips and wits, to exclude certain discourses from the domain of the sayable. The struggles that ensue 'are not exactly for or against the "individual" but rather they are struggles against the "government of individualization" '.[21] And the archives reveal evidence of the 'agonism' produced in the tension between the forces of such governance and the inevitable dissenting 'counter-conduct' of 'critical subjects', subjects whom Jana Sawicki describes as 'capable of critical historical reflection, refusal and invention'.[22]

We see such reflection, refusal and invention in the responses of various English subjects to Reformation imperatives. Despite the widespread compliance with the universal oath swearing of 1534, for example, there was clearly some doubt as to the efficacy of these illocutionary speech acts. Bishop Hugh Latimer writes to Cromwell that 'If you might make progress throughout England, you should find how acts declares hearts'; the implication, argues Elton, is that the existence of the 'universal acquiescence beloved by historians'[23] is doubtful, that in fact such coercively elicited 'acts' do not necessarily 'declare hearts' at all.[24]

Elizabeth Barton clearly refuses acquiescence as well, in the role cast for her as sovereign subject. Her utterances and actions are displaced by her from the sovereign centre of individualized speech where the law would situate them and onto the divine as

[19] M. Foucault, *Discipline and Punish: The Birth of the Prison* (Alan Sheridan (trans.), New York, 1978), 194.
[20] Foucault, *Discipline and Punish*, n. 19 above, 305.
[21] Foucault, 'The Subject', n. 12 above, 781.
[22] J. Sawicki, *Disciplining Foucault: Feminism, Power, and the Body* (New York, 1991), 103.   [23] Elton, *Policy*, n. 4 above, 6.
[24] *Ibid.*

well as back onto a long history of English political prophecy. The king would foreclose on her mode of prophetic discourse, her connection to both the past and the present, in order to cite her words as individual acts emanating from a sovereign, autonomous, treasonous personage. She instead speaks from a pre- and anti-sovereigntist position, offering ritualized performatives saturated in history and community.

The government certainly was successful in its censoring of Barton's words and words about Barton, through its enactment of the sovereign power of death and destruction. Through its production of Reformation discourse, it also aimed and succeeded in foreclosing upon the truth value of some modes of public speech (such as prophecy and mystical utterance) that had allowed women and some members of the lower orders to have a voice in public affairs. The operation of foreclosure was not entirely successful however. I suggest that the performative force exerted by Barton gets transcoded by the government from the field of the theological onto the field of the theatrical. It does so by accusing Barton and her followers of secrecy, of being duplicitous, of being guilty of a criminal discrepancy between what they are thinking and what they are saying; in short of 'acting'. Thus, the government inadvertently associates the theatrical with that which is 'unspeakable' in lawful social discourse and, significantly, with forms of public speech with incredible social and political power. Moreover, the government itself, as we shall see, attempts to appropriate some of the most felicitous and 'performative' practices from the cult of the Holy Maid for its own governmental purposes.

Recent attention has been directed by both historians and literary critics to late medieval and early modern women prophets and mystics, to the particular case of English political prophecy and to the role of women in political dissent in general in the period.[25]

[25] For some recent general studies of women, religion and politics see Tina Krontiris, *Oppositional Voices: Women as Writers and Translators of Literature in the English Renaissance* (London, 1992); Patricia Crawford, *Women and Religion in England 1500–1720* (London, 1993); Rosalynn Voaden (ed.), *Prophets Abroad: The Reception of Continental Holy Women in Late-Medieval England* (Cambridge, 1996). Especially important to work that problematizes the incidents in which transgressive women are offered a public space in which to speak by the government institutions that at the same time convict them, see Francis Dolan ' "Gentlemen, I have one thing more to say": Women on Scaffolds in England, 1563–1680' (1994) 92, 2 *Modern Philology* 157–78.

Barton's case has been cited across this range of research interests. She clearly practised a unique, hybrid form of European mysticism and English prophecy, both of which had been producing an increasingly politicized discourse from early in the previous century.

Diane Watt aims to amend the comparative lack of attention paid to English women's significant involvement in religious and political issues in the period. She has explored Barton's relation to such continental women mystics as St Bridget of Sweden, St Catherine of Siena and St Teresa of Avila, all of whom directed their religious and mystical practices towards ameliorating injustice in the world. She observes that 'prophecy could offer women a rare opportunity for direct involvement in the political sphere',[26] and she has recently linked Barton genealogically to other English women religious prophets from the middle ages through to the civil war period.[27] Phyllis Mack concurs that 'women as prophets enjoyed virtually the only taste of public authority they would ever know' and that 'the visionary's experience was profoundly *social*. Her enlightened condition did not imply detachment from the world but connectedness'.[28] Michel de Certeau, in his study of continental mystics in the turbulence of the Reformation centuries, explores the political threat to secular powers of these mystical movements.[29] He observes the many cases in which humble holy people (often women) were raised up to the status of erudite fonts of spiritual knowledge: 'maids, cowherds, villagers . . . characters, real or fictitious were like pilgrimages to an alternative "illumination" '. Learned clerics, he observes, 'became exegetes of female bodies, speaking bodies, living Bibles spread here and there in the countryside or in the little shops, ephemeral outbursts of the "Word" '.[30] The nature of the spiritual experience made possible by these meetings, outside churches, in private homes and humble cottages was, de Certeau argues, in fact highly personal and extra-institutionalized experience and '[t]his proliferation of private

---

[26] D. Watt, 'Reconstructing the Word' (1997) L:1 *Renaissance Quarterly* 138.
[27] See D. Watt, *Secretaries of God: Women Prophets in Late Medieval and Early Modern England* (Cambridge, 1997).
[28] Phyllis Mack, *Visionary Women: Ecstatic Prophecy in Seventeenth-Century England* (Berkeley, 1992) 5, 8.
[29] M. de Certeau, *The Mystic Fable: Volume One The Sixteenth and Seventeenth Centuries* (Michael B. Smith (trans.), Chicago, 1992).
[30] De Certeau, *The Mystic Fable*, n. 29 above, 26.

experiences, which was tied to the individualization of practices (from the development of the auricular confession to personal devotions), appeared dangerous'.[31] It is this dangerously private spiritual experience that Henry VIII and his Council would foreclose upon, expropriate in fact in the interest of setting into motion their own varied and highly personal relationships with English subjects.

If late medieval mysticism was both highly personal and highly political, political prophecy in late medieval England also linked communal narrative, personal inspiration, and political protest. Alistair Fox observes that such prophecies

> had circulated in the fifteenth century and even earlier, but after the accession of Henry Tudor [Henry VII] . . . they seem to have been collected and refurbished with particular zeal. Indeed, several of the most important extant compilations date from the last three decades of Henry VIII's reign . . . Indeed, political prophecy was exploited to create a myth of destiny which foreshadowed, and perhaps even promoted, the later idea of England as the elect nation.[32]

Fox proceeds to demonstrate how the same prophecies were appropriated and reinterpreted in the interest of rival factions in the 1530s and like Sharon Jansen, sees them as a 'sub-literary genre'[33] in need of re-evaluation.[34] In Jansen's careful study *Political Protest and Prophecy under Henry VIII*, she argues that Barton 'was very much aware of the form and language of contemporary political prophecy',[35] such as the old prophecy '9, 9, 9, the reign of a king how long he shall reign' which, Barton claimed, meant that Henry's reign would end in its twenty-seventh year—1535. Speaking a prophecy is clearly a citational act; one becomes a prophet by performing a novel and locally significant interpretation of a text that originates, not from a sovereign self, but from a shared history and the 'reading', like the prophecy, thus belongs to the community from which it sprang.

---

[31] De Certeau, *The Mystic Fable*, n. 29 above, 86.

[32] Alistair Fox, *Reassessing the Henrician Age* (Oxford, 1986), 80–1.

[33] Fox, *Henrician Age*, n. 32 above, 77.

[34] Any study of early modern prophecy owes a debt to Keith Thomas's chapter 'Ancient Prophecies' in his massive and important work *Religion and the Decline of Magic* (London, 1971).

[35] S. Jansen, *Political Protest and Prophecy under Henry VIII* (Woodbridge, 1991), 70.

Women figured prominently among mystics and prophets, as they did among those actively protesting the Reformation in the reign of Henry VIII. Operating within a vibrant culture of resistance, such women, including Barton, practised what Sharon Jansen calls 'dangerous talk and strange behaviour' that at the very least disturbed and worried the government. Jansen complains that: '[t]he presence of so many women in the popular resistance to Henry's reforms has been largely overlooked, even in revisionist analyses of the Tudor revolution and Reformation'.[36] She makes the important observation that Barton's case was not unique, not as 'singular as it has seemed to historians'.[37] What is unique about Barton, however, is the effect her 'revelations' exerted on the nation and consequently, the range of extant documents that deal with her case.

This is the context in which individualizing forces that appropriated sovereign selves for government interests worked to exclude women from the public sphere.[38] The counter-reform conceived of by those clustered around Barton is figured as a particularly feminizing force, however, and one with broad social ramifications. Henry Gold, vicar of Ospringe, soon to be a follower of Barton and one who would die with her, preaches in 1522 that 'trew religion is wonderfully dekayed from her old state of perfection'.[39] In a similar vein, Barton's follower Henry Mann writes to her confessor Dr Bocking: 'Let us magnify the name of the Lord, who has raised up this holy virgin, a mother indeed to me, and a daughter to thee, for our salvation. She has raised a fire in some hearts that you would think like the opera-

---

[36] S. Jansen, *Dangerous Talk and Strange Behavior: Women and Popular Resistance to the Reforms of Henry VIII* (New York, 1996), 3.

[37] Jansen, *Dangerous Talk*, n. 36 above, 70.

[38] Several Henrician imperatives worked to accomplish this end. In the general iconoclasm that accompanied the Reformation, images of Mary and the feminine saints are disqualified and destroyed. Both convents and legal brothels are closed, as women are subjugated as always and only wives or waiting to become wives. Inside the institution of marriage, women's status as non-persons is supported by such legislation as the Statute of Wills (32 Henry VIII, c. 38), which put the state firmly in charge of property issues and limited married women's ability to write wills. In 1543 the first legislation against witchcraft (34 Henry VIII, c.8) brings this mostly feminine category of transgressor into civil discourse.

[39] L. E. Whatmore (ed.), 'A Sermon of Henry Gold, Vicar of Ospringe, 1525–27, Preached Before Archbishop Warham' (1944) lvii *Archaeologia Cantiana: Being Transactions of the Kent Archaeological Society* 38.

tion of the Holy Spirit in the Primitive Church'.[40] The insurrection Barton aimed to generate would effect the daily and secular lives of English subjects. Reading one of the lost pamphlets about Barton, an Elizabethan writes that she 'preached frankly against the corruption of maners and civill life'.[41] The movement inspired by Barton clearly conceives of itself as a renewal, a return to a pre-lapsarian past. On the other hand, those who had been influenced by Barton are described by the Act of Attainder against her as 'inclyned to newfangilness'.[42] Clearly, the struggle at this time was over the nature of inevitable reform of both religious and secular life and the struggle worked itself out at the level of discourse through rhetorical claims on the past and the future.

Certainly, explicit, overt forms of government censorship were highly successful in Barton's case. Those texts about Barton's miracles (likely in the thousands) were called in for destruction by the parliamentary Act and the subsequent proclamation that convicted her of treason. We have been left no physical trace of any of these texts, nor one word that we can attribute to her with complete confidence. More than simple censorship occurs however. 'A subject who speaks at the border of the speakable', argues Butler, 'takes the risk of redrawing the distinction between what is and is not speakable, the risk of being cast out into the unspeakable'.[43] Barton herself, her words and the discourse of reform that was produced by, around, and through her are indeed cast out. Yet the archive leaves a record of struggle. In particular, the 'Act of Attainder', the St Paul's Cross sermon and *Hall's Chronicle* leave no doubt that Barton was an extremely well-known and powerful figure and that her prophecies became increasingly political as her career advanced. By 1526, her prophecies were already widely known. When she announced that she had instructions from 'Our Lady' to attend the chapel at Court-at-Street on a certain day to be cured of her affliction—the 'falling sickness'—she was followed by a crowd of between two and three thousand people of all social

---

[40] J. S. Brewer *et al.* (eds.), *Letters and Papers, Foreign and Domestic, of the Reign of Henry VIII, 1509–1547*, 21 vols. and *Addenda* [*L&P*] (London, 1862), VI, letter number 835.

[41] W. Lambarde, *A Perambulation of Kent* (Bath, 1970), 171.

[42] *Statutes*, n. 9 above, 451.

[43] Butler, *Excitable Speech*, n. 2 above, 139.

classes, who, with Thomas Cranmer, witnessed Barton's ecstasy. As the sermon puts it, 'the King's Grace's people went in procession with this false and dissembling person . . . [all] singing the litany and saying divers psalms and orations by the way'.[44] An Elizabethan historian of Kent, William Lambarde, relates that at the shrine of Court-at-Street she lit 'candels without fire, moisten[ed] womens breastes that before were drie and wanted milke, resort[ed] all sort of sicke to perfect health, reduc[ed] the dead to life againe . . . finally dooing al good'.[45] She is alleged to have performed a great many such miracles from out-of-body transport to invisibility and telepathy. A Cromwellian spy reports the story of some monks fleeing England to join Tyndale. Barton 'by hur prayer'[46] rendered the ship powerless to leave the harbour. While her secrets were not yielded up, she claimed jurisdiction over the secrets of others, from the state of Wolsey's soul (arrested in purgatory), to, as we have seen, the future of the house of Tudor.

By repeating her miracles and her fame, however, these government documents are caught in their own discursive trap. Like all censors, they are compelled to reiterate the speech they would eradicate. They complain that Barton 'was brought into a mervelous fame credit and good opynyon of a great multitude of the people of this Realme'.[47] They speak of 'sondry bokes, bothe greate and small both prynted and wrytyn'.[48] By these books, the Act complains, Barton 'was brought into a greate brute and fame of the people in sondre partes of this Realme',[49] putting 'the nobles and commons of this realm in continual strife, dissension, and mutual effusion of blood'.[50] The events involving Barton, relates Lambarde were 'manifested to al men in bookes abroad'.[51] If she had not been discovered, 'this realm . . . might have been brought to utter confusion and destruction'.[52] Clearly she rivalled the King and Cromwell in her breadth of

[44] L. E. Whatmore (ed.), 'The Sermon against the Holy Maid of Kent and her Adherents, delivered at Paul's Cross, November the 23rd, 1533, and at Canterbury, December the 7th' (1943) lviii *The English Historical Review* 465.
[45] Lambarde, *Perambulation*, n. 41 above, 174.
[46] Thomas Wright (ed.), *Three Chapters of Letters Relating to the Suppression of Monasteries* (London, 1843), 16.   [47] *Statutes*, n. 9 above, 448.
[48] *Ibid.*   [49] *Statutes*, n. 9 above, 449.
[50] *Statutes*, n. 9 above, 464.
[51] Lambarde, *Perambulation*, n. 41 above, 170.
[52] Whatmore, 'Sermon . . . at Paul's Cross', n. 44 above, 469.

influence and did so with far fewer resources, as either she, or the array of written material about her, followed the same routes around the realm as the government's many printed statutes, injunctions, articles of interrogation, sermons, and proclamations.

To counter such power, such charisma, such press, the government aimed to discredit Barton by accusing her of not being what she seemed, of being something else entirely, something secret and, predictably, something sexual, something steeped in Catholic carnality. The Attainder Act declares that when she entered the convent at St Sepulchre, her newly appointed confessor 'had commenly hys resort, not without probable vehement and vyolent suspicion of incontinency, pretendyng to be hir gostly father by Godys appoyntment'.[53] Hall reiterates the theory that she stole forth at night to fornicate 'for bodely communication & plasure with her frendes'.[54] She is a whore secretly playing the part of a nun. Thus, she is accused of criminal 'feigning' and this verb 'to feign' becomes a keyword in government discourse in association with the accusation of culpable secrecy.

Hall accuses Barton and her followers of travelling 'to divers places in this realme [making] secrete relacion of thesayd false fayned hypocrysie and revelacions of thesayd Elizabeth'.[55] The official investigators Roland Lee and Thomas Bedyll report of their visit to Barton at her convent that '[t]he crafty nuune kept herself very secrete here, and shewed her marchandise more openly when she war far from home'.[56] The Act of Attainder lists those who knew about the many books but kept quiet while they 'traytrously beleved in theire hartys' that the prophecy had come true, that is that the king was not now the true king

in the reputacion of Almyghty God: wherby in theire hertes and wylles they trayterously withdrewe from his Highnes theire naturall dueties of obedience, and secretely taught and moved other persons . . . to thyntent to sow a secrete murmur and gruge in the hartys of the Kynges subjectis agenst the Majestie of our seid soveraigne Lorde.[57]

---

[53] *Statutes*, n. 9 above, 448.
[54] *Hall's Chronicle*, n. 3 above, 810.
[55] *Hall's Chronicle*, n. 3 above, 815.
[56] Wright, *Three Chapters*, n. 46 above, 25.
[57] *Statutes*, n. 9 above, 449.

Richard Morison aims to reveal the trickery and depravity of Barton; he claims that she and the friars duped the people who came to her for prayers, advice, and information. They would be shriven by a priest who relayed their secrets to Barton. Morison inadvertently offers an intriguing scene in which the fiery Barton chastises a series of men:

[s]he took the opportunity to rail most bitterly against the particular sins of the man she was addressing. Thus—You should not have done such and such a thing at such and such a time.—You should not have disgraced such and such widow.—You should not have ravished such and such a girl's reputation for chastity. And so [complains Morison] she brought every one of the wretch's sins to mind. The sinner sees that nothing however hidden, nothing however secret, can be done without being known to God and to those whom God favours.[58]

Clearly, this claim on the space and time of the secrecy of the subject is usurping the jurisdiction of More's shepherd/king and the new Treason Act is a tactic to resecure that jurisdiction, through its conceptual collapse of intent, speech, and conduct.

In this discourse, theatricality becomes the play between the individual, their secret 'wish, will or desire' and the external forces that would know and prosecute those secrets and desires. Salcott claims that Dr Bocking 'daily rehearsed matter enough unto her, out of St. Bridget and St. Catherine of Senys [Siena's] revelations'.[59] The claim is that she studies in order to imitate the ecstatic trances of these beloved women saints. Similarly, Edward Hall relates that she bases the gestural form of her feigned trances on her own bouts of the 'falling sickness' as directed by Edward Bocking: 'when the said Elizabeth had used this false, feigned counterfeatyng for a ceason and was perfecte therein', Hall reports, they went on tour.[60] Lambarde calls Barton's entire career a 'pageant'. The sermon claims that 'She feigned herself to be in a trance and disfigured'; that 'she feigned and spake divers sentences as though she had been in another world'.[61] The Act of Attainder accuses her of 'craftely utteryng in her seid feyned and false traunses dyverse and many vertous and holy wordes . . . and heresies'.[62] Lambarde,

[58] Morison quoted in Neame, n. 8 above, 142.
[59] Whatmore, 'Sermon . . . at Paul's Cross', n. 44 above, 469.
[60] *Hall's Chronicle*, n. 3 above, 809.
[61] Whatmore, 'Sermon . . . at Paul's Cross', n. 44 above, 466.
[62] *Statutes*, n. 9 above, 447.

reading a now lost pamphlet describes how she 'fell . . . into a marveilous passion . . . utter[ing] sundry metricall and rhyming speeches'.[63] Barton's words and actions, these writers contend, were composed, scripted, studied, rehearsed, and performed.

While these government writers associate theatricality with criminality in their narration of these events, at the very height of Barton's power, the government attempts to use theatrical spectacle itself in order to counter what they saw as the force of dissent wielded by Barton and others' performative acts. Nowhere is this use of sensationalism by the government better marked than in the fascinating case of 'corporate idolatry'[64] that was Anne Boleyn's coronation. This was to be the last of the Henrician mega-spectacles, as polemicism was to replace splendour as a tactic in the solicitation of the acquiescence of the people.[65] The four-day celebration in early June 1533 is described by a range of eye witnesses in *Letters and Papers*, as well as by Edward Hall. Again, there is evidence that subjects refused to acquiesce to the crown's expectations. As one of Cromwell's clerk's put it, 'many of the inconstant commons be not therewith satisfied [with the divorce and remarriage]. And though they forbear to speak at large for fear of punishment, yet they mutter together secretly . . . which doth not a little embolden the King's adversaries without the realm'.[66] It is clearly a question of national security that the people be brought to demonstrably accept the marriage and Boleyn's coronation was designed to have a perlocutionary effect in this regard.

Nothing was spared for the spectacle, as the extensive lists of purchases for the event in *Letters and Papers* demonstrates. Hall reports that on 29 May, the days of celebration leading up to the coronation on 2 June were launched by a procession on the river of fifty barges followed by 200 smaller boats to bring Anne from Greenwich to the Tower. 'The whole river was covered', reports one writer.[67] Another witness claims that '[i]t was a marvellous sight how the barges kept such good order and space between them that every man could see the decking and garnishing of cloth of gold'.[68] Before the first barge, the mayor's, there was 'a great

---

    [63] Lambarde, *Perambulation*, n. 41 above, 173.
    [64] E. W. Ives, *Anne Boleyn* (Oxford, 1986), 218.
    [65] S. Anglo, *Spectacle Pageantry, and Early Tudor Policy* (2nd edn, Oxford, 1997), 261.   [66] *L&P*, n. 40 above, VI, 738.
    [67] *L&P*, n. 40 above, VI, 584.   [68] *L&P*, n. 40 above, VI, 563.

Dragon continually movynge, & castyng wyldfyer . . . [and with] terrible monsters and wylde men castying fyer, and makyng hideous noyses'.[69] After such chaos comes the order of the official personages in their stately, dazzling procession with its glorious musical accompaniment: 'shalmes, shagbushes & divers other instruments, whiche continually made goodly [h]armony';[70] this provision was 'a thinge of a nother world'.[71]

The day before the coronation itself, Anne left the Tower accompanied by all the principal justices in England (reports one of those judges commanded to be present):

[Her dress was] the same fashion as those of France. She mounted a litter covered inside and out with white satin. Over her was borne a canopy of cloth of gold. Then followed twelve ladies on hackneys, all clothed in cloth of gold. Next came a chariot [with the duchess of Norfolk and the queen's mother]. Next, twelve young ladies on horseback, arrayed in crimson velvet. Next three gilded coaches, in which were many young ladies; and, lastly twenty or thirty others on horseback, in black velvet . . . Before all, marched the French merchants, in violet velvet, each wearing one sleeve of the Queen's colours; their horses being caparisoned in violet taffeta with white crosses. In all open places . . . were scaffolds, on which mysteries were played; and fountains poured forth wine . . . On Sunday morning . . . she went on foot from her lodging to the church, the whole of the road being covered with cloth . . . the length of the garden of Chantilly . . . After hearing mass [she was] crowned by the archbishop of Canterbury.[72]

Despite the spectacle designed to legitimate and to produce awe, however, there are reports that all the people did not respond on cue:

Though it was customary to kneel, uncover, and cry 'God save the King, God save the Queen,' whenever they appeared in public, no one in London or the suburbs, not even women and children, did so on this occasion. One of the Queen's servants told the mayor to command the people to make the customary shouts, and was answered that he could not command people's hearts, and that even the King could not make them do so. Her fool, who has been to Jerusalem and spakes several languages, seeing the little honor they showed to her, cried out, 'I think you have all scurvy heads and dare not uncover'.[73]

---

[69] *Hall's Chronicle*, n. 3 above, 799.   [70] *Ibid.*
[71] *L&P*, n. 40 above, VI, 563.   [72] *L&P*, n. 40 above, VI, 584.
[73] *L&P*, n. 40 above, VI, 585.

Order and magnificence meet resistance and refusal. The writer above also reports on her dress, but not as French fashion; rather as the livery of terror, '[h]er dress was covered with tongues pierced with nails, to show the treatment which those who spoke against her might expect'.[74] Tongues and torture: a more blatant association of forms of speech and state retribution could not be made. The tongues attending the coronation did not transgress by commission, however, but rather they cleverly transgressed by omission; they offered only silence when they were meant to be crying their *aves*.

Five months later, the government designed and produced another spectacle, this time at St Paul's Cross with Elizabeth Barton cast as the lead. The imperial ambassador calls this event a 'comedy . . . to blot out of people's minds the impression they have that the Nun is a saint and a prophet'[75] and notes that each of the principals will 'play the same part' on the next two Sundays in different locations.[76] This event, with its own scripted text, props, and stage directions, announces that it is being presented so that 'people shall plainly understand the beginning, the progress, and final intent of this false, forged, and feigned matter'.[77] Theatricality aims to show the inherent treachery of theatricality.

I want to conclude by returning to Archbishop Cranmer's report of Barton's 'cure' at the chapel of 'Our Lady of Court-at-Street'. Despite himself, Cranmer is moved by this vision and chooses the word 'ravish' (a legal synonym for rape in the period) to describe the effect of this seemingly grotesque image of a disfigured, Picasso-esque body with its ventriloquized yet enthralling voice. This image calls into question the notion of an uninterrupted drive from autonomous thought to considered speech to determined effect, pointing instead to what Eve Sedgwick and Andrew Taylor call 'the torsion, the mutual perversion . . . of reference and performativity'.[78] In speaking from her belly in rhyming verse, Barton challenges, consciously or not, the king's

[74] *L&P*, n. 40 above, VI, 585. The Queen's daughter, when Queen herself, would wear a dress with a message as well; in the famous 'Rainbow Portrait', Elizabeth I's gown is embroidered with a multitude of eyes and ears.
[75] Quoted in Whatmore's introduction to 'Sermon . . . at Paul's Cross', n. 44 above, 461.   [76] *L&P*, n. 40 above, VI, 1445.
[77] Whatmore, 'Sermon . . . at Paul's Cross', n. 44 above, 465.
[78] Andrew Parker and Eve Kosofsy Sedgwick (eds.), *Performativity and Performance* (New York, 1995), 3.

premise that there is an easily determinable relation between intent and the effect of speech acts. Barton's voice speaks from elsewhere, like the murmur of discourse, its form precedes and exceeds the vulnerable body through which it lives. As Foucault frames the relation between the subject and discourse 'discourse is not life; its time is not yours'[79] and as Butler paraphrases Foucault, 'The time of discourse is not the time of the subject'.[80] Paradoxically, on the border of the unspeakable, Barton is granted agency (in the form of the performative force of the theatre) by the very source that would seek to disarm her. It is her audience, in fact specifically her male audience, that is rendered passive, ravished even, in Archbishop Cranmer's figuration.

Yet even when she is reported to have been fully conscious, Barton confounds identification as a subject whose intentions are easily determinable. We learn that after her confession of fraudulence under interrogation, she claimed that her annunciatory angel had appeared to her in what she knew to be a final vision.[81] She was instructed to make the denial of her former revelations because the world was not ready, the time had not come for her message. In this denial of her denial, the truth of her motivations and her estimation of these strange events is deferred once more, this time onto the angel of history, within whose jurisdiction her story still lies.

[79] 'Politics and the Study of Discourse' in *The Foucault Effect*, n. 13 above, 71. [80] Butler, *Excitable Speech*, n. 2 above, 31.
[81] See Whatmore, 'Sermon . . . at Paul's Cross', n. 44 above, 474 and Wright, *Three Chapters*, n. 46 above, 18.

THE GUERNSEY WITCHCRAFT TRIALS OF 1617: THE CASE OF COLLETE BECQUET

Matthew McGuinness

Introduction

The primary source for the study of early modern witch trials in Guernsey is a series of Royal Court registers relating to criminal trials of all kinds, known as 'Livre en Crime'.[1] Le Patourel explains that trials were registered in this series by virtue of the nature of the alleged act, rather than by virtue of having come all from a single division of the court dedicated to criminal law.[2] It does not apparently follow, however, that all acts of the same kind are to be found in the same set of registers. There are thirty-seven cases of witchcraft registered in the volumes known as 'Jugements et Ordonnances'.[3] Seven of these are supplementary materials relating to cases registered in 'Livre en Crime'. Even allowing for the fact that the first volume of 'Jugements et Ordonnances' (1527–81) plainly contains an incorrectly bound section of 'Livre en Crime' (1529–81), overlapping with the first two identified volumes of 'Livre en Crime' (1563–9 and 1580–1617), containing a number of witchcraft trials, the remaining sections of the first two 'Jugements et Ordonnances' volumes contain twenty-three witchcraft trials, two of which are supplementary materials relating to cases registered in 'Livre en Crime'.

Guernsey experienced 167 trials in the secular court connected

---

[1] The Guernsey Greffe, Livre en Crime MS, list i/32/26, i–v (1563–1660).
[2] J. le Patourel, 'Introduction', in *List of the Records in the Greffe Guernsey*, Special Series, 2 vols. (List and Index Society, 1969), II, 1–26 (18).
[3] The Guernsey Greffe, Jugements et Ordonnances MS, list i/33/27, i–ii (1527–1631).

with witchcraft between 1563 and 1650, including public prosecutions, private prosecutions of a suspected witch, and slander cases in which the complainant was responding to an informal accusation or insult. Of the 116 public prosecutions, eighty-seven are known to have resulted in punishment of some kind, although in forty-one of these cases banishment was inflicted rather than execution (one private prosecution also resulted in banishment), usually because the court only entertained 'vehement suspicions'. Thus about 40 per cent of prosecutions resulted in executions. Eighteen suspects in public prosecutions were freed, and no verdict is known in the remaining eleven public prosecutions. The majority of private prosecutions appear to have been actions against informal witchcraft accusations or insults, and the slander seems commonly to have been refuted. It is certainly noteworthy, therefore, that by contrast only eighteen public prosecutions are known to have ended with the suspect being set free.[4]

The Witchcraft Trials of 1617

I have selected 1617 for discussion for a number of reasons. It was the year with the largest total number of prosecutions, fourteen, all of which were public prosecutions. This peak appeared after four years during which there were apparently no prosecutions at all. It is a year with a larger than normal differential between female and male suspects—twelve and two respectively. It is also one of only two years from which we have transcripts of confessions available to us. Throughout much of the late sixteenth and early seventeenth centuries witch-hunting seems to have been low level and endemic, and it is precisely for that reason that these features of the year 1617 all seem to be deserving of explanation. If we take the three obvious peak years of prosecution, 1617, 1622, and 1631 we get quite a different impression of witch-hunting in Guernsey. Forty of the prosecutions for witchcraft occurred in these three years, thirty-seven of which were public prosecutions, about 31 per cent. Seventeen of these prosecutions ended in executions. At about 46 per cent, this is in fact not very different to the proportion of executions in the totality of years. Perhaps unexpectedly also, six of the eight instances of a suspect being

---

[4] Greffe, Crime MS, n. 1 above, i–v.

freed occurred in these three peak years (none in 1617, two in 1622, and four in 1631). The extraordinary factors evidently—though equivocally—at work during the three peak years may have provoked a crisis of confidence within the Royal Court, resulting in acquittals. After 1631 there were only ten more public prosecutions, one of which resulted in another acquittal, one in a banishment for crimes other than witchcraft even though the court was not convinced of the witchcraft charge, and four of which have no recorded verdict. The exceptional nature of these peak years suggests that they may require different explanations than would be appropriate to the phenomenon of witchcraft prosecution in general.

The trials of 1617 are to be found mainly in volume two of 'Livre en Crime', though with some material appearing in volume three. Volumes two and three overlap by six years, and it can be surmised that the binding of the volumes reflects a difference in the class of documents to be found in the two volumes. Volumes one and two contain long transcripts of depositions presented in criminal trials, whereas volumes three and onwards contain only references to the stages of each trial process. During the overlap period the materials in volumes two and three relate to the same trials.

The witch trials of 1617 lasted from 29 March until 31 January. There were fourteen people accused, two of whom were men. Eight were executed and five banished. One verdict is unknown. The method of execution was normally hanging and burning, although Jeane Guignon (alias de Callais) was burned alive. Banishment in all cases was perpetual. In this paper I focus on the case of Collete Becquet, tried and eventually executed. I describe some of the features of her confession and of the depositions against her, suggesting that in order to understand the meanings of the evidence against this woman, for all concerned in her trial, we should see it as a dialogue between a legal culture, the beliefs of the accused and those of deponents.

The Case of Collete Becquet

A summary of the procedure used in Collete Becquet's trial given in her sentencing, together with two other women, explains that she had been found guilty on the basis of the deposition evidence against her, and that before being strangled and burnt she should be tortured to reveal the names of her accomplices.

A large number of very incriminating depositions having been produced against them by the said officers, it is clear and evident that they have for many years practised the aforesaid diabolic art . . . the said women will presently be led, with nooses around their necks, to the usual place of execution, and there attached by the criminal officer to a gibbet, hanged by the neck, burned in the fire until their bones be reduced to ashes, their ashes scattered to the winds, and their goods, chattels and heritage, if there be any, forfit to his majesty. Also it is ordered that, in order to make them confess their accomplices, they shall be put to the question in the torture chamber before being executed.[5]

This use of torture as part of a sentence gives the confession of Collete Becquet a fascinating paralegal status. It is one of the few features of the Guernsey trials which have heretofore attracted the attention of serious scholars. As Soman notes,[6] Brian Levack has remarked on it as an unusual feature of Guernsey's procedures in witchcraft trials. There are in fact a few precedents for such a procedure in French practice, as Robin Briggs notes. Thus Collete's confession was not a proof of guilt so much as an arena for testing theories about the nature of witchcraft. It is hardly surprising, therefore, that the confession is full of the *topoi* of witchcraft so often related in late medieval and early modern demonologies.

The witches' sabbat is described quite fully in the confession:

The devil came to collect her to take her to the sabbat, and called on her without anyone seeing. He gave her a black unguent, with which (after stripping herself) she rubbed her stomach and chest. Having dressed herself she went out of the house and was suddenly carried far away at

[5] 'vn grand nombre de trespregnantes depositions faites et produites a lencontre deux par les dyts officiers par lesquelles est clair et euident quauroyent par longues annees praticque le susdyt diabolicque art—les djtes femes seront presentement conduites la hart au coul au lieu de suplice accoustume et la par lofficier criminel attachees a vn posteau pendues, estranglees arses & bruslees iusqua ce que leur chair et ossements soyent reduits en cendre leur cendres esparses par les vents leur biens meubles & heritage si aulcuns en ont acquis a sa Majeste Et ordonne que pour leur faire confesser leur complices quelles seront mises a la question en jehenne auant que destre executees' Greffe, Crime MS, n. 1 above, iii, 90. (Italics mark words expanded from abbreviations.)

[6] Brian P. Levack, *The Witch-hunt in Early Modern Europe* (London and New York, 1987), 14; A. Soman, 'Trente procès de sorcellerie dans la Perche' in Brian P. Levack (ed.), *Articles on Witchcraft, Magic and Demonology*, 12 vols. (New York and London, 1992), V, 56 at 66.

great speed, and found herself in an instant at the place of the sabbat, which was sometimes by the cemetery of the parish, and other times by the sea shore in the area of Rocquaine Castle. At that place she often encountered fifteen or sixteen wizards and witches along with devils, who were in the form of cats and hares. She did not recognize the wizards and witches, because they were all blackened and disfigured. It is true to say that she heard the devil call them by name, and she remembers amongst others Madame Callais and Madame Hardie. She also confesses that at the start of the sabbat the devil sometimes started the roll call with her. Her daughter Marie, the wife of Piere Massy, presently condemned for the same crime, is a witch, and she took her to the sabbat with her twice. She does not know where the devil marked her. At the sabbat, after having worshipped the devil, who was standing on his hind legs, they had sex with him in the form of a dog, then danced back to back, and after having danced they drank some wine (does not know of what colour) which the devil poured out of a pot into a silver or pewter goblet. The wine did not seem so good to her as that which one ordinarily drinks. She also ate some white bread which was given to her. She never saw any salt at the sabbat.[7]

Any number of literary authorities can be cited for the details of flying to a distant location,[8] the company of devils in animal

---

[7] 'Que le diable l'estant venüe querir pour aller au Sabath l'appelloit sans qu'on s'en apperceust; et luy bailloit vng certain onguent noir duquel (appres s'estre despouillée) elle se frotoit le dos ventre et estomac; et s'estant reuestüe sortoit hors son huis lors estoit incontinent emportée *par* loin d'une grande vitesse; et se trouuoit a l'instant au lieu du sabath quj estoit q*u*elque fois pres le cimetiere de sa *paroisse*; et quelques autres fois pres le riuage de la mer, aux enuirons du chasteau de Rocquaine la ou estant ariuée sy rencontroit souuent quinze ou saize sorciers et sorcieres auec les diables quj estoient la en forme de chiens chats et lieures; lesquels sorciers et sorcieres elle n'a peu recognoistre; *parce* qu'ils estoyent tous noircis et deffigures bien est vray auoir ouy le diable les euocquez *par* leur noms et se souuient entre autres de la Callaise et dela hardie/Et confesse qu'a l'entrée du sabath; le diable les voulant esuocquer com*m*encoit *par* elle q*u*elque fois/Que sa fille marie fem*m*e de Massy *present* condamnée pour *pareill* crime est sorciere; et quelle la menée *par* deux fois au sabath auec elle; ne scait *par* ou le diable la merchee; Qu'au sabath appres auoir adore le diable lequell se tenoit de bout sur ses pieds de derriere ils auoyent copula*t*ion auec luy en forme de chien, puis dansoyent dos a dos et appres auoir danse beuuoyent du vin (ne scait de q*u*elle couleur que le diable versoit hors d'un pot en vng gobelet d'argent ou d'estain lequell vin ne luy sembloit sy bon que celuy qu'on boit ordinaire*m*ent, mangeoist aussy du pain blanc quj leur presentoit n'a jamais veu de sell au Sabath' Greffe, Crime MS, n. 1 above, ii, 110r.

[8] Jean Bodin, *De la demonomanie des sorciers* (Paris, 1580), ff. 81r–81v; Henri Boguet, *An Examen of Witches* (E. A. Ashwin (trans.), Montague Summers (ed.), London, 1929), 41; Lambert Daneau, *A Dialogue of Witches* R. W. (trans.) (London, 1575), F VII r; Pierre de l'Ancre, *Tableau de l'inconstance des mauuais anges et demons* (Paris, 1612), 80; Jacques Fontaine, *Discours des marques des sorciers* (Paris, 1611), 22–3; James VI/I, *Daemonologie* (Edinburgh, 1597), 38.

forms,[9] marking by the devil,[10] obeisance to the devil,[11] demonic sexual activity,[12] and a meal.[13] No single source can be identified. Guernsey did not have a resident demonological theorist whose theorizing enjoyed a symbiotic relationship with the practice of witch-hunting, as the Franche-Comté had an Henri Boguet, or Lorraine had a Nicolas Remy. Rather we seem to have here a conservative selection of the elements of sabbat accounts in continental demonologies and trials.

By contrast the depositions upon which the guilty verdict against Collete Becquet was based revolve largely around narratives of harm to animals and human beings. The following deposition by Jeane Totevin is a good example.

Jeane Totevin deposes that about seven years ago she bought a cow from the heirs of Thomas du Prey. Collete Becquet came to ask for some milk. This was about the month of March. And she was told to come back on the following day, since they didn't have any for the time being. With that the cow was taken with a terrible illness, such that it couldn't eat.[14]

No mention of the devil is made by deponents in this kind of narrative, in contrast to the confession cited above. However, it would be too easy, in discussing the differences between confessions and deposition material, to make black and white distinctions between the court officers' understanding of witchcraft in terms of demonic apostasy and the deponents' accounts of witchcraft focusing on the harmful activities of the witch (*maleficium*). In fact there are a number of demonic motifs in the depositions against Collete Becquet, as well as motifs suggestive of the elements of the sabbat as described in the confession. But it should

---

[9] Boguet, *Examen*, n. 8 above, 5; Nicolas Remy, *Demonolatry* (E. A. Ashwin (trans.), Montague Summers (ed.), London, 1929), 27–8; de l'Ancre, *Tableau*, n. 8 above, 73; F. Pierre Crespet, *Devx livres de la hayne de sathan et malins esprits* (Paris, 1590), f. 230v.

[10] James VI/I, *Daemonologie*, n. 8 above, 33; Alexander Roberts, *A Treatise of Witchcraft* (London, 1616), 14; Thomas Cooper, *The Mystery of Witch-craft* (London, 1617), 88–9.

[11] Boguet, *Examen*, n. 8 above, 56; Daneau, *Dialogue*, n. 8 above, D VI r; Remy, *Demonolatry*, n. 8 above, 65; James VI/I, *Daemonologie*, n. 8 above, 37; Cooper, *Mystery*, n. 10 above, 90.

[12] Daneau, *Dialogue*, n. 8 above, F VII v; Remy, *Demonolatry*, n. 9 above, 61; Crespet, *Devx livres*, n. 8 above, 236v; Cooper, *Mystery*, n. 10 above, 92; Bodin, *Demonomanie*, n. 8 above, ff. 83r–84v; de l'Ancre, *Tableau*, n. 7 above, 94, 126.

[13] Boguet, *Examen*, n. 8 above, 61; de l'Ancre, *Tableau*, n. 8 above, 453–4.

[14] Greffe, Crime MS, n. 1 above, ii, 99r.

be noted that the sabbat was by no means essential even to the orthodox demonological conception of witchcraft as a matter of the pact, that is to say, demonic apostasy. In fact the earliest and most influential of demonologies, Kramer and Sprenger's *Malleus Maleficiarum* (1487), contained no account of the witches' sabbat, although the demonic pact was a constant in orthodox accounts of the nature and meaning of witchcraft. Furthermore there are details of the harmful activities of witches present in all three confessions of 1617. Demonological authors themselves were certainly not unconcerned with the issue of *maleficium*, often linking it to the demonic pact.

In Collete Becquet's confession the idea of witchcraft as apostasy, the worship of the devil, is dovetailed neatly with the idea of witchcraft as *maleficium*. We are told that '[a]t the end of the sabbat the devil incited her to perform many evil deeds, and to that end gave her certain black powders, which he commanded her to throw on any persons or animals whom she wanted to'.[15] Several specific instances when Collete used the black powder are identified. One of them is in fact the harm allegedly done to Jeane Totevin's cow cited above as an instance of the typical deposition narrative of *maleficium*.

At the end of the sabbat the devil incited her to perform many evil deeds, and to that end gave her certain black powders, which he commanded her to throw on any persons or animals whom she wanted to. With the powder she performed many evil deeds. Amongst others she remembers that she threw it on Monsieur Dolbell the parish minister, which brought about his death. With the same powder she bewitched the wife of Jean Manques. She persistently denies that she died by her hand. She touched the side of and threw powder on the deceased wife of Jean Perchard, the successor of Monsieur Dolbell as minister in the parish. She became housebound and died, as did her offspring. She does not know what occasion the said woman gave her.

When the wife of Collas Tottevin refused her some milk she dried up her cow by throwing some of the powder on it. She saw the cow afterwards and made it eat some bran and herbs which the devil gave her.[16]

Demonological texts in fact prefigure this kind of link between *maleficium* and encounters with the devil at the sabbat. Daneau,

---

[15] Greffe, Crime MS, n. 1 above, ii, 110v.
[16] Greffe, Crime MS, n. 1 above, ii, 110v.

for example, explains that the devil distributes the means of harming in the form of powders and poisons at the sabbat, and Remy observes likewise.[17] Clearly the location of the confession in a paralegal space after the sentencing of Collete Becquet may indicate that this demonic understanding of *maleficium* had the status only of an experimental testing of demonological theory. However, the identification of particular episodes from the depositions as instances of the use of the black powder raises a question as to whether the maleficial evidence which provided a basis for Collete's conviction did so because it was viewed by the court officers in a demonic light. Certainly the court officers refer in sentencing summaries of trial proceedings, including Collete's, to the diabolic nature of their crimes, and refer only to maleficial charges. 'It is clear and evident that they have for some time practised the aforesaid diabolic art. They have not only cast spells on inanimate objects, but also made people and animals suffer with strange illnesses.'[18]

Of course, the term 'diabolicque' need not be any more than a reference to the wickedness of the suspect's crimes. Certainly it would be placing too great an interpretive burden on this one word to suggest that the court officers necessarily had in mind the kind of relationship between the suspect and the devil for the purpose of doing harm elaborated in the confession, namely the provision of harming powders. Although the sabbat as described in demonological literature does elaborate themes in the orthodox understanding of witchcraft, most significantly in providing a representation of the occasion of the pact, the sabbat was by no means central to demonology of the pact, as I have indicated. In fact the pact and its relationship to the practice of *maleficium* were elaborated in demonological texts without reference to the sabbat or the provision of harmful powders. The activities of witches are often presented in demonological literature as ciphers for the influence of the devil. This idea often had nothing to do with the direct provision of unguents or any other substances by the devil at the sabbat, and could even spring from a conviction

---

[17] Daneau, *Dialogue*, n. 8 above, F VI r; Remy, *Demonolatry*, n. 9 above, 3.

[18] 'est clair et euident quauroyent par longues annees praticque le susdyt diabolicque art pour auoir nonseulement ietté leur sort sur les choses insensibles, mais aussy tenu en langeur par maladies estranges plusieurs personnes & bestes' Greffe, Crime MS, n. 1 above, iii, 90.

that the witches were being duped by the devil; that their magical means did not possess the powers that they believed them to possess. Cotta, for example, suggests that 'Some receiue power and vertue from the Diuell vnto their Diabolical preparations, by certaine inchanted herbs, or medecines which they mixe and gather'. He indicates that the devil is behind the witches' powers, but does not indicate the level of confederacy between witch and devil. Some formulations of diabolic involvement in witchcraft clearly indicate that it is the existence of a pact with the devil which gives efficacy to the witches' magical means. King James explains that the mechanisms used by witches ape the sacraments in that they are not themselves efficacious without supernatural aid. As Cooper puts it, magical elements are only 'Signes and Watch-wordes to Satan to worke his wonders by'. There is still some ambiguity over the level of confederacy between Satan and the witch, although Cooper's language in particular implies conspiracy on the part of the witch. Elsewhere Cooper does indicate that the efficacy of charms derives directly from the pact. Cotta in fact describes a direct link between the pact and the efficacy of harmful witchcraft, suggesting that 'Some bring their cursed Sorcery vnto their wished end, by sacrificing vnto the Diuell some liuing creatures'. Perkins also states quite clearly that acts of witchcraft are 'brought into execution by vertue of mutuall confederacie, between him and the Magician'.[19]

The relationship between the demonic pact and the efficacy of *maleficium* is so close in many demonological works that they are sometimes considered to be one and the same action. Both Roberts and Perkins suggest that attempting anything known to be impossible, or using a superstitious prayer, can in itself initiate an implicit, rather than an explicit pact. Cooper also suggests that the use of certain magical mechanisms effectively initiates a form of pact.[20] Thus it is entirely conceivable that reports of maleficial activity amounted to evidence of the pact in the eyes of the court officers.

The criteria of proof, and thus the status of particular items of

[19] John Cotta, *The Triall of Witch-craft* (London, 1616), 89, 122; James VI/I, *Daemonologie*, n. 8 above, 12; Cooper, *Mystery*, n. 10 above, 65, 161–2; William Perkins, *A Discourse of the Damned Art of Witchcraft* (Cambridge, 1608), 12.

[20] Roberts, *Treatise*, n. 10 above, 27; Perkins, *Discourse*, n. 19 above, 51–2; Cooper, *Mystery*, n. 10 above, 68–70.

potential evidence, in the Royal Court's trials for witchcraft are by no means clear from the legal records. In part this is a function of widespread legal attitudes to witchcraft. Across Europe jurisdictions struggled with the problem of demonstrating the occurrence of this covert crime. By designating witchcraft as a *crimen exceptum* demonological theorists were able to propose exceptional criteria of proof. The absence of a confession prior to Collete Becquet's conviction suggests that, as per the recommendations of the demonological authors, other forms of evidence were deemed to be sufficient substitutes. Witness testimony was allowable as a substitute for a confession according to many theorists. For Perkins, 'true' proofs included free and voluntary confession, or the testimony of two witnesses as to the pact or witchcraft practices. These witchcraft practices might include invocation of the devil, entertaining a familiar, a testimony under oath that the accused has done anything implying the pact, such as using enchantment or raising storms. By contrast Perkins specifically identified narratives which describe an argument with the suspect prior to some misfortune as inadequate evidence for conviction. The kinds of testimony approved by Perkins in fact seem to assume the acceptability of another form of non-standard procedure, the use of the evidence of convicted accomplices. Boguet even put a figure of five on the number of accomplices' testimonies required for a conviction.[21] If Perkins' rejection of testimony concerned with misfortune after an argument describes the Royal Court's attitude to deposition accounts of *maleficium*, then the confession accounts of *maleficium* performed with a demonic unguent would seem definitely to have the status of demonological experiments, and no more.

The confession narratives themselves, with their accounts of demonic involvement in *maleficium*, need not be seen as purely the products of the demonological beliefs of the legal elite. There is some evidence that Collete herself had access to an understanding of *maleficium* in terms of demonic agency, though different in important respects from that explored in the context of the sabbat narratives of the confessions. She seems to have launched into an initial account of meeting the devil in the neighbouring parish without very much persuasion whereas her interrogators apparently

[21] Perkins, *Discourse*, 205–14; Boguet, *Examen*, n. 8 above, 159.

had to force her to come to a rather different account of receiving powders at the sabbat. The confession transcript notes at the start that after sentencing and before leaving the courtroom she confessed to being a witch, and so was taken away to give a full account of herself. Her confession then begins with an account of temptation by the devil in everyday circumstances. She describes meeting the devil on her way back from seeing to her cows, whereupon he persuaded her to take revenge on neighbours with whom she was in conflict.

To begin with the said Collete, immediately after the said sentence had been given, and before leaving the courtroom, freely recognized that she was a witch. Not wanting to particularize her crimes she was taken, with the others, to the place of interrogation, and interrogation having been applied she confessed that when she was young the devil appeared to her in the form of a cat in the parish of Torteval as she was returning from her animals, during the day. He took the opportunity to seduce her by inciting her to take revenge on one of her neighbours with whom she was just then engaged in a quarrel over some damage done by the neighbour's animals to her property. Thereafter, whenever she had a quarrel with someone, he appeared to her in the aforesaid form, and sometimes in the form of a dog, inciting her to take revenge on those with whom she was angry, persuading her to kill animals and human beings.[22]

There are important contrasts between this episode and Collete's subsequent description of having been provided with harmful powders by the devil at the sabbat. In the earlier episode Collete described having met the devil in a familiar setting, in the neighbouring parish, rather than at the sabbat, when he persuaded her to take revenge on a neighbour with whom she had argued over some damage caused to Collete's property by his animals. No means of doing harm is mentioned, and certainly no black powder. The earlier episode suggests a conception of the devil as a tempter, exploiting existing moral pressures of a familiar and unexceptional kind. The sabbat episode suggests an idea of the devil providing practical if not supernatural help to those who worship him. This difference might indicate that Collete could make a link between demonic witchcraft and *maleficium* without the persuasions of her interrogators, although, as we have seen, there was a degree of latitude in demonological theorists' views

---

[22] Greffe, Crime MS, n. 1 above, ii, 110r.

about the mechanism of demonic influence through the actions of witches. The kind of pact narrative with an everyday setting which I have tentatively identified with Collete's own beliefs was certainly not unknown in demonological literature, although Collete apparently gave her version a personal location in time and place. Thus the differences between this part of the confession and the sabbat section may bear witness to nothing more than the diversity of the demonological texts underlying the preconceptions of Collete's interrogators.

Potentially, a popular commitment to a pact-centred understanding of witchcraft could be ascribed to the influence of literate members of social elites—perhaps legal or ecclesiastical—on popular perceptions of witchcraft prior to the trials of 1617. This seems possible, since, although Collete embarked on her account of the pact in an everyday setting before going on to describe the sabbat, we are told that she did not want to enumerate her crimes to start with at all. Clearly some degree of coercion was required to elicit even this initial pact narrative, which would be consistent with the idea that Collete Becquet and others had been the objects of acculturation with an unfamiliar demonic understanding of witchcraft. However, there is no way of knowing what degree of coercion was necessary, and thus whether or not Collete had access to even an undigested narrative of the pact prior to her interrogation.

As I have indicated, one occasionally sees demonic motifs in deposition evidence, in Collete Becquet's as in other suspects' cases. This would seem to bear witness to a degree of penetration of popular belief with a demonic understanding of witchcraft, or perhaps the existence of a popular tradition of demonic beliefs. The former seems more likely given the small numbers of these depositions containing motifs that could be associated with orthodox imagery of the demonic. Furthermore, the fact that this kind of evidence seems to have exercised a high degree of influence over the court might seem to indicate that, by contrast, they did not view the mass of maleficial deposition narratives as evidence of the pact. The influence of demonic motifs on the verdicts of the Royal Court can be seen in the trials of two sisters, Marie and Thomasse de Callais, in 1617. Marie was executed, whereas Thomasse was only banished on vehement suspicion. Although there were far fewer depositions against Thomasse than against Marie, that fact alone may not explain the difference in the fates of the two women. Rather it seems significant that there was a suggestion of demonic involvement in the evidence against Marie, but none detectable in the evidence against Thomasse. A group of school-boy friends appear to have shared a rumour that Marie kept a black sheep in a cellar under her bed. There are four depositions to that effect among the sixteen depositions against her.[23] This is suggestive of English beliefs concerning animal familiars. In a pamphlet relating to trials in Chelmsford, it is stated that Elizabeth Francis was persuaded by her grandmother to give her blood to Satan in the form of a white cat, and to renounce God. The cat is evidently to be seen as a kind of familiar, since it could be willed to perform harmful acts if it was given some blood, though in this example we see the propensity for familiar beliefs to gather overtones of the pact.[24] Given this propensity of English familiar beliefs it would not be surprising if the rumour concerning the black sheep suggested, in the Guernsey context, the idea that Marie had dealings with a 'little master', a demonic seducer or tempter as described in continental demonologies. Remy, for example, states that sometimes demons, or 'little masters' appear as an animal such as a black dog. The name 'little master' suggests a personal identification with a witch in a manner similar to English familiars, though a somewhat different power relationship between the two parties is implied.[25]

Similarly, there are features of the deposition evidence against Collete Becquet which are suggestive of the demonic imagery of orthodox demonological texts, in particular imagery of the sabbat. It should be remembered that the sabbat was not intrinsic to literary diabolism, though apparently its elements had a wide appeal. Thus it could not be argued that these fragments of the sabbat scattered around the deposition evidence against Collete demonstrate that any deponent subscribed to pact beliefs about witchcraft. A deposition by Collas le Hurey provides a good example.

Collas le Hurey reports that about four years ago, coming from the town to his house, he encountered Collete Becquet in a lane. Passing by her he resumed his way, saying to her "I hope you don't mind if I go before you

---

[23] Greffe, Crime MS, n. 1 above, ii, 128r, 128v.
[24] Alan C. Kors and Edward Peters (eds.), *Witchcraft in Europe 1100–1700: A Documentary History* (Philadelphia, 1973), 229.
[25] Remy, *Demonolatry*, n. 9 above, 27–8.

Collete" and carried on directly. Further on he came across the said Collete in front of her house, at which he was astonished. He stared at her and noted particularly that it was her talking to her family, dressed in the same clothes that he had seen her in before. He believes that that was not possible without witchcraft. The said Collete, examined on the said deposition, says with arms folded that she came by horse.[26]

The idea of travelling so fast that it is not easily explicable in natural terms seems to anticipate the account in Collete's confession of the flight to the sabbat at great speed. The motif has no connection to the sabbat and no overt demonic explanation in le Hurey's deposition, but the fact that it diverges so sharply from the accounts of harmful witchcraft which dominate the depositions at least implies that it requires special explanation. Perhaps it is explicable in terms of common literary influences on both deponents and court officers. This scenario poses many difficult questions about the social class of deponents and their access to literacy. Perhaps the rolling momentum of the trials themselves, educating deponents with literary demonological concepts offers a more plausible explanation. But the last registered sabbat account in the Guernsey material prior to 1617 was in 1563. Other more recent years of prosecution may have yielded unregistered confessions which informed the deponents of 1617 with demonological ideas and images, but that cannot be verified. In any case the direct influence of literature or of other witchcraft trials would seem unlikely, given the absence of any demonic rationale for the fast travel in le Hurey's deposition. Collete was not going to the sabbat, and she was not overtly enabled to travel quickly by the devil or any substance provided by him as in the confession. Le Hurey's isolated and ambiguous account of unnaturally fast travel could be either a fragment of elite beliefs about witches, shorn of its demonic context, or perhaps the tip of an iceberg of popular beliefs about witches and their marvellous, though not necessarily demonic powers, which for the most part remained submerged in *maleficium*. Curiously, le Hurey's deposition seems to contain a remnant of a conflict-and-misfortune type of narrative. He notes that he apologized for going ahead of Collete on the road. The detail is left hanging; a potential explanation of a subsequent misfortune which never appears. Instead, an idea of the witch as

[26] Greffe, Crime MS, n. 1 above, ii, 97r.

capable of marvellous acts has apparently replaced the concept of the harmful witch. The narrative may at some point have been the object of an acculturation process. It has been brought into a kind of conformity with literary demonological images of flying witches, in so far as the basic features of the narrative allowed that to happen. In practice such literary images, the unfamiliar products of acculturation, were probably unlikely to receive popular expression without the presence of courtroom pressures or pretexts for doing so. Hence, when they were expressed by deponents, characteristically literary ideas, like the notion that witches could fly, might be expected to appear only occasionally and in a piecemeal fashion, as seems to be the case in le Hurey's narrative.

This would seem to argue quite the opposite to my earlier suggestion that Collete's apparent reluctance to confess to sabbat attendance can be put down to a popular, though tacit commitment to the idea of the pact without any sabbat corollary. However, types of narrative may be part of the repertoire of a community or class without necessarily being deemed appropriate for indiscriminate utterance in any given context. The initial non-sabbat pact narrative related by Collete in her confession seems to have been a type of account which, if it represented part of the narrative repertoire of the non-elite at all, would almost certainly only have been related in extreme circumstances such as interrogation and torture. The pact was the kernel of orthodox demonology, and it is not surprising that a narrative which addressed itself to the interrogator's central concern should be forthcoming under torture. But in the context of deposing against a suspect, it is also hardly surprising that the more lurid aspects of the elite demonology, or something analogous to it in popular belief, should be used occasionally to spice up the drama of developing hostility, suspicion and accusation.

The influence of the courtroom context on the shaping of demonic evidence should not be stressed at the expense of considering the development of diabolic beliefs about a suspect prior to formal accusation. It could be argued that Collete Becquet, who as we know became a witchcraft suspect, may initially have been seen as a possible demoniac. Understandings of demonic possession cases available in demonological texts sometimes had blurred borders with understandings of the nature of witches. If Collete Becquet was located by her accusers in such a blurred region we may have a case for identifying a degree of congruity prior to formal accusation between popular and elite notions of witchcraft as a matter of the demonic pact. The wife of Richard le Roy described having seen Collete Becquet rolling around, naked, like the Gadarene demoniac perhaps, on her floor, crying that she was burned.

The wife of the said le Roy reports that one morning, at about nine o'clock, passing before the said Collete's house, she heard her cry, saying 'I'm burning'. She was totally naked, lying on the floor twisting and turning. Thereafter the husband of the said Collete arrived on the scene and said to Collete 'You're certainly playing silly devils. I'm going to Collas le Marinel's place.' Having told all this to Mauger's wife, the deponent returned to find her dressed.[27]

It might be argued that Collete was thought to be undergoing the effects of a counter-magical riposte to a bewitching perpetrated by her, perhaps a counter-magical action involving the heating or burning of either the suspect's or a victim's property such as we hear about in a number of other depositions. However, Collete's symptoms are remarkably similar to the classic symptoms of demonic possession, particularly the bizarre and uncontrolled movements typical of French possession accounts. Collete is said to have been 'desroulant & contournant'. The behaviour or symptoms of a possessed person, as described in Blendecq's *Cinq histoires admirables*,[28] might include levitation, murderous attacks, and the seeing of strange visions. All authors who handle the subject indicate that possession cases were associated with bizarre and uncontrolled movements, particularly in the abdominal region and in the face. King James also describes typical symptoms of possession similar to those described in French works; unnatural strength, agitations in breast and belly, speaking languages, and so on.[29] While the agitations, convulsions, and

---

[27] 'La feme du dyt le roy raport qvn mattin viron les neuf heures passant par deuant la maison de la dyte Collete elle louit crier disant, ie suis bruslee et estoit toute nue couchee en son aire se desroulant & contournant que la dessus le mary de la dyte Collete y ariuant *comme* la deposante estoit presente se print a dire a la dyte Collete tu fais bien les gambades, je men vay ches Coll*as* le Marinel, quayant la deposant raporte cela a la feme de mauger icelle y courut et la trouua vestue' Greffe, Crime MS, n. 1 above, ii, 97r.

[28] D. Charles Blendecq, *Cinq histoires admirables* (Paris, 1582).

[29] James VI/I, *Daemonologie*, 70–1.

levitation described in English and French sources find parallels in the Guernsey narratives cited, there is obviously much detail that does not appear in any deposition of 1617. This would seem to suggest that, in the case of Guernsey's possession beliefs, an ideological propensity for blurring the distinction between demoniacs and witches was compounded by a certain amount of ignorance about the nature of demoniacs. Kaplan makes the point that demoniacs were often ambiguous figures, susceptible to at least three other diagnoses—melancholia, epilepsy, or hysteria—and who had perhaps submitted voluntarily to the devil.[30]

It is obviously problematic to suggest that this deposition shows Collete to have been interpreted as a demoniac before she was interpreted conclusively as a witch, since there would be no reason for the narrative to survive and be told at a witchcraft trial if the consensus had settled on a demoniac interpretation. However, the moral tone of Madame le Roy's deposition is markedly different from that of a 'typical' *maleficium* narrative directed against a suspected witch. Although the deponent's husband had access to narratives which clearly depict Collete as a witch capable of inflicting misfortune, with, for example, a curse, it is difficult to tell whether, if Collete was at one point viewed as potentially either a witch or a demoniac, she was at that time viewed in a morally negative or positive or even a neutral light. It seems unlikely that the story would have survived alongside more damning *maleficium* narratives concerning Collete if her earlier indistinct state had been read in a morally positive way.

There was more than one moral framework within which possession cases could be viewed in international witchcraft culture. There is a widespread tradition in French literature of seeing possessed individuals as victims of a type of *maleficium*, caused by a witch. This was often understood to place possession victims on a superior moral footing, along with other victims of *maleficium*. This model of possession was often reflected in the courts of the French speaking world. Monter suggests that, in Geneva, possession was considered to be just another form of bewitching. After 1605 possession was the single most common Genevan *maleficium* in fact. He does not offer an interpretation of

---

[30] Benjamin J. Kaplan 'Possessed by the Devil? A Very Public Dispute in Utrecht' *Renaissance Quarterly* 49 (winter 1996), 720, 738–9.

the moral meaning of the phenomenon.[31] Briggs argues that the popular view of possession in France was that witches caused it to happen, and that this in fact placed the possessed person in a morally superior position. By contrast, he argues, theologians were inclined to define possession as a punishment for sinful individuals, and thus to place the possessed person in a morally inferior position.[32] This moral understanding of possession would be more in keeping with the possible reinterpretation of Collete Becquet from demoniac to witch. Both Marescot and d'Alexis adopted the view that God allows possession to happen, as with other types of *maleficium*. As d'Alexis puts it, possession is intended by God to be both an evil and a medicine. One assumes that this is for the chastening of the possessed individual, and that the devil is the agent of the affliction with the witch as a necessary tool. Benedicti puts forward the idea that possession is an affliction for the sinful, or a temptation for the good, for which the devil is responsible, but does not mention the agency of witches. He uses the figure of Job to describe the demoniac, a *locus* usually reserved for the victims of bewitching, suggesting that he was actually more engaged with the idea of possession as a temptation than with the idea that it could function as a punishment for the sinful. It was extremely common for writers to adopt the Job image in this context.[33]

Like Monter, Kittredge argues that, in England, the difference between bewitching and demonic possession was a matter of 'psychical hair-splitting' unlikely to concern the layman.[34] Sharpe states that possession was established in the popular imagination in Britain by the 1570s. The Warboys case, with the pamphlet response to it, seems to have been a significant factor in spreading possession beliefs.[35] Possession is quite definitely presented in this

---

[31] E. William Monter, *Witchcraft in France and Switzerland: The Borderlands During the Reformation* (Ithaca, 1976), 59–60.

[32] Robin Briggs, *Witches and Neighbours: The Social and Cultural Context of European Witchcraft* (London, 1996), 81.

[33] Michel Marescot, *Discours veritable sur le faict de Marthe Brossier de Romorantin, pretendue demoniaque* (Paris, 1599), 2; Leon d'Alexis, *Traicté des energumenes* (Troyes, 1599), f. 36v; I. Benedicti, *La Triomphante victoire de la Vierge Marie* (Lyon, 1611), 24–5.

[34] George Lyman Kittredge, *Witchcraft in Old and New England* (Cambridge Mass., 1929), 124.

[35] James Sharpe, *Instruments of Darkness: Witchcraft in England 1550–1750* (London, 1996), 191, 208.

pamphlet as a misfortune inflicted by a witch, and not as a punishment or test. Lady Cromwell experienced distressing dreams about Mother Samuel, for example.[36] This understanding of possession is hardly applicable to the demoniac-like antics of Collete Becquet, who seems always to have been seen as morally suspect, whether as a demoniac or as a witch.

Interestingly, French witchcraft material, like the narrative concerning Collete Becquet cited above, seems to bear witness to a stage early in some episodes of possession when public opinion might easily have branded the victimized demoniac as a victimizing witch. There may even have been some technical confusion in certain quarters about the proper distinction between demoniacs and witches (rather than the bewitched), even leading to some uncertainty about their relative moral status. Both Marescot and Fontaine relate how the demoniacs with whom they were concerned were pricked just as if they were suspected of witchcraft. Later in Marescot's *discours* there is some indication given of a rather different rationale; namely that only a demoniac could have endured the pain of pricking without crying out, but one suspects that the similarity of treatment betrays a confusion.[37] Perhaps a factor in this confusion was the bizarre and frightening behaviour of demoniacs. The confusion could be realized in life. Mandrou identifies an instance of genuine confusion over the affliction of a girl in a convent thought to have been the victim in some sense of the convicted witchcraft suspect Father Louis Gaufridy. He quotes the words of the President of the Parlement concerned, Provence, to Gaufridy, 'the girl who was debauched by you, made to become a witch and taken to the sabbat for conversion, has been found to be possessed, the spirit having declared that he will not come out unless the magician who put him there is either dead or converted'.

She is referred to as having been made to become a witch and as having been possessed. It is not absolutely clear whether in this case, since they are both states of affliction, being a witch and being possessed are morally equivalent; if so they are states that are morally equivalent in a positive sense, strangely enough, since

---

[36] Barbara Rosen, *Witchcraft* (London, 1969), 254.
[37] Fontaine, *Discours des marques*, n. 8 above, 30; Marescot, *Discours veritable*, n. 33 above, 7.

she is quite definitely presented as Gaufridy's victim.[38] Cotta, by contrast, points out that both possessed and witch are 'habitacles of Diuels' and so will have similar habits, such as the haunting of graveyards by night. This implies a negative moral equivalence of the possessed and the witch, if anything.[39] Cotta's formula is therefore morally appropriate to Collete Becquet, who came to be accused in court by Madame le Roy. In so far as the negative moral equivalence of witch and demoniac had a diabolic rationale for Cotta, the negative moral implications of Collete's ambiguous state may also imply that a diabolic understanding of the witch-stereotype had attached itself to Collete Becquet by the time Madame le Roy delivered her deposition in court. Her deposition may therefore be seen as not just playing into the hands of the court officers' diabolic understandings of witchcraft, but as actually fostering this kind of ideology. There is no direct evidence, however, to indicate that such a demonic rationale was applied to Collete Becquet as a result of her ambiguous demoniac/witch identity. The metaphysics of this confusion, as I have already suggested, may simply have sprung from the bizarre and frightening antics of a demoniac.

Conclusion

To summarize, we see in the Guernsey material a complex interplay between the witchcraft beliefs of the legal elite and the beliefs both of deponents and of suspects. The court officers seem to have been eager to reconcile the maleficial charges in the depositions with the demonic conception of witchcraft explored in the confession, having almost certainly identified the alleged acts of *maleficium* with demonic agency. This was a recognized literary stance. These links forged in confessions between the pact and specific acts of *maleficium* perhaps imply that the Royal Court was engaged in a campaign of moral cleansing intended to legitimize the Calvinist order in the island. The dovetailing of *maleficium* into the sabbat accounts perhaps reflects a desire to restore the pact to the sphere of moral conduct in society, which the sabbat

---

[38] Robert Mandrou, *Magistrats et sorciers en France Au XVIIe siècle* (Paris, 1968), 200.
[39] Cotta, *Triall*, n. 19 above, 96.

setting is inclined to diminish. Furthermore, the specific maleficial depositions with which Collete Becquet's confession to the pact links up is perhaps revealing as regards the motivation of the officers of the court. The episodes identified as having been enacted with the black substance received from the devil, as we have seen, are the death of Monsieur Dolbel, the minister of St Piere du Bois parish, the illness of the wife of Jean Manques—although Collete denies causing her death—the death of the wife of Jean Perchard, Dolbel's successor, and the drying up of Jeane Tottevin's cow. It is possible that the episodes relating to Dolbel and Perchard direct the maleficial view of witchcraft to moral cleansing by dramatizing the conception of witchcraft as apostasy, a rejection of God and the Church. The Perchard episode is the only one identified by Collete which does not have a corresponding deposition. The selection of an ecclesiastical victim of *maleficium* seems to have overridden the use of any one of the attested cases of *maleficium* described in the depositions. Collete could not come up with a reason given her by Perchard's wife for the bewitching, and the registering of this fact in the confession probably bespeaks the influence of the interrogator, seeking to substantiate a case of *maleficium* that suggested apostasy.

The acculturation of popular maleficial conceptions of witchcraft might well have been an accompaniment to such a campaign of moral cleansing. The categorical definition of witchcraft as a matter of apostasy by literate social elites may have placed this perennial crime in the new context of an apocalyptic struggle between the devil and his enemy, the true church. The promotion of this pact-centred understanding of witchcraft, through secular and ecclesiastical trials of maleficial witches, and trials of men and women consulted as healers, but also perhaps through more diffuse channels such as the sermons of the parish ministry, may have encouraged the non-elite to see the church and the godly as actors in an apocalyptic drama. There is not a great deal of evidence that such a campaign of acculturation had been undertaken either by the sacred or secular authorities in Guernsey, at least with any degree of success. Although there are some indications that certain individuals may have been viewed as 'habitacles of devils' prior to formal accusation in the courts, we have seen that rather special circumstances were probably required before members of the non-elite would enter into anything like an orthodox discourse of demonic witchcraft. In fact those who deposed against Collete Becquet seem on occasion to have been moved only to reshape their maleficial narratives using the more highly tellable, but demonologically peripheral elements of sabbat accounts. There were depositions which seemed to display some awareness of the more central issue of demonic apostasy, deploying imagery suggestive of Satan's conventional animal manifestations, but these are few in number, and by no means unimpeachable as evidence of acculturation. In a narrative like that concerned with the black sheep allegedly kept by Marie de Callais, the concept of the witch's familiar, itself only tangentially related to pact beliefs in the English context, is suggested only obliquely. Thus the whole idea of animal apparitions might seem, as far as the Guernsey deponents were concerned, to have been a hazy and ill-defined mix of concepts, some foreign and even literary in origin, but some probably native and popular. That very vagueness almost certainly allowed the court officers to bring such a deposition into agreement with their pact-centred preconceptions of witchcraft.

THE HIDDEN TRUTH OF AUTOPOIESIS

It is the apparent functionality of organisms which has misled us the most. (Elias Canetti, *Die Fliegenpein* (Munich, 1992))

Willem J. Witteveen

The Problem of Irreducible Rationalities

In interpretations of the 'postmodern condition', it is often stated that there are in our time sharply differentiated and irreducible rationalities that complicate human communications and interactions. Economic rationality, legal rationality, political rationality, and technical rationality are all indispensable for functioning social systems but they each employ a different 'logic', they speak different languages, and their central terms and categories are mutually untranslatable.[1] As a result, human actors functioning in social systems are forced to speak just one of these languages and exclusively to follow the dictates of its rationality—to view a problem only in economic terms, or as a matter of law, or as a political issue, or as a technical problem. Alternatively, they are forced to switch rationalities as the situation demands and are then left with irresolvable problems of translation and integration—the economic factors do not fit into legal categories, political considerations have no exact counterpart in technical expertise. There is no common standard that can be used to compare relevance across rationalities. In effect, this means that individual rationality, or deliberation by an autonomous and

---

[1] The thesis of irreducible rationalities is derived from theories of law and of society that are in other respects in disagreement, such as J. Habermas, *Theorie des kommunikativen Handelns*, 2 vols. (Frankfurt am Main, 1981); N. Luhmann, *Ausdifferenzierung des rechts* (Frankfurt am Main, 1981); N. Luhmann, *Das Recht der Gesellschaft* (Frankfurt am Main, 1995).

reflective subject weighing all relevant considerations, is made virtually impossible. The different rationalities are both used by human actors and they determine what these actors can meaningfully think and say. In this conflict, the postmodern idea is that the divergent rationalities win out over individual deliberation and that the idea of concerted social action between autonomous deliberating persons—the old ideal of politics in an Aristotelian sense—loses its meaning.

This problem of irreducible rationalities is of great interest to law and literature scholarship. It is through language that different rationalities are constructed and reconstructed. Literary texts may mirror (and distort) these processes of language and may so provide persons involved in social systems, struggling to manage problems in terms of different rationalities, with an opportunity for reflection. Literature may provide insights that facilitate a critical attitude towards these rationalities and one's personal involvement in their operation.

The theories law and literature scholarship develops are likewise suited to stimulate reflection on the problem of irreducible rationalities. As an example, think of James Boyd White's incisive criticisms of the language of economics. Those engaged in the language games of economics tend to uncritically 'assume that everything can be said in its terms', in a purely representational approach to language. Economics is then supposed to be 'a transparent system . . . existing above or beyond language itself.'

The language of economics is thus assumed to be a super-language, or an authoritative meta-language, and this in two dimensions: it describes the world in the only way the world can be described; and it creates a set of conceptual structures which, if they meet the tests of economics themselves, are the only accurate conceptual structures for thinking about the world. Everything that is real can be said in, or translated into, this language.[2]

Opposing this, White claims that 'the literary view of language', embodied in the law, recognizes the limits of languages, understands that 'none says the whole truth' and acknowledges that 'full translation from one to the other is always in a deep sense impossible'. As a result, one can never evade responsibility for one's use of the language of economics, as of any other language.

[2] James Boyd White, *Justice as Translation: An Essay in Cultural and Legal Criticism* (Chicago, 1990), 81.

This means that the most profound obligation of each of us in using his or her language is to try to recognize what it leaves out, pointing to the silence that surrounds it—to acknowledge the terrible incompleteness of all speech, and thus to leave oneself open to hearing other truths, in other languages.[3]

This line of reasoning leads to an awareness of the problems of irreducible rationalities, not to their dissolution. In this paper an approach to systems theory will be discussed that starts with recognition of the problem, but tries to develop a model of communication that explains and accepts, even justifies the discursive power of different rationalities. This approach is called autopoiesis. Having introduced this theory, we will then turn to a literary text that effectively brings out the problems inherent in the autopoietic view of social life.

Autopoiesis as a Model of Law and Society

The word 'autopoiesis' is a neologism combining two Greek words: *autos* meaning self and *poiein* meaning to make. It was coined by the biologists Maturana and Varela, in order to describe living systems (such as organisms) as self-contained unities whose only reference is to themselves. Autopoiesis characterizes living as a process of cognition in which an organism reproduces itself. Direct communication with another organism is not possible (there are no common codes); the meaning accorded to an outside stimulus is always constructed self-referentially.[4]

Already the inventors of the idea of autopoiesis have thought of applications to social systems. Maturana, for instance, states that 'what determines the constitution of a social system are the recurrent interactions of the same autopoietic systems'.[5] Awareness of the functioning of autopoietic systems in society, according to the same author, leads to a preference for an anarchic rather than a hierarchic organization of society, since this is 'a society made for and by observers that would not surrender their condition of observers as their only claim to social freedom and mutual respect'.[6]

---

[3] James Boyd White, *Justice as Translation*, n. 2 above, 81.
[4] Humberto R. Maturana and Francisco J. Varela, *Autopoiesis and Cognition: The Realization of the Living* (Dordrecht and Boston, 1980).
[5] Maturana, *Autopoiesis*, n. 4 above, xxvi.
[6] Maturana, *Autopoiesis*, n. 4 above, xxx.

The meaning of this last statement will become clearer when we turn to later applications of autopoiesis to law and society. The sociologists Luhmann and Teubner further adapted autopoiesis into a model for describing the functioning of law as a subsystem of society. According to Teubner, law is a second-order autopoietic system, that distinguishes itself from society (the first-order autopoietic system) by constituting its components in a self-referential way and linking them together in a hypercycle.[7] Law is not immune to influences from the outside, just as living organisms are not immunized from them. But typically there is in social regulation through law a combination of operative closure and cognitive openness to the environment.

On the one hand, by generating knowledge within the system itself, law produces an 'autonomous legal reality'. It orients its operations according to this, without any real contact with the outside world. On the other hand, the law is connected with its social environments through mechanisms of interference which operate between systems.[8]

At this point it must, of course, be asked what exactly are the entities, the organisms, of law as a system that is supposedly operating in this way? This is Teubner's answer:

Social systems, including face-to-face interactions, formal organizations, and society as a whole, reproduce themselves on the basis of meaning. The components of all these social systems are communications, not individual human beings. Communications as a unity of communication, information, and understanding constitute social systems by reproducing recursive communications.[9]

So, the systems that are behaving in an autopoietic way, selectively translating inputs from their environments using the code that is already established within them, are not organisms in a literal sense, but consist of 'communications'. An act of reconstruction, performed by an observer, is needed to conceive of such systems of communications; they are not present to the unenlightened eye. During this exposition of his theory, Teubner manages to resist the temptation to provide extended and detailed examples of systems of communications that are both operatively closed and

---

[7] Gunther Teubner, *Law as an Autopoietic System* (Oxford, 1993), 25.
[8] Teubner, *Law as an Autopoietic System*, n. 7 above, 65.
[9] Teubner, *Law as an Autopoietic System*, n. 7 above, 30.

cognitively open. The theory must apparently be explained at a high level of abstraction, perhaps because Teubner wants to formulate a general model, applicable to law, regardless of time and place. His is a universally applicable model. The model mirrors reality, just as autopoiesis as a model reflects the reality of cognitive processes in living organisms. It provides a picture of what goes on out there, in the world where communications reproduce themselves.

Questions and Answers

Two questions immediately come up when we see that the theory of autopoiesis provides a model of this mimetic kind. First, whether it can ever be true that law in society is literally operating according to the same laws as an organism in its natural environment. When autopoiesis is transferred from the world of biology to 'law's empire', does this not rather mean that a metaphor is being formed, that we are invited to think in terms of an analogy, which is never literally true?[10] And second, when the basic unit of the system of law is taken to be 'communications', what happens in this model or this metaphor with the human beings themselves, without whose interactions there cannot be any meaningful communications? What about the systematic social relations between interacting human beings? Is autopoiesis, as Frankenberg remarked cynically, 'as postmodern as the neutron bomb which eliminates the subject while leaving everything else as it was?'[11]

It is important to note that Teubner, against these and other critics, argues that a focus on the communications rather than on human beings affords a liberating point of view. Indeed, 'autopoiesis breathes new life into the individual'. By seeing man at the mercy of autonomous processes which reproduce themselves

---

[10] This question was first raised by Hubert Rottleuthner in a paper surveying the use of biological metaphors for law in the 19th century and reaching rather sceptical conclusions about the prospects for new organicist metaphors such as autopoiesis. Hubert Rottleuthner, 'Biological Metaphors in Legal Thought' in Gunther Teubner (ed.), *Autopoietic Law: A New Approach to Law and Society* (Berlin, 1988), 97–127.

[11] G. Frankenberg, 'Down by Law: Irony, Seriousness, and Reason' in C. Joerges and D. Trubeck (eds.), *Critical Legal Thought: An American-German Debate* (Baden-Baden, 1989), 336.

according to a logic of their own, we can gain a better understanding of human existence.

Despite premature reports to the contrary, the autonomous reflecting subject is still with us. It has certainly not been deconstructed, merely decentred. In its unique position it is threatened by communicating social systems, law among them, which have at their disposal independent (communicative) mechanisms for understanding the world and for self-reflection. Herein lies one of the most important innovations of systems theory, one which makes it so relevant, particularly for law. Law is not identical with the sum of lawyers' consciousnesses. Rather, it is the product of an emergent reality, the inner dynamics of legal communications.[12]

This is a key passage. It shows us how a model intended for observation of the law as a functioning system, from the outside as it were, requires a conceptual move that makes human beings into actors at the periphery of law, in the margins, under the spell of its 'inner dynamics', even while human actions are necessary for the continuing operation of autopoietic systems. The individual is marginalized, or, as Teubner puts it, he is 'decentred'. Remembering Maturana's remark about the freedom inherent in being an observer, we can say that the decentred subject in conditions of autopoiesis is first, foremost, and in the last instance, looking at law and society from the outside.

Gains and Losses

In this autopoietic picture of law there is both gain and loss. To see some of the gain, we have to look at the analysis, finally becoming somewhat more realistic, of social regulation through law that Teubner gives after the autopoietic system has been introduced in abstract and general terms. Imagine two autopoietic systems, the law and the economy. Through a legislative measure a price-freeze is imposed on the economy. Is this a direct intervention of law into the economic system, which after all will now presumably change its functioning in accordance with a legal norm? Autopoietic theory denies this common-sense insight altogether. What is at stake is an act of observation. 'The law observes the economy through a legal ruling on price control . . . What was

---

[12] Teubner, *Law as an Autopoietic System*, n. 7 above, 45.

an ambitious piece of external regulation becomes mere self-observation.'[13] At the same time, the economic system also performs an act of self-observation, seeing the input from law in its own terms.

The interventions of law in the economy have to be regarded as reciprocal observations between two autonomous, hermetically sealed communication systems. The law 'invents' an image of the economy, and formulates its norms by reference to this image. The economy 'invents' an image of the law and processes its payment procedures by reference to it.[14]

Autopoiesis, as a model of what really goes on in law and society, in a useful way draws attention to the resilience of social systems to change. As a result of the model one can accurately predict that there are inherent limits to efforts to regulate autopoietic systems from the outside, because their operative closure in combination with their cognitive openness make for mechanisms that turn all other rationalities into the particular rationality already contained in the system of legal communications. It is easy to imagine how these reciprocal acts of observation lead to distorted pictures, to translations that do not match. By reacting according to the logic of the functioning economic system, the purpose of the price-freeze as defined in legal terms may well be circumvented, without the legal system being able adequately to conceptualize this development. Autopoietic processes limit feedback possibilities between systems.

It is important to see the limits to social regulation through law resulting from operative closure and cognitive openness. Seeing these limits may even influence legislative strategy, as it has briefly done in the Netherlands when, during the 1980s, the strategy of legally-conditioned self-regulation was contemplated and even tried out.[15] But the price paid for this insight is a lack of understanding

---

[13] Teubner, *Law as an Autopoietic System*, n. 7 above, 77.
[14] Teubner, *Law as an Autopoietic System*, n. 7 above, 79.
[15] The strategy of legally-conditioned self-regulation means that the government, in order to achieve its regulative purposes, appeals to the self-regulative potential of organized sectors of society (such as the educational system or the agrarian economy). It is hoped that rules will come about that are easier to monitor because they emerge from within functioning social systems. The price to be paid for this is lack of fit with official purposes of the government. Through procedural law this lack of fit can be minimized and evaluated. At the same time, the government accepts limits to its lawmaking and law-enforcing potential. For a spirited defence of this legislative strategy, see Philip Eijlander, *De wet stellen* (Zwolle, 1993), 1–255.

of what human action and interaction really can achieve through
law as a language. What Teubner does is to describe the law as if
he came from Mars. While pursuing a thoroughly 'external point
of view', there is no room in autopoiesis for what Hart calls 'the
internal aspect of rules'.[16] The 'internal point of view' presupposes
that at least some members of a community of law show 'a critical
reflective attitude' in using 'common standards'. They must, in
other words, be able self-consciously to follow rules rather than
share a social habit of obedience to them. In any given society,
there will be those that take the internal point of view alongside
those that primarily look upon law from an external point of
view. 'One of the difficulties facing any legal theory anxious to do
justice to the complexity of the facts is to remember the presence
of both these points of view and not to define them out of existence.'[17] If autopoiesis excludes the important social phenomenon
of adherence to law from an internal point of view, even more
does it exclude Fuller's 'internal morality of law', which posits the
existence of moral criteria inherent in forms of social order (such
as legislation or contract) that are not only accessible to participants in the practices of law but even play a constitutive role in
determining whether a given legal act is 'really' a specimen of the
intended type of social order (for example, under what circumstances words on paper count as an act of legislation addressing
the community of law).[18] There is in autopoiesis no hermeneutical
understanding of law and because of this there can be no meaningful advice to lawyers participating in the functioning of law as
a practice, at most there may be advice directed at the designers of
systems for society.

What is a 'System of Communications'?

Autopoiesis is presented as an innovation of systems theory. So it
must articulate a coherent conception of law as a system. But
what exactly is a 'system of communications'? There are at least
four candidates for such systems of communications and all of
them can be studied for the way they reproduce themselves. A

[16] H. L. A. Hart, *The Concept of Law* (2nd edn, Oxford, 1994), 56.
[17] Hart, *Concept of Law*, n. 16 above, 91.
[18] Lon L. Fuller, *The Morality of Law* (revised edn, New Haven, 1969).

social system can be a (reconstructed) set of communications, an institution, a sector of society, and a semi-autonomous social field. In talking about a social system understood as a 'set of communications', we are dealing with a sociological reconstruction of those communicative acts that are operative in a practice of law, eliminating all other aspects of this practice; it is a theoretical reconstruction that isolates certain data. In the case of institutions, we face such familiar instances as the family, the firm, the hospital, and the court. In order to see systematic communications in these institutions, again some kind of reconstruction in a theoretical framework is necessary, abstracting from the day-to-day interactions that go on in these institutions. Sometimes a social system is referred to in a more abstract sense, as a 'sector of society', such as the economy, politics, culture, religion. Because of its interest in the unbridgeable gaps between various kinds of rationality, much of systems theory is actually practised at this abstract level of analysis. Systems in the sense of 'semi-autonomous social fields' require somewhat more explanation, since here we meet a technical term coined by anthropologist of law Sally Moore (and further elaborated by legal sociologist John Griffiths) in order to indicate any conglomerate of interacting individuals with different roles and differing interests and points of view. The field is semi-autonomous in being able to produce rules, as a result of the interactions going on inside it, that are to some extent binding on all participants, but at the same time it is open to external influence by rules that are imposed from outside or are invoked by participants when deemed useful. Analysing such diverse semi-autonomous social fields as the New York dress industry, the agricultural economy of the Chaggo of Mount Kilimanjaro (Moore), and Dutch euthanasia practices in hospitals (Griffiths), these theoretical statements are underpinned with empirical research material.[19]

These four kinds of systems are so different from each other as to make even stable classification impossible. For those who want to make general statements about the way systems function in society, the abstract categories of the 'set of communications', the 'institution' or the 'sector of society' are more attractive, but there

---

[19] Sally Falk Moore, *Law as Process: An Anthropological Approach* (London, 1978), 54–81; John Griffiths, *De sociale werking van recht* (Nijmegen, 1996), 469–513.

is no clear reason to prefer one or other of these conceptions when it comes to the discovery of autopoietic processes of self-reproduction. Indeed, there is a danger in mixing statements about one kind of system with statements relating only to one of the others. When one wants to observe actual interactions between people involving law, the semi-autonomous social field has obvious attractions because it offers an empirical research language. Meanwhile, semi-autonomous fields do not coincide with the boundaries of the other three social systems; as a 'field', after all, is a stylized place of meeting.

When 'systems of communications' are the business of autopoietic theory, it is important that autopoiesis can deal with all four kinds of systems (or that it explicitly exclude one kind of system). In order to be a convincing approach to law and society, the model of autopoiesis should minimally be applicable for law practices going on in semi-autonomous social fields. It should not limit itself to theoretical reconstructions and abstract speculations but should show how interacting individuals in their semi-autonomous social field have no choice but to reproduce this system and its constructions of reality. This remains, unfortunately, an unfulfilled agenda.[20] Even if this were seriously attempted, the issue of the lack of a hermeneutical understanding would remain unresolved. In order to understand law in its functioning as a system, it would be necessary to bring in the internal aspect of rules (Hart), in other words to pay attention to what Teubner ironically calls 'the sum of lawyers' consciousnesses'. It is even desirable to go one step further and agree with Fuller that in order to know how the law can be a system that produces 'good order and workable social arrangements', it is necessary to study the actual expectations that people belonging to a legal culture have of their legal institutions, such as courts, that perform their function well according to both a morality internal to the institution and moralities that are not intimately bound up with the institution in question.[21] For example,

---

[20] Teubner seems to think that autopoiesis is not in need of application to situations in which semi-autonomous social fields are at work, but on theoretical grounds provides a better alternative theory explaining the resistance of social autonomy to legislation and other outside interventions: Teubner, *Law as an Autopoietic System*, n. 7 above, 76.

[21] Lon L. Fuller, *The Principles of Social Order: Selected Essays of Lon L. Fuller* (Durham, NC, 1981), part 1.

the internal morality of legislation demands that laws be understandable and consistent and that there is not a large gap between their formulation on paper and their practical application. These canons of the internal morality of law have no place in autopoietic reconstructions of how the law functions. But they clearly do affect law as a system of communication: laws which systematically flout minimum levels of these and other canons constituting the morality of legislation are not even perceived or accepted as proper laws that require respect on the side of the citizen. (But they could theoretically achieve high operative closure.)

Literature and Autopoiesis

It seems there are a number of reasons to be critical of attempts to model legal communication on the picture autopoiesis derives from the cognitive processes of living organisms. Meanwhile, there is a hidden truth of autopoiesis. This becomes visible when we drop the idea that autopoiesis is a model of communication and rather attempt to see the story autopoiesis tells about operative closure in combination with cognitive openness, as a metaphor. And I believe the force of autopoiesis as a metaphor for human communication, seen in a certain light, can be better understood by turning to certain literary works that have brought out the truth hidden in autopoiesis, unintentionally no doubt, much more clearly than an abstract theory can ever do.

The Palace is the Ear of the King

I now turn to a short story by Italo Calvino, entitled 'A king listens'.[22] The king of this story is portrayed as a man whose exercise of the royal prerogative is at the same time the prison in which he is captive. His omnipotence makes him impotent. His very power keeps him in place. The rituals of court life, celebrated in his presence on the throne, are both the expression of his exalted position in the kingdom and the mark of his total subordination to its minutest details. The king's every wish will be immediately obeyed, it is true, but at the same time the king can never

---

[22] All quotations are from Italo Calvino, *Under the Jaguar Sun* (San Diego, 1986), 31–64.

know what intrigues are going on behind his back. While his predecessor is in jail, in the cellars of the palace, his successor may be plotting against him in the many spaces surrounding the central hall of the palace. In this condition, the king is both autonomous and unfree, both the centre of all attention and completely alone. The need to be on the alert all the time, to guess what is going on from the sounds he hears, makes his freedom, which is theoretically without bounds, a chimera. All he can do is listen. And while it is a quality of good kings to listen attentively to their subjects in order to pronounce on their troubles and conflicts (the king as the speaking law), this king does not listen in order to communicate with the citizens but in order to make sure everything is still in order and his undoing is not at hand. The king does not take part in the ordinary interactions between humans, and yet he is truly the centre around which the daily life of the kingdom is organized.

Here are some passages in which the listening King is described, occupying the centre of the palace, all ears.

The throne, once you have been crowned, is where you had best remain seated, without moving, day and night. All your previous life has been only a waiting to become king; now you are king; you have only to reign. And what is reigning if not this long wait? Waiting for the moment when you will be deposed, when you will have to take leave of the throne, the scepter, the crown, and your head.

Kings do not have watches: it is assumed that they are the ones who govern the flow of time; submission to the rules of a mechanical device would be incompatible with regal majesty. The minutes' uniform expanse threatens to bury you like an avalanche of sand: but you know how to elude it. You have only to prick up your ears in order to recognize the sounds of the palace, which change from hour to hour . . . The palace is a clock: its ciphered sounds follow the course of the sun; invisible arrows point to the change of the guard on the ramparts with a scuffle of hobnailed boots, a slamming of rifle-butts, answered by the crunch of gravel under the tanks kept ready on the forecourt. If the sounds are repeated in the customary order, at the proper intervals, you can be reassured, your reign is in no danger: for the moment, for this hour, for this day still.

The palace is a great ear . . . You are crouched at the bottom, in the innermost zone of the palace-ear, of your own ear; the palace is the ear of the king.

Here the walls have ears. Spies are stationed behind every drapery,

curtain, arras . . . And you know that every secret service has been infil-
trated by agents of the opposing secret service . . . What the spies' eaves-
dropping records, whether at your command or your enemies', is the
maximum that can be translated into the code formulas, inserted into
programs specifically devised to produce secret reports conforming to the
official models. Threatening or comforting as it may be, the future that
unfolds on these pages no longer belongs to you, it does not resolve your
uncertainty. What you want revealed is something quite different, the fear
and the hope that keep you awake, holding your breath, in the night:
what your ears try to learn, about yourself, about your fate.

If we take the king to be the decentred subject autopoiesis tells us
about, the one confronted with an 'emerging reality' that he both
sets into motion but cannot prevent from overwhelming him, we
can see that the experience of such a decentred subject, such an
autonomous but powerless figure, is not one of new freedom but
one of hope and fear in self-imposed captivity, more like the experience of a prisoner than of a free agent.

The next two passages are more explicit on this point, showing
how reality in an autopoietic system ('the palace-ear') is being
reconstructed.

While your palace remains unknown to you and unknowable, you can try
to reconstruct it bit by bit, locating every shuffle, every cough at a point
in space, imagining walls around each acoustical sign, ceilings, pave-
ments, giving form to the void in which the sounds spread and to the
obstacles they encounter, allowing the sounds themselves to become the
images . . . The palace is a construction of sounds that expands one
moment and contracts the next, tightens like a tangle of chains.

What process is at work in this vivid picture of royal activity?
Clearly, here we have operative closure coupled with cognitive
openness.

Next, the story explicitly explores the organic nature of the
system the king is operating. Not in a neutral way, however. A
danger manifests itself.

The palace is the body of the king. Your body sends you mysterious
images, which you receive with fear, with anxiety. In an unknown part of
this body, a menace is lurking, your death is already stationed there; the
signals that reach you warn you perhaps of a danger buried in your own
interior. The body seated askew on the throne is no longer yours, you
have been deprived of its use ever since the crown encircled your head;
now your person is spread out through this dark, alien residence that

speaks to you in riddles. But has anything really changed? Even before, you knew little or nothing about what you were. And you were afraid of it, as you are now.

This is autopoiesis as body language. The king motionless on his throne, all ears, frantically reconstructing in his imagination the world around him but knowing he fails to capture what is really there, fails to immunize himself against the final intervention that is still not at hand.

The Duplicity of the Narrative Voice

We have come to the point where we think we see how the autopoietic universe of kingship works. A picture, such as this one, is a frozen sight. But a story cannot remain in this state of description. The king cannot remain motionless. The readers of the story demand action. Something must change, must fight against the all-powerful mechanisms of operative closure and cognitive openness. And Calvino makes this happen, in distinction from the really rather static metaphor of autopoiesis which portrays a condition that is always recreated, no matter what interventions and interactions take place (unless the system ceases to be autopoietic, that is: ceases to be a living organism). This is how Calvino makes an opening towards real drama. 'The palace is a weft of regular sounds, always the same, like the heart's beat, from which other sounds stand out, discordant, unexpected.' And these 'discordant sounds', these signals that may be connected but may also be isolated, prompt on the part of the king the search for meaning, the desire to truly get into contact with an Other.

A door slams. Where? Someone runs down steps, a stifled cry is heard. Long, tense minutes pass. A prolonged, shrill whistle resounds, perhaps from a window in the tower. Another whistle replies, from below. Then silence. Does some story link one sound to another? You cannot help looking for a meaning, concealed perhaps not in single, isolated noises but between them, in the pauses that separate them. And if there is a story, does that story concern you? Will some series of consequences involve you finally?

We have now reached the crucial question: the one of personal involvement in a story, in a sequence of events made meaningful, in human interactions between individuals struggling to be both free and involved. A love story perhaps, as the sequence of isolated sounds may be taken to suggest.

At this point, we will have to postpone the satisfaction of our curiosity about what is happening, what is going to happen. We must now pay attention to the narrative voice in this story, the voice through which we come to form us a picture of the listening king in his palace-ear. There is something peculiar about this narrator, who seems to speak to the king, telling him how proper kings behave, how this king must behave, how the king actually feels, what the king is listening to so intently. It is a narrative voice talking to us by addressing the king. It makes both the king and us into listeners, since we, as listeners, want to hear about the king who listens. It is a narrative voice that duplicates the position the king is in: the voice is advising the king who in his regal majesty is the autonomous subject deciding his fate, and the voice is capturing at the same time all the king's very thoughts and so compels the king to listen.

We note a change in register, so to speak, when the action starts interfering with the hyperstability of autopoiesis in the palace-ear. The narrative voice has begun in the traditional vein of the advice to kings, it sounds like the kind of voice you can find in treatises on the topic of how the king must behave to be a good or effective king, say by Erasmus or by Machiavelli, the 'mirrors of princes' dating from the late Renaissance.[23] It is an educative voice, telling the king how to hold the sceptre, how to deal with the heavy crown on his head, how to satisfy all his bodily needs while seated. This advice has a tinge of the technical about it. But from this traditional advisory function, the narrative voice develops into a self-reflective voice, impersonating the king, speaking the musings going on in his mind. The voice is that of a sympathetic observer who is both wise in the ways of the world and privy to understanding what really goes on in the king's mind. The voice, emphasizing now the one, now the other register, shows a true autonomy as a speaking voice, as the voice of a teller of tales, that contrasts with the impotent power of the king.

In the passages just considered, there is ample evidence of this double nature of the narrative voice, speaking both to the king

---

[23] Quentin Skinner, *The Foundations of Modern Political Thought, Volume I: The Renaissance* (Cambridge, 1978), 118–38.

and from inside him. This is how life must be for a decentred subject: there are constant exhortations that are indistinguishable from one's very own thoughts.

Erasmus and Machiavelli on the Princely Art of Listening

Digressing within this digression on narrative voice, the question comes up whether Erasmus and Machiavelli, who published their treatises on royal government within a few years from each other, and who argue such diametrically opposed visions—Erasmus advocating the Christian responsibilities of kings and Machiavelli returning to 'pagan' virtues that belie Christian precepts of morality—have addressed the autopoietic predicament of listening kings. It turns out they have, albeit in a limited way. Both Machiavelli and Erasmus are concerned that flatterers, of whom there are always many about in a princely court, will get the better of the king and will cause the king to overestimate his own greatness and thereby to get out of touch with reality. In court life, the language of flattery is in a way obligatory and it is self-reproducing. The prince will be spoken to, using epithets that express his exalted status. While this is a social convention, it nevertheless appeals to the king's vanity. And this is still an innocent aspect of flattering. Court rules and rituals are impregnated with flattery. 'The King can do no wrong.' This legal maxim makes it possible to let government proceed in name of the king but without his actual participation, except in a marginal sense. Yet, at the same time, there is clearly the suggestion that the king is above the law. Machiavelli and Erasmus see great dangers in the language of flattery, precisely because the prince will never be able to escape from it. It is the lingua franca in court. But while Machiavelli sees the danger in strategic terms—a king who is flattered, loses his cool judgment and may lose his position of power—Erasmus is more concerned for the well-being of the Christian prince's soul and for the pernicious results flattery will have for the interests of the subjects.

Consequently, they advocate quite different precautions. The prince must make it clear, according to Machiavelli, that in principle people at court are to speak the truth (for its reality-effect), but this 'right' must not be used regularly by many persons, since this would entail loss of respect for the king. The solution is to appoint a small number of wise men as advisers and allow freedom of opinion only to them. The king himself should decide when advice is called for, thus occupying a position of power in the stream of communication. How to know when to ask advice and when to forgo this? 'Here is an infallible rule: a prince who is not himself wise cannot be well advised.'[24] A kind of autopoiesis of the second degree, quite similar to the situation the king in Calvino's story is in when deciding what messages from spies and counter-spies to judge credible. Only Calvino's king does not have the judgmental powers to make accurate discriminations. Erasmus points out that the prince can avoid the moral degeneration resulting from flattery by an act of deliberate reinterpretation of the flattering title. Honorary titles remind the king of his office and of his duties. For instance, when the prince is called 'invincible', the prince must remind himself that 'a man who is conquered by anger, a slave to lust every single day', cannot rightfully be called invincible. And when the prince is called 'the famous', he should remind himself that only integrity and good actions make such a title deserved.[25] Again, this supposes that the prince exerts power over the streams of communication coming his way. While autopoietic self-reproduction of flattery threatens, there is an escape into a pure language of virtue open to all true Christians. In both cases—Machiavelli's strategic advice and Erasmus' moral exhortations—the voice used in advising the king is not duplicitous. It respectfully presupposes a listening king who is autonomous, who is not captive in his palace and in court life as in a body.

Action, an End to Digressions

We return to Italo Calvino's story about the listening king. We left him at the prospect of dramatic change in his static situation. But then, at the prospect of human interaction and of meaning to be found in a story, the voice addresses the king in a disrespectful way, as if the adviser cannot bear to see the way the king is acting. 'Stop raving.' Or is this the despair of the raving king speaking to

---

[24] N. Machiavelli, *The Prince* (1514) (Harmondsworth, 1981), 127.
[25] D. Erasmus, *The Education of a Christian Prince* (1516) (Lisa Jardine (ed.), Cambridge, 1997), 59–60.

himself and fighting to overcome the inaction that has become his life? This is what follows:

Everything heard moving in the palace corresponds precisely to the rules you have laid down: the army obeys your orders like a prompt machine: the ritual of the palace does not allow the slightest variation in setting and clearing the table, in drawing the curtains or unrolling the ceremonial carpets according to the instructions received; the radio programs are those you decreed once and for all. The situation is in your grip; nothing eludes your will or control. Even the frog that croaks in the basin, even the uproar of the children playing blind-man's buff, even the old chamberlain's sprawl down the stairs: everything corresponds to your plan, everything has been thought out by you, decided, pondered, before it became audible to your ear. Not even a fly buzzes here if you do not wish it.

But perhaps you have never been so close to losing everything as you are now, when you think you have everything in your grip. The responsibility of conceiving the palace in its every detail, of containing it in your mind, subjects you to an exhausting strain. The obstinacy on which power is based is never so fragile as in the moment of its triumph.

Both readings are equally plausible: the exhortation to escape from the blind cycle of reconstruction of social reality and the attempt to keep everything under one's control; and the desperate insight that even power and control, even the exercise of the regal majesty, are powerless in their moment of triumph.

How about the drama? Is there going to be drama, or even any action at all? The king hears rapping against the walls, fists beating. Are these raps signals, he wonders. He tries to find a code that gives meaning to the sequence of sounds, perhaps originating from the cellars where the prisoners are held. He seems to understand a threat being made to his life. Then imagines that this is all his imagination really, because he does not know the code, has no access to the language. The king tries rapping himself, but is uncertain what the listener on the other side, if there is such a listener, will make of this. And who is responding to the rapping king? Is it the former king, captive in the cellars? Is the king making all of this up in the prison of his own mind? Is he communicating merely with himself? It can never be proved that he really is listening to the former king.

Every palace stands on cellars where someone is buried alive or where some dead man cannot find peace. You need not bother covering your ears with your hands: you will go on hearing them all the same.

Again, as this is both concluded and admonished, the narrative voice issues a warning to take action: 'Run away!'

The king finds himself in the city, or in the images he can form—seated on the throne—of life outside the palace. There he meets his Other. He hears a singing woman's voice.

That voice comes certainly from a person, unique, inimitable like every person; a voice, however, is not a person, it is suspended in the air, detached from the solidity of things.

The king wants to respond to this singing voice, and suddenly he discovers that his voice has already started to sing too.

It is you who are singing, no doubt about it: this is your voice, which you can listen to at last without alienation or irritation.

This is not the prelude to a happy ending. Immediately, the reality of life as an autopoietic system takes over. As the king imagines he can order a singing contest in which all the women of the city must participate and how this will lead to the meeting of their voices, he also understands that this plan will not work. A woman singing in court would have to sing like all other women singing in court, she would have to obey the rules for correct singing in the royal presence. That would make the voice unrecognizably different. And when the king would choose to sing to these women, his voice would not be heard as it really is either.

They would be listening to the king, in the way a king must be listened to, receiving what comes from above and has no meaning beyond the unchanging relationship between him who is above and those who are below. Even she, the sole addressee of your song, could not hear you: yours would not be the voice she hears; she would listen to the king, her body frozen in a curtsey, with the smile prescribed by protocol masking a preconceived rejection.

So the king, or the adviser talking to the king, concludes:

Your every attempt to get out of the cage is destined to fail: it is futile to seek yourself in a world that does not belong to you, that perhaps does not exist.

It could be the epitaph of the story, its true moral. But the story ends beyond this passage. The king hears the woman's song and then he hears how his own song is sung in response by the voice of the captive king. Human interaction, at last. But the decentred subject has no part of it, or rather: has the worst part of it.

The two voices move toward each other, become superimposed, blend, as you had already heard them joined in the night of the city, certain that it was you singing with her. Now surely she has reached him, you hear their voices, your voices, going off together. It is useless for you to try to follow them: they are becoming a murmur, a whisper; they vanish.

After this moment of estrangement and insight, the king's world ends in a 'roar that occupies all space, absorbs all sighs, calls, sobs'.

The Hidden Truth of Autopoiesis

Is there something we can learn from this remarkable story about the realities of autopoiesis, about decentred subjects and, perhaps, about law and society? 'A king listens' serves to articulate concern in these respects: it suggests that the realities of autopoiesis are harsh, that decentred subjects do not lead free and autonomous lives, and that even if law can be decreed with absolute power, there is no knowing what comes of this and there is no effective intervention in society. The hidden truth of autopoiesis is that, indeed, it is possible to be a participant, even the major partici-pant, in a legal system and yet to have no real influence on its functioning, which involves your own functioning and your own personality. This is a moral that lawyers are rightly reminded of. But it must also be noted that the autopoietic experience is not the universal condition of man. If 'A king listens' is taken as a cautionary tale which is highly informative about the pitfalls of communication, this does not mean that the conditions autopoiesis describes, or metaphorically draws attention to, are the ordinary ones for people involved in law, nor even that they are very frequently realized. The experience of kings is certainly not representative of the experiences of ordinary men.

It is nevertheless important to take in the bitter truths of autopoiesis. For two new issues arise as a consequence. First, the thesis that it is empirically possible to be autonomous and yet disempowered, to be a truly decentred subject, raises the question how people in their interactions, making use of the law and being used by the law, can be empowered.[26] Second, the corollary of

---

[26] This concern animates Joseph Vining's attempts to restore the authentic voice of people enaging in the practices of the law. Joseph Vining, *The Authoritative and the Authoritarian* (Chicago, 1986), especially part 2.

what the role of lawyers can be in assisting these processes, making law more communicative (as Fuller and Habermas hope for) and more responsive (witness Selznick's 'progressive elimination of injustice').[27] Anthony Kronman has argued that the nineteenth-century American ideal of the lawyer-statesman, the ideal that makes the lawyer into a person of practical wisdom at the service of his community, is in decline.[28] That is another way of raising the same issue: how must lawyers think of themselves (what kinds of kings are they) in order to serve the interests of the community at large and its citizens.

It is not only the problems of decentred subjects, however, that are involved. Regulatory activities in the welfare state show often enough that they work according to the dictates of autopoietic self-reproduction. When it is systems of rules and bureaucratic organizations working with such systems of rules, the lawyer can and must be a mediator, who strives to bring in those points of view and those languages and those pressing concerns that the autopoietic system excludes or defuses into its own reduced language. So that, in the end, the lawyer coming upon the harsh realities of autopoiesis should engage in what James Boyd White calls 'justice as translation'.

The central truths of translation are the central truths of human interaction. To say this suggests an excellence of mind and character, that of the good translator, to which we can aspire: an attempt to be oneself in relation to an always imperfectly known and imperfectly knowable other who is entitled to a respect equal to our own.[29]

That is the challenge: translation between languages and systems, between rationalities and cultures, using the language of law as a working language to come to understandings that are based on mutual respect. And as law is used as such a mediator's language and tool, as the concepts, rules, principles, and ideals are formulated that may assist such an undertaking, the law comes more and more to resemble not the autopoietic systems so much as the medium for a justly-constituted and well-managed social order.

---

[27] Philip Selznick, *The Moral Commonwealth* (Berkeley, 1992), 428–76.
[28] Anthony Kronman, *The Lost Lawyer* (Cambridge, Mass., 1993).
[29] White, *Justice as Translation*, n. 2 above, 258.

WHAT FREDERICK DOUGLASS SAYS TO KANT, WITH HELP FROM EINSTEIN

Wai Chee Dimock

What sort of things are rights? Are they the bedrock ingredients of our humanity, a class of objects coming into being with the birth of every life? And are they so basic, so much the cornerstone of our moral fabric, as to be ontologically prior to all other features of human association, all measures that we might take to give definition to our being?

Ronald Dworkin, making a case for just this sort of ontological priority, has put forward what he calls a 'deep theory' of rights.[1] Rights, he says, 'are not simply the product of deliberate legislation or explicit social custom, but are independent grounds for judging legislation and custom'.[2] Rights come before any social and political arrangements we might see fit to devise. They inhere in the fact of being human, and, as a prior fact, they come ready-made, they owe nothing to human hands. They are foundational in the sense that they are not derived, not negotiable, not a part of the shifting currents of human affairs. They are a given rather than an effect.

This foundational claim made on behalf on rights would seem to put Dworkin on the same side with Kant, a philosopher with even grander foundational ambitions. Dworkin acknowledges this kinship, but he is also anxious to put as much distance between himself and Kant as possible. And so, rather than making the usual distinction that philosophers make between two kinds of moral theories—between the 'teleological' and the 'deontological'—Dworkin proposes instead a threefold division. According to

---

[1] Ronald Dworkin, 'Rights and Justice' in *Taking Rights Seriously* (Cambridge, Mass., 1978), 169.
[2] Dworkin, 'Rights and Justice', n. 1 above, 177.

him, there are, first of all, those theories that are based on goals, such as Bentham's. Then there are those theories that are based on duty, such as Kant's. Finally, there are those theories that are based on rights, and this is how he would characterize his own work.[3] This threefold division amounts to a taxonomic declaration of independence. A line is drawn now between the concept of rights and the moral absolutism that we usually associate with Kant. However, since that line is probably not apparent to everyone, Dworkin is at pains to enlarge on this point. 'A theory that takes rights as fundamental is a theory of a different character from one that takes duties as fundamental', he writes.[4] And he goes on to explain why that is. Duty-based theories, he says, are predicated on an absolute moral code, and 'the man at their center is the man who must conform to such a code'.[5] Right-based theories, on the other hand, are predicated only on the sanctity of the individual, and 'the man at their center is the man who benefits from others' compliance, not the man who leads the life of virtue by complying himself'.[6] Kant wants us to bow to the moral law, Dworkin wants us only to bow to each other. There is a big difference between the two, he says, and nowhere is it more striking than when it comes to penal law. A duty-based theory would dispense punishment according to the principle of retribution, whereas a right-based theory would 'reject the retributive argument', insisting only that 'individual rights must be served even at some cost to the general welfare'.[7]

To make the same distinction that Dworkin is making, but using a different language, we can say that, in a duty-based theory, the absolute moral space is assigned to a transcendent injunction, whereas, in a right-based theory, the absolute moral space is assigned to each and every human being. The difference between these two is certainly not trivial. And yet, in their equal reliance on a foundational postulate, in their designation of a space that is given ahead of time and that must always remain a given, anterior to circumstances and independent of circumstances, perhaps the two also have more in common than Dworkin would like to admit.

---

[3] Dworkin, 'Rights and Justice', n. 1 above, 171.   [4] *Ibid.*
[5] Dworkin, 'Rights and Justice', n. 1 above, 172.   [6] *Ibid.*
[7] Dworkin, 'Rights and Justice', n. 1 above, 173.

What I would like to do in this paper, then, is to look more closely at this foundational postulate, this common thread which binds Dworkin to Kant, and which binds the concept of rights to a more general Kantian moral theory. I will analyse what kind of foundation this is, what underlying premises go into its making. As suggested earlier, I see these premises as primarily spatial in nature. They are especially spatial in a Newtonian sense, in the sense that they are based on an *a priori* grid of the world, a geometry that is formally antecedent, not shaped by every particular context. I will be looking critically at this *a priori* grid and, in bringing to bear on it the modern scientific debate about the nature of space, I want to suggest that a similar debate might be helpful in our thinking about law and ethics. Like twentieth-century scientists, we too might do well to look beyond Newton, beyond the notion of absolute space. Only then, perhaps, can we come up with a theory of rights that can free itself from another kind of absolutism, the moral absolutism that is so much a legacy of Kant.

Without further ado, I proceed directly to Kant, to an unforgettable moment in his *Philosophy of Law* (sometimes also translated as *The Metaphysical Elements of Justice*).[8] Here, Kant is making an all-out argument in favour of the death penalty. The death penalty is necessary, he says, because the 'penal law is a Categorical Imperative,'[9] and, as such, it demands an absolute form of retribution, one that is the exact equivalent of the crime:

This is the Right of retaliation (jus talionis) . . . whoever has committed Murder, must *die*. There is, in this case, no juridical substitute or surrogate, that can be given or taken for the satisfaction of justice. There is no *Likeness* or proportion between Life, however painful, and Death; and therefore there is no equality between the crime of Murder and the retaliation of it but what is judicially accomplished by the execution of the criminal. . . . Even if a Civil Society resolved to dissolve itself with the consent of all its members—as might be supposed in the case of a People

8 Immanuel Kant, *The Philosophy of Law* (W. Hastie (trans.)), is the Edinburgh edition of Kant's *Metaphysische Anfangsgrunde der Rechslehre* (1796). The Hastie translation is more complete than the 1965 John Ladd translation, which appeared under the title of *The Metaphysical Elements of Justice* (Indianapolis, 1965).

9 Immanuel Kant, *The Philosophy of Law: An Exposition of the Fundamental Principles of Jurisprudence as the Science of Right* (1796) (W. Hastie (trans.), Edinburgh, 1887), 195.

inhabiting an island resolving to separate and scatter themselves throughout the whole world—the last Murderer lying in the prison ought to be
executed before the resolution was carried out. This ought to be done in
order that every one may realize the desert of his deeds, and the blood-
guiltiness may not remain upon the people.[10]

Without question, this is the voice of moral absolutism. The
murderer has to die: not because he is dangerous to others, but
because he has made someone else die. His crime has violated a
transcendent fiat, and the harm can be undone only by an
absolute form of retribution. Only such retribution will affirm the
sanctity of the moral law, make it once again supreme, once again
inviolate. And only then will the criminal serve the cause of
justice. The blood that he has shed will now be wiped clean with
his own blood.

This is the Kant from whom Dworkin would like to distance
himself. What is interesting, though, is that on this occasion Kant
is actually talking not about duty but about rights. The duty to
execute the criminal is expressed here as the 'right of retaliation'.
This right is vested in the state, to be sure, it is not an individual
right. However, there is no question that it is a right, a form of
moral entitlement, indeed a coercive power. And it is a right
because it is simply the enactment of the duty of every private citizen. Its absoluteness flows from the absolute obligation—enjoined
upon every individual and collectively implemented by the state—
to uphold a transcendent moral law, a law given to us unnegoti-
ated, and remaining forever unnegotiable.

Kant's moral theory is indeed duty-based, as Dworkin says, but
this duty is directly correlated with, and indeed directly translatable
into, a right.[11] This should not surprise us too much. After all,

----

10 Kant, *The Philosophy of Law*, n. 9 above, 196, 198.

11 The 'correlativity' of rights and duties is, of course, a major issue in moral
and legal theory. Bentham, for example, writes: 'It is by imposing obligations, or
by abstaining from imposing them, that rights are established or granted ... All
rights rest therefore upon the idea of obligation as their necessary foundation.' See
Bentham, *Works* (John Bowring (ed.), repr. New York, 1962), III, 181. Wesley
Newcomb Hohfeld, while classifying rights into four well-known categories—
liberty rights, claim rights, power rights, and immunity rights—also argues that
only claim rights can be discussed in a manner that is not 'nebulous' and so
commits himself to a positivist notion of rights that resembles Bentham's. See his
influential *Fundamental Legal Conceptions* (New Haven, 1919), 38–9. For the
relation between Bentham and Hohfeld, see H. L. A. Hart, 'Bentham on Legal
Rights' in *Oxford Essays in Jurisprudence*, 2nd ser. (A. W. B. Simpson (ed.),

right and duty for Kant are just two faces of the same coin, alternate expressions of the same foundational principle. Both are categorical imperatives. And both refer us back to an anterior moral domain, the home of these categorical imperatives. This anterior moral domain is, quite literally, an absolute space for Kant. In the *Critique of Practical Reason* (1788), he explicitly links the formal composition of this space to the formal composition of geometry:

Pure geometry has postulates as practical propositions, which, however, contain nothing more than the proposition that one *can* do something and that, when some result is needed, one *should* do it. . . . One ought absolutely to act in a certain way. The practical rule is therefore unconditional and thus is thought of *a priori* as a categorically practical proposition . . . this principle of morality, on account of the universality of its legislation which makes it the formal supreme determining ground of the will regardless of any subjective differences among men, is declared by reason to be a law for all rational beings.[12]

The moral domain, some of us might think, is a hopelessly grey area. Not so for Kant. In this breath-taking, stunningly counter-intuitive passage, he says that the moral domain, the domain of practical reason, is the *only* domain that is not grey, but clear-cut in its boundaries, visible to all, absolutely self-evident. The self-evidence comes about because, unlike other cognitive phenomena (which are only epiphenomenal and not to be trusted), the moral law is grounded in its own logical necessity. If we were to believe in human beings as free and rational beings, freely and rationally choosing between right and wrong, we would *have to* believe in a moral law as the antecedent ground for these choices. The prior existence of the moral domain, in short, is the only thing that can be established with the rigours of logic, the only thing that lends itself to the claim of cognitive certainty. And, in that cognitive certainty, it is also the only domain that can be formalized into a set of

Oxford, 1973), 171–201, and Joseph Singer, 'The Legal Rights Debate in Analytical Jurisprudence from Bentham to Hohfeld' (1982) *Wisconsin Law Review* 975. Many political theorists, I should also point out, have vigorously disagreed with the notion of 'correlativity'. For them, rights and duties are neither substantively nor even structurally symmetrical. See, for example, David Lyons, 'The Correlativity of Rights and Duties' (1970) 4 *Nous* 45. I mean only to acknowledge this large body of material, not to engage it.

[12] Immanuel Kant, *Critique of Practical Reason* (1788) (Lewis White Beck (trans.), New York, 1993), 31.

maxims, giving unconditional weight to the word 'must'. The moral law is thus the only article of reason that is analogous to geometry, since its propositions, like geometrical propositions, are formally self-sufficient. This is why the moral law can be said to occupy a transcendent realm, not intersecting with and not affected by circumstances. This is why its rule is simply that, a rule, 'an imperative, commanding categorically because it is unconditioned'.[13]

The formalization of ethics into an absolute space is a great intellectual triumph for Kant. This is his tribute to Newton and— more ambitiously—his revision of Newton. Like a good many Enlightenment thinkers, including d'Alembert and Condorcet, Kant had started out as a student of science before he turned to philosophy. He had done work in physics, astronomy, geology, and meteorology, and, as a lecturer at the University of Konigsberg, had taught not only ethics but also logic, mathematics, and the natural sciences, including the new subject of physical geography.[14] He was not alone in his high esteem for Newton, or in his hope that Newtonian science might be extended to serve other ends. In England, Newton's ideas had long been extended in just that way, disseminated as they were by Anglican divines lecturing in popular fora such as the Boyle lectures.[15] To these popularizers and their audience, the natural order was a manifestation of the divine order, and from Newton's accounts of the former, they could extrapolate 'a set of ethical prescriptions about how to conduct oneself on earth'.[16] The laws of physics seemed translatable into the laws of ethics; natural philosophy underwrote a civic religion. There was such a thing as 'cultural Newtonianism', a broad intellectual mantle that fell far beyond the technical spheres of science.[17] Under its auspices, many began

[13] Kant, *Critique of Practical Reason*, n. 12 above, 32.

[14] Friedrich Paulsen, *Immanuel Kant: His Life and Doctrine* (J. E. Creighton and Albert Lefevre (trans.), New York, 1963), 35.

[15] The Boyle Lectures were named after Robert Boyle, who left £350 in his will to endow lectures defending Christianity. The Rev. Samuel Clarke, who defended Newton in the Leibniz–Clarke debates, was one such Boyle Lecturer.

[16] Steven Shapin, 'Of Gods and Kings: Natural Philosophy and Politics in the Leibniz–Clarke Disputes' (1981) 72 *Isis* 192.

[17] For a reading of Newtonian natural philosophy as 'justification for the pursuit of sober self-interest, for a Christianized capitalist ethics', see Margaret C. Jacob, *Newtonians and the English Revolution* (Ithaca, 1976), 160. For the broad cultural influence of Newton, see Betty Jo Teeter Dobbs and Margaret C. Jacob, *Newton and the Culture of Newtonianism* (Atlantic Heights, New Jersey, 1995).

to think that human society itself might prove to be rule-governed, harmonized by a prior design, and running according to a fixed plan, as the natural world seemed to be. It was to this noble dream that Hume paid tribute when, in the *History of England*, he sang the praises of Newton in this uncharacteristically rhapsodic note: 'In Newton this island may boast of having produced the greatest and rarest genius that ever arose for the ornament and instruction of the species'.[18]

Nor was the worship of Newton limited to the British Isles. Newton was the 'demi-God' of the Enlightenment, Peter Gay points out, and, throughout the eighteenth century, his 'deification' proceeded as briskly on the Continent as it did in England.[19] Voltaire spoke for an entire age when, in *Elemens de la philosophie de Neuton*, he put his subject at the very centre of Western civilization: 'This philosopher gathered in during his lifetime all the glory he deserved; he aroused no envy because he could have no rival. The learned world were his disciples, the rest admired him without daring to claim that they understood him'.[20] In France, in the Netherlands, and in Germany, Newton's authority was 'unsurpassed and unsurpassable'.[21] And so the abbé Jacques Delille surprised no one when, in the second half of the eighteenth century, nearly fifty years after Newton's death, he saw fit to adapt Pope's famous couplet for his French audience:

> O pouvoir d'un grand homme et d'une âme divine!
> Ce que Dieu seul a fait, Newton seul l'imagine,
> Et chaque astre répéte en proclamant leur nom:
> Gloire à Dieu qui crea les mondes et Newton![22]

Such was the adulation from the religious-minded. Those more scientifically inclined did not lag behind. Indeed, for Enlightenment thinkers generally, Newtonian physics was nothing less than the pivot of all knowledge. But it was Kant, more than

---

[18] David Hume, *History of England* (1688), 6 vols. (Boston, 1856), VI, 374.

[19] For a detailed account of Newton's centrality to the Enlightenment, see Peter Gay, *The Enlightenment: The Science of Freedom* (New York, 1977), 126–87.

[20] Voltaire, *Elements de la philosophie de Neuton, Oeuvres* (1738), XXII, 402, quoted in Gay, *The Enlightenment*, n. 19 above, 139.

[21] Gay, *The Enlightenment*, n. 19 above, 129.

[22] Jacques Delille, *Oeuvres*, IX, 7, quoted in Gay, *The Enlightenment*, n. 19 above, 132.

anyone else, who would try to graft a metaphysics onto the back of this physics, gathering the two into a formal ethical theory.

What Kant especially liked was Newton's idea of absolute space. In the *Principia* (1686), Newton had distinguished between 'absolute and relative, true and apparent, mathematical and common' space and time.[23] 'Absolute, true, and mathematical time', according to him, 'flows equably without relation to anything external', just as 'absolute space, in its own nature, without relation to anything external, remains always similar and immovable'.[24] Newtonian space and time are absolute because they are simply a given, a preassigned fact. They make up an *a priori* grid of the world. Only such a grid would guarantee that there would always be true relations among things, relations neither circumstantial nor negotiable, relations that, 'from infinity to infinity, do all retain the same given position one to another'.[25]

For Newton, absolute space is a necessary postulate if the world is to have a proper foundation. This Newtonian tenet Kant embraced almost wholesale in his early, pre-critical writings. In an essay entitled 'Concerning the Ultimate Foundations of the Differentiations of Regions in Space', Kant simply said, 'Absolute space had its own reality independently of the existence of matter', and 'is itself the ultimate foundation of the possibility of its composition'.[26] The statement had all the authority of Newton behind it. Indeed it could have come from Newton himself. However, Kant is not one to move slavishly in another's orbit. Thirteen years later, in *The Critique of Pure Reason* (1781), he would amend his position, putting his own stamp on it.

Here, Kant once again insists on the '*a priori* necessity of space', but, departing from Newton, he now insists that, for space to be truly *a priori*, it cannot be taken as an objective fact, not a physical dimension of the world, 'not an empirical concept at all'.[27] Nothing *a priori* can come from the empirical. And so, for

[23] Isaac Newton, *Mathematical Principles of Natural Philosophy* (1686) (Florian Cajori (ed.) and Andrew Motte (trans.), Berkeley, 1934), 6. This is commonly referred to as the *Principia*. [24] *Ibid.*

[25] Newton, *Mathematical Principles*, n. 23 above, 9.

[26] Immanuel Kant, 'Concerning the Ultimate Foundation of the Differentiation of Regions in Space' (1768) in *Kant: Selected Pre-critical Writings* (G. B. Kerferd and D. E. Walford (eds. and trans.), Manchester, 1968), 37.

[27] Immanuel Kant, *Critique of Pure Reason* (1781) (Norman Kemp Smith (trans.), New York, 1965), 68.

Kant, Newtonian space must now be turned on its head, which is to say, it must be transposed from a physical fact into a form of intuition, antecedently given to us, 'prior to any perception of an object'.[28] Not indebted to the world, it is also not limited by our limited knowledge of the world. It is simply an innate form of the mind, the form that reasoning takes when it processes the chaotic array of sensory data into a mental unity. The 'space' of cognition is thus logical rather than empirical. Its existence can be proven, and can be proven on the grounds of logic alone. Here, then, is a domain in which human reason is adequate unto itself; here, we are guaranteed the same kind of certainty that is guaranteed by geometry, because, where space is concerned, 'reason is the faculty which supplies the principles of *a priori* knowledge'.[29] And, once the autonomy of reason is established in this one particular realm, the foundation is laid for an ethics that can lay claim to it, declare itself the privileged occupant. This is an ethics unified by its own logical givenness and, in that givenness, also occupying a point of antecedence, as a mental domain at once sequentially prior and spatially integral. Its laws, as Kant says, 'are valid as Laws, in so far as they can be rationally established *a priori* and compre-hended as necessary'.[30]

Kant's ethics, in short, is an ethics that fancies itself to have transcended the limits of epistemology. It stands entirely on its own, a space unto itself, not mixed up with the other problems of human cognition. Its truth-claims are unburdened by the limits of human knowledge. Everything else in Kant, including his uncom-promising position on the death penalty, follows from this attribu-tion of spatial absoluteness to ethics. Fenced off from epistemology, this ethics is integrated as a kind of cognitive sanc-tum. Here, 'knowing' is not a problem; here, good and evil are concepts intuitively given to us. Here, any choice that we make is made in the fullness of knowledge and with full responsibility for its consequences, for to choose at all is to do so in a cognitive realm in which epistemology is by definition not an issue, a realm in which human reason is supposed to act with what Kant calls 'apodeictic certainty'.[31] This moral absolute space, I have tried to

[28] Kant, *Critique of Pure Reason*, n. 27 above, 70.
[29] Kant, *Critique of Pure Reason*, n. 27 above, 58.
[30] Kant, *The Philosophy of Law*, n. 9 above, 27.
[31] Kant, *Critique of Pure Reason*, n. 27 above, 68.

argue, is a version of Newtonian absolute space. Given its centrality not only to Kant but also to so much of our legal and ethical
thinking, it is worth taking a closer look at this Newtonian
concept, to see how well it is holding up, what some objections
might be, and to ask what a moral theory might look like if it
were to abandon such a foundation.

It is helpful, then, to go beyond our own disciplines and to
consider, very briefly, some of the developments in modern
physics. Here, we will find a quite unambiguous rejection of
absolute space. The concept has been demolished by Einstein.
Einstein begins, in fact, with an explicit critique of Newton.
'Absolute space' and 'absolute time', he says, are not meaningful
concepts. It is not meaningful to talk about either distance or
duration without specifying the states of motion from which that
distance and that duration are being measured. Using the example
of a moving train against the background of the embankment,
Einstein shows that, given these two different frames of reference,
one moving and the other at rest, there can be no absolute agreement between the units of space and time measured from each.
The time interval between two events will have a different length
measured on the train from that measured on the embankment; so
too will the space interval between two points. It is this non-
absoluteness of distance and duration that Einstein calls the 'relativity of space and time'.[32]

The world summoned into being by Einstein is not a preassigned grid but an operational consequence. Its geometry is not
'purely axiomatic geometry', a geometry which remains invariant
on logical grounds; rather, it is what Einstein calls 'practical
geometry', a geometry whose axioms can take alternate forms,
being differently specified by different frames of reference. For
such a geometry,

Affirmations rest essentially on induction from experience, but not on
logical inferences only. We will call this completed geometry 'practical
geometry', and shall distinguish it in what follows from 'purely axiomatic
geometry' . . . I attach special importance to the view of geometry which I
have just set forth, because without it I should have been unable to
formulate the theory of relativity. Without it the following reflection

[32] Albert Einstein, *Relativity: The Special and the General Theory* (15th edn,
New York, 1961), 3–64, 155–78.

would have been impossible: in a system of reference rotating relatively to an inertial system, the laws of disposition of rigid bodies do not correspond to the rules of Euclidean geometry on account of the Lorentz contraction; thus if we admit non-inertial systems on an equal footing, we must abandon Euclidean geometry.[33]

For Einstein, geometry, as a set of logical axioms, is indeed self-enclosed and self-sufficient. But such a geometry can give us no actual knowledge about the physical world. To know something about the physical world, geometry needs to be guided by more than logic. It needs to come under the constraints of the empirical, which is to say, it must conceive of itself as subject to the specifications issuing from different contexts, its different axiomizations being called forth by the physics of different events. The very form that geometry takes turns out to be frame-dependent. And, in some frames, for example, in the relative motion of bodies in non-inertial systems, Euclidean geometry will have to be abandoned altogether. It will have to be replaced by a host of non-Euclidean geometries: the hyperbolic geometry of Karl Friedrich Gauss, Janos Bolyai, and Nikolai Lobachevsky, the spherical geometry of Bernhard Riemann.[34] Rather than being formally prior, knowable in advance of any actual event, space is contingent upon that event, induced by it to yield different geometries. It is anything but absolute.

This rejection of absolute space has tremendous implications for physics. It would seem to have some implications for ethics as well. Einstein is quite aware of this. In an essay entitled 'The Law of Science and the Law of Ethics', he sets out expressly to tackle the relation between the two. With characteristic bluntness, however, he begins by cautioning against any hope that ethics might find its grounding in physics. 'Scientific statements of facts and relations', he says, 'cannot produce ethical directives'.[35] Physics, in other words, is not directly translatable into ethics. It

---

[33] Einstein, 'Geometry and Experience' in his *Ideas and Opinions* (New York, 1954), 235. By 'Lorentz contraction', Einstein refers to the slightly shortened unit lengths of moving bodies in an electromagnetic field.

[34] For useful accounts of Euclidean and non-Euclidean geometries and their relations to relativity, see Bas C. Van Fraassen, *An Introduction to the Philosophy of Time and Space* (New York, 1985), 108–69; Lawrence Sklar, *Space, Time, and Spacetime* (Berkeley, 1974).

[35] Einstein, 'The Laws of Science and the Laws of Ethics', Preface to Philipp Frank, *Relativity: A Richer Truth* (New York, 1950), vi.

cannot serve as a foundation for our human affairs. And yet, in refusing to serve as a foundation, it nonetheless issues a challenge which, Einstein says, ethics cannot afford to ignore.

And here, striking a distinctly un-Kantian note, Einstein suggests that the challenge of physics to ethics is the challenge of *empiricism*. Ethics, like physics, cannot pretend to be a transcendent body of knowledge, cannot imagine itself to be spatially prior to the actual problems it confronts. No such spatial priority inheres in any cognitive domain. Ethics, like everything else, is simply a candidate for our allegiance, and the status of its candidacy will have to be scrutinized like any other, continually thought and rethought. For, just as scientific theories 'cannot claim an unlimited domain of validity',[36] neither can ethics. Its axioms should thus be 'tested not very differently from the axioms of science',[37] which is to say, they should be tested as a set of as-yet-incomplete postulates. Their domains of validity will have to be mapped with greater precision, their contents will have to be revised and supplemented. There can be no categorical imperatives here, no axioms formalizable ahead of time. Einstein, who has been reading *The Critique of Pure Reason* since the tender age of 13,[38] knows what he is rejecting, and is emphatic in rejecting it: 'I have never been able to understand the quest of the *a priori* in the Kantian sense'.[39]

Understood as a challenge to the *a priori*, Einstein's physics suggests that the privilege of foundational certitude might not be ours to claim. No article of reason can hope to transcend the limits of reason. Fallibility is our common lot, and the shadow it casts is cast, without exception, upon the full spectrum of cognitive activities. No space of the mind can free itself enough to come

---

[36] Einstein, *Relativity*, n. 32 above, 85.

[37] Einstein, 'The Laws of Science', n. 35 above, vi.

[38] As Gerald Holton reports, Einstein 'at the tender age of thirteen was introduced to Immanuel Kant's philosophy, starting with *The Critique of Pure Reason*, through his contacts with a regular guest at the Einstein home, Max Talmey. He reread Kant's book at the age of sixteen and enrolled in a lecture course on Kant while at the Technical Institute in Zurich ... [A]t the Institute in Princeton his favorite topic of discussion with his friend Kurt Godel was, again, Kant'. However, as Holton also points out, 'All this, typically, did not make Einstein a Kantian at all', for 'Einstein objected to the central point of Kant's transcendental idealism by denying the existence of the synthetic *a priori*.' See Holton, 'Einstein and the Cultural Roots of Modern Science' (1998) 127 *Daedalus* 18–19.

[39] Einstein, 'The Problem of Space, Ether, and Field in Physics' in *Ideas and Opinions* (New York, 1954), 278.

clean, to ground itself in its own logical necessity, to constitute itself as a formal given. This new humility, taken in stride, has led to some spirited critiques of Kant within the philosophy of science, most notably by Hans Reichenbach and Rudolf Carnap. Carnap, following Einstein, takes Kant to task for his faith in geometry as a vehicle of *a priori* knowledge. That faith, Carnap says, 'involve[s] a fundamental confusion between two fields of quite different character'.[40] Mathematical geometry is indeed *a priori*, as Kant says, but, as such, it might or might not describe the physical geometry of existing objects. There is no one-to-one correspondence between the logical consistency of a mathematical proposition and the actual composition of the world. Any foundational claim issuing from the former must fall through this slippage. Carnap goes on: 'Kant held that *a priori* knowledge is certain knowledge . . . Relativity theory made it clear, to all who understood, that, if geometry is taken in this *a priori* sense, it tells us nothing about reality'.[41] Hans Reichenbach, likewise, points to the 'dissolution of the *synthetic a priori* [as] one of the significant features of the philosophy of our time'.[42] This dissolution, he says, more or less takes apart the entire Kantian project:

Kant believed himself to possess a proof for his assertion that his *synthetic a priori* principles were necessary truths: According to him these principles were necessary conditions of knowledge. He overlooked the fact that such a proof can demonstrate the truth of the principles only if it is taken for granted that knowledge within the frame of these principles will always be possible. What has happened, then, in Einstein's theory is a proof that knowledge within the framework of Kantian principles is not possible.[43]

Knowledge that transcends the limits of reason—knowledge that is absolute and foundational—turns out to be a knowledge that is literally beyond us, outside of our grasp. That fact, tragic to some, is to Einstein a cause for celebration. Indeed, the development of science, as he sees it, is motivated precisely by the non-absoluteness

---

[40] Rudolf Carnap, 'Kant's synthetic *a priori*' in his *An Introduction to the Philosophy of Science* (1966) (Martin Garner (ed.), New York, 1995), 182–3.

[41] *Ibid.*

[42] Hans Reichenbach, 'The Philosophical Significance of the Theory of Relativity' in *Albert Einstein: Philosopher-Scientist* (Paul Arthur Schilpp (ed.), La Salle, Illinois, 1991), 308.

[43] Reichenbach, 'The Philosophical Significance', n. 42 above, 309.

of scientific knowledge, by its endless fallibility. Such fallible knowledge needs to be continually supplemented, and the supplements too will eventually fall short. Here, every 'foundation' will be shown, sooner or later, to be not foundational enough, not broad enough in its scope or deep enough in its explanations. Here, every truth-claim will end up losing its initial self-sufficiency, its discrete frame of reference giving way to a broader web of connections, previously unknown, unsuspected. The world ushered in by Einstein is a world in which human thought is daily plagued by its inadequacies and daily inspired by those inadequacies. It is a world in which the limits of reason mark not the end of knowledge but many yet-to-be-tested new beginnings. Reichenbach concludes: 'It is the philosophy of empiricism, therefore, into which Einstein's relativity belongs'.[44]

American pragmatists, exponents of a 'radical empiricism', could not agree more.[45] Many of Einstein's objections to Kant have actually been anticipated by Charles Sanders Peirce. Peirce indeed, like Einstein, has immersed himself in the work of his adversary: 'I devoted two hours a day to the study of Kant's *Critique of Pure Reason* for more than three years, until I almost knew the whole book by heart, and had critically examined every section of it'.[46] His disagreement with Kant, again like Einstein's, focuses on one specific point: Kant's commitment to the *a priori*. For Peirce, what is especially objectionable is Kant's 'confusion of *a priori* reason with conscience'.[47] Conscience so conceived, he says, 'refuses to submit its dicta to experiment, and makes an absolute dual distinction between right and wrong'.[48] Rather than following Kant in his quest to ground the moral in the *a priori*, Peirce proposes an alternate approach, what he calls a 'doctrine of fallibilism'.[49] This doctrine, as its name suggests, begins with the limits of human reason and, not unhappy with this state of affairs, refuses to imagine a space outside it, free from its cognitive failings. Not imagining such a space, it extends to ethics no basis for

[44] Reichenbach, 'The Philosophical Significance', n. 42 above, 309.
[45] The phrase 'radical empiricism' is coined by William James. See James, *Essays in Radical Empiricism* (Ralph Barton Perry (ed.), Lincoln, Nebraska, 1996).
[46] Charles Sanders Peirce, 'Concerning the Author' (1940) in *Philosophical Writings of Peirce* (Justus Buchler (ed.), New York, 1955), 2.
[47] Charles Sanders Peirce, 'The Scientific Attitude and Fallibilism' in *Philosophical Writings of Peirce*, n. 46 above, 46.   [48] *Ibid.*
[49] Peirce, 'The Scientific Attitude', n. 47 above, 58–9.

transcendence. Ethics, in other words, is granted no immunity from all the problems that afflict epistemology. Its domain, not enclosed by its own logical necessity, does not constitute an absolute space of its own. Its axioms cannot be antecedently formalized, cannot be located beyond doubt.

William James, following Peirce, makes an even more emphatic case against the 'philosophy of the absolute', arguing instead for a variety of relational and contextual spaces, a 'pluralistic universe'. And it is in the name of reason, in the name of a 'radical empiricism', that he goes about challenging the absolute.[50] 'The great claim made for the absolute is that by supposing it we make the world appear more rational', James writes.[51] Driven by that ambition, 'monistic idealists after Kant have invariably sought relief from the supposed contradictions of our world of sense by looking forward toward an *ens rationis* as its integration or logical completion'.[52] Radical empiricists, on the other hand, find the notion of 'logical completion' itself unpersuasive. Mindful of the finitude of reason, they are struck instead by the provisionality of thought itself, the fact that all mental spaces can be compounded, enlarged, reconfigured:

Everything you can think of, however vast or inclusive, has on the pluralistic view a genuinely 'external' environment of some sort or amount. Things are 'with' one another in many ways, but nothing includes everything, or dominates over everything. The word 'and' trails along after every sentence. Something always escapes. 'Ever not quite' has to be said of the best attempts made anywhere in the universe at attaining all-inclusiveness.[53]

Every cognitive domain, however rigorously defined, carries with it a residuum, a trailing 'and' that opens up its boundaries to the vexations of other domains, and breaks down any assumption of an *a priori*, a logical space free from contextual specifications.

---

[50] The distinction between the monist and the pluralistic—between the philosophy of the absolute and the philosophy of radical empiricism—is central to James. See especially 'The Types of Philosophic Thinking', Lecture I of *The Pluralistic Universe*, in *William James: Writings 1902–1910* (Bruce Kuklick (ed.), New York, 1987), 631–48.

[51] James, *The Pluralistic Universe*, n. 50 above, 680. The immediate reference is Hegel, but the statement applies equally well to Kant.

[52] James, *The Pluralistic Universe*, n. 50 above, 738. Again, the figure James has in mind is Hegel, but Hegel seen as a continuation of Kant.

[53] James, *The Pluralistic Universe*, n. 50 above, 776.

Radical empiricism, understood in this sense, is a theory about the extension, conjunction, and permeation of spaces. It is a challenge to any formalism based on 'partition of territories'.[54] This challenge, carried forward by John Dewey in the 1920s and with a direct reference to Einstein, takes the form of a critique, not only of Newton's absolute space and time, but also of Kant's epistemology and ethics.[55]

More recently, in law, a scepticism toward the *a priori* has also led to some stimulating arguments. In an essay entitled 'The Curvature of Constitutional Space: What Lawyers can Learn from Modern Physics', Laurence Tribe directly invokes Einstein to argue for a legal paradigm forthright about its less than discrete, less than transcendent ontology. 'Just as space cannot extricate itself from the unfolding story of physical reality', Tribe writes, 'so also the law cannot extract itself from social structures'.[56] The rule of law, in other words, does not emanate from anything that might be called absolute space. Law does not stand 'above' human conflict. It does not have the privilege of antecedence over what it adjudicates. Rather, it is a party to the grievances that come before it, a shaping force and an active contributor to that very fabric of relations that give rise to that grievance.

For Tribe, then, the crucial point is that law is not neutral. But his rejection of absolute space also seems to suggest another line of inquiry. Indeed, what especially strikes me, in this context, is a question that leads directly back to the question with which we began, namely, the spatial ontology of rights, and Dworkin's argument on behalf of its absolute priority. Are rights antecedently vested in us, grounded in our humanity, in such a way as to transcend all circumstances? Or are they a party to those circumstances, permeated and compounded by them, deriving their very shapes from that shifting matrix? Do rights intersect at all with the limits of human reason? If so, how are they affected by this entanglement between ethics and epistemology? What consequences does this entanglement have for either cognitive domain?

[54] John Dewey, *The Later Works, 1925–1953. Vol. 4. The Quest for Certainty* (Jo Ann Boydston (ed.), Carbondale, Illinois, 1981), 47.

[55] Dewey, *The Quest for Certainty*, n. 54 above, 47–50, 89–104, 113–17, 137–45.

[56] Laurence Tribe, 'The Curvature of Constitutional Space: What Lawyers can Learn from Modern Physics' (1989) 103 *Harvard Law Review* 7.

I want to explore these questions by looking beyond both law and science—through a tradition which, though rarely seen in conjunction with Newton, Kant, and Einstein, nonetheless has something to say to each. This is the tradition of African-American literature, a tradition born out of the very entanglement between ethics and epistemology. And no one is more keenly aware of that entanglement than Frederick Douglass. Born a slave in Maryland, Douglass managed, against all odds, to teach himself to read and write, eventually running away to become a writer, orator, and statesman, a towering figure in nineteenth-century American public life. Here was someone who knew the institution of slavery, knew it in all its intimate and dehumanizing details, and knew it as the purveyor of a deep and quite inescapable kind of ignorance. 'I never saw my mother, to know her as such, more than four or five times in my life'; when she died, 'I was not allowed to be present during her illness, her death, or burial. She was gone long before I knew anything about it'.[57] To be a slave was to be robbed of some vital cores of knowledge, a deprivation of which illiteracy was only the most obvious marker. For Douglass, this enforced ignorance was of a piece with the physical violence inflicted on the slave. It was less spectacular, but no less brutalizing than the beatings of his aunt Hester, or the summary execution of a field hand. Douglass himself seemed fated to become a victim of this enforced ignorance. And, in overcoming that fate, he would seem to have overcome slavery itself, reducing it instead to an object of knowledge, as naked and as self-evident an object as one might hope to find.

This epistemological privilege, one might think, ought to put Douglass in a moral absolute space, an ethical domain unburdened by imperfect knowledge. It ought to give him a right of judgment. This right Douglass expressly renounced. When he went South after the Civil War to have a final meeting with his former master, it was not to flaunt his cognitive authority, not to speak from a moral high ground, but to lower himself, surprisingly, into the unedifying and unenviable company of the man who was no longer his master and perhaps never truly his master. The two of them, Douglass said, were kindred in more than one

[57] Frederick Douglass, *The Narrative and Selective Writing* (Michael Meyer (ed.), New York, 1984), 19.

sense, equally limited in the extent of their powers. Just as the master could no longer lay claim to an inherent racial superiority, so too the slave could not lay claim to an inherent moral privilege:

He was to me no longer a slaveholder either in fact or in spirit, and I regarded him as I did myself, a victim of the circumstances of birth, education, law, and custom. Our courses had been determined for us, not by us. We had both been flung, by powers that did not ask our consent, upon a mighty current of life, which we could neither resist nor control. By this current he was a master, and I a slave; but now our lives were verging towards a point where differences disappear, where even the constancy of hate breaks down . . . on this occasion there was to this rule no transgression on either side.[58]

If there is a geometry in Douglass's landscape, it is anything but an *a priori* grid, anything but a basis of knowledge given ahead of time. No such knowledge exists under slavery. For, as Douglass has shown over and over again, this institution is an institution of enforced ignorance, an ignorance that takes roots in the slave no less than in the master. Both are at sea, flung into the 'mighty current of life', a current swift, all-ensnaring, more powerful than the reason of any single individual, and quite unfathomable to those caught up in it and swept along by it. This current of life puts master and slave on the same footing, and denies to both the guarantee of a firm and solid foundation. Ethical action, on either side, cannot be said to proceed from the vantage point of knowledge, an unproblematic access to what is good and evil. It proceeds, rather, from a necessary ignorance, necessary, because what each knows is to a large extent determined, as Douglass says, by 'birth, education, law, and custom'. The institution of slavery puts a complicated set of blinkers—segregated but also interrelated—on both master and slave. Both are fallible as actors, and fallible as knowers.

The fallibility of the slave does not exonerate the master. But it does cast the evil of slavery in a somewhat different light. This evil, it turns out, is more epistemological than it is ethical, a problem sprung out of the cognitive limits of an entire society, rather than the moral choices exercised by a single person. To acknowledge this epistemological problem—to acknowledge the unavoidable

---

[58] Frederick Douglass, *Life and Times of Frederick Douglass* (1892; repr. New York, 1962), 441–2. This is the last of Douglass's autobiographies.

blindfold of a slave-owning society—is to take ethics out of its self-sufficient domain, and to put it in the thick of what William James calls its 'external environment'. It is to take the blame out of the hands of a single individual, loosening it and spreading it out across a blinkered collectivity. Blame, spread out in this way, can no longer support a firm division between master and slave. It points instead to a common ground between these two, a common lack of moral transcendence, not peculiar to either side, and not to be condemned on either side. Both are victims of that least escapable form of ignorance, an environmental ignorance. Neither side knows enough to be capable of conduct that can be called an absolute good. There is only goodness so-called, goodness as it is capable of being practised within the limits of slavery and as it is comprehensible to those whose minds are formed by that institution. Such was the conduct of an overseer named Mr Hopkins, who replaced a predecessor, fittingly (if improbably) named Mr Severe:

Mr Severe's place was filled by a Mr Hopkins. He was a very different man. He was less cruel, less profane, and made less noise, than Mr Severe. His course was characterized by no extraordinary demonstrations of cruelty. He whipped, but seemed to take no pleasure in it. He was called by the slaves a good overseer.[59]

Douglass's point is not that good and evil are just names, just matters of denomination. The names go with a felt reality, but it is a reality felt as such, and named as such, only within a particular context. If name-calling suggests a degree of knowledge, it is a knowledge predicated on and ultimately indistinguishable from a collective ignorance. The slaves could not have known better than to call Mr Hopkins a 'good' overseer, just as Mr Hopkins could not have known better than to be the 'good' overseer he imagined himself to be. The cognitive limits of each meet in a continuum, a continuum that breaks down the absolute division between master and slave, even as it breaks down the absolute division between good and evil.

And it breaks down yet another division as well. In the entanglement between knowledge so-called and goodness so-called, Douglass makes it clear that the boundaries between ethics and

[59] Frederick Douglass, *The Narrative and Selective Writing*, n. 57 above, 27.

epistemology are less than discrete, less than sustainable. Both are permeated by the current of life, borne along by it, churning with its contending forces. The cognitive horizon of each extends no farther than the horizons of that current. In this way, each bears witness not to the autonomy of reason but to its environmental limits. And, to the extent that those limits are shared, jointly operative in each, ethics and epistemology are bound together as Siamese twins, the failings in the former being conditioned by, and to that extent also excused by, the failing in the latter. It is the transitive relation between these two cognitive domains—and the mitigating circumstances generated by that transitiveness—that removes from Douglass's landscape the notion of absolute guilt. That notion would have required a wrongdoer acting in the fullness of knowledge and fully punishable for his action. Such a wrongdoer would have been the target of Kantian justice. No such target exists for Douglass. Where all knowledge is filtered through a blindfold, and good and evil environmentally variable, there can be no right of retaliation, because there is no absolute space to hold the blame.

SINGULAR AND AGGREGATE VOICES: AUDIENCES AND AUTHORITY IN LAW & LITERATURE AND IN LAW & FEMINISM

Judith Resnik

Law &s, and Audiences

This essay is written for a segment devoted to 'Theory' in a 'Law and Literature Colloquium'. Such a title is an invitation to be self-conscious, but self-conscious about what? The concept of 'Law & Literature' could be understood as either marvellously capacious or vacuous.[1] A central issue *internally* is whether 'Law & Literature' merits acceptance as a field of study or instead refers to an analytically disparate set of interests, temporarily sharing a moniker but not having much in common. The question *externally* is whether anyone, save those inside, cares. 'Anyone' is a large category; as a member of a law faculty in the United States, I focus on how, if at all, Law & Literature has fared over the past decades in law. At issue is whether sets of ideas grouped under 'Law & Literature' have had much effect other than on those affiliated with these labels.[2]

In addition to engaging with Law & Literature, I am affiliated with another Law &—Law & Feminism. A decade ago, Carolyn

---

[1] Jane B. Baron and Julia Epstein, 'Language and the Law: Literature, Narrative, and Legal Theory' in David Kairys (ed.), *The Politics of Law: A Progressive Critique* (3rd edn, New York, 1998), 662.

[2] Austin Sarat, 'Traditions and Trajectories in Law and Humanities Scholarship' (1998) 10 *Yale Journal of Law and the Humanities* 401; Judith Resnik, 'On the Margin: Humanities and Law' (1998) 10 *Yale Journal of Law and the Humanities* 416.

Heilbrun and I taught and wrote about the interrelationships among law, literature, and feminism.[3] While it was surely not news in 1989 that Law (as a discipline) and Literature (as a discipline) had historically excluded women from various forms of authorship and authority, it was interesting to consider the ways in which the newly-formed joint endeavour 'Law & Literature' (aspiring to be another discipline) was indifferent to the rich infusion of feminist theory in literature departments and to the claims that feminist jurisprudence was making in law. Consideration of the intersection of these two '&s' was therefore (in 1989) a discussion about voice and authority, about the efforts at constructions of a field of endeavour (Law & Literature) that seemed to mimic unselfconsciously either Law or Literature as they had existed in the decades before the 1970s.

While less has changed within the confines of Law & Literature than I had hoped, what intrigues me here is another aspect of the convergence between Law & Literature and Law & Feminism: these two '&'s' share similar aspirations *vis-à-vis* law and legal education in the United States. For those within both, the insights proffered are constitutive of how to think, write, and teach about law. Yet, both fields quest for more—acceptance or acknowledgement or engagement by those outside their parameters that the endeavour is necessary or helpful in understanding the enterprises of law. I term this a search for an 'authorizing audience'. Not only do both fields hope for an impact, opposition to both &s sometimes is expressed in similar terms—that the insights are soft instead of hard-edged, too particularistic to be offering guidance, or too general to be instructive. Yet both fields can point to successes, such as the creation of new journals,[4] books, and conferences, and an increasing number of courses offered. Moreover, the effects of feminist thought can be found in the tangible operations of law, in terms of statutes, judicial decisions, and court-based efforts to improve fair treatment of women. Law & Literature has had a less obvious impact; it remains peripheral to both legal education and decision-making.

What limits Law & Literature in its hopes for a wide audience?

---

[3] Carolyn Heilbrun and Judith Resnik, 'Convergences: Law, Literature, and Feminism' (1990) 99 *Yale Law Journal* 1913.

[4] Two in the United States relate to Law & Literature; the Index to Legal Periodicals, available through online databases, lists seventeen journals of feminism, women's issues, or gender and the law.

What are the possible relationships among audiences and enthusi-asts of either domain? What efforts to gain narrative authority have been deployed and with what reception? Below, I consider the reliance of Law & Literature on singular narratives, the issues of representativeness raised by deployment of specific stories, the turn by Law & Feminism to polyphonic aggregated narratives, and the forms of resistance encountered in response.

One example of the engagement of feminism with law is inven-tive; projects termed 'task forces' on gender, race, and ethnicity have been launched around the United States. These projects should be of special interest to Law & Literature scholars for a variety of reasons; they have relied on a range of narrative techniques (such as first-person narratives, plays, and videos), have used both singular personal narratives and a multitude of anonymous aggregate and individual voices, and have invented another legal–literary form in United States law, something called a 'bias task force report', all in an effort to obtain and to hold an audience and thereby to shift understandings of the current state of law and legal processes. Through examination of the interactions among these storytellers and audiences, I identify issues—of giving and gaining authority in law—central to Law & Literature's engagement with law.

The Specific Contexts of Literature and of Law

LITERATURE, AND THE INVOCATION OF A NARRATIVE

Law & Literature aficionados want people in law to understand that Law & Literature has something to teach and that it needs to be heard. A principal method is the deployment of stories—novels, plays, poems, first-person narratives, films. These stories are selected with the view that they carry meaning beyond the individ-ual instance to which they call attention.

An elegant illustration of that aspiration is provided at the outset of this volume, as Professor James Boyd White, one of the first architects of this field, offers a poem by William Carlos Williams to be read in conjunction with the First Amendment of the United States Constitution.[5] Conversation and dialogue, lead-

---

[5] James Boyd White, 'Writing and Reading in Philosophy, Law and Poetry' in this book, 1.

ing to new insights, are his goals. Others, such as those who adhere to what Jane Baron and Julia Epstein term 'Law & Narrative', make an express claim to alter the *status quo* through the introduction of particular stories.[6] They argue that law has failed to acknowledge 'outsiders', affected by and subjected *to law* but not often acknowledged as authoritative speakers *of law*.

But why should any particular story be the occasion for thick description and elaborate discussion? Which stories should be the ones to which attention is paid? In the 'old days' (not that long ago) of 'the canon', Law & Literature had a ready response. The canon offered the possibility of self-authentication.[7] The very status of a specific text as a part of the 'great works' seemed to (was supposed to) suffice to establish its didactic worth. If one was reading a play by Shakespeare, for example, one knew that the particular text was plainly more than 'a' story or 'one' example. Its stature as a part of the canon was a self-verifying method of demonstrating that it was about 'the human condition' and able to give insight to generation after generation.[8]

Similarly, when Law & Literature—in its mode of Law *as* Literature—interpreted Supreme Court decisions as texts, any given ruling was not just 'a case'. Rather, it came wrapped with the authority of the highest court in the United States. From that status, decisions laid claim to being larger than any particular instance because Supreme Court rulings were generalized into 'the law', making specific stories specially privileged.

When shared agreements among *cognoscenti* authorized certain authors as powerful speakers of the universal, Law & Literature had a lighter burden of proof/persuasion that any given text ought to be read. Had such a vision prevailed, Law & Literature might have gained authority, either as a standard form of pondering Supreme Court rulings or as a supplement to law schools' standard curriculum to spark imagination and to enhance moral insight.

But the comfort of the canon is gone. From within and without

---

[6] Baron and Epstein, n. 1 above, 670–2.

[7] J. M. Balkin and Sanford Levinson, 'The Canons of Constitutional Law' (1998) 111 *Harvard Law Review* 963, 979.

[8] The most frequently assigned works of fiction in Law & Literature courses in the United States continue that tradition; Melville's *Billy Budd* and Shakespeare's *Measure for Measure* top the list at 30 and 23 listings: Elizabeth Villiers Gemmette, 'Law and Literature: Joining the Class Action' (1995) 29 *Valparaiso University Law Review* 665.

the legal academy, an array of challengers (with intersecting views based in feminist, critical race, postmodern, and other perspectives) has made plain the contest over who establishes authoritative texts. Law & Literature, self-proclaimed as expanding law's horizons, has been challenged as itself exclusive and closed.[9] The claim was not only that more books from a diverse authorship were needed, but that the multitude of voices within law had been silenced by reliance on Supreme Court opinions as the basis for literary interpretation of law. For some, *outsider* voices were needed;[10] for others, *insiders* (lower court judges, witnesses, lawyers) were being ignored.[11] In short, and in part through the practice of Law & Literature, the wealth of possible stories to which to draw attention became plain, as did the question of why any particular story ought to have central stage.

LAW, AND ITS SELF-REGARD

Those seeking to engage law's readers need to be attentive to features of law that form its background culture. While several aspects of law are relevant here, one is that law is self-celebratory, proud of its efforts to secure fair treatment and ready to assume success about that to which it aspires. A vivid example of such expression in United States legal culture comes from a 1987 Supreme Court decision, *McCleskey* v. *Kemp*,[12] in which an individual African-American man sought to overturn a jury's imposition of the death penalty on the grounds of discrimination. As proof, he offered a social science study that demonstrated that defendants convicted of killing white victims were four times more likely to be sentenced to death than were defendants found guilty of killing African-Americans.[13]

---

[9] Heilbrun and Resnik, n. 3 above; Judith Resnik, 'Changing the Topic' (1996) 8 *Cardozo Journal of Law and Literature* 339; also published at (1996) 7 *Australian Feminist Law Journal* 95.

[10] Richard Delgado and Jean Stefanic, 'Norms and Narratives: Can Judges Avoid Serious Moral Error?' (1991) 69 *Texas Law Review* 1929, 1954–8.

[11] Judith Resnik, 'Constructing the Canon' (1990) 2 *Yale Journal of Law and the Humanities* 221, 222–8 (discussing Robert Ferguson's reading of *Minersville School Dist.* v. *Gobitis*, 310 US 586 (1994) and *West Virginia State Bd of Educ.* v. *Barnette*, 319 US 624 (1943)). [12] 481 US 279 (1987).

[13] 481 US at 285, citing a study commonly called the 'Baldus' study. David C. Baldus, George Woodworth, David Zuckerman, Neil Alan Weiner, Barbara Broffitt, 'Racial Discrimination and the Death Penalty in the Post-*Furman* Era: An Empirical and Legal Overview, with Recent Findings from Philadelphia' (1998) 83 *Cornell Law Review* 1638.

The Supreme Court rejected Warren McCleskey's argument that inferences from general studies showing a discriminatory pattern were acceptable; McCleskey had to 'prove that the decision makers in his case acted with discriminatory purpose'.[14] In an oft-quoted section of the decision, Justice Powell, writing for the majority, insisted on contextuality when considering questions of bias. Given the discretionary authority judges were accorded in sentencing, he opined, 'exceptionally clear proof' would be required.[15] Then, enlarging the context from sentencing to the criminal justice system in general, the Court commented on the significance of McCleskey's argument, as if to explain why it had to be rejected.

[T]aken to its logical conclusion [McCleskey's claim] throws into serious question the principles that underlie our entire criminal justice system . . . Thus, if we accepted McCleskey's claim that racial bias has impermissibly tainted the capital sentencing decision, we could soon be faced with similar claims as to other types of penalties [and with challenges] that correlate to membership in other minority groups, and even to gender.[16]

The *McCleskey* case (and what I will here call 'the *McCleskey* Problem') provides a conceptual placeholder for a salient aspect of law. Legal culture's self-regard and self-celebration pose a general difficulty for storytellers whose stories are at variance with law's self-satisfaction. The *McCleskey* ruling shows how difficult it is to convince the unconvinced in law of a relationship between an individual instance and a larger social phenomenon, when both the individual instance and the larger social phenomenon are claimed to betray liberal democracy's legal commitments to fairness and inclusion. The *McCleskey* Problem, presented in that case in the context of race discrimination in the criminal justice system, can arise any time the legal culture's faithfulness to its promises of equal treatment and fair process are challenged and the legal system responds by refusing to entertain the question of its own failings.[17] The *McCleskey* Problem is also not limited to a particular form of the challenge, such as the way in

---

[14] 481 US at 292.   [15] 481 US at 297.
[16] 481 US at 313.
[17] Susan Bandes, 'Patterns of Injustice: Police Brutality in the Courts' (manuscript, on file with author) (also invoking *McCleskey* in reviewing how to challenge the *status quo*).

which the discrimination claim was presented in the *McCleskey* case itself, by an individual arguing from social science data on discrimination to the particulars of his case. Rather, the *McCleskey* Problem is about backdrop assumptions, about beliefs that individual examples of discrimination could be illustrative of larger social phenomena or that larger social phenomena could in turn be part of the proof of individual instances of unfairness. Further, while the *McCleskey* Problem may arise in other settings, it has special significance in law because legal professionals make express commitments to a constitutionally fair regime. Thus, the *McCleskey* opinion illustrates an important aspect of legal ideology in the United States.

To the extent that many of the stories deployed by Law & Literature adherents are efforts to teach law of its own moral failings, limited insights, or insufficiently thick narrative techniques, Law & Literature often faces (but rarely acknowledges) the *McCleskey* Problem. In contrast, Law & Feminism—starting from the position of law as a means of oppressing women—has always known that it has a *McCleskey* Problem. Below, I sketch the contours of one form of activity that feminism has taken in law, projects aimed at educating judges and lawyers about the problems of bias towards and unfair treatment of women. These polyphonic projects engage directly with the problem of representativeness of specific stories about unfairness in law.

Feminist Responses to Law's Self-Regard: The Invention of Bias Task Forces

VIVID NARRATIVES

In the 1960s and 1970s, as litigators in the United States pursued lawsuits to combat discrimination against women, they found that judges—like the rest of the society—thought in terms of stereotypes based on gender, and that those stereotypes limited opportunities for women. The litigators thought that the problem stemmed, at least in part, from a lack of understanding, and they turned to education as a response. In the late 1970s, the Legal Defense and Education Fund of the National Organization of Women sponsored a new project, the 'National Judicial Education

Program',[18] which worked in cooperation with the National Association of Women Judges to organize educational programmes for judges about women.

Gaining podiums at a few conferences, panellists gave examples of vivid narratives from cases that illustrated judicial stereotypes and bias. The educators did not rely on the time-honoured legal tradition of deploying a hypothetical; to turn to fiction was to risk accusations of exaggeration. Rather, the educators cited 'facts' of a particular kind, those detailed by specific judges, juries, or lawyers, on the record. Judicial opinions were the texts of preference; transcripts and/or newspaper reports of judicial proceedings were the fall-backs. Purposefully didactic, the educators quoted judges' decisions to judges in the audience, oftentimes through the voices of other judges who served as educators-lecturers.

I provide one such example here, not from a case actually used in the 1970s[19] but from the 1990s. A young woman plaintiff, Marie Catchpole, was a freshman in college; she received some scholarship support from a hamburger franchise, for which she also had to work, part time. Ms Catchpole was physically and sexually accosted by the manager.[20] At the bench trial of her lawsuit alleging sexual harassment, assault and battery, and intentional and negligent infliction of emotional distress, the dispute centred not around the underlying events but about whether the assaults were work-related.[21] Ms Catchpole testified; she was cross-examined not only by defendants' lawyers but also by the

---

[18] Norma Juliet Wikler, 'On the Judicial Agenda for the 80's: Equal Treatment for Men and Women in the Courts' (1980) 64 *Judicature* 202; Norma J. Wikler, 'Water on Stone: A Perspective on the Movement to Eliminate Gender Bias in the Courts' (Fall 1989) 26 *Court Review* 6.

[19] Examples then invoked included 'a Colorado judge dismissing as "an attempted seduction" a sexual assault charge against a man who broke into a woman's trailer, threw her to the floor, and put his hand inside "her clothing and into her body"' and a 'California judge [who] told a rape victim that by hitchhiking she had invited sexual intercourse': Lynn Hecht Schafran, 'Educating the Judiciary about Gender Bias: The National Judicial Education Program to Promote Equality for Women and Men in the Courts and the New Jersey Supreme Court Task Force on Women in the Courts' (1985) 9 *Women's Rights Law Reporter* 109, 112.

[20] A police officer testified at trial that the defendant admitted the assault to him: *Catchpole v. Brannon*, 36 Cal. App. 4th 237, 242 (Cal. App. 1 Dist. 1995).

[21] 36 Cal. App. 4th at 258.

trial judge. The record, excerpted by a California appellate court, included the judge asking this young female plaintiff:

[Your father] somehow blames you for what happened, is that right? . . . Is this suit in any way connected with how your father feels about the situation? You want to prove something to him? . . .

    You stated at one point . . . that once he [the assailant] had taken your clothes off, that you were constantly trying to get them on and leave. Did you ever consider just leaving without your clothes?[22]

The educators had hoped that such specific examples of gender bias by judges in courts would enable their audience to understand that (a) a problem of fair treatment existed in courts and (b) judges had a role in correcting the problem.[23] But it did not work.

AUDIENCE RESISTANCE: DISCOUNTING AND DISCREDITING

The audiences' resistance to such vivid narratives was complex, with varying calibrations of distance and differing forms of rebuff, some aimed at the particular story and others at the speakers. To capture one distinction, some rejections of narratives may rely on *discounting* the import of a story, while others *discredit* the story and its speaker. Discounting can exist on an imagined continuum of openness. When not embracing a text as deeply insightful and instructive, members of audiences can entertain a range of assumptions, from a sympathetic stance that what has been presented is unusual to a less friendly act of trivialization. An individual story can be rejected based on a belief that it is not true, or, if true, not troubling, or if troubling, not common but a singular event that is aberrant rather than abhorrent. In contrast, to discredit a story is always to attempt affirmatively to dislodge authority. While some efforts to discredit may be based on good-faith beliefs that an error has occurred (the story is 'false') and may be accompanied by some efforts at discounting, the more hostile versions of discrediting are accompanied by efforts to

---

[22] 36 Cal. App. 4th at 250, 257.

[23] Were they cognitive psychologists, the educators might have described themselves as deliberately choosing 'vivid' examples in an effort to anchor different 'schemas' and 'scripts' and thereby to reorganize legal professionals' understanding of court processes. Richard E. Nisbett & Lee Ross, *Human Inference: Strategies and Shortcomings of Social Judgment* (Englewood Cliffs, NJ, 1980).

disempower the speaker, to disable her/him from having any authority in that venue, and sometimes in other places as well.

In addition to a continuum of open embrace to disaffection and hostility, a range of techniques is available to make a rebuff, be it aimed at discounting or discrediting. One could describe a given 'true' example as an 'anecdote', by which is currently (not intrinsically) meant that, while true once, the 'story' was not generally true but rather an idiosyncratic event.[24] In Stephen Greenblatt's words, the insistence here is on the 'singularity of the event' (as a *petite histoire*) in contrast to what the presenters proposed, that the specific case's 'representative' qualities link it to a *grand récit*, a 'history that knows where it is going'.[25] A related rebuff might acknowledge some representational aspects but claim them dated, that, to the extent the case exemplified more than a particular instance, it was of historical, not contemporary, interest. The specific case proffered is pushed away as an 'old story', described as relating events that 'used to happen' but do not happen 'any more'.

Negating stories' import through discounting and discrediting is a possible response to any form of narration; distancing oneself from judicial narratives has some wrinkles. For example, a generic mode of discrediting is to claim that a false story has been told; rejection is based on forthright disbelief. Such a strategy is difficult in the face of a text that has the imprimatur of a 'judgment'. Here discrediting requires a more circuitous route, such as suggesting that only part of the story has been told, and that missing aspects of the specific narrative would change its interpretative potential.

Two techniques for rejecting the link between specific instance and larger picture are particular to law. One is what I call the 'jurisdictional rebuff'. When told, for example, about the 1995 decision I described from California, an audience of judges or lawyers from outside California might respond: Well, that's all very interesting, but your example comes from California, not

---

[24] The word is defined by the *Oxford English Dictionary*, 2nd edn, *sub nom.*, Vol. I, at 454 as 'secret, private or hitherto unpublished', as well as the 'narrative of a detached incident, or of a single event, told as being in itself interesting or striking'. Anecdotes are often assumed to have entertainment value, an attribute sometimes linked to a diminished claim of authenticity. Clifton Fadiman, 'Introduction' in *The Little, Brown Book of Anecdotes* (Boston, 1985), xii–xxii.

[25] Stephen Greenblatt, *Marvelous Possessions* (Chicago, 1991), 2–3.

here (in, for example, Nevada). That may be the way judges treat people in California, but we, professionals here in Nevada, do not behave like that.

Another peculiarly legal form of rebuff is based on the legal professional culture's own self-regard. United States legal cultural *aspirations* of fairness translate, for some, into *assumptions* of fairness. This ideology of fairness makes difficult an appreciation that at least some people neither perceive themselves to be nor are fully included as participants. While aware of problems of discrimination in the world at large, legal professionals in the United States partake of a judicial system conceived as distinct and special, a part *of* but apart *from* general government.[26] The paradigmatic heroic judge is, after all, speaking truth to power.[27] Legal culture enacts these assumptions through reliance on a series of rituals peculiar to courts.[28] Judges wear odd clothes (robes); some sit elevated; normal rules of conversation are suspended. The institution of the court is obliged under ethical rules and constraints to be fair. Further, as the French put it, *l'être et le paraître*;[29] law must be and seem to be fair. Judicial canons call not only for avoidance of partiality but also for sensitivity to even the appearance of partiality.[30]

Thus, when presented with judicially authored examples of unfairness, many legal professionals fell back on their socially honed intuition that courts were somehow different, transformative spaces in which ordinary biases and stereotypes were not admitted. They argued not only that such events could not happen 'here', in the sense of a particular jurisdiction, but rather that such events do not happen 'here', in the larger sense of law as an ideological and

---

[26] This feature is emphasized in the United States federal system with a conception of the federal judiciary as an 'independent' branch of government. How free life-tenured judges are from control of other branches is discussed in Judith Resnik, 'The Federal Courts and Congress: Additional Sources, Alternative Texts, and Altered Aspirations' (1998) 86 *Georgetown Law Journal* 2589.

[27] Robert M. Cover, 'Folktales of Jurisdiction' (1985) 14 *Capital University Law Review* 179.

[28] Pierre Bourdieu, *Language and Symbolic Power* (John B. Thompson (ed.), Gino Raymond and Matthew Adamson (trans.), Cambridge, Mass., 1991), 105–36.

[29] Robert Jacob, *Images de la justice: essai sur l'iconographie judiciare de moyen age à l'age classique* (Paris, 1994), 9.

[30] American Bar Association, *Model Code of Judicial Conduct* (1990), Canon 3.

social space. The *McCleskey* case provides the paradigmatic gesture of dismissal. For many judicial audiences, stories like the *Catchpole* case had nothing to say.

AGGREGATE AUTHORSHIP

Ever optimistic (the footnote here being that optimism is a hallmark of feminism under-appreciated in a world busily painting feminists as dour, radical avengers), the educators engaged with the *McCleskey* Problem by concluding that they needed a stronger form of 'true fact', a thicker version of the story, to counteract the rejections that had greeted them. Instead of a 'true' case from anywhere in the United States, they wanted instead to rely on 'true facts' from the specific jurisdiction from which their audiences hailed. Instead of singular stories, they wanted an amalgam of stories, to bring the problems 'home' and up to date, to prove their representativeness through evidence of their recurrence.

The National Association of Women Judges and the National Judicial Education Program urged courts to set up research projects, calling them 'task forces' and coining the phrase, 'the gender bias task force'.[31] Their first success came in New Jersey; in 1982 Chief Justice Robert N. Wilentz of that state's Supreme Court created the first such task force.[32] Two years later, in 1984, he established the first task force on minorities in the courts.[33] While sought by entities often identified as 'women's groups', these projects were (and are) official, specially commissioned by the government, usually by the Chief Justice of a state court or by the governing judicial council of a federal circuit. Take, for example, the mandate issued in Connecticut, my current home state. In her capacity as Chief Justice, the Honorable Ellen Peters in

---

[31] Lynn Hecht Schafran, 'Educating the Judiciary about Gender Bias' (1986) 9 *Women's Rights Law Reporter* 109, 124 (as Executive Director of the NJEP, describing its 'dream' to be 'a task force in every state'); Lynn Hecht Schafran, 'Documenting Gender Bias in the Courts: The Task Force Approach' (1987) 70 *Judicature* 280, 281.

[32] The New Jersey Supreme Court Task Force on Women in the Courts, *First Year Report of the New Jersey Supreme Court Task Force on Women in the Courts* (New Jersey, 1984), 4.

[33] New Jersey Judiciary, Supreme Court Task Force on Minority Concerns, *Differential Use of Courts by Minority and Non-Minority Populations in New Jersey* (New Jersey, 1993), vi.

1989 charged the Connecticut court-appointed task force as follows: 'It is the duty of this task force to determine the presence and extent of gender bias in Connecticut courts and to develop strategies for its eradication.'[34]

Chartering specially-commissioned reports is not novel within law. In the United States such ad hoc bodies are sometimes called 'blue ribbon' commissions, while in England the term is a Royal Commission, which may lead to a 'White Paper'.[35] Gender and race bias task forces hoped to associate with these traditions by invoking familiar images of specially-convened and impeccably authorized ad hoc committees.[36] Further, like such commissions, the gender and race task forces operated pursuant to a mandate or charge, gathered information, and produced reports.[37] And many such commissions are products of political struggles, in which efforts are made to provide and disseminate knowledge of certain conditions to enable reform.

Yet gender and race bias task forces differ, in terms of who is authorized to speak, their methods of investigation, the kinds of reports generated, and in their very multitude and repetition. While deliberately linked to the ordinary format, they also deliberately altered it. First consider who is authorized to report. Unlike a blue ribbon commission of a few senior professionals with name recognition and pre-existing authority,[38] task forces often have

[34] Connecticut Task Force, *Gender, Justice, and the Courts* (Connecticut, 1991), 6.

[35] As explained in Norman Wilding and Philip Laundy's *An Encyclopedia of Parliament* (New York, 1971), 787, a White Paper is a 'colloquial term for a government report, statement of policy or similar document, which is not of sufficient thickness to require the stout blue covers which would transform it into a Blue Book'.

[36] '[T]hese colloquia of honorary statesmen, with the help of civil service secretariats, produce reports that receive the state's imprimatur and are ordained as officially recognised discourses': Frank Burton and Pat Carlen, *Official Discourse: On Discourse Analysis, Government Publications, and the State* (London, 1979), 2.

[37] See Richard A. Chapman, 'Commissions in Policy-Making' in Richard Chapman (ed.), *The Role of Commissions in Policy Making* (London, 1973), 174–84.

[38] T. J. Cartwright, *Royal Commissions and Departmental Committees in Britain* (London, 1975), ch. 5, 'Choosing the Right People', 62, 69, 71 ('The most obvious characteristics of committee chairmen are that they are almost all men and that most of them have reached a relatively advanced age' and also that 'chairmen tend to be peers, judges, or lawyers.'). As a prologue to their book, Burton and Carlen, n. 36 above, ix–x, reproduce a 1934 poem by A. P. Herbert, which includes the lines: 'And the Government courageously decided that the Crown/Should appoint a score of gentlemen to track the trouble down.'

larger numbers and an amalgam of speakers, not all of whom have high profiles. Most members are judges, lawyers, or academics, often female and/or of colour. Given their professional stature, they should not be conceived as actual 'outsiders', yet they are less 'insiders' than many appointees to commissions. While pre-ordained authoritative elders (chief justices or judicial councils) provide mandates, and some powerful judges, lawyers, and academics do participate, a good many named participants are selected because they share the characteristics—legal professionals of both genders and diverse races and ethnicities—that are the subject of discussion in the reports.

Second, this eclectic group of authors produces a different kind of document from that produced by blue ribbon commissions, which typically offer their members' corporate vision on the subject of inquiry from a lofty perch. In contrast, gender and race bias task force reports claim authority by capturing hundreds and thousands of voices, the stories of individual women and men in courts. These task forces use social science methods to obtain aggregate data about a range of topics, from courtroom interactions to the application of substantive law.[39] A good deal of the information comes from responses to questionnaires by hundreds of judges and thousands of lawyers. Those surveys are specially developed to elicit views about how courts respond to participants of both genders and to those of all colours. For example, in the federal system, six circuits (consisting of twenty-two states and the District of Columbia) have conducted task forces in which questionnaires were sent to judges, lawyers, staff personnel, a few litigants, and some jurors. The reports present views from more than 13,150 attorneys, about 600 active and senior judges (district and appellate, bankruptcy, and magistrate judges), 90 administrative law judges from one region, more than 4,000 court employees, and (note the professional tilt), some 1,250 jurors, 190 bankruptcy

---

[39] The reports took on a set of topics related to courts, including courtroom interactions and related activities, such as discovery and settlement; women and men who are professionals in courts; their work life and some information about family life; the court as an institution and as an employer; committee appointments, conferences, educational programmes; staff and employee relations; the application of legal doctrine or issues in particular areas of law, such as sentencing guidelines, prosecutorial discretion and race, language barriers, women as victims of violence, employment law, family law, immigration, federal benefits, or bankruptcy.

debtors, about 95 convicted criminal defendants, and some 35 detained or incarcerated women.[40] Thus, and third, gender and race bias reports do not share the distance, typical in the blue ribbon commission, between the authors and the subject of inquiry.

COLLECTIVE ANONYMITY AND DRAMA

Compare such task force reports with the array of texts that are usually the subject of Law & Literature. Included are judicial opinions, interpreted as texts; fictional accounts (novels, plays, short stories, poems, films) deployed for didactic purposes; testimony or other first-person narratives of litigants and other participants; and commentary on all of these works by scholars. Task force reports do not fit any of these forms. Two features of this particular legal–literary genre are of special interest: its array of authorial strategies and its efforts to cope with its own volume and potentially tedious qualities.

A persistent stance adopted by task forces is reliance on a range of authors, some identified and others participating through collective anonymity. Each task force begins with a listing of the individual members (described above) who officially form 'the' task force, followed by lists of names of those who sat on special committees or who undertook specific research, and then by the names of many individuals thanked for their assistance. Thereafter, a foreword or introduction is provided by the chief judicial officer of the jurisdiction or by the chair of the task force. These official introductions serve a function associated with slave narratives, in which whites would write prefaces to establish 'the narrator's veracity and the reliability of the account'.[41] While sharing that validating purpose, the typically brief introductory endorsements of task forces do less speaking and writing 'for' task forces than do many of the introductions of slave narratives. Rather, most of the substantive information comes from reports of

---

[40] See Tara Veazey, 'An Analysis of the Methodologies of the Federal Task Forces on Gender, Race, and Ethnicity' (working draft, June 1998, on file with author) (These data do not include individuals surveyed from the First or Eleventh Circuit or, to avoid double counting of individuals, the Second and Ninth Circuits' task forces on race, religion and/or ethnicity).

[41] Valerie Smith, *Self-Discovery and Authority in Afro-American Narrative* (Cambridge, Mass., 1987), 38.

data collected from the samples of lawyers, judges, and court staff and the occasional litigants and jurors. These reporters, in turn, are identified only by one or two descriptors, such as gender or age and kind of practice or level of court. Race is used less frequently because, given the relatively few judges and lawyers of colour, race becomes one means of identification and attribution. Such aggregate data precludes individual identification and, in theory, promotes frank reporting.

Anonymity is not novel in law, social science, literature, or politics. Police and the press regularly turn to anonymous informants. Occasionally (albeit warily), actors in court proceedings are unnamed, as John or Jane Doe plaintiffs or defendants. While judges in the United States are individually identified, many civil law countries require judicial anonymity, linked to unanimity.[42] Contemporary social scientists, as well as marketeers, often collect quantitative information from individuals, identified by characteristics salient to the issue at hand. In literature, women authors have sometimes assumed men's names and have done so for a range of reasons, including to gain readership and to avoid personal criticism.[43] By changing names, writers tried to pass through gender, class, race, or ethnic lines,[44] thereby undermining associations between authorial capacity and such categories.[45] When authorized by their demographic position to speak, some political pamphleteers invoked names associated with the republics of Athens or Rome in an effort to historicize and politicize their

[42] Ruth Bader Ginsburg, 'Remarks on Writing Separately' (1990) 65 *Washington Law Review* 133.

[43] Elaine Showalter, *A Literature of Their Own: British Women Novelists from Bronte to Lessing* (London, 1982), 58–93; Sandra M. Gilbert and Susan Gubar, *The Madwoman in the Attic: The Woman Writer and the Nineteenth-Century Literary Imagination* (New Haven, Conn., 1979).

[44] Lurana Donnels O'Malley, 'Masks of the Empress: Polyphony of Personae in Catherine the Great's "Oh Those Times!" ' (1997) 31 *Comparative Drama* 65.

[45] See the discussion of Georges Sand as 'a great man', the vocabulary then available to capture her accomplishments, in Carolyn Heilbrun, *Writing a Woman's Life* (New York, 1988), 35. Compare Saul Levmore, 'The Anonymity Tool' (1996) 144 *University of Pennsylvania Law Review* 2191, 2192, 2198, 2208–10 (discussing the 'puzzle of why and when anonymity is acceptable'; contrasting 'honest disclosure' and 'deception', and arguing that 'anonymity is a less acceptable social practice where the informer can use an intermediary to avoid confrontation with the recipient and to convey information about the reliability of the source').

views.[46] But while authors may be anonymous or disguised, the events described and other actors are usually identified. One-sided anonymity is the norm.

In contrast, anonymity in bias task forces is two-directional. Not only are the authors unidentified, the stories they tell are edited to make unavailable identification of persons who might be seen either as biased or as subjected to bias. Unlike the *Catchpole* case example, in which the individual actors are specified, named 'culprits' do not dot the thousands of pages of task force reports. When episodes are detailed, clues such as the specific place or level of court may be deleted, all in an effort to avoid identification of individual actors.

In addition, and again unlike case law reports, the plot line moves away from narratives of *blame* to ones of *description* in which all participate and none are culpable. In many of the reports, the focus is not on bias or discrimination, in the current legal sense,[47] but rather on the relevance of or the effects and impact of gender, race, and ethnicity. The reports seek to understand if and how respondents' experiences of courts vary with gender, race, age, social status, and the like. Seeking wide audiences, words like 'fairness' and 'equity' or 'equality' appear in many titles of these reports. (Such a deferential, system-supporting vocabulary is not the only choice available, as is illustrated by looking to a government-based project in Ontario, Canada, called 'The Commission on Systemic Racism in the Criminal Justice System in Ontario.')[48]

The actual contents of reports also vary; some are friendly, didactic, mild-mannered, while others are more unabashed. Further, within a single volume might come differing voices,

---

[46] The obvious reference here is *The Federalist Papers*, n. 75 below, with three authors (James Madison, John Jay, and Alexander Hamilton) all relying on a single pen-name, Publius. Their choice has served to enable a wide range of arguments, all claiming parentage in the *Federalist Papers*.

[47] See, e.g., *Adarand Constructors* v. *Pena*, 515 US 200 (1995); *McCleskey* v. *Kemp*, 481 US 279 (1987).

[48] Commission on Systemic Racism in the Ontario Criminal Justice System, *Report of the Commission on Systemic Bias in the Ontario Criminal Justice System* (Ontario, 1995), ii (defining 'systemic racism' as the 'social processes that produce racial inequality in decisions about people and in the treatment they receive. It is revealed by specific consequences, incidents, and acts that indicate differential decisions or unequal treatment, but it is the underlying processes that make such events "systemic".').

reflecting chapters drafted by various authors or committee members' editorial revisions. Thus, headline and content can vary, such as the hortatory title of Connecticut's report, *Gender, Justice, and the Courts*, accompanying the less upbeat conclusion, that 'women are treated differently from men in the justice system and, because of it, many suffer from unfairness, embarrassment, emotional pain, professional deprivation and economic hardship'.[49]

By shaping these narratives without identified villains and by relying on thick layers of detailed descriptions, task force reports sought to avoid the problems associated with the singular individual narratives and to increase their own acceptability, thereby enlisting proponents for implementing recommended changes. But their very lack of drama puts these reports at risk of losing audiences. The dense, statistically-encrusted texts, with hundreds of pages of text, appendices, and charts providing a dry rendition of the aggregate 'facts' may help authenticity but produce another problem—readership.

In response (atop the authorizing introduction, the anonymous aggregate voice, the melange of emphatic and dry tones), another literary decision can be found within the pages of task force reports: movement back and forth from an aggregate voice to disaggregated, individual episodes. The hundreds of pages are peppered with brief first-person narratives. These anonymous first-person testimonials quote 'margin comments' written as part of responses to the anonymous surveys, 'focus group' discussions, testimony taken at public hearings, and reported cases. These narratives are piled one upon another to enliven the materials and also to translate statistical information into accessible knowledge.[50]

But the very denseness and quantity, even with individual stories, proved problematic. Who would take the time to read it all? So task forces turned to dramatic enactments as a means of translation. Task forces wrote plays, sang songs, and made movies—all to 'tell stories' that turn the wealth of data back into manageable narrative units, albeit now in a composite form. For

[49] Connecticut Task Force, *Gender, Justice, and the Courts*, n. 34 above, 12.

[50] Deborah R. Hensler, 'Studying Gender Bias in the Courts: Stories and Statistics' (1993) 45 *Stanford Law Review* 2187.

the Eighth Circuit's conference on its report on gender fairness,[51] the Mixed Blood Theatre of Minneapolis, Minnesota, put on a play entitled *Is it Something I Said?: A Play About Gender Fairness in the Eighth Judicial Circuit*, with music adapted from *West Side Story* and featuring a series of incidents in which women judges and lawyers address the audience and struggle with issues of gender equality. One of the opening voice-overs is:

The Eighth Circuit ... 83 judges ... 8 white women ... 5 African American men ... one African American woman ... zero Latinos ... zero Asian Americans ... zero native judges (*a lightning bolt as the organ crescendos, then returns to its low groan*).

The words set to a song, ('Something's Coming') include:

> Can we be ... fair to all ...
> Is the system ... on the ball?
> What if it's not? ...
> Times are changin'
> women and men—are equal in—the law today
> we shouldn't play—by different rules!

A closing narration states:

What you've seen here are all things that have actually happened recently in the courts of the Eighth Circuit. Are you surprised? Does it bother you? Or did you know it happens and didn't think it mattered? Should someone do something about it? Who and What?[52]

To ensure that attention was paid at a conference of the Eleventh Circuit on gender bias, a short film was shown in which actual judges and lawyers from the Eleventh Circuit (Alabama, Florida, and Georgia) turned themselves into actors, playing lawyers and judges in a series of 'vignettes' about gender bias.[53] In Connecticut, a play relied on the device of role reversals, as if women judges would discuss men's looks or invoke

---

[51] Eighth Circuit Gender Fairness Task Force, 'Final Report and Recommendations of the Eighth Circuit Gender Fairness Task Force' (1997) 31 *Creighton Law Review* 1.

[52] Syl Jones, playwright with the Mixed Blood Theatre Company, with Additional Scenes and Dialogue by Laura Cooper, Carol Jackson, and Leslie Freeman, *Is it Something I Said?: A Play About Gender Fairness in the Eighth Judicial Circuit* (the latter three being, respectively, a lawyer, a judge, and the executive director of the Eighth Judicial Circuit).

[53] Eleventh Circuit, Video (1995) (on file with the author).

clubby connections to exclude men lawyers and make them as uncomfortable as women lawyers reported that male judges had done.[54]

The introduction to the Connecticut play, proffered by a male 'Superior Court Judge and a Deputy Chief Court Administrator for Connecticut's Courts' who was also a co-chair of the Task Force on Gender Justice and the Courts, bears examination. He began with a 'we' (implicitly, we, the State of Connecticut, its judges, its lawyers, its people). 'We found':

We found, as did the states that preceded us and the states which followed, that there is an unjustified differential treatment of men and women in the justice system ... The discovery ... should come as no surprise. Judges, attorneys, and judicial staff are a product of their environment ... The law, the judicial selection process and the court proceedings through the words used convey the impression that the standard is that of the male. The female is presented as an exception to the standard ... Imagine if you will a world of law in which women are the predominant players and where the male is the exception to the norm. The play which follows is a dramatization of this idea ...[55]

'We found'. Through the commission from judiciaries, task force reports became vehicles by which new narratives were heard and adopted, shared, joined with officialdom's voice. These efforts made a space for claims that gender matters, to women's detriment, that race matters, to racial minorities' detriment, and that they mattered in courts, in which all were to be treated as equal.

New Audiences and Some Authority

Thus, the aggregate polyphonic narratives worked. While New Jersey courts were the pioneers in 1982, they were not long alone; by 1988, the Chief Justices of all the state courts adopted a resolution calling for the study of gender, racial, and ethnic bias. Activity in the federal courts began in the 1990s, with more than half the circuits authorizing projects and the official body of

---

[54] Connecticut Judicial Branch, 'The Nice Suit,' a one act play on video, in *Gender and Justice: Approaching the Bench* (Connecticut, 1992), (on file with the author).

[55] The Hon. Francis X. Hennessy, 'Introduction to "The Nice Suit" ' in Connecticut Judicial Branch, *Gender and Justice*, n. 54 above.

federal judges—the Judicial Conference of the United States—
approving of such inquiries. As of 1998, thirty-seven reports have
been published on gender, sixteen on race, seven combined
reports, stemming from thirty-nine states, Puerto Rico, the District
of Columbia, and six federal circuits.

Several state reports contained summary conclusions that incorporated the claims made by the educators who had, a decade
before, attempted to convince judges through individual narratives
exemplifying gender bias: that the system of courts, dedicated to
fair and equal treatment, was not as fair or equal in the treatment
of women or of people of colour than had been hoped. For example, New York's Task Force on Gender found in 1986 that,
'[w]omen uniquely, disproportionately and with unacceptable
frequency must endure a climate of condescension, indifference
and hostility'.[56] From Tennessee, in January of 1997, came the
words 'The Commission finds that gender bias in Tennessee's legal
system prevents the full participation of women therein. While
many corrective measures have been taken . . . evidence of gender
bias persists.'[57] The Second Circuit (the federal courts for the
states of Connecticut, New York and Vermont) in June 1997
commented that '[s]ome biased conduct toward parties and
witnesses based on gender or race or ethnicity has occurred on the
part of both judges and lawyers'.[58]

When the focus is on race and ethnicity, the reports contain
parallel statements. Michigan's 1989 report stated that 'there is
evidence that bias does occur with disturbing frequency at every
level of the legal profession and court system'.[59] From Florida, in
1990, came concerns 'that the rights of non-English speaking
defendants are systematically being compromised due to the lack

[56] New York Task Force on Women in the Courts, 'Report of the New York
Task Force on Women in the Courts' (1986–7) 15 *Fordham Urban Law Journal* 1,
17–18.

[57] Commission on Gender Fairness, *Report of the Commission on Gender
Fairness* (Tennessee, 1997), 1 (submitted to the Tennessee Supreme Court January
15, 1997).

[58] Second Circuit Task Force on Gender, Racial, and Ethnic Fairness in the
Courts, *Report of the Second Circuit Task Force on Gender, Racial, and Ethnic
Fairness in the Courts* (New York, 1997), 43 republished in (1997) 1/2 *Annual
Survey of American Law* 9, 51.

[59] Michigan Supreme Court Task Force on Racial/Ethnic Issues in the Courts,
*Final Report of the Michigan Supreme Court Task Force on Racial/Ethic Issues in
the Courts* (Michigan, 1989), 2.

of trained, qualified court interpreters'.[60] New Jersey found in 1992 that '[m]inority litigants, minority witnesses, and minority attorneys are subjected to racial and ethnic slights from all levels of court and security personnel—from the bailiff to the bench'.[61] Minnesota reported in 1993, '[d]espite the fact that racial discrimination in the courts is often subtle, its ultimate effects are anything but'.[62]

Not only did the task forces generate a thick literature and multiple conversations, they also resulted in a series of actions, ranging from changing modes of appointing judges to altering procedures when women are the victims of violence, from writing policies on sexual harassment that applied to judges to revising canons of ethics and local rules to create methods to address bias and discrimination in courts. Yet other literature was spawned. Handbooks on fairness in the courts provided 'how to' manuals with guidelines about modes of addressing people in court, such as reminding participants not to use first names or call anyone 'hon'. Manuals about how to conduct gender and race bias task forces came into being,[63] a law review symposium was published summarizing federal efforts,[64] and the activity of doing such studies moved from courts and the legal profession into law schools.[65]

And judicial opinions changed. A small body of reported decisions now exist in which judges label a behaviour 'gender' bias or 'race' bias and reverse judgments or impose sanctions on participants for

---

[60] Florida Supreme Court Racial and Ethnic Bias Study Commission, *Where the Injured Fly for Justice: Report of the Florida Supreme Court Racial and Ethnic Bias Study Commission* (Florida, 1992), Vol. II, viii.

[61] New Jersey Task Force on Minority Concerns, 'Final Report' (1992) 1 *New Jersey Lawyer* 1225, 1230.

[62] Minnesota Supreme Court Task Force on Racial Bias in the Judicial System, *Final Report* (Minnesota, 1993), S–3.

[63] Lynn Hecht Schafran and Norma Juliet Wikler, *Operating a Task Force on Gender Bias in the Courts: A Manual for Action* (Washington, DC, n.d.); Molly Treadway Johnson, *Studying the Role of Gender in the Federal Courts: A Research Guide* (Washington, DC, 1995).

[64] Symposium, 'The Federal Courts' (1998) 32 *University of Richmond Law Review* 603.

[65] American Bar Association Commission on Women, *Elusive Equality: The Experiences of Women in Legal Education* (Chicago, 1996); Lani Guinier, Michelle Fine, Jane Balin, Ann Bartow, and Deborah Lee Statchel, 'Becoming Gentlemen: Women's Experiences at One Ivy League Law School' (1994) 143 *University of Pennsylvania Law Review* 1.

displaying such bias.[66] The example with which I began, about the judge who had so aggressively and hostilely questioned a young woman plaintiff, came from a 1995 California appellate decision, reversing that decision for the judge's treatment of Marie Catchpole.[67]

One ending of this narrative should thus be marked; two others will follow. The denouement here is that an aspect of Law & Feminism succeeded in responding to the *McCleskey* Problem. By bringing forbidden questions of fairness into the halls of justice and relying on a *mélange* of literary genres, social science, and inventive revision of the legally-commissioned report, new authority was obtained for authors formerly discounted. Through plays and dramatic enactments, anchored by a multitude of polyphonic stories, the idea that law could be unfair came to be understood. From within and without, a joinder of official and outsider voices, in a chorus of challenges, undertook a painful self-assessment. Social action followed. A sector of legal professionals in the United States acknowledged that its culture did not produce all the fairness and equality to which it aspired and tried to make justice good on its promises. Further, during this, the third decade of such work, new areas of concern are starting to come into focus: the intersection of gender, race and ethnicity, and hence 'women of color in the justice system',[68] the problems in courts faced by gay men and lesbians,[69] and the obstacles to justice for those with disabilities.[70]

---

[66] Vicki C. Jackson, 'Gender Bias in the Courts: What Can Judges Do?' (1997) 81 *Judicature* 15.

[67] *Catchpole* v. *Brannon*, 36 Cal. App. 4th 237, 262 (Cal. App. 1 Dist. 1995) ('The [trial] court's remarks throughout the trial show that its conception of the circumstances that may constitute sexual harassment were based on stereotyped thinking about the nature and the roles of women and myths and misconception about the economic and social realities of women's lives.').

[68] Judicial Council of California, Administrative Office of the Courts, *Roundtable on Women of Color and the Courts* (California, 1998); Judith Resnik, 'Asking About Gender in Courts' (1996) 21 *Signs* 952, 973–7.

[69] New Jersey and California have such projects.

[70] Judicial Council of California, *Leading Justice into the Future: Judicial Council of California Long-Range Strategic Plan and Fiscal Year 1998–99 Administrative Office of the Courts/Advisory Committee Action Plan* (California, 1997), 38 (available at http://www.courtinfo.ca.gov/onlinereference/index.htm#leading justice).

DISCOUNTING, AGAIN

But the *McCleskey* case and the culture of law that it illuminates are also robust, and hence two other, conflicting denouements, need to be played out. Moreover, 'denouement' may be the wrong term. Relying on feminist possibilities of breaking the 'masterplot line' by writing different stories,[71] I should characterize the three endings more as way-stations than conclusions. Further, as Tony Sharpe explained,[72] much of what is interesting in narrative comes before the tidying-up of a denouement. In that sense, what is unfolding should surely be situated as not-yet-the-end. One such non-ending, described above, is of expanding concerns and self-consciousness about the failures or limits of fair treatment. The second and third focus on legal audiences' means of discounting and discrediting these aggregate voices.

To return to the voluminous literature that I have described, while some may have affection for serial romances or the familiar narrative structures of detective fiction, these bias reports do not have such cachet. Rare is the reader of all sixty such reports. Moving from potential readership to the authors of these volumes, notice the time and energy (most of it donated by individuals already fulfilling a multitude of demands) required to produce each report. The sheer joy of writing and the invigoration from commitment to such projects may account for some of the quantity, but all sixty?

Note further that the underlying conclusions seem not at all hard; courts look like society, and society is organized by gender, race, and ethnicity more than it should be. More than that: courts were themselves vehicles of discrimination. As the judge who introduced the play based on the Connecticut task force explained, finding 'unjustified differential treatment of men and women in the justice system . . . should come as no surprise. Judges, attorneys, and judicial staff are a product of their environment.'[73] Racial segregation existed *de jure* until the middle of the twentieth century, sanctioned by courts. Formal

---

[71] Susan Winnett, 'Coming Unstrung: Women, Men, Narrative, and Principles of Pleasure' (1990) 105 *Proceedings of the Modern Language Association* 505; Heilbrun, *Writing*, n. 45 above.

[72] Tony Sharpe, '(Per)versions of Literature' in this volume, 91.

[73] Connecticut Judicial Branch, *Approaching the Bench*, n. 54 above.

discrimination against women was lawful, not illegal, through the 1990s.[74]

The saga of these reports can therefore be read not only as a victorious march across boundaries but also as an oddly long-winded tale. What required the tedious slogging through scores of jurisdictions, taking large investments of human capital to prove the obvious, time and again? Answers come from returning to the travails of the individual vivid narrative of unfairness and its reception as (at best) a *petite histoire*, and more often as idiosyncratic, out of date, jurisdictionally-limited, and implausible in law. The polyphonic, aggregate task force report (or five of them) faced audiences primed to discount or discredit stories of law's unfairness. Only one in each and every jurisdiction, anew, and again, begins to respond to the legal culture's impulse toward self-satisfaction.

And, while one of the non-endings overcomes such impulses, two others do not. While negating such aggregate polyphonic stories, endorsed by officialdom, is complex, audiences found means to discount and discredit them as they had the singular story. Some of the devices used to distance from the individual narrative—such as its very singularity—are not available when so many iterations are linked together in one and then many official reports. Different means were needed.

One way to discount the reports has been to confine their problematic aspects through assimilation into a professional discourse on 'civility', a topic of increasing concern within United States legal culture. The discussion of task forces moved away from a focus on unfairness and towards the professional mainstream, in which courts and bar associations are preoccupied with the question of legal 'professionalism'. What were seen as problems of 'discrimination' and 'bias' are relocated into a discourse of manners.

Such assimilation occurs from within task forces and without. Re-reading these projects as a piece with ordinary professional exchanges is enabled by one of the authorial decisions made by many task force writers: keeping the conversation on a positive note to avoid being seen as challenging. That tone does not necessarily entail a shift in substance, but a shift in substance can also be found within some reports. As opponents of self-conscious remedial work (some of which bears the label 'affirmative action')

---

[74] *United States* v. *Virginia*, 518 US 515 (1996) (finding unconstitutional the all-male admissions policy of the Virginia Military Institute).

increased, the composition of task forces changed. Judges and lawyers who registered scepticism or opposition were sometimes appointed to membership on task forces; the resulting documents reflect (to borrow Clinton Rossiter's descriptor for *The Federalist Papers*) a 'bundle of compromises'.[75]

The conclusions that I cited earlier—of systemic unfairness—exemplify the first wave of task forces on gender, race, and ethnicity, in which state court task forces announced problems of discrimination (so-labelled) and called for new laws and serious reconsideration of rules and procedures. In contrast, several recent reports stress the 'positive' (here meaning self-affirming) side, that few overt instances of gender bias have been reported or that claimed problems of discrimination are not borne out in the data.[76] Over the past few years, some of the reports—attesting to law's basic fairness and arguing that only a few imperfections exist—sound more like blue ribbon commissions than innovative reinterpretations.

Thus, the many gender, race, and ethnic bias task force reports can be read as a series of chapters in which, over time, judges and lawyers have become increasingly self-absorbed in studies of themselves as professionals. The examination and documentation of bias and discrimination have become subsumed under and transformed into generic discussions of civility and professionalism. Task force reports turn into 'novels of manners'. But just as that genre has within it both self-satisfied as well as subversive iterations,[77] so do task force reports. While some reports adopt the rhetoric of professionalism and civility, they make it plain that the absence of civility takes a particular toll on women.[78] And, while

---

[75] Clinton Rossiter, 'Introduction' in Clinton Rossiter (ed.), *The Federalist Papers* (New York, 1961), xv.

[76] As one participant views the Third Circuit process, 'the report was understood by many to make the finding that there was no bias—as opposed to the finding that there was no *systemic* bias, which was the Report's conclusion. I believe that this understanding allowed many to breathe a sigh of relief and to conclude that no changes need be made. Anyone who reads the Task Force report in its entirety could scarcely come to such a conclusion, but many will not undertake that task': Letter from Professor JoAnne A. Epps to Professor Judith Resnik (6 May 1998) (on file with author).

[77] Bege K. Bowers and Barbara Brothers (eds.), *Reading and Writing Women's Lives: A Study of the Novel of Manners* (Ann Arbor, Mich., 1990).

[78] Eighth Circuit Task Force, 'Final Report and Recommendations', n. 51 above, 125–36 (discussing differing forms of 'incivility' in the courts and that women suffer from three kinds: generalized, gender-based, and sexualized incivility).

the *McCleskey* Problem is not solved by civil discourse but by reallocations of power (hopefully through civil discourse), the professionalism–civility veneer to gender and race task force reports still legitimates discussion of race, gender, and ethnicity in courts, and thereby makes possible some space in which authority may be gained.

DISCREDITING, AGAIN

Another non-ending moves from discounting to discrediting, within which space for dialogue, exchange, and remediation is lost. At first, one found individual objections—diffused by the larger context of a friendly audience—to a given task force project. Handwritten comments, attached to questionnaires, complained that such projects were 'a complete waste of time and money!'; 'a pile of garbage'; 'much ado about nothing'.[79] Such responses echoed the rejection of individual narratives but could not suffice to undermine these polyphonic, authorized, detailed reports. A different, but parallel, set of oppositional stances had to be developed.

One technique, again specific to law, stressed law's concern with boundaries. Critics raised a jurisdictional objection—that the task forces had wandered too far afield. While the singular narrative was rejected because it came *from another* jurisdiction, the task force efforts were attacked on the grounds that these committees *reached outside* their jurisdiction, such as making inquiries into the practices of law firms and of prison officials.[80]

Another mode of rebuff addressed the very collectivity of task forces, dependent on joint accord and official support. For example, a few judges on the United States Court of Appeal for the District of Columbia protested against the fact of a task force; they attempted de-authorization. When unable to stop the reports, they sought to discredit them by a dissent, 'disassociating' themselves

[79] Ninth Circuit Gender Bias Task Force, 'The Effects of Gender in the Federal Courts: The Final Report of the Ninth Circuit Gender Bias Task Force' (1994) 67 *Southern California Law Review* 731, 960.

[80] Laurence H. Silberman, 'The D.C. Circuit Task Force on Gender, Race, and Ethnic Bias: Political Correctness Rebuffed' (1996) 19 *Harvard Journal of Law and Public Policy* 759.

from the reports and their recommendations.[81] Yet another means of undoing was to de-fund. While much of the collective work was undertaken *pro bono*, some court resources (such as staff time) were inevitably implicated. In 1995, three Republican Senators then in charge of judicial oversight and budget attempted to halt such support. Despite a federal statute approving the projects,[82] they put into the Congressional Record a 'colloquy' (an odd legal form, itself worthy of study) in which they called for an end to all federal funds for 'race-gender bias studies'.[83]

When dissociation and de-funding failed to stop such projects, critics attacked those participating in them. While the etiquette of judging made difficult challenges directly to colleagues on a court, questions were raised about judges and lawyers (presumably upright) choosing to associate with others on the task force,[84] and specifically 'law professors . . . who have made it their primary business to wage ideological struggles unceasingly'.[85] Moving from the named participants to the anonymous ones, efforts were made to undermine their voices as well. The use of aggregate data was termed 'an anonymous plebiscite',[86] obtained by inappropriate deployment of social science methods.

After challenging collectivity and its participants, critics moved to the substance of the reports. While individual narrative could be dismissed as 'idiosyncratic', aggregate narratives had to be reframed as potentially exaggerated, fictional. Critics argued that task force reports presented not truth but only 'perceptions'. For example, a 1996 state task force report bears the title *A Difference in Perceptions*, which is explained as meaning not that 'one group is right while the other group is wrong; it simply provides an opportunity to see a situation from different vantage

---

[81] 'Statement of Disassociation by Circuit Judges Buckley, Ginsburg, and Randolph' in The DC Circuit Task Force on Gender, Race, and Ethnic Bias, *The Gender, Race, and Ethnic Bias Task Force Project in the D.C. Circuit* (Washington, DC, 1995), Vol. I, V1–V8; Lynn Hecht Schafran, 'Will Inquiry Produce Action? Studying Gender in the Federal Courts' (1998) 32 *University of Richmond Law Review* 615, 626–7.

[82] 42 USC §14001 (a) (1998).

[83] Cong. Rec. S14691, 29 Sept. 1995.

[84] Silberman, n. 80 above, 763 ('[o]ne wonders why such people would lend their names but not their convictions to such a process').

[85] Silberman, n. 80 above, 764.

[86] Silberman, n. 80 above, 763.

points'.[87] Or, as the General Accounting Office of the United States put it: 'Perceptions of differential treatment are important and may be used as a baseline data on participants' observations of fairness of various court processes and operations. But data on perceptions are not necessarily evidence that gender and/or racial bias exists.'[88] Critics distinguished thus between 'objective' reality and 'subjective' perceptions of that reality. Through the implicit invocation of Rashomon's multiple points of view, the information proffered by task forces (with their polyphonic voices and their location as court-authorized inquiries) was not rejected outright but reduced to a not-very-useful pile of 'perceptions', no longer authoritative, possibly not even interesting, and arguably imaginative.

A different way to try to command the interpretative space was to read the reports as congratulatory. A predicate to that reading relies on the transposition of the recent narrowing definitions of discrimination used in litigation—the requirement of specific proof of intentional actions by individual actors (*McCleskey* again)—into the baseline against which task force findings were to be measured. The myriad reports of people's experiences of differential treatment did not constitute anything about which to be concerned. As one of the most visible and active critics, a judge sitting on a federal circuit court, explained:

It is comforting, although hardly surprising, to hear from one of the social scientists who provided services to the Task Force that the basic data,

---

[87] 'A Difference in Perceptions: The Final Report of the North Dakota Commission on Gender Fairness in the Courts' (1996) 72 *North Dakota Law Review* 1115, 1140 (submitted to the North Dakota Supreme Court by the North Dakota Commission on Gender Fairness in the Courts, October 1996, and implemented on 5 March 1997 *per* Administrative Order 7). The text of the report is more complex, reflecting the 'split personalities' of multiply authored documents (a term Rossiter applied to the *Federalist Papers*, Rossiter, n. 74 above, xv); the Commission also noted that 'perceptions are often realities' and further that courts should be particularly concerned with perception data: 'A Difference in Perceptions', above, 1143.

[88] See Letter from Norman J. Rabkin (Director, Administration of Justice Issues, General Accounting Office of the United States) to the Honorable Charles E. Grassley (Chairman of the Subcommittee on Administrative Oversight and the Courts, Committee of the Judiciary, US Senate) of 8 March 1996, GAO/GGD 96–71R 7 (Circuit Bias Task Force Reports); and General Accounting Office, The Federal Judiciary: Observations on Selected Issues (Sept. 1995), GAO/GGD 95–236BR at 62–71.

even taking into account the flawed methodology, shows no statistically significant incidents of bias (as normally defined) in our courts.[89]

The keys here are the phrases 'bias (as normally defined)' and 'in our courts'. Whose definition constitutes the 'normal'? Who speaks for others? His assertion of authority displaces the reported experiences of participants within 'his'/the court. Ignore the fact that a third of black women attorneys reported that judges assumed they were not lawyers;[90] no 'statistically significant incidents of bias (as normally defined)' have occurred 'in our courts'. Further, such critics argued that other judges would agree, had they not been stilled by 'speech police' who have silenced opposition.[91] (Here, the *McCleskey* Problem is flipped; powerful ideologues have cast law as unfair and individuals need speak out against such a misconception of law.)

A final mode of negation builds on the critique of individual narratives as *implausible in law* because 'law' does not behave in an unfair manner. As the dissociators to the DC federal task force reports argued, such projects were 'fundamentally at odds with judicial impartiality'.[92] When feminist aggregated voices responded by linking *petites histoires* to a *grand récit* through the quantity of first-person narratives and a resort to social science methods, charges of implausibility and unrepresentativeness were diffused. But negation then moved to another front: that the inquiry itself was *harmful to law*. By studying gender, race, and ethnicity, a few United States Senators argued, task forces undermined the independence and fairness of the courts.[93] As one Senator put it: 'In my view, [these studies] threaten the independence of the Federal judiciary.'[94]

This comment echoed the prominent judicial critic, who similarly framed task forces as generating 'improper' activities,

---

[89] Silberman, n. 80 above, 765.

[90] DC Report, n. 81 above, IVA47, n. 26.

[91] Silberman, n. 80 above, 763, claiming to speak for unnamed others ('At least a score of federal judges have told me privately that they disapproved of the Ninth Circuit Task Force').

[92] 'Statement of Disassociation by Circuit Judges Buckley, Ginsburg, and Randolph', n. 81 above, V3.

[93] Such an attack is odd, given that task forces are quintessentially affectionate projects, populated by friends of courts who are committed to equal justice and seeking to make true the claims of the rule of law through law-based activities.

[94] Cong. Rec., S14691 (Senator Hatch).

antithetical to law. The words used are aggressive. The task force for the District of Columbia was 'lurching out of control';[95] it generated a 'three-year long period of turmoil' aimed at 'bludgeon[ing]' federal judges into altering 'substantive decisions'.[96] While 'dodging the bullet',[97] it was nevertheless 'frightening that a powerful ideological movement with hard political overtones could have come so close in its efforts to intimidate the federal judiciary'.[98]

This narrative of collective voices under attack should miss neither the individual nor the institutional level. In terms of personal attacks, some critics of task forces attempted to limit the professional opportunities of some who had participated in task force work.[99] On the institutional side, the conflict about the task forces is but a part of a major broader effort, within legal circles, to limit the authority of professional organizations that have, over the past decades, evidenced concern about equal treatment within the law.[100]

As the opposition grew more vocal, the vocabulary became increasingly familiar, reminiscent of 'the culture wars' and other disputes about identity, politics, and culture. The judge so hostile to this work named his oppositional essay 'Political Correctness Rebuffed';[101] in it, he warned that efforts at 're-education programs' were in the wings.[102] Note that he, a prime resister who claimed fear of bludgeoning, is a life-tenured judge. Given salary protections and a lifetime job, what prompts his shrill tone? The judge, accustomed to asserting narrative authority ('no bias (as normally defined) in our courts') was unused to being the

---

[95] Silberman, n. 80 above, 763.　　　　　　　　　[96] *Ibid.*

[97] Silberman, n. 80 above, 760.　　　　[98] Silberman, n. 80 above, 765.

[99] See, for example, the efforts to stop the nomination of one woman, Margaret McKeown, who had been appointed by the courts to serve as a member of a task force and then was attacked for such service: Robert T. Nelson, 'Conservatives Make an Example of Seattle Lawyer: Past Liberal Activism Haunts Federal Appeals Court Nominee', *Seattle Times B1*, 24 March 1997.

[100] One specific target is the American Bar Association. A publication of the Federalist Society, entitled 'ABA Watch' provides critiques, including a speech by Senator Orrin Hatch describing the ABA as no longer a 'trade organization, limiting itself to advancing positions which affect the economic health of lawyers' but addressing issues of the administration of justice and constitutional values, and hence acting as a 'political interest group.' 'Senator Orrin Hatch Ends ABA Official Role in Judicial Confirmation Process' (March 1997) 3 *ABA Watch*.

[101] Silberman, n. 80 above.　　　　　　[102] Silberman, n. 80 above, 569.

object of the gaze; he was startled to find himself potentially in full view.[103] No matter that the task force had not named names; no matter that the inquiry was mild-mannered, avoiding charges of discrimination and attempting to be reassuring. It impermissibly intruded on his understandings of judicial prerogatives, thereby unleashing emotive and energetic rebuffs.

To summarize, the polyphonic, authorized narratives raising the *McCleskey* Problem bring forth a range of techniques to discount or discredit them. Individual stories are rebuffed as idiosyncratic or out-of-date anecdotes superseded by modern antidiscrimination principles, or as jurisdictionally land-locked examples with no capacity to provide insight beyond the territorial parameters from whence they issued, or simply as incompatible with norms of judicial impartiality. Aggregate voices are rebuffed by claims of jurisdictional excess, capture by outsiders with political agendas, misuse of public funds, undertaking the wrong kinds of inquiries, obtaining insufficient data of only limited value, relying on 'perceptions' veering toward the fictional as contrasted with objective reality that defines the parameters of bias, and of causing harm to law.

The form taken to raise the *McCleskey* Problem does not itself avoid all rebuffs, for it is the content that is so painful to take in. In both individual adjudication and in group endeavours like task forces, struggles in law persist about equality within law. Task forces parallel judicial opinion-writing. In both venues, judges debate the meaning of equality. In decisions, the issues are framed in terms of levels of intent required to show discriminatory purpose or effect and whether remedies should be 'colour blind'. In task forces, the questions are about whether judges in their administrative capacity should report information about the gender or race of their employees and of their appointments, cooperate in inquiries addressing their own institutions, or license and support such inquiries at all.

The struggle for narrative authority is sometimes harsh, as the lawyers, judges, and politicians hostile to task forces attempt to reconstruct the identities of the judges and lawyers who have

---

[103] Linda Nochlin's display of 'Achetez des Bananes', contrasted with 'Achetez des Pommes', comes to mind. See Linda Nochlin, 'Eroticism and Female Imagery in Nineteenth-Century Art' in Thomas B. Hess and Linda Nochlin (eds.), *Woman as Sex Object: Studies in Erotic Art, 1730–1970* (New York, 1972), 8, 12–13.

sponsored or worked on task forces. The effort is to make such insiders into kinds of 'outsiders', to marginalize and to demonize them as policing speech and engaging in 'identity politics'. The goal is to make it harder to have discussions of even perceptions of unequal or disparate treatment. The underlying struggle is for control over the narrative; at stake is whether the potential of task forces to address the *McCleskey* Problem will be fulfilled, diffused, or rejected.

Lessons for Law and Literature

New Texts, This Context: The Distinctive Ideologies of the Judicial

A first lesson *from* Law & Feminism *for* Law & Literature is self-evident. The study of Law & Literature in the United States, currently preoccupied with analysis of only a few forms,[104] misses texts that could and should be the object of analysis. Gender, race, and ethnic bias task force reports are but one, albeit particularly rich, given the polyglot of authorized and anonymous speakers providing polyphonic texts from in- and outside officialdom. They offer a template for questions about the search for authority, the use of different identities, the narrative power of different voices, the blurring of voices, the role of authorizing introductions, and the turn to anonymity. Much more could be added to the repertoire, colloquia and legislative reports among them; the mining of the relationships between legal and literary forms is far from complete.[105]

A second conclusion builds on the evidence, provided by the task forces and the stories of their making, about the complex and distinctive culture of courts. The struggles over the *McCleskey* Problem and the distinctive means of discounting and discrediting within courts should prompt more exploration into the peculiar features of legal culture. Bob Cover movingly reminded us that

---

[104] Gemmette, 'Joining the Class Action', n. 8 above. See also Elizabeth Villiers Gemmette, 'Law and Literature: An Unnecessarily Suspect Class in the Liberal Arts Component of the Law School Curriculum' (1989) 23 *Valparaiso Law Review* 267.

[105] Compare J. M. Balkin and Sanford Levinson, 'Law as Performance', in this volume, 729.

courts are institutions of violence.[106] Here, I have stressed another aspect of their specificity, a self-image as a uniquely-situated public institution obliged to behave differently from other institutions.

At times self-satisfied and at rare moments self-reflective, courts have ideological commitments that literary analysis of their products needs to, but does not always, take into account. How should a commitment to 'due process' affect theories of voices in courts? What should be made of courts' interests in 'the appearance' of impropriety as well as the fact of such impropriety? What about courts' roles as civic spaces, as places in which collective identities are built? Narrative theories often assume interactions among readers, text, and authors: do a designated spot for 'the public' and presumptive rights of access alter that interaction?[107] Yet courts are also institutions filled with interactive but quasi-private exchanges.[108] While I share Sandy Levinson's and Jack Balkin's call for attention to courts as performative spaces, performance is no longer their centrepiece. In the United States, less than 5 per cent of civil cases end through trials. While interactive and participatory, much of what judges and lawyers do occurs in chambers and offices, not in view.

By working within the spaces of courts, Law & Feminism has taken on the specifics of law, making possible in turn debates about whether law can plausibly take on feminist commitments or is antithetical to them.[109] Some within Law & Literature have often assumed that literature can nest in law without exploring the ideologies and mores of law's culture.

GIVING AUTHORITY: WHAT VOICES? WHICH NARRATIVES?

The next issue is about the voices to which those currently practising Law & Literature in the United States now turn. Who is read?

---

[106] Robert M. Cover, 'Violence and the Word' (1986) 95 *Yale Law Journal* 1601.

[107] Judith Resnik, 'Due Process: A Public Dimension' (1987) 39 *University of Florida Law Review* 405.

[108] Judith Resnik, 'Managerial Judges' (1982) 96 *Harvard Law Review* 374.

[109] Compare Carol Smart's observation, that law 'disqualified women's experiences of knowledge', with some of the conclusions from task forces: Carol Smart, *Feminism and the Power of Law* (London, 1989), 2.

According to recent research about works of non-fiction assigned in classes of Law & Literature, the expositor on Law & Literature most often assigned to students is the legal economist, Richard Posner, whose connection to literature stems from two editions of one book, *Law and Literature: A Misunderstood Relation*, arguing the limited use of the linkage.[110] Of twenty-two non-fiction works assigned more than three times, a book by Richard Posner comes first, followed by names more familiar to the literary–legal world, specifically Henry David Thoreau, Richard Weisberg, and James Boyd White.[111]

Unquestionably, students in Law & Literature courses should be exposed to what critics of such perspectives think. Hence, it is of no surprise to find Posner or other critics among the list of works assigned. It is, however, curious that Posner heads the list. Not only has his book received a good deal of commentary that it fundamentally misunderstands that which it sets out to critique[112] but, given that much of what Richard Posner has written comes in response to Robin West,[113] the absence of frequent references to her voice is both surprising and disheartening.[114]

The ceding of so much space to Posner is paralleled by the discussion (just had) about gender bias task forces, in which, in

[110] Richard Posner, *Law and Literature: A Misunderstood Relation* (Cambridge, Mass., 1988, new edn 1998). The 1988 edition built on a series of articles written in exchange with Professor Robin West, see n. 113 below. In 1998, a 'new and enlarged edition' was published, the result of 'reconsideration in light of the intervening decade of scholarship': Preface to the 1998 edition (ix). Judge Posner also warned readers (7), that despite his 'emphasis on the limitations', he supports the 'law and literature movement . . . and wish[es] to see it flourish'.

[111] Gemmette, 'Joining the Class Action', n. 8 above, 693, n. 46 (reviewing assignments made by the 84 teachers reporting such classes).

[112] See, e.g., Stanley Fish, ' "Don't Know Much About the Middle Ages": Posner on Law and Literature' (1988) 99 *Yale Law Journal* 777; Jack M. Balkin, 'The Domestication of Law and Literature' (1989) 14 *Law & Social Inquiry* 787.

[113] See, e.g., Robin West, 'Authority, Autonomy, and Choice: The Role of Consent in the Moral and Political Visions of Franz Kafka and Richard Posner' (1985) 99 *Harvard Law Review* 384; Richard A. Posner, 'The Ethical Significance of Free Choice: A Reply to Professor West' (1986) 99 *Harvard Law Review* 1431; Robin West, 'Submission, Choice, and Ethics: A Rejoinder to Judge Posner' (1986) 99 *Harvard Law Review* 1449; Robin West, 'Economic Man and Literary Woman: One Contrast' (1988) 39 *Mercer Law Review* 867.

[114] West is not listed as an author of the twenty-two non-fiction works assigned more than three times: Gemmette, 'Joining the Class Action', n. 8 above, 693, n. 46. West appears on six of the 46 syllabi provided in the appendices: Gemmette at 694–794.

one of the non-endings, a few nay-sayers (inveighing in that context against task forces on gender, race, and ethnicity) loom large. Of the sixty task force reports written, to my knowledge only one—that of the federal courts for the District of Columbia— has been accompanied by 'dissociation' from some of the appellate judges of the court. One of those judges is the source of most of the vivid quotes cited above. How much space should these few voices be given in the narratives of task force work? Should counter-quotes be provided? Or recent endorsements by other high level judges?[115] What 'plurality of consciousness, voices, and language'[116] should herein be engendered?

These are the questions to be asked by Law & Literature. How and why do Richard Posner's words gain attention? Is it the depth of his insight or the joy of an argument? The need for a foil or gratitude for being the object of attention by such a visible figure? Who else is invoked and who ignored? Elizabeth Gemmette's recent empirical work reminds us that the contours of Law & Literature are not fixed; that within the last half-dozen years, some changes have occurred, such as the assignment of works of fiction by women that now appear on a few reading lists, mostly in courses taught by women.[117] Yet the changes are only a trickle,[118] and women as professors of the metier, as critics shaping the

---

[115] For example, in May 1998, Justice Ginsburg described a recent federal report as evidencing 'both how far we have come and the distance still before us as we work to achieve our aspirations of equality and fairness for the federal courts': Hon. Ruth Bader Ginsburg, 'Foreword' to the *Report of the Second Circuit Task Force on Gender, Racial, and Ethnic Fairness in the Courts* (1997) 1/2 *Annual Survey of American Law* 1, 7.

[116] Milner S. Ball, 'Stories of Origin and Constitutional Possibilities' (1989) 87 *Michigan Law Review* 2280, 2289 (explaining Bakhtin's views of Dostoevsky's achievement as realizing that characters and authors were 'equally independent and engaged in dialogue. The whole is polyphonic.')

[117] Gemmette, 'Joining the Class Action', n. 8 above, 687–8 reports that both Toni Morrison's *Beloved* (New York, 1987) and Susan Glaspell's *A Jury of Her Peers* (first published in a collection of short stories in 1917), reprinted in Robert M. Cover, Owen M. Fiss, and Judith Resnik, *Procedure* (Westbury, NY, 1988) are now used occasionally. Glaspell's story, also made into a video, has garnered a good deal of attention. See Patricia L. Bryan, 'Stories in Fiction and in Fact: Susan Glaspell's A Jury of her Peers and the 1902 Murder Trial of Margaret Hossack' (1997) 49 *Stanford Law Review* 1293; Marina Angel, 'Criminal Law and Women: Giving the Abused Woman Who Kills a Jury of her Peers Who Appreciate Trifles' (1996) 33 *American Criminal Law Review* 229.

[118] Such works may be mentioned 'only once or twice'. Gemmette, 'Joining the Class Action', n. 8 above, 686–7.

discourse, remain unrecognized as authoritative by teachers within the domain.[119] Bringing into Law & Literature the discussion of Feminism & Law is one way in which to invite self-conscious reappraisal, not only about to whom authority is given but also about whose voices are assumed already to be authoritative.

GAINING AUTHORITY

The next issue is about the authority of Law & Literature. While Richard Weisberg offers an upbeat overview of its audiences,[120] fewer than half of the law schools in the United States offer courses in the arena.[121] A recent study of new course offerings in United States law schools does not include Law & Literature as among the 'top 25 areas of curricular growth'.[122] The American Association of Law Schools' directory has no separate listing of law professors as teachers of Law & Literature; they are included as teachers of 'jurisprudence'.[123] While the number of such classes has increased over the years,[124] no claim to centrality in law can be made.

Why so little voice, more than two decades after James Boyd White wrote *The Legal Imagination*, a text also cited as establishing

---

[119] Of the top twenty-two works of non-fiction, only one woman—Patricia Williams—made the list: Gemmette, 'Joining the Class Action', n. 8 above, 671, n. 46.

[120] Richard Weisberg, 'Literature's Twenty-Year Crossing into the Domain of Law: Continuing Trespass or Right by Adverse Possession?' in this volume, 47.

[121] Of 199 law schools in the United States queried in the middle of the 1990s about whether any such course is offered, eighty-four responded affirmatively: Gemmette, 'Joining the Class Action', n. 8 above, 666. Missing points of comparison are the number of courses offered in Law and Economics and a measurement of 'mainstream' offerings, that is courses denominated 'Property' or 'Torts' in which materials from either discipline are used in a systematic fashion.

[122] Deborah Jones Merritt and Jennifer Cihon, 'New Course Offerings in the Upper-Level Curriculum: Report of the AALS Survey' (1997) 47 *Journal of American Legal Education* 524, 536–8, 562 (but noting that 'law and literature' was a field in which 'more specialization is possible during the coming years').

[123] 574 people are so listed. American Association of Law Schools (AALS), *Directory of Law Teachers, 1997* (Westbury, NY, 1997), 1199–1205, including lists of the 165 teachers of Law & Economics, the 140 of Women & the Law, as well as categories of Computers & the Law, Jurisprudence, Law & Medicine, Law & Psychiatry, Law & Science, and Law & Social Sciences. See at 1213–14, 1291–3, 1097–8, 1214–16, 1216–17, 1217–18, 1218–20.

[124] Gemmette, 'Joining the Class Action', n. 8 above, 666 (the percentage of law schools reporting such courses in 1993–4 was 43 per cent, as contrasted with 28 per cent reporting such courses in 1987).

what some term the Law & Literature 'movement'? Law & Literature shares the problem that feminist panellists had, as they stood before judges in the early 1980s, and offered singular examples of egregious treatment of women in courts by judges. 'Law's stories' (to borrow the phrase from a recent book title[125]) have such a range that the questions raised to feminist narratives are apt here as well: why this anecdote? Is it dated? Particular to a given jurisdiction? In sync with law's culture? The polyphonic plasticity that Milner Ball celebrates as making the 'aesthetics of narrative' sympathetic to 'the dynamics of the American legal order'[126] proves less of a virtue than anticipated. Moreover, while not all of Law & Literature's texts are instances of systemic unfairness, a subset of them are, and hence fit specifically within the *McCleskey* Problem.[127] Law & Feminism always knew it had a *McCleskey* Problem, but some within Law & Literature may be surprised to learn that they have it too, that they are grouped as outsiders in the conflating commentaries of the critics.[128]

Given the fragility of canonicity as a means of authenticity, Law & Literature currently lacks a means of showing that the singular text proffered is more than a *petite histoire*, worthy of attention either as an alternative means of knowledge or as representative of anything in the world at large. No longer can the study of Herman Melville's *Billy Budd*, decisions of the United States Supreme Court, and the deployment of varying forms of literary theory, be they traditional or the continental sort that is linked to (and equates) Derrida, Lacan, and Foucault, save Law & Literature from the marginal status in which it now sits. And, ironically, proponents and/or allies of Law & Literature have been *a* source (careful, not too much agency here) of its limited authority. By arguing that 'the canon' was at best incomplete and at worst harmfully fictive, they helped to undermine one source of Law & Literature's claim to authority.

---

[125] Peter Brooks and Paul Gewirtz (eds.), *Law's Stories: Narrative & Rhetoric in the Law* (New Haven, Conn., 1996).

[126] Ball, n. 116 above, 2290.

[127] For example, Posner's central critique of 'oppositionalist storytellers' is that the 'significance of a story of oppression depends on its representativeness'. Posner (1998 edn), n. 110 above, 349.

[128] See, e.g., Suzanna Sherry, 'The Sleep of Reason' (1996) 84 *Georgetown Law Journal* 453, conflating various forms of critical theory to create a 'unified' version then critiqued. See also Daniel A. Farber and Suzanna Sherry, *Beyond All Reason: The Radical Assault on Truth in American Law* (New York, 1997).

Further, lacking much by way of theoretical requirements, Law & Literature's status as an all-covering umbrella under which fits an array of methods and ideas may prompt dismissal more than dialogue. Whatever the delight in what Milner Ball calls 'narrative multiplicity',[129] Law & Literature needs some 'stories' or 'theories' of selection and content to gain a claim to audiences' attention. Rehabilitative efforts, insisting on literature's powers of moral edification,[130] resemble the effort to assimilate task forces by also framing them as rehabilitative tools, civilizing attorneys. Becoming a part of a vague *mélange* of professional equipage provides only small opportunities for generativity.

Another factor, here coming back to shared problems of Law & Literature and Law & Feminism, is an instability from within, an ambivalent attitude towards the intellectual projects of which we are a part. At times, both fields celebrate the individual, claim the right to set forth particular instances, narratives, and stories without a requirement of explanation. These aspects of both &s are linked to a range of postmodern stances, as that term is loosely used. At other points, both fields display impulses toward their own *grand récit*,[131] albeit oftentimes a metanarrative of distressing unfairness, quintessentially painful in (but not limited to) venues like courts that are explicitly committed to fairness. Yet, while radical in critique, many of the claims are aligned in content with the state's aspirations. Nuanced, caveated stories are what we have to tell, some not cohering to related, let alone singular, theoretical stances. And the 'we' here is itself tenuous, a loose affiliation unsure of having a common moment. (This ambivalence from within is not unique to either Law & Literature or Law & Feminism; introspection about methodology is underway in anthropology, history, and sociology, themselves engaged in what Lawrence Stone terms 'The Revival of Narrative'.[132])

---

[129] Ball, n. 116 above, 2311.
[130] Martha C. Nussbaum, *Poetic Justice: The Literary Imagination and Public Life* (Boston, 1996).
[131] See, e.g., Nancy Fraser, 'False Antitheses: A Response to Seyla Benhabib and Judith Butler' (1991) 11 *Praxis International* 166; Seyla Benhabib, Judith Butler, Drucilla Cornell and Nancy Fraser, *Feminist Contentions* (New York, 1995), 59, 61–2; Tracy E. Higgins, ' "By Reason of their Sex:" Feminist Theory, Postmodernism, and Justice' (1995) 80 *Cornell Law Review* 1536.
[132] Lawrence Stone, 'The Revival of Narrative' (1979) 89 *Past and Present* 3, 22–4.

But even were Law & Literature to develop theoretical paradigms and gain a sense of its own identifying characteristics, it is facing—in United States law schools—other difficulties. Above, I explored the ideology of courts, with a self-conception as uniquely fair. Law schools too have a self-image. Law schools have spent this passing century attempting to cast law as a discipline with its own integrity, situated along with political theory, government, philosophy, economics, and business, but uniquely equipped to engage in the 'real' world while simultaneously reflecting on the shape and meaning of that world, as understood through its laws—to be at the centre of governance within the United States.[133]

Yet law itself is a very local enterprise, both in terms of its method of analysing particular cases and in terms of its interest in specific governing regimes. Law is parochial in many of its enactments. Further, a prime technique of teaching law—reading cases—is reading narratives. Given the official—albeit increasingly superficial[134]—commitment to the case method, one might have thought that law schools would embrace those intrigued by narrative as 'within the fold', and perhaps attempt to subsume them as within the ordinary workings of 'the legal mind'. One might then have thought that, even if lacking authority in legal culture in general, Law & Literature would have a special place in law schools' vocabulary.

But during the same decades (the 1970s through the 1990s) when classes and ideas called 'Law & Literature' were pushing themselves forward, many law schools saw themselves as in need not so much of the particular as the grand. They turned to philosophy and economics (or more correctly, small subsets of both of these fields) as sources of advancing law schools' own claims to authority within the academy. Moreover, competition for authority occurs both within universities and beyond. Outside the academy,

---

[133] Here carrying the heritage of 'law is king' examined in Robert A. Ferguson, *Law and Letters in American Culture* (Cambridge, Mass., 1984).

[134] Many casebooks are comprised of such truncated versions of original opinions as to provide little by way of factual specificity or legal argument to permit intense engagement with the specifics of the reprinted case or to enable students to engage or disagree with the stance provided either by casebook editor or classroom teacher. One rebellion—cumbersome in length—against that trajectory can be found in Cover, Fiss, and Resnik, n. 117 above, which in some instances offers many readings and multiple opinions from the 'same' case.

the turn towards the 'global' has exacerbated law schools' anxiety. As globalization of markets makes national governance less salient,[135] law has less primacy. Yet law schools' aspirations to participate in worldwide governance is unabated. Globalization becomes a source of pressure towards simplifying metanarratives and sweeping generalizations, not the thick descriptions of specific texts that much of Law & Literature represents. The quest for authorizing audiences has, over the past decade, become harder.

In Medias Res

Stephen Greenblatt tells us that if we know where we are going, it may be less interesting than finding out where we are.[136] Susan Winnett reminds us that the 'Masterplot' is but one form, and that not all stories come with 'awakening, an arousal, the birth of an appetency, ambition, desire or intention . . . and significant discharge'.[137] Having offered three non-endings to the embedded tale of feminist encounters with law, I stop the larger narration with the beginning of George Eliot's *Daniel Deronda*, 'in medias res'.[138]

Men can do nothing without the make-believe of a beginning. Even Science, the strict measurer, is obliged to start with a make-believe unit, and must fix a point in the stars' unceasing journey when his sidereal clock shall pretend that time is at Nought. His less accurate grandmother Poetry has always been understood to start in the middle; but on reflection it appears that her proceeding is not very different from his; since Science, too, reckons backwards as well as forwards, divides his unit into billions, and with his clock-finger at Nought really sets off *in medias res* . . .*

---

[135] See Jean-Marie Guehenno, *The End of the Nation State* (Victoria Elliot (trans.), Minneapolis, 1995).

[136] Greenblatt, *Marvelous Possessions*, n. 25 above, 2.

[137] Winnett, n. 71 above, 506, quoting Peter Brook, *Reading for the Plot: Design and Intention in Narrative* (New York, 1984), 90–112.

[138] George Eliot, *Daniel Deronda* (Harmondsworth, 1983), 35.

* My thanks to Denny Curtis, Carolyn Heilbrun, and Vicki Jackson, ever willing to think with me; to Susan Bandes and Jane Baron, for helpful comments on this essay; and to Yale Law School class of 2000 students, Kim Demarchi, Megan Johnson, and Tara Veazey, for insightful and companionable assistance.

Since this essay is self-conscious about voice, position, and authority, I want to acknowledge the roles that I play. Not only do I narrate, on occasion I have participated in the projects I describe, including as a teacher of classes on law, literature, and on feminism, a critic of particular stances taken by some proponents of Law & Literature, and as a member and/or adviser to task forces on gender, race, and ethnicity, and hence as a respondent to criticism of those enterprises.

LAW AS PERFORMANCE

J. M. Balkin and Sanford Levinson

Introduction

The analogy between law and the literary text has been central to
the law-as-literature movement since its inception. Both of us have
contributed to the development of this analogy,[1] and both of us
have learned much from it. Yet every analogy has its limitations,
and we think it is time to move on. We believe that the comparison between law and the literary text interpreted by an individual
reader is inadequate in important respects. A much better analogy,
we think, is to the performing arts—music and drama—and to the
collectivities and institutions that are charged with the responsibilities and duties of public performance. In other words, we think it
is time to replace the study of law as literature with the more
general study of law as a performing art.

Law, like music or drama, is best understood as performance—
the acting out of texts rather than the texts themselves. The
American Legal Realists distinguished 'law on the books' from 'law
in action'. Our claim takes this distinction one step further: 'laws
on the books'—that is, legal texts—by themselves do not constitute
the social practice of law, just as music on a page does not constitute the social practice of music. Law and music require transforming the ink on the page into the enacted behaviour of others. In an
important sense, there is *only* 'law (or music, or drama) in action',
in contrast to poetry or fiction, whose texts do not require performance but can be read silently to oneself. Like music and drama,
law takes place before a public audience to whom the interpreter
owes special responsibilities. Legal, musical, and dramatic interpreters must persuade others that the conception of the work put
before them is, in some sense, authoritative. And whether or not
their performances do persuade, they have effects on the audience.

---

[1] See, e.g., Sanford Levinson, 'Law as Literature' (1982) 60 *Texas Law
Review* 273; J. M. Balkin, 'Deconstructive Practice and Legal Theory' (1987) 96
Yale Law Journal 783.

For this reason, the best examples of legal performers are not law professors, but persons at the cusp of decision, who must determine—often under highly imperfect circumstances—how a text should be given concrete meaning in the social context before them. That context must include the political and institutional constraints of the moment as well as the capacities of the other performers in the legal system. Most judges, like most directors, are not blessed with all-star casts of Callases and Oliviers guaranteed to give thoughtful and inspired performances, or with subtle and sophisticated audiences, eager to receive the latest and most daring interpretations. Like actors and directors, judges must take into account the interpretive abilities and predilections of others. Judicial performances depend on further performances by lower court judges and executive officials; the efficacy of their work often depends on acceptance by others: not only by other government officials, but by the people as a whole. The wise judge, like the wise director, understands the limitations and the interests of her co-performers and her audience and tailors her interpretations accordingly.

How to Perform (or not Perform) an Offensive Text

One of the best ways to understand the responsibilities of performance is through the problem of offensive texts. In important ways, the decision about whether and how to perform an offensive text raises difficulties similar to interpreting and enforcing an unjust law. We begin our discussion with a hymn by Sydney Carter entitled 'Lord of the Dance'. The words are set to the lovely Shaker tune 'Simple Gifts',[2] best known to many through

---

[2] See Raymond F. Glover, 3B *The Hymnal* 1982, (New York, 1994), 1027–8 for the history of the song. The original lyrics of 'Simple Gifts' are set out in Edward D. Andrews, *The Gift to be Simple: Songs, Dances and Rituals of the American Shakers* (New York, 1940), 136:

'Tis the gift to be simple, 'tis the gift to be free,
'Tis the gift to come down where we ought to be.
And when we find ourselves in the place just right,
'Twill be in the valley of love and delight.
When true simplicity is gain'd
To bow and to bend we shan't be asham'd.
To turn, turn will be our delight
'Till by turning, turning we come round right.

We are grateful to David Hunter for providing us the sources quoted in this footnote and in the text immediately following.

its appearance in Aaron Copland's ballet *Appalachian Spring*. The lyrics are as follows:[3]

1. I danced in the morning when the world was begun,
And I danced in the moon and the stars and the sun,
And I came down from heaven and I danced on the earth;
At Bethlehem I had my birth.
Refrain:
Dance then wherever you may be;
I am the Lord of the Dance, said he,
And I'll lead you all, wherever you may be,
And I'll lead you all in the dance said he.

2. I danced for the scribe and the pharisee,
But they would not dance and they wouldn't follow me;
I danced for the fisherman, for James and John;
They came with me and the dance went on:
Refrain

3. I danced on the Sabbath and I cured the lame:
The holy people said it was a shame.
They whipped and they stripped and they hung me high,
And they left me there on a cross to die:
Refrain

4. They cut me down and I leap up high;
I am the life that'll never, never die;
I live in you if you'll live in me:
I am the Lord of the Dance, said he.
Refrain

Although the music is lovely, the verses get progressively troublesome. Simply put, verse three of the song is anti-Semitic, and the descriptions it offers have a long and unfortunate history. Recurrent portrayals of 'the holy people . . . whipp[ing] and . . . stripp[ing] and . . . h[anging Jesus] high' go back as far as the Gospels, especially the Gospel of St John. As the Catholic Church has recently acknowledged, these religiously-sanctioned depictions of Jews and Judaism were major contributing factors to the pervasive anti-Semitism that resulted in a history of discrimination, pogroms, and eventually the Holocaust. Similar problems haunt many other musical works, the most famous of which is probably

---

[3] We quote from the text as found in *Hymns for Today* (Norwich, 1983), No. 42.

Bach's *St John Passion*, which includes many troublesome passages taken from the Gospel most overtly hostile to Judaism.[4]

What is most important for our purposes, however, is that 'Lord of the Dance' is not simply a text that one reads to oneself, but a song to be performed in front of an audience. 'Performance' encompasses many different kinds of activities. A song can be performed before a secular audience, or as part of a religious service. It can be performed live or recorded for future performance. These recordings, in turn, can be played on a home stereo system or they can be broadcast to large numbers of people. In fact Levinson first became aware of 'Lord of the Dance' while listening to his favourite Austin radio station, a 'public radio' station operated by the University of Texas that plays an important role in shaping local culture. People who decide to sing the song before a live audience, perform it in a religious ceremony, record it for mass consumption, or broadcast it to the public, are in a somewhat different position from people who simply read the text silently to themselves. Because performers are associated with what they perform, questions naturally arise about not only how to perform a particular work, but whether to perform it at all.

Moreover, performances usually exist within traditions and institutions of performance. 'The Lord of the Dance' is not just a song, it is also a religious hymn. In 1996 the General Conference Hymnal Oversight Committee of the Society of Friends decided to include the 'Lord of the Dance' in its newly revised hymnal. The decision did not go unnoticed; it caused a remarkable debate in the pages of *The Friends Journal*. One anguished Quaker wrote a letter decrying the song as 'anti-Semitic' and concluding that '[i]t is a sacrilege that "The Lord of the Dance" has been included in *Songs of the Spirit* and other Quaker song books. It will be a continuing disgrace and a sin for the Religious Society of Friends to continue to disseminate this song.'[5] Whatever might be said about reading anti-Semitic lyrics silently to oneself, the protester

---

[4] Indeed, this is the subject of a recent book by Michael Marissen, *Lutheranism, Anti-Judaism and Bach's St. John Passion* (Oxford, 1998), discussed in James R. Oestreich, 'Of Bach and Jews in the "St. John Passion" ', *New York Times*, 26 April 1998, §2, 33.

[5] 42 *Friends Journal*, No. 9 (September 1996), at 5 (letter of Joseph W. Letson). We are grateful to Professor Larry Ingle, of the University of Tennessee—Chatanooga, for bringing this exchange to our attention.

recognized that the Society of Friends took on additional responsibilities when they authorized public performances as part of their canon of officially approved materials.

The Hymnal Oversight Committee understood that the song might be controversial. They had contacted the author, Sydney Carter, and 'engaged in discussions with [him] about his song', but Mr Carter refused to alter the words. Even so, the Committee might have authorized a redacted version for the hymnal despite Mr Carter's objections. For example, they could have replaced the words 'The holy people' with 'The faithless people' or even 'The unbelievers'. Apparently, however, they felt that this was unwise, either out of respect for the author's creative authority, fear of copyright infringement, or because they felt they lacked the institutional authority to require redaction. Instead, the Committee chose another strategy. They denied that the lyrics, properly understood, were anti-Semitic at all. The Committee added a footnote in the hymnal stating that the expression ' "They" refers to the authorities responsible for the crucifixion, mainly the Romans.' In addition, '[an] historical note further clarifies "the ambiguous 'they' " and notes the different parties involved: the Pharisees, the Romans, the Sanhedrin, and the Sadducees'.[6]

Not everyone in the Quaker community was persuaded, judging by other letters sent to the *Friends Journal*. David Rush wrote to the editors that '[n]o one in the world would mistake the Romans for the "holy people" '.[7] Of course, the Oversight Committee might have meant that the word 'They' appearing after the words 'The holy people' did not refer to 'the holy people' but to a different group of persons. If so, it is not a very persuasive reading; it is hard to see whom else the 'they' could refer to. Another letter from Paul Thompson took a different approach in defence of the lyrics: he argued that 'Jesus' first followers were Jewish. So were his opponents. The latter came from the hereditary and professional priesthood, etc.' Thus, he argued, 'Any attempt by anyone to read more into the phrase "the Holy People" in Carter's song "Lord of the Dance" than that is ludicrous, even paranoid. Any attempt to cast the

---

[6] *Friends Journal*, n. 5 above, 5–6.
[7] 43 *Friends Journal*, No. 3 (March 1997), 5 (letter of David Rush).

composer as anti-Semitic is unjustifiable.'[8] Accusations of paranoia, of course, depend on the plausibility of the 'reasonable' alternative: most specialists in American constitutional law remember the Supreme Court's famous dismissal of the claim that 'enforced separation of the two races stamps the colored race with a badge of inferiority' in the 1896 case of *Plessy* v. *Ferguson*. This suggestion was preposterous, Justice Brown argued: 'If this be so, it is not by reason of anything found in the act, but solely because the [paranoid?] colored race chooses to put that construction upon it.'[9]

Whether one sides with the Hymnal Oversight Committee or its critics, both sides shared the view that performance of a text before an audience carries distinctive responsibilities for interpreters. The question was not what was the 'best' interpretation of the text in the abstract, but what the text should fairly be read to mean given the institutional context of performance and the social consequences of performing it. The two sides simply disagreed over whether the responsibilities of performance had been met.

Unlike the solitary interpreter-as-reader, the interpreter-as-performer is often faced with the question whether a text should be altered, redacted or not performed at all. Consider Sir Charles Mackerras's 1992 recording of a new version of Gilbert and Sullivan's *The Mikado* with the Welsh National Opera Orchestra and Chorus.[10] Mackerras's recording was hailed by the critics for sweeping away cobwebs of previous tradition. The authors of *The Penguin Guide to Compact Discs* awarded it not only three stars for 'an outstanding performance and recording in every way', but also a 'rosette'—their highest recommendation, signifying a performance of special excellence and quality.[11]

Yet, as *The Penguin Guide*'s authors noted, Mackerras's performance was unusual in many ways. Because he wanted to fit the entire work on to a single compact disc, the entire performance

---

[8]   43 *Friends Journal*, No. 5 (May 1997), 6 (letter of Paul Thompson).

[9]   *Plessy* v. *Ferguson*, 163 US 537 (1896).

[10]   See W. S. Gilbert and Sir Arthur Sullivan, *The Mikado, or the Town of Titipu*, performed by Sir Charles Mackerras, Orchestra and Chorus of the Welsh National Opera, CD–80284, (Telarc International Corporation 1992). [Hereinafter cited as Mackerras, *The Mikado*.]

[11]   Ivan March, Edward Greenfield and Robert Layton, *The Penguin Guide to Compact Discs*, New Edition, (Harmondsworth, 1996), viii–ix, 1314–15 [hereinafter *The Penguin Guide*].

had to last less than eighty minutes.[12] As a result, Mackerras omitted a great deal that one would hear at a live performance. In particular, he dispensed with the overture and the whole of the dialogue. The omission of the overture might easily be defended on the ground that the overture was not in fact by Sullivan himself, but was a pastiche of themes from the operetta strung together by another hand.[13] No such defence could be offered of Mackerras's decision to omit all of W. S. Gilbert's witty dialogue. One might defend the latter on grounds of the changed context of performance: many people listening at home might wish to skip the dialogue and go straight to the musical numbers. But tailoring the CD for those listeners merely begs larger questions about recording works originally crafted for the stage: has Mackerras done justice to a piece intended for performance in front of a live audience? One might object that when it is offered as a series of unconnected musical numbers, *The Mikado* begins to sound more like a comic oratorio than an operetta.

Finally, and most important for our purposes, Mackerras made two alterations that one strongly suspects were motivated by something other than the desire to save valuable time. The listener simply will not hear the middle verse of Ko-Ko's famous aria 'I've got a little list'. As Gilbert and Sullivan fans know, Ko-Ko, the Lord High Executioner, describes his list '[o]f society offenders who might well be underground, and who never would be missed'. In W. S. Gilbert's original 1885 libretto, the second verse begins by counting as disposable 'the nigger serenader, and the others of his race . . .'.[14] Mackerras presumably omitted these

[12] The recorded performance lasts 79 minutes and ten seconds. See Mackerras, *The Mikado*, n. 10 above. [13] *The Penguin Guide*, n. 11 above, 1314.
[14] The entire verse is as follows:

> There's the nigger serenader, and the others of his race,
> And the piano-organist, I've got him on the list!
> And the people who eat peppermint and puff it in your face,
> They never would be missed, they never would be missed!
> Then the idiot who praises, with enthusiastic tone,
> All centuries but this, and every country but his own;
> And the lady from the provinces, who dresses like a guy,
> And who 'doesn't think she waltzes, but would rather like to try';
> And that singular anomaly, the lady novelist,
> I don't think she'd be missed, I'm *sure* she'd not he missed!

W. S. Gilbert and Sir Arthur Seymour Sullivan, *The Mikado, or The Town of Titipu*, in *The Complete Plays of Gilbert and Sullivan* (New York, 1941), 305–6

words on the grounds that they are offensive (or as *The Penguin Guide* delicately puts it, 'unpalatable') to today's audiences.[15] (Of course this raises the question whether the entire work should be considered offensive to the Japanese.)[16] Nevertheless, given that there are only three verses in the entire song, one has to agree that this is a significant omission: Mackerras has literally chopped a third out of the piece![17]

Nor is this the only editorial change to the libretto. In the Mikado's famous Act II aria, where his 'object all sublime' is to 'let the punishment fit the crime', Mackerras alters the following verse:

> The lady who dyes a chemical yellow
> Or stains her grey hair puce,
> Or pinches her figger,
> Is blacked like a nigger
> With permanent walnut juice.

by substituting for the last three lines:

> Or pinches her figger,
> Is painted with vigour
> And permanent walnut juice.[18]

[hereinafter Gilbert and Sullivan, *The Complete Plays*]. Needless to say, one could say much more about the social assumptions behind this verse. While no one has yet raised objection to dispatching the cross-dressing lady, Ian Bradley tells us that: 'Even within Gilbert's lifetime there ceased to be anything either singular or anomalous about the lady novelist (if indeed there ever had been), and for Edwardian revivals he variously substituted "the critic dramatist", "the scorching bicyclist" and "the scorching motorist". Throughout the 1920s and the 1930s Sir Henry Lytton sang of "that singular anomaly, the prohibitionist", while in 1942 it became "the clothing rationist".' Ian Bradley (ed.), *The Annotated Gilbert and Sullivan* (1982), 274 [hereinafter *The Annotated Gilbert and Sullivan*].

[15] *The Penguin Guide*, n. 11 above, 1314; Mackerras, *The Mikado*, n. 10 above, at track 7. Compare liner notes to *id.*, 15–16 (omitting second verse) with Gilbert and Sullivan, *The Complete Plays*, n. 14 above, 305–6 (including second verse).

[16] The usual defence is that 'everyone' understands that the Japanese in Gilbert's libretto are thinly disguised caricatures of persons in British society. Ironically, by 1907 the music from *The Mikado* was sufficiently popular in Japan that it formed part of the regular repertoire of the Japanese Imperial Army and Navy bands, while the British had stopped performing it temporarily for fear of giving offence. See *The Annotated Gilbert and Sullivan*, n. 14 above, 259.

[17] Not all recordings have omitted the offending verse. See, e.g., the libretto to Sir Arthur Sullivan and William Schwenck Gilbert, *The Mikado*, Arabesque Recordings Z8051-2 (1986), 9. Here, too, we are indebted to David Hunter for tracking down this source.

[18] Compare Gilbert and Sullivan, *The Complete Plays*, n. 14 above, 331–2, with liner notes to Mackerras, *The Mikado*, n. 10 above, 27.

Mackerras could have cited a tradition of past performance to justify the second alteration, if not the first. Apparently in response to repeated objections from American audiences, the D'Oyly Carte Opera Company, the original performer and artistic custodian of the operettas, asked A. P. Herbert to alter the lyrics for American performances of *The Mikado* in 1948.[19] Herbert inserted the new lyrics in the Mikado's song and changed 'the nigger serenader and the others of his race' in Ko-Ko's list song to 'the banjo serenader and the others of his race'. Apparently Herbert and D'Oyly Carte judged the latter line no longer racist or otherwise offensive, though one certainly doubts if 1998 audiences would be so easily appeased. In any event, it has remained in official D'Oyly Carte libretti and performances ever since.[20] Nevertheless, Mackerras decided that the verse was still offensive and he omitted it.

Given these cuts, it is quite interesting that the authors of *The Penguin Guide* lavished such praise on Mackerras's performance. Usually they are quite finicky in their demands for textual authenticity and completeness. For example, they praise Mackerras on another occasion for offering the complete original version of Janacek's *Glagolitic Mass*,[21] and they commend Claudio Abbado for recording Schubert's original melody in the slow movement of the Great C major symphony, not the familiar version resulting from editorial changes by Brahms.[22] Even more to the point, they offer a rosette to John McGlinn for 'faithfully offering the original score' of Kern and Hammerstein's *Showboat*, a score whose lyrics can surely raise hackles as much as anything found in *The Mikado*.[23] Finally, they downgrade many performances for employing cuts, even those of long standing or ones sanctioned by the composer.[24] Indeed,

---

[19] *The Annotated Gilbert and Sullivan*, n. 14 above, 274.
[20] *Ibid.*   [21] *The Penguin Guide*, n. 11 above, 650.
[22] *The Penguin Guide*, n. 11 above, 1125.
[23] *The Penguin Guide*, n. 11 above, 658.
[24] See, e.g., Ivan March, Edward Greenfield and Robert Layton, *The Penguin Guide to Compact Discs: Yearbook 1997/98* (Harmondsworth, 1997), 329 [hereinafter *Yearbook*] (downgrading Earl Wild's performance of Rachmaninoff's Piano Concerto No. 3 because of cuts in the text); and 442 (noting that the 'one snag' in the Academy of St Martin in the Fields' performance of Tchaikovsky's Souvenir is that 'their version has been subjected to some tactful cutting'); *The Penguin Guide*, at 1334 (expressing disappointment at Emil Gilels' performance of Tchaikovsky's Piano Concerto No. 2 because it uses the truncated Siloti edition).

sometimes they criticize performances for failing to observe repeats.[25]

Given their scruples in these cases, what best explains their award of a rosette, their highest honour, to Mackerras's version of *The Mikado*? Should not the omission of the dialogue, and the offending verses of Ko-Ko's and the Mikado's arias make the performance less acceptable on grounds of authenticity? Of course, this raises the question whether 'authenticity'—whether defined in terms of the composer's original intentions, fidelity to the text, or adherence to the conditions of performance when the work was premiered—is a worthy touchstone for judging performances. Perhaps, on the contrary, Mackerras did precisely what a conscientious conductor/performer should do in recording this work for contemporary audiences. Faced with a text that is undeniably offensive by today's standards, the conductor excises or redacts it to produce a rewarding aesthetic experience. In one sense altering the work may be more faithful to its best qualities; it also increases the chance that a work like *The Mikado* will maintain its place within the canon of performed works and therefore carry the fame of Gilbert and Sullivan forward to future generations.

Indeed, Rupert D'Oyly Carte justified hiring A. P. Herbert to revise Gilbert's lyrics on the ground that 'Gilbert would surely have approved' of Herbert's changes.[26] Although this sounds like an appeal to original intention, D'Oyly Carte offered no evidence or argument to support his assertion. Perhaps D'Oyly Carte was practising an altogether justifiable principle of charity in interpretation: he assumed that Gilbert was a man of his times; the original lyrics manifested mere parochialism rather than conscious malevolence. Surely, it might be argued, a decent person would change a lyric when its offensiveness was brought to his attention, and if the person in question is dead, one ought to act on this assumption in the interests of charity. Indeed, if Gilbert were alive today, he would probably never have written such racist lyrics in the first place. In this sense, D'Oyly Carte was more fortunate

---

[25] See, e.g., *Yearbook*, n. 24 above, 144 (noting that Christoph von Dohnanyi's performance of Dvorak's 'New World' Symphony 'should by rights, be a first recommendation, but it fails to observe the first-movement exposition repeat').

[26] *The Annotated Gilbert and Sullivan*, n. 14 above, at 274.

than the Hymnal Oversight Committee of the Society of Friends, who were able to ask Sydney Carter if he would mind changing his lyrics to 'Lord of the Dance' and were met with a firm refusal.

Performing Legal Texts

Many of these issues should sound altogether familiar to lawyers who have sparred over the proper interpretation of legal texts, who have fought over the authority of original intention or who have debated the possibility, or desirability, of separating legal from moral reasoning. We argued several years ago that lawyers could learn a great deal from looking at performing arts like music and drama.[27] Part of our argument, which may have been more implicit than explicit, is that having mined much of what there is to learn from the analogy of 'law-as-literature' more illumination lies in thinking about 'law-as-a-performance-art'.

Every analogy is imperfect (including the one we propose in this essay). Each illuminates certain aspects of the thing to be explained while making others less salient. Nevertheless, we think that the analogy to the performing arts is much superior to the analogy to poetry or novels. The analogy of law to literature tends to hide three important features of legal practice.

First, legal practice features a triangular relationship between the institutions that create law, the institutions that interpret law, and the persons affected by the interpretation. Although the lawmaker and the law interpreter can be one—as in the case of common law judges—the two categories are analytically distinct. Indeed, in the contemporary administrative and regulatory state, judges spend much of their time interpreting the statutes and regulations made by others. In the performing arts, there is also a triangular relationship between the creator of the text, the performer, and the audience. Reading a poem or novel to oneself tends to disguise this triangular relationship, because the role of interpreter and audience are merged into one. For this reason, many of us think of reading literature as a 'private' experience, in which we curl up in our study with the book or poem in question and try to enter into the imaginative world created by the

[27] Sanford Levinson and J. M. Balkin, 'Law, Music, and Other Performing Arts' (1991) 139 *University of Pennsylvania Law Review* 1597.

author. Music and drama, by contrast, seem more overtly 'public'.

To be sure, the distinction between 'public' and 'private' can easily be problematized and even deconstructed. The seemingly isolated reader of the poem lives within a complex social world of language, shared values, common expectations, publishing distribution networks, and the like. Moreover, literary figures sometimes read their poetry, short stories, and novels aloud in front of audiences, and so become performance artists. Conversely, music can be played in the privacy of one's own home, just as a group of friends can read a play aloud for their own amusement. Even so, the triangular relationship between the text, performer and audience is more salient in music and drama than in the interpretation of poetry. And it is this salience that we are most interested in exploring and pursuing.

Second, law is a social practice that consists of not only texts but the enforcement and implementation of these texts in practice. Indeed, some of the legal realists argued that legal texts were not law but only sources of law. In this respect music and drama provide a particularly apt analogy. Though both involve texts, whether scores or scripts, these texts need to be brought to life through action. A Bach score is merely a set of directions for performance. Moreover, in order to be realized, music and drama usually require the coordinated efforts of many different individuals. Often performance occurs under the explicit leadership of a conductor or director, who tries to instantiate an interpretation of the work in the actions of the orchestra or cast of the play.

Third, legal interpretation—which includes adjudication, enforcement, and offering legal advice—is a social activity that shapes, directs, and normalizes the thought and behaviour of others. Legal interpretation affects its 'audience': it does things with them and to them. Hence performance always brings with it special responsibilities to the audience.[28] The analogy of law to literature tends to underemphasize the responsibility that the legal

---

[28] Lawyers who advise clients perform law before at least two different audiences—their clients and the legal officials whose behaviour they are trying to predict. The lives and fortunes of clients are surely affected by the interpretations lawyers offer. But lawyerly interpretations also aim at another audience; lawyers offer advice based on the likely response of judges, jurors, or executive officials to their client's proposed course of action.

actor or interpreter bears to the audience affected by what he or she does. We do not claim that these performative aspects are wholly absent when people read poems or novels to themselves, only that these aspects are less salient. Surely a person who reads a poem to herself is affected thereby, and people may well have ethical responsibilities to themselves when they read and interpret literature. (Consider the debate about whether one should even read pornographic literature, let alone sell it or distribute it.) Yet here again, the model of literature and poetry seems to merge the roles of interpreter and audience into one, whereas the great advantage of the analogy to the performing arts is that these roles are more clearly separated.[29] This separation is important precisely because the performer's interpretations can have effects on others for which the performer can be held morally if not legally responsible.[30]

Our point is well illustrated by a conversation one of us had with a very prominent, theoretically sophisticated, American constitutional scholar about the political problems of performing *The Mikado* and the choices that Mackerras made in his 1992 recording. The constitutional scholar rejected the idea of redaction as a solution; indeed, he would *insist* on purchasing a CD that contained the original version of the operetta to listen to in his own home. When asked if he would be willing to perform *The Mikado* in its original version, he quickly responded 'Of course not'. He explained that he would feel 'responsible' for the use of the racist lyrics in a public performance, whereas no such responsibility attached to listening to them in the privacy of his own study. Nothing better confirms the intuitive, albeit under-theorized, distinction between 'private' consumption through reading or listening, and participating in public performance, with its attendant responsibilities to an audience. Indeed, we wonder if this scholar, well known as a man of the left and a critic of the public–private distinction, would even feel comfortable being observed walking into a concert hall advertising an 'authentic' production of *The Mikado* (especially if the entrance involved

[29] Perhaps the closest analogy to the performing artist is the literary critic whose criticisms are read by others.
[30] Consider the dilemma facing an actor about whether she should perform in a production of the Marquis de Sade's *Justine*, or in a production of *The Merchant of Venice* that the actor believes underscores its antisemitism.

crossing the almost inevitable picket line to do so). The public performer (and even the public listener) faces a situation quite different from the phenomenologically isolated consumer of cultural objects. Tending one's own garden is different from putting one's flowers into the stream of (cultural) commerce.

We should not ignore important differences between legal, musical, and dramatic performances. Conductors do more than produce different interpretations of a score. Often they refuse to follow clear textual commands, for example, directions in the score to repeat a certain section or to play at a certain metronome marking. Stage directors are even more liberal in their revisions. For example, almost no one—including the Royal Shakespeare Company—performs the entire text of *King Lear*. Apparently excising verses from one of the greatest plays in the English language is not *per se* illegitimate.

Lawyers and judges, on the other hand, normally are estopped from forthrightly stating that they will choose to regard a given patch of legal text as no longer authoritative, unless, of course, it has been held unconstitutional or, if part of the constitution itself, has been repealed by later amendment. Instead, legal interpreters usually evade the force of a particular text by reading it narrowly or in novel ways. But in a deeper sense the similarity remains, for both redaction and interpretation are ways to 'perform' a work of art or a body of law. A conductor like Mackerras performs *The Mikado* by leaving out Ko-Ko's second verse and all of Gilbert's dialogue; a jurist like Justice Miller in *The Slaughterhouse Cases*[31] 'performs' the United States Constitution by reading the Privileges or Immunities clause of the fourteenth amendment so narrowly that it has no legal importance and can safely be ignored in future litigation and legal discussions.[32] This is not editing or redaction in a technical sense, but it is in a practical sense. It is likely that significant parts of the Constitution have, as a practical matter, been read out of existence by subsequent judicial interpretations. In addition to the Privileges and Immunities clause, the most obvious examples would be the second amendment and the

---

[31] 83 US (16 Wall.) 36 (1873).

[32] Judges' ability to redact through interpretation is only an example of a more general feature of legal precedent: judicial doctrine is important precisely because it directs lawyers' attention to judicial decisions and away from either the text or the original understandings behind the text.

Republican Form of Government clause. Almost no practising lawyer or court-oriented academic seems to think it necessary to worry about these textual patches, given their practical irrelevance as part of court-oriented legal argument. Though the language itself obviously remains as part of the text of Constitution, it is almost never used in ordinary legal argument or taught to aspiring law students as doctrinally significant.[33]

It is tempting but incorrect to argue that the difference between legal interpretation and musical or dramatic redaction lies in the fact that the language of the Privileges or Immunities clause remains in the Constitution, while Ko-Ko's second verse has actually been removed from *The Mikado*. This argument confuses musical texts with performances of music; it also confuses legal texts (and sources of law) with performances of law. Mackerras's performance does not change the text of *The Mikado*. That text remains as it was before his performance. His performance is simply one that omits parts of that text, although if he is successful and influential, a tradition of performance may arise that routinely adopts similar cuts. Likewise, an interpretation of the Privileges or Immunities clause that reads it out of practical existence does not alter the text of the Constitution as a source of law; it merely produces an interpretation that has the force of law and itself becomes a source of law. The textual provisions of the Privileges or Immunities clause lay dormant to be discovered and made use of by future judges willing to overrule *Slaughterhouse*.[34] In the same way the original text of Gilbert's libretto lies available for use by a future conductor mounting a future production.

With these considerations in mind, imagine the situation of a

---

[33] These are not, of course, the only such examples. The post-New Deal Constitution gave diminished vitality to the Contract Clauses of Article 1, paras. 9 and 10 of the Constitution. Before the New Deal, these had served as important constitutional protections of private property. Similarly, the tenth amendment, with its reminder that the powers of the national government are delegated, and thus limited, was dismissed as a basically irrelevant 'truism', without genuine performative import, in the heady days following the New Deal. Nevertheless, the tenth amendment has enjoyed a revival in the past decade, as conservative judges on the federal bench have tried to promote the values of federalism. See *Printz* v. *United States*, 117 S. Ct. 2365; *New York* v. *United States*, 505 US 144 (1992); *Gregory* v. *Ashcroft*, 501 US 452 (1991).

[34] And the tenth amendment, dismissed in *US* v. *Darby*, 312 US 100 (1941), as a mere 'truism', has also resurfaced due to a conservative majority on the Supreme Court. See, e.g., *US* v. *Lopez*, 514 US 549 (1995).

musical artist faced with the decision whether (and how) to perform *The Mikado* or 'Lord of the Dance'. Should the intention of the composer be dispositive? Recall that the author of 'Lord of the Dance', Sydney Carter, was consulted about the possibility of changing his text and that he refused to allow any changes. Even so, why should this matter? Once the text leaves his hands, should he retain a veto over subsequent interpretations?

Lawyers might respond that copyright stands in the way of revising Carter's song. But this is too clever a response. Long-dead composers or authors (or their estates) may have no legal rights at all. It does not follow that performers have no moral obligations to perform their works faithfully. Surely the absence of copyright restrictions does not mean that performers of Beethoven and Shakespeare bear no aesthetic responsibilities towards authorial intention, while performers of Sydney Carter do? To clarify the issue, then, let us assume away the particular impediment of copyright law. Could a performer who believes that 'Lord of the Dance', when excised of the offensive language, is worth preserving and singing as a way of praising the glory of God, simply go ahead and omit the verses in question or, indeed, rewrite them to contain more suitable sentiments? Or would this mean that whatever is being preserved is *not* 'Lord of the Dance', but, rather, a *faux*-version?

The questions raised by 'Lord of the Dance' and by Mackerras's interpretation of *The Mikado* are strikingly similar to questions that lawyers might ask about legal interpretation. Does faithful performance of a legal text require that we hew strictly to the intentions of its framers and the plain meaning of the text? Does faithful performance require that we treat all of the authors' intentions and all parts of the text as equally binding on us? Or does legal interpretation permit or even demand some degree of flexibility and selectivity in textual exegesis in the interests of justice?

Authenticity and Traditions of Performance

Before answering these questions, we offer one other example of a piece written for the glory of God, a motet by Anthoine Busnois, recently recorded by the early music group Pomerium. Busnois, the ' "first singer" at the Court of Charles the Bold, the Duke of

Burgundy',[35] died in 1492, leaving as his legacy some extraordinarily beautiful music. One of the most striking compositions on the CD is the motet *Victimae paschali*, described by Alexander Blachly, the director of Pomerium, as 'the most adventurous of all his creations'.[36] *Victimae paschali* is a setting of traditional Catholic liturgy. It begins, 'Let Christians offer praises to the paschal victim'. The key verses ask Mary Magdalene to tell what she saw, to which she answers 'The tomb of the living Christ, the glory of the Resurrected One. . . . Christ our hope has risen and will precede his followers to Galilee.' At this point the liturgy set by Busnois reads: *Credendum est magis soli Marie veraci/quam Judeorum turbe fallaci*, helpfully translated in the album notes as 'More trust is to be put in honest Mary alone than in the lying crowd of Jews.'[37] Interestingly enough, Blachly notes that '[t]his verse has long been abolished from the Catholic liturgy, but', he insists, 'to excise it here would render the piece unperformable. Despite misgivings, we have left the text intact.'[38]

Blachly took a path quite different from Sir Charles Mackerras or, for that matter, Rupert D'Oyly Carte. Where they thought it important to redact W. S. Gilbert's text for contemporary audiences, Blachly believed it incumbent upon him to present the motet in all its offensiveness, regardless of the Church's subsequent recognition of its pernicious aspects.

Blachly's defence seems to suggest that one simply could not perform the piece without the offending lines. Perhaps this might be true if one excised them while offering nothing in their place. But does Blachly present us with the only viable alternative? Reviewing the disc, the musicologist Richard Taruskin, himself an active performer of medieval music (and the editor of some key works of Busnois), strongly disagreed. One need scarcely eliminate the entire line; it would be sufficient, Taruskin notes, simply to substitute the word ' *peccatorum*, "of sinners", for *Judeorum*'.[39] So revised, the motet would proclaim that Mary is more trustworthy than the lying crowd of sinners. The number of syllables in the two Latin words is the same, and there is no reason to doubt

---

[35] See Richard Taruskin, *Text and Act: Essays on Music and Performance* (New York and Oxford, 1995), 354.
[36] Album notes of *Antoine Busnoy: In Hydraulis & Other Works* 5 (Dorian recording DOR–90184) 5.   [37] *Idem*.
[38] *Idem*, n. 36.   [39] Taruskin, 356.

Taruskin's assurance that the revised version would be eminently 'performable'. (This is, of course, precisely what A. P. Herbert did for Gilbert's lyrics.) Perhaps Blachly simply didn't think of this possibility, but no future performer, having read Taruskin (or, for that matter, this essay) can take refuge in that excuse. Hence if future singers insist on adherence to the original text, it must be for reasons other than technical performance considerations.

Pomerium is part of the authentic performance movement, and so it is possible that Blachly's decision rests on a particular vision of what 'authentic' performance requires. Perhaps Blachly believed that fidelity to the musical score requires singing about 'the lying crowd of Jews'. A performer has no authority to change the text of a score or a libretto and, indeed, the conductor or director is under an injunction to repeat exactly, or in more legal terms, to 'enforce', what has been written on the page. Perhaps Blachly believed he was also honouring original intention by presuming that composers would desire that their lyrics would be performed exactly as written indefinitely into the future. Nevertheless, this may hardly constitute charity in interpretation, and it may wrench the music from its original context of performance. Busnois's motet was originally religious music, and not, as it has now become, a source of entertainment for devotees of ancient music in a pervasively secular age. The Catholic Church viewed, and continues to view, its liturgy as performative—as having beneficial effects on its intended audience. If Busnois was in fact a loyal son of the Church, would he not, at the very least, have acquiesced and even applauded the Church's later decision to reject the liturgical text he originally set? Is not Blachly *insulting* Busnois by inferring that he would prefer to be known to twentieth-century audiences as a thoughtless anti-Semite at variance with the Church's own teachings?

Yet Blachly's hesitation to innovate might stem from yet another source. Performers often feel comfortable in revising works of art for performance because they are part of a tradition of performance that connects them with the work of art and hence authorizes and empowers their interpretations. Thus a pianist in the early twentieth century could feel connected to the work of Chopin because he or she was immersed in a tradition of romantic performance that extended back for a century or more, and because he or she was part of a long line of students and teachers organically connected to this tradition. Being within this tradition gives a performer the freedom and the authority to improvise and innovate within it. An excellent example is the tradition of performing Gilbert and Sullivan operettas. This tradition has produced many accretions to the libretto and score, and there is a long practice of altering lyrics to make satirical points about contemporary issues. Within such an organic tradition the argument for rigorous textual fidelity to the original libretto or even to the conditions of original performance becomes much less persuasive. Quite the contrary: no 'authentic' Gilbert and Sullivan performance would be complete without a little horsing around on stage.

Indeed, as we have pointed out in previous work, arguments for textual rigidity and hewing to original intention arise only after one no longer feels part of an organic tradition of performance.[40] Within an ongoing tradition, authentic performance is assured by living and working within that tradition. Only when that tradition dies and people feel isolated and separated from the past do they attempt to cling to concrete exemplars of the tradition as guarantees of authenticity. And, ironically, the more people cling to these concrete exemplars rather than to the world that fostered them, the less likely they are to be authentic to that former world. Surely one can play Bach on a baroque trumpet, but this hardly ensures the authenticity of what one plays.[41] We no longer live in Bach's world, a world in which music was written for religious purposes, a world in which all performances were live, offered in religious contexts before an audience of believers, a world in which any particular piece might be performed only a few times in the composer's lifetime. Today's 'authentic' performances are usually recorded so that they can be played anywhere at anytime for the amusement of secular audiences. Today we can listen to 'authentic' performances of Bach in our underwear, working in our office cubicle, or speeding down the highway at 70 miles per hour. The notion that using a baroque trumpet in a Bach Cantata somehow guarantees 'authenticity' threatens to make a mockery of that word.

Perhaps then Blachly might argue that he is powerless to change

---

[40] 'Law, Music and Other Performing Arts', n. 27 above, 1637.
[41] *Idem*, 1621–2.

the text of Busnois's motet precisely because we no longer live in an organic tradition of performance of Renaissance polyphony. But this too, begs an important question. For even if Blachly and Pomerium are not part of Busnois's traditions, they do seem to be part of a contemporary tradition of 'authentic performance'. The authentic performance movement hoped to discover old and forgotten music and make well-known music fresh and alive by adopting the instrumental and performance practices of the past. It is this tradition of performance, and not some transhistorical principle of fidelity to text, that seems to counsel that Pomerium preserve Busnois's original language. Precisely because Blachly and Pomerium form part of this tradition, they are also free to improvise within it, to make this music fresh and alive through a creative use of authentic practices. For example, because many musical works were performed in alternative versions, authenticists have sometimes combined them to produce the most aesthetically satisfying version for modern audiences.[42] It by no means follows from the principles or commitments of authentic performance or the authentic performance movement that Busnois's motet must be sung in all of its textual ugliness.[43] As the constitutional scholar in

---

[42] See, e.g., Donald Burrows, 'A Fine Entertainment', Liner notes to *George Frideric Handel, Messiah*, The English Concert and Choir, Trevor Pinnock, conductor, DG Archiv 423–630–2 (1988), 18 (noting that 'the combination of solo voices in this recording is not precisely the same as that available for any of Handel's performances').

[43] Blachly's position about the Busnois text also seems based on a notion of artistic criteria of integrity in performance that are largely independent of moral or political considerations. There is an interesting analogy to law. Just as a jurist might argue that the rule of law requires us to be bound by law regardless of its justice in the individual case, so too, Blachly seems to be arguing that artists and performers like himself are bound by principles of artistic performance that require him to obey the text regardless of its offensiveness or injustices. Blachly is offering an artistic equivalent to a version of what is now called legal positivism. Positivism claims that there is a discourse of law and legality that is in principle separate from the discourse of individual and political morality. But Blachly is offering something more than a positivist definition of artistic performance. He is also making a normative claim about what existing conventions dictate and how one should interpret music. This is by no means required by legal positivism. Many positivists believe that legal interpreters may look to morality to help them solve legal questions as long as the conventions of their particular society permit it. In the same way, someone like Mackerras might contend that a person deciding how best to perform *The Mikado* can take political and moral consequences into account. Our conventions of appropriate musical and dramatic performance permit considering these questions even though there is much more to good performance than political morality.

the earlier anecdote suggested, performers are indeed 'responsible' for the choices they make. It is not enough to plead that one must perform the texts as written by the author, or even—as in the case of Sydney Carter—that the author explicitly rejected the changes in question.[44]

Conclusion: Performance and Canonicity

The problems of performance we have described in this essay all rely on the assumption that there are good reasons to perform the text in the first place. If a song or play is mediocre artistically, we are much less likely to want to perform it. Conversely, the question of how to perform *The Mikado,* the *St John Passion,* or *The Merchant of Venice* is likely to stem from the performer's belief that, on the whole, the work is artistically meritorious. Thus the problems of performance are deeply connected to the canonical status of the work to be performed. If Shakespeare were merely a minor figure of mediocre talent, directors would not be so obsessed about navigating the shoals of *The Merchant of Venice.* Similarly, one doubts that the Oxford University Press would publish a book about, or that the *New York Times* devote a full column to, the possible anti-Semitism of some long-forgotten hack composer.[45] If the composer is Bach, however, everyone recognizes that something important is at stake. It surely occasions no surprise to learn that Michael Marissen's recent book on the *St John Passion* argues that a suitably deep analysis of Bach's musical structures reveals him to be a critic of anti-Semitism—at least

---

[44] We emphasize that these considerations do not depend on whether one regards the work in question as 'high' or 'low' culture, or—as in the case of Gilbert and Sullivan—an indeterminate 'middle brow' that has changed its status over time. Indeed, we think that the high/low culture distinction is a red herring. Our earlier essay used examples from Schubert and Beethoven, higher than which, presumably, musical culture cannot go. Rock and roll performers often change and revise lyrics for performance. But that is not because they constitute 'low' culture. It is because they are immersed in an ongoing tradition of performance in which revisions are permissible and even expected features of artistic creativity. Nevertheless, we predict that as time passes, and future generations are increasingly distanced from those traditions, an 'authentic performance' movement may well spring up, demanding that 'Thunder Road' be performed exactly as Bruce Springsteen originally performed it in the middle 1970s. The irony, of course, will be delicious, since Springsteen prided himself on revising his music continually in live concerts.

[45] See Oestreich, 'Of Bach and Jews', n. 4 above.

given the confines of his own culture—rather than one of its most talented manifestations.[46] If people regard a particular song or play as part of the artistic canon, or, what often amounts to the same thing, an indelible part of our cultural heritage, the obligation to perform it becomes strong. In that case people are much more likely to make excuses for the work's political shortcomings. On the other hand, the canonicity of a work may also lead, as in the case of *The Mikado*, to continuous attempts at ameliorating it through a tradition of performances and glosses on previous performances.[47] If we have little choice in jettisoning canonical works, we will tend either to accept them too generously, attempt to interpret them in their best possible light, or else to edit or rearrange them closer to our heart's desire. Yet our ability to revise the work depends on existing traditions and institutions of performance. As we have seen, it is much easier to revise Gilbert and Sullivan lyrics within the traditions of the D'Oyly Carte Opera Company than to revise lyrics among devotees of the authentic performance movement. The Catholic Church felt able to revise its liturgy in ways that the Society of Friends did not. The more rigid the sanctions against redaction in the traditions of performance, the more one must fall back on claims that the canonical work, properly interpreted, is not really so bad after all. That, of course, is precisely what the Hymnal Oversight Committee did in the case of 'Lord of the Dance'. In short, not only are there important relationships between a work's canonical status and the tendency to downplay its evils or embarrassments, there are also important connections between the inability to redact a canonical work overtly, and attempts to revise it through the use of interpretive glosses.[48]

---

[46]   Marissen, *Lutheranism*, n. 4 above.

[47]   Consider that if we had to excise all sexism from Shakespeare's plays, we might have little left. Shakespeare's values pervade his work. But what can be said of Shakespeare can also be said of much of Western art and music, and not only of past works: if we attempted to rid contemporary music of its sexism, we might have little contemporary music left. Much the same is true, we think, with respect to our constitutional tradition. The injustices of the past are embedded in our constitutional tradition, in ways we do not always understand.

[48]   The political scientist Albert Hirshman noted a similar, although not identical, triangular relationship between the ability to exit from an institution, voice in governing the institution, and loyalty to the institution. Easy exit and less voice may produce less loyalty; difficult exit and increased voice may produce greater loyalty. Albert Hirschman, *Exit, Voice, and Loyalty*.

There is an important analogy here to laws, and especially to constitutions. Precisely because legal texts have the force of law, we do not usually think that we can disregard them like mediocre works of art from the past. Rather, we have to live with them, just as we have to live with *The Merchant of Venice* or *The Magic Flute*, whatever their imperfections. Moreover, the Constitution, at least in the United States, is not only a legal text but a symbol of national identity and national pride, and for some even an object of veneration.[49] As a result Americans tend to adopt one of two approaches to its defects. On the one hand, they tend to overlook its shortcomings, promote its achievements and regard critics as nitpicking, unpatriotic, or worse. On the other hand, they may tend to read better values into the Constitution through doctrinal glosses or creative interpretations.[50] Both of these practices of performances are likely responses when people are faced with a canonical work of art. And, we think, they are the most likely responses to the performance of constitutive legal texts.

[49] See Sanford Levinson, *Constitutional Faith* (Princeton, NJ, 1988).
[50] See J. M. Balkin, 'Agreements with Hell and Other Objects of Our Faith' (1997) 65 *Fordham University Law Review* 1703.

INDEX

760 *Index*